THE CONSTANT F

THE CONSTANT FLUX

*A Study of Class Mobility in
Industrial Societies*

ROBERT ERIKSON
AND
JOHN H. GOLDTHORPE

CLARENDON PRESS · OXFORD

Oxford University Press, Walton Street, Oxford OX2 6DP
Oxford   New York   Toronto
Delhi   Bombay   Calcutta   Madras   Karachi
Kuala Lumpur   Singapore   Hong Kong   Tokyo
Nairobi   Dar es Salaam   Cape Town
Melbourne   Auckland   Madrid
and associated companies in
Berlin   Ibadan

Oxford is a trade mark of Oxford University Press

Published in the United States
by Oxford University Press Inc., New York

British Library Cataloguing in Publication Data
Data available

Library of Congress Cataloging in Publication Data
Erikson, Robert, 1938–
The constant flux: a study of class mobility in industrial
societies / Robert Erikson and John H. Goldthorpe.
p.   cm.
Includes bibliographical references and index.
1. Social mobility—Europe—History—20th century.   2. Social
mobility—History—20th century.   3. Social classes—Europe—
History—20th century.   4. Social classes—History—20th century.
5. Europe—Economic conditions—1945–   I. Goldthorpe, John H.
II. Title.
HN380.Z9S654   1992   305.5'13'09045—dc20   91–30724
ISBN 0–19–827908–6

3 5 7 9 10 8 6 4 2

Printed in Great Britain
on acid-free paper by
Bookcraft (Bath) Ltd., Midsomer Norton, Avon

For Margareta and Rhiannon

PREFACE

From the conception to the completion of this study we have depended upon the support and co-operation of several institutions and a great many individuals. The main purpose of this Preface is to acknowledge their contribution and to express our thanks to them.

The study was conducted under the auspices of the CASMIN (Comparative Analysis of Social Mobility in Industrial Nations) Project, directed by Walter Müller and John H. Goldthorpe from the Institut für Sozialwissenschaften of the University of Mannheim. The project was financed between 1983 and 1988 by grants from the Stiftung Volkswagenwerk, and our first and largest debt of gratitude is to the Stiftung for making our work possible. Dr Helga Junkers was a model foundation administrator: unobtrusive yet unfailingly efficient and helpful. We can only hope that this, and the wide range of other publications that have resulted from the CASMIN project, will play their part in encouraging the Stiftung to continue with its programmes of support for the social sciences.

We would also like to express our warm thanks to Walter Müller and his colleagues at the Institut für Sozialwissenschaften for so often taking us beneath their roof and invariably providing both excellent working conditions and a most convivial atmosphere. We shall always retain happy memories of the 'old days' of the Institut at Tattersallstrasse 2.

Likewise essential to our enterprise were two other academic bodies—those to which we are personally affiliated: the Swedish Institute for Social Research at the University of Stockholm and Nuffield College, Oxford. They afforded us contrasting, yet equally congenial, intellectual milieux between which we could shuttle, and also a variety of infrastructural services, the total cost of which over the years of our collaboration we would not care to calculate (and trust that no one else will either). Of particular value to us were our ever-willing secretaries: Ulla Carlstedt in Stockholm, who was responsible, among many other things, for drawing most of the figures in the book; and Audrey Skeats in Oxford, who became expert in managing communications between us by all methods known to the late twentieth century.

Our study is one based on secondary analysis, and thus other institutions to which we are endebted are all those that carried out, or facilitated, the original enquiries on which we have drawn. In this respect, however, we are most keenly aware of the thanks that we owe to the individuals who were our chief 'contacts' with these enquiries. They assisted us, first of all, in acquiring the data-sets and in finding our way around the tapes and documentation; and subsequently by answering what must to them have seemed strings of tedious questions. Into this category fall: Rudolf Andorka,

David Featherman, Bob Hauser, Frank Lancaster Jones, Robert Miller, Walter Müller, Geoff Payne, Claude Thélot, Ken'ichi Tominaga, and Krzysztof Zagórski. Additional material was also at various stages of our work generously made available to us by Marek Boguszak, Antonio Cobalti, Harry Ganzeboom, John L. Hammond, Anthony Heath, Sören Holmberg, Mike Hout, Knud Knudsen, Tamás Kolosi, Karin Kurz, Håkon Leiulfsrud, Gordon Marshall, Roger Sapsford, and Bernhard Schimpl-Neimanns.

At the stage of organizing and processing the volume of data that we accumulated, we were dependent on extensive research assistance and on aid and guidance from a variety of specialists. In the construction of the CASMIN data archive at Mannheim and the preparation of our International Mobility Superfile, a key role was played by Wolfgang König, whose industry was prodigious. At various times we also enjoyed the assistance of Karin Kurz and Paul Lüttinger. Subsequently, the bulk of our computing was undertaken at Stockholm, and here the main burden of our usually extravagant and occasionally, we suspect, not entirely coherent demands for support fell upon Miljan Vuksanovic. He viewed us tolerantly and invariably applied his great expertise to producing what we wanted, if not something better. We also received welcome help from Ingemar Kåreholt. In some part, the costs of research assistance in Stockholm were met by grants from the Swedish Council for Social Research. At the Oxford end, computing support was provided, with their usual efficiency, by Clive Payne, Martin Range, and Jane Roberts of the Faculty of Social Studies Computing Unit.

We also found ourselves recurrently in need of guidance on statistical questions, and here our ever-present help in trouble was Jan Hoem. He made his time and knowledge available to us with remarkable generosity and has contributed a valuable annex to one of our chapters. We also benefited greatly from admonition and advice received at various points from Richard Breen, Sir David Cox, Leo Goodman, Shelby J. Haberman, Clive Payne, Joseph Schwartz, and Jan Selén.

A further need of which we were aware from the time we first sought to grapple with our national data-sets, and which intensified as we reached the stage of interpreting and writing up the results of our analyses, was that for instruction on the more detailed aspects of the history and sociology of the various societies with which we were concerned. We imposed upon a large number of colleagues with our queries, and the following, at least, responded —some, in addition, preparing written commentaries on our treatment of particular nations for a CASMIN project conference held at Schloss Reisensburg in March 1988: Rudolf Andorka, Daniel Bertaux, Ronald Dore, Carl le Grand, Johann Handl, Bob Hauser, Mike Hout, John Jackson, Frank Lancaster Jones, Harold Kerbo, Tamás Kolosi, Jadwiga Koralewicz, Walter Korpi, Bogdan Mach, Karl-Ulrich Mayer, Robert Miller, Geoff Payne, Sawako Shirahase, Kazimierz Słomczyński, Aage Sørensen, Ryszard Szulkin, Ken'ichi Tominaga, Peter Travers, Wout Ultee, and Krzysztof Zagórski.

In regard to our work on Japan, special mention should be made of the part played by Hiroshi Ishida. Since, of all the nations we sought to cover, Japan was that about which we knew least, his collaboration and the access he provided to the large amount of relevant literature available only in Japanese was vital to the inclusion of this singularly important case in our study. Chapter 10 is substantially based on a journal article written jointly with him.

From the time when we began to produce our first drafts, we further benefited from the interest and goodwill of those colleagues who were prepared to read and respond to them. Many of those already mentioned above deserve our thanks in this respect also, but to Mike Hout and Walter Korpi, whose comments were unusually extensive and helpful, these thanks should be expressly repeated. Others who contributed—and perhaps more than they were aware—with criticism, suggestions, information etc. include Göran Ahrne, Erik Allardt, Tom Colbjørnsen, Peter Flora, Max Haller, Carl-Gunnar Janson, Janne Jonsson, Susan McRae, Colin Mills, Joakim Palme, Seppo Pöntinen, Lucienne Portocarero, John Ridge, Natalie Rogoff-Ramsøy, Albert Simkus, Göran Therborn, Hannu Uusitalo, Jelle Visser, Carolyn Vogler, Karin Widerberg, and Włodek Wesołowski.

These acknowledgements of professional indebtedness would not be complete without mention of the particular research community to which we have the good fortune to belong—that is, what to outsiders must seem the rather strange freemasonry of mobility researchers. Perhaps its most distinctive and attractive feature is the way in which it combines traditions of mutual helpfulness—of which the foregoing gives ample evidence—with those of vigorous criticism. It will come as no surprise to those familiar with this community that many of those thanked above should reappear in the text that follows as authors with whom we take issue—nor that they are likely to appear yet again as those whose responses to this book will, let us say, be among the most spirited.

Finally, we must here recognize the extent of the personal as well as the professional support that we have received over the years of the CASMIN project. On our frequent visits to Germany our usual lodging was at the *Halber Mond* in Heppenheim under the genial proprietorship of Herr and Frau Homm; but our second home was with Gigi and Walter Müller at Laudenbach. Lady Eden once complained that the Suez Canal ran through her drawing-room; very often, the CASMIN project ran through most of the rooms at Kirchstrasse 7a, but Gigi never complained, despite the inevitable disruption to her own professional as well as domestic life. Rather, she and Walter dispensed the splendid hospitality that has indeed made their house famous around the world as a haven for itinerant sociologists.

Which brings us to the somewhat more modest establishments in Mälarhöjden and North Oxford. These too, we must accept, have felt the effects of the CASMIN project. Our frequent absences from the premises may not have been experienced by our wives *entirely* as periods of deprivation, absolute or relative (though we never, we feel, fully persuaded them of the hardships that our travels entailed). But there were also, of course, the many occasions when the exigencies of our collaboration meant that one wife had to cope with the two of us together. And a recurrent lodger—however retiring in personality, however skilled in the domestic arts—can never count as a quite unproblematic addition to a dual-career family. We do therefore acknowledge, with love and thanks, the contribution that our wives have made to this book, most obviously, but not only, by accepting with great good humour the many inconveniences that its writing has imposed upon them; and, as a very modest recompense, we dedicate it to them.

R.E.
J.H.G.

May 1991
Stockholm and Oxford

CONTENTS

FIGURES

TABLES

1
Introduction: Industrial Society and Social Mobility

The ultimate concern of this study is with the sociology of industrial nations. Its focus on social mobility reflects the centrality that this topic holds in prevailing theories of industrialism and in debates on various aspects of industrial society that have been prompted by both academic and socio-political interests. Social mobility research has often been criticized for setting a higher value on displays of statistical virtuosity than on contributions of substantive interest. There is, we believe, some truth in this charge. None the less, it should not be allowed to obscure the prime sociological importance of the phenomenon of mobility itself.

In the most general terms, we would maintain the following. It must be a leading task of any theory of industrial society to elucidate the relationships that exist between, on the one hand, the structure of the division of labour that is taken to characterize this form of society and, on the other hand, the main patterns of social action that are observable within industrial societies. Discussion of social action requires reference to actors who have, in the last analysis, to be recognized as individual men and women: we must, as Stinchcombe has put it, see the social structure as being 'peopled' (1983: ch. 5).[1] And, once this view is taken, then the relevance of mobility, in the sense of the movement of individuals among positions defined by the structure of the division of labour, should be apparent enough. If we are to understand how the distribution of individuals within this structure is related to the creation of the identities and interests that are the mainsprings of action, both individual and collective and in both the private and the public spheres, mobility has to become an issue of major interest.

[1] We here, of course, imply an acceptance of the principle of methodological individualism: that is, of the principle that all social phenomena are ultimately explicable in terms of the actions of individuals and of their intended and unintended consequences (cf. Popper 1945: ch. 14; Elster 1985: ch. 1). This principle has often been attacked by sociologists but nearly always on the basis of a misunderstanding: it is supposed that methodological individualism entails *ontological* individualism—the claim that only individuals *exist*. It is, however, entirely possible to accept, as we clearly would, that social positions, relations, structures, etc., have their own independent existence or 'reality', which in various ways influences individual action, and yet still to maintain that, in the last analysis, these phenomena can only be understood as the product, intended or unintended, of preceding action by individuals (cf. Popper 1972: ch. 4). What methodological individualism denies is not the reality of social phenomena but rather that there are supraindividual actors or ('subjects')—for example, 'humanity', 'the nation', 'capital in general', 'the working class'—whose action can or must be understood independently of, and prior to, that of individuals in the context of, say, some theory of history or of the functioning of social systems.

Most obviously, the degree of permanence or impermanence with which individuals are associated with different positions, and their rates and patterns of movement among them, may be expected to condition both the formation of identities and the recognition of interests and, in turn, to determine where, and with what degree of sharpness, lines of cultural, social, and political, as well as economic division are drawn. At the same time, the nature and extent of mobility can be expected to influence the evaluations that individuals make of the social order under which they live and, in particular, concerning the legitimacy or otherwise of the inequalities of both opportunity and condition that it entails. In short, mobility rates and patterns may be seen as a persisting and pervasive factor shaping the ways in which the members of a society define themselves, and in turn the goals they pursue and the beliefs and values that they seek to uphold or contest. In attempting to establish connections between structure and action in industrial societies, mobility must, therefore, be regarded as a crucial mediating process—and, one could add, it has in fact become so regarded from a variety of theoretical standpoints.[2]

In this study, we should emphasize, we do not aim to address the entire range of questions that are implied in the above programmatic outline. We shall concentrate on what we take to be the primary tasks of describing, and of gaining some analytic understanding of, the rates and patterns of social mobility that are found in industrial societies, with special reference to the extent of change and variation, constancy and commonality, that they display. These tasks *are* primary, in our view, not only because they are those to which our present resources as regards both data and techniques would seem most adequate, but further because they are ones that must be accomplished before we can move forward to serious attempts at tracing in any detail either the determinants of mobility or its likely concomitants and consequences within different social contexts.

In this introductory chapter our aims are straightforward. We seek, first of all, to present a series of arguments about social mobility that are integral to the most developed and influential theory of industrial society so far available—what we shall call 'the liberal theory of industrialism'. It will be seen that the treatment of mobility in this theory is rather comprehensive, even though our account will reflect the priorities of interest that we have declared above. Secondly, we trace out, with similar emphases, a number of rival arguments which vary widely in both the nature and the extent of their theoretical grounding and which, moreover, since they confront the liberal theory from very different approaches, quite often come into opposition with each other.

[2] Note, for example, the similarities in this respect in the otherwise widely differing positions of Giddens (1973: esp. chs. 6, 7), Wright (1989*b*; and cf. also Wright and Shin 1988) and Runciman (1989). At an empirical level, one may also note the long tradition of enquiry into the effects of social mobility on different forms of political action, extending from the early work of Lipset (1960) through to such sophisticated analyses as De Graaf and Ultee (1990).

We have attempted to carry out this work of exegesis with some care, because it is the competing and conflicting claims about mobility rates and patterns, trends and processes, that we here review that provide the main frame of reference for the central chapters of the book. That is to say, our examination of empirical evidence will be aimed, directly or indirectly, at assessing the validity of these claims and, in turn, of the theoretical positions from which they derive—with a final evaluation of the latter being presented in our concluding chapter. One difficulty that we have encountered should, however, be noted. Among the arguments we consider, some are several decades old and thus antedate various important technical advances in the analysis of social mobility, while others are relatively new and draw directly on conceptual distinctions and refinements that such advances have only recently made possible. To have presented both old and new arguments entirely in their original terminology would have obscured the extent to which they do in fact address the same issues and, without rather elaborate commentary, could well have been confusing to non-specialist readers. We have, therefore, sought to achieve a more-or-less uniform mode of expression—though no doubt at cost of some precision—by sometimes giving the older arguments a rather modern gloss, while presenting the newer ones, at this stage, in an entirely non-technical form.

SOCIAL MOBILITY AND THE LIBERAL THEORY OF INDUSTRIALISM

What we propose to call the liberal theory of industrialism is in fact a construct, based on the work of a number of mainly North American social scientists, active from the 1960s through to the 1980s. Although differing in their disciplinary allegiances, in the focus of their substantive interests, and in their theoretical idiom, these authors arrive at positions so similar in their essentials that a collective treatment would seem not merely warranted but desirable. For our present purposes, however, two contributions stand out as being of particular importance, and it is to these that we shall chiefly attend: namely, that made over a period of twenty years or more by Kerr and his associates (Kerr *et al.* 1960/1973; Dunlop *et al.* 1975; Kerr 1969, 1983), and that which is to be found in the later writings of Parsons (1960: esp. chs. 3 and 4, 1967: esp. chs. 4 and 15, 1971).[3]

---

[3] Others whose work could, with greater or less qualification, be associated with the theory include Galbraith (1971) and proponents of both 'modernization theory' (e.g. Moore 1963, 1967, 1979) and the theory of 'post-industrial' society (e.g. Bell 1973). It might, however, be noted that, in contrast with their US counterparts, European exponents of the idea of industrialism or industrial society (e.g. Aron 1962, 1964, 1967; Dahrendorf 1959) appear to have been attracted more by the purely critical potential that was provided—*vis-à-vis* Marxist analyses of capitalism—than by the basis offered for the building of new macrosociological theory, at all events of a developmental kind.

We refer to the theory developed by these authors as being a 'liberal' one in recognition of the political commitment which they have in common and do not attempt to conceal: that is, to the form of liberal, or pluralist, democracy that operates, at least in principle, in the nations of the Western world. This commitment is related to the theory they advance, in that it is an ultimate objective of the latter to endow liberal democracy with a special significance: to present it as that form of polity which is most compatible with—and indeed as that which in the long term is necessitated by—the requirements of a viable industrial economy.

The model for the enterprise in which exponents of the liberal theory are engaged is, in fact, none other than that provided by Marx in his attempt to reveal 'the laws of motion of capitalist society' and to demonstrate that these must finally lead, through class conflict and revolution, to the realization of communism. The concern of liberal theorists is, first of all, to establish the failure of Marx's analysis and of the predictions based upon it; but then to replace it by a new account of the developmental tendencies of industrial, rather than of simply capitalist, society, and one which shows that, out of whatever political context the initial impetus to industrialization may have come, it is liberal democracy that represents the goal towards which the evolution of all industrial societies is moving.[4]

The problems raised by the historicism that the liberal theory thus takes over from that of Marx (cf. Goldthorpe 1971, 1979, 1991b) may at this point be passed over. But what has to be emphasized is that the theory also inherits the functionalist character of Marx's analysis (cf. Cohen 1978; Elster 1985). It starts from the assumption that, implicit in the transition from pre-industrial to industrial society, is an irreversible commitment to technical and economic rationality: the progressive exploitation of material resources and the sustained increase in real income *per capita* which characterize industrialization are founded upon this commitment. Thus, the possibility arises of defining the distinctive 'properties' of industrial societies in terms of the essential prerequisites for, or necessary consequences of, the operation of technical and economic rationality. For Marx, the process of social development was to be explained by reference to the functional exigencies imposed by the forces of production on relations of production—and periodic discontinuities were to be seen as marking the points at which the growth of the former outran the capacity of the latter to respond. But, for exponents of the liberal theory, industrialism imposes its inherent 'logic' on its social context in a gradual but unremitting and pervasive way—reinforcing features which are functionally consistent with it and undermining those

---

[4] In the work of Kerr and his associates the influence of the Marxian model is openly acknowledged (see, e.g., Kerr *et al.* 1960/1973: ch. 1; Kerr 1983: ch. 1). In Parsons's work, on the other hand, the influence of this model is less immediately apparent but, on examination, emerges clearly enough (see, e.g., 1967: ch. 4, 1971: ch. 1).

which are not, so as to bring all industrial societies on to convergent developmental paths.

It is, then, in terms of this functionalist analysis that claims made by liberal theorists regarding social mobility—and the importance of these claims to the liberal theory as a whole—must be understood. What is maintained factually, with more-or-less complete unanimity, is straightforward, and may be put in the form of the following three-part proposition.

In industrial societies, in comparison with pre-industrial ones:

1. rates of social mobility are high, and upward mobility—i.e. from less to more advantaged social positions—predominates over downward mobility;
2. mobility opportunities are more equal, in the sense that individuals of differing social origins compete on more equal terms to attain (or to avoid) particular destinations;
3. both rates of mobility and the degree of equality of opportunity tend to increase.

To explain *why* these contrasts between mobility in pre-industrial and industrial society should arise, liberal theorists then turn to a range of arguments which have, moreover, been elaborated and extended in the specialist literature by other authors generally sympathetic to the liberal position. Of particular importance here are the contributions of Blau and Duncan (1967: esp. ch. 12) and Treiman (1970). While all the arguments in question take on a functionalist form, we may, with our later purposes in mind, usefully distinguish between those relating to three different kinds of effect—structural, processual, and compositional—and treat each type of argument in turn.

First, it is held that within industrial society the dynamism of a rationally developed technology calls for continuous, and often rapid, change in the structure of the social division of labour, which also tends to become increasingly differentiated. High rates of mobility thus follow as, from generation to generation and in the course of individual lifetimes, the redistribution of the active population is required: that is, among economic sectors—first, from agriculture to manufacturing and then from manufacturing to services—and, in turn, among industries and among a growing diversity of occupations. Furthermore, the overall tendency is for advancing technology to *upgrade* levels of employment. Although some skills are rendered obsolete, new ones are created, and the *net* effect is a reduction in the number of merely labouring and routine occupations and a rising demand for technically and professionally qualified personnel. At the same time, both the increasing scale of production, dictated by economic rationality, and the expansion of the services sector of the economy promote the growth of large bureaucratic organizations in which managerial and administrative positions also multiply. Industrial societies become increasingly 'middle-class', or at least 'middle-mass', societies. Consequently, upward mobility is more likely than downward in both intergenerational and work-life perspective. Under industrialism, the chances of 'success' are steadily improved for all.[5]

Secondly, it is further claimed that, as well as thus reshaping the objective structure of opportunity, industrialism transforms the processes through which particular individuals are allocated to different positions within the division of labour. Most fundamentally, rational procedures of social selection require a shift away from *ascription* and towards *achievement* as the leading criterion. What counts is increasingly what individuals can do, and not who they are. Moreover, the growing demand for highly qualified personnel promotes the expansion of education and training, and also the reform of educational institutions so as to increase their accessibility to individuals of all social backgrounds. Human resources cannot be wasted; talent must be fully exploited wherever it is to be found. Thus, as, within a society of widening educational provision, 'meritocratic' selection comes to predominate, the association between individuals' social origins and their eventual destinations tends steadily to weaken; or, in other words, relative mobility chances become more equal and the society takes on a more 'open' character. And, at the same time, various other features of industrialism also serve to reduce the influence of social origins on individuals' future lives. For example, urbanization and greater geographical mobility loosen ties of kinship and community; mass communications spread information, enlarge horizons, and raise aspirations; and a greater equality of condition—that is, in incomes and living standards—means that the resources necessary for the realization of ambition are more widely available.

Thirdly, it is argued that the foregoing effects interact with each other, in that the emphasis on achievement as the basis for social selection will be strongest within the expanding sectors of the economy—that is, the more technologically advanced manufacturing industries and services—and within the increasingly dominant form of large-scale bureaucratic organization. Conversely, ascriptive tendencies will persist chiefly within declining sectors and organizational forms—for example, within agriculture or small-scale, family-based business enterprise. In other words, compositional effects on mobility occur in that, once a society begins to industrialize, the proportion of its population that is subject to the new 'mobility regime' characteristic of industrialism increases not only as that regime imposes itself, but further as those areas and modes of economic activity that are most resistant to it become in any event ever more marginal.

Having thus sought to show how high and increasing levels of mobility and openness are integral to the functioning of industrialism, liberal theorists

---

[5] The influence of the analyses of economic growth advanced by Clark (1957), Rostow (1960), and Kuznets (1966) is in this respect manifest, as also is the interpretation of Western industrialization found in the work of historians such as Landes (1965/1972).

then complete their analysis by turning to the consequences of mobility for the political order of industrial societies. In this respect, their main concern has been to bring out the ways in which, in societies where a liberal democratic polity is established, mobility serves to sustain it and, in particular, to protect it against threats from the left that might be raised by labour movements under 'ideological'—that is, radical socialist—leadership.

The rates and patterns of mobility characteristic of industrial society are seen as contributing to the stability of liberal democracy in two different ways. First, they help legitimate prevailing class and status inequalities. Where mobility is high and linked to educational attainment, differences in rewards, both material and symbolic, can be better represented and understood as fair returns for differing abilities and contributions than where families maintain the same relative positions over generations. Moreover, since the changing structure of employment ensures that upward mobility will predominate over downward, there will still under meritocratic procedures be more 'winners' than 'losers', and thus a large number of individuals who will be inclined to regard the system of social selection favourably—as, in fact, confirming their own worth—than who are likely to feel resentment against it.

Secondly, high mobility is also regarded as being protective of liberal democracy in that it reduces the potential for collective action of a class-based kind. As earlier indicated, liberal theorists, even in the 1960s, still retained fears that in Europe, if not in the United States, working-class movements and parties which had not accepted social-democratic 'revisionism' might undermine democracy or otherwise disrupt the appropriate developmental pattern of industrial societies. However, increasing mobility—and especially increasing upward mobility from working-class origins—is taken as a crucial countervailing factor in that it tends both to weaken class identification and to encourage individual rather than collective efforts at social betterment. As Blau and Duncan put it in a revealing passage:

Men who see little opportunity for improvement in their own economic status or, at least, that of their children, have greater inducements than those anticipating advancements in status to organize a union to raise wages or to vote for a party that advocates higher taxes for the wealthy, though many other factors unquestionably play a part. . . . Inasmuch as high chances of mobility make men less dissatisfied with the system of social differentiation in their society and less inclined to organize in opposition to it, they help to perpetuate this stratification system, and they simultaneously stabilize the political institutions that support it . . .[6] (1967: 440)

---

[6] This passage occurs in a subsection of Blau and Duncan (1967), with the heading 'Opportunity and Democracy'. As is illustrated, however, the thrust of the argument seems directed towards showing how high chances of (upward) mobility not only help sustain democracy *per se* but further how, in tending to reduce support for trade unionism and redistributive fiscal and social policies, they help prevent democracy from finding expression in other than its 'liberal' form.

From this last argument in particular, it might appear that high levels of mobility, with a bias towards upward movement, would favour the stability of the prevailing political order whatever its form. But, in fact, in further considering state socialist regimes, or at all events those of post-war Eastern Europe, liberal theorists have seen the mobility processes of industrialism as having, in this case, subversive effects. Social selection on the basis of ideological reliability or of 'appropriate' class origins—peasant or worker—as was often practised in the immediate post-revolutionary stage of 'socialist reconstruction', did not, it was held, represent a sustainable policy. The more rational, non-discriminatory, achievement-oriented procedures that operate elsewhere in the industrial world were inevitably introduced. Thus, with the extensive recruitment required by the expansion of professional, administrative, and managerial positions in the 'secondary stage' of socialist development, the ideological purity of the former élite of revolutionary intellectuals and Party officials was compromised. The 'new men' were modern bureaucrats and technocrats, the products of the system of higher education and training, rather than simply *cadres* who had gained their advancement through the Party itself. And, in turn, it is these new élite groups who have come to play the leading role in the drive towards liberalization; it is they who have both the power and the motivation to challenge Party dominance, and to demand more decentralized and democratic forms of decision-making in the economy and polity alike.[7]

It should, then, be apparent that in the liberal theory of industrial society arguments relating to mobility play a pivotal role. On the one hand, high and rising levels of mobility and openness are represented as functional imperatives of industrial development—as being necessitated by the rational technology and economy that are the constitutive features of industrialism. On the other hand, both the actual experience of mobility and the availability of mobility opportunities are taken as key factors shaping individuals' response to the industrial societies in which they live, and, in particular, to their stratification and their political systems. In other words, within the liberal theory, the treatment of mobility serves as a major connecting link between its macrosociological and microsociological elements—as indeed we have argued must be the case in any theory of comparable ambition.

We shall subsequently criticize the liberal theory on a variety of grounds, and indeed conclude that its claims regarding mobility are in large part mistaken. None the less, it is, we believe, appropriate to underline here its

---

[7] Interesting Eastern European versions or analogues of the arguments of liberal theorists have been advanced. For example, Ossowski (1957) suggested that the long-term effect of socialist revolutions in increasing mobility would come via the stimulus they gave to industrialization rather than from any transformation of values; and, on the potentially destabilizing role of new élites created by high rates of mobility, see especially Gellner's (1971) review of the work of Pavel Machonin and his associates in the context of events in Czechoslovakia in 1968–9, and also Konrad and Szelényi (1979).

very considerable merits. As well as being impressive in its scope and coherence, it can—unlike much of what today passes for sociological theory—make a genuine claim to explanatory and predictive potential; and it is, of course, precisely in virtue of this fact that it is open to the kind of empirically grounded critique that we wish to undertake. The justification for giving this theory the primacy that we do in a study of mobility in industrial society will, we believe, become more evident as we go on to consider alternative possibilities.

THE MARXIST RESPONSE

As we earlier remarked, the liberal theory of industrialism was developed with the more-or-less explicit objective of undermining and superseding the Marxist theory of capitalism. Liberal theorists rejected the idea of contradictions between the forces and relations of production that would inevitably intensify class consciousness and conflict, and lead to the revolutionary overthrow of the existing order. Rather, they saw technological and economic progress as together reducing class differences and inequalities, and thus— at least within the Western democracies—removing both the motivation and the social bases for oppositional class action. Within this liberal scenario, as we have sought to show, mobility rates, processes, and trends that are represented as characteristic of industrial society take on a central importance. It would, therefore, seem of obvious interest for us to ask what response to the liberal theory has been forthcoming from the Marxist side, and to what extent rival arguments concerning mobility are entailed.

In fact, the Marxist response must be judged, on any critical examination, to have been extraordinarily weak. Although Marxist authors have tended to adopt attitudes of intellectual as well as moral superiority towards liberal theorists, their attempts to meet the challenge posed by the latter have been recurrently unconvincing, and would appear by the present time to have more or less collapsed.

During the 1970s leading Marxists did indeed write extensively on class analysis. But, under the then dominant influence of 'structuralist' theory, their attention was given almost exclusively to elaborating the criteria by which class locations and class boundaries were to be determined. Although much of this activity was prompted by problems of the class location of salaried white-collar groupings, whose growth was emphasized by liberal theorists, and although an evident concern was with socialist strategy and the possibilities for 'class alliances', the question of the relationship between class structure and class action was left almost entirely unconsidered. It was, it appears, regarded as one not amenable to theoretical discussion, *either* because it was simply axiomatic that 'agents' were the bearers of the class interests and forces implicit in their structural locations *or* because the relationship was quite indeterminate![8] For such authors, then, social mobility was obviously of no great interest. It could be dismissed empirically as a phenomenon of little actual importance, or theoretically as one of relevance only within a 'bourgeois problematic' (cf. Poulantzas 1974: 37).

However, from other than quite sectarian standpoints, such arguments could scarcely be acceptable. They suggested a concern more to evade than to take up the liberal challenge. Out of recognition, one suspects, of their inadequacies, Marxists who were in somewhat closer touch with contemporary sociology—and social reality—did then make one rather more serious effort to provide, at least in part, an alternative to the liberal position. This took the form of a revival of the theory of proletarianization.

For Marx himself, proletarianization was the 'driving-down' of small proprietors and independent artisans into the ranks of wage labour; it referred, that is, to a particular kind of mobility. In the earlier twentieth century the concept was extended, notably by German Marxists, to refer also to the decline in pay and working conditions of clerical and other white-collar employees which, it was held, brought their 'objective' situation close to that of manual workers (see, e.g., Klingender 1935; cf. Speier 1934, 1986; Mills 1951). In the new theory, however, the meaning of proletarianization was still further widened. Under the influence chiefly of the work of Braverman (1974) what was now implied was a form of structural change through which, within capitalist societies, employment of all kinds tended to be 'deskilled' and 'degraded', so that a steady expansion occurred in the proportion of proletarian—that is, of non-skilled, entirely subordinate—positions within the division of labour as a whole.

In other words, a direct contradiction was here involved of the liberal view that in the course of industrial development the structure of employment is progressively upgraded. Against the argument that such upgrading is the necessary consequence of technological advance, the new Marxist theory maintained that, under capitalism, work must be organized in such a way as to meet the requirements not simply of productive efficiency but further of the social control and economic exploitation of labour. Thus, the possibility of using new technology and managerial methods in order to remove skill, and in turn autonomy and discretion, from the mass of employees and to concentrate them in the hands of their own agents is one that employers will seek always to realize.

Clearly, then, to the extent that this argument could be upheld, key liberal claims would be invalidated—that industrial societies become increasingly 'middle class', that mobility shows an upward bias, that the need to develop resources as fully as possible encourages a greater equality of opportunity. Rather, the contention was that the 'logic' of capitalist industrialism destroys skill at all levels of employment, and thus, especially in the case of white-

[8] See, e.g., Johnson (1977). A cogent critique of the treatment of social action in 'structuralist' Marxism can be found in Lockwood (1981).

collar workers, generates large-scale downward mobility of a collective kind and, in turn, a society in which wage labour is the fate of a growing majority.[9] In Braverman's words:

The problem of the so-called employee or white-collar worker which so bothered earlier generations of Marxists, and which was hailed by anti-Marxists as proof of the falsity of the 'proletarianization' thesis, has thus been unambiguously clarified by the polarization of office employment and the growth at one pole of an immense mass of *wage-workers*. The apparent trend to a large nonproletarian 'middle class' has resolved itself into the creation of a large proletariat in a new form. (1974: 355; cf. also Carchedi 1977: 73)

In fact, though, while the new theory of proletarianization lacked nothing in the vigour of its expression, to provide it with a convincing empirical basis was, and has remained, a major difficulty.

Such evidence as could be produced in favour of Braverman's original 'deskilling' thesis came from case-studies of particular enterprises. But such studies were of little relevance to the question of the direction of change in the structure of employment as a whole. Liberal theorists had never sought to deny that new technologies and managerial practices did in many instances eliminate skills: the case for upgrading turned on *net* effects, and could thus be judged only on the basis of data that related to the entire economy. Moreover, such data in the form of national census statistics have consistently lent support to the liberal, and contradicted the Marxist, position. In all economically advanced nations, the tendency is for the proportion of the work-force in professional, administrative, and managerial occupations to rise, while the proportion in occupations at the lowest skill levels, both manual and non-manual, either remains stable or falls. In addition, there is little indication from survey findings of a widening experience of 'degraded' work: where trend data are available, these show employees reporting higher levels of work-related education and training, and work-tasks that are more demanding mentally, if not physically (see, esp., Åberg 1984, 1987; also Gallie 1988).

In the face of such evidence, one sophisticated attempt was made at 'saving' the proletarianization theory which is worthy of further note—not least because of its eventual outcome. Wright and Singelmann (1982) correctly observed that the trends indicated by official statistics *could* come about through changes taking place in the structure of employment at the societal level which were independent of changes in the actual organization

---

[9] It could then also be argued that, where rising upward mobility was apparently demonstrated in survey-based enquiries, much of this was illusory, since the professional, administrative, and managerial positions to which such mobility was seen as leading would themselves often be degraded—i.e. entirely routinized and subordinated—and thus only nominally comparable to such positions in previous periods. See, e.g., Crompton (1980) and, for a reply, Goldthorpe (1980*b*).

of production. Thus, the increasing proportion of professionals, administrators, and managers could be the result largely, or entirely, of the growth of industries—for example, service industries—in which such occupations had always been more prominent than in industries now in decline. Consequently, it was possible that, behind the masking effect of these inter-industry shifts, the 'degrading' of labour was indeed occurring at the level of actual factories and offices. Wright and Singelmann were able to present analyses of data for the United States in the 1960s that at least kept this possibility alive, and they anticipated that evidence of proletarianization would be more readily apparent once data were available for the period after the ending of the 'long boom' of the post-war years.

However, in later papers these same authors have reported that exactly the opposite to what they had expected proves to be the case (Singelmann and Tienda 1985; Wright and Martin 1987). Further analyses of US data extending to 1980 rather decisively show that overall changes in the structure of employment *cannot* be accounted for simply in terms of inter-industry shifts, but must be seen as resulting also from technological, organizational, and other changes which in fact *up*grade the occupational 'mix' *within* production units. And essentially similar results, it may be added, have also been produced for several Western European nations (see, e.g., Gershuny 1983; Marshall and Rose 1988). Thus, the failure of the proletarianization theory has come to be recognized even by those who have been its most resourceful defenders. Wright and Martin conclude that 'it is quite problematic to claim that a process of sustained and systematic proletarianization exists in advanced capitalist countries', and that indeed 'these countries are likely to witness a continued expansion of nonproletarian locations in their class structures' (1987: 25).[10]

If, then, the theory can still claim any vitality, it would appear to be in only one, quite restricted, version: that is, as applying specifically to *women* workers. Braverman himself saw the growth of women's employment—in largely deskilled work—as offsetting the tendency for the numbers of male manual workers to fall, and as thus preserving working-class organizational potential. Subsequently, a somewhat similar argument has been taken up by *marxisant* feminist authors (e.g. West 1978; Crompton and Jones 1984; Stanworth 1984) who have seen the channelling of the new cohorts of women workers into degraded jobs as leading to the formation of a new *female* proletariat, even while increasing numbers of men, who have been the main beneficiaries of upgrading, may be found in higher-level white-collar positions. Overall, though, it is clear enough that the Marxist attempt to provide a viable alternative to the liberal perspective on issues of stratification and mobility has lost its force. The claim of a general upgrading

[10] A Marxist interpretation of this situation is preserved in that it is seen as an aspect of the 'globalization' of capital—one consequence of which is that advanced capitalist nations increasingly locate their proletariats in the Third World rather than within their own frontiers.

in employment may not be one that can withstand all qualification (see further Goldthorpe 1991*b*); none the less, it has sufficient empirical support to prevent it from being simply stood on its head, as its Marxist opponents sought in effect to do.[11] If, therefore, we hope to find responses to the liberal theory of industrialism that can more usefully inform our analyses of mobility rates and patterns, we must move on from Marxist efforts to consider a number of other more plausible, if more eclectic, positions.

THEORIES OF CROSS-NATIONAL VARIATION IN MOBILITY

Under this heading we outline a number of arguments concerning mobility in industrial societies which stand in opposition, implicit or explicit, to those found in the liberal theory in the emphasis that they give to cross-national differences in mobility rates. According to the liberal theory, some such differences are in fact to be expected—but only in so far as nations have attained different levels of industrialism. Specifically, more advanced societies should show higher rates of mobility and greater openness than those less advanced, but the latter should, in this as in other respects, steadily converge in their development on the model which the former already approximate. In contrast, it has from several different standpoints been maintained that either particular industrial societies or industrial societies of a certain type are distinctive in their mobility patterns, and on account of factors which have little to do with their developmental stage or which, at all events, have proved highly resistant to the effects of economic change.

Such claims, it might be added, are not always ones derived from elaborated theoretical positions, but in some cases take more the form of *ad hoc* hypotheses. None the less, what all in some degree reflect is a scepticism concerning the operation, or at least the cogency, of the functional 'logic' of industrialism, on which, as we have sought to show, the liberal theory depends. If such a logic is at work at all, then, it is implied, it is one that faces countervailing forces and can be overridden by them. Two such forces are chiefly invoked: culture and politics. Thus, one set of arguments stresses the persisting effect that may be exerted on mobility, despite the progress of industrialism, by aspects of national culture, historically formed and expressed both in popular beliefs and values and in national institutions. A second set reverses the causal primacy that is supposed by the liberal theory and, instead of seeing industrialism as ultimately requiring a liberal democratic

---

[11] It should, moreover, be noted that, in order to sustain a serious proletarianization theory, whether restricted to women workers or not, more than just evidence of the degrading of work is required. Data on, precisely, the mobility of individuals is also needed. It has to be shown *both* that degraded jobs are held by individuals 'forced down' from more advantaged positions *and* that these individuals then have little chance of escaping from such jobs. It would in fact appear that for many workers, men and women, in lower-grade non-manual jobs especially, one or other of these conditions does not apply. Cf. Stewart, Prandy, and Blackburn (1980), Goldthorpe (1985*a*), Prandy (1986).

polity, asserts that other forms of polity can coexist with industrialism and may, moreover, impose a distinctive shape on industrial societies that is expressed in their stratification and mobility patterns. We may usefully consider these two kinds of argument in turn.

The culturalist position has in fact been adopted most often in support of claims of national 'exceptionalism'. The paradigm case here is, of course, provided by the long-standing argument that the industrial society that has emerged in the United States is of a distinctively more mobile and open kind than that found in the older nations of Europe. While Marx saw high rates of mobility in the United States of the mid-nineteenth century as a transient phenomenon which would fade once the frontier was closed and large-scale industrial enterprise developed, a succession of other commentators have taken their lead rather from Tocqueville and have viewed American society, and its form of stratification in particular, as being *sui generis*. The absence of a feudal tradition, the rejection of deference in interpersonal relations, the generalization of ambition, and the pervasive influence of the 'American Dream' of material success—all these have been seen as aspects of the American way of life which promote unusually high levels of mobility.[12] It is of interest to note that even Blau and Duncan, despite their support for the liberal theory and their insistence that high rates of mobility in the United States are to be understood essentially as a consequence of advanced industrialism rather than of the peculiarities of American history, still cannot entirely resist the attractions of the exceptionalist stance. At least in one respect—the openness of élite positions and the amount of upward mobility of a 'long-range' kind—they raise the possibility that the United States *is* in fact distinctive, and thus that 'there is a grain of truth in the Horatio Alger myth' (1967: 435).[13]

There are, however, various other cases that could be cited of national societies being represented as exceptional in the mobility opportunities that they offer on account of a favourable—that is, in some sense or other, egalitarian—culture that has been created in specific historical circumstances. Thus, Australia, as Encel (1970) and others have noted, has often been taken as a case comparable to that of the United States of a 'new' society which from its origins was free of traditional barriers to mobility, which attracted individuals in search of opportunity, and which has in some degree been able to preserve the egalitarian ethos of its pioneering days. Again, within the European context, Scotland has been widely regarded, among native commentators at least, as having developed a precocious, pre-industrial form of meritocracy which continued to produce a distinctive degree of social fluidity, at all events until compromised by external, namely

---

[12] These and other arguments concerning US—and also Australian—exceptionalism are considered at greater length in Chapter 9.

[13] Horatio Alger (1834–99) was a prolific author of children's books in which the hero 'made good' against the odds. But there is in fact a good deal of myth about the myth (see Wohl 1953).

English, influences (cf. Maclaren 1976; McCrone, Bechhofer, and Kendrick 1982; Gray, McPherson, and Raffe 1983: pt. 2). And, finally, it may be noted that, more recently, the FRG has become represented as a nation of distinctive openness (see, e.g., Ardagh 1988: 145–6) on account, it is believed, of the major cultural *disjuncture* that followed from the Second World War and its aftermath: that is, the destruction of the former sharply defined status order of German society and its hierarchical institutional forms and the emergence of a new 'ethos of democratic equality enshrined in the Constitution'.

Rather less common are cases where exceptionalism is claimed in the opposite sense—that is, of a society displaying unusually restricted mobility. However, one instance at least may be noted. Olson (1982: esp. 82–7, 143–5) has suggested that, while in the period of its early industrialization Britain possessed a more open form of society than that characteristic of continental Europe, by the present time the situation is reversed and Britain is now excep-tionally 'sclerotic'. This reversal is attributable, in Olson's view, to the relative tranquillity of modern British history. While on the Continent—as the German case can well illustrate—pre-industrial cultural patterns and associated institutions have been effectively destroyed by two centuries of revolution, war, totalitarianism, military defeat, and enemy occupation, the 'unique stability of British life since the early eighteenth century' has allowed many pre-industrial values and attitudes to remain more or less unchanged and, in addition, has permitted a long-term build-up of defensive associations and restrictive practices on the part of more privileged groups and strata. In this connection, Olson refers, for example, to the dominant influence at the higher levels of the British educational system of the 'public' schools and ancient universities and to the degree of control that both professional bodies and craft unions are able to exercise over recruitment procedures.

Olson's hypothesis of British exceptionalism is of particular interest in that it does derive from, or at least is an extension of, a more general theory of 'social rigidities'.[14] It thus poses a potentially stronger challenge to the liberal theory than arguments for exceptionalism which entail no more than the invocation of cultural specificities and which then, in their very nature, invite accommodation as referring simply to 'deviant' cases. Although Olson has much in common with liberal theorists in believing that the

---

[14] Olson's central concern is in fact with the rigidities in the operation of markets that result from various forms of collective action on the part of unions, cartels, professional and trade associations, etc., and which, in his view, undermine the standards of performance of national economies. In extending his theory to restrictions on mobility, he recognizes that it does not cover all factors that are at work here—for example, the association between the positions of parents and children created by the intergenerational transmission of capital, human and otherwise. None the less, he would still wish to see rigidities of the kind that the theory does address as contributing importantly to what he takes to be the distinctive impermeability of the British class structure.

efficient operation of a modern economy implies a high level of mobility and openness, he does not share their conviction that the requirements of efficiency must always prevail. His starting-point is in fact with the observation that industrial societies show widely varying standards of economic performance. Rather than being impressed by the force of some inherent functional logic of industrialism, Olson seeks to show how individuals and collectivities are always likely to resist change and to act in pursuit of their own interests in ways that, whether intended or not, promote immobility and other kinds of social rigidity that are damaging to the welfare of society as a whole. No developmental tendency can be assumed through which such problems will be automatically reduced. On the contrary, the mere passage of time will, in the absence of disrupting factors, simply allow cultural patterns to become entrenched and rigidities to accumulate and intensify. Under Olson's theory, Britain is thus an exceptional case because an extreme one—in that in modern British history so little in the way of social disruption has occurred.

Turning now to arguments which see cross-national variation in social mobility as resulting from political factors, we may begin with the response that has emerged to the views of liberal theorists on mobility in state socialist societies. In this respect, the most considered and detailed position, so far as post-war Eastern European nations are concerned, is that developed by Parkin (1969, 1971*a*: chs. 5 and 6; 1971*b*; cf. also Giddens 1973: ch. 12).[15]

To an extent, Parkin would accept that the processes of social selection typical of the period of 'socialist reconstruction' were later modified, as ideological considerations became outweighed by those of technological and economic rationality. Thus, it might well be misleading to claim a distinctive state socialist pattern of mobility on the evidence of such heroic periods alone. However, Parkin would still maintain that the influence on mobility of persisting ideological and institutional differences between socialist and capitalist societies is underestimated in the liberal theory, and that there are in fact good grounds for believing that mobility patterns in the two types of society have in fact remained differentiated in some degree throughout the post-war era.

Most obviously, under socialist regimes the direct intergenerational transmission of property and accumulated wealth must play a far less important part in determining chances of mobility—or immobility—than under capitalism. Not only is the private ownership of property, whether productive or otherwise, tightly controlled, but, further, the 'new men' who make their way into professional, administrative, and managerial positions have to do so more exclusively than their counterparts in the West on the basis of their

---

[15] The fact that, at the time of writing, state socialist regimes in most Eastern European nations have collapsed or appear about to do so does not detract from the significance of the historical experience of these nations for sociological analysis—although it may well of course affect just what that significance is taken to be.

'cultural' capital—which is then far less surely transmissible to the next generation than capital of a more conventional kind. The 'intelligentsia' of socialist societies thus represents a relatively more permeable upper stratum than the 'bourgeoisie' or 'middle class' of capitalist societies.

In addition, Parkin would maintain that, largely for ideological reasons, state socialist regimes created a significantly different reward system from that generated under capitalism. In particular, a much greater overlap was established between the incomes and living standards of manual and non-manual workers. Several consequences for mobility then follow. To begin with, the children of manual and non-manual workers compete on a more equal basis so far as the material resources of their families are concerned. And, further, they are likely to have more comparable levels of ambition: socialist societies display in this respect far less 'normative differentiation' along class lines than do capitalist ones. Thus, the aspiring children of manual workers will not, as often occurs in the West, seek merely to enter lower-level non-manual employment—since this could scarcely count as advancement—but will, rather, aim for higher education and positions within the intelligentsia. In sum, then, there is for Parkin one quite specific way in which mobility rates under state socialism and capitalism could be expected to diverge and, on his reading of the evidence, have indeed done so: while in capitalist societies mobility is found to be predominantly 'short range', in socialist societies it has more often implied 'large-scale movements across the entire range of the reward hierarchy, not merely the interchange of personnel at the class margins' (1971a: 157).

Finally, in this connection it may also be noted that, although Parkin himself remained somewhat ambivalent on the question of the long-term future of state socialist regimes, other authors were ready to see in the distinctive mobility pattern to which he pointed a major source of their stability—in this way, of course, further controverting the liberal view. Thus, according to Bauman (1971) and Johnson (1981), for example, the extensive recruitment of peasants and workers—and of their children—into the bureaucracies of the police, the security forces, local government, and large industrial enterprises, as well as of the Party, served to create a widespread sense of achievement *made possible by* the regime. In other words, the generation of satisfaction with, and support for, the prevailing order as a result of upward mobility is not to be thought of as a process confined to the liberal democracies; regimes of a quite different political character can also benefit from it, and indeed perhaps to a greater extent if they are better able to promote such mobility.[16]

---

[16] Bauman's paper triggered a lively debate. A strongly opposing view is to be found in Kolakowski (1971). The demise of Eastern European socialist regimes, it should be said, does not necessarily mean that arguments such as those of Bauman and Johnson were entirely mistaken. Several commentators have regarded the failure of these regimes, from around the mid-1970s onwards, to *maintain* the previous high level of mobility opportunities as one factor

So far as the possibility of 'politically induced' variation in mobility is concerned, it is undoubtedly in regard to state socialist societies that the strongest challenge to the liberal theory has been mounted. However, the further issue has been raised of whether such variation is not also apparent among capitalist societies. In effect, this issue turns on the experience of those nations—Sweden and Norway being the leading examples—in which social democratic parties became politically dominant in the post-war years and have pursued a range of policies specifically aimed at the reduction of the social inequalities that are produced by the operation of a 'free-market' economy (cf. Esping Andersen 1985; Erikson et al. 1987).

Parkin's work (1971a: ch. 4) is again of relevance here. The extent of inequality in capitalist societies—for example, in the distribution of incomes—varies sufficiently widely, he maintains, to confirm doubts about the cogency of any logic of industrialism and to suggest that significant scope may exist for political intervention. However, he further argues that, when in government, social democratic parties are more attracted to a 'meritocratic' version of socialism, emphasizing equality of opportunity—and entirely compatible with the prevailing form of economy—than to more radical versions emphasizing equality of condition. He would, therefore, expect that societies in which social democratic parties have been dominant will show a somewhat greater degree of openness than others—chiefly in fact as a result of their more egalitarian educational policies; and, in his assessment, this expectation is borne out so far as the available evidence goes. In Parkin's view, one might then say, a difference is created because social democrats have a more serious commitment to the logic of industrialism—or of capitalism—than do their conservative opponents.

A rather stronger position has been adopted by Stephens (1979: esp. ch. 4), with reference primarily to the Swedish case. Stephens accepts the attractiveness of 'mobility politics' to social democratic governments, but sees no serious problem in the goals of greater equality of opportunity and greater equality of condition being pursued together. Indeed, these goals are complementary: greater openness requires greater equality among individuals and families in the resources they can command and, once achieved, should itself imply greater distributional equality as a result of the removal of restrictions on the supply side of the labour market. In Stephens's view, the evidence suggests that where, as in Sweden, a social democratic government has been able to act in concert with a strong, centralized labour movement, the possibility arises of integrating macroeconomic, labour-market, and social policies in such a way as to create a form of democratic socialist society that is more open and equal, and thus more rational in its functioning, than that of liberal capitalism.

that undermined their legitimacy and encouraged support for oppositional movements. See, e.g., Wesołowski and Mach (1986) and Garton Ash (1989).

In conclusion, then, one might say that the arguments reviewed in this section have all, in one way or another, implied criticism of the liberal theory for being too simplified and over-general; or, in other words, for lacking sensitivity to the range of factors, and especially ones of a cultural and political kind, that can shape the extent and pattern of mobility within a society, even if one launched into industrialism. However, this is not the only possible line of attack. In the following section we turn to arguments which could be taken, rather, to suggest that the liberal theory is *in*sufficiently generalized—that it attaches too great an importance to the distinctiveness of industrial society or at all events to its supposed developmental tendencies.

THEORIES OF 'NO TREND' AND OF CROSS-NATIONAL SIMILARITY IN MOBILITY

Under the liberal theory, as we have remarked, cross-national variation in mobility is to be expected along one particular dimension: societies should show greater mobility and openness the further their industrial development has proceeded. What is perhaps not always appreciated is the extent to which, when first advanced, this view marked a departure from prevailing opinion. Not only did it constitute a quite explicit challenge to Marxist orthodoxy but, at the same time, it went contrary to the position represented in the one major academic treatise on social mobility then extant, that of Sorokin (1927/1959)—in which a highly critical stance was adopted towards *all* unilinear evolutionary or developmental theories of stratification and mobility, whether Marxist or otherwise. In this section we first outline Sorokin's position and then go on to consider more recent arguments that have some degree of affinity with it.

Sorokin's approach to his subject was above all a synoptic one, dependent as much on historical and ethnographic materials as on the results of contemporary social research. In the light of his assembled evidence, he was led to the conclusion that in modern Western societies mobility was at a relatively high level, and he was further ready to acknowledge the possibility that, from the eighteenth century onwards, mobility rates had in general shown a tendency to rise. However, he was at the same time much concerned to reject the idea—which, he believed, was stimulated by 'the dynamism of our age'—that what was here manifested was in effect 'the end of history' and the start of a 'perpetual and "eternal" increase of vertical mobility'. Rather, Sorokin argued, once ethnocentrism was set aside, the only view possible was that the present situation represented no more than a specific historical phase; in some societies in some periods mobility increased, while in other periods it declined. Overall, no 'definite perpetual trend' was to be seen towards either greater or less mobility, but only 'trendless fluctuation'. Those who were impressed by the distinctiveness of the modern era knew too little about historical societies and their diversity: 'What has been happening is only an alternation—the waves of greater mobility superseded by the cycles of greater immobility—and that is all' (1927/1959: 152–4).

It might from the foregoing appear that Sorokin's position was merely negative. But, in fact, underlying his denial of developmental trends in mobility and his preference for a cyclical view, at least the elements of a theory can be discerned. In arguing against the supposition that rates of mobility in the modern period are quite unprecedented, one of the points Sorokin most stresses is that, while certain barriers to mobility have been largely removed—for example, juridical and religious ones—it is important to recognize that other barriers have become more severe or have been newly introduced—for example, those represented by systems of educational selection and occupational qualification (1927/1959: 153–4, 169–79). This, moreover, is what must always be expected. Sorokin, one could say, never overlooked the fact that the forms of social stratification which provide the context for mobility are themselves structures expressing differential power and advantage, and thus possess important self-maintaining properties. Those who hold privileged positions will not readily cede them and, in the nature of the case, can draw on superior resources in their defence. Indeed, Sorokin remarks that, if he *had* to believe in the existence of a permanent trend in mobility, it would be in a declining one, since social strata are often observed to become more 'closed' over time as the cumulative result of those in superior positions using their power and advantage to restrict entry from below (1927/1959: 158–60). However, this propensity for closure, which we may understand as being *endogenous* to all forms of stratification, is not the only influence on mobility rates. A further point that Sorokin several times makes (see, e.g., 1927/1959: 141–52, 466–72) is that in periods of both political and economic upheaval—associated, say, with revolution or war or with rapid commercial, industrial, and technological change—marked surges in mobility are typically produced as the social structure as a whole, including the previously existing distribution of power and advantage, is disrupted. In other words, increased mobility here results from the impact of factors that are *exogenous* to the stratification order.

In effect, then, Sorokin does indicate a way—though he never sets it out systematically—in which the trendless fluctuation in mobility rates that he believes must be empirically accepted might actually be produced: periods of relative social stability in which the inherent tendency for stratification to become more rigid is unimpeded are punctuated by bursts of increased mobility and openness occurring in times of social uncertainty and dislocation. This implicit theory might appear as a forerunner of that of Olson, to which we have previously referred; but, while similarities exist, they are in fact rather superficial,[17] and it is other positions represented by contemporary authors that stand in a more direct line of descent.

[17] As earlier remarked (see n. 14 above), Olson concentrates his attention on the creation—and removal—of rigidities associated with collective action via 'special-interest' organizations

More or less contemporaneously with the development of the liberal theory, Lipset and Zetterberg (1956, 1959) took up what they saw as the urgent task of reappraising the sociology of mobility in the light of the new empirical materials produced in the post-war years. Their starting-point was a rejection of the idea of American exceptionalism. The evidence now available, they argued, made it clear that the level of mobility found in the United States was not substantially different from that observed in a number of European nations. Sorokin would seem to have been correct (cf. 1959: 443 ff.) in maintaining that all modern Western societies show relatively high mobility rates, and that the United States is in no way unusual. The main conclusion to which Lipset and Zetterberg were eventually led was in fact that, across the nations of the Western industrial world, 'the overall pattern of social mobility appears to be much the same' (1959: 13). In this way, they then went beyond Sorokin in two main respects: first, in suggesting that Western societies not only had high, but further similarly high, mobility rates; and, secondly, in wishing to speak of these societies as being 'industrial' and to regard their high mobility as a specific feature of their industrialization. In consequence of this latter view, their position has often been assimilated to that of the liberal theorists;[18] but it is important that a number of major differences are recognized.

To begin with, Lipset and Zetterberg, unlike liberal theorists, do not seek to argue that mobility steadily *increases with* industrial development. Indeed they remark that, among industrial societies, there does not appear to be any association between mobility rates and rates of economic growth. They should rather be understood as proposing a 'threshold' effect as they write, 'our tentative interpretation is that the social mobility of societies becomes relatively high once their industrialization, and hence their economic expansion, reaches a certain level' (1959: 13). Lipset and Zetterberg in fact draw attention to the high rates of mobility that appear already to have prevailed in many Western societies from the end of the nineteenth century, and that are found at least in the urban centres of presently 'developing' nations (1959: 28–38). In other words, the suggestion is that the threshold at which mobility rises comes rather early in the industrialization process.

Again, it is necessary to recognize that Lipset and Zetterberg are concerned specifically with mobility and not with openness—or equality of mobility chances. They are at pains to point out that 'the fact that one country contains a greater percentage of mobile individuals than another does *not*

rather than on rigidities resulting directly from the actions of individuals and families under the influence of motivations and constraints implicit in the phenomenon of social stratification itself. For perceptive comments on the way in which Sorokin's interest in mobility processes centres precisely on competition among individuals and families and on 'the chances of a given group *relative* to other groups', see Carlsson (1963).

[18] Thus, Kerr himself (1983: 53) apparently wishes to regard Lipset's and Zetterberg's work on mobility as being supportive of his own position.

mean that that country approximates a model of equal opportunity more closely' (1959: 27); and it is not part of their case that the high mobility that is characteristic of industrial societies reflects greater openness or that openness tends to increase. In this respect, it may also be noted that, although, like the liberal theorists, Lipset and Zetterberg have an interest in the effects of mobility on political action, this is not primarily with the way in which popular recognition of greater openness furthers the stability of democratic institutions. It is, rather, with how the actual *occurrence* of mobility—whatever its causation or its direction—may be socially disruptive and psychologically damaging, and thus a possible source of anti-democratic political extremism of either a left-wing *or* a right-wing kind.[19]

Finally, not only do Lipset and Zetterberg make far more limited empirical claims about mobility trends than do liberal theorists; they also pursue a quite different explanatory approach. For them, observed mobility rates can be largely accounted for in terms of just two factors—the 'structural' and the 'motivational'. The former is, on a broad historical view, the variable factor. The objective opportunities for mobility will be greater or less depending on the degree of differentiation of the social division of labour, its rate and pattern of change, the proportion of positions within it to which access is not formally restricted, and the degree of competition for available positions as determined by demographic trends. The second factor is a constant one. Lipset and Zetterberg maintain that every form of social stratification, industrial or otherwise, generates similar mobility motivations. This is because the positions that individuals hold within the stratification order are reflected in their self-evaluations; consequently, they strive to protect their positions, if these are at all advantaged, in order to protect their egos and, likewise, to improve their positions in order to enhance their egos (cf. 1956: 162–3; 1959: 57–64).

From this standpoint, therefore, Lipset and Zetterberg can explain the similarly high rates of mobility which, in their view, all Western industrial societies display, simply by saying that the structural changes associated with industrialization produce a similar expansion of opportunities for social advancement, and that ever-present mobility motivations then ensure that these opportunities are taken up. They have no need to invoke the functional exigencies of industrialism as a source of increased—and continually increasing—mobility, nor to attach explanatory importance in this respect to the impact of industrialism on goals, values, and norms. Given their view that mobility motivations are located 'in the realm of more or less universal egoneeds operating within stratified societies' (1956: 163), they are sceptical of the relevance of all culturalist explanations of mobility, whether advanced in

---

[19] This concern is developed in Lipset's work with Bendix (1959: esp. ch. x) and in much of his own subsequent political sociology. For further discussion see Goldthorpe (1980a/1987: 17–20).

order to account for supposedly exceptional cases or within the context of developmental scenarios.[20]

The affinity with Sorokin's position is thus twofold. Like Sorokin, Lipset and Zetterberg prefer to regard the high levels of mobility evident in modern societies as expressing a historic shift rather than a permanent trend that is in some way generated by the very functioning of these societies. And, again like Sorokin, they recognize, through their distinction between structural and motivational factors, influences on mobility that are both exogenous and endogenous to the phenomenon of social stratification itself—and in turn, then, influences that make both for change and variation in mobility rates *and* for constancy and similarity.

From the time it was first advanced, the LZ hypothesis (as we shall term it) that the overall pattern of mobility in Western industrial societies is 'much the same' was taken as a point of reference for further comparative analyses. In the event, however, these analyses for the most part failed to provide confirmatory results. Thus, Miller (1960), working with much of the same data as Lipset and Zetterberg but applying somewhat more refined methods of comparison, was able to endorse their position only with very heavy qualification; and Jones (1969) pointed to serious deficiencies in Lipset's and Zetterberg's treatment of their data which, once corrected, made cross-national variation a good deal more apparent. Furthermore, the existence of such variation has been quite consistently revealed in studies that have been able to draw on the findings of more recent national mobility enquiries and that have also introduced higher standards of data comparability (see, e.g., Broom and Jones 1969; Featherman, Jones, and Hauser 1975; Erikson, Goldthorpe, and Portocarero 1979, 1983; Pöntinen 1983).[21]

Thus, while Lipset himself (1982) would still seem to find the LZ hypothesis valid, and indeed extendible to state socialist societies, the more generally accepted view would now be that, among industrial—or even capitalist—nations, far from negligible differences do exist in (to use Miller's term) their 'mobility profiles'. Perhaps the most obvious source of the difficulties that the hypothesis has encountered lies in the fact that, contrary to what Lipset and Zetterberg need to assume (cf. 1959: 73), structural effects may produce generally higher rates of mobility at a certain level of industrialization *without* thereby creating mobility rates that follow a similar pattern in all societies that have reached this level. In particular, it is relevant to note the ample evidence of wide variation in the employment and occupational structures of industrial nations and in the rate and phasing of

---

[20] The importance of cultural variation, Lipset and Zetterberg would argue, lies rather in the different values and interpretations that may be attached to mobility across societies whose actual rates are similar—for it is via these subjective responses that the political consequences of mobility are necessarily mediated.

[21] The few comparative analyses that could be held to lend some support to the LZ hypothesis were all of earlier date than those referred to in the text. Perhaps the most influential was that by Svalastoga (1965), which, however, referred to Western European nations only.

their development (see, e.g., OECD 1970–1; Garnsey 1975; Gagliani, 1985). For the expectation must then be—and especially if constant mobility motivations are to be supposed—that this structural variation will be closely reflected in variation in mobility flows.

The cumulation of empirical results damaging to the LZ hypothesis has not, however, been without more positive outcome. Most notably, Featherman, Jones, and Hauser (1975) have attempted a reformulation of the hypothesis that has attracted considerable interest. Their argument is that the claim of cross-national similarity should be taken as applying not at the 'phenotypical' level of actually observed mobility rates but rather at the 'genotypical' level of the pattern of relative mobility chances that underlies these rates. If mobility is considered at the former level, cross-national similarity can scarcely be anticipated—precisely because observed rates are greatly influenced by the structure of the division of labour, and in turn by effects deriving from a range of economic, technological, and demographic circumstances, which are known to vary and which, so far as particular individuals and families are concerned, must be regarded as 'exogenously determined'. If, however, mobility is considered net of all such effects, the likelihood of cross-national similarity being found becomes much greater. For at this level only those factors are involved that bear on the relative chances of individuals of differing social origin achieving or avoiding, in competition with each other, particular destination positions among those that are structurally given; and there is reason to suppose that in modern societies the conditions under which such endogenous 'mobility regimes' operate may not show wide variation. Most importantly, there is evidence that the organization of work activities and resultant occupational hierarchies show a large degree of cross-national commonality—which is, in turn, reflected in broad similarities in both the desirability or prestige of different occupational groupings and their objective 'socio-economic' attributes: for example, in educational and income relativities. Thus, Featherman, Jones, and Hauser would propose replacing the LZ hypothesis with one which claims that, assuming a market economy and (at a minimum) a nuclear family system, it is the pattern of 'genotypical' mobility, in the above sense, that will in all industrial societies prove to be 'basically the same' (1975: 340).[22]

In the light of what has earlier been said, the FJH hypothesis might in fact be regarded as an updating of Sorokin's position as much as a restatement of Lipset's and Zetterberg's; and, in one respect, it is without doubt closer to the former. The factors endogenous to the stratification of industrial societies

[22] The theoretical arguments underlying the hypothesis are unfortunately not developed at any great length and several important issues are left open. Thus, our indication in the text that the condition of a nuclear family is a minimum one—i.e. in a society where extended families were the norm, the hypothesis would be taken to apply *a fortiori*—is based on personal communication with Frank Lancaster Jones and Robert Hauser.

that create similarity in their mobility regimes are taken to operate through social, and not only psychological, processes: that is, through processes of competition among individuals and families with differing socio-economic resources rather than simply through personal attempts at satisfying ego-needs.

However, the more important point, for present purposes at least, is that it is now the FJH rather than the LZ hypothesis that poses the serious challenge to the claims of the liberal theorists. On the one hand, so far as observed mobility rates are concerned, it implies a basic scepticism about the possibility of *any* long-term, developmentally driven trend; while, on the other hand, it stands directly opposed to the proposition that under indus-trialism a steady increase in openness occurs. Although some initial develop-mental effect in this direction early in the industrialization process might be compatible with the hypothesis, any continuing change in relative mobility chances is clearly precluded (cf. Grusky and Hauser 1984: 20). In other words, once societies can be deemed to have become industrial, their mobility regimes should stabilize in some approximation to the common pattern, and should not thereafter reveal any specific or persistent tendencies, whether towards convergence on greater openness or otherwise. No forces inherent in industrialism which work to transform the pattern of mobility opportunities are recognized.

At the same time, the FJH hypothesis does, of course, also come into conflict, to some degree or other, with most of the positions that were considered in the previous section. Thus, while the argument from which the hypothesis stems would indeed lead to an expectation of cross-national variation at the level of observed mobility rates, it suggests no reason for this variation to be in any way *systematic*—that is, to be correlated with particular types of industrial society as might be defined in economic, cultural, or political terms. Rather, given the diversity of the exogenous factors that are seen to be involved, *all* nations might well be in some degree 'exceptional'—or, that is, show certain distinctive features in the mobility rates that they display.[23]

Moreover, as regards relative mobility chances, there is an evident tension between the FJH hypothesis and the suggestion that capitalist societies in which social democratic parties have achieved political domin-ance may be more open than others. The common mobility regime that the hypothesis proposes has obviously to be understood as one that is highly resistant to change—being modifiable in an egalitarian direction only if significant alteration can be made in the occupational and associated

---

[23] Grusky and Hauser (1984) call for research into the factors influencing cross-national differences in structural effects on mobility, since—if the FJH hypothesis is accepted—it is these that are the immediate source of most cross-national variation in observed rates. However, they make no suggestions as to what theoretical expectations might guide such research.

socio-economic hierarchies that are characteristic of capitalism. Thus, from the standpoint of the FJH hypothesis, it must be expected that, if social democratic governments pursue merely the kind of 'mobility politics' that Parkin would see as typical, they will in fact achieve little; while more radical programmes of the kind envisaged by Stephens, which aim at reducing inequalities of opportunity and condition together, will encounter problems of economic as well as of political viability.[24]

Finally, in this connection the issue must arise of whether the FJH hypothesis is applicable to state socialist societies. As initially presented, it would seem rather clearly restricted to the capitalist world or, at least, to those societies that have market economies. However, Featherman, Jones, and Hauser conclude (1975: 358) by suggesting the possibility that the hypothesis might be extended to non-capitalist societies, and this suggestion has subsequently been taken up by Grusky and Hauser (1984). If the hypothesis is well founded, what should in fact follow is that, in so far as in state socialist societies links between occupational and socio-economic hierarchies correspond to those of capitalist societies, a similar distribution of relative mobility chances will occur—regardless of how market-oriented their economies might be. Thus, if it is the case that, in the 'secondary stage' of socialist development, egalitarian ideologies and policies aimed at creating a different social order to that of capitalism have been abandoned, then any deviations that might have emerged from the mobility regime generic to Western societies should subsequently be reduced. In this particular respect, therefore, the FJH hypothesis would become aligned with the liberal theory in implying a degree of 'convergence', as against a persistingly distinctive socialist mobility pattern. What would permit such a *rapprochement*, one might say, is the refusal embodied in the liberal theory and the FJH hypothesis alike to allow to political action the capacity to achieve any substantial and lasting modification of social processes which are grounded in the industrial form of the division of labour and in the inequalities it generates—even though liberal theorists would see these processes as themselves evolving, while exponents of the FJH hypothesis are impressed rather by their constant features.

We come thus to the end of our review but, at the same time, to some questions that can scarcely be avoided. Most obviously: how is it that such a range of different, and often contradictory, arguments can persist in regard to issues which are, after all, in large part empirical ones? There are indeed certain positions which, as we have noted, have by now rather few defenders —for example, that taken up by Marxists aiming to revive the theory of proletarianization, or that of Lipset and Zetterberg on the cross-national

---

[24] At the same time, one might add, the FJH hypothesis must also imply scepticism as regards neo-Conservative thinking which supposes that both greater equality of opportunity and greater *in*equality of condition can be promoted simultaneously.

similarity of observed mobility rates. None the less, this still leaves us with large and, it would appear, long-standing areas of disagreement. Why should this be so? Why have not more of the contending claims been eliminated from serious discussion?

The answer is, we believe, that, while for several decades now high quality studies of social mobility have been carried out on a national basis, comparative work in the field has not, or not until quite recently, attained a similar level of methodological sophistication. Thus, in seeking to establish comparative results in order to test rival arguments, investigators have laboured under serious difficulties, the full extent of which, moreover, they seem not always to have appreciated. The national enquiries that have served as data sources were ones prompted by diverse theoretical and practical concerns, and conducted within often widely differing conceptual contexts. Consequently, the data they provide, at least in their published form, have been of such a limited degree of comparability that serious doubts must arise over whether any useful purpose at all can be served by bringing them together. In our judgement, even 'preliminary' conclusions based upon them would be as likely to mislead as to inform further enquiry.[25] In addition, advances that have been made in the course of national studies in techniques of data analysis have not always proved to be readily applicable in comparative work; and comparative analysis does in any event have its own distinctive problems which remain to be overcome—including ones which call for more than simply technical expertise.

In sum, then, the issues that we have surveyed have for the most part remained unresolved because we have not thus far had available anything like the quantity or *quality* of empirical evidence that would be required to subject them to serious examination. In this book we hope to contribute to making good this deficiency. If we are to do so, though, we must first of all devote a good deal of attention to the methodological problems to which we have alluded. This is our concern in the chapter that follows.

---

[25] We argue this point at greater length in the following chapter. However, we may note here that it is because of our radical doubts about the data they utilize that we have given little attention in this introductory chapter, or indeed elsewhere, to the *substantive* results reported in such studies of comparative mobility as Miller (1960), Cutright (1968), Hazelrigg (1974), Hazelrigg and Garnier (1976), Hardy and Hazelrigg (1978), Tyree, Semyonov, and Hodge (1979), McClendon (1980), Heath (1981), Grusky and Hauser (1984), Strmiska (1987), and Kelley (1990)—although we would certainly wish to recognize that several of these studies have made valuable contributions to the development of theory and technique from which we have ourselves benefited.

2
Concepts, Data, and Strategies
of Enquiry

In this chapter we consider a variety of methodological issues which range from ones of a quasi-philosophical character through to others of statistical technique. To some readers, our discussion of these issues may seem to constitute an excessively lengthy preamble to the treatment of the substantive matters that are of ultimate importance. If so, we must remain unrepentant. We do not believe that the way in which in a sociological study methodological problems are defined and resolved can be seen as simply a 'backstage' operation, to be reported on, if at all, only in the decent obscurity of an appendix. The treatment of methodological and of substantive problems is in fact often difficult to separate, and this should not be concealed. Moreover, as we have argued at the end of the previous chapter, the unsatisfactory state of comparative mobility research, as regards the persistence of large areas of disagreement on essentially empirical questions, has to be attributed largely to methodological difficulties, and there is then a particular need for these to be explicitly identified and addressed.

We begin the chapter with a discussion of the different conceptual contexts within which the study of social mobility may be undertaken, and we explain our decision to adopt a class-structural perspective. We then give an account of the class schema through which we have attempted to make this decision operational, and which provides the basis for the numerous mobility tables that we shall subsequently construct. From such problems of concepts and their representation, we move on to those of data and, most importantly, to those associated with achieving data of an adequate standard of cross-national comparability. We describe the approach that we have taken to these problems and the procedures that we have followed in constituting the data-set on which our empirical analyses rest. Our next concern is with analytical techniques. We seek to show why, following the conceptual approach that we have adopted, we may most appropriately work through the analysis of mobility tables, using—in addition to simple percentaging—techniques of log-linear modelling, and how in this way we can implement what is for us a crucial distinction between *absolute* and *relative* mobility rates. Finally, we take up large, yet highly consequential, issues of the methodology of comparative studies. We note the sharp divergencies of opinion and practice that here exist, and explain the 'combined' or 'mixed' strategy that we will ourselves attempt to follow.

THE CHOICE OF CONCEPTUAL CONTEXT

As will have become apparent enough from the previous chapter, the study of social mobility has been prompted by a range of different, and often conflicting, interests, socio-political as well as academic (see, further, Goldthorpe 1980*a*/1987: ch. 1). It is thus scarcely surprising to find a similarly wide range of variation in the conceptual approaches that have been followed by those actively engaged in investigating and analysing mobility. The most basic divergence which, as recounted elsewhere (Goldthorpe, 1985*a*), can be traced back to nineteenth-century origins, relates to the conceptual context within which mobility is to be defined and, in turn, observed and measured. Two main traditions can here be distinguished: one in which mobility is envisaged as occurring within a *class structure*, and the other in which it is envisaged as occurring within some form of *social hierarchy*. For those who follow the first tradition, mobility refers to the movement of individuals as between *social positions* that are identified in terms of relationships within labour markets and production units; for those who follow the second, mobility refers to the movement of individuals as between *social groupings or aggregates* that are ranked according to such criteria as their members' prestige, status, economic resources, etc.[1]

To be sure, particular mobility studies may not always neatly fall into one rather than the other of these two traditions. Some investigators appear to shift between a class-structural and a hierarchical context more or less unknowingly, while others have sought deliberately to work within both. However, what may be said is that in any study one conceptual approach or

---

[1] As regards the origins of these different conceptual traditions, a comparison of passages from Marx and John Stuart Mill is of interest. Marx, in one of the rather few instances in which he discusses social mobility directly, alludes to the ease with which in the United States of the mid-nineteenth century wage-labourers were able to turn themselves into 'independent self-sustaining peasants'—so that the position of wage-labourer was for the majority of those who occupied it 'but a probationary state which they are sure to leave within a longer or a shorter term' (1865/1958: 444). And what is then for Marx of chief significance about this mobility is not that it represents any form of social ascent—he makes no attempt to characterize it in 'vertical' terms—but rather that it serves to prevent what he elsewhere refers to as 'a developed formation of classes'. Because of the prevailing high rate of mobility, Marx argued, classes in American society 'have not yet become fixed but continually change and interchange their elements in constant flux' (1852/1958: 255).

Mill, on the other hand, has a quite different perspective on mobility. Anticipating liberal theorists, he emphasized the way in which advancing industrialism in mid-nineteenth-century England was beginning to break down the barriers that had traditionally existed to movement between different levels or grades of employment. Hitherto, the demarcation between these grades had been 'almost equivalent to an hereditary distinction of castes, each employment being chiefly recruited from the children of those already employed in it, or in employments of the same rank with it in social estimation . . .'. But currently, according to Mill, 'the habits and disabilities which chained people to their hereditary conditions are fast wearing away, and every class is exposed to increased and increasing competition from at least the class immediately below it' (1848: 462–3). Thus, although Mill here uses the language of class, he clearly sees the context of mobility as being in fact a social hierarchy: that is, one determined by the type of work performed and its 'social estimation'.

the other tends to be dominant; and this is, in our view, to be expected, since the two approaches are directed towards the treatment of different, even though overlapping, sets of problems.

For our own part, we have chosen here to take up the class-structural perspective, on the grounds that it would appear to be the more encompassing and, in any event, the more promising overall as regards the range of problems on which, as we have indicated, we intend to concentrate our attention. In what follows, we seek to explain this choice in more detail and what is entailed by it.

If mobility is studied within the conceptual context of a social hierarchy, it may be supposed that a prime focus of interest is on mobility in some 'vertical' sense—that is, on social ascent or descent in terms of prestige, status, or whatever is taken as the ordering principle of the hierarchy; for it is such upward or downward movement that will, of course, be implied in each individual instance of mobility. Such an approach has an obvious relevance for the examination of a number of major issues within the field of mobility research. It is, for example, well suited to treating questions concerning the determinants of individual 'success' or 'failure'—or, in other words, questions of 'who gets ahead—and why?' Thus, scales of occupational prestige or of 'socio-economic' status have formed the basis for most studies carried out within what has become known as the 'status-attainment' paradigm (see, e.g., Blau and Duncan 1967; Jencks 1972, 1979). And in turn, then, a hierarchical perspective can also be taken up in macrosociological and comparative analyses where the aim is to characterize societies as being more or less 'open' according to the relative importance of ascription and achievement—as represented, say, by 'family' and 'education'—in promoting success or guarding against failure.

However, what must at the same time be noted is that occupations that are found in close proximity to each other on scales of prestige or status need not, and often do not, have much else in common with each other, and may indeed hold quite disparate locations within the social division of labour. Thus, within the same narrow band of scale values one may find, say, groupings of skilled industrial workers brought together with certain types of small proprietor and minor official; or, again, farmers and smallholders placed alongside artisans, industrial labourers, and personal service workers.[2]

---

[2] For instance, in the case of the Duncan Index of Occupational Status (Duncan 1961; Blau and Duncan 1967: 122–3), one finds within the score interval 55–9 electrotypers and stereotypers and locomotive engineers grouped together with funeral directors and wholesale proprietors, railroad conductors, and certain types of foremen; or again, in the interval 10–14, farmers and fishermen bracketed with shoemakers and repairers (non-factory), longshoremen and stevedores, labourers in machinery manufacturing, hospital attendants, and taxi-drivers. Inspection of the more detailed Hope–Goldthorpe scale of the prestige or 'general desirability' of occupations (Goldthorpe and Hope 1974: 96–109) would provide still more numerous examples of such heterogeneity. It should be emphasized that the aim here is not to question the validity of these scales. The point is, rather, that, where occupations are brought together according to their

In consequence, where mobility is analysed in a hierarchical context as represented by occupational prestige or status scales, it becomes difficult for the structural influences that bear on mobility rates and patterns to be adequately isolated and displayed. Occupational groupings that are treated as equivalent will in fact often be ones that are affected in quite different ways by, for example, shifts in demand, technological innovation, or the policies of national governments, and that may thus be following, within the overall course of economic development, quite divergent trajectories of expansion or decline (cf. Westergaard and Resler 1975: 287–8).

If, in contrast, mobility is studied in the conceptual context of a class structure, it is not 'vertical' movement on some social scale that will be at the centre of attention but, rather, mobility understood in terms of *relational* changes: specifically, changes in the nature of individuals' involvement in relations within labour markets and production units. Such changes may not, in fact, be readily interpretable as implying social ascent or descent. For, while the relationships that constitute a class structure can be seen as expressing differential social advantage and power, they do so in quite varying ways; and class positions need not therefore be ordered in any consistent unidimensional fashion (cf. Carlsson 1958: ch. 3; Dahrendorf 1959: 74–7; Giddens 1973: 106).[3] Further, though, within a class-structural approach individual chances of mobility, whether vertical or otherwise, are unlikely to be the only issue raised. In contrast with the social groupings found at similar levels of prestige or status, classes—in the minimal sense of collectivities defined by their common class locations—can be expected to show some degree of homogeneity not only in the kinds and levels of resources that their members command but further in their exposure to structural changes and, in turn, in the range of at least potential interests that they may seek to uphold. Thus, within a class perspective, it becomes possible for the investigation of mobility chances to be included within a larger concern. While the significance of such chances in themselves—and in actually revealing the inequalities in advantage and power associated with different class locations—can be fully recognized, other issues can also

status, prestige, etc., there is no reason why they should also be homogeneous in terms of their structural locations and that, in all probability, they will not be.

[3] Our position here does, however, differ significantly from that of Runciman. Although Runciman initially defines classes as 'sets of roles whose common location in social space is a function of the *nature* and degree of economic power (or lack of it) attaching to them through their relation to the institutional processes of production, distribution and exchange' (1990: 377; emphasis added), he then wishes to treat as *equivalent*, on a single dimension, 'roles whose shared level of economic power derives from different institutional relations . . .' (1990: 380). Whether or not it is the case that the idea of such equivalence 'is in principle familiar enough to sociologists of all theoretical schools', we find it difficult to understand why Runciman should go on to concern himself with the question of 'How many classes are there?' For it would seem far more consistent with his general position for him to conceptualize the differing degree of economic power attaching to class roles—its differing nature being effectively discounted—as forming a continuum.

be addressed: on the one hand, those of how the mobility of individuals also reflects the structural aspects of economic development and, on the other, those of how mobility rates, as both endogenously and exogenously determined, help to create or to undermine the conditions under which class identities are formed and class interests pursued.

Given, then, that in this study our major aim is to evaluate theories which in various ways seek to establish connections between mobility and economic development—specifically, the development of industrial societies—the attractions for us of the class-structural as against the hierarchical approach should not be difficult to appreciate. To put the matter more concretely, we would, for the task in hand, see a decided advantage in being able to discuss mobility rates and patterns in terms of class categories—such as, say, those of industrial wage-workers, peasants or farmers, salaried employees, proprietors and self-employed workers, etc.—rather than in terms of categories which represent simply levels distinguished within a prestige or status continuum. For it is, we would maintain, far more as members of categories of the former than of the latter kind that individuals have in fact experienced the processes—political as well as economic—through which their societies have developed as industrial ones, and have in turn responded to, and participated in, these processes.[4]

To argue thus, we would stress, does not require us to claim that classes are more 'real' than collectivities distinguished by reference to prestige or status, nor to regard a class-structural approach as being superior to a hierarchical one in any absolute sense. As we have sought to make clear, our preference for the former approach is entirely a matter of choosing one conceptualization over another because we believe that, on balance, it is the more suited to our purposes. Accordingly, we would not seek to deny that, along with the advantages offered, certain disadvantages are also entailed. Most obviously, within a class-structural perspective the possibility is lost of treating mobility systematically in terms of social ascent or descent, and further, then, the possibility of applying various elegant analytical techniques which depend upon the adoption of categories ordered within a social hierarchy.

At the same time, though, we would reject the implication of arguments such as those of Kelley (1990) to the effect that a class-structural context for the study of mobility is in some way less 'natural'—or conceptually more arbitrary—than a hierarchical one in being less securely grounded in the ways in which mobility is typically thought of and 'lived through' by the 'lay members' of a society. While we would not, of course, question that popular conceptions of mobility do often imply a hierarchical context, the idea of

---

[4] We would regard it as significant that it is in fact in terms of classes, rather than of prestige or status levels, that historians of the modern period have usually wished to discuss social cleavages, conflicts, and movements; and working within essentially the same conceptual framework as they have done is itself an advantage that we will seek to exploit.

mobility between class positions which cannot be readily characterized in vertical terms is *also*, we believe, one that finds a wide correspondence at the level of actual social experience.

For example, in the course of industrialization the most important of all mobility flows, numerically at least, are those of peasants and small farmers and of their offspring into semi- and unskilled wage-earning jobs in industry; and there can be little doubt that radical changes thus ensue not only in the market and work relationships in which these individuals are involved but further in their entire way of life and its social setting. Yet perhaps one of the *least* revealing questions to be asked about such mobility, whether from the standpoint of the sociologist or from that of the social actors in question, is whether it is 'upward' or 'downward' in direction. Typically, such mobility would appear to bring, and to be experienced as bringing, varying kinds of both gains and losses for which no common denominator is readily available: for example, increased income and shorter hours of work but devaluation of previously acquired skills and reduced autonomy; the chance of entering 'modern' affluent society but also the risk of cultural and social impoverishment (cf. Smelser and Lipset 1966; Johnson 1981).[5] Moreover, other instances of mobility in which similar trade-offs seem often present—and likewise ambivalence on the part of those contemplating, or who have made, the transition—are not difficult to cite: for example, that from employee to 'independent', self-employed status or from a rank-and-file to a first-line supervisory position (see, e.g., Chinoy 1955: chs. 5 and 7; Goldthorpe *et al.* 1968: ch. 6; Mayer 1977; Bland, Elliott, and Bechhofer 1978; Crossick and Haupt 1984). And here again what would appear from the monographic

---

[5] Johnson has written as follows on the implications of mobility from the peasantry into industrial work in Eastern European societies in the post-war period.

It should be stressed that the move from the village to the town or city represented an enormous change in nearly every aspect of the lives of those involved. It was not simply a case of changing one 'job' for another. An enormous gulf separated the relatively 'modern' lifestyle of the industrial centers from the age-old patterns and traditions of the relatively isolated peasant communities. The urban migrant left behind the emotional support and the economic security (however tenuous) provided by multibonded ties of familial relationship and lifelong acquaintance for the anonymity and impersonality of life among strangers. Instead of the relatively self-sufficient patterns of consumption characteristic of subsistence agriculture and handicraft production, he now found it necessary to depend . . . upon his capacity to acquire the cash to purchase [commodities] by selling his labor. Instead of the autonomous, self-scheduled and periodically varied patterns of work characteristic of small-scale agriculture, he now had to accustom himself to the unfamiliar discipline of the foreman, the punch-clock and a minutely specialized and routinized task on the assembly line. With his skills as a farmer and husbandryman essentially useless in his new setting, and lacking in formal education, he almost necessarily had to settle for the low wages and often unpleasant working conditions of an unskilled or semiskilled laborer; yet at the same time the example of his acquaintances and the proximity and visibility of amenities and 'luxury' commodities almost unknown in the village stimulated him towards acquisitiveness and a consumption-oriented mentality that linked the sense of self-worth with the outward trappings of material prosperity. (1981: 33–4)

literature to be of chief significance is the *relational* changes that are involved rather than movement along some 'vertical', attributional dimension.

Since our main aim thus far has been to bring out as clearly as possible the differences between the class-structural and hierarchical approaches to the study of mobility and to show how these have been developed in regard to different sets of problems, we have in effect represented the two approaches as alternative paradigms between which a choice must, implicitly or explicitly, be made. In conclusion, however, we should qualify this account by recognizing rather more fully that the two approaches are not entirely incompatible and that, in practice, some degree of compromise between them may be sought.

Thus, in the case of investigators taking up a hierarchical perspective on the basis of prestige or status scales, it is notable that, while, for example, Glass (1954) and Svalastoga (1959) made little or no attempt to reduce the heterogeneity of occupations that were placed at the same hierarchical level, later exponents of this approach have often been concerned to do so. At least for the purposes of mobility-table analysis, the practice has become quite regular of *starting with* a set of occupational categories—derived, say, from official statistics—that are relatively homogeneous in their structural locations and of *then ordering these categories* in the light of some average of the scale values of their constituent occupations (see, e.g., Blau and Duncan 1967: 26–9; Featherman and Hauser 1978: 25–30). Indeed, it may also be the case that the ranking thus produced is itself subject to further *ad hoc* modification, with the aim, it would seem, of bringing it into yet closer accord with what might be described as 'class-like' criteria.[6] This latter step is, however, one which, in our view, risks achieving compromise at too great a cost in terms of conceptual consistency: it becomes unclear just what the context of mobility is taken to be.

In turn, where a class-structural perspective is adopted, the most obvious way of attempting to capture some of the hierarchical aspects of mobility is then to order the classes distinguished by reference to prestige, status, or some other appropriate criterion of an 'external' kind. This is, in fact, the strategy that we shall ourselves take up, as described in the section that follows. None the less, we shall pursue it to only a rather limited extent. While at an empirical level a fairly high correlation may be expected

---

[6] Thus, for example, Blau and Duncan, having ranked seventeen occupational categories according to socio-economic status on the basis of median income and years of schooling, then modify the order by moving 'Salesmen, retail' above three categories of craftsmen so as 'to maintain the nonmanual–manual distinction' (1967: 26). (They appear, however, to forget making this adjustment when later seeking to argue (1967: 71–5) that the multidimensional scaling of mobility flows confirms the centrality of socio-economic status.) Likewise, Featherman, and Hauser modify their socio-economic ranking of the same seventeen categories, invoking 'conventional distinctions among major occupational strata and the supplemental information provided by other rank criteria' (1978: 27). 'Salesmen, retail' are again promoted, this time above two categories of craftsmen, so as to be included in the second—'lower nonmanual'—of five strata into which the seventeen categories are for some purposes aggregated.

between the social inequalities that are conceptualized in terms either of a class-structure or of a prestige or status hierarchy, it is, we believe, still the case that no perfect mapping from one conceptualization to the other can be achieved and that—to return to the point from which we began—there is good reason why, in any particular study, one or the other should be privileged.[7]

THE CLASS SCHEMA

Having opted to conduct our analyses of mobility within a class-structural context, we need then to translate this decision into practice by establishing some set of class categories which will provide the basis for our empirical work. However, there is no obvious and uncontroversial way in which this may be done: to the contrary, the concept of class is a notoriously contested one. Our position in the face of this difficulty is the following. We take the view that concepts—like all other ideas—should be judged by their consequences, not by their antecedents. Thus, we have little interest in arguments about class that are of a merely doctrinal nature. The class schema that we have developed in connection with the present and previous (Erikson, Goldthorpe, and Portocarero 1979) comparative investigations possesses a theoretical rationale which, we trust, endows it with a measure of internal consistency. But, as will become apparent, it is in its inspiration rather eclectic. We have drawn on ideas, whatever their source, that appeared to us helpful in forming class categories capable of displaying the salient features of mobility among the populations of modern industrial societies—and within the limits set by the data available to us. Correspondingly, it is by reference to this objective that, we would hope, the value of the schema will be assessed.

Table 2.1 provides a description of the categories of the schema. The most extended version, shown in the first column of the table, is presented, together with the diagrammatic account of Figure 2.1, primarily to help readers follow the rationale of the schema that we set out—thematically rather than class by class—in the remainder of this section. It is actually the seven-class version of the schema, found in the second column of Table 2.1, that will for the most part serve as the basis of our empirical analyses, since, as we report in the next section, some collapsing of categories was necessary in order to maintain standards of cross-national comparability in our data. The explanation below of features of the full version of the schema that we cannot in fact utilize should enable readers to make their own judgement of

[7] In principle, a complete reconciliation of the two approaches might be thought possible simply through the elaboration of a sufficiently large number of categories: for example, through distinguishing prestige or status strata *within* each of a set of classes. In practice, however, very large samples would then be required in order to have reliable cell counts in mobility tables based on such a categorization, and questions of the theoretical focus of particular analyses would in any event remain.

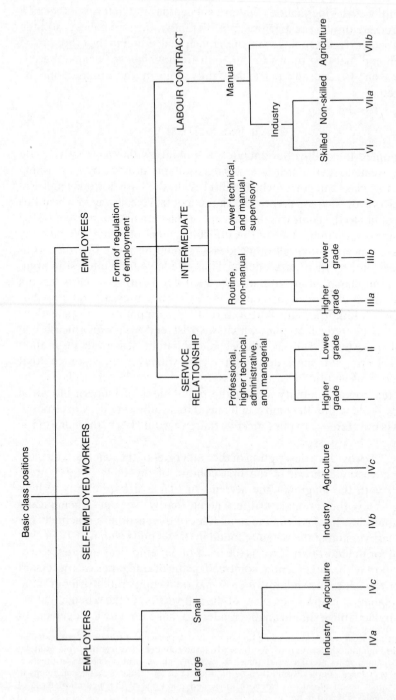

FIGURE 2.1. *The derivation of the class schema*

how far in its seven-class form its underlying principles are compromise. The five- and three-class collapses that are also shown in Table 2.1 are clearly less satisfactory but were unavoidable in a number of more complex analyses where cell counts would otherwise have become unreliably low.[8]

The aim of the class schema is to differentiate positions within *labour markets* and *production units* or, more specifically, one could say, to differentiate such positions in terms of the *employment relations* that they entail.[9] The principles of differentiation that we adopt have been mainly derived from classic sources, in particular, from Marx and Max Weber. But these principles have been adapted, under the influence of various later authors, to try to meet the specific requirements of analysing class mobility within the total populations of mid-twentieth-century industrial nations, both capitalist and state socialist.

For Marx and Weber alike, it could be said that employment relations are crucial to the delineation of the structure of class positions within modern society—even though these authors would accord a somewhat differing significance to these relations.[10] From both sources, we can derive a basic, threefold division of class positions, as follows:

1. employers: i.e. those who buy the labour of others and thus assume some degree of authority and control over them;
2. self-employed workers without employees: those who neither buy the labour of others nor sell their own;

---

[8] The origins of the present schema lie in one devised by Goldthorpe and Llewellyn (1977) for use on British data. This was then modified for purposes of the comparative mobility analyses reported in Erikson, Goldthorpe, and Portocarero (1979) at the same time as Erikson was involved in revising a Swedish classification (Andersson, Erikson, and Wärneryd 1981) which already in its original form (Carlsson *et al.* 1974) had close similarities with that of Goldthorpe and Llewellyn. Further refinements were proposed in the course of later British work by Goldthorpe and Payne (1986) in collaboration with Anthony Heath. The rather cumbersome labelling of classes by combinations of roman numerals and letters is here retained, since this enables earlier and later versions of the schema to be systematically related.

[9] In earlier presentations we have referred to the class schema as aiming to bring together individuals holding similar market and work situations. The revised formulation here used seeks to bring out more clearly that the schema is intended ultimately to apply to *positions*, as defined by social relationships, rather than to *persons*, although, for purposes of describing the classes distinguished, it is difficult to avoid referring to actual incumbents—e.g. managers, proprietors, workers, etc. We might also add here that, while we then allocate individuals to class positions within our schema, we do not thereby commit ourselves—logically or sociologically—to the view that the class of all individuals alike will be most validly determined by reference to their *own* employment. Questions of 'derived' class, turning on whether the individual or the family is the more appropriate unit of class composition, will be taken up at length in discussing the class mobility of women in Chapter 7.

[10] We would, in fact, believe that the opposition between Marxian and Weberian conceptions of class that is by now enshrined in sociology textbooks is in many respects exaggerated, and especially in view of the fact that the work of neither author can be regarded as providing a canonical statement of his position. Our own approach has been often referred to and discusssed as 'Weberian', but we would not regard this as particularly informative or otherwise helpful: to repeat, it is consequences, not antecedents, that matter.

TABLE 2.1. *The class schema*

Full version	Collapsed versions		
	Seven-class*	Five-class	Three-class
I Higher-grade professionals, administrators, and officials; managers in large industrial establishments; large proprietors	I+II Service class: professionals, administrators and managers; higher-grade technicians; supervisors of non-manual workers	I–III White-collar workers	Non-manual workers
II Lower-grade professionals, administrators, and officials; higher-grade technicians; managers in small industrial establishments; supervisors of non-manual employees			
IIIa Routine non-manual employees, higher grade (administration and commerce)	III Routine non-manual workers: routine non-manual employees in administration and commerce; sales personnel; other rank-and-file service workers		
IIIb Routine non-manual employees, lower grade (sales and services)			

Class	Description	Aggregation		Aggregation	
IVa	Small proprietors, artisans, etc., with employees	IVa+b	Petty bourgeoisie: small proprietors and artisans, etc., with and without employees	IVa+b	Petty bourgeoisie
IVb	Small proprietors, artisans, etc., without employees				
IVc	Farmers and smallholders; other self-employed workers in primary production	IVc	Farmers: farmers and smallholders and other self-employed workers in primary production	IVc+VIIb	Farm workers
V	Lower-grade technicians; supervisors of manual workers	V+VI	Skilled workers: lower-grade technicians; supervisors of manual workers; skilled manual workers	V+VI	Skilled workers
VI	Skilled manual workers				
VIIa	Semi- and unskilled manual workers (not in agriculture, etc.)	VIIa	Non-skilled workers: semi- and unskilled manual workers (not in agriculture, etc.)	VIIa	Non-skilled workers
VIIb	Agricultural and other workers in primary production	VIIb	Agricultural labourers: agricultural and other workers in primary production		

Right-hand groupings:

- Petty bourgeoisie
- Farm workers
- Manual workers (Skilled workers + Non-skilled workers)

Note:

* As indicated in the text, the seven-class version of the schema is the one we shall most frequently use in our analyses. We give here the name —'service class', etc.—by which we will usually refer to each class.

3. employees: those who sell their labour to employers and thus place
   themselves to some degree under their authority and control.

In the construction of the class schema, this threefold division may be
regarded as the starting-point, as Figure 2.1 illustrates. However, considerable modification and elaboration then follow, in respect chiefly of two
closely related developments within the twentieth-century industrial world:
first, the transformation of property into corporate forms, whether private
or public, which has resulted in most major employers being *organizations*
rather than individuals; and, secondly, the growth of employees as a
proportion of the total active population, accompanied by a greater differentiation of the forms of employer–employee relations as employing organizations have become increasingly bureaucratized.

As regards, first, the now predominantly corporate—or, in socialist
societies, state-owned—nature of productive property, the main implication is
that the class of 'employer' becomes one made up overwhelmingly of *small*
employers with, say, work-forces that number at most in tens rather than in
hundreds. Such small proprietors are comprised by Class IV*a* of our schema,
while Class IV*b* covers self-employed workers without employees—apart in
both cases from those engaged in primary production, who go together in
Class IV*c*.

As can, then, be seen from Table 2.1, no separate class of large employers
is provided for. Large proprietors are in fact included in Class I, where they
might appear to constitute a rather anomalous element. However, more
detailed examination of the cases in question, which we have been able to
make in several of our national samples, suggests that, as well as being few in
number,[11] they are also less straightforward than they might seem.

To begin with, it should be emphasized that we are *not* dealing here, other
than quite exceptionally, with members of a capitalist élite or leaders of
industry. Rather, 'large' proprietors turn out to be most typically the owners
of stores, hotels, restaurants, garages, small factories, or building or trans-
portation firms. Indeed, it might be argued that, since their operations tend
to be on only a slightly more ambitious scale than those of the small
proprietors of Class IV*a*, little is gained in seeking to separate them from the
latter. The main reason for so doing, and for including them in Class I, is
that, in so far as such large proprietors tend to be quite extensively involved
in managerial as well as entrepreneurial activities, they may be regarded as
having a yet greater affinity with those salaried managers to be found in
Class I who have a substantial share in the ownership of the enterprises in
which they work. Most often, the difference here will be simply one of

---

[11] We would estimate that, across the Western industrial societies that we consider, 'large
employers' account for only around 5–10 per cent of all men allocated to Class I, which itself
makes up only around the same proportion of the total work-force. For our two Eastern
European societies the category will not, of course, be relevant, except, perhaps, as regards
class origins.

whether enterprises of very much the same kind as was indicated above—that is, relatively modest ones—have become incorporated or not: a matter which will be of somewhat varying consequence cross-nationally, depending on prevailing company law and business practice, but in any event more from a legal, financial, and fiscal than from a sociological standpoint.[12]

It might further be noted at this point that considerations similar to the foregoing underlie the inclusion in Classes I and II of the schema of *all* professionals, whether reportedly self-employed or employees. Among professionals, a variety of legal and conventional arrangements is to be found through which independent practice and salaried employment are combined or the distinction between them is effectively blurred; and, even where it might be possible for 'true' independents to be identified, it would then seem likely that in most of the national samples at our disposal their numbers would be too small to allow separate analysis.[13]

When we turn, secondly, to the growth in numbers of employees and the increased differentiation in their relations with employers (usually, employing organizations), what we are clearly forced to recognize is the inadequacy of treating all employees alike as holding similar class positions. It is apparent that, in consequence of employer–employee relations being based on quite heterogeneous principles, employees in fact occupy a range of different labour-market and work situations, among which meaningful distinctions can and should be made in class terms.

The line of division to which we would here give greatest emphasis—following Weber and in turn Renner (1953) and Dahrendorf (1959, 1964)—is that which stems from differences between, on the one hand, the labour contract and, on the other, the conditions of employment which typically obtain within organizational bureaucracies, both public and private. Employment relationships regulated by a labour contract entail a relatively short-term and specific exchange of money for effort. Employees supply more-or-less discrete amounts of labour, under the supervision of the employer or of the employer's agents, in return for wages which are calculated on a 'piece' or time basis. In contrast, employment relationships within a bureaucratic context involve a longer-term and generally more diffuse exchange. Employees render service to their employing organization in return for 'compensation',

[12] It should be noted that, where in truly large-scale enterprises managers have a share in ownership, this will typically amount to only a very small fraction of the total equity and—even if sufficient to give these individuals considerable personal wealth—will still not constitute the basis of their authority, which will remain bureaucratic. In other words, the wealth of such managers derives from their positions of authority and not vice versa, as with the entrepreneur in the 'heroic' phase of capitalist industry.

[13] Thus, for example, in England, where self-employed professionals include, for largely technical reasons, all general medical practitioners working for the National Health Service and many Church of England clergymen, the category still accounts for only a little over 1 per cent of all men within the work-force and for about 5 per cent of all allocated to Classes I and II together; while in Sweden, where a stricter definition of self-employment applies, the corresponding percentages are roughly halved.

which takes the form not only of reward for work done, through a salary and various perquisites, but also comprises important *prospective* elements—for example, salary increments on an established scale, assurances of security both in employment and, through pensions rights, after retirement, and, above all, well-defined career opportunities.

As argued at greater length elsewhere (Goldthorpe 1982), a 'service' relationship, rather than one formulated in terms of a labour contract, is likely to be found where it is required of employees that they exercise *delegated authority* or *specialized knowledge and expertise* in the interests of their employing organization. In the nature of the case, such employees must then be accorded a legitimate area of autonomy and discretion and, to this extent, their performance will depend on the degree of moral commitment that they feel towards the organization rather than on the efficacy of external sanctions. A service relationship can thus be understood as the means through which an employing organization seeks to create and sustain such commitment; or, that is, as a functional alternative to direct control in regard to those employees whom the organization must to some significant extent *trust* to make decisions and to carry them through in ways that are consistent with organizational values and goals.[14]

It is, therefore, the distinction between employees involved in a service relationship with their employer and those whose employment relationships are essentially regulated by a labour contract that underlies the way in which, within our class schema, different employee classes have been delineated. The most obvious division to be made in this respect is that between the predominantly salaried professional, higher technical, administrative, and managerial positions of Classes I and II and the predominantly wage-earning manual occupations of Classes VI and VII. The former may be taken as those positions with which a service relationship is most characteristically associated, and thus as constituting the basis of the 'service class' or 'salariat' of modern industrial societies; the latter, as those where the labour contract usually prevails, and which thus constitute the basis of the working class. We find it of interest and significance that something close to this division receives rather widespread linguistic recognition: for example, in the distinction made in English between 'staff' and 'workers'; in French, between *cadres* or *employés* and *ouvriers*; in German, between *Beamte* or *Angestellte* and *Arbeiter*; or in Swedish between *tjänstemän* (literally, 'service men') and *arbetare*. We would, furthermore, see a reflection of a similar division in the distinction drawn in state socialist societies between 'intellig-

---

[14] While one would, then, from this point of view, expect to find a close association between type of employment relationship and the content of work tasks and roles, it should be emphasized that it is the *former* rather than the latter that, for us, is decisive in determining class position. Thus, in the case suggested by some exponents of the proletarianization thesis (e.g. Crompton 1980) of employees who are performing routine administrative work although with the 'cosmetic' title of manager, the crucial question is whether this title does or does not carry with it the advantages of a service relationship with the employing organization.

entsia' and 'workers' (cf. Szczepański 1970; Hardin 1976), even though the historical context and wider connotations are here of course in some respects very different.[15]

We have, though, at the same time to recognize that the contrast that we have set up between a service relationship and employment regulated via a labour contract is one of an ideal-typical kind, and that actual employment relationships will often only approximate one type or the other, or may indeed fall rather ambiguously between them. Consequently, and as Figure 2.1 again brings out, we elaborate on our basic division of employees in two ways.

First, the distinctions between Classes I and II and Classes VI and VII are made within the service class and the working class respectively. Positions covered by Class I may be taken as those to which the largest responsibilities in decision-making attach and which will in turn offer the fullest range of beneficial conditions associated with the service relationship; while in the case of the lower-level positions of Class II, certain of these features may be attenuated. Conversely, it is with non-skilled labour as represented by Class VII, where there is least need for employees to be allowed autonomy and discretion and where external controls can be most fully relied on, that the labour contract will tend to operate in its purest form; while, with skilled labour as represented by Class VI, modifications directed towards making the 'money-for-effort' exchange somewhat less specific and short term are more likely to be found.[16]

Secondly, we distinguish two classes which may be regarded as 'intermediate' in the sense that they comprise positions with associated employment relationships that would appear characteristically to take on a very mixed form. Class III covers the range of routine non-manual positions, usually involving clerical, sales, or personal-service tasks, which exist, so to speak, on the fringes of professional, administrative, and managerial bureaucracies; and Class V takes in lower-grade technical and first-line supervisory positions whose incumbents usually work closely with rank-and-file manual employees, although being in certain respects differentiated from them. In both cases, the extent to which a service relationship could be said to prevail over the

---

[15] For debates on the 'class' role of the intelligentsia in Eastern European nations, see Konrad and Szelényi (1979), Starski (1982), and Frentzel-Zagórska and Zagórski (1989).

[16] For example, workers in Class VI could be regarded as more likely than those in Class VII to be included in 'internal' or 'craft-specific' labour markets. It might be added here that employers appear increasingly prepared to introduce 'service' elements into the employment relationships of various grades of manual worker in positions involving high levels of skill or responsibility, so that the latter might then be more appropriately allocated to Class V (see following text). And, certainly, we would not regard the 'manuality' or otherwise of work performed as being in itself relevant to class allocation—consistently with the position taken in n. 14 above. However, over the period to which our data relate, which, as will be seen, extends several decades back from the mid-1970s, the manual–non-manual division does in fact appear to have corresponded rather closely with that we have noted of 'workers' versus 'staff', etc., so far as employment relations are concerned.

presuppositions of a labour contract is problematic. Employing organizations appear to display a frequent uncertainty over whether the roles performed by such personnel are ones that would justify 'staff' status or whether they are to be treated essentially as labour. It is notable that difficulties arising from this uncertainty—in regard, say, to methods of remuneration, time-keeping, promotion chances, union representation, etc.—have been a recurrent theme in studies of employer–employee relations concerning the groups in question.[17]

It should be added that the subdivision of Class III into III*a* and III*b* that is further indicated in Table 2.1 was prompted by the application of the schema in studies of women's mobility, and is used only in analyses where women are involved. The purpose of the subdivision is to isolate in Class III*b* a range of routine and very low-skill non-manual positions which are largely occupied by women and to which (especially *when* held by women) very little ambiguity in fact attaches. That is to say, these positions tend, in contrast to those retained in Class III*a*, to be more-or-less undifferentiated in their conditions of employment from those of non-skilled manual workers. Thus, in analyses in which the subdivision is applied, Class III*b* is usually collapsed with Class VII*a*.

There remains one other feature of the class schema on which some comment should be made: namely, the sectoral division through which proprietors and wage-workers in agriculture and other primary production are separately identified as Classes IV*c* and VII*b*. This elaboration would seem necessary in view of various distinctive aspects assumed by class relations within primary production—in consequence, for example, of the major form of property ownership being in land, of the organization of production remaining often family-based, and of the frequent substitution, even in the case of labour drawn from outside the family, of payment-in-kind for money wages. Ideally, we would also have wished to introduce into the schema some degree of differentiation among agricultural proprietors, in regard to form of tenure, size and value of holding, etc. However, there appeared little point in so doing, since relevant information, at least in a form that would permit cross-national comparisons, is not sufficiently available in the data-sets on which we rely.

From what has already been said in this and the preceding section it will be apparent that the class schema is not constructed around any single hierarchical principle from which a regular ordering of the classes could be derived. If, therefore, for particular analytical purposes, such an ordering would seem desirable, it must be produced by reference to external criteria. As we have already remarked, we would doubt if any very ambitious moves in this

[17] See, for example, on clerical workers, Mills (1951), Lockwood (1958/1989), Crozier (1965), Kocka (1980*a*, 1981); on foremen and supervisors, Thurley and Wirdenius (1973) and Child (1976); and on technicians, Roberts, Loveridge, and Gennard (1972) and Low-Beer (1978).

direction could be justified. However, good grounds would appear to exist for introducing within the seven-class version of the schema a threefold hierarchical division which could be more-or-less equally well taken as ordering class positions in terms of their prestige, socio-economic status, or 'general desirability'. We would, in fact, regard scales purporting to rank occupations according to such criteria as all reflecting in a rather similar way differences in, on the one hand, levels of job rewards and, on the other, job-entry requirements (cf. Goldthorpe and Hope 1972, 1974).

In Table 2.2 we show the results achieved if we assign scores to the classes of the schema on the Treiman international occupational prestige scale (Treiman 1977a) and also on a number of scales available for individual nations that will be represented in our subsequent analyses. On each scale we have obtained a score for every occupational and employment status grouping comprised by a particular class—to the extent that a mapping between the categories of the scale and those of the class schema proved

TABLE 2.2. *Scores for classes of the schema on different occupational scales as a basis for a threefold hierarchical division*

Scale*	Class						
	I+II	III	IVa+b	IVc	V+VI	VIIa	VIIb
Treiman	56	35	42	44	35	29	24
Hope–Goldthorpe (England)	63	36	39	47	40	29	31
Wegener (FRG)	92	50	49	50	49	39	30
Irish Occupational Index (all Ireland)	58	30	42	42	37	24	26
de Lillo–Schizzerotto (Italy)	71	41	51	48	34	20	11
Naoi (Japan)	62	41	37	37	41	33	30
Duncan (USA)	66	27	46	25	33	17	14
Division	1	2				3	

Note:
  *· The international Treiman scale and those for the FRG, Ireland, and Japan are intended as scales of occupational prestige, although constructed in different ways; the English scale and also, it would seem, the Italian, are intended as ones of the general desirability of occupations in popular estimation; and the US scale, while originally constructed as a proxy for a prestige scale, is now generally interpreted as one of the socio-economic status of occupations. For further details, see Treiman (1977a), Goldthorpe and Hope (1974), Wegener (1988), Boyle (1976), de Lillo and Schizzerotto (1985), Naoi (1979), and Duncan (1961).

possible—and we have then taken the median of these values as the overall class score. Although scores are not, of course, directly comparable from scale to scale, it is still evident enough that Class I+II, the service class or salariat, consistently ranks above all others, and that Classes VIIa and VIIb, those of non-skilled workers in industry and of agricultural workers, consistently rank below all others, while the relative positions of the remaining classes are cross-nationally rather variable. A threefold hierarchical division of the schema guided by these results, and as indicated in Table 2.2, would therefore seem well founded.

There is, however, one modification that we would wish to make in the case of the class of farmers, IVc. In the course of industrialization, agriculture typically undergoes a radical transformation. Peasant, or other kinds of largely subsistence, farming give way to more decisively market-oriented forms of production, and then in turn commercialized family farming is in part superseded by relatively large-scale 'agribusiness'. In this process, a substantial decline in the number of farmers goes together with a steady increase in the average size of farms and in levels of capital investment and sales values (see, e.g., Renborg 1969; Newby 1978). As we have mentioned above, we cannot, with the data at our disposal, differentiate among farmers in such a way that would allow us to capture these changes directly in our analyses. But in those cases where we utilize our hierarchical division, we can, even if only crudely, still try to give some recognition to what is in effect the *collective upward mobility* of farmers by treating Class IVc differently as a class of origin and of destination. That is to say, we can take Class IVc, following Table 2.2., as falling in the intermediate division when considered as a destination class, but then relegate it to the lowest division, along with Classes VIIa and VIIb, when considered as an origin class.

In conclusion of this section, we would again wish to emphasize that the schema we have presented is to be regarded not as an attempt at providing a definitive 'map' of the class structures of individual societies but essentially as an *instrument de travail*.[18] As we have sought to make clear, its construction and adaptation have indeed been guided by theoretical ideas—but *also* by more practical considerations of the context in which, and purposes for which, it is to be used and of the nature of the data to which it is to be applied. In turn, the crucial test of the schema, as of any other conceptual device, must lie in its performance: it must be judged by the value that it proves to have in enquiry and analysis. But any such judgement, we would then suggest, will need to meet two requirements: first it must be made across the entire range of applications in which the schema is involved—and, as will be

[18] Thus, it does not aim at responding to the question posed by Runciman (1990) of 'How many classes are there?'—the only sensible answer to which is, we would believe, 'As many as it proves empirically useful to distinguish for the analytical purposes in hand.' Even while preserving the underlying idea of the schema that classes are to be defined in terms of employment relations, the differentiation of these, following the pattern of Figure 2.1, could obviously be much further extended, were there good reason to do so.

seen, these are rather diverse; and, secondly, it should be made in comparison with what might be offered by the available alternatives.[19]

DATA

At the end of the previous chapter we argued that one major reason for the unsatisfactory state of comparative mobility research is that data of the kind that have been typically utilized are seriously inadequate: in particular, they *lack* comparability from one national case to another, and indeed to such an extent that one might question the value of basing any analysis upon them. In this section we seek first of all to amplify this point and then to describe how, for the purposes of the present work, we have attempted to generate data to which greater reliability might attach.

Until recently, most comparative research has been based on the published results of national mobility enquiries: that is, on the results of these enquiries as reported in books and journal articles. Such data are, of course, readily accessed and, as their range has widened, they have offered tempting possibilities to the quantitatively oriented macrosociologist. It would, none the less, seem clear that with such data severe, and in fact largely intractable, problems of comparability are encountered in (at least) two respects.

First, national enquiries, as might be expected, differ in many of the technical details of their design and conduct: for example, in their precise population coverage, in their sampling and weighting procedures, in the wording of questionnaire items, etc. In the literature to which we here refer, such problems have in fact received little attention—whether because it has been bravely, but unjustifiably, assumed that they can be of no great consequence or because, in working with already processed data, what can be done to overcome them is in any event very limited.

Secondly, as we have been concerned to emphasize above, mobility can be studied from different conceptual standpoints, and attempts to render these operational in different national contexts have created great diversity in the social categorizations by reference to which mobility has been defined, observed, and measured. In the face of this difficulty, the standard practice

[19] The most obvious extant alternatives are the two different class schemata proposed by Wright (1978, 1985) of an explicitly Marxist character (and see also the further comments of interest in Wright, 1989b). We do not ourselves find the theoretical basis of either of these sociologically convincing; and, furthermore, serious problems arise in implementing at least the earlier version in intergenerational mobility studies, since class allocation in part depends on interview data on individuals' subjective assessments of their degree of authority and autonomy in work, which are unlikely to be available for the parental generation. However, comparisons made between the results of using our own and Wright's schemata across a range of issues in the field of class analysis must form the main basis of any competitive evaluation (cf. Goldthorpe 1990: 406–9). In this respect, the major contribution thus far is that of Marshall and his colleagues (Marshall *et al.* 1988; Marshall and Rose 1990), which indicates that a version of the class schema here used performs appreciably better in displaying a variety of 'class effects' than does either of Wright's proposals.

has been to try to produce cross-nationally comparable data by the progressive collapsing of the categories of different enquiries until some 'lowest
common denominator' is reached. This has in fact usually turned out to be a
simple twofold non-manual/manual occupational division or, at best, a
threefold non-manual/manual/farm one.[20] On examination, however, such
collapsing turns out to be of very doubtful advantage. The comparability
that is thus produced can be of only a *nominal* kind, and the extent to which a
high standard of *real* comparability is achieved remains entirely problematic
(Treiman 1975; Goldthorpe 1985*a*). There is, in other words, no reason for
supposing that the two or three categories that are ultimately distinguished
will be comparable in their actual content—that is, in the particular occupations that they comprise—and, indeed, it would seem highly likely that this
will *not* be the case. As is shown in some detail elsewhere (Goldthorpe
1985*b*: Appendix), the non-manual/manual division especially is one that is
open to very variable interpretations, with the result that certain occupational
groupings may be—and in national mobility studies regularly have been—
allocated to either one category or the other or split in differing ways
between them. Moreover, these 'borderline' groupings are not small. They
include foremen and other supervisors, technicians, lower-grade service
workers, self-employed artisans, and small working proprietors. Together,
they could be reckoned to account for a fifth to a quarter of the total work-
forces of most of the societies for which nationally based mobility data are
available.

Our point is, then, that comparative mobility analyses dependent on the
already processed data of published accounts are vitiated not because of the
simple presence of error due to non-comparability of one kind of another,
but rather because of the potential magnitude of this error and of the
difficulties of identifying its sources and of estimating and allowing for its
effects. It would seem highly probable that in such analyses variation in
mobility rates and patterns could be displayed *as a result solely of the non-
comparability of data* which would be *of a size similar to, or indeed larger
than, any genuine differences that one might reasonably expect to discover.*
Yet there is no way of knowing if, when, and where such distortions are
occurring. Those who have presented analyses of the kind in question have .
usually been ready enough to acknowledge the shortcomings of the data
they use. But they have then typically resorted to the argument that,
imperfect though they may be, these data are 'better than nothing' and
permit at least some 'preliminary' or 'provisional' conclusions to be drawn.
This is not, we believe, a tenable position. The possibility can never be
discounted—and in the case at issue is all too real—that, beyond a certain
point, defects in data will give rise to results which, rather than serving as a
useful first approximation, will in fact simply confuse and mislead.

[20] See, for example, the studies cited in Chapter 1, n. 25.

Our own approach to questions of data quality starts from the conviction that, in comparative work above all, these are ones of fundamental importance and should be recognized as such in the attention and resources that are devoted to them. In an ideal design, cross-national analysis would be based on the results of research carried out specifically for this purpose and with high standards of data comparability being thus a goal from the first. In practice, of course, the difficulties that stand in the way of organizing and conducting research of this kind are formidable, and it is only rather infrequently accomplished; in the field of social mobility, it has not so far been seriously attempted.[21] We have, therefore, to turn to some alternative means of constituting comparative data-sets, through which the ideal can at least be approximated.

Such an approximation is, in our view, best sought by working with the data of existing national mobility enquiries but in their raw rather than their processed form—that is, through 'secondary analysis'; and, further, by undertaking, preparatory to such analysis, the extensive recoding of these data at unit-record level to new categories of a standardized kind. In this way it is possible to adjust the original data so as to remove, or at least reduce, cross-national differences resulting from variation in research design and protocols; and a data-set for mobility analyses can then be created which provides for high standards of real, rather than simply nominal, cross-national comparability, and without the necessity for categories to be drastically collapsed.[22]

In the empirical parts of the present study we work essentially with a data-set that has been constituted by the procedures outlined. Specifically, we have recoded the original data of twelve national enquiries, details of which are given in Table 2.3.[23] All these enquiries, as is indicated, took place during the early or mid-1970s and were ones which either were focused directly on social mobility or led to the collection of substantial amounts of information relevant to mobility as part of wider-ranging concerns. All were

[21] The closest approximation to a mobility study of the kind in question is that of Pöntinen (1983), who was able to use data for Denmark, Finland, Norway, and Sweden from a common source, the Scandinavian Welfare Survey, 1972. However, as its name indicates, this survey was not one specifically concerned with stratification and mobility and, moreover, the national sample sizes were rather small—c.1,000 men and women aged 15–64. The Comparative Project on Class Structure and Class Consciousness, organized by Erik Olin Wright, aims to collect strictly comparable data across a wide range of nations but is not in fact designed to have class mobility as one of its central concerns.

[22] We developed this methodology in earlier comparative work covering England, France, and Sweden (Erikson, Goldthorpe, and Portocarero 1979, 1982, 1983).

[23] Additional material utilized is of two kinds. First, in Chapter 5 we analyse intergenerational class mobility tables for three other nations than those covered in Table 2.3 (Czechoslovakia, Italy, and the Netherlands), which were produced by independent researchers who have, however, adopted our class schema; and, secondly, we are at various points led by our arguments to reanalyse data-sets placed in the public domain by other mobility researchers whose conceptual or methodological approaches are different from ours.

TABLE 2.3. *National enquiries used as data sources*

Nation	Enquiry	Date	References for survey details
Australia (AUS)	Social Mobility in Australia Project	1973–4	Broom *et al.* (1977)
England & Wales (ENG)	Oxford National Occupational Mobility Enquiry	1972	Goldthorpe (1980*a*)
France (FRA)	INSEE Enquête Formation-Qualification Professionelle	1970	Pohl, Thélot, and Jousset (1974)
Federal Republic of Germany (FRG)	ZUMA Superfile	1976–8	Erikson *et al.* (1988)
Hungary (HUN)	Social Mobility and Occupational Change in Hungary	1973	Andorka and Zagórski (1980)
Irish Republic (IRL)	Determinants of Occupational Mobility	1973–4	O'Muircheartaigh and Wiggins (1977)
Japan (JAP)	Social Stratification and Social Mobility Survey	1975	Ando (1978); Tominaga (1979*a*)
Northern Ireland (NIR)	Determinants of Occupational Mobility	1973–4	O'Muircheartaigh and Wiggins (1977)
Poland (POL)	Change in the Socio-Occupational Structure	1972	Zagórski (1977–8)
Scotland (SCO)	Scottish Mobility Study	1974–5	Payne (1987)
Sweden (SWE)	Level of Living Survey	1974	Andersson (1987)
United States (USA)	Occupational Change in a Generation Replicate	1973	Featherman and Hauser (1978)

conducted from reputable institutions and by competent research teams, who were able to provide clean data-tapes and adequate documentation.

A leading aim of the recoding exercise that was carried out was, of course, to allow mobility to be analysed on the basis of the class schema that we have previously described. To achieve this end, the method regularly adopted was the following. A two-way table was drawn up for each national case in which the most detailed occupational classification used in the national enquiry was crossed with an employment status classification constructed so as to distinguish between employers, self-employed workers, and employees, and also in some way between rank-and-file, supervisory, and managerial grades of employee. Each cell within this table (apart from those which remained empty on all variables of interest—respondent's class, father's class, etc.) was then allocated to one or other class of our schema, and in this way a recoding algorithm was established which could be subsequently applied by computer to all unit records within the data-set.

In carrying out this allocation, we should emphasize, our overriding concern was not to treat particular occupation and employment status combinations themselves in exactly the same way from nation to nation. It was, rather, to allocate such combinations to the appropriate class in each national case *in the light of the employment relations which, in that case, were typically associated with the positions comprised.* While, in fact, similar combinations were very largely placed in the same class across all nations alike, certain exceptions did arise—most often with workers in lower-level administrative, clerical, and service occupations, whose characteristic employment relations appeared to be unusually variable.

No claim could be made that this recoding of data to the categories of the class schema was undertaken by reference to formal decision-rules: our own judgements were clearly paramount. We did, however, attempt to make these judgements as systematic and informed as possible. We drew heavily on national experts both for guidance on the principles and idiosyncracies of different classificatory systems and for information on aspects of employment relations—for example, levels and methods of pay and other 'conditions of service', fringe benefits, career structures, etc.—within different occupations, industries, and types of enterprise. Other investigators appear not to have found great difficulty in implementing our procedures (see p. 166) and we can, moreover, report one instance in which a useful check on them has been provided. Davis (Jones and Davis 1986: 17) independently recoded the Australian data that we use and arrived at an allocation of individual cases to the classes of the schema that is almost identical to our own.[24] Thus, while further checks might not, of course, prove so entirely satisfactory, we are encouraged to believe that our recodings are ones that would in very large part be reproduced by other sociologists who were similarly informed and similarly conversant with the ideas that underlie the class schema.

The data-set that will form the basis of our subsequent analyses does then, in our view, represent a clear improvement on those previously used in cross-national mobility research so far as standards of comparability are concerned. To be more specific, the procedures we have followed should mean that, where in our analyses significant differences in mobility rates and patterns are revealed between nations, it will in most instances be the reasonable *presumption* that these differences are real rather than simply artefactual; and, in so far as some amount of non-comparability remains—

---

[24] These data were made available to us by Professor Frank Lancaster Jones, to whom we are duly grateful.

as it undoubtedly does—our recoding exercise has given us the further advantage of a good deal of insight into its sources and location. The data-set is now in the public domain and detailed documentation is provided in Erikson *et al.* (1988).[25]

Finally, though, in conclusion of this section, we have to acknowledge a number of ways in which our efforts to achieve high standards of data comparability have, unfortunately, led to limitations being imposed on our analyses in other respects. First, to return to a point mentioned earlier, we should note that, while in recoding data to the class schema we did in fact work with the most extended version, as shown in Table 2.1, the standard of comparability that was attainable at this level of differentiation fell below our expectations. Collapses of classes of the schema appeared to be called for in three respects, giving rise—in the way indicated in Table 2.1—to the seven-class version, which has then provided the main basis of our analyses. Classes IV*a* and IV*b* had to be combined simply on account of inadequate information for several nations on whether or not self-employed workers had employees. The collapse of Classes I and II appeared advisable because, while we could draw a meaningful dividing line between these classes in each national case, differences in the original classificatory systems prevented this from being the *same* line from one case to another. And Classes V and VI were likewise collapsed because they could not be separated in a cross-nationally comparable way, although here it seems likely that the problems encountered were ones not only of incongruent classifications but further of real cross-national differences in the organization of first-line supervision, especially in manufacturing industry (cf. Maurice, Sorge, and Warner 1980; Maurice, Sellier, and Silvestre 1982).[26]

Secondly, the combined effects of deficiencies and incompatibilities in the national enquiries mean that, although we have been able to create a data-set on which comparative work can be reliably carried out, it is one that offers rather uneven possibilities for the study of different aspects of mobility. Specifically, we have better data on intergenerational than on

[25] The collection, recoding, and subsequent analysis of the data in question were, as noted in the Preface to this volume, carried out under the auspices of the CASMIN Project, funded by the Stiftung Volkswagenwerk and based at the Institut für Sozialwissenschaften of the University of Mannheim. Copies of the data-set—the International Mobility Superfile (IMS)—together with supporting documentation including all recoding algorithms—are available on request to Abteilung Microdaten, ZUMA, B2,1, D-6800 Mannheim, Federal Republic of Germany. It should be noted that a number of—very minor—corrections were made to the IMS in the final stages of its preparation. Thus, results derived from it may not always correspond exactly with those reported in the present text. However, all discrepancies should be quite trivial and without consequence for any substantive conclusions.

[26] Although, then, the IMS data will be found coded to as full a version of the class schema as possible—and with, in fact, a further division of 'large' from 'small' farmers added—this is intended simply as a facility for users who might be interested in the analysis of data for *single* nations. For the reasons set out in the text, the application in cross-national analyses of more extended versions of the schema than the seven-class one, as, for example, by Hout and Hauser (1991), is not, in our view, defensible.

intragenerational, or work-life, mobility, for men than for women, and for European than for non-European nations. It is for this reason that in what follows our central comparative analyses will, in fact, be concentrated on the intergenerational mobility of men in the nine European nations included in the listing of Table 2.3. Questions of the mobility of women, of work-life mobility, and of mobility rates and patterns in the three non-European nations in the data-set, in regard to which our data are for one reason or another somewhat more problematic, will then be treated separately.

Thirdly, the recoding of data to standardized categories for the purposes of secondary analysis is a time-consuming and expensive procedure, and one that can in any event only be usefully applied where the original data are themselves of a relatively high standard. Thus, in following this approach, greater data comparability is likely to be achieved at the cost of a less extensive coverage of nations than would typically be found in a cross-national mobility study based on published results. We do in fact work with a rather restricted sample of nations and one, moreover, that could only be described as 'accidental'. By chance, it does comprise industrial nations that are highly diverse as regards their levels and paths of economic development, their socio-cultural traditions, and their political evolution and status. In this latter respect, not only liberal democratic but also the post-war state socialist nations of Hungary and Poland are included, and, in the case of England and Wales, Northern Ireland, and Scotland, we have nations that are the component parts of a larger, multinational state. However, while we can seek to exploit this range of variation wherever it appears of value to do so, we still, of course, have no grounds for treating the nations we consider as being representative of all within the industrial world. The evident limitations of our sample of national cases must, therefore, be a factor in shaping our comparative strategy, which we will outline in the last section of this chapter.[27] First, though, we must turn to a consideration of analytical techniques.

[27] We may at this point note a further approach to the problems of data and comparative strategy in the field of mobility research that has been followed by Ganzeboom, Luijkx, and Treiman (1989). The aim here is to accumulate data-sets allowing the construction of *multiple* mobility tables for as many nations as possible, by dint of relaxing standards of recoding to comparable categories and of accepting data-sets from very small samples (for example, ones of only a few hundred respondents). Each mobility table thus produced is treated as a 'data-point', subject to error; and analyses are then undertaken in which attempts are made to test for the extent of error, due to non-comparability and other deficiencies of the data, at the same time as substantive issues are addressed.

While recognizing the considerable ingenuity underlying this approach and indeed its validity in principle, we remain highly sceptical about the way in which it has so far been implemented. First, the theory of measurement by which it is informed crucially requires that the entries in the several tables for each nation comprise the true values plus *random* error and represent entirely *independent* observations. In fact, the tables often derive from enquiries carried out by the same research organization or are based on the same national occupational classification. And in this connection Ganzeboom, Luijkx, and Treiman do not introduce appropriate 'quality controls' (see, further, ch. 3, n. 32). Secondly, while such controls are introduced in regard to coding comparability, sample bias (in terms of age), and cross-national study effects, it is still

ANALYTICAL TECHNIQUES

It is not perhaps surprising that mobility research should be the field in which 'analytical developments come faster and more furiously . . . than in any other in sociology' (Hout 1983: 7). For, as well as having the major substantive importance that we have stressed in the previous chapter, mobility is an inherently quantitative phenomenon which lends itself readily and rewardingly to statistical treatment, ranging from simple description through to various kinds of formal modelling. It is, in fact, now a major problem for students of mobility to know how to choose among the array of possible techniques that are open to them and enthusiastically recommended by devotees. In this section we seek to explain why, in the analyses that follow, we have actually employed only a rather limited number of the techniques currently on offer, and by no means the most avant garde. As will be seen, the primary criterion by which we have been guided has been not statistical elegance or sophistication but rather aptness to our sociological concerns.

Probably the first technical decision that has to be made by the mobility analyst is that of whether—or when—to work on the basis of mobility tables or through regression and related methods, such as path analysis. Fortunately, there is by now a good deal of agreement on the relative merits of these two approaches.

If interest centres not primarily on mobility, or immobility, in the sense of the degree of association between social origins and destinations, but rather on elucidating the various factors that are involved in 'success' or 'achievement', then regression methods are generally to be preferred. Evident affinities indeed exist between the conceptual choice of a social hierarchy as the context for studying mobility, which puts the emphasis on vertical movement, and the technical choice of regression as a means of exploring the determinants of such movement. The dependent variable is the individual's present position on a usually interval-level prestige or status scale, and the explanatory variables are the individual's origin, and perhaps subsequent positions on this scale, plus measures of a range of other 'background' or 'personal' characteristics. If, however, the focus of interest does indeed rest on the association between origins and destinations itself—on its detailed pattern and, further, on how far this pattern and its variation over time and place reflect endogenous as against exogenous, 'structural' influences—then a tabular approach has obvious advantages. It permits analysis both of actual mobility flows and of mobility 'propensities' as

disturbing that each mobility table is otherwise given equal weight in their analyses, despite great differences in sample size and also, one may reasonably suppose, in quality in such other respects as response rate and data collection and preparation. The reason given for not taking account of differences in sample size—that larger tables would then considerably outweigh smaller ones—is scarcely persuasive.

between all origin and destination categories that are distinguished; and, further, no particular difficulties arise where these categories are unordered or only partially ordered, as they are likely to be where the conceptual context is that of a class structure.

It will, then, be apparent enough from all that we have previously said that, for us, it is the tabular approach that must commend itself. As we have indeed already indicated, we will work essentially from mobility tables constructed on the basis of the class schema which we have described, and by reference to which we have recoded the data of our source enquiries in order to achieve relatively high standards of cross-national comparability.

Mobility table analysis is a special case of the analysis of contingency tables. What is special about it is simply that the kinds of analysis undertaken reflect the particular interests of mobility researchers, as in turn then do the substantive interpretations that are given to the results produced. In the present case what we chiefly seek from tabular analysis are means of establishing and implementing a distinction that will in fact prove crucial to the discussion of most of the chapters that follow: namely, that between *absolute* and *relative* mobility rates.

Absolute mobility (or immobility) rates refer to the proportions of individuals in some base category who are mobile (or immobile), and these rates are thus most readily expressed by percentaging values in particular cells within the mobility table. The three kinds of absolute rate that we shall consider are total rates, inflow rates, and outflow rates, all of which have, of course, been in use from the early days of mobility research. Total rates are given by the percentage of all individuals represented in the mobility table who are found in cells off the main diagonal—that is, whose categories of origin and destination are not the same. Inflow rates show the percentage by origin of individuals of a given category of destination; and outflow rates show the percentage by destination of individuals of a given category of origin.

Relative rates, as might be supposed, are then produced by in some way setting different absolute rates against each other. We will here follow what has by now become the standard practice of treating relative rates in terms of (second order) odds ratios: that is, ratios which show the relative odds of individuals in two different categories of origin being found in one rather than another of two different categories of destination. In the simplest possible case of a 2×2 mobility table, the one odds ratio calculable would thus be given by

$$\frac{f_{11}/f_{12}}{f_{21}/f_{22}}$$

where f_{11} is the number of cases immobile in category 1, f_{12}, the number mobile from category 1 origins to category 2 destinations, and so on. In mobility tables with more than two categories, more than one odds ratio will, of course, be calculable—in fact, one for every possible pair of origin categories considered in relation to every possible pair of destination categories. Thus, the number of odds ratios implicit in a (square) mobility table with k categories will be given by

$$\frac{(k^2 - k)^2}{4}$$

although it can be shown that a 'basic set' (cf. Goodman 1979) of $(k - 1)^2$ odds ratios can be specified which will determine the remainder.

The relative rates, as expressed by odds ratios, that are embodied in a mobility table have been aptly described in their totality as 'the endogenous mobility regime' (Hauser 1978). We will ourselves take up this terminology but will also, following our earlier practice (Erikson, Goldthorpe, and Portocarero 1982, 1983), speak synonymously of 'the pattern of social fluidity'—thus seeking to give the ideas of mobility and fluidity a sharper differentiation than in much previous usage; that is to say, we will take fluidity as referring specifically to *relative* rates.

Another way in which odds ratios can be interpreted is as expressing the pattern of *net* association between categories of origin and destination—that is, the pattern of association considered net of the effects of the marginal distributions of these categories. An odds ratio of 1 implies complete statistical independence of the origin and destination categories involved— or, that is, a situation of 'perfect mobility'—while the further an odds ratio departs from 1, the stronger the association that is indicated.[28] Odds ratios are able to capture such net association because they are what has been termed (Bishop, Fienberg, and Holland 1975) 'margin-insensitive' measures: that is, they remain unaltered under the multiplication of the rows or columns of a contingency table by (non-zero) constants. An important implication so far as the analysis of mobility is concerned is, therefore, that two or more mobility tables could in fact possess the same underlying pattern of relative rates, as expressed by odds ratios—or, that is, the same endogenous mobility regime—even though they have different marginal distributions and thus display different absolute rates.

One further major advantage of thinking of relative rates in terms of odds ratios is that these ratios constitute the elements of log-linear models. Such models have emerged as the sociologist's most flexible yet powerful means for the analysis of contingency tables of any kind (for introductions see, e.g., Payne 1977; Hauser 1979; Knoke and Burke 1980; Gilbert 1981). In the context of mobility research the major advantage obtained from log-linear

---

[28] In the context of mobility analysis, the interpretation of odds ratios greater than and less than 1 will depend on the classes, or other categories, involved and also on their ordering, if one is assumed. In the simplest case of a 2 × 2 table, an odds ratio greater than 1 will, of course, imply mobility below the independence or 'perfect-mobility' level and a ratio less than 1, mobility above this level

modelling is that it thus becomes possible to express hypotheses on relative rates—for example, concerning temporal stability or cross-national similarity—in a form in which they both have precise meaning and are readily available for empirical test. In addition, though, log-linear models have been increasingly applied, usually in a more exploratory mode, in order to investigate the more detailed features of relative rates, and it is indeed in this respect that technical innovation has of late been most rapid of all.

One family of recent models consists of those developed specifically for application to mobility tables with ordered categories. Their defining characteristic is the assumption they embody that, other things being equal, mobility between two categories will vary—inversely—with the 'social distance' that separates them, as measured by prestige, status, etc. While this assumption undoubtedly makes for parsimony, models of the kind in question have tended, in fact, to give only rather poor fits to mobility tables unless other, non-hierarchical, effects are in some way suppressed or the models are elaborated to allow these effects to be accommodated (see, further, Erikson and Goldthorpe 1989).[29] But, in any event, such models are not those most appropriate to our own approach and concerns. Rather, we turn to another family of models which have been labelled as 'topological' (Hout 1983: 37; cf. Hauser 1978, 1979) and which are also known, somewhat more modestly perhaps, as 'levels models'.

These models are especially suited to the analysis of mobility within a class-structural context in that they do not require any ordering in the categories of the mobility table. What they aim to do is to elucidate the pattern of relative rates—or, as we would wish to say, of social fluidity—by allocating the internal cells of the mobility table to a number of subsets, and by then requiring all cells in a subset to show the same level of net association (or 'interaction') as between the origin and the destination categories involved. In other words, one could say that topological or levels models seek to divide up the mobility table into a number of 'regions', distinguished from each other by differing 'propensities' for the transitions that their constituent cells define.[30] The adaptability of these models is such that no problems arise in fitting the data, should this be the only objective. However,

---

[29] It might be added here that, while models based on some notion of social distance between categories do not actually require the assumption that this distance is unidimensional and 'vertical', it is, none the less, such an interpretation that is generally introduced, whether the attempt is made to justify it *a priori* or—as, say, in the case of 'scaled association' models—*a posteriori*.

[30] It can be shown (see Goldthorpe 1980*a*/1987: 119) that, under a topological model, the relationship of the interaction parameters for any tetrad of cells within the mobility table to the expected odds ratio for that tetrad is simply

$$\frac{F_{ik}/F_{il}}{F_{jk}/F_{jl}} = \frac{I_{ik}/I_{il}}{I_{jk}/I_{jl}}$$

where i,j are a pair of origin classes and k,l a pair of destination classes, and F and I refer to expected cell values and cell-interaction parameters respectively.

little is in fact thus gained unless the design of models—that is, the allocation of cells to different subsets and levels—is invested with some theoretical rationale, rather then being merely *ad hoc*, so that the analyst has a basis for choosing among different models which show a similar goodness of fit or indeed among models with different designs but which are in fact formally equivalent (cf. Macdonald 1981; Pöntinen 1982). In the present study the main technical innovation that we will ourselves propose, in Chapter 4, is a new form of topological model in which the ultimate allocation of cells to different levels is the outcome of a series of more specific decisions that the analyst is called upon to make in some systematic way.

To recapitulate, then, we will pursue our interests in mobility within a class-structural context through tabular analysis and on the basis of the distinction between absolute and relative rates. The former can be treated in simple percentage terms; the latter we will express as odds ratios and analyse by certain kinds of log-linear modelling. There is, however, one remaining issue on which we should here set out our position. We should make it clear that we would regard the distinction between absolute and relative mobility rates as effectively superseding that used in much previous mobility research between 'structural' and 'exchange' mobility.

The latter distinction was prompted by an awareness of the fact that where, as is usually the case, the marginal distributions of a mobility table are not identical, some amount of mobility is necessitated by this discrepancy alone: it is arithmetically impossible that all cases should be found on the main diagonal. Consequently, various attempts were made to find ways of measuring such structural—or 'forced'—mobility separately from that which might be thought of as occurring, independently of any marginal discrepancy, in the form of entirely compensating exchange—or 'circulation'—mobility between different categories. The accounting identity underlying most of these efforts was

$$\text{total mobility} - \text{structural mobility} \equiv \text{exchange mobility}$$

where total mobility was represented by the proportion of all cases found in cells off the main diagonal of the table, and structural mobility by, for example, the index of dissimilarity for the marginal distributions. However, in all such procedures a basic confusion of levels of analysis would appear to be present. As argued elsewhere:

What is being attempted is to use the straightforward partitioning of recorded instances of individual mobility as a means of expressing a distinction which can have meaning only at a supra-individual or 'macrosociological' level. Structural and exchange mobility are in effect being treated as if they were two different kinds of mobility, between which the movements of individuals may be divided up—when the distinction between them must be understood, if it is to have sociological significance at all, as relating to two aspects of mobility which are variable properties of societies, taken as units of analysis. (Goldthorpe 1980a/1987: 75)

Not surprisingly, then, a series of both technical and interpretive problems arose and remained unresolved (cf. Bertaux 1969).

In our view, those substantive issues which led to the concern to isolate exchange from structural or total mobility—that is, issues of social fluidity and openness—are ones that, as we have already argued, can now be in all respects better treated by distinguishing relative from absolute rates. And, in place of the identity given above, one may more usefully think of a set of relative rates once embodied—as odds ratios—within given marginal distributions as then entailing a set of absolute rates: that is

$$\text{marginal distributions, relative rates} \Rightarrow \text{absolute rates.}$$

Proposals for reviving the distinction between structural and exchange mobility have been advanced by Sobel, Hout, and Duncan (1985). These authors abandon the idea of a deterministic partitioning of individual instances of mobility into two types, and seek rather to implement the distinction stochastically within a log-linear modelling approach. Thus, structural mobility is modelled as a factor that raises or lowers the odds, across all categories of origin uniformly, of individuals being found in a given category of destination, while exchange mobility is understood as that part of the mobility process that produces 'equal flows' between pairs of origin and destination categories.

This approach is evidently far more sophisticated than previous ones; none the less, we still do not find it convincing. As Sobel, Hout, and Duncan acknowledge, their reformulated concepts of structural and exchange mobility can give an adequate account of the mobility table *only if* certain *empirical* conditions are met: that is, if the pattern of net association between pairs of origin and destination categories is *symmetrical*; otherwise, the entirely *ad hoc* notion of 'non-reciprocated exchanges' has to be introduced. We can see no good sociological reasons for privileging symmetrical association in this way, and it would in any event appear unsatisfactory—above all from the standpoint of comparative research—that the applicability of a conceptual scheme for the analysis of mobility tables should in fact be dependent upon one of their quite contingent features.[31] We find no difficulty, we should stress, with the idea of structural *effects* on (absolute) mobility rates, in the sense of effects that are mediated via the marginal distributions of the mobility table; and, indeed, we will in this respect later exploit the proposals that Sobel, Hout, and Duncan put forward. But, as regards attempts to distinguish between structural and exchange mobility *per se*, we would underwrite the conclusion reached by Sobel in an earlier paper (1983) that these are by now outmoded and unhelpful and should no longer be pursued.

---

[31] A log-linear model proposing symmetrical association fails in fact to give an adequate fit to four out of the twelve intergenerational mobility tables in our data-set (those for Australia, the FRG, Japan, and Scotland) even when we standardize on the size of the smallest (N = 1,991).

COMPARATIVE STRATEGY

As Ragin (1987) has noted, comparative, cross-national research in sociology would at the present time seem to be characterized by a sharp methodological division. On the one side are those comparativists who work primarily with 'qualitative' materials, derived mainly from historical or anthropological sources, and who wish to treat national societies or other mascrosocial units 'holistically'—that is, as so many separate case-studies that are to be interpreted. On the other side are those who work primarily with 'quantitative' data, derived from survey research or official statistics, and whose strategy is essentially that of taking nations (cf. Kohn 1989) not simply as providing the *context* of analysis but as being in fact the *units* of analysis, differences among which are then to be explained through the same multivariate techniques as would be applied in regard to differences among individuals. Thus, while adherents of the former approach tend to be highly sensitive to the specificities of national histories and cultures—sometimes to the point at which their general arguments may no longer be easy to discern—adherents of the latter approach are guided by the radical programme of conceptually transcending all such specificities or, as expressed in the well-known phrase inspired by Przeworski and Teune (1970), of 'replacing the names of nations with the names of variables'.

However, despite the clear conflict between the two approaches—ultimately, perhaps, over what sociological analysis can and should hope to achieve—they may, as Ragin further suggests, still be regarded as in some degree complementary. For example, the typical emphasis in case-studies on the part played by particular actors, individual or collective, in given historical contexts can help offset the tendency of 'variable-oriented' analyses to produce explanations of an excessively abstract and 'black-box' kind—while this emphasis is itself usefully qualified by the ability of wider-ranging and more systematic analyses to bring out the more general structural constraints to which human agency and historical process may be subject. From such complementarity there does then arise the possibility that 'combined' or 'mixed' comparative strategies of various kinds may be developed; and it is, in fact, this possibility that, for our present purposes, appears to us to have the greatest attraction.[32]

We shall, of course, wish to treat class mobility within the nations that we consider in quantitative terms: that is, by distinguishing and measuring absolute and relative rates in the way we have indicated in the preceding section. Moreover, we shall also wish to make direct quantitative comparisons of mobility rates, patterns, and trends among nations. Thus, we are clearly committed to the assumption—apart from all technical questions of data

---

[32] Ragin (1987: ch. 5) would himself rather recommend what he calls 'synthetic' strategies. However, the particular proposals that he makes under this head—for, in effect, comparisons based on the logic of Boolean algebra—do not appear well suited to our own concerns.

comparability—that at a conceptual level our class schema does have valid cross-national applicability. In other words, we must reject the argument, which some sociologists appear ready to maintain, that national class structures have to be regarded as entirely *sui generis* and can be compared, if at all, only in some holistic fashion and not through quantitative analyses dependent on concepts and categories formed at a high level of generality.[33] To this extent, therefore, it is clearly the quantitative and variable-oriented approach that we will take up.

However, when we come to consider the results of our quantitative comparisons of mobility, we shall not until a very late stage—and even then with some amount of scepticism—attempt to explain such cross-national differences as may be revealed by relating these systematically to differences displayed by our nations in other of their macrosocial attributes. That is to say, we shall not be primarily concerned with the kind of multivariate analysis, by now quite common in comparative mobility research, in which measures of mobility serve as the dependent variables and the independent variables are indicators of such national characteristics as level of industrialization, degree of educational opportunity, degree of income inequality, political complexion of governments, etc.[34] Rather, in seeking to account for cross-national differences in mobility, we shall for the most part rely on analyses of a more 'internal' and historical kind. Thus, the explanations we will suggest for features of mobility of special interest to us in particular nations will often be ones couched in terms of the more immediate effects of events, conjunctures, and social processes occurring within these nations; and, instead of assuming that multivariate analysis is here the 'natural' approach to follow, we will treat as essentially open the question of whether the factors we identify are ones that *could* be usefully subsumed under variable names. In this respect, then, we shall opt for a version of the qualitative, case-study approach, and the names of nations will certainly not disappear from our text.

Our reasons for favouring a mixed strategy on the lines indicated are, we must acknowledge, of differing kinds. To begin with, some are no more than pragmatic. As we previously remarked, in constituting our comparative data-set through the detailed recoding of information from reputable national studies, we have in effect traded off coverage for reliability. Thus, apart from all questions of their representativeness, the number of national cases that we have available to us is clearly a good deal less than would be desirable for the purposes of multivariate analysis, and sets narrow limits on the range of independent variables that could be sensibly introduced.

We would also wish to emphasize that all the reservations we earlier expressed concerning the quality of comparative data on mobility taken

[33] See, for example, Burawoy (1977)—and also the very effective reply by Treiman (1977*b*). We will return to this issue more specifically in Chapter 10 in considering the case of Japan.
[34] Various examples are again provided by the studies citied in Chapter 1, n. 25.

directly from published sources could be reiterated with no less force as regards measures of the independent variables that have most often been considered in relation to cross-national differences in mobility. It is not just that there is much room for disagreement on exactly how level of industrialization, degree of educational opportunity, economic inequality, etc., are to be measured, but that the data available for doing so on a comparative basis, in whatever way may be chosen, are still for the most part highly unsatisfactory. In our judgement, major improvements will in this respect need to be made before *any* comparative analysis that incorporates such variables can produce results that warrant being taken seriously other than in their crudest outline.[35]

At the same time, though, we would still wish to regard the choice of strategy that we have made as being something more than simply a *pis aller*. There are, in fact, three considerations which lead us to believe that it may, in present circumstances, offer positive advantages.

It is, first of all, relevant to recall from Chapter 1 that a number of the arguments concerning mobility that we aim to assess, as embodied both in the liberal theory of industrialism and in certain rival positions, are ones claiming very strong regularities in the form of 'univariate' tendencies or indeed of *in*variances. Thus, the liberal theory proposes that both absolute and relative mobility rates (as we might now say) will rise steadily in relation to just one, overriding factor: namely, the progress of a society's industrial development. According to the LZ hypothesis, however, in all industrial societies, at whatever developmental stage they may be, absolute rates of intergenerational mobility between manual and non-manual positions will be found at much the same level. Or, according to the FJH hypothesis, all such societies will display relative rates that are on a basically similar pattern. Where, then, we are dealing with arguments of this degree of boldness, multivariate analysis is scarcely required: as Popper has emphasized (see, e.g., 1972: ch. 1), the stronger a hypothesis, the more easily it may be tested. Provided that we do, in fact, have good grounds for trusting our data, 'deviant' cases, if they exist, should be readily identifiable, and any such that emerge will be sufficient to show that the hypothesis in question should be rejected or, at all events, should to some degree or other be qualified—on lines which close examination of the deviant cases might in turn help to suggest.

---

[35] To illustrate our point here, we may take the case of comparative data on the personal distribution of incomes, which have been widely used in constructing indices of economic inequality. The inadequacies of such data as may be found in official compilations and standard source books are clearly revealed by results from the Luxembourg Income Study (LIS) (Smeeding and Schmaus 1990; cf. also O'Higgins, Schmaus, and Stephenson 1990), which represents the first attempt to raise standards of cross-national comparability in this respect by reprocessing unit-record data, in a way analogous to that we have followed in the case of mobility. Correspondingly, though, the LIS data-set is not all that extensive.

Secondly, to the extent that regularities of both a strong and a straight-forward kind fail to be demonstrated, and some more complex understanding of mobility rates, patterns, and trends is evidently required, it still does not necessarily follow that one should move directly to multivariate analysis. It may yet be of greater value to maintain a focus on particular cases, with the aim of developing the insights that can thus be gained into hypotheses bearing directly on the actual generation of the variation that is to be observed. Certainly, it would not be difficult to argue that the multivariate analyses of cross-national differences in mobility that have so far been undertaken have tended to be theoretically underdeveloped, if not quite premature, with the result that the specification of the models applied would appear often rather arbitrary and their—far from consistent—results very difficult to interpret.

Thirdly, the possibility has always to be kept in mind—and it is one that will in fact grow in importance as this study proceeds—that, even where cross-national variation in mobility is apparent enough, it may still not be open to macrosociological explanation or, at least, not of the kind that multivariate analysis can offer. That is to say, some aspects of the variation at least may simply not be generated in ways that are universal across the range of societies in question but rather in ways that are specific to particular societies and, perhaps, particular times. And to the extent, then, that this is so, little is likely to be achieved through a programme in which the names of variables are to be substituted for those of nations. Thus, it may be argued, attention to variation in mobility as it arises in particular national contexts will be of value in determining the scope that does in fact exist for multi-variate analysis to be validly deployed.[36]

In sum, then, we would see our mixed strategy as one that is not inappropriate to the aims—and limitations—of our present study and indeed to the present 'state of the art' in comparative mobility research. In the circumstances, we do not find it unduly eclectic to link together a quantitative and variable-oriented approach to the study of mobility within nations where the units of our analysis will be individuals or families, and a largely qualitative and case-oriented approach when we compare mobility rates and patterns among nations. Such a strategy will in some instances undoubtedly restrict the kinds of conclusion that we can reach, and we must, in particular, resist the temptation of engaging in 'verbal multivariate analysis' in the absence of the real thing. But we will, on the other hand, as we have sought to show, have various opportunities to exploit the advantage we gain from our relatively small number of cases in being able to acquire, and draw on, a rather detailed knowledge of each individually.

[36] Note here that to try to determine this matter simply from the results of multivariate analyses—for example, in terms of 'variance explained'—would be especially dubious in view both of the lack of any detailed theoretical basis for model specifications and of the small number of cases likely to be involved.

After this extended excursion into methodology, we are now ready to turn to our substantive concerns. Questions of method, however, should not, and will not, henceforth disappear from view. In the foregoing we have indicated in necessarily rather general terms the positions that we shall adopt on a range of—often contentious—issues of conceptualization, data, technique, and comparative strategy. In the following, the options that we take up will be given more specific expression in the way that we attempt to realize the programme set out in our introductory chapter: that is, the testing of a variety of arguments on mobility rates, patterns, and trends within industrial societies. As this attempt proceeds, the full implications of our methodological commitments will become more apparent, and the reader will thus be provided with a far better basis than the present chapter alone for forming judgements as to their merits or otherwise.

3
Trends in Class Mobility

We begin our treatment of substantive matters by considering those arguments outlined in Chapter 1 which relate to mobility *trends*. We have shown that, within what we have called the liberal theory of industrialism, such arguments play a pivotal role. The central claim is that, in consequence of various functional exigencies of developing industrialism, mobility rates are not only pushed to a generally higher level than in pre-industrial societies—and with a bias towards upward movement—but, moreover, tend steadily to increase. And, following our discussion of analytical issues in the preceding chapter, we can now further say that the mobility trend that the liberal theory envisages has to be understood as applying to absolute and relative rates alike. Absolute rates increase because of the mounting rapidity of structural change in industrial economies and societies, but also because evolving processes of social selection favour achievement over ascription and thus make for greater openness—or, that is, for progressively more equal relative chances of mobility—and especially within 'leading sectors'.

Among the arguments that could in this respect be ranged against the liberal theory, some would appear clearly less forceful than others. For example, the Marxist attempt to replace the liberal view of a progressive upgrading of employment under industrialism with a directly contrary one of the 'degradation of labour' and the proletarianization of the work-force has proved to be empirically untenable. And, again, suggestions that mobility rates and patterns in particular societies or types of society are exceptional or distinctive could, even if validated, offer a basis for only a partial or indirect critique of the liberal position in regard to trends.[1] However, at least three other arguments were earlier identified which do raise a challenge to this position of a more immediate and serious kind.

First, there is Sorokin's contention that, when a long-term view is taken, mobility rates will be seen to display no continuous direction of change but merely 'trendless fluctuation'. If any endogenous tendency does exist, it is for all forms of social stratification to become more rigid; but changes in levels of mobility result primarily from the impact on stratifying processes of

---

[1] The liberal theory of industrialism—in much the same way as the Marxist theory of capitalism—can be rather readily protected against what would appear at any one time as difficult cases by arguments that exploit its developmental form: such cases can be represented as only 'transitional' or 'temporary' and as destined eventually to disappear as the theory works itself out. Critiques that focus on the actual course of change are less easily dealt with in this way, although it is true that developmental theories can in the end always be 'saved' by arguments to the effect that they will 'come good' at some unspecified future stage.

a diversity of exogenous factors, and it is in this way that fluctuation in rates is produced.

Secondly, there is the argument of Lipset and Zetterberg that, at a certain stage in the industrialization of a society, (absolute) mobility rates rise to a new historic 'high'. This is essentially the result of structural change—that is, of the emergence of a more differentiated social division of labour—rather than of any necessary increase in equality of opportunity. Since mobility motivations are an effective constant, mobility then tends to remain at this same high level across all societies that have entered the industrial world. As was noted in Chapter 1, this last step in the argument—the hypothesis of cross-national similarity in absolute rates—appears difficult to sustain either logically or factually. However, in the present context Lipset's and Zetterberg's initial idea—that industrialization may have a 'threshold' effect on mobility rates rather than a continuous one—is still of potential importance.

Thirdly, there is the reformulation of the hypothesis of cross-national similarity, due to Featherman, Jones, and Hauser, which locates this similarity at the level not of absolute but of relative rates. The FJH hypothesis thus stands in clear opposition to the liberal expectation that, in consequence of the inherent dynamics of industrialism, more advanced industrial societies will show more equal relative rates than those less advanced. The emphasis is rather placed on the highly stable nature of inequalities of opportunity and condition alike. Furthermore, the FJH hypothesis would appear to imply radical doubts about the possibility of trends in absolute rates also. For, in much the same way as Sorokin, its authors point to the wide range of exogenous factors that bear, directly or indirectly, on such rates and generate change and variation in them.

These, then, are the claims and counter-claims which in this chapter we shall seek to assess. First, though, we must say something about the geographical and historical context from which the data of our analyses derive.

THE RELEVANCE OF THE EUROPEAN EXPERIENCE

As indicated in Chapter 2, we intend, to begin with, to base our analyses on those of our comparative data which are of highest quality. In this chapter, therefore, we shall examine questions of trends by considering the class mobility of men, and with reference chiefly to intergenerational rather than to work-life mobility. We shall also restrict our attention to the nine European nations that are included in our sample. However, we would believe that in this last respect at least the narrowing of focus that is entailed does bring with it certain compensating advantages. This is so because, in discussion thus far of mobility trends in the course of industrial development, the specific importance of the European experience would seem to us to have been insufficiently appreciated.

It is not difficult to detect within the liberal theory of industrialism a degree of American, or, more accurately perhaps, Anglo-American, ethno-centrism. Historically, the origins of modern industrial society are traced back to late-eighteenth- and early nineteenth-century England; and other Western nations, including the United States, are then seen as having successively followed England's lead in breaking free of the constraints of a traditional social order and entering the industrial world.[2] Contemporaneously, it is the United States rather than England that is recognized as the vanguard nation; and, with industrialization now on the global agenda, the major differences between industrial and pre-industrial, or modern and traditional, society are seen as best revealed through explicit or implicit USA–Third World comparisons. Within these perspectives, therefore, the experience of industrialization of the mainland European nations is viewed in only a rather restrictive way. It tends either to be taken for granted, as fitting unproblematically into the trajectories defined by the two paradigm cases, or, alternatively, as providing interesting instances of 'deviations', over which, however, the logic of industrialism has eventually to prevail.[3]

This schematic background to the liberal theory must be regarded as excessively simplified, and possibly misleading, in at least two respects. On the one hand, while England did indeed industrialize early, the supposition that other Western nations then followed along the same path, being differentiated only by the degree of their 'retardation', is one that has no sound historiographic basis. What is chiefly significant about the process of industrialization in England is that—in part *because* of England's priority, but for other reasons too—it took on a quite distinctive character which subsequent cases could scarcely reflect (cf. Kemp 1978: esp. ch. 1). Rather than having simply followed in England's wake, other European nations do in fact display in their recent economic histories a great diversity of developmental paths; and it is, furthermore, important to recognize that later industrialization and economic retardation should not always be equated—as, for example, the French case can well illustrate (cf. O'Brien and Keyder 1978).

---

[2] The influence here of the 'stages-of-growth' model of Rostow (1960: see, esp., Chart 1) would seem to be of particular importance and also, perhaps—though the evidence is indirect—the interpretation of European industrial development provided by Landes (1957, 1965/1972), which places major emphasis upon the rate and pattern of diffusion of techniques of production from Britain to the more 'backward' economies of the European mainland.

[3] Thus, for example, in Kerr *et al.* (1960/1973) discussion of France and Italy is largely concerned with the impediments to industrial development that result from the persisting importance of 'family-dominated enterprises' with 'patrimonial management' (see, e.g. 1960/1973: 80, 141–2; and cf. Landes 1957); and discussion of Germany, with difficulties of social rigidity and authoritarianism, following from the promotion of industrialization by a dynastic elite (e.g. 1960/1973: 54–5, 150–1).

On the other hand, it would also be mistaken to suppose that by the end of the nineteenth century the industrialization of Europe was essentially completed. This would be to neglect the great economic and social import- ance that agriculture and also artisanal and other 'pre-industrial' forms of production continued to have throughout the nineteenth, and for well into the twentieth century—and in many of the more advanced European nations as well as in those on the 'periphery'. It was, in fact, as Bell has remarked (1980: 233), only in the period *after* the Second World War that Europe as a whole became an industrial society. Indeed, various interpreta- tions of the 'long boom' of this period have seen it as reflecting aspects of this culmination—for example, as being driven by the final phase of the supply of surplus rural labour (Kindleberger 1967) or as marking the ultimate overcoming of the dualism of traditional and modern sectors within European economies (Lutz 1984).[4]

The fact, then, that we here concentrate on the nine European nations included in our study by no means implies that we will be treating questions of mobility trends within an unduly limited context. To the contrary, we have the advantage that, while these nations can supply us with high quality data (far better, for example, than those usually available from Third World nations), they do also display a remarkably wide range of variation in their levels and patterns of industrial development—and even if we consider only that time-span to which our mobility data have some reference: that is, from the 1970s back to the first two decades of the century, in which the oldest respondents within our national samples were born. This point may be illustrated, as in Figure 3.1, on the basis of a simple, but defensible, indicator of industrial development (ILO 1977; Gagliani 1985)—the proportion of the total labour force engaged outside agriculture.

From Figure 3.1 it would in fact appear that among our nine nations we should be ready to recognize at least three different types of trajectory.[5] First, England and Wales (henceforth 'England'), along with Scotland, can be taken as cases of 'early' industrializing nations in which the proportion of the labour force outside agriculture was not only high, but indeed already close to its maximum, by the start of the twentieth century. A second developmental pattern of what we may call 'late' industrialization is then represented by France, Germany, Northern Ireland, and Sweden. These nations show a substantial agricultural work-force persisting throughout the

---

[4] It is of interest that Bell should refer to the situation on which he comments as one 'that has gone relatively unexamined'. This statement may well be true for American theorists of industrialism, but it can scarcely hold in the case of European economic and social historians. See, for example, the discussion of issues central to the 'reperiodization' of the development of industrial society in Europe that are found in Wrigley (1972) and Mayer (1981).

[5] We have, of course, the problem here that several of the nations in our sample do not retain the same political identity and frontiers over the entire period covered by Figure 3.1. Major differences occur in the cases of the FRG, Hungary, Ireland, Northern Ireland, and Poland. However, as noted, the data are adjusted so that they refer throughout the period to post-Second-World-War territories.

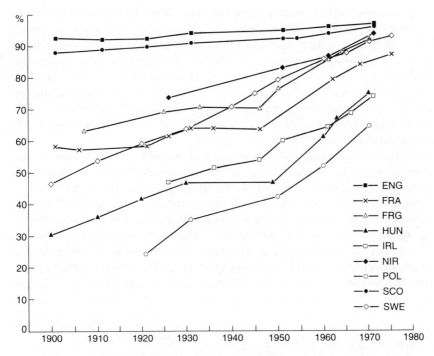

FIGURE 3.1. *Total labour force engaged outside agriculture*

first half of the century, and being reduced to something approximating the British level only towards the end of the long-boom period. And, thirdly, Hungary, the Republic of Ireland (henceforth 'Ireland'), and Poland appear as nations of 'delayed' industrialization, whose economies and societies remained—at least in terms of the distribution of the work-force—*predominantly* agrarian up to the time of the Second World War, and saw decisive industrial development only in the period after 1950.

For our present purposes, therefore, one implication of obvious interest may be noted. If it is the case, as Lipset and Zetterberg have suggested, that there is a stage in the emergence of an industrial society at which absolute mobility rates shift upwards to a new high level, then we might reasonably expect to find evidence of this shift—and even were it to occur quite early in the industrializing process—within the mobility patterns displayed by men in certain of the national samples that we consider.

However, while the range of variation in the developmental paths that our nations reveal is thus a valuable resource for us, it is also important that these nations do share, albeit in differing ways, in a *common* experience of industrial advance and of concomitant economic growth. This experience is indicated, for the period to which our mobility data relate, in Figure 3.2, which shows trends in real GNP *per capita*. As is clearly reflected, the period comprises two rather distinct economic eras. From the First World War to around 1950 European economies grew, but their growth was interrupted and held back by both the First and then the Second World Wars and by the intervening economic crises. But from 1950 through to the early 1970s the long boom prevailed. Across Western and Eastern Europe, also, high rates of growth were sustained in a quite unprecedented way, and the structures of national economies underwent more rapid transformation than at any time previously (cf. Postan 1967; Maddison 1973; Bairoch 1976; Pollard 1981; Tipton and Aldrich, 1987).

In this way too, then, the European experience provides a context well suited to our purposes. If, as the liberal theory claims, mobility and openness tend alike to increase as the development of industrial societies proceeds, trends of this kind should be readily discernible within our data-set. In particular, we might expect to find such increases among the younger age-groups within our national samples—that is, among those made up of men whose working lives have fallen largely or entirely within the post-war years. Furthermore, as Figure 3.1 suggests, over the period covered by our data the nations we consider became progressively more like each other in having essentially industrial economies. And thus, following the liberal

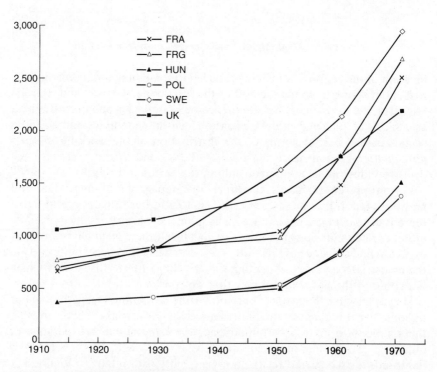

FIGURE 3.2. *Real GNP per capita (1960 US$ and prices)*

theory, we might expect that, under the influence of the logic of industrialism, some degree of convergence would also be apparent in their mobility rates: that is to say, the mobility displayed by the younger age-groups in our samples, as well as being at a higher level than that of older age-groups, should also reveal a greater cross-national similarity.

Conversely, we could of course regard the European experience during the period in question as providing an unusually stern test of those positions earlier reviewed that entail scepticism about mobility trends, at least as these might be generated by economic development. If, over the years of the long boom especially—when all indicators of such development tend to march in lockstep—change in mobility rates of a directional kind should prove hard to detect within our European nations, then theories of 'no trend' might indeed be thought robust.

It will from the foregoing have become evident that, in seeking to exploit the historical richness of our European data, we are prepared to make a large assumption: namely, that valid inferences about the presence or absence of mobility trends can be drawn from the data of single enquiries. What we are in effect proposing is that age-groups distinguished within our samples from the 1970s can be treated as successive birth-cohorts, and that the mobility experience of their members can then be taken as indicative of whether or not change over time has occurred in mobility rates and patterns. In such an approach certain well-known difficulties arise, above all in treating intergenerational mobility, and in conclusion of this section we should therefore give these some attention.

To begin with, we must recognize that we are not in fact dealing with true birth-cohorts within the nations we consider but only with what might better be called 'quasi-cohorts': that is, with the survivors of true cohorts, following on losses due to mortality and emigration, to whom immigrants will then be added. In such cases as those of the FRG, Ireland, and Poland, the numbers here involved will obviously be substantial. This, however, is a situation that we can do little to remedy; we can only trust that no serious distortions will be introduced into our data of a kind that might affect our conclusions regarding trends.[6]

Further, there is the so-called 'identification problem'. If, for the members of a national sample, one compares their present class position (i.e. at time of enquiry) with their class of origin (i.e. father's class), the mobility experience of the individuals within successive 'quasi-cohorts' will be likely to reflect several different effects: not only those of the historical period through which they have lived but also those of their age and of their cohort membership *per se*. Thus, the problem is that of how we can assess 'period' effects—which are those relevant to questions of mobility trends—separately

---

[6] So far as emigration is concerned, a detailed review of the possible and likely effects on mobility rates and propensities is provided by Hout (1989), with special reference to the Irish case.

from effects of the other kinds. No clear-cut solution is, or can be, available (cf. Glenn 1977), since birth-cohorts and age-groups are inescapably 'embedded' in historical time. However, several considerations would lead us to believe that, in pursuing our present purposes, we need not in fact be at so great a disadvantage in this respect as might initially appear.

First, it would seem empirically defensible to regard men of around 30–35 years of age as having reached a stage of 'occupational maturity', beyond which further major changes in their class positions become relatively unlikely (Goldthorpe 1980*a*/1987: ch. 3; cf. also Blossfeld 1986). Thus, we may take results for cohorts of this age or older as giving a reasonably reliable indication of the 'completed' pattern of the collective class mobility of their members.

Secondly, for all of our European nations except one, the FRG, we have information on individuals' experience of mobility from their class of origin to their class of *first* employment. For this transition, therefore, age effects at least will obviously be much reduced, since attention is focused on a fairly well-defined life-cycle stage. We would not wish to regard data on this transition as a very satisfactory basis for cross-national comparisons of intergenerational mobility—on grounds that we will discuss at some length in Chapter 8. None the less, we are thus provided with the possibility of checking whether or not the conclusions that we reach on trends, or their absence, in mobility from class of origin to present class are consistent with ones that pertain to mobility rates of a more age-specific kind.[7]

Thirdly, it is important for us to emphasize that, in the analyses that follow, our concern will be not so much with the actual empirical description of mobility trends as with the evaluation of particular claims about such trends. What, therefore, we can always consider is whether, if we were to suppose some confounding of effects in our results, these would be of a kind that would tend unduly to favour or disfavour a given position. Thus, for example, in the case of the liberal claim that within industrial nations mobility and openness tend steadily to increase, it is difficult to see why any confounding of period effects by age effects should produce unfairly *negative* results: that is to say, it would appear unlikely that an actual increase in openness and mobility among the more recent cohorts within our national samples would be concealed by the fact that these cohorts are made up of young persons. If anything, one might expect the contrary, since younger persons will have benefited more widely from the expansion of educational provision which, according to the liberal theory, is one of the major sources of greater mobility and equality of opportunity. Likewise, there would seem no reason why age effects should obscure any trends within our data for the mobility rates of different nations to converge—as would be expected under

---

[7] For our present purposes, it is the confounding of period by age effects that is most likely to create problems. To the extent that cohort effects are present in the data, this may be regarded as valid evidence against the occurrence of secular trends.

the liberal theory as differences between nations' levels of industrial development are reduced. For if, as the theory maintains, the determinants and
processes of mobility become increasingly standardized through the logic of
industrialism, then convergence in mobility rates should, presumably, be
more apparent among the younger than the older age-groups in our samples
(for an elaboration of this point, see Erikson, Goldthorpe, and Portocarero
1983: 307–10 and Figure 1).

As Glenn has observed (1977: 17), cohort analysis should never be a
mechanical exercise, uninformed by theory and by additional 'external'
evidence; and this point obviously applies *a fortiori* in the case of analyses,
such as those we shall present, which rest only on 'quasi-cohorts'. But, since
we do have some knowledge about both the historical setting of the mobility
that we consider and its life-course phasing, and since we are addressing a
number of more-or-less specific and theoretically grounded hypotheses
rather than proceeding quite empirically, our strategy is, we believe, one
capable of producing results that can be interpreted in a reasonably reliable
and consequential way. It is to these results that we now turn.

ABSOLUTE RATES

In seeking to assess the arguments that we have earlier reviewed, we start
with evidence on intergenerational class mobility in the form of absolute
rates: that is, rates expressed in simple percentage terms. So as to avoid
marked age effects in considering the transition from class of origin to
present class, we restrict our attention to men in our national samples who
were over age 30 at the time of enquiry (i.e. at some point in the early or mid-
1970s; cf. Table 2.3). These men, we suppose, would be approaching, or
would have attained, a stage of relative occupational maturity. The maximum
age-limit that we apply here—and in all subsequent analyses—is 64.[8]

First of all, we consider *total* mobility rates: that is, the percentage of all
men in our national samples found in cells off the main diagonal of the
intergenerational mobility table, based on the sevenfold version of our class
schema; or, in other words, the percentage of all men whose 'present', or
destination, class was different from their class of origin—the latter being
indexed by the respondent's *father's* class at the time of the respondent's
early adolescence.[9] In Figure 3.3 we seek to plot the course followed by the
total mobility rate in each of our nine European nations on the basis of
moving weighted averages of this rate for men *in successive birth years*, using

[8] This is in fact the highest maximum age that we could apply across all nine of our national
samples.
[9] The wording of the questions from which this information was derived varied somewhat
from one national enquiry to another but not, we believe, in ways likely to have any significant
effects on the comparability of data. In this and all similar instances full details of question
wording, construction of variables, etc., are to be found in the documentation to the CASMIN
International Social Mobility Superfile (Erikson *et al.* 1988).

a method of graduation that has been developed by Hoem and Linneman (1987) and that is further described and extended by Hoem in an annex to this chapter.[10]

From inspection of Figure 3.3 the general impression gained must be one of support for the contention that absolute mobility rates display merely trendless change. It would, at all events, be difficult to ally the data here presented with the idea of mobility increasing steadily as industrialism advances. No regular tendency is apparent for the mobility of older respondents—of men born, say, in the first two decades of the century—to be exceeded by that of respondents who were born some twenty years later, and who would have reached occupational maturity during the long boom of the post-war years. And we may add that no essentially different picture emerges if, using the same technique, we plot total mobility rates from class of origin to class of *first* employment.[11] It would thus seem improbable that

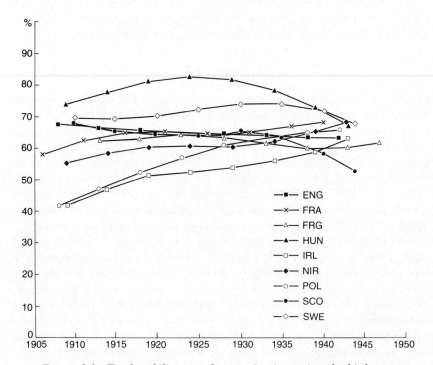

FIGURE 3.3. *Total mobility rates for men in nine nations by birth year*

[10] We are greatly endebted to Jan Hoem for his most generous help in this aspect of our work.

[11] These plots are not shown, but in what follows it may be assumed that, where no reference is made to rates of mobility from class origins to class of first employment, our findings in this respect would not lead us seriously to qualify those we have obtained for rates from class origins to present class.

the failure of the graphs of Figure 3.3 to move upwards to the right, as would be expected from the liberal theory, can be explained simply in terms of the confounding of period by age effects.

The one possible pattern that might be discerned in Figure 3.3 is some tendency for total mobility rates to converge—even if not while steadily rising. That is to say, some narrowing down could be claimed in the cross-national range of mobility levels as between those displayed by the oldest and the youngest cohorts in our samples. For the former, as can be seen, the range of total mobility rates is from around 40 to over 70 per cent, while for the latter it is from 50 to under 70 per cent—and, one might add, would be some ten percentage points narrower still if the one case of Scotland were to be discounted.

However, it is important to note how this convergence comes about. It is, in fact, to a large extent the result of an increase in total mobility in two nations, Ireland and Poland, in which the rate among older cohorts, at around the 40 per cent mark, was substantially lower than in other nations. Ireland and Poland are—together with Hungary—those nations in our sample in which, as we have earlier indicated, industrialization was most delayed. An alternative interpretation of Figure 3.3 would, therefore, be that, instead of revealing a general tendency towards convergence in mobility rates, it rather supports a hypothesis of the kind suggested by Lipset and Zetterberg: that is, of a specific upturn in mobility occurring at a stage relatively early in the industrialization process when the first major impact of structural change is felt.

That Hungary would then appear as deviant, in showing a high total mobility rate even among the oldest men considered, need not be found surprising. This could be seen as the result of the quite exceptional amount of mobility imposed upon the Hungarian agricultural work-force through direct political intervention, and which is thus reflected across the experience of all age-groups alike. In the period immediately following the Second World War, the land reforms of the provisional government created over half a million new peasant proprietors; but then, under the subsequent state socialist regime, agriculture was, within a decade, almost entirely collectivized through the establishment of co-operatives or state farms (Kulcsár 1984: 78–84, 96–100; Brus 1986a, 1986b). Thus, respondents to our 1973 survey who were the sons of agricultural proprietors—over a quarter of the total—held different class positions from their fathers more or less of necessity, and even, in fact, where they continued to work the same land.[12]

---

[12] The results that we report here for Hungary do of course depend on our treating workers on agricultural co-operatives or state farms as having a different class position (VII*b*) from that of peasant proprietors (IV*c*). Some analysts of mobility in Hungary have not made this distinction, but we would argue the desirability of so doing, wherever it is practically feasible. It was, after all, precisely the aim both of the immediate post-war land reform and of the subsequent collectivization programme to *change* agrarian class relations. In the Polish case, it

These findings on total mobility do, we believe, carry significant implications, to which we shall wish to return. It is, however, of further interest here to try to obtain a somewhat more detailed picture of tendencies in absolute rates by considering also intergenerational *outflow* rates. Unfortunately, the relative smallness of the sizes of certain of our national samples means that we cannot reliably base our examination of such rates on the seven-class version of our schema but must, for the most part, resort to the three-class version, as given in Table 2.1, which distinguishes simply between non-manual, manual, and farm classes.[13]

Figures 3.4–3.8, which are produced via the same procedures as Figure 3.3, show the course followed in each of our nations by five different outflow

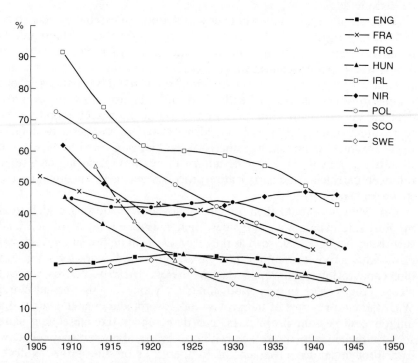

FIGURE 3.4. *Outflow rates from farm origins to farm destinations for men in nine nations by birth year*

should be noted, the attempt that the regime launched at the end of the 1940s to collectivize agriculture met with fierce peasant opposition and was finally abandoned in 1956 (cf. Lewis 1973).

[13] Although, then, we are here forced back to the three-class basis of the earlier comparative research that we have criticized in Chapter 2, we must stress that we do still retain from our recoding exercise a much higher standard of data comparability. In other words, we have a reasonable assurance that the categories of 'non-manual', 'manual', and 'farm' are being applied in a consistent manner from nation to nation, rather than providing comparability of a merely nominal kind.

rates calculated from 3 × 3 intergenerational mobility tables (again for men aged 30–64). As is indicated, the rates in question are those for intergenerational immobility within the farm class, for mobility from farm origins to manual and to non-manual destinations, and for mobility from manual origins to non-manual destinations, and vice versa. Of the other transitions possible within the 3 × 3 tables, those from manual and non-manual origins to farm positions were generally followed by too few individuals to allow any reliable rates to be established; and the fact that the numbers involved here are more-or-less negligible means, in turn, that trends in the remaining rates—that is, rates of immobility within the manual and non-manual classes—need scarcely be plotted separately, since they will be essentially the complements of those already examined of mobility between these two classes.

Figure 3.4 displays the changing proportions of men across birth-cohorts in our nine nations who were of farm origins and who were themselves found in farm work. A broad tendency is apparent for such intergenerational immobility to decline, which might be expected in consequence of the general contraction of agricultural employment, as illustrated in Figure 3.1. The decline in the cases of Ireland and Poland from farm immobility rates of upwards of 70 per cent in the oldest cohorts is of particular interest in view of the interpretation we have suggested of the increases in total mobility in these nations revealed in Figure 3.3. By resorting to the raw data, we can, in fact, show that changes within the farm sector here played a crucial part. Thus, the contribution of this sector to the total *im*mobility rate (i.e. the proportion of all cases in the mobility table found in cells on the main diagonal) fell in the Irish case from 69 per cent for men born before 1925 to only 27 per cent for those born after 1940, while in the Polish case the corresponding decline was from 77 to 35 per cent.

In two other nations, France and Hungary, the decline in farm immobility is also more-or-less continuous over the period to which our data refer. However, the cases of England, Scotland, and Northern Ireland, and likewise that of the FRG, would suggest that, once the decline of agriculture has reached a certain point, rates of farm immobility tend to level out or to become rather variable. And Sweden appears quite distinctive, in that farm immobility is shown at a low level—never more than 25 per cent—throughout the decades in which agricultural employment was falling. Here, though, we do have evidence to suggest some distortion in our results. Our corresponding plot for the transition to class of first employment indicates a strong decline in farm immobility; but, on account perhaps of the very rapidity of agricultural contraction in the post-war years, it would seem that many men also left the farm work-force at a quite late age, thus obscuring the downward trend when the transition to present class is considered.

Finally, it may be observed that in Figure 3.4, as in Figure 3.3, any impression of converging rates is created essentially by the rather dramatic

Irish and Polish graphs. If these are disregarded, the cross-national range in
rates of farm immobility merely fluctuates, being, for example, no narrower—
at around 15–50 per cent—for men born from the mid-1930s onwards than it
was for men born around 1920.

Figures 3.5 and 3.6 then display the course of outflow rates from farm
origins to manual and non-manual destinations respectively. Figure 3.5
would suggest that, in those cases where declining trends in intergenerational
immobility in farming were revealed in Figure 3.4, their counterpart has
been increased outflows from farm origins into manual wage-earning positions in industry. France, Hungary, Ireland, and Poland all show such
increases of a continuous kind. In the remaining nations, however, trends
are less readily discerned. In the cases of the FRG and Sweden, increasing
proportions of men in the cohorts born up to about 1930 moved from farm
origins into manual work—following what might perhaps be taken as a
characteristic tendency of the drive to 'mature' industrialism. But in later
cohorts this tendency is clearly not sustained, although for Sweden there is
probably some underestimation of the rate in question as the converse of the

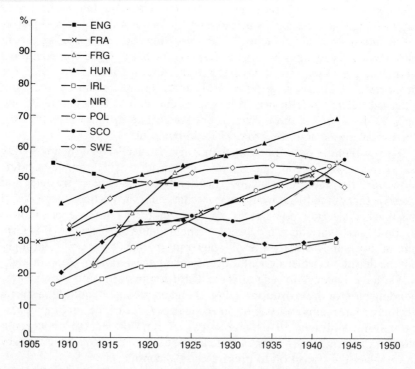

FIGURE 3.5. *Outflow rates from farm origins to manual destinations for men in nine
nations by birth year*

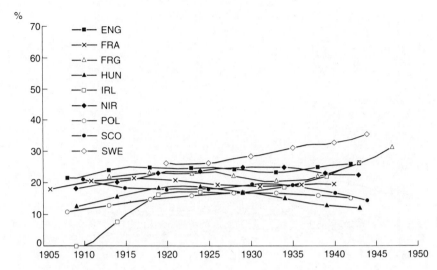

FIGURE 3.6. *Outflow rates from farm origins to non-manual destinations for men in nine nations by birth year*

distortion noted in regard to farm immobility. For England, Northern Ireland, and Scotland the graphs undulate in no readily interpretable way. Turning to the outflow rates from farm origins to non-manual destinations presented in Figure 3.6, we find that trendless change is here still more manifest. The most remarkable feature of the graphs displayed is indeed their flatness apart from the early rise from a near-zero level in the Irish case.[14] The remaining point to be observed from Figures 3.5 and 3.6 together is that we find little indication at all of national mobility rates converging. Over the period covered, the cross-national range for farm-to-manual outflows shifts upwards, but with little narrowing, from around 10–55 per cent to 30–70 per cent; while the rates for farm-to-non-manual outflows are notable for being almost entirely confined within a range of 10–25 per cent.

The last two figures in the series, 3.7 and 3.8, show changes in rates of intergenerational mobility between the broad manual and non-manual classes that we distinguish. From inspection of the graphs it would once again seem difficult to avoid the conclusion that no clear trends emerge. Although some impression may perhaps be given that, overall, mobility from manual origins to non-manual destinations has decreased while that in the reverse direction has increased, it is in fact only in the Polish case that

[14] It may be noted that in Figure 3.6 the left tail of the curve for Sweden has been deleted. This is on account of its unreliability, as determined by the test described in the Annex to this chapter. For the same reason, we have also deleted the left tail of the curve for Northern Ireland in Figure 3.10.

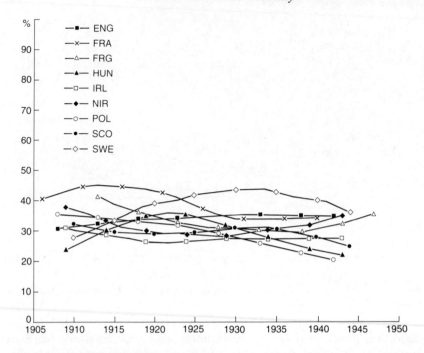

FIGURE 3.7. *Outflow rates from manual origins to non-manual destinations for men in nine nations by birth year*

monotonic trends in these directions can be found. In general, fluctuating rates are displayed, and the graphs for different nations frequently cross. Moreover, as earlier remarked, the negligible volume of outflows from both manual and non-manual origins to farm destinations means that the plots of Figures 3.7 and 3.8 can be taken as essentially the obverses of those relating to *im*mobility within our manual and non-manual classes; so in the case of these rates too an absence of trends may be claimed.

Finally, Figures 3.7 and 3.8 again fail to provide evidence of cross-national convergence in mobility rates. Over the period covered, the cross-national range for rates of mobility from manual origins to non-manual destinations narrows only slightly as it falls from around 30–55 per cent for the oldest cohorts down to 20–40 per cent for the youngest; and the range for mobility in the reverse direction shows no narrowing at all in moving from 20–45 up to 30–55 per cent.[15]

[15] These results are of direct relevance to the LZ hypothesis of cross-national similarity in absolute rates, since this was in fact formulated in terms of outflow rates from non-manual to manual positions and vice versa. However, since this hypothesis does not in itself refer to mobility trends, we defer detailed consideration of it to Chapter 6.

It is the results contained in these last two figures—and also in Figure
3.6—that may occasion most surprise among those presented so far. It
would be generally accepted that non-manual work tends to grow and
manual work to contract as industrial societies reach the more advanced
stages of their development—regardless of whether this is seen as contributing to a net degrading or upgrading of the employment structure overall.
And thus, within the context of the three-class version of our schema,
increasing mobility into non-manual destinations from farm and manual
origins alike should be 'structurally' favoured. Yet, in our data, no consistent
indication of such tendencies is to be found, even within the more advanced
nations or among the younger cohorts.

However, it must in this connection be noted that (as Table 2.1 shows) our
non-manual class is very widely defined. It includes some groupings, such as
routine non-manual employees in administration, commerce, and services,
which have grown primarily through the greater work-force participation of
women; and others, such as small proprietors and other self-employed
workers, which, over the period that our data cover, were typically in
decline. If, then, we wish to consider mobility flows into the non-manual

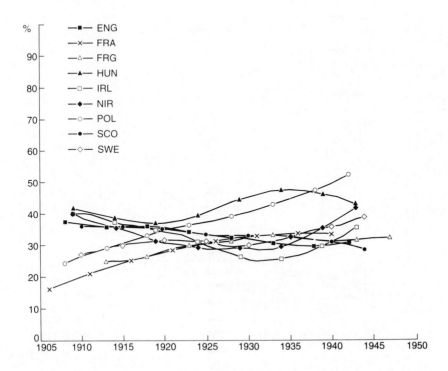

FIGURE 3.8. *Outflow rates from non-manual origins to manual destinations for men in
nine nations by birth year*

groupings that have most clearly expanded among the male work-force, which, as noted in Chapter 1, are in fact mostly at the higher levels of the white-collar range (and cf. also the discussion in Chapter 6, pp. 204–7), we need to draw on data from mobility tables of a more elaborated kind. Although, as we have explained, we cannot go over entirely to the seven-class version of our schema, we can, for present purposes, make a useful compromise: we can construct mobility tables that apply the seven-class version to destinations while retaining the three-class version for origins.

In Figures 3.9 and 3.10 we show the course followed by two outflow rates derived from such 3 × 7 tables: that is, outflow rates from farm and from manual origins respectively into Class I+II of the seven-class version—the service class of primarily professional, higher technical, administrative, and managerial employees. In other words, we here focus on subsets of the rates presented in Figures 3.6 and 3.7 where the mobility in question is into types of employment that *have* been in general expansion. Furthermore, we can also in this way examine changes in mobility flows which, in the light of our earlier discussion of the hierarchical aspects of our class schema, could be

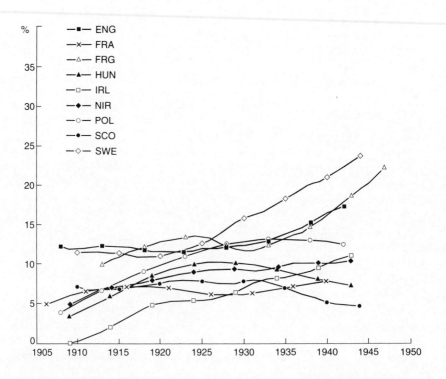

FIGURE 3.9. *Outflow rates from farm origins to service-class destinations for men in nine nations by birth year*

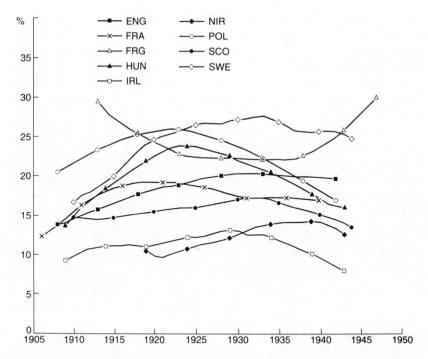

FIGURE 3.10. *Outflow rates from manual origins to service-class destinations for men in nine nations by birth year*

regarded as representing mobility *upwards* from less to more advantaged class positions.[16]

A preliminary point to be noted about Figures 3.9 and 3.10 is that, because the rates we are here concerned with are generally lower and less differentiated than those presented in previous figures, we have doubled the vertical scale, thus, of course, 'enlarging' the changes that are depicted. Even so, they do not appear as highly dramatic.

In Figure 3.9 some increase in mobility from farm origins into the service class is shown up among younger cohorts in several nations—that is, in England, the FRG, and Sweden and, more weakly, in Ireland. But in the remainder any increase that can be detected occurs among older cohorts, and the trend then fades out—so that cross-national differences in rates in fact *widen*. In Figure 3.10 rates of mobility from manual origins into the service class likewise display an increase in England and Sweden which is at least held, and in the FRG they turn sharply upwards among the youngest cohorts. But again, too, the other nations differ, with the most common

---

[16] See pp. 44–6. Following the hierarchical levels that we propose, a further upward flow—that our 3 × 7 tables do not enable us to distinguish—would be represented by men entering Class I+II positions from Class III origins.

tendency being for rates first to rise but then at some later point to decline. It is of interest to note that this tendency is most marked in Figure 3.10, and also appears in Figure 3.9, in the graphs for our two Eastern European nations. Upward mobility into the service class among Hungarian and Polish men born in the early 1920s—who would reach occupational maturity in the period of post-war 'socialist construction'—rose to a level that later cohorts quite fail to match.

Where, among younger cohorts, the graphs of Figures 3.9 and 3.10 level out or turn down, we cannot preclude the possibility that this is in some part the result of age effects—so that in fact, as the men in these cohorts become older, a larger proportion will enter into service-class positions. However, what we would doubt is that such effects are likely to an extent that would make the graphs seriously misleading. There are good empirical grounds for supposing—and the liberal theory would certainly predict—that, the younger the men in our samples, the more probable it is that they will achieve upward mobility through education, so that this mobility will be apparent at a relatively early stage in their working lives. And, in this connection, it is then further relevant to emphasize that the graphs corresponding to those of Figures 3.9 and 3.10 which depict mobility to class of first employment similarly fail to reveal consistently rising trends. It emerges rather that, even if one considers only men born from the 1920s onwards, a steady increase in mobility into the service class from farm and manual origins alike is found in just one nation—namely, Sweden.

What, we believe, should be emphasized here is that, although the service class does show a general tendency to expand within modern societies, it does not do so at a steady pace simply in response to the exigencies of industrial development. Periods of relatively rapid growth and of stasis will alternate under the influence of other factors, not least political ones, thus producing rises and falls in rates of upward mobility into this class of a kind which the Hungarian and Polish cases do no more perhaps than exemplify at their most striking.[17]

How, then, can we best sum up the foregoing findings in regard to trends in absolute rates? To begin with, we can say that our investigation of outflow rates points to certain trends which seem likely to have occurred in most, if not all, of the nations we consider at *some* stage of their industrial development:

1. a decline in intergenerational immobility within the farm sector;

[17] Thus, for example, in the English case the more-or-less continuous rise in upward mobility into the service class across the cohorts we distinguish can be related to a corresponding steady expansion of this class from a time somewhere between 1931 and 1951 (there was no 1941 Census)—following, however, on several decades in which it grew scarcely at all (see Goldthorpe 1980*a*/1987: esp. ch. 2). As regards socialist societies, it may further be noted that evidence of a 'parabolic' curve for upward mobility, similar to that we record in Hungary and Poland, is also found for post-war Czechoslovakia in data from a survey conducted in 1984 (personal communication from Marek Boguszak, and cf. Boguszak 1990).

2. an increase in mobility from farm origins into manual employment in industry;
3. some upturn in mobility from farm and manual origins into service-class positions.

To this extent, therefore, we might stop short of an extreme antinomianism of the kind that Sorokin could be taken to represent, and recognize that industrialism does carry typical implications for the direction of several broad mobility flows—as, indeed, Carlsson (1963) argued some time ago in a critique of Sorokin's position.

However, we must then also say that the trends that we are able to identify have rarely appeared as continuous over the period to which our data refer; that from nation to nation their phasing within the developmental process evidently differs; and, moreover, that changes in all other rates that we have examined would appear to be essentially directionless. In turn, therefore, we can produce little evidence that within our European nations mobility rates overall are moving steadily towards some relatively well-defined 'industrial' pattern in the way that the liberal theory would suggest—and certainly not towards one that is characterized by steadily rising mobility. The outflow rates that we have considered show no clear tendency to converge; and, whatever course they may follow, they are not associated with any consistent upward trend in total mobility rates. In the light of the evidence presented, and in particular of that of Figure 3.3, it could not be claimed that men in our national samples whose working lives began, say, after the Second World War have generally lived in more mobile societies than those who first entered employment in the 1920s.

The one possible qualification that might here be made is suggested by our findings for Ireland and Poland. These could be taken as meeting the expectation that an upward shift in the level of total mobility will occur in the course of industrialization where a rapid decline in agricultural employment or, more specifically perhaps, the break-up of a predominantly peasant economy, goes together with a rising demand for industrial labour. But, even if, as Lipset and Zetterberg would hold, a shift of this kind can be regarded as a general characteristic of the emergence of industrial societies, at least two further points would still, on our evidence, need to be made. First, the upturn in mobility has to be seen as being of a delimited, once-and-for-all kind; and, secondly, it still leaves ample room for subsequent variation in absolute mobility rates and patterns as nations proceed to the further stages of their development.[18]

---

[18] It would, moreover, be mistaken simply to equate a peasant economy—or society—with a 'traditional' one. Thus, while one may with justification speak of a peasant economy existing in substantial areas of Ireland at least up to the 1940s, many of its key institutional features—most importantly, perhaps, non-partible inheritance—were relatively new (cf. Hannan 1979). The Irish peasant community, as classically depicted by Arensberg and Kimball (1940/1968), has in fact to be seen as the historical product of economic and social conditions in Ireland

RELATIVE RATES

We move on now to consider trends in intergenerational class mobility from the standpoint of relative rates. As indicated in the previous chapter, we propose to treat relative rates in terms of odds ratios—that is, ratios which show the relative odds of individuals in two different classes of origin being found in one rather than another of two different classes of destination; or, alternatively, one could say, which show the degree of *net* association that exists between the classes of origin and of destination involved. In our earlier discussion of odds ratios two other points of present relevance were also made.

First, the total set of such ratios that can be calculated within a mobility table may be taken as representing the 'endogenous mobility regime' or 'pattern of social fluidity' that the table embodies. Since odds ratios are 'margin insensitive' measures, it is then possible for this underlying regime or pattern to remain unaltered as between two or more mobility tables, even though their marginal distributions differ and, thus, all absolute rates that can be derived from them. And, we might add, it would be possible for relative rates as expressed by odds ratios to differ from table to table in some systematic way without this being readily apparent from an inspection of absolute rates.

Secondly, odds ratios are the elements of log-linear models; and, thus, where these ratios are taken as the measure of relative mobility rates, hypotheses about the latter can be presented and formally tested through the application of such models. This is the approach that we shall here follow.

In examining relative rates, we shall attempt, in the same way as we did with absolute rates, to make inferences about the extent of changes over time from the mobility experience of successive birth-cohorts within our national samples. However, instead of here working with yearly cohorts, we distinguish four ten-year birth-cohorts, which can then be regarded, given the closeness of the dates of the enquiries from which the samples derive, as having more-or-less comparable locations within the broad sweep of recent European economic history.

The first—that is, the earliest—of these cohorts comprises men aged 55–64, who were thus mostly born in the first two decades of the century, and who entered employment before or during the inter-war depression years. The second is of men aged 45–54, the majority of whom were born in the 1920s and entered employment in the later 1930s or the war years. The third is that of men aged 35–44, who were born between the late 1920s and the early 1940s, and whose working lives have fallen very largely within the post-

following the Great Famine of 1846–9 and then of the land-reform legislation introduced between 1870 and the First World War.

war period. And, finally, the fourth cohort is that of men aged 25–34, who were born from the end of the 1930s onwards and who mostly entered employment while the long boom was in train. This last cohort is clearly made up of respondents who could not be generally assumed to have reached a stage of occupational maturity, and this we must recall where it might be relevant to the interpretation of our results.

When we thus divide our national samples into cohorts, we again have a potential problem of unduly low cell counts in the mobility tables for each cohort. To obviate this, we base our analyses throughout on the five-class version of our schema as shown in Table 2.1.

As regards relative rates, there is, as we have noted, an obvious opposition between the expectations that follow from the liberal theory and those that may be derived from the FJH hypothesis. According to the former, a tendency should be found in the course of the development of industrial societies for relative rates to become more equal—or, one could say, for all odds ratios to move closer to the value of 1, which signifies the complete independence of class origins and destinations or 'perfect mobility'. According to the latter, relative rates will be basically the same across all societies that have market economies and (at least) nuclear family systems, whatever stage their level of industrial development may have reached; and thus, when examined over time within particular industrial societies, relative rates should reveal little change at all.

We may then start off from an attempt at evaluating these rival positions, and, to this end, we first introduce a rather simple log-linear model, which is, however, able to provide a direct representation of expectations under the FJH hypothesis, at least if this is taken *stricto sensu*. This model, which we have earlier labelled the 'constant social fluidity' (CnSF) model (Goldthorpe 1980*a*/1987: ch. 3; Erikson,' Goldthorpe, and Portocarero 1983) may, for present purposes, be written as

$$\log F_{ijk} = \mu + \lambda_i^O + \lambda_j^D + \lambda_k^C + \lambda_{ik}^{OC} + \lambda_{jk}^{DC} + \lambda_{ij}^{OD} \quad (3.1)$$

where F_{ijk} is the expected frequency in cell ijk of a three-way table comprising class of origin (O), class of destination (D), and cohort (C) and, on the right-hand side of the equation, μ is a scale factor, λ_i^O, λ_j^D, and λ_k^C represent the 'main' effects of the distribution of individuals over origins, destinations, and cohorts respectively, and the remaining terms represent the effects for the three possible two-way associations in the table.

Thus, the model entails a number of substantive propositions, most of which are unproblematic: for example, that an association exists between class of origin and class of destination; and that further associations exist between class of origin and cohort and between class of destination and cohort—in other words, men in different cohorts have different origin and destination distributions. It is, however, a further proposition that is critical. Since no *three-way* association is provided for in the model (the λ_{ijk}^{ODC} term does not appear), it is also entailed that the level of association between class of origin and of destination is *constant across cohorts* or, one could alternatively say, that over the mobility tables for successive cohorts all corresponding relative rates, as measured by odds ratios, are identical.

We can then consider our nine nations separately, and in each case fit the above CnSF model to a three-way table which comprises the five classes of origin, five classes of destination, and four cohorts that we propose to distinguish. The results of so doing are present in Table 3.1.

In this table we also report the results of applying a model that represents the hypothesis of the (conditional) independence of class origins and destinations; that is, the CnSF model minus the λ_{ij}^{OD} term. We do not expect this independence model to fit the data—and, as can be seen, in no case does it; but it serves as a useful baseline, by reference to which we can assess, through the rG^2 statistic in the fourth column of the table, how much of the total association between class of origin and class of destination the CnSF model is able to account for.[19]

Also in addition to the more usual 'goodness-of-fit' statistics, we give in the last column of Table 3.1 values for the statistic $G^2(S)$. This we introduce here, and subsequently in this study, to attempt to deal with a difficulty arising from the large variation in the sizes of our national samples. In consequence of this variation, our national mobility tables differ quite widely in their capacity to show up as statistically significant relatively small deviations from models that we fit to them. It is as if we were looking at slides through microscopes of greatly differing power: we have the possibility of seeing far more detail in some cases than in others. Thus, there is the evident danger that we do not evaluate a model in an even-handed way from nation to nation. We could, for example, be led to reject a model in the Polish case on account of deviations which, were they present also in the case of, say, Ireland, we would simply not observe. Thus, we evidently need some measure of goodness of fit that is standardized by sample size. One possibility would be to take G^2/N. However, we prefer, as a more refined measure, Schwartz's suggestion of $G^2(S)$ which is given by $((G^2-df)/N) \times K + df$, where K is the sample size which is to be taken as standard.[20] We will

---

[19] It is important that rG^2, referred to by Goodman (1972) as the 'coefficient of multiple determination', should be interpreted within the particular context of log-linear modelling, rather than being taken as the equivalent of the perhaps more familiar R^2 of regression analysis. As Schwartz has pointed out (1985), the fact that R^2s are typically much lower than rG^2s reflects the fact that in regression the units of analysis are usually individuals while in log-linear modelling they are the cells of cross-tabulations and the scores are the number of individuals in a cell. Such aggregate data must then be expected to reveal stronger regularities than individual-level data. Schwartz's summary (1985: 2–3) is apt: rG^2 'measures how adequately a model accounts for the observed *associations* among a pre-specified set of variables while R^2 and Eta^2 measure the amount of *variation* in one variable that can be accounted for by its (linear) association with specified independent variables'. The point may be added that the substantive meaning of rG^2 will, of course, depend on the model that is chosen as baseline.

[20] This suggestion was made to us by Joseph E. Schwartz in a personal communication, for which we are duly grateful.

TABLE 3.1. *Results of fitting the CnSF model to intergenerational class mobility for four birth-cohorts*

Model*	G^2	df	p	rG²[†]	Δ[‡]	$G^2(S)$ (1,746)
ENG (N = 8,343)						
OC DC (con. ind.)	1,695.0	64	0.00	—	16.1	405
OC DC OD (CnSF)	53.1	48	0.28	96.9	2.6	49
FRA (N = 16,431)						
OC DC	6,370.6	64	0.00	—	24.7	734
OC DC OD	96.7	48	0.00	98.5	2.0	53
FRG (N = 3,570)						
OC DC	1,092.0	64	0.00	—	21.2	567
OC DC OD	81.9	48	0.00	92.5	4.4	65
HUN (N = 10,319)						
OC DC	2,386.0	64	0.00	—	19.2	457
OC DC OD	69.9	48	0.02	97.1	2.4	52
IRL (N = 1,746)						
OC DC	902.3	64	0.00	—	29.2	902
OC DC OD	60.2	48	0.11	93.3	5.2	60
NIR (N = 1,808)						
OC DC	780.6	64	0.00	—	25.5	756
OC DC OD	44.5	48	>0.50	94.3	5.0	45
POL (N = 27,993)						
OC DC	7,357.7	64	0.00	—	19.6	519
OC DC OD	66.7	48	0.04	99.1	1.4	49
SCO (N = 3,985)						
OC DC	1,146.6	64	0.00	—	18.1	538
OC DC OD	66.3	48	0.04	94.2	4.4	56
SWE (N = 1,882)						
OC DC	403.9	64	0.00	—	17.3	379
OC DC OD	45.2	48	>0.50	88.8	5.1	45

Notes:

  * O = origin class; D = destination class; C = cohort.

  [†] rG² shows the percentage reduction in the G^2 for a model taken as baseline (here the conditional independence model) that is achieved by a more complex model (here the CnSF model). For further discussion of this statistic, see n. 19.

  [‡] Δ is the dissimilarity index, showing the percentage of all cases in the table analysed that are misclassified—that is, allocated to the wrong cell—by a particular model.

throughout follow the conservative practice of setting K equal to the size of the *smallest* of the national samples with which we are concerned—and thus, in Table 3.1, at 1,746. To help remind the reader of the hypothetical nature of $G^2(S)$—that it is the G^2 value that we would expect from a sample of size K, all other things being equal—we report it only to the nearest integer.

What, then, can we learn from the content of Table 3.1? It would in fact appear that the CnSF model performs fairly well. It is true that the p values reported indicate that in only four of the nine nations—England, Ireland, Northern Ireland, and Sweden—would one retain this model, taken as the null hypothesis, according to the conventional 0.05 criterion. However, it is also evident that much of the variation in the G^2 and p values returned is attributable to differences in sample size. When one examines the $G^2(S)$ values in the final column of the table, one finds that these are in fact contained within a rather narrow range, and moreover that in no case do they exceed the 65 mark, thus implying, with df = 48, p values of above 0.05. In other words, if we were restricted throughout to sample sizes of 1,746, such as that we have for Ireland, we would find it difficult to reject the CnSF model for any nation—although the FRG would have to be regarded as a borderline case.

What could, therefore, be claimed on the basis of the foregoing is that, while significant deviations from the CnSF model do have to be recognized in some at least of our nations, such deviations would not appear to be at all substantial. In this connection, it is of further relevance to note that in all cases but one the CnSF model accounts for more than 90 per cent of the total association existing between class of origin and class of destination—the exception being Sweden, where the independence model fits least badly; and, again, that within the different national mobility tables the CnSF model leads to the misclassification of, at most, only a little over 5 per cent of all cases.[21]

At the same time, though, it must be acknowledged that the test of the hypothesis of constant social fluidity that we have undertaken via our CnSF model is one of a very generalized or 'global' kind—with, therefore, only a low power to detect shifts that may have taken place in more particular aspects of mobility regimes. That is to say, even where the hypothesis as represented by the CnSF model cannot be safely rejected, the possibility still remains that certain changes over cohorts could have occurred which, while on an overall view quite small, might none the less be of substantive interest. And, in this connection, we must clearly recognize that the liberal theory

---

[21] We may add that results from equivalent analyses of data referring to mobility from class of origin to class of first employment are essentially similar. In only one case, that of Ireland, would the CnSF model be rejected on the basis of the $G^2(S)$ statistic; and again only in the Swedish case does the model not account for at least 90 per cent of the total origin–destination association, while at most only a little over 5 per cent of all cases are misclassified. It should, however, be recalled that we cannot undertake an analysis of the kind in question for the FRG, owing to lack of information on first employment.

claims not simply that fluidity patterns change, but that they do so *in a particular direction*, namely, towards increased fluidity. Thus, if we are to do full justice to this theory, we need to test as specifically as we can for trends of the kind in question.

A shift towards increased fluidity would mean that the odds ratios defining the association between classes of origin and destination tend to move closer to the value of 1 that implies complete independence.[22] Within the context of the CnSF model as represented by equation (3.1), it is not possible to provide for such a shift in any straightforward way. If we simply add the term for the interaction between class origins, class destinations, and cohorts— λ_{ijk}^{ODC}—we then 'saturate' the model; that is, we constrain the values expected under it to be the same as the observed values, and we can thus learn little at all from it. We have in fact experimented with a number of different approaches to the problem that we here encounter and we would now believe that the following is the most satisfactory.[23]

We may start from the assumption—for which the fit of the CnSF model as shown in Table 3.1 provides good grounds—that in each of our nations there is at all events a general pattern to the net associations between classes of origin and destination (as defined by odds ratios) which persists over cohorts, even though the overall strength of this association may vary from one cohort to another. This then suggests a model of the form

$$\log F_{ijk}^{'} = \mu + \lambda_i^{O} + \lambda_j^{D} + \lambda_k^{C} + \lambda_{ik}^{OC} + \lambda_{jk}^{DC} + \beta_k\, X_{ij} \quad (3.2)$$

where X_{ij} represents the general pattern of association and β_k the relative strength of association that is specific to a cohort. In order to fit this model to the data for a given nation, we first of all equate X_{ij} with the values for λ_{ij}^{OD} that are derived from fitting the CnSF model, and, in turn, β_k can be estimated through a standard log-linear analysis. From the starting values thus obtained, we then work with a simple iterative procedure in order to improve the fit and, we believe, to approximate a Maximum Likelihood estimator.[24]

---

[22] As indicated in Chapter 2, from the conception of social fluidity that we adopt such movement could in principle be from values either above or below 1.

[23] One of the alternative possibilities—based on a model that allows for linear trends in individual odds ratios—is taken up in our paper with Hiroshi Ishida (Ishida, Goldthorpe, and Erikson 1991) on class mobility in post-war Japan, on which we draw in Chapter 10. While this approach does in fact appear to lead very consistently to the same substantive conclusions as that we adopt in the present study, the latter is the more direct. In developing the model that we here use, we started from a suggestion made to us by Jan Hoem, and we have benefited greatly from his subsequent comments and advice and likewise from those of David Cox.

[24] In more detail, the fitting procedure is as follows. We set $X_{ij} = \lambda_{ij}^{OD}$, where the latter term is estimated under the CnSF model of equation (3.1). The model

$$\log F_{ijk} = \mu + \lambda_i^{O} + \lambda_j^{D} + \lambda_k^{C} + \lambda_{ik}^{OC} + \lambda_{jk}^{DC} + \beta X_{ij}$$

will thus be exactly equivalent to that of (3.1) with $\beta = 1$. A version of the model of equation (3.2) is first fitted with these initial values for X and varying β_k and then in the next step we fit the model

Under the fitted model, the differences between the β parameters will show in which direction and to what extent the overall strength of the association between origin and destination classes differs across cohorts. If the difference between the β parameter for a younger cohort and for an older one is negative, then all expected odds ratios in the younger cohort are closer to 1 than are the corresponding odds ratios in the older, with the size of the change in association from one cohort to the other being a function of the absolute size of the difference between the two parameters. We may, therefore, call the model of equation (3.2) one of uniform change or, more generally, of uniform difference—uniform, that is, in the sense that all odds ratios expected under the model for different cohorts will differ uniformly (though not by a constant amount) in moving together either towards or away from independence.[25]

$$\log F_{ijk} = \mu + \lambda_i^O + \lambda_j^D + \lambda_k^C + \lambda_{ik}^{OC} + \lambda_{jk}^{DC} + \lambda_{ij}^{OD} + \beta_k X_{ij}.$$

If an improvement in fit is thus obtained, the model of equation (3.2) is again fitted with X_{ij} being replaced by $X'_{ij} = \lambda_{ij}^{OD} + X_{ij}$, and the same procedure is followed until no further improvement in fit is produced. In fact, the number of iterations needed before this stabilization was reached did not exceed three for any of our nations.

We cannot rule out the possibility that there may be other models that are likewise based on a uniform change in odds ratios and that fit better than that of (3.2). We have not, however, been able to develop any such model. As suggested in the text, the procedure here described may be regarded as an attempt to achieve an iterative estimating procedure which converges on a Maximum-Likelihood (M-L) estimator. Intuitively, we believe that parameter estimates produced by the model of (3.2) will be close to M-L estimates in cases where the CnSF model fits fairly well—as it does in the present application. We would have less confidence in the iterative procedure in cases where, in spite of a substantial association between origins and destination, the CnSF model could achieve little improvement in fit over that of conditional independence.

[25] The odds ratios expected under the model of equation (3.2) will depend only on X and β. Thus, the logged odds ratio (θ) for the tetrad of cells determined by the two rows i and i' and the two columns j and j' in cohort k will be $\theta_k = \beta_k (X_{ij} + X_{i'j'} - X_{ij'} - X_{i'j})$; and the difference between a logged odds ratio in, say cohort 3 and the corresponding logged odds ratio in cohort 2 will be $\theta_3 - \theta_2 = (\beta_3 - \beta_2)(X_{ij} + X_{i'j'} - X_{ij'} - X_{i'j})$. Let the odds ratio be Q (Q = $\exp(\theta)$), and Z_{ij} = $\exp(X_{ij})$. Then the ratio of this odds ratio in cohort 3 to the corresponding odds ratio in cohort 2 will be Q raised to the power of $(\beta_3 - \beta_2)$, and thus $Q_3/Q_2 = Q^{\beta_3 - \beta_2}$ where $Q = Z_{ij} Z_{i'j'}/Z_{ij'} Z_{i'j}$. Assume that Q = 2 and $(\beta_3 - \beta_2)$ = -0.20. Then the 'cross-cohort' quotient will be equal to $2^{-0.20}$ = 0.87, indicating a decrease in association from cohort 2 to cohort 3. If we were to reverse the order between, say, the two columns involved, Q would be equal to 1/2 = 0.5 and the cross-cohort quotient would take the value of $0.5^{-0.20}$ = 1.15, likewise indicating a decrease in association: 1/1.15 = 0.87. Thus, if the difference $(\beta_3 - \beta_2)$ is negative, odds ratios that are greater than 1 will decrease and those that are less than one will increase, which means that the measure of change we adopt is not dependent upon the order of rows and columns. In other words, the 'change parameters', the βs, are invariant under permutations of rows and columns, in the sense that differences between them will under any permutation indicate the same rate of change of the odds ratios towards or away from independence.

That the change in odds ratios is dependent upon Q means that a given difference in the β parameters implies a greater change in odds ratios the more that Q deviates from 1. To take an example from Table 3.2, the β parameter difference between cohort 2 and cohort 1 for Ireland is -0.15. Given this difference, the quotient of expected odds ratios in cohort 2 to the corresponding odds ratios in cohort 1 (Q_2/Q_1 for Q > 1 and Q_1/Q_2 for Q ≤ 1) varies in fact between 0.45 and 1.00, with the median quotient being 0.84. If, however, we consider the difference between cohort 4 and cohort 1, for which the β parameter is (absolutely) smaller

In addition to thus testing for change in a certain direction over all odds ratios defining the association between class origins and destinations, we can also test for changes in fluidity as these may show up *in particular cells* of the mobility table. Of special theoretical interest here are, of course, cells on the main diagonal which imply class immobility. In the light of the liberal theory, one would anticipate that relative rates would so change over time that the propensity for class immobility would decline. Can we then detect any such tendency across cohorts distinguished within our various national tables? To attempt an answer to this question, we need to extend our CnSF model as in equation (3.1) by adding a further term that is specifically designed to capture any shifts in fluidity that might bear on the main diagonal cells. The model thus becomes

$$\log F_{ijk} = \mu + \lambda_i^O + \lambda_j^D + \lambda_k^C + \lambda_{ik}^{OC} + \lambda_{jk}^{DC} + \lambda_{ik}^{OD} + \alpha_k \, \delta_{ij}$$

$$(3.3)$$

where the term that is added to the CnSF model is a parameter α_k multiplied by the Kronecker δ, which partitions the internal cells of the mobility table into two levels of association, one level for the cells on the main diagonal and one level for the off-diagonal cells (cf. Hauser 1978).[26] The difference in fit between the CnSF model and that of equation (3.3), when applied to tables for different cohorts, will then reveal to what extent association within cells on the main diagonal varies across cohorts, and the signs and values of the α parameters will show the direction and size of any changes in the same manner as with the β parameters in the model of equation (3.2).

The results of fitting the models of equations (3.2) and (3.3) are given in Table 3.2. Since we still do not test quite specifically for monotonic change, we show here for each of our nations both the improvement in fit produced by these models and the uniform- or diagonal-change parameters that are estimated for each cohort. Should the latter indicate monotonic change, it

(-0.09), the range of quotients is then narrower, varying between 0.64 and 1.00 with a median of 0.91.

Parameters can, of course, be compared directly only within particular applications of the model. Thus, for example, the parameter difference between cohort 4 and cohort 1 for Sweden happens to be the same as that between cohort 2 and cohort 1 for Ireland (-0.15). But the resulting Swedish quotients vary between 0.54 and 1.00 with a median of 0.90—that is, are larger than the Irish equivalents given above. This implies, then, that on average the Swedish odds ratios are closer to 1 than are the Irish.

Our model, it should thus be observed, is not one of *constant* change in expected odds ratios: i.e. $Q_k/Q_{k'}$ is not constant over tetrads of cells. A model of constant change over odds ratios could *not* be a model of uniform change towards or away from independence, since with such a model both odds ratios greater than 1 and less than 1 would increase or decrease by the same amount from cohort to cohort, and consequently some odds ratios would move towards independence while others moved away from it. However, our model does imply constant change in logged odds ratios: i.e. $\theta_k/\theta_{k'} = \beta_k/\beta_{k'}$ for all tetrads.

[26] This is equivalent to the Kronecker $\delta = 1$ for cells on the main diagonal, i.e. where $i = j$, and $\delta = 0$ otherwise.

TABLE 3.2. *Improvement in fit (ΔG^2) over the CnSF model and parameters for (i) the model of uniform change in association between class origins and destinations, and (ii) the model of change in level of association in main diagonal cells*

Nation	(i) Uniform change				(ii) Diagonal change			
		Parameter for cohort*				Parameter for cohort*		
	$\Delta G^{2\dagger}$	2	3	4	$\Delta G^{2\dagger}$	2	3	4
ENG	1.3	0.01	0.07	0.05	1.6	0.06	0.08	0.07
FRA	14.0‡	0.10	0.13	0.15	7.4	0.08	0.13	0.15
FRG	12.8‡	−0.13	0.18	−0.05	4.6	−0.11	0.09	−0.06
HUN	8.4‡	−0.08	−0.19	−0.16	8.1‡	−0.05	−0.23	−0.15
IRL	4.3	−0.15	0.07	−0.09	3.5	−0.29	−0.03	−0.20
NIR	1.8	0.02	−0.12	−0.10	3.8	0.08	−0.04	−0.20
POL	1.0	0.03	0.04	0.04	2.0	0.06	−0.00	−0.01
SCO	1.3	0.04	0.05	0.11	7.5	0.03	0.02	0.23
SWE	8.6‡	0.35	0.14	−0.15	5.1	0.17	−0.08	−0.19

Notes:
  * Parameters for cohort 1 (oldest) are set at zero.
  † We assume that each model takes up an additional 3 degrees of freedom over the CnSF model, although, for reasons explained in n. 27 to this chapter, a conservative test of significance would assume 4 degrees.
  ‡ Significant at 5 per cent level.

would be unwise to discount this, even if the improvement in fit falls short of significance.[27]

From Table 3.2 it may be observed, first of all, that in no instance do both models give a significant improvement in fit *and* produce parameter estimates that point to a steady increase in fluidity and to a general decline in the propensity for class immobility. The nearest approximation to such a result occurs in the case of Hungary, where a trend towards greater openness over the first three cohorts appears, however, to level out in the fourth. This finding is, in fact, in line with those of several other enquiries into mobility in Hungary in the post-war period which have used data sources different, in part at least, from our own and have followed different conceptual and analytical approaches (Simkus 1981; Andorka, Csicsman, and Keleti 1982;

---

[27] Both models require the addition of three further terms to the CnSF model—that is, the β_k or α_k terms for each of three cohorts, with the other of our four cohorts (in fact, the oldest) serving as the baseline. However, it should be noted that in the case of the uniform-difference model the 'change' parameters—i.e. the βs—are not independent of each other since, as we have described, they are estimated through an iterative procedure starting from values derived from the data. Thus, it should be recognized that somewhat more than three degrees of freedom are taken up, and a conservative test of significance would be based on four degrees. But, so as to give the benefit of the doubt to the liberal theory, in Table 3.2 we calculate significance with reference to three degrees only.

Ganzeboom and Luijkx 1986; Wong 1988; Andorka 1990; Simkus *et al.* 1990).

Turning to the three other nations for which the uniform-change model produces an improved fit, we find that in one case, that of France, the change parameters show steadily *decreasing* fluidity—as also do the parameters from the diagonal-change model[28]—while with the FRG and Sweden the parameters do not display any consistent trend. The relatively poor fit of the CnSF model to the German data that we previously noted would seem to result from an increase in fluidity within the second cohort being followed by a sharp decrease in the third; while in the Swedish case the indication is that, consistently with other quite independent results (Jonsson 1991) fluidity increased notably in the fourth cohort—for which, it can also be seen, the diagonal-change parameter correspondingly suggests a decline in class immobility.

With the remaining nations, the important point to note for present purposes is that, as well as both of our new models failing to improve on the fit of the CnSF model, the parameters estimated under them do not in general suggest any steady movement towards greater fluidity which yet more sensitive modelling might be capable of revealing as significant. Only perhaps in the case of Ireland could this idea be entertained. We have seen from Figure 3.3 above that in Ireland a rather dramatic increase occurred over the period covered by our data in the rate of total mobility. The possibility that a shift in relative rates played some, albeit slight, part in this upturn cannot be precluded. In contrast, though, in the case of Poland, where a similar increase in total mobility occurred, we can now rather safely say that this had no parallel in rising fluidity. In other words, the structural influences to which we earlier alluded—most obviously, the rapid rate of contraction of the agricultural sector—can in fact be regarded as solely responsible.[29]

---

[28] Our results for France appear somewhat out of line with those reported in an earlier analysis (Goldthorpe and Portocarero 1981), which compared data from the 1970 survey with those from an enquiry of 1953 and found some weakening in the propensity for immobility. However, through using the 1953 data, this analysis covered a much longer period—so as in fact to include the experience of men born at the end of the last century—and was also based on a different categorization from that employed here. It should further be noted that the significant improvement in fit obtained for France with the uniform-change model—as also for Hungary—in some part reflects the relatively large samples that we have for these nations. Thus, if we were again to consider $G^2(S)$ with the standard sample size at 1,746, a significant improvement in fit would be obtained only for the FRG and Sweden. We are inclined to give more weight to the result for Hungary than to that for France on account of the degree of corroboration from other studies.

In this connection, it might be added that our findings of no trend towards greater fluidity in England is also confirmed by other analyses using in part different class categories, techniques, and data. See Goldthorpe (1980a/1987: chs. 3 and 9) and Macdonald and Ridge (1987).

[29] It should, however, be noted that the structural influences of the decline of agriculture, at least, will be of two different kinds. As well as what could be called 'discrepancy' effects, resulting from fewer opportunities to enter farm employment for sons than for their fathers, there will also be 'compositional' effects, resulting from the interaction between the decline of

If, then, we review the findings so far presented in this section, it is undoubtedly expectations that may be derived from the FJH hypothesis rather than those of the liberal theory that are the better supported. We do have evidence that a considerable degree of stability in relative rates has underlain the mobility experience of men in successive birth-cohorts within our nine nations; and the contrast may be underlined between the rather slight nature of such shifts as we are able to detect in relative rates and the much larger and more rapid changes that we could often trace in absolute, total and outflow, rates. Furthermore, where movement in relative rates is to be found, there is no indication that this is regularly in the direction of more equal rates, whether expressed in a weakening overall in the net association between class origins and destinations or in the propensity for class immobility.

However, still to pursue our quest for trends in relative rates, we may go on to consider one further possibility: namely, that, even if no general tendency towards greater social fluidity is in train within industrial nations, their relative rates might still be moving into closer similarity on some *other* lines. Although entailing a major modification of the liberal position, this would still represent an alternative to what must, strictly speaking, be envisaged from the standpoint of the FJH hypothesis. For the implication of the latter clearly is that such convergent trends, whether towards greater fluidity or otherwise, are unlikely to be observed, since all industrial societies will already possess endogenous mobility regimes that show little variation.

To proceed in this respect, we need to introduce a further model which we have previously labelled (Erikson, Goldthorpe, and Portocarero 1983) as that of 'common social fluidity'. This model is in fact formally equivalent to the CnSF model; but, while the latter proposes identical relative rates over time (that is, in the present application, across cohorts), the common social fluidity (CmSF) model proposes identical relative rates over different populations (in the present case, national populations). We may then write the CmSF model as

$$\log F_{ijk} = \mu + \lambda_i^O + \lambda_j^D + \lambda_k^N + \lambda_{ik}^{ON} + \lambda_{jk}^{DN} + \lambda_{ij}^{OD} \quad (3.4)$$

where F_{ijk} is the expected frequency in cell ijk of a three-way table comprising class of origin (O), class of destination (D), and nation (N).

Previously, we treated our nine nations separately, and applied the CnSF model to four cohort-specific mobility tables constructed within each nation. We may now take our four cohorts separately, and apply the CmSF model to nine national mobility tables constructed within each cohort. In this way we may hope to gain some idea of the extent of variation in relative rates among

---

agriculture and the pattern of relative rates, even though the latter may itself be unchanging: that is, total mobility will increase as a result of the decline overall in the size of a class that possesses—as the farm class does—an unusually high propensity for immobility.

our nations and, of chief interest in the present context, of whether from cohort to cohort such variation is narrowing or widening.

From Table 3.3, in which the results of thus fitting the CmSF model are presented, two main results are apparent. First, for no cohort does the model reproduce the data in an entirely acceptable way. Certainly, for each cohort alike, it accounts for around 95 per cent of the association between class of origin and class of destination, and misclassifies less than 4 per cent of all cases. None the less, statistically significant deviations are clearly present. Secondly, it could scarcely be said that the fit of the model tends to improve across successive cohorts. Although the $G^2(S)$ returned in the case of the youngest cohort—that of men aged 25–34—is the lowest, it would still seem that a judgement of 'no trend' is the only one that could be safely made. It may, moreover, be added that, when the corresponding analysis is undertaken on our data for mobility from origin to first employment, the $G^2(S)$ for this youngest cohort then turns out to be the *largest* of the four. Whether or not the CmSF model fits well enough to our data to uphold the FJH hypothesis of a 'basic' cross-national similarity in relative rates is a matter that we will not take up here, but defer to our two next chapters. For

TABLE 3.3. *Results of fitting the CmSF model to intergenerational class mobility tables by nation for four ten-year birth-cohorts*

Model*	G^2	df	p	rG^2	Δ	$G^2(S)$ (13,840)
Cohort 1 (oldest) (N = 13,840)						
ON DN (con. ind.)	4,442.7	144	0.00	—	22.2	4,443
ON DN OD (CmSF)	217.6	128	0.00	95.1	3.5	218
Cohort 2 (N = 19,368)						
ON DN	5,805.4	144	0.00	—	20.8	4,190
ON DN OD	300.7	128	0.00	94.8	3.9	251
Cohort 3 (N = 22,007)						
ON DN	6,371.7	144	0.00	—	20.1	4,061
ON DN OD	309.9	128	0.00	95.1	3.3	242
Cohort 4 (N = 20,861)						
ON DN	5,514.8	144	0.00	—	19.6	3,707
ON DN OD	255.2	128	0.00	95.4	3.1	212

Note:
 * O = origin class; D = destination class; N = nation.

our present concerns, what emerges from Table 3.3 of greatest relevance is that, while *some* scope for cross-national convergence in relative rates of mobility may be recognized, there is little reason to suppose that any such convergence is in fact taking place.

Following from this, it is of interest to carry out one last analysis in which the CnSF and CmSF models are applied together. In this case, we need to consider our data in the form of a single four-way ($5 \times 5 \times 4 \times 9$) table of class of origin by class of destination by cohort by nation, which will thus comprise thirty-six different mobility tables, each of a cohort- *and* nation-specific kind. To this array we can then fit either the CnSF or the CmSF model, or both simultaneously, or a further model which allows for variable fluidity both among cohorts and among nations. The results of an exercise on these lines are shown in Table 3.4.

From Table 3.4 it should be noted first of all that even model E, that providing for cross-cohort *and* cross-national variation in fluidity, still shows a significant lack of fit to the data—thus implying that, strictly speaking, we need to move to a 'saturated' model by including the four-way interaction

TABLE 3.4. *Results of fitting different models of social fluidity to intergenerational class mobility tables by nation and birth-cohort* (N = 76,076)

Model*	G^2	df	p	rG^2	Δ
A. OCN DCN					
(con. ind.)	22,133	576	0.00	—	20.5
B. OCN DCN OD					
(CnSF and CmSF)	1,174.9	560	0.00	94.7	3.6
C. OCN DCN ODN					
(CnSF)	584.9	432	0.00	97.4	2.3
D. OCN DCN ODC					
(CmSF)	1,083.4	512	0.00	95.1	3.4
E. OCN DCN ODN ODC					
(variable)	501.5	384	0.00	97.7	2.0
				$G^2/df^\dagger$	
B–C (ODN)	590.5	128	0.00	4.6	
D–E (ODN)	581.9	128	0.00	4.5	
B–D (ODC)	91.5	48	0.00	1.9	
C–E (ODC)	82.9	48	0.00	1.7	

Notes:
* O = origin class; D = destination class; C = cohort; N = nation.
† We use this statistic as a descriptive measure of the comparative goodness of fit of models in the sense indicated by Hagenaars (1990: 65).

term.[30] However, with a total N of over 76,000—giving an average of over eighty observations in each cell—this is not perhaps an entirely surprising outcome; and, in the light of the other indicators reported, we propose to take model E as at all events fitting well enough for the purposes we have in hand.

Our interest focuses in fact on the results given in the lower panel of Table 3.4. Here we compare the performance of the CnSF and CmSF models, that is, models C and D, as against model E and also as against model B, which is that requiring both constant and common social fluidity together. It is the CnSF model that clearly shows to advantage—which would, therefore, point to an important conclusion: namely, that variation in relative rates of class mobility across cohorts is *less* than is such variation across nations. We should recognize that the G^2s returned by non-fitting models will reflect not only deviations between the odds ratios required by the model and those actually found in the data but, further, compositional effects: that is, effects of the numbers of cases in the cells that are involved in particular odds ratios. Such 'weighting' does of course have its own logic; but, in order to check that compositional effects are not unduly distorting our judgements about differences in relative rates *per se*, we can also look directly at their variance. If we calculate the average variance of logged odds ratios from cell values expected under model E, which we would be ready to accept as giving an adequate fit to our data, the results do in fact strongly confirm our above conclusion. The average variance among nations and within cohorts is 0.22, while the average variance among cohorts and within nations is 0.03.[31]

We would, then, take these results as further supporting the suggestion that, instead of convergence in relative rates being seen as precluded by the degree of cross-national similarity that already prevails, the emphasis may better be placed on the degree of stability of relative rates over time and on the lack of any consistent direction in such changes as may occur. Whatever view may eventually be reached about the extent, nature, and significance of cross-national variation in social fluidity—to which questions we will devote much further discussion—the point here to be underlined is that such variation as does exist appears to be quite persistent; or, in other words, that differentiation among national mobility regimes shows no overall tendency to diminish.

Finally in this section, and in view especially of the rather well-defined results that we would claim, some comment would seem necessary on a recent study likewise concerned with trends in relative rates of class mobility but which leads its authors to conclusions that are in important respects at

---

[30] This term could be taken to imply that the degree of variation in fluidity over cohorts varies significantly across nations or, alternatively, that the degree of variation in fluidity across nations varies significantly over cohorts.

[31] Since each of the thirty-six cohort- and nation-specific mobility tables involved in the analysis of Table 3.3 is based on the five-class version of the schema, each comprises $(5^2 - 5)^2/4 = 100$ odds ratios.

variance with our own. Ganzeboom, Luijkx, and Treiman (1989) report an analysis of 149 mobility tables drawn from thirty-five nations over the period 1947–87 that are based on a sixfold version of our class schema (i.e. the standard seven-class version but with the two farm classes, IV*c* and VII*b*, collapsed). This analysis leads them to the view that, while the industrial— and 'developing'—nations that they consider show 'a basic similarity in mobility *patterns*', there are at the same time 'substantial cross-national and cross-temporal differences in the *extent* of mobility' and, furthermore, that one element in the latter is in fact 'a trend towards increasing openness over time' (1989: 47; emphases in original).

In Chapter 2 (see n. 27) we have already noted problems with the approach to comparative enquiry that Ganzeboom, Luijkx, and Treiman (henceforth GLT) pursue, and these problems do, in our judgement, render their data base a far less reliable one for their purposes than they are willing to acknowledge. In addition, though, various difficulties can be shown to arise with their analysis itself, so that our scepticism as to the results that they report is reinforced.

First of all, the 'world wide secular trend towards increased societal openness' that GLT claim to detect is, on their own account, a fairly weak one and shows up significantly only with parameters for the overall association between class origins and destinations and not with parameters (under a model where these can be estimated) for class immobility—which must count as a rather puzzling outcome, at least from the standpoint of the liberal theory. Moreover, our own reanalyses of GLT's data would suggest that their finding of such a trend is not in fact as robust, in the face of controls for data quality, as GLT would wish to believe.[32]

Secondly, credence in the parameters in question must in any event be strained by the fact that they are estimated under highly parsimonious (scaled association) models which, according to conventional criteria, are far from fitting the total data array and also many of the mobility tables for individual nations.[33] GLT accept such models in part, it would seem, simply because the whole strategy of their analysis would be undermined if they were to be rejected; but they seek also to legitimate their choice by reference

[32] As argued in Chapter 2 (n. 27), from the standpoint of the measurement theory that GLT adopt, it would seem important that they should take account *inter alia* of the possibility of design effects from studies replicated over time *within* nations. In one reanalysis of their data we have carried out in which we introduce such a factor, we find no significant decline in parameters either for the overall association of class origins and destinations or for class immobility. We are grateful to Harry Ganzeboom for making the relevant data available to us.

[33] As regards tables for individual nations, GLT report that their most favoured model fits more than half of these—actually, 57 per cent—'according to the criterion of classical statistical inference'. This is, however, if the 1 per cent level of significance is adopted. Taking the 5 per cent level, which has in fact been the convention in the modelling of mobility tables, it can then be determined from the results that GLT present (1989: Table 2) that the model can be accepted as fitting in only 44 per cent of cases.

to the *bic* statistic (Raftery 1986*a*, 1986*b*) which favours these models over other, more complex, ones that they consider.

Thirdly, though, reanalysis of GLT's data further reveals that, if they are indeed committed to this statistic as their criterion of selection, then there is at least one other model, even simpler than those they favour, which they should rather adopt—that is, which returns an even more preferable *bic* value. This is none other than our model B of Table 3.4 above, which in effect combines the CnSF and CmSF models into one or, in other words, proposes—and quite contrary, of course, to what GLT would seek to argue—exactly the same set of relative mobility rates over time and over nations *alike*.[34] We do not ourselves, we should make clear, have any belief in the validity of this model; we did indeed readily reject it for our own data. What we wish rather to bring out is just how misleading a reliance on *bic* can be—above all, on account of its evident bias in favour of parsimony as against fit—and how GLT are thus led into a decidedly awkward position. If they stand by *bic*, then they must, it seems, accept a model that neither they nor any one else would wish to take seriously; but if they abandon *bic*, why then should anyone be content with the models that they do accept and that provide the parameter estimates on which their entire argument rests?[35]

Finally, it may be noted that, even if, despite all of the foregoing, GLT's evidence of a general trend over time towards greater fluidity were to be taken at face value, this still would not mean that the liberal theory receives unambiguous support from their work. In addition to testing for trends in relative rates, GLT's analyses also yield estimates of specific 'nation' effects, which they have not so far sought to interpret. However, as reported (1989: Table 5), these effects show no general consistency with the idea that more industrialized nations will be more open than less industrialized ones. Thus, for example, nations such as Finland, the Philippines, Poland, and Taiwan are represented as more open than France, the FRG, and the Netherlands. It would then appear that, in any attempt at accounting for these cross-national differences, level of industrialization could at all events be only one factor among others of quite comparable importance.

We have sought in this chapter to use data from European nations in order to evaluate various arguments concerning mobility trends within industrial societies. The major outcome, it might be said, has been a negative one: that is, considerable doubt has been thrown on claims associated with what we

---

[34] For their most favoured model, GLT report a *bic* value of −33,712 (1989: Table 3, Model D). From their data as we have them, we cannot reproduce this figure exactly, obtaining rather a *bic* of −33,618. However, our combined CnSF and CmSF model returns a clearly lower—and, therefore, preferable—*bic* value of −34,230. A further model that GLT consider (1989: Table 2, Model E) gives by their account a *bic* value that is in fact identical to that of their preferred model (i.e. −33,712) but which we calculate at −33,702.

[35] For further comment in similar vein on problems of consistency in GLT's choice of models, see Jones (1991).

have called the liberal theory of industrialism. We have found no evidence of general and abiding trends towards higher levels either of total mobility or of social fluidity within the nations we have considered; nor evidence that mobility rates, whether absolute or relative, are changing in any other consistent direction; nor again evidence that such rates show a tendency over time to become cross-nationally more similar. The most that could be said on the side of arguments proposing some linkage between industrial development and increased and more standardized mobility rates would be that structural changes—most importantly, the decline in agriculture—appear likely to generate upturns in total, and also perhaps in certain outflow rates over periods of limited duration and of very variable phasing.

Such results are all the more damaging to the liberal theory since, as we earlier emphasized, Europe over the middle decades of the twentieth century, and above all in the post-war era, provides a context in which the theory should have every chance of showing its force. Furthermore, we may reiterate the point that any distortions in our findings that derive from our reliance on (quasi-)cohort analysis, and in particular from the confounding of age and period effects, are unlikely to be ones that tell unfairly against liberal claims: if anything, the contrary should be supposed.

We would, therefore, believe that the attempt to represent changes in mobility rates in modern societies as displaying regular developmental patterns, driven by a functional logic of industrialism, is one that faces serious empirical difficulties; and, in turn, we would argue that the need must be recognized to search for ways in which these changes might be more satisfactorily understood. In this connection, there is then one further outcome of the analyses of the present chapter which should, in our judgement be seen as having major significance: namely, that while it appears that liberal expectations of directional tendencies in absolute and relative mobility rates are in both respects largely unfounded, *the nature of the contrary evidence is quite different from one case to the other: with absolute rates it is evidence of trendless, though often quite wide, fluctuation, but with relative rates it is evidence of considerable stability.* What is thus suggested is that, in attempts to go beyond the liberal theory, the treatment of absolute and of relative rates is likely to set quite different kinds of problem and of analytical task.

As regards absolute rates, liberal expectations most obviously fail, we would suggest, because changes in structural influences on mobility do not themselves have the regularity that liberal theorists have been wont to suppose. As noted in Chapter 1, the analyses of economic growth advanced in the 1950s and 1960s by authors such as Clark, Rostow, and Kuznets were taken as demonstrating clear sequences of change in the sectoral and occupational, and hence in the class composition of labour forces. However, it would by now be widely accepted that, whatever theoretical insights the work of these authors may provide, it does *not* allow one to think, at a historical level, in terms of a well-defined series of developmental stages through which the structure of the labour forces of different nations will pass in turn as industrialization proceeds. While certain very general tendencies of change may in this respect be identified, considerable variation still prevails from case to case in relation to the speed with which change occurs and the extent to which different aspects of change are separated in time or overlap (Singelmann 1978; Gagliani 1985).

The European experience of industrialization, which has provided the setting for our analyses in this chapter, itself well illustrates the variety of paths that the development of labour forces may follow; and it does, moreover, bring out the diversity of the causal factors at work here—by no means all of which can be plausibly taken as part of some englobing developmental process. Thus, the historical formation of national class structures has to be seen as reflecting not only early or late industrialization but, in addition, important influences stemming, on the one hand, from the international political economy and, on the other, from the various strategies pursued by national governments in response to both external and internal pressures. To take but one example here, the contraction of agriculture— which we have found to play a major part in the pattern of change in absolute class-mobility rates—cannot be understood, as it has occurred in particular cases, simply in terms of the shifting marginal productivity of sectors and differences in the elasticities of demand for their products that the theory of economic growth would emphasize. As the agrarian histories of our nations can amply show (see, e.g., Priebe 1976), the pace and timing of agricultural contraction also—and often far more decisively—reflect whether nations were at the centre or on the periphery of international trading relations, in a position of economic dominance or dependence; and, further, the policies that their governments adopted towards agriculture in regard to both its social organization and its protection against or exposure to market forces.[36]

Once, therefore, the variability and complexity of the determination of the structural contexts of mobility is appreciated, the extent to which the movement of absolute rates over time appears as merely trendless can no longer be found especially surprising. If changes in such rates do largely express the shifting conjunctures of a diversity of exogenous effects, then 'trendlessness' is indeed what must be expected. It is noteworthy that it is essentially an argument on these lines that has been pursued by the several European economic and social historians who have sought to join in the sociological debate. In rejecting 'the idea of a sustained growth in social

[36] Moreover, while we would believe that 'demand-side' factors are generally of major importance in promoting structural change, 'supply-side' ones may also have to be taken into account—for example, the effects of demographic change, including in- and out-migration, and of changes in the work-force paticipation rates of women and of different age-groups. And in these respects, too, political intervention may obviously play a crucial role.

mobility during industrialization', these authors have emphasized the 'multitude of factors' which affect mobility levels; and, in place of developmental stages, they have sought rather to establish empirically a number of different 'eras' or 'phases' of both rising *and falling* mobility within the period in which European industrialization has occurred (see, esp., Kaelble 1984: 490; also Kaelble 1981; Mendels 1976; Kocka 1980*b*).

Thus, we would maintain, the crucial issue that arises so far as absolute rates of mobility are concerned is that of whether, or how far, the course of change they follow is in fact a phenomenon open to explanation in macrosociological terms. Investigators who have been impressed by the degree of temporal variation in absolute, as compared with relative, rates have gone on to conclude that the dynamism of the former must lie primarily in structural effects; and, in turn, they have urged that these should not be treated as merely a 'nuisance factor' but should become themselves the focus of enquiry (e.g. Hauser *et al.* 1975; Grusky and Hauser 1984; Goldthorpe 1985*b*). However, while this argument has an evident logic, it does leave quite undecided the question of just what *kind* of understanding of structural effects—and thence of change in absolute rates—it might be possible to achieve. In so far as generalizations about such effects can be made, will they prove to be of any great explanatory value when applied to particular instances? Or may one in this respect be forced back willy-nilly to a reliance largely on specific historical descriptions—as a position such as that of Sorokin would in effect imply? Or again are there perhaps intermediate possibilities? These are among the central problems which will confront us, and to which we shall need to respond, when in Chapter 6 we return to the matter of absolute rates and examine in some greater detail the patterns that our nine European nations display.

Turning now to relative rates, we meet a very different situation. In this case, the liberal theory is undermined because, instead of the anticipated trend of change, in the direction of greater equality, we find evidence of an essential stability. Although shifts in relative rates can in some cases be detected, these are not only ones that go in various directions but, more importantly, ones which, as against those observed in absolute rates, are of very limited magnitude—so that one might wish to speak more of 'oscillation' than of fluctuation. In other words, the liberal theory would here appear to fail because the logic of industrialism has not in fact automatically generated the changes within processes of social selection which were expected of it, and through which a steady increase in fluidity and openness would be promoted.

The stability in relative rates that we can demonstrate gains in significance, we may add, not only because, as earlier argued, the period that our data cover is one that would seem especially favourable to the validation of the liberal theory. As well as comprising decades of unprecedented economic growth, the period was also, of course, one of major political upheavals, in which, in the train of war and revolution, national frontiers were redrawn and massive shifts of population occurred.[37] The fact that the relative rates underlying the mobility experience of cohorts within our national samples should then reveal so little change—whether directional or otherwise—becomes all the more remarkable. While we have not been able to support the claim of a sustained developmental trend, we have, it appears, found indications of something of no less sociological interest: that is, of a constancy in social process prevailing within our several nations over decades that would in general have to be characterized in terms of the transformation and turbulence that they witnessed.

Furthermore, this finding is, as we have already indicated, one which may be related to a larger sociological argument, namely, that represented by the FJH hypothesis. In this chapter we have presented analyses which indicate that *some* variation in fluidity patterns does in fact occur among nations—indeed, more than within nations over time—and also that this variation shows no tendency to diminish. Thus, expectations of convergence are not met. However, neither would cross-national variation appear to be increasing; and, more importantly, on the evidence so far examined, it could not be reckoned as sufficiently wide to rule out the possibility that the 'basic' similarity in relative rates that the FJH hypothesis claims is, at all events, the *major* source of the temporal stability that we have observed. In short, it could still be the case that *constancy* above all reflects *commonality*.

Thus, in so far as the degree of similarity proposed by the FJH hypothesis could be established, we might wish to think of temporal shifts in fluidity within nations as being no more than oscillations occurring around the standard pattern that the hypothesis implies or, at all events, as being restricted in their frequency and extent by whatever set of effects it is that generates this pattern. But, conversely, if the amount of cross-national variation in relative rates were found to be too great to allow the hypothesis to remain plausible, one might then be inclined to think rather of the stability of such rates within nations as reflecting aspects of their abiding distinctiveness; or, that is, to favour theories of the kind reviewed in Chapter 1 which envisage that particular societies, or types of society, will display mobility regimes that are differentiated in relation to their distinctive cultural, political, or other characteristics.

In this respect, then, our way ahead is not difficult to see: clearly, what is needed is investigation of the FJH hypothesis in greater depth. In particular,

---

[37] Most importantly, in the aftermath of the Second World War the FRG was created out of the division of the Third Reich, and Poland's frontiers were moved some 150–200 miles to the west—both changes being accompanied by large population movements. In addition, one may note the truncation of Hungary in 1920 (with the loss of almost 70 per cent of its area and 60 per cent of its population); and the partition of Ireland in 1920–2, following the War of Independence and the Civil War, so as to create the Irish Free State (which became the Republic of Ireland in 1949) and the six counties of Northern Ireland, a constituent element of the United Kingdom with, up to 1973, its own parliament and executive.

we must consider not simply whether a 'basic' cross-national similarity in relative rates exists but, first of all, what this might be taken to mean and, subsequently, what are the nature and the significance of such deviations from it as may be found. It is to these tasks that Chapters 4 and 5 will be devoted.

ANNEX: The Moving Average Graduation Method

Jan M. Hoem

The curves of intergenerational outflow mobility rates in Chapter 3 have been smoothed by a symmetric twenty-one-term minimum-R_1 moving-weighted-average method that is exact for straight lines, Borgan-optimal for thirty-five curve points, and smoothly extended to the tails by a method proposed by Hoem and Linnemann (1988). The purpose of this annex is to explain how this graduation method works and what its main properties are.

Figure 3.6 above can be taken as displaying some typical output. The points on the horizontal axis represent single-year birth-cohorts of men whose fathers had occupations in farming. Thus, the Swedish cohorts were born from 1910 to 1944. In Figure A3.1 the corresponding data have been plotted before and after graduation. Each ordinate on the curve marked 'raw' in that figure is the fraction of the corresponding cohort of sons observed to end up in non-manual class destinations. The smoothed value corresponding to a raw data-point is a weighted average of that point itself and ten points on each side of it, with modifications in each tail of the curve. (When a data-point has less than ten neighbouring points to the left or to the right, only the points actually available can be used and the weights must be adjusted.) We see how well the graduation method brings out the general trend across cohorts, even when there are only thirty-five data-points and each (ten-point) tail is as much as almost one-third of the whole curve.

For most of the many graduated curves shown in Figures 3.3–3.10, the central part can be approximated reasonably well by a straight line, and for the great majority of such curves this line can be extended through the left tail without any problem. On an occasional curve, however, such as the one for Sweden in Figure 3.6, the left tail is best approximated by a different straight line which is at an angle with the central part of the curve. One may ask whether a 'fluttering tail' like that of Figure A3.1 is a real phenomenon or whether it could be due to random variation, caused perhaps by higher variances of the points in the tail than in the central part of the smoothed curve. If a deviant tail is just an effect of random variation, then one may as well leave it out of the curve plot and base no further substantive analysis on it.[1]

---

[1] No plot has displayed a fluttering right tail, so we will concentrate on the left tail here. The curves for Hungary and Poland tend to be more parabolic than curves for other countries, and often look more like a bullet trajectory.

The purpose of the smoothing exercise is to bring out the main structure of the curves and to avoid being confused by all the ragged variation of the raw data, without making very strong assumptions about the underlying social or behavioural features. Once the main structure has been displayed, the sociologist can look for understandable patterns that confirm or revise his insight into the societal processes at work, in this case features of inter-generational social mobility. The operational question raised by the left tail of the smoothed curve in Figure A3.1 is whether the sociologist needs to look for an explanation of why these Swedish mobility rates seem to have fallen across the cohorts born in the second decade of this century. The answer is *no*,[2] and we will show how we have come to this conclusion. We suggest a simple general test and illustrate it by an application to the data that initiated this excursion.[3] Before we do so, we briefly explain the particular notions and terminology of moving average graduation.

The curve marked 'smooth' in Figure A3.1 has been produced in the following manner.

Let n_k be the number of sons who had fathers in farming occupations in cohort number k of the Swedish data-set, and let X_k be the number of those sons who end up in non-manual class destinations. Then the corresponding outflow rate is $f_k = X_k/n_k$, and the raw curve in Figure A3.1 is a plot of the set $\{f_k\}$. The central part of the smoothed curve (i.e. the points for k = 11, 12, . . ., 25) is a plot of

$$f_k^* = \sum_{-10}^{10} r_i f_{k+i},$$

where the $\{r_i\}$ are suitably selected graduating coefficients, listed in the final column of Table A3.1. As we see, the graduated value for cohort k is a weighted average of the raw values of all cohorts between number k−10 to number k+10, i.e. twenty-one cohorts in all. In the left tail of the curve (i.e. for k = 1, 2, . . ., 10), this formula cannot be used, for there are not data for ten cohorts to the left of any left tail cohort. For each such cohort k, we use a special set of graduating coefficients $\{r_{ki}: i = -k+1, -k+2, . . ., 10\}$ and get the smoothed value

$$f_k^* = \sum_{i=-k+1}^{10} r_{ki} f_{k+i}.$$

Thus, for k = 1, 2, . . ., 10, the graduated value for cohort number k is a weighted average of the raw values for cohorts 1, 2, . . ., k+10, with weights that depend on the cohort number. The weights are given in the ten first columns of Table A3.1.

Similarly, the original twenty-one-point formula cannot be used in the right tail, i.e. for k = 26, 27, . . ., 35. Graduated values for the right tail are computed symmetrically using the weights for the left tail 'backwards'.

---

[2] Correspondingly, the fluttering left tail has been left out of the curve for Sweden in Figure 3.6. Similar tails have been deleted from curves in other figures.
[3] Some selected further examples have been given elsewhere (Hoem 1991).

TABLE A3.1. *Graduation coefficients for the symmetric twenty-one-term minimum-R_1 moving average, smoothly extended to the tails by the method of Hoem and Linnemann, exact for straight lines, and Borgan-optimal for thirty-five curve points*

Tail*										Central moving average
k=1	k=2	k=3	k=4	k=5	k=6	k=7	k=8	k=9	k=10	
30,750	26,653	22,923	19,500	16,339	13,404	10,669	8,111	5,714	3,463	1,346
26,884	23,561	20,506	17,681	15,056	12,610	10,324	8,182	6,172	4,284	2,509
22,842	20,294	17,913	15,686	13,599	11,642	9,804	8,078	6,455	4,930	3,497
18,635	16,862	15,155	13,525	11,976	10,507	9,119	7,808	6,572	5,410	4,318
14,271	13,272	12,240	11,208	10,196	9,216	8,276	7,381	6,533	5,733	4,984
9,761	9,537	9,179	8,744	8,270	7,779	7,288	6,808	6,347	5,911	5,503
5,115	5,666	5,983	6,146	6,209	6,206	6,165	6,100	6,027	5,953	5,887
347	1,672	2,663	3,424	4,024	4,511	4,918	5,269	5,583	5,872	6,147
-4,532	-2,433	-767	592	1,729	2,705	3,561	4,328	5,029	5,681	6,298
-9,508	-6,634	-4,294	-2,337	-662	802	2,107	3,289	4,377	5,393	6,351
-14,566	-10,917	-7,903	-5,348	-3,136	-1,183	570	2,169	3,644	5,022	6,322
	2,466	4,199	5,394	6,187	6,672	6,918	6,975	6,882	6,666	6,351
		2,202	3,791	4,916	5,686	6,176	6,444	6,533	6,475	6,298
			1,995	3,467	4,534	5,282	5,775	6,060	6,175	6,147
				1,831	3,209	4,227	4,957	5,451	5,750	5,887
					1,700	3,001	3,980	4,695	5,191	5,503
						1,595	2,835	3,782	4,485	4,984
							1,511	2,701	3,623	4,318
								1,443	2,594	3,497
									1,389	2,509
										1,346

Note:

* The coefficients for the left tail (k=1, 2, . ., 10) are used symmetrically in the right tail, in such a manner that the coefficients in column k are used for point number k as well as (in reverse order) for point number 36−k.

It pays to choose the weights $\{r_i\}$ and $\{r_{ki}\}$ with care. The ones used here have been selected by the following criteria.

Each f_k is the usual estimate of a corresponding underlying binomial probability p_k, and its variance is $p_k(1-p_k)/n_k$. By the nature of the data-set, the various f_k are stochastically independent. While the plot of $\{f_k\}$ can be very ragged, as in Figure A3.1, there is no reason to believe that a plot of the $\{p_k\}$ would be the same, if we only knew these 'true' outflow probabilities. In fact, as a first approximation, the $\{p_k\}$ should lie pretty much on a straight line in most cases, at least locally, i.e. over segments of the curve. A smoothing procedure should take this into account. If the p_k do lie on a straight line, then applying the graduation procedure to that line should give the same straight line as output.[4] In addition, the procedure should take into account that the investigator is interested in the *gradient* as well as in the *level* of the curve.

A statistician can pick up both of these considerations by offering graduation coefficients essentially selected so as to minimize the quantity

$$L = \sum_{k=1}^{34} (\Delta f_k^* - \Delta p_k)^2$$

under the side condition that the graduation leave straight lines untouched. Here, Δ is the first-difference operator, i.e. $\Delta p_k = p_{k+1} - p_k$, and such first differences appear in L to accommodate the substantive interest in the curve gradient. This criterion was first developed by Borgan (1979), so we call the set of graduation coefficients that it produces *Borgan-optimal*.[5] The coefficients will be Borgan-optimal for the estimation of the curve gradient, and they will be very good (though not quite optimal) for estimating the level p_k of the curve at each point as well (Borgan 1979: Table 4).

A simple test can then be provided of whether the left tail of a curve has any significant deviation from the direction of the rest of the curve. On the basis of the consistent observation of graduated curves that are roughly linear, or that consist of two roughly linear pieces joined together at some 'splicing point' s (in our case cohort 11),[6] we make the following specification of p_k:

$$p_k = \begin{cases} a + bk \text{ for } k=1, 2, \ldots, s \\ A + Bk \text{ for } k=s, s+1, \ldots, 35 \end{cases}$$

Since the lines meet at the splicing point, we get $a = A+(B-b)s$, and the three parameters (A,B,b) are sufficient to define the possibly broken

---

[4] This may seem as a trite restriction on the smoothing procedure, but procedures without this property exist and are in use.

[5] To be more precise, the expected value of N·L converges to some limiting quantity as the number $N = \Sigma\, n_k$ increases to infinity. The technical criterion is to minimize this quantity under the side condition that locally linear curves remain unchanged by the graduation.

[6] Note that this is where the graduation switches from the set $\{r_i\}$ of coefficients used in the central part of the curve, to the special coefficients used in the tail.

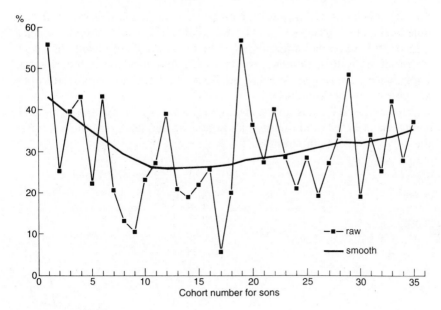

FIGURE A3.1. *Raw and graduated Swedish outflow rates from farm origins to non-manual destinations, by cohort number*

polygonal line that approximates the underlying 'true' curve $\{p_k : k=1, 2, \ldots, 35\}$.

The polygonal line is not broken and the two line segments form a single straight line if $b=B$. To check whether the fluttering of a left tail is a real or a random phenomenon, one suitable procedure may therefore be to carry out a formal statistical test of the hypothesis

$$H_0: b = B$$

which can be done as follows.

Define

$$Q = Q(A,B,b) = \sum_{k=1}^{s} w_k(f_k - a - bk)^2 + \sum_{k=s+1}^{35} w_k(f_k - A - Bk)^2$$

with $a = A + (B-b)s$ and $w_k = n_k/[f_k^*(1-f_k^*)]$. The weight w_k is the reciprocal of an estimate of the variance of f_k. (We let $w_k = 0$, if the numerator is 0.) Let Q_1 be the minimum of $Q(A,B,b)$ with respect to free variation in (A,B,b), and let Q_0 be the corresponding minimum of $Q(A,B,B)$ under free variation of A and B, i.e. Q_0 is the minimum of Q when H_0 is assumed to hold.[7] Then

---

[7] For the minimization, note that under our broken-line specification, $E(f_k) = A + (k-s)\alpha(k)b + [k-(k-s)\alpha(k)]B$, with $\alpha(k)=1$ for $k=1, 2, \ldots, s$, and $\alpha(k)=0$ for $k = s+1, s+2, \ldots, 35$. When $b=B$, $E(f_k)=A+Bk$.

the difference $D = Q_1 - Q_0$ approximately has a chi-square distribution with a single degree of freedom when $b=B$, and it can be used to test H_0, which is rejected if D exceeds a suitable percentage point in the relevant chi-square distribution. If this happens, we conclude that $b \neq B$, that the two line segments are at an angle with each other, and that the 'fluttering' of the tail is a non-random phenomenon.

Conversely, if D does not exceed the relevant percentage point, then H_0 cannot be rejected, and the sociologist may as well disregard the left tail of the curve if this fits his purpose.

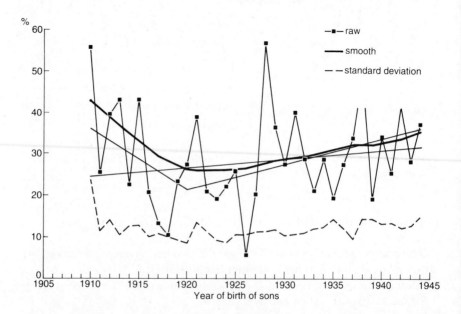

FIGURE A3.2. *Polygonal representations of Swedish outflow rates from farm origins to non-manual destinations*

An application of the above procedure to the Swedish data of Figure A3.1 gives results which are plotted in Figure A3.2. The stippled curve gives the estimated standard deviations of the raw values. The plot also contains a straight line fitted to the whole set of raw points and a two-piece broken polygonal line fitted to the two parts of the data. The test statistic is $D = 3.89$, which is slightly larger than the 95th percentage point of the chi-square distribution with one degree of freedom ($=3.84$), but much smaller than the corresponding 97.5 percentage point ($=5.02$), say. Given the need for some caution in the choice between rejecting and accepting the null hypothesis, the empirical investigator may feel justified in leaving the left tail of this curve out of account and paying it little attention in his substantive discussion.

The sociologist need not make much effort to explain why outflow rates from farm origins to non-manual destinations in Sweden seem to have *fallen* over the cohorts born in the second decade of this century. There may not have been a real decline in these outflow rates.

Finally, it may be noted that the test method just suggested can be used for purposes other than those for which it was originally developed. As mentioned in our note 1, several of the curves for Hungary and Poland, for example in Figures 3.6, 3.7, and 3.10, look more like (skew) parabolas than like (a combination of) straight lines. These Eastern European curves tend to have a maximum (or a minimum, as the case may be) at or close to cohort number 14, that of men born in 1922. One such case is shown in Figure A3.3. Our test procedure with a 'splicing-point' at $s=14$ for this data-segment gives a test statistic of $D=24.03$, which is far beyond any percentage point normally used in hypothesis testing in the chi-square distribution with one degree of freedom. As indicated in Chapter 3 (p. 84 and n. 17), it is of substantive interest that the curves for Eastern European countries should show such a distinctive pattern in evident association with the period of post-war 'socialist reconstruction'. Rather than checking for a fluttering tail due to the graduation method, the test here serves to confirm the idea of a parabolic curve. Thus, for the curve of Figure A3.3, the splicing point is not at cohort 11, where we change over from the special graduation coefficients for the tails, but at cohort 14, as generated by the real curve pattern.

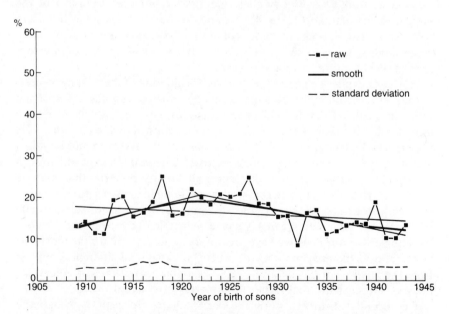

FIGURE A3.3. *Hungarian outflow rates from farm origins to non-manual destinations, by birth year*

4

Social Fluidity within Class Structures: Modelling the FJH Hypothesis

In Chapter 1 we have described how the FJH hypothesis was advanced as a reformulation of that earlier suggested by Lipset and Zetterberg. The latter had proposed a basic similarity among industrial nations in actually observed, or absolute, rates of social mobility: the FJH hypothesis, however, claims that such a similarity will be found not at the 'phenotypical' level represented by absolute rates but, rather, at the 'genotypical' level of relative rates—or, as we would wish to say, in patterns of social fluidity.

As we then sought to show, this reformulation is one of great potential importance. If valid, the FJH hypothesis must controvert, on the one hand, the liberal expectation of steadily increasing fluidity in the course of the development of industrial societies and, on the other, all arguments which maintain or imply that across such societies fluidity reveals significant variation in relation to differences in cultural tradition, political regime, etc. Furthermore, as observed in the preceding chapter, acceptance of the FJH hypothesis would be directly consequential for our understanding of the large measure of temporal stability that fluidity patterns can in fact be shown to possess: that is, such constancy could then be seen as a derivative of the commonality that is to be found in such patterns across a range of developmental levels and institutional settings.

However, while the need for a thorough evaluation of the FJH hypothesis is thus evident enough, to achieve this has not proved easy. Two main difficulties can be identified. The first is that of data quality which we have already discussed in Chapter 2. For the empirical testing of the FJH hypothesis, high standards of cross-national comparability in mobility data are of particular importance. There is clearly little point in engaging in such testing if any cross-national differences in fluidity patterns that may be shown up are as likely to reflect non-comparability in data as actual variation in social processes. However, this difficulty is, we believe, substantially overcome with the data-set that we have been able to construct through our recoding procedures. As we have previously argued, it will for the most part be the reasonable presumption that, where cross-national differences emerge from the analysis of this data-set, whether in fluidity patterns or otherwise, these differences are real rather than merely artefactual.

The second difficulty concerns the exact meaning that is to be given to the FJH hypothesis and in turn the way in which, for purposes of empirical testing, it is to be modelled. It is with this difficulty, and its resolution, that the present chapter is concerned. In the section that follows we outline the problems that arise in interpreting the hypothesis, and propose a new approach in which we introduce the idea of a 'core' pattern of social fluidity. We further show how a possible empirical representation of this core pattern may be arrived at. In the next section we then seek to develop a sociologically meaningful model of 'core' fluidity which can adequately reproduce the empirical representation, and which at the same time provides a basis for testing the FJH hypothesis and for assessing the substantive as well as statistical significance of any departures from expectations under the hypothesis. In the final section we consider certain emergent features of the model and their implications.

THE FJH HYPOTHESIS AND THE IDEA OF 'CORE' FLUIDITY

As originally presented by its authors (Featherman, Jones, and Hauser 1975: 337–9), the FJH hypothesis is embodied in what in the previous chapter we have called the 'common social fluidity' (CmSF) model: that is, the model which states that across a set of national mobility tables all corresponding relative rates, as measured by odds ratios, will be identical. Any such attempt to express a hypothesis in a form in which it is readily available for empirical testing is to be applauded. None the less, it has to be recognized that in the particular case in question problems have ensued since the verbal and the formal versions of the hypothesis are not in fact in complete accordance. The former, as we have noted, claims that across all modern societies relative mobility rates will prove to be 'basically' the same; while the latter requires that (underlying any sampling fluctuation) these rates be *exactly* the same. As a result, then, of this discrepancy, empirical tests of the FJH hypothesis, as represented by the CmSF model, have tended to be rather inconclusive—in a way that can be well illustrated on the basis of our own data-set.

We have already in the previous chapter utilized the CmSF model in investigating the extent of cross-national variation in fluidity within and across birth-cohorts. For our present purposes, however, we may simply fit the model to the standard intergenerational mobility tables for our nine nations, which cover all men aged 20–64. The results of so doing are given in Table 4.1. As can be seen from the first three columns of the table, the model fails to reproduce the data within the limits of sampling error. We must, in other words, accept that significant cross-national differences in relative rates—or in patterns of social fluidity—do occur. At the same time, though, it is also indicated by the results in the last two columns of the table that these differences are rather small. The CmSF model accounts for almost 95 per cent of all of the association between class of origin and class of destination

TABLE 4.1. *Results of fitting the CmSF model to intergenerational class mobility tables for nine nations*

Model* (N = 86,913)	G^2	df	p	rG^2	Δ
ON DN (con. ind.)	29,810	324	0.00	—	21.5
ON DN OD (CmSF)	1,567.0	288	0.00	94.7	4.2

Δs for each nation separately under the CmSF model, based on Ns standardized to 10,000[†]

ENG	2.5	NIR	5.0
FRA	3.3	POL	5.0
FRG	4.8	SCO	5.3
HUN	4.9	SWE	6.0
IRL	5.5		

Notes:
* O = origin class; D = destination class; N = nation.
[†] Using unstandardized Ns, the expected values produced under the model fitted, and hence Δ values, are unduly affected by sample size—i.e. 'in favour' of nations with large samples. Thus, in this case, Poland has, not surprisingly, the lowest Δ (3.2), and, furthermore, the Δs for other countries are then, in turn, much influenced by how closely their patterns of fluidity correspond to the Polish.

and, overall, misallocates only a little over 4 per cent of all individual cases.[1]

Thus, the following troublesome considerations arise. If the FJH hypothesis is to be identified with the CmSF model, then we must, by conventional standards of hypothesis testing, clearly reject it: relative rates of class mobility are *not* identical from nation to nation. But, if we do reject the hypothesis in this very strict form, are we not in real danger of throwing out the sociological baby with the statistical bathwater—that is, of ignoring the considerable degree of commonality that would still seem to be present in relative rates, and to which the 'basic similarity' in the verbal expression of the hypothesis might be taken to refer? But then again, if we should opt for the hypothesis in this weaker—albeit far more plausible—version, does this not undermine the possibility of ever being able to reach a satisfactory appraisal of it? How is a 'basic' similarity in relative rates to be recognized? What would cross-national variation in fluidity have to be like in its degree and kind for the hypothesis in this form to be invalidated?

The difficulties here indicated are not ones that can be overcome through statistical technique alone. What is first of all required is some way of explicating the FJH hypothesis which can, on the one hand, remove the

[1] Such an outcome is of course directly anticipated in Table 3.3, in which we report the results of fitting the CmSF model to the mobility data for our nine nations, but with the national samples divided up into four ten-year birth-cohorts and omitting those aged 20–24.

danger of its premature rejection but which will, on the other, still allow it to be critically assessed and, if need be, refined or qualified or indeed discarded after all. To this end, we would suggest thinking on the following lines.

The hypothesis that, within the modern world, relative mobility rates have a 'basic' cross-national similarity may be taken to mean that a particular pattern of such rates is identifiable, to which the patterns actually found in different national societies will all approximate even though any, or indeed all, of these societies may show some amount of deviation. There is, in other words, a strong and well-defined theme, but one on which national variations may be played. Construed in this way, therefore, the hypothesis will not be disconfirmed simply by the fact that cross-national differences in relative rates can be detected. It will, however, be undermined in so far as these differences are either of such an extent that no one pattern which is generally approximated can be specified *or* prove to be of a systematic character: that is, to represent not merely a series of specific deviations from a common pattern but rather a number of patterns distinguishable from each other in a way that would suggest some kind of societal typology or, at all events, the regular covariation of fluidity with other generalizable attributes of national societies. In these circumstances, the idea of cross-national differences in fluidity as representing variations on a single theme would then be likely to give way to alternative hypotheses—drawn perhaps from among those reviewed in Chapter 1—that would be more adequate to the regularities in question.

If, therefore, this approach to evaluating the FJH hypothesis is to be implemented, what is obviously necessary is that a representation of the putative common or 'core' pattern of fluidity should in some way be produced, against which observed patterns within our sample of nations can be compared.

One means of thus identifying 'core' fluidity would in fact suggest itself from the application of the CmSF model to our comparative data on which we have already reported: that is, to take the core pattern as being defined by the set of *expected* odds ratios that results from the fitting of this model, and then to regard the size and location of national deviations as being indicated by the appropriate residuals. However, while straightforward and formally attractive, this procedure would, we believe, carry a serious disadvantage. It must be remembered that the set of expected odds ratios under the CmSF model is simply the result of an averaging process applied to the sets of odds ratios implicit in the actual mobility tables to which the model is fitted.[2] It follows, therefore, that, if these empirical data were to be changed—for example, by the introduction of mobility tables for further nations—then, in all probability, the expected odds ratios that are to be taken as defining the core pattern would themselves change. In other words,

---

[2] The averages of odds ratios taken are in fact weighted geometric means (cf. Payne 1977: 116–17).

we could not in this way obtain a *stable* representation of this pattern, and neither therefore, could we securely establish deviations from it.

An alternative method of obtaining a representation of core fluidity that we would ourselves favour is the following. We start from the supposition that variation in fluidity patterns among industrial societies will occur along a number of different dimensions, which together define a certain 'space'. In terms of their overall fluidity patterns, some nations can then be thought of as being positioned towards the edges of this space, while others will be close to its centre. The former nations are ones which deviate relatively widely from the core pattern of fluidity, while the latter are those which conform to this pattern quite closely. If, therefore, we could establish the space in question and, further, find a number of more-or-less 'central' societies within it, we should then be able, by reference to these latter cases, to arrive at a fairly accurate picture of what core fluidity should be taken to be.

A rather direct way in which this conceptualization can be realized is available. We fit the CmSF model not to our nine national mobility tables simultaneously, as we did before, but instead to these nine tables *taken in all pairwise combinations*—and with their total number of observations standardized (i.e. N is taken as 10,000 in all cases). In this way, we obtain from the G^2s returned a set of comparable measures of the goodness of fit to each possible pair of nations of the model which states that their patterns of social fluidity are identical. This set of G^2s—thirty-six in all—may thus be understood as a 'dissimilarity matrix' (or, to be precise, half-matrix) which reflects the 'distances' between each pair of nations in terms of their fluidity patterns; and in turn these data can then be used as input to a multidimensional scaling (MDSCAL) exercise. Such an exercise is one designed specifically to show in what kind of space the distances in question—and hence the variation in fluidity patterns that they represent—can best be seen as occurring; and further how, within this space, different nations are positioned relative to each other.

In Figure 4.1 we show the results thus obtained. As is indicated, a satisfactory fit of the distances implied between the nations was achieved by a three-dimensional solution; and it is further apparent from the plot that there are in fact two nations, England and France, which do hold rather central positions within the space that is constituted.[3] If we calculate (Euclidean) distances, in terms of co-ordinate units, from the centroid of the total configuration, these prove to be 0.43 and 0.49 for England and France

[3] We should add here that it is not, for our purposes, necessary to interpret the dimensions of Figure 4.1, nor even that they should be interpretable. As Shepard has observed in a standard text on multidimensional scaling:

The discovery of interpretable axes is not . . . the only way in which a meaningful pattern can be found in a spatial representation. In many cases is has turned out that a quite different aspect of the spatial configuration—such as the way the points are ordered around the perimeter of a circle—constitutes the most interpretable aspect of that configuration. (1972: 4)

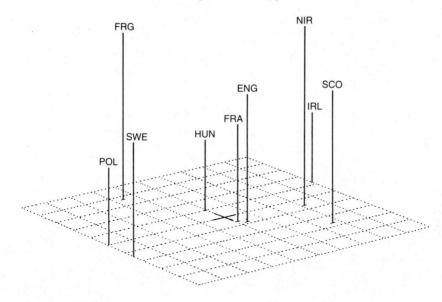

FIGURE 4.1. *Three-dimensional (ALSCAL) solution for distances between national patterns of social fluidity for nine nations, Kruskal's stress formula 1 = 0.066.*

respectively, while the distance for the next closest nation, Hungary, is 0.82. This finding is consistent with England and France showing in Table 4.1 the lowest Δ values when the CmSF model is fitted to all our nine nations simultaneously. And since its robustness is obviously a matter of some consequence, it is reassuring to be able to report further that the centrality of England and France was found to persist if we repeated our MDSCAL exercise but with a dissimilarity matrix of corresponding Δ values in place of the original G^2s; and also, as is shown in Figure 4.2, if we extended the initial exercise so as to take in appropriate mobility tables that we could obtain for three other European nations (Czechoslovakia, the Netherlands, and Italy, see pp. 165–7) plus those for the three non-European nations represented in our own data-set.[4]

[4] As a further check on the centrality of England and France, one other exercise was undertaken. We compared the set of odds ratios produced when the CmSF model is fitted to the English and French tables alone—i.e. our preferred empirical representation of core fluidity—with the set produced when the CmSF model is fitted to the tables for the *other seven* of our European nations. If England and France do indeed hold a central position within the overall variation in patterns of social fluidity, then these two sets of odds ratios should be very similar. For, in this case, England and France will approximate the 'average' pattern, and removing them should thus have little effect on the average for the remaining nations. In fact, we obtain a

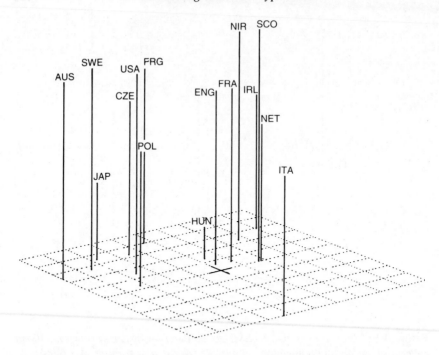

FIGURE 4.2. *Three-dimensional (ALSCAL) solution for distances between national patterns of social fluidity for fifteen nations, Kruskal's stress formula 1 = 0.111.*

In pursuing the strategy earlier outlined, it would, therefore, seem clear that it is the fluidity patterns of England and France that we should take as offering the best basis on which to form our understanding of core fluidity— and thus to obtain a *fixed* standard against which the extent and significance

correlation ratio for the two sets of (logged) odds ratios of 0.96. It is then made still more apparent that our representation of core fluidity is very close indeed to that we would have obtained by taking the odds ratios implicit in expected values under the CmSF model when this is fitted simultaneously to all our nations, while of course our representation retains the avantage of being a fixed one. This result is further reassuring in that it suggests that our MDSCAL exercises are not unduly distorted by the fact that—as Albert Simkus has pointed out to us—the G^2s on which they are based will reflect 'compositional' effects as well as simply differences in odds ratios: i.e. effects resulting from the interaction of differences in odds ratios and differences in the sizes of classes of origin and destination across our nations. What we cannot rule out is the possibility that, if we had based our MDSCAL exercises on different nations from those in our 'accidental' sample, different nations might then have appeared as central. Thus, a sample containing, say, several Southern European nations might have produced some other outcome. Our judgement is that the nations we consider are in fact sufficiently varied in their economic, political, cultural, and institutional characteristics to be able to provide a more-or-less effective coverage of the space into which variation in social fluidity across all industrial nations extends. But whether or not this judgement is correct must, of course, remain open to further empirical investigation.

of cross-national variation may be assessed. To this end, the most obvious next step is then to 'average' the relative mobility rates of our two central nations, and this we can in fact aptly do in the following way. We may fit the CmSF model *to the English and French mobility tables alone* (standardized to the same N)[5] and take as our empirically derived representation of core social fluidity *the set of odds ratios that are implicit in the expected cell values under this model*.

Having arrived at this representation, it would of course be possible to use it *directly* as a basis for determining how far and in what ways the social fluidity displayed within our nations deviates from the core pattern. We could, for example, construct for each nation a 'counterfactual' mobility table which preserves the marginal distributions of the original but embodies the set of odds ratios that we have taken as defining core fluidity. Such tables would thus serve to show what mobility in each nation would be like if core fluidity, on our understanding of it, *were* universally to prevail. And by comparing these tables with the actually observed ones, the degree of approximation to, or deviation from, core fluidity expectations could in each case be examined in detail.

However, while results of some interest might in this way be achieved, our representation of core fluidity will, we believe, be yet more effectively exploited if it is first subjected to some refinement. That is to say, rather than applying this empirically produced pattern immediately to the task of assessing cross-national commonality and variation in relative mobility rates, we will do better by taking it as the basis for constructing an explicit model of core fluidity. In proceeding thus we can, first of all, hope to remove from our representation of core fluidity any features that might reflect mere peculiarities of the English and French cases from which it derives—as distinct from their 'centrality'; and, secondly, and more importantly, we can aim to provide some insight into why our representation of core fluidity should be as it is—or, in other words, to make core fluidity more sociologically intelligible.

A MODEL OF CORE FLUIDITY

We have already argued in Chapter 2 that our conceptual choice to study mobility within the context of a class structure, rather than that of a social hierarchy, has direct implications for the kind of model of relative rates that we will prefer. It will be clearly more appropriate to our interests for us to adopt a topological or 'levels' model, which does not, in principle, presuppose any ordering of the categories of the mobility table, rather than a model

---

[5] The fit is, as might be expected, a close one. The G^2 returned, with 36 degrees of freedom, is 75.1, Ns being standardized to 10,000; and, while this implies statistically significant variation, the model still accounts for 99.2 per cent of the G^2 obtained under the independence model and misclassifies only 1.4 per cent of all cases.

constructed around some notion of 'social distance' as the crucial determinant of mobility. As we further noted, the main attraction of topological models is the flexibility with which they can be used to partition mobility tables into regions of (net) association, or interaction, as between origin and destination categories, and in this way, then, directly to define patterns of social fluidity. But, we recognized, difficulties are likely to occur in interpreting, and in choosing between, topological models in so far as the allocation of cells to different interaction levels is determined *ad hoc*, with the aim simply of fitting the data, rather than being guided by some theoretical rationale.

In an attempt to minimize such difficulties, we propose here a topological model of the mobility table of a more sophisticated kind than has been used hitherto. That is, one based not on a single levels matrix but rather on a number of such matrices, *each of which is designed, in a theoretically informed way, in order to capture a specific effect exerted on the pattern of relative rates*. A standard topological model of the mobility table can be written as

$$\log F_{ij} = \mu + \lambda_i^O + \lambda_j^D + \lambda_{a(ij)}^I \tag{4.1}$$

where F_{ij} is the expected frequency in cell ij of the table and, on the right-hand side of the equation, μ is a scale factor, λ_i^O and λ_j^D are the main effects of the distribution of individuals over classes of origin and destination respectively, and the $\lambda_{a(ij)}^I$ term refers to the particular interaction level to which the ijth cell is allocated within the levels matrix. However, in the model we suggest $\lambda_{a(ij)}^I$ is decomposed into a set of more specific terms, each of which has to be represented by its own levels matrix, and it is then through the summation of these terms that the interaction levels of the cells of the table are determined. To develop a topological model of this more differentiated kind thus calls for some fairly explicit rationale and, in turn, such a model should, when applied, give results that are open to more direct and unambiguous interpretation.

A further consequence of our opting to study mobility within the context of a class structure is that we do not view the latter as being, so to speak, merely a framework for mobility, but are rather committed to the view that positions defined within this structure, that is, by class relations, will themselves exercise a distinctive influence on mobility propensities (cf. Mach and Wesołowski 1986: ch. 2). The general considerations that we would see as relevant in this respect are those earlier set out by Goldthorpe (1980*a*/1987: 99), and may be grouped under three heads:

1. the relative desirability of different class positions, considered as destinations;
2. the relative advantages afforded to individuals by different class origins—in the form of economic, cultural, and social resources;

3. the relative barriers that face individuals in gaining access to different class positions—which may be thought of in terms of requirements corresponding to the resources indicated under (2): for example, requirements for capital, qualifications, 'knowing people', etc.

In efforts that we have previously made to give conventional topological models some theoretical grounding, we have drawn on these ideas of desirability, advantages, and barriers in order to suggest why particular cells of an intergenerational mobility table—or in other words, particular intergenerational transitions—might plausibly be allocated to one interaction level rather than another (Goldthorpe, 1980*a*/1987: 100–4; Erikson, Goldthorpe, and Portocarero 1982; Erikson and Pöntinen 1985). However, these attempts have been of an undeniably impressionistic kind and, for many features of the models in question, we could scarcely claim to have shown that they follow unequivocally from our guiding concepts. In developing a multi-matrix model, we hope to achieve a significant improvement in this respect.

We begin by considering the several kinds of effect on the patterning of social fluidity that can be associated with differences in desirability, advantages, and barriers within a structure of class positions—as represented for present purposes by the sevenfold version of our class schema. We distinguish four such effects, which we label as those of *hierarchy*, *inheritance*, *sector*, and *affinity*. The task that follows, therefore, is to devise, in as explicit a way as possible, separate levels matrices for each of these effects which, when combined in a single model, will adequately reproduce the pattern of core fluidity that we have earlier reached by empirical means. The following designs are proposed.

Hierarchy

In conceptualizing social mobility, as we have sought earlier to show, a class-structural context stands as an alternative to that of a social hierarchy; and it is, of course, within the latter that hierarchical—or 'social distance'—effects will be most readily invoked in explaining mobility patterns. Lines of class demarcation, however, must be understood in relational terms, and do not necessarily translate into differences on some 'vertical' scale. Correspondingly, we have emphasized that our class schema does not embody a central hierarchical principle from which a regular ordering of the classes might be derived. At the same time, though, it is evident that, at least by reference to external criteria, hierarchical aspects of the scheme can be recognized, and we have in fact aimed to represent the most salient of these by the threefold division of the schema that is presented in Table 2.2. This division, as we have described, is obtained from the ranking of the constituent elements of the classes of the schema on various occupational scales, which we would interpret as essentially reflecting differences in rewards and in entry requirements (cf. Goldthorpe and Hope 1972, 1974). Hence, we would suppose that, as well as marking broad differences in the general desirability of class positions, the division will also capture other hierarchical features of the classes that exert an influence on fluidity patterns: ones, that is, pertaining to their relative advantages, considered as classes of origin, and to their relative accessibility, considered as classes of destination.

Thus, we would see Class I+II of our schema, which makes up the highest hierarchical division, as covering what are generally the most desirable positions within modern societies—that is, primarily salaried professional, administrative, and managerial positions; and, further, as the class that offers the greatest resources as a class of origin and for which entry requirements are most demanding. On the other hand, Classes VIIa and VIIb, which form the lowest hierarchical division, cover the least desirable positions, those of non-skilled manual wage-workers, and also, we would suggest, provide the least advantages as classes of origin and present the fewest barriers to access—for anyone, that is, who should actually seek to move into them. The remaining classes, which are included in the intermediate hierarchical division—that is, those of routine non-manual workers, small proprietors and artisans, and lower-level technicians, supervisors, and skilled manual workers—can then be regarded as likewise intermediate as regards the advantages and accessibility as well as the desirability of the positions they comprise, with the exception that, on grounds earlier explained (p. 46), we would wish to treat Class IVc, that of farmers, as falling in the lowest division when taken as a class of *origin*.

Our specification of hierarchy effects on fluidity patterns is then directly dictated by this threefold division made within the class schema, as reference back to Table 2.2 will confirm. Treating each *shift* in level separately, we obtain the two 'hierarchy' matrices that are given below—the term above each matrix being that by which it is indexed in our final model. In the first

HI1 (a(i, j))								HI2 (b(i, j))						
I+II	1	2	2	2	2	2	2	1	1	1	1	1	2	2
III	2	1	1	1	1	2	2	1	1	1	1	1	1	1
IVa+b	2	1	1	1	1	2	2	1	1	1	1	1	1	1
IVc	2	2	2	2	2	1	1	2	1	1	1	1	1	1
V+VI	2	1	1	1	1	2	2	1	1	1	1	1	1	1
VIIa	2	2	2	2	2	1	1	2	1	1	1	1	1	1
VIIb	2	2	2	2	2	1	1	2	1	1	1	1	1	1

matrix, HI1, we put at a base level 1 cells which imply no hierarchical mobility—that is, the classes of origin and destination to which they refer fall within the same hierarchical division; while we put at level 2 those cells which do imply such mobility, since the classes involved fall in different divisions. Our expectation is, of course, that there will be a lower propensity for the 'vertical' movement that the latter cells define; or, in other words, that there will *ceteris paribus* be a reduced probability of individual cases being observed in those cells where the intergenerational crossing of lines of hierarchical division is involved. Then in the second matrix, HI2, we put at level 2 only those cells which imply a *two-step* hierarchical movement—that is, from a position in the highest of our three divisions to one in the lowest or vice versa—all other cells now going to level 1. Here, we anticipate that the propensity for mobility of the kind indicated by the level 2 cells, that is, 'long-range' vertical mobility, will be at an especially low level.[6]

Inheritance

Inheritance effects we interpret as all those that increase the likelihood of individuals being found in positions in the same class as that in which they originated. A tendency towards inheritance in this sense could be expected as a result of the special attractiveness to individuals of positions falling within their class of origin, and also, of course, as a result of distinctive opportunities and constraints. And, indeed, that such a tendency prevails might be reckoned as one of the most secure findings of mobility research to date. This points, therefore, to the most obvious way in which inheritance effects can be represented in our model: that is—as shown in the first 'inheritance' matrix, IN1, below—by placing all cells on the main diagonal of the mobility table at a different interaction level from the remainder. We set the latter at the base level 1 and the former at level 2, so as to accommodate what we would anticipate as being a generally greater propensity for individuals to be found in their class of origin than in any other. However, since class inheritance can result from a number of quite different social processes, it may further be expected that the propensity for inter-generational immobility will vary from one class to another, and this should also be reflected in our modelling.

First of all in this connection, we should recognize that immobility may in some instances result from class positions being inherited in a relatively strict sense. This possibility is most evident within our Classes IV*a*+*b* and IV*c*, those of the petty bourgeoisie and farmers, in that fathers may be able to

---

[6] In other words, in these, and in the further design matrices subsequently presented, level 1 always represents a base level, and level 2 a shift from this base level. Thus, where cells are allocated to level 1, it will not always be the case that a *higher* level of interaction is expected in those cells than in ones allocated to level 2—as would follow from what has become the practice in numbering levels in conventional models; rather, level 1 *or* level 2 may refer to the higher expected interaction, depending on the particular contrast that is being modelled. It might also be noted here that where, in constructing our levels matrices, we in effect put cells on the same level—as, for example, in treating all one-step or all two-step hierarchical shifts as being equivalent—we typically do so in the interests of parsimony or, that is, for want of good theoretical reasons for proceeding otherwise.

	IN1 $(c(i, j))$							IN2 $(d(i, j))$						
I+II	2	1	1	1	1	1	1	2	1	1	1	1	1	1
III	1	2	1	1	1	1	1	1	1	1	1	1	1	1
IVa+b	1	1	2	1	1	1	1	1	1	2	1	1	1	1
IVc	1	1	1	2	1	1	1	1	1	1	2	1	1	1
V+VI	1	1	1	1	2	1	1	1	1	1	1	1	1	1
VIIa	1	1	1	1	1	2	1	1	1	1	1	1	1	1
VIIb	1	1	1	1	1	1	2	1	1	1	1	1	1	1

	IN3 $(e(i, j))$						
I+II	1	1	1	1	1	1	1
III	1	1	1	1	1	1	1
IVa+b	1	1	1	1	1	1	1
IVc	1	1	1	2	1	1	1
V+VI	1	1	1	1	1	1	1
VIIa	1	1	1	1	1	1	1
VIIb	1	1	1	1	1	1	1

pass on a 'going concern' directly to their sons or, alternatively, to endow them with the capital necessary for them to 'start up on their own' (cf. Stinchcombe 1961; Robinson 1984; Simkus 1984). Further, though, within Class I+II the retention of—highly desirable—class positions can likewise be favoured by the intergenerational transmission of capital, in the form both of accumulated wealth and also of 'cultural' capital (Bourdieu and Passeron 1964, 1972). Through such familial resources, the recipient generation can obtain a considerable advantage in acquiring the education and training, and in turn the credentials, that are the main requirements for access to the positions comprised by the service class (cf. Goldthorpe 1982). We are, therefore, led to our second 'inheritance' matrix, IN2, in which we allow for a distinctive—we would expect, distinctively high—propensity for immobility within Classes IVa+b, IVc, and I+II alike; that is, we now put at level 2 only the diagonal cells of the mobility table that relate to these three classes.

Finally, with inheritance as with hierarchy effects, the class of farmers would appear to require special treatment—that is, over and above that provided for in IN2. There are in fact several grounds for expecting that the propensity for immobility will be still higher in this class than in any other. To begin with, the most important kind of capital to be passed on intergenerationally will be 'fixed' capital in the form of land. And father-to-son succession in farming is likely to be further encouraged, on the one hand, by the highly specific nature of the skills that are transmitted within farming families and, on the other, by a wider cultural inheritance expressed in an 'attachment to the land which increases the relative desirability of farming for farm sons even where other opportunities exist (cf. Franklin 1969; Gasson 1969). Thus, as can be seen, in our third inheritance matrix, IN3, we use level 2 in order to differentiate the diagonal cell for Class IVc from all others.[7]

Sector

As earlier described, we have, in fact, built into our class schema a sectoral division so that proprietors and wage-workers in agriculture and other forms of primary production are separately identified. We saw this division as necessary in order to take account of various distinctive features of class relations within primary production, but we would envisage class mobility as being patterned by sector in ways that extend beyond those that may be captured through the hierarchy and inheritance effects already proposed. That is, we would suppose that further relative advantages and barriers will operate so as to increase the probability of movements of an intrasectoral as against those of intersectoral kind. For example, mobility between agricultural and non-agricultural class positions will often also entail geographical and cultural relocation; and thus, in comparison with intrasectoral mobility, it is less likely to be facilitated by transferable skills, knowledge of employment opportunities, or personal contacts, while being more likely to be impeded by controls on job entry or by rehousing problems (cf. Bishop 1969; Franklin 1971). It is then such effects that we seek to capture in our model by the 'sectoral' matrix, SE, shown below, which follows directly from the division made within our class schema. Cells of the mobility table that imply movement between our agricultural classes, IVc and VIIb, and non-agricultural classes are differentiated from the remainder; while the latter are at base level 1, the former are set at level 2, with the expectation that there will here be a lower propensity for the intergenerational transitions that these level-2 cells define.

$$\text{SE } (f(i, j))$$

I+II	1	1	1	2	1	1	2
III	1	1	1	2	1	1	2
IVa+b	1	1	1	2	1	1	2
IVc	2	2	2	1	2	2	1
V+VI	1	1	1	2	1	1	2
VIIa	1	1	1	2	1	1	2
VIIb	2	2	2	1	2	2	1

[7] It should, of course, be remembered that men found in this cell of the mobility table—i.e. men who have succeeded their fathers as farmers—are also viewed as upwardly mobile; that is, as a result of our decision to treat Class IVc as falling in the lowest level of the hierarchy as a class of origin but in the intermediate level as a class of destination. This might at first appear contradictory but, we would suggest, is in fact quite consistent with what we take to be the social

Affinity

Under the label of affinity we try to capture effects on mobility which derive from specific linkages *or* discontinuities between classes, and which operate *additionally to* the more generalized effects that we have so far considered. In suggesting such affinity—or disaffinity—effects, there is an obvious danger of *ad hoc* argumentation directed simply towards producing a model through which an approximation to our empirical version of core fluidity can be generated. We have, therefore, tried to keep these effects to a minimum, and to give as clear a rationale as possible for those that we do include.[8]

First of all, we propose a disaffinity: that is, between our Class I+II, the service class, and Class VIIb, that of agricultural workers. We have already recognized barriers to mobility between these classes in the form of both hierarchical and sectoral effects. But it would seem appropriate to recognize further the particular disadvantages that the sons of agricultural workers are likely to face in seeking to qualify for entry into service-class positions and the particular improbability of the downwardly mobile sons of service-class families being found as wage-workers in agriculture rather than elsewhere. On the one hand, educational provision in rural areas has often been left below generally prevailing national standards, and the economic and cultural circumstances of agricultural workers' children have tended to be especially far removed from those of the *famille educogène* (Franklin 1971; Connor 1979: 207–11). On the other hand, for those men of service-class origins who have failed to exploit the advantages of their birth and have little to offer but their labour, agricultural work may be expected to be still less desirable than unskilled work in manufacturing or service industry, since, apart from its cultural remoteness, it must appear ,to hold out still fewer chances of subsequent 'counter-mobility' back to higher-level positions. Thus, as can be seen below, in our first 'affinity' matrix, AF1, we differentiate, at level 2, the two cells indicating mobility between Classes I+II and VIIb, in the expectation of there being a distinctively low propensity for such movement.

reality of *collective* upward mobility on the part of farmers. Those men who have stayed in farming, in the context of the general exodus from the land, can be assumed to have, on average, more substantial enterprises than their fathers; and it is not in turn inappropriate to regard them as having had to surmount 'hierarchical' barriers—e.g. that of finding funds for capital investment—in order thus to maintain their position within their class of origin.

[8] Hout (1989: 148), in discussing the model as previously presented in Erikson and Goldthorpe (1987), appears to regard the affinity terms as entirely *ad hoc* and to be based 'mostly on a ransacking of the British [*sic*] and French mobility tables'. In response, two points must be made. First, Hout does not mention either the general or the specific grounds that we give for the introduction of affinity terms (and which we shall here spell out rather more fully); and, secondly, he does not make clear *why* not just the affinity terms but indeed the model *as a whole* is influenced by the English and French tables or, more precisely, by the expected values that result when the CmSF model is fitted to these tables: that is, because, as earlier described, our MDSCAL exercises would indicate that it is in this way that the most satisfactory empirical representation of core fluidity can be obtained.

	AF1 (g(i, j))							AF2 (h(i, j))						
I+II	1	1	1	1	1	1	2	1	2	2	1	1	1	1
III	1	1	1	1	1	1	1	2	1	1	1	1	1	1
IV*a+b*	1	1	1	1	1	1	1	2	1	1	2	1	1	1
IV*c*	1	1	1	1	1	1	1	1	1	2	1	1	2	1
V+VI	1	1	1	1	1	1	1	1	1	1	1	1	2	1
VII*a*	1	1	1	1	1	1	1	1	1	1	1	2	1	1
VII*b*	2	1	1	1	1	1	1	1	1	1	1	1	2	1

The second affinity matrix that we develop, AF2, then relates to instances where we would see affinities of various kinds working to *offset* barriers to mobility that are captured by our hierarchical and sector effects. We would suggest the existence of such affinities in three aspects.

To begin with, we would enter an affinity between Class I+II and Class III, the class of routine non-manual employees; and again between Class V+VI and Class VII*a*, the two classes of largely industrial wage-workers. In both these cases alike, we see the affinity as lying in the evident 'closeness' of the classes in question within the *status* structures of modern societies, understood *stricto sensu*, in relational rather than attributional terms—which, it should be stressed, we would *not* regard as being adequately reflected in occupational scales of the kind from which the hierarchical division of our class schema is derived.[9] It has, for example, been a consistent finding of studies of differential association in friendship, leisure activities, etc., that routine non-manual employees have relatively frequent social ties with members of the service class and form together with them what is, in terms of status, a rather well-defined 'white-collar bloc'; while such ties are also relatively frequent among industrial workers of differing skill level, thus giving rise to a corresponding 'blue-collar bloc' (see, for a valuable study and literature review, Mitchell and Critchley 1985). Thus, we would envisage mobility between the classes within these two blocs as being facilitated through the participation of their members in extensively shared subcultural norms and life-styles and informational and social networks.

Next, we would propose two affinities arising out of the possession—and hence the possibility of *transfer*—of capital, which we have so far considered only as a source of *im*mobility. The first of these affinities is between Class IV*a+b* and Class IV*c*, the two classes of small proprietors—where shared ideologies of 'independence' or even personality traits (cf. Miller and Swanson 1958; Kohn 1969; Hout 1986) may also be important

---

[9] What is in effect involved here is the distinction between status in the classic European sense, in which the reference is to relations expressing deference, acceptance, and derogation, and the prevalent American notion of status, or prestige, which refers to a ranking of individuals—whether by the sociological observer or in public opinion—in terms of some set of attributes of a loosely 'socio-economic' character. On the empirical discrepancy that tends to emerge between these two kinds of ordering, see further pp. 138–9, and n. 16 below.

in influencing ideas of desirable class positions. And the second is between Class IVa+b and Class I+II, in regard to which it should be recalled from our discussion of the class schema in Chapter 2 that within the service class there will be some number of individuals who, to a greater or lesser degree, share in the ownership of professional practices or of business enterprises.

Finally, we would introduce into our model two other affinities, which, in contrast to the foregoing, are of an *asymmetrical* kind: that is, between the two agricultural classes—Class IVc or VIIb—considered as classes of origin and Class VIIa, that of non-skilled wage-workers outside agriculture, considered as a class of destination. Men who are mobile from agricultural origins may be regarded as particularly likely to enter Class VIIa jobs, in that these will be ones that are most readily available to them in not requiring 'industrial' skills or experience nor always, perhaps, long-range geographical mobility—as, say, in the case of unskilled jobs in transport, distribution, or construction (cf. Bishop 1965, 1969; Johnson 1981).

As in the AF1—disaffinity—matrix, we again in the AF2 matrix set the differentiated cells at level 2; but, whereas in the former case the effect supposed is for a reduction in the propensity for mobility of the kind indicated, we would of course envisage that the mobility indicated by the level-2 cells in AF2 will show an increased propensity.[10]

In the foregoing, we have then identified four different kinds of effect that we would expect to influence patterns of social fluidity within the class structures of industrial societies, and we have represented these effects by eight separate matrices which may be incorporated into an elaborated topological model. This model may be written as

$$\log F_{ij} = \mu + \lambda_i^O + \lambda_j^D + \lambda_{a(i,j)}^{HI1} + \lambda_{b(i,j)}^{HI2} + \lambda_{c(i,j)}^{IN1} + \lambda_{d(i,j)}^{IN2} + \lambda_{e(i,j)}^{IN3} + \lambda_{f(i,j)}^{SE} + \lambda_{g(i,j)}^{AF1} + \lambda_{h(i,j)}^{AF2} \qquad (4.2)$$

where, as in the standard model earlier presented, F_{ij} is the expected frequency in cell ij, μ is a scale factor, and λ_i^O and λ_j^D are the main effects of origin and destination, while the remaining eight terms correspond to the matrices set out above.

---

[10] In the light of our subsequent experience in applying our core model and of the discussion that has followed the publication of preliminary results (Erikson and Goldthorpe 1987), we would now believe that some advantage might have been gained, at all events in terms of interpretation, if we had treated *separately* the three kinds of (positive) affinity here distinguished; i.e. by allowing each to be represented in the model by a separate effect. On the other hand, though, this would, of course, have entailed a loss of two degrees of freedom and we have no theoretically grounded expectation that these different kinds of affinity should be of differing strength.

Since these matrices in fact result in thirteen different combinations of effect being specified for the cells of the 7 × 7 mobility table (cf. Table 4.3), it might be thought that our model is simply the equivalent of a standard topological one in which thirteen different levels are distinguished. It should, however, be observed that this is not the case. Such a single-matrix, thirteen-level model would have twenty-four degrees of freedom, whereas our multi-matrix model has twenty-eight as a result of the constraints that are imposed on *differences between* cell-interaction parameters.[11]

Having then spelt out the way in which we would wish to model core fluidity, we must of course go on to consider how well our model performs: that is, in the first instance, how well it can reproduce the empirical representation of the core pattern that we arrived at following our MDSCAL exercise. Since this representation takes the form simply of a set of odds ratios (those expected under the CmSF model applied to the data of our two 'central' nations England and France), it is of a somewhat abstract nature: like the Holy Ghost, it is fully realized only in conjunction with the Father and the Son—that is, with the two marginal distributions of a mobility table. Thus, what we must in fact examine are the results of fitting our model of core fluidity to our nine national mobility tables *as they would be* if core fluidity according to our empirical representation were in operation—or, in other words, to counterfactual tables of the kind we mentioned earlier. The results of so doing are given in Table 4.2.

From these results, it is apparent that our model does in fact recover the counterfactual tables rather satisfactorily. There is some variation in the sizes of the G^2s returned, which, since all tables have the same odds ratios, must come from compositional effects or, that is, from cross-national differences in the sizes of classes. But in all cases the model accounts for between 98.5 and 99.5 per cent of the G^2 returned by the independence model or, in other words, for this amount of the total association between class of origin and class of destination, and the proportion of cases misclassified ranges from only 1–2 per cent. What, therefore, we may reasonably conclude is that, if we were right in supposing that our empirical representation of core fluidity is more-or-less central to the multidimensional space within which all cross-national variation in fluidity occurs, then so too is the pattern of fluidity that our model generates.

EMERGENT FEATURES OF THE MODEL

Since we may accept our model as one that adequately reproduces core fluidity as we have sought to identify it empirically, we may in turn consider

---

[11] Thus, for example, if one examines Table 4.3, entries of HI1+SE, HI1, SE, and neutral fluidity (—) can each be found in one or more cells of the mobility table, and with a conventional model each would then have an independent parameter. But in our model the difference in interaction level between cells with HI1+SE and those with HI1 only must of course be the same as that arising between cells with SE only and those with neutral fluidity.

TABLE 4.2. *Results of fitting the model of core social fluidity to counterfactual tables showing mobility in nine nations as it would be under core fluidity as empirically derived*

Nation	G^2 for ind. model (df = 36)	G^2 for core model* (df = 28)	rG^2	Δ
ENG	2,376	31.1	98.7	1.5
FRA	4,478	42.0	99.1	2.0
FRG	3,058	27.6	99.1	1.5
HUN	2,875	27.4	99.0	1.8
IRL	5,577	44.5	99.2	1.9
NIR	4,185	39.4	99.1	1.9
POL	4,564	25.8	99.4	1.1
SCO	2,696	39.7	98.5	1.6
SWE	3,101	28.1	99.1	1.8

Note:
  * The G^2s here reported are not comparable to those that are obtained when our model is applied to actually observed mobility tables. Apart from the standardization of Ns to 10,000, the derivation of the counterfactual tables from values expected under the CmSF model when fitted to the English and French data means that random variation will already have been much reduced. Thus, no p values are reported and, as indicated in the text, the G^2s are taken simply as indicating how closely our empirical representation of core fluidity can be reproduced by our model.

what the model can further tell us about the nature of the core pattern. That is to say, we may examine features of the model which are, so to speak, emergent from our specification of hierarchy, inheritance, sector, and affinity effects, and which were often not—and indeed hardly could have been—ones that we envisaged in advance. To begin with, it will be helpful if, as in Table 4.3, we integrate the information given in the eight matrices earlier presented, and show how the effects that our model proposes apply to each of the individual cells of the 7 × 7 class mobility table.

From Table 4.3 an initial point to note is that in seven of these cells, which are marked by dashes, our model provides for *no* interaction effects at all. In other words, the model here entails that the numbers of individuals following the transitions defined by these cells will be determined solely by generalized 'structural' effects relating to classes of origin and of destination. As can be seen, one of the seven cells is that indicating mobility from farm origins into the class of agricultural workers, which we do not, it should be recalled, treat as downward mobility. The remaining six cells are those which indicate all possible intergenerational mobility transitions between Classes III, IVa+b, and V+VI. Our model can, therefore, be taken as saying that, as between non-agricultural classes within the intermediate ranges of the class structure—that is, the routine non-manual class, the petty

TABLE 4.3. *Postulated effects of hierarchy, inheritance, sector, and affinity in the cells of the 7 × 7 intergenerational class mobility table*

	I+II	III	IVa+b	IVc*	V+VI	VIIa	VIIb
I+II	IN1 +IN2	HI1 +AF2	HI1 +AF2	HI1 +SE	HI1	HI1 +HI2	HI1+ HI2+SE +AF1
III	HI1 +AF2	IN1	—	SE	—	HI1	HI1+SE
IVa+b	HI1 +AF2	—	IN1 +IN2	SE +AF2	—	HI1	HI1+SE
IVc*	HI1+ HI2+SE	HI1 +SE	HI1+ SE+AF2	HI1+IN1 +IN2+IN3	HI1 +SE	SE +AF2	—
V+VI	HI1	—	—	SE	IN1	HI1 +AF2	HI1+SE
VIIa	HI1 +HI2	HI1	HI1	HI1 +SE	HI1 +AF2	IN1	SE
VIIb	HI1+ HI2+SE +AF1	HI1 +SE	HI1 +SE	HI1	HI1 +SE	SE +AF2	IN1

Notes:
-------- = hierarchical divisions (shown horizontally).
. . . . = sectoral divisions (shown vertically).
 * Class IVc, that of farmers, is treated as being in the lowest level of the hierarchy as a class of origin but in the middle level as a class of destination (see text).

bourgeoisie, and the skilled working class—an area of what might be called 'neutral' fluidity prevails: there are no factors that particularly inhibit propensities to move between the classes in question, though neither are there any that particularly enhance such propensities.[12]

Once this feature of core fluidity, according to our model, has been remarked, it is then natural to ask further which are the areas of the mobility table where the effects we postulate generate, on the one hand, 'positive' and, on the other hand, 'negative' interactions between classes of origin and destination, as compared to the neutral-fluidity level. This cannot be fully ascertained from Table 4.3, since in some cells hierarchy and sector effects, representing barriers to mobility, are offset by affinity effects. We need, therefore, to know about the relative strengths of these effects, or, in other words, we need to have estimates of the parameters of the model. Such estimates can, in fact, be produced from the fitting of our core model to the counterfactual national tables, as reported on in Table 4.2, in the form of

[12] While the idea of 'neutral fluidity' may be thought of as cognate with that of 'perfect mobility', it should be noted that they are not statistically equivalent.

averages over the small differences that are shown up from nation to nation in consequence of slight variations in the goodness of fit. In the first row of Table 4.4 we give these average parameters, in log-additive form, and it may be noted that all take their expected sign: that is, hierarchy, sector, and disaffinity effects are negative while inheritance and affinity effects are positive. We then show the interaction parameters which result in each cell of the mobility table when all effects that apply to that cell are summed. For example, it can be seen from Table 4.3 that in the first cell of the mobility table, that indicating immobility in Class I+II, the effects that operate are IN1+IN2; the parameters for these effects are given in the first row of Table 4.4 as 0.43 and 0.81, and thus in the corresponding cell of the mobility table below the value of 1.24 appears.[13]

It should be noted here that we work throughout with the system of parameter estimation of the GLIM program. This would appear the most apt to the nature of our model in that—as is more fully explained in the annex to Chapter 5—it allows the cells that we would wish to treat as ones of neutral fluidity always to take an interaction parameter of zero, which would not be possible with other systems, for example, that of the ECTA or LOGLIN programs. However, it is important to keep in mind that we are thus merely opting for one rather than another equally valid way of imposing constraints on the log-linear model in order to make estimates of parameters possible; and that, for purposes of interpretation, attention should focus not on the absolute values of the estimates, which will depend on the particular system used, but on the *differences between them*, which will remain unaffected. Thus, in what follows we always, explicitly or implicitly, interpret cell parameters by reference to the neutral-fluidity level: that is, as indicating mobility (or immobility) propensities so many times greater or less than this level would imply. The fact that the parameter for this level is always zero is, to repeat, simply a convenience.

From the content of Table 4.4 it is not difficult to perceive that the distribution of cells displaying positive and negative parameter values, relative to neutral fluidity, follows rather well-defined lines—which we bring out by the arrow-shaped figure drawn on the mobility table. Cells with positive values are those on the main diagonal, implying of course tendencies towards *im*mobility, plus four in the top-left corner of the table indicative of high fluidity between Class I+II and Classes III and IVa+b, and two more towards the bottom-right corner indicative of high fluidity between Class V+VI and Class VIIa. In other words, apart from indicating a generally high propensity for immobility, our model presents as further features of the core

---

[13] Parameters are, of course, also returned for the λ_i^O and λ_j^D terms in the model, or, that is, for the 'main effects' of class of origin and class of destination. Although in the present context they are of no direct relevance, we do make use of these elements of the model, as applied to the *actual* mobility data of our several nations, in our analyses of absolute rates presented in Chapter 6.

TABLE 4.4. *Parameters (in log-additive form) for effects in the model of core social fluidity and resulting interaction parameters in the cells of the 7 × 7 intergenerational class mobility table*

			Effect parameers				
HI1	HI2	IN1	IN2	IN3	SE	AF1	AF2
−0.22	−0.42	0.43	0.81	0.96	−1.03	−0.77	0.46

			Cell parameters*			
	I+II	III	IVa+b	IVc	V+VI	VIIa	VIIb
I+II	1.24	0.24	0.24	−1.25	−0.22	−0.64	−2.44
III	0.24	0.43	0.00	−1.03	0.00	−0.22	−1.25
IVa+b	0.24	0.00	1.24	−0.57	0.00	−0.22	−1.25
IVc	−1.67	−1.25	−0.79	1.98	−1.25	−0.57	0.00
V+VI	−0.22	0.00	0.00	−1.03	0.43	0.24	−1.25
VIIa	−0.64	−0.22	−0.22	−1.25	0.24	0.43	−1.03
VIIb	−2.44	−1.25	−1.25	−0.22	−1.25	−0.57	0.43

Note:
  * As indicated in the text, parameters should be interpreted by reference to the neutral-fluidity level (= 0). Thus, the value of 1.24 in the I+II–I+II cell indicates that the propensity for immobility in the service class is about three-and-a-half times greater ($e^{1.24} = 3.46$) than it would be if neutral fluidity prevailed in that cell or, that is, in the absence of the two effect parameters, IN1 and IN2, that are in fact taken to operate. Likewise, in the IVc–I+II cell the propensity for mobility is shown to be only one-fifth ($e^{-1.67} = 0.19$) of what it would be under neutral fluidity.

pattern what one might think of as two areas of distinctive 'white-collar' and 'blue-collar' fluidity respectively (cf. Erikson and Pöntinen 1985: 157). In turn, cells having negative parameter values are all off-diagonal cells other than the six just noted and the seven neutral-fluidity cells that were referred to earlier. Or, in more substantive terms, our model states that in a clear majority of the possible intergenerational transitions that would imply class mobility (29 out of 42), barriers operate to keep the actual rate to a greater or lesser extent below the neutral-fluidity level.

On the basis of Table 4.4, we can then, so to speak, map out the contours of the interaction parameters that our model proposes within the mobility table. However, the multi-matrix design of the model means that we can, in fact, go beyond this and also obtain some insight into how these contours are actually formed. Thus, from the parameter estimates given in Table 4.4, it can be seen that the largest single effect is that for sector, while the three inheritance effects amount to the most important set. In comparison, affinity and, especially, hierarchy effects appear as only modest. Furthermore, if we take the details of Table 4.4 in conjunction with those of Table 4.3, we can gain some idea of how these relative strengths of the four effects are reflected within the overall pattern of fluidity that our model describes.

On the one hand, it is obviously inheritance effects that produce all the larger positive interaction parameters, that is, in cells on the main diagonal of the mobility table—although one should at the same time note the wide range of values in these cells. One could say that immobility within Classes III, V+VI, VIIa, and VIIb, where only IN1 operates, is one-and-a-half times greater ($e^{0.43} = 1.54$) than it would be in the absence of any inheritance effect or, in other words, under neutral fluidity; but that immobility is about three-and-a-half times greater ($e^{1.24} = 3.46$) within Classes I+II and IVa+b, the service class and the petty bourgeoisie, where IN1 *and* IN2 operate, and is as much as seven times greater ($e^{1.98} = 7.24$) within Class IVc, that of farmers, where all three IN terms apply (though also HI1).

On the other hand, it can be seen that it is sector effects—barriers to mobility between agricultural and non-agricultural classes—that play by far the major role in producing negative interaction parameters. Of the twenty-nine cells of the mobility table in which negative values appear (Table 4.4), twenty are those in which the SE term occurs (Table 4.3). Moreover, because the effect of sectoral barriers is so strong, implying that mobility between sectors is only about a third ($e^{-1.03} = 0.36$) of what it would be in the absence of such barriers, even in cases where the SE term is accompanied by that indicating a positive affinity (AF2), the offsetting is only partial and a negative value still results. This is what one finds, for example, in the cells indicating mobility from petty-bourgeois origins into farming, or from farm-worker origins into the ranks of unskilled industrial labour. And, of course, where other barriers to mobility are *added to* those of sector, particularly large negative interactions are generated. Thus, for instance, under our model mobility from Class IVc to Class I+II, that is, from farm origins into the service class, which is constrained by both sectoral and hierarchical barriers, is only one-fifth of what it would be in their absence ($e^{-1.67} = 0.19$).

However, in those cases where the barriers to mobility that are postulated are simply ones of hierarchy, the negative parameter values that arise are much closer to zero—or, that is, to the neutral-fluidity level—than where the sector effect operates, since even the HI1 and HI2 terms together imply only a halving of mobility ($e^{-0.64} = 0.53$); and, in turn, where the HI1 term is countered by the AF2 term, a positive value is produced. Again from comparison of Tables 4.3 and 4.4, it can be seen that it is, in fact, through such an offsetting of hierarchy by affinity effects that the previously noted areas of high white-collar and high blue-collar fluidity are created.

As a general conclusion, we might then say that, while the account of core fluidity that emerges from our model does in certain respects conform with standard expectations, it is in others rather deviant. Thus, it is in no way surprising to find that, according to our model, the highest positive interactions occur in cells on the main diagonal of the mobility table, nor again that off-diagonal cells showing positive interactions—or being neutral-fluidity cells—are ones indicative of mobility that is, in some sense or other, 'short range'. But what fits much less well with prevailing views is the conception of fluidity as being, overall, less powerfully shaped by hierarchy effects than by those of inheritance and sector. It is these latter effects which, under our model, create the really strong contrasts in fluidity or, one could say, which generate the most striking inequalities in class-mobility chances.[14] And to accept this implication of the model does, therefore, mean breaking with the assumption, which has underlain much previous research, that the pattern of fluidity will primarily reflect the influence of a social hierarchy of some kind. Indeed, we should note that Featherman, Jones, and Hauser themselves, though recognizing some evidence of what we would treat as sectoral effects, would still see as the main source of the similarity of mobility regimes that they hypothesize a common structure of 'occupational socio-economic status', extending across 'all capitalist (and possibly other) societies' (1975: 357).

To be sure the issue that arises here is in part simply one of conceptual preference: the results that we have reported are clearly conditioned by the fact that, for reasons we have explained in Chapter 2, we *choose* to view mobility within a class-structural rather than a hierarchical context. Thus, there can be no doubt that some of the effects on fluidity that we have captured as ones of inheritance or sector—or again of affinity—could alternatively be represented as ones of hierarchy. As Pöntinen (1982) and Hauser (1984), among others, have observed, models of fluidity patterns developed within different conceptual perspectives are still likely to involve

---

[14] We may add that we have investigated the effects of replacing the two hierarchy matrices within our model with the kind of 'linear-by-linear' interaction term proposed by Hout (1984: 1388). This, it might be argued, would be better able to capture the full extent to which the classes of our schema are hierarchically differentiated. For this purpose, we assigned to each class the scores derived from three of the scales drawn on in Table 2.2 above, i.e. the Treiman, Hope–Goldthorpe, and Duncan scales, except that, in order not to weight the test unduly against the model with a linear-by-linear term, we preserved our distinction between IVc as a class of origin and of destination by using median scores for 'small' farmers in the former case and for 'large' farmers in the latter (these pairs of scores being 36.5/55, 37/58, and 14/25 for the three scales respectively). Whichever scale was used to provide scores, the model with the linear-by-linear term substituted for HI1 and HI2 gave a clearly less good fit than the original to our tables representing empirical core fluidity in the context of different national marginals. As compared with the G^2s reported in Table 4.2, which range from 28.5 (POL) to 44.5 (IRL) with 28 degrees of freedom, the G^2s for the model with the linear-by-linear term based on Duncan scores—which give overall the best results—range from 56.0 (POL) to 100.6 (FRA), with 29 degrees of freedom. What would seem important to note in understanding the better performance of our hierarchy terms is that the effects they capture are *not* linear. As can be seen from the parameter values reported in Table 4.4, the increment of HI2 on HI1 tends to be almost twice as large as HI1 itself.

overlapping contrasts, and thus it may well not be possible to decide conclusively between them on empirical grounds alone. In this case, therefore, the important question must be that of which conceptual approach—and keeping in mind always the specific limitations of the available data—will prove most revealing in regard to the sociological problems that are the investigator's chief concern.

However, this is not perhaps all that can usefully be said. There are features of our model of core fluidity that we have described which, we believe, do indicate certain substantive problems with the view that the structure of mobility propensities can be understood in an essentially hierarchical way. To begin with, we would question whether it is possible for the strong sectoral barriers that our model expresses to be fully, or even largely, 'translated' into hierarchical terms in any plausible fashion. To seek to achieve this—as seems often (implicitly) to be done—by placing such agricultural classes as are distinguished together at the bottom of the hierarchical ordering has not so far been given convincing justification by reference to any specific hierarchical principle. Thus, if it is 'prestige' or 'general desirability' that is invoked, then farmers should certainly be distinguished from farm workers, and should in fact be located somewhere in the middle ranges of the hierarchy (cf. Table 2.2); and if, rather, 'socioeconomic status' is the favoured criterion, it should be noted (see, e.g., Featherman and Hauser 1978: 27–30) that much weight has then to be given to the low—reported—money incomes of farmers. However, serious doubts must arise here not only concerning possible underestimation and the neglect of income in kind but, further, concerning the determination of the socio-economic status of self-employed groups by reference only to income and education and without regard to property ownership.[15]

Further, to the extent that fluidity patterns can be seen as shaped by hierarchical effects, experience with our model would lead us to suggest that such effects are not homogeneous; or, in other words, that effects deriving from more than one 'vertical' dimension must be recognized. Thus, we may re-emphasize that the areas of both 'white-collar' and 'blue-collar' fluidity that are a feature of the model do not result from 'closeness' within the threefold hierarchical division that we have introduced into the class schema and take as reflecting differences in rewards and entry requirements; rather, they are produced mainly by *countervailing* affinity effects which have then

---

[15] In the debate that has gone on, chiefly among US sociologists, over the respective merits of scales of occupational prestige or of socio-economic status in the analysis of mobility (see, e.g., Treiman 1975; Featherman, Jones, and Hauser 1975), it is difficult to avoid the suspicion that what has chiefly favoured the latter is the legitimation they would appear to provide for *not* having farmers as a middle-ranking category, where income and education are the only socio-economic attributes considered. For further analyses, quite different in approach from our own but which likewise underline the importance of recognizing a sectoral as distinct from a hierarchical 'dimension' of mobility, see Domański and Sawiński (1987) and Sawiński and Domański (1989).

to be understood in terms of closeness within another hierarchy, that of status *stricto sensu*. For, despite practices that have obfuscated the matter (see ch. 2 n. 6), it is well documented that hierarchies based on occupational prestige, socio-economic status, or general desirability (which provide the empirical basis for our threefold division) by no means map perfectly on to those of social status defined in a relational rather than an attributional sense. And a major discrepancy is that, while the latter tend to show a fairly clear white-collar/blue-collar or non-manual/manual divide, the former do not: certain more skilled and better-paid manual workers rank, quite appropriately, above routine and relatively poorly paid grades of non-manual employee.[16]

What, therefore, must clearly follow is that, if, in the light of the application of our model, we do come to underwrite the FJH hypothesis in some degree or other, we will in any event wish to see the pattern of fluidity that is common to industrial nations as being generated in more complex ways than the authors of the hypothesis themselves would envisage. Propensities for mobility within class structures, whether cross-nationally common or variant, must, in our view, be treated as being more than one-dimensional.[17]

In the course of this chapter we have suggested a new way of explicating and in turn of modelling the FJH hypothesis, with the aim of making possible a more satisfactory evaluation of it than has so far been achieved. Instead of the hypothesis being embodied in the simple CmSF model—in which form it may be surely but rather unfairly and perhaps wastefully rejected—we have proposed that it be modelled in a way that is, in fact, closer to its verbal formulation: that is, as claiming a common or core pattern of social fluidity that is generic to industrial societies, although one on which particular national variations may occur. On the basis of an initial, empirically derived representation, we have developed a model of core fluidity, of an elaborated topological kind, which we would see as possessing a number of specific advantages for the purposes we have in hand.

[16] Thus, it is apparent from Table 2.2 that, in respect of scales of occupational prestige, socio-economic status, or general desirability alike, little warrant can exist for ranking Class III of our schema, that of routine non-manual employees above Class V+VI, that of skilled manual workers. However, when the schema is used in what might be regarded as the analysis of status *stricto sensu*, a far sharper differentiation of these two classes emerges, with Class III being clearly the higher—in the sense, that is, of the closer to Class I+II (see Goldthorpe 1981–2; Mitchell and Critchley 1985).

[17] We would, of course, expect that if, without compromising standards of comparability, we could have made more hierarchical divisions within our class schema—including, for example, one between Classes I and II—we would have needed to give a greater importance to hierarchical effects. But it should then be noted that one might argue analogously in regard to the sectoral differentiation of the schema. Thus, an explicit self-employed employee distinction might be made; or again, with appropriate data, a manufacturing/services or a public/private distinction could be introduced. Both these points are neglected in the critique offered by Hout and Hauser (1991).

First of all, as we have emphasized, the model provides a representation of core fluidity that is stable and independent of the data under analysis—unlike that implicitly introduced if the FJH hypothesis is tested by fitting the CmSF model. Although our model obviously requires that mobility data be organized on the basis of our class schema (in its seven-class version), it is not tied to any particular cross-national data-set, and can indeed be applied directly to the mobility table for any single nation. Secondly, the way in which the model is constructed, with different effects being expressed through separate levels matrices, makes the rationale for the allocation of individual cells to different interaction levels far more explicit than with a standard topological model. This means that, while the way in which we have sought to understand core fluidity is, of course, open to challenge, critics will need to go beyond charges of mere arbitrariness and address themselves to substantive issues. And, thirdly, it should be noted that, as well as providing a representation of core fluidity, our model is readily modifiable or extendable so as to represent deviations also. If in the mobility data for a particular nation significant deviations from core fluidity are revealed, hypotheses concerning the nature of these deviations can be tested in a systematic way simply by changing the matrices of the model, or by adding new ones, so as to try to capture the distinctive effects that are thought to be at work in the case in question.

As will be seen, this last facility will prove to have a special importance as, in the chapter that follows, we apply our model to our comparative mobility data. We will seek to test the FJH hypothesis by asking whether such national deviations as are revealed are ones that can be plausibly accounted for as nationally specific variations on a common theme or, rather, ones which are either so large or so systematic in their extent as to require that the idea of such a commonality be abandoned.

5

Social Fluidity within Class Structures: Commonality and Variation

Having now developed our model of core social fluidity, we seek in the present chapter to apply it to our comparative data on intergenerational class mobility and, on this basis, to arrive at a more thorough and considered assessment of the FJH hypothesis than has hitherto been available. Our model is such that we can use it to test the hypothesis with differing degrees of strictness; and further, as we have noted, the model can be readily adapted in order to represent specific deviations from core fluidity in different national cases.

In the first section of the chapter we report the results we obtain when we apply the model, without modification, to the data for each of the nine European nations within our data-set. In the following section we then propose, in so far as this would seem necessary, 'national variants' of the model; and, in the case of each such variant model, we discuss the grounds for, and the significance of, the changes to the core pattern that we introduce. In the third section of the chapter we go on to consider in a similar fashion the fit of the core model to mobility tables for three further European nations, which were not covered in our own recoding exercise but for which data have been subsequently produced by other investigators, who have independently taken up our class schema. Finally, we return to the FJH hypothesis and, in the light of the analyses presented, we reappraise the question of whether or not it may be usefully retained and, if so, with what degree of refinement and qualification.

THE FIT OF THE CORE MODEL TO NATIONAL MOBILITY TABLES

In Table 5.1 we show the results of fitting our model of core social fluidity to intergenerational mobility tables for the nine European nations represented in our data-set. In each case the tables refer to the experience of men aged 20–64, and are drawn up on the basis of the sevenfold version of our class schema. In the present section we will be chiefly concerned with the results given in the first two rows of each national panel within Table 5.1: that is, the results produced when the model is fitted to each national case (i) with fixed, cross-nationally common parameters and (ii) with its parameters being estimated separately for each nation.

In Table 4.4 we have given parameters for the effects comprised by our

TABLE 5.1. *Results of fitting the model of core social fluidity to national mobility tables (i) with cross-nationally common parameters; (ii) with nation-specific parameters; (iii) with effects modified or added (national variant model)*

Nation		G^2	df	p	rG^2	Δ	$G^2(S)$ (1,991)
ENG	(i)	85.9	36*	0.00	96.1	2.3	47
(N = 9,434)	(ii)	68.3	28	0.00	96.9	1.7	37
FRA	(i)	106.8	36	0.00	98.8	2.7	44
(N = 18,671)	(ii)	82.1	28	0.00	99.0	2.4	34
FRG	(i)	133.0	36	0.00	89.6	6.0	86
(N = 3,890)	(ii)	101.6	28	0.00	92.1	5.3	66
	(iii)	45.4	28	0.02	96.5	2.8	37
HUN	(i)	440.4	36	0.00	85.2	7.4	103
(N = 12,005)	(ii)	245.6	28	0.00	91.7	5.7	64
	(iii)	76.0	28	0.00	97.4	2.7	36
IRL	(i)	81.1	36	0.00	93.2	6.5	81
(N = 1,991)	(ii)	67.9	28	0.00	94.3	5.8	68
	(iii)	40.3	29	0.08	96.6	4.6	40
NIR	(i)	58.2	36	0.01	93.9	5.7	57
(N = 2,068)	(ii)	47.3	28	0.01	95.1	4.6	47
	(iii)	37.0	28	0.12	96.1	4.0	37
POL	(i)	1,229.5	36	0.00	88.6	5.4	110
(N = 32,109)	(ii)	379.0	28	0.00	96.5	3.2	50
	(iii)	186.2	29	0.00	98.3	1.9	39
SCO	(i)	104.5	36	0.00	92.7	4.6	66
(N = 4,583)	(ii)	74.6	28	0.00	94.8	3.3	48
	(iii)	60.5	29	0.00	95.8	2.5	43
SWE	(i)	78.0	36	0.00	82.3	6.1	76
(N = 2,097)	(ii)	33.0	28	0.24	92.5	3.8	33
	(iii)	33.7	29	0.25	92.4	3.9	33

Note:
   * Since, as described in the text, the interaction parameters of the model are in this case included as offsets, rather than being estimated from the data, the degrees of freedom are the same as they would be for the independence model.

model (estimated by applying the model to counterfactual mobility tables showing what each national table would look like if it embodied the odds ratios of our empirical representation of core fluidity); and in this table we further show the interaction parameters that result in each of the cells of the 7×7 mobility table when all the effects that operate in that cell are summed. We may then fit the model to each of our observed national tables with these latter parameters included as constants known *a priori* (or, in the language of the GLIM program, as 'offsets') so that each table is required to have exactly the same pattern of odds ratios.

When this is done, it can be seen from Table 5.1 that only for England and France do the various goodness-of-fit statistics suggest that the model comes at all close to being satisfactory. This is scarcely surprising, since we already know from the results reported in Table 4.1 that a model which simply proposes 'common social fluidity'—without specifying the pattern that this should take—itself shows a significant lack of fit if applied to our nine nations simultaneously; and the present test of the FJH hypothesis is, of course, a more demanding one. Nor is it surprising that our model should appear better suited to the English and French tables than to any others; for, as we have described in Chapter 4, it is from the English and French cases that we derive the empirical representation of core fluidity that our model seeks to render more sociologically intelligible.

Thus, what we can say about the fit of our model with fixed parameters does little more than restate the problem that we outlined at the start of Chapter 4. On the one hand, the results can lend some support to the FJH hypothesis if this is taken in its less strict form of claiming only a 'basic' similarity in patterns of social fluidity. For only one nation, Hungary, do we misclassify more than 7 per cent of all cases, as indicated by the Δ values; and again for only one nation, Sweden, does the model account for less than 85 per cent of the total association between class of origin and destination, as shown by the rG^2 values. On the other hand, though, the lack of fit of the model, by all the indicators used, is still clearly such that cross-national variation in fluidity of a sociologically as well as a statistically significant kind could well be present.

When we move on to fit our model with its parameters estimated separately for each nation, we of course make less stringent demands. In this case, we require that the pattern of effects, or of combinations of effects, over the cells of the mobility table should be the same for all nations—that is, as specified in Table 4.3—but the strength of these effects is allowed to vary. To revert to the metaphor we introduced at the end of the previous chapter, we could say that we expect the contours of interaction parameters to follow the same lines in all nations, but the heights attached to the contours can differ.

In this way we necessarily achieve better fits. As Table 5.1 shows, $G^2(S)$, with K set at 1,991, the size of our smallest national sample, now falls below the 40 mark—which gives a p value of above 0.05—for England and France and also for Sweden. Likewise, Δ is now below 6 for all nations, and rG^2 indicates that always more than 90 per cent of the association between class origins and destinations is accounted for under the model. Moreover, if we examine the parameter estimates returned for each nation, we find that they always take the same, and expected, sign: that is, hierarchy, sector, and disaffinity effects are always negative, and inheritance and affinity effects are always positive. In other words, our model would at all events appear to identify effects that do consistently either inhibit or favour specific inter-generational transitions, even if they operate from nation to nation with differing force.

When the model is fitted in this way, we can also test whether the differences that show up between effect parameters for particular nations and those estimated for the core model are statistically significant. The results of so doing are summarized in Table 5.2.[1] It can be seen that no significant differences are found for Northern Ireland as well as for England and France, while only one effect is significantly different in the cases of Ireland, Scotland, and Sweden. However, the FRG has two significantly different parameters, Poland has three, and Hungary, four.

TABLE 5.2. *Results of testing for the significance of differences between values of effect parameters estimated for nine nations and for the core model**

Nation	HI1	HI2	IN1	IN2	IN3	SE	AF1	AF2
ENG								
FRA								
FRG					+	−		
HUN	+		−			−		−
IRL			+					
NIR								
POL					−	−		−
SCO	−							
SWE						−		

Note:
* A plus sign (+) indicates significantly stronger than core value; a minus sign (−) indicates significantly weaker than core value, at 5 per cent level.

We must view these latter results with some caution, since we are considering parameters for models that in most cases we would not be ready to accept as fitting adequately. But, in fact, together with the results reported in the previous paragraph, they serve chiefly to reinforce the rather ambiguous position that we have so far been obliged to adopt. Further

[1] These tests were carried out in the following way. For each national table, the G^2 produced when the core model was fitted with its parameters being allowed to vary (as in (ii) in Table 5.1) was subtracted from the G^2 produced when the model was fitted with one parameter in turn being fixed at the core value and the remainder being allowed to vary. The difference between the two G^2s could then be related to the chi-square distribution with one degree of freedom (cf. Bishop, Fienberg, and Holland 1975: 129). As noted in the text below, to the extent that the fit of the model with nationally specific parameters is poor, these tests should be regarded as indicative only, since the estimates of the parameters that we are comparing with the fixed core value may be unreliable.

support is certainly provided for the idea of a substantial commonality in cross-national fluidity patterns; but again, too, the reality of far from negligible cross-national variation is brought out. In order to advance our evaluation of the FJH hypothesis, what would then seem necessary is that we should go on to examine the nature of this variation in greater detail.

In so far as our model does not give a satisfactory fit to the observed mobility data for a particular nation, our aim must be to modify it so as to capture the 'deviation' from core fluidity that occurs. This we can seek to do in two main ways: by making changes in the distribution of effects over the cells of the mobility table, as these were set out in Table 4.3, or by adding new effects. Of course, once we allow such modifications to the model, it will in the end be possible to obtain a fit with any given set of mobility data. We shall, therefore, improve our chances of obtaining sociologically interpretable results if we restrict alterations or additions to the model to a minimum, and if we try so far as possible to make modifications for which there are grounds *other than* those of our model-fitting requirements.

The procedure we have adopted is the following. For those nations where we cannot accept our model as adequate, even with nationally specific parameters, we have begun by examining the residuals produced under the model, and have thus identified cells where its fit is especially poor. We have then attempted to obtain a more acceptable fit by the introduction of successive small changes to the model, *and* by giving preference to changes *for which we could find some support in existing sociological or historical studies of the national society in question*. We have regarded a 'national variant' model as being adequate to our data, and have not introduced further modifications, once a $G^2(S)$ of *c*.40 was returned. Through thus developing and then interpreting national variant models, we have sought to implement the comparative strategy that we outlined in Chapter 2: that is, one in which the sources of cross-national variation in mobility—or fluidity—patterns that are quantitatively established are then explored through the 'internal' analysis of particular national cases.

In the following section the several national models that we develop are specified, and at the same time we consider both the basis and the implications of the deviations from core fluidity that are thus represented. The point that remains here to be noted, by reference to row (iii) in the panels of Table 5.1, is that, as well as each of these models now giving, by design, an acceptable $G^2(S)$, the highest Δ returned is 4.6 (for Ireland) and the lowest proportion of association accounted for is 92.4 (for Sweden).[2] In other words, even if the models fitted do not capture in their entirety the national patterns of fluidity that they seek to describe—and we are in fact in some

---

[2] It should be noted that this proportion is depressed in the Swedish case in that the independence model, which serves here as our baseline, fits less badly for Sweden than for any other of our nations.

instances knowingly underfitting the data[3]—we can at all events say that what escapes them is not of major quantitative importance.

NATIONAL VARIATION IN SOCIAL FLUIDITY

In this section we treat our national cases in turn. We first indicate any modifications to the core model that we have made so as to fit the mobility data for a particular nation, and also our grounds for seeking a variant model on these lines. We then go on to consider the full implications of the model that we fit for the pattern of fluidity in the nation in question. This we do by reference chiefly to the effect parameters that we estimate for the model. These parameters are presented for all nine of our nations in Table 5.3, in which we also indicate where parameters are affected by modifications to the core model, where new parameters have been added, and where insignificant ones have been dropped. Since national variant models do, of course, differ from the core model—and from each other—we cannot now test for the statistical significance of differences between parameters. Rather, our discussion of such differences must be at the level of the substantive interpretation of the models that we accept. We can, however, also consider the implications of our national variant models by reference to the cell-interaction parameters to which they give rise, when these are taken together with the corresponding parameters resulting from the core model that were given in Table 4.4. We cannot properly compare the *absolute* values of such parameters, whether between the core pattern and a particular nation or between nations (see pp. 133–4), but we *can* compare *differences between* parameters. Thus, we shall also refer to an annex to this chapter in which we show (Table A5.1) the extent to which cell parameters under our various national models differ from neutral fluidity in relation to the corresponding differences under the core model.[4]

We may further note here that, in order to test the stability of our national variant models, we have also fitted them to the mobility data for

---

[3] This is, of course, the consequence of taking the $G^2(S)$ value as our chief criterion in accepting models—which, as we have noted in Chapter 2, is forced upon us by the wide variation in the sample sizes of the national enquiries from which our data derive.

[4] In a previous paper (Erikson and Goldthorpe 1987), we used symmetrical odds ratios calculated under different national variant models as a basis for discussing differences among the patterns of fluidity that they represented. Such odds ratios—that is, ones where the pair of origin and the pair of destination classes involved are the same—lend themselves readily to sociological interpretation as indicating the degree of inequality in mobility chances between two classes or, alternatively, the 'social distance', in terms of mobility chances, that separates them. However, as we previously recognized, the set of symmetrical odds ratios implicit in a mobility table does not constitute a 'basic set' in the sense of one from which all other implicit odds ratios can be calculated; and we have further become aware of the way in which symmetrical odds ratios may be misleading as regards the overall pattern of social fluidity through reflecting compositional effects. The approach we take here to comparing national variant models is, we believe, an improvement, and has led to several changes, though chiefly minor ones, in the interpretations of models that we suggest.

two broad birth-cohorts distinguished within each national sample: one of men aged 25–44, the other of men aged 45–64 (in other words, a twofold collapse of the four cohorts used in Chapter 3). We found that allowing parameter estimates to vary between the two cohorts gave a significant improvement in fit only for two of the nations with the largest sample sizes, that is, Hungary and Poland. We refer to the main sources of the shifts observed in discussing these nations below.

England and France

We may take these two nations together, since it is from their—very similar—patterns of social fluidity that our core model ultimately derives. We are thus able to accept the model as fitting their mobility data without modification; and, as can be seen from Table 5.3, when the parameters of the model are estimated separately for each nation, they do not in fact differ very widely. Hierarchy and inheritance effects appear somewhat stronger in France than in England, while the reverse holds with sector effects. In other words, the account that we gave in the previous chapter (pp. 132–6) of the pattern of social fluidity under the core model could in turn be taken as a largely accurate characterization of the actually prevailing English and French patterns. The one way in which this conclusion might be qualified is

TABLE 5.3. *Effect parameters of accepted models**

Nation	HI1	HI2	IN1	IN2	IN3	SE	AF1	AF2	AFX
ENG	−0.16	−0.35	0.47	0.71	0.77	−1.22	−0.76	0.44	
FRA	−0.24	−0.47	0.41	0.92	1.00	−0.89	−0.75	0.47	
FRG	−0.33	−0.57	0.49	*1.17*	2.17	−0.43	*−0.50**	*0.39*	
HUN	−0.33	−0.64	0.50	ns	*1.01*	−0.50	−0.58	*0.40*	*0.89*
IRL	ns	−0.43	0.90	0.68	0.80	−0.85	−0.93	*0.62*	
NIR	−0.29	−0.38	0.48	0.72	1.45	−1.04	ns	0.38	*0.66*
POL	ns	−0.14	0.75	1.23	−0.37	−0.55	−0.45	*0.49*	
SCO	ns	−0.30	*0.63*	0.90	0.83	−1.37	−0.48	0.50	
SWE	−0.16	−0.45	0.28	0.65	0.78	−0.62	ns	0.37	
CORE	−0.22	−0.42	0.43	0.81	0.96	−1.03	−0.77	0.46	

Note:
   * Parameters directly affected by modifications to the core model are in italic type; instances where a parameter initially returned a non-significant value at the 5 per cent level and has then been omitted in re-estimating the model are indicated by ns.
   It should be remembered that, as described in the previous chapter (pp. 124–7), the parameters for hierarchy and inheritance effects are presented *incrementally*: i.e. the values given for HI2 represent increments on those for HI1, those for IN2 increments on IN1, and those for IN3 increments on IN2. However, this is *not* the case with the parameters for affinity effects, since AF1 refers to negative affinities and AF2 to positive affinities.

by noting that, chiefly as a result of the strength of sectoral barriers, England quite often appears as an outlier in Table A5.1 where transitions involving agricultural classes are concerned.[5]

The question must of course arise as to why it should be England and France that emerge from the analysis of Figure 4.1 as those of our nations that are most 'central' to the multidimensional variation of social fluidity, and thus the nations on which we have based our conception of the core pattern. However, our discussion of this question will be better deferred until towards the end of this chapter. For the present we will only make *en passant* the negative point that the centrality of England goes contrary to Olson's expectation of English society being highly 'sclerotic', on account of its having escaped major political upheavals. In the following, we will concentrate our attention on the extent of deviations from the core pattern of fluidity that are to be found in the other nations we consider.

The Federal Republic of Germany

In contrast with England and France, the FRG is among those of our nations that show the greatest deviation from core social fluidity as we would represent it. As can be seen from Table 5.1, the fits of our unmodified model to the German data, whether with common or nationally specific parameters, are quite poor. But what is chiefly distinctive about the German case is the extent of the changes that we have found it necessary to make to the model in order to obtain a more satisfactory version. In all, eight of the forty-nine cells of the mobility table are involved, while no more than six cells are affected by the changes made for any other of the nations in our data-set.

The modifications introduced are as given below, and—as with the specifications of other national variant models—will most usefully be read in conjunction with Table 4.3:

1. the IN2 term is omitted from the cell indicating immobility in the service class, I+II;
2. the AF2 term (positive affinity) is included in the pair of cells indicating mobility between the class of routine non-manual employees, III, and that of the petty bourgeoisie, IVa+b;
3. the AF1 term (negative affinity) is included in the three cells indicating upward mobility from the non-skilled manual origins of Class VIIa into the white-collar positions of Classes I+II, III, and IVa+b; and likewise in the two cells indicating upward mobility from farm worker, Class VIIb, origins into Class III and IVa+b positions. (A negative

[5] In particular, the propensity for the sons of both farmers and farm workers to move either into non-manual positions (i.e. those of Classes I+II, III, and IVa+b together) or into skilled manual positions falls further below the neutral-fluidity level in England than in all other nations.

affinity in the VII*b*–I+II cell, it may be recalled, is already present in the core model.)

Although extensive, these modifications still follow a rather clear pattern. Their effect is essentially twofold. On the one hand, the area of white-collar fluidity of the core model is, so to speak, spread out, so that, while immobility within the service class is relatively low, this area also takes in exchanges between the routine non-manual employees and the petty bourgeoisie. On the other hand, distinctive barriers to upward mobility are implied, not only to movement from the class of agricultural workers into the service class, as in the core model, but, more generally, to movement from *all* non-skilled manual origins into *all* of the white-collar classes.

To produce an acceptable model of the German pattern of social fluidity on these lines is, we would suggest, consistent with two well-established themes in analyses of the German class structure. First, a series of authors from Geiger (1932) onwards have pointed to the relatively high degree of socio-cultural homogeneity that has historically prevailed among white-collar groupings in Germany, and to the unusual extent to which differences in employment relations between white-collar and manual workers have been institutionalized. The conditions of employment of public officials (*Beamte*) provided the model for those of 'staff' employees in private enterprises (*Angestellte*, or earlier and significantly, *Privatbeamte*), so that the latter, even if no more than routine clerks or sales personnel, were clearly set apart from wage-workers (Kocka 1980*a*, 1981; Rutter 1986). In addition, it has been observed that closer affinities have prevailed in Germany than elsewhere between the 'new middle class' of non-manual employees and the 'old middle class' of small employers and proprietors, since *Angestellte* were often regarded, if only for ideological reasons, as themselves performing entrepreneurial functions (cf. Kaelble 1978; Speier 1986: ch. 5). Thus, it has been claimed (cf. Lipset 1960: 143–9; Dahrendorf 1968: ch. 6; Kocka 1980*a*; Rutter 1986), these various groupings within the *Mittelstand* remained, through into the post-war years, less divided by their differing market and work situations than united in their common concern to maintain their status and material advantages as against the threat posed by the organized working class.

Secondly, a more recent but still more securely documented argument concerns the division that arises *within* the German working class, as between its skilled and non-skilled components, largely as the result of the distinctive 'dual system' of vocational education and training. The possession or non-possession of an apprenticeship has been shown to be especially consequential for German workers as regards both their occupational life-chances and their standard and style of living (Maurice, Sellier, and Silvestre 1982: ch. 1; Müller 1986; König and Müller 1986); and it might then be expected that in the German case the chances of upward mobility of the sons of non-skilled workers would be unusually restricted, in particular relative to those of skilled workers.[6]

If we now go on to examine the parameters estimated for our variant model for the FRG (as presented in Table 5.3), several points of further interest emerge. To begin with, it may be noted that the additional disaffinities that we have included in the model operate on top of already strong hierarchical effects. From the table it can be seen that these effects are stronger in the FRG than under core fluidity and indeed than under any other national variant model apart from that for Hungary. For intergenerational transitions where both HI1 and HI2 apply, mobility is at only two-fifths of what it would have been in the absence of these effects ($e^{-0.90}$ = 0.41) as compared with around half under the core model ($e^{-0.64}$ = 0.53). It is not then surprising to discover from Table A5.1 that, as a result of disaffinity and hierarchical effects together, the relative chances of men of Class VII*a*, non-skilled manual, origins are clearly less favourable in the FRG than in any other nation that we consider.

Furthermore, with our German model, inheritance effects are also unusually strong in some instances. In the case of the petty bourgeoisie, where IN1 and IN2 apply, immobility is more than five times above the neutral-fluidity level ($e^{1.66}$ = 5.26), as compared with less than three-and-a-half times under the core model ($e^{1.42}$ = 3.46). And inheritance effects among German farmers are far in excess of those of the core (cf. Table 5.2) or of any other national model—indeed, to an extent that should perhaps be regarded as freakish.[7]

Finally, though, one major exception to this tendency towards low fluidity has also to be recognized. Our model for the FRG returns a lower estimate for sectoral effects than does that for any other nation, implying that in Germany sectoral barriers reduce mobility to only around two-thirds of what it would otherwise be ($e^{-0.43}$ = 0.65) as against a reduction to around one-third ($e^{-1.03}$ = 0.36) under the core model (again cf. Table 5.2). Our model, we would suggest, here reflects what one author has called 'the historic binary character of peasant society' in Germany—that is, its basis in both agriculture and artisanal crafts—which facilitated the transition to industrialism 'without a wholesale derooting of the rural population' (Franklin

---

[6] In this connection, two further points may be noted. First, our sample for the FRG omits immigrants without citizenship status; had *Gastarbeiter* been included, it may be supposed that a still stronger impression of inequality in mobility chances between non-skilled and skilled workers would have been created (cf. Müller 1986). Secondly, though, in the German case Class V comprises *Werkmeister*, a grade of worker for which in most of our other nations there is no exact equivalent, and which could arguably have been allocated to Class II. It is, therefore, possible that this German peculiarity, and the way that we have dealt with it, has the effect of exaggerating somewhat the contrast between the mobility chances of men of Class V+VI and Class VII*a* origins.

[7] Under the German model the propensity for immobility among farmers is in fact over thirty times what it would be at the neutral-fluidity level ($e^{3.50}$ = 33.12) as compared with seven-and-a-quarter times ($e^{1.98}$ = 7.24) under the core model.

1969: 22; cf. also Mellor 1978; Catt 1986; Kaschuba 1986); or, again, the fact that, in the words of another commentator, 'historically German farmers have never constituted a society apart to the same degree as the French peasantry' (Ardagh 1988: 128). In the modern period, still vital rural communities, in which part-time farming and commuting to adjacent industrial districts are frequent practices, have given a distinctive character to German agriculture, and at the same time have served to mitigate the problems of geographic and cultural relocation through which, as we suggested in developing the rationale of the core model, sectoral barriers to mobility are largely constituted.[8]

In sum, then, we could say that what for our present purposes is chiefly of interest about fluidity within the German class structure is that it deviates from core expectations not so much in being generally greater or less, but rather in showing in various respects a more strongly differentiated pattern. Quite contrary to the suggestions we noted in Chapter 1—that, following on the trauma of the Second World War and the *Stunde Null* of 1945, a new 'semi-classless' form of society and a 'land of fluidity' were created (see, e.g., Ardagh 1988: 145–6)—it would appear that historically formed influences on class-mobility chances have very largely retained their power.

Hungary

As Table 5.1 shows, Hungary is, like the FRG, a nation for which our model of core social fluidity does not fit well in unmodified form. However, in the Hungarian case the deviations from core fluidity are far more specific than in the German and in turn more readily accommodated. The changes we introduce into the model bear in fact on only four cells of the mobility table:

1. the IN3 term is included in the cell indicating immobility in the petty bourgeoisie, IV$a+b$;[9]
2. the AF2 term (positive affinity) is omitted from the pair of cells indicating mobility between the petty bourgeoisie and the service class, I+II;
3. an additional positive affinity term (AFX in Table 5.3) is included in

---

[8] It should, however, be further observed that the weakness of sectoral barriers in the FRG may to some extent be exaggerated as a result of the influx into the country of refugees from the East after the end of the Second World War. Many of the latter were of farm origins but found little alternative within the FRG to entering manual jobs in industry (cf. Janowitz 1958). It is noteworthy that, when we fit our German model to the two cohorts of men aged 25–44 and 45–64 with parameters being allowed to vary, we just fail to obtain a significant improvement in fit, but that the greatest difference appears in the sector effect, which is much less weak for the younger cohort.

[9] Since it turns out that the IN2 term is then insignificant and is thus dropped from the final version of our Hungarian variant, we could alternatively say that we here modify the model by omitting the IN2 term from the cell indicating immobility within Class I+II and omitting the IN3 term altogether.

the cell indicating mobility from the class of farmers, IV*c*, to that of agricultural workers, VII*b*.

These modifications to our model are all ones that we would see as being warranted by major changes in the Hungarian class structure following the establishment of the state socialist regime after the end of the Second World War. On the one hand, only a fraction of the former petty bourgeoisie was allowed to remain in existence (men in this class amount to just 2 per cent of our Hungarian sample); and, under the new order, not only were strict limitations placed on private entrepreneurship and its attractiveness much diminished (Andorka 1988) but, further, persons of petty bourgeois origins were more likely to be regarded as ideologically suspect than to be treated with favour. In these circumstances, therefore, the affinity proposed in the core model between the petty bourgeoisie and the service class—or, in an Eastern European context, the intelligentsia—of professionals, administrators, and managers would seem clearly inapt. And, in turn, both the reduced chances of upward mobility for the sons of the petty bourgeoisie and the reduced opportunities and motivation for entry into this class could be expected to heighten the propensity for intergenerational immobility within it.

On the other hand, in the agricultural sector, as we have earlier noted (p. 75), the creation of large numbers of new independent proprietors through land reforms was followed in the 1950s by large-scale collectivization. By the end of the decade the status of the overwhelming majority of former proprietors had been converted to that of employees in either so-called peasant co-operatives or state farms. The special affinity term that we introduce into the IV*c*–VII*b* cell is then intended to take account of this process of collective and largely forced mobility, which meant that the 'inheritance' of many men who grew up as farmers' sons—and who perhaps still worked the same land as their fathers—was in fact a different class location. It should, however, be noted that one of the main reasons why we get a significant improvement in fit when we allow the parameters of our Hungarian model to vary between two birth-cohorts is that this special affinity term is much weaker—and would not, in fact, be needed to produce a fitting model—for the younger cohort, that of men born between 1929 and 1948.

If we turn, then, to Table 5.3, we may note, to begin with, a feature that might be anticipated as the counterpart of this special treatment of the IV*c*–VII*b* cell. Since the IN2 effect is insignificant and the other inheritance effects are not especially strong, the propensity for immobility among Hungarian farmers is clearly weaker than elsewhere, implying immobility at only three-and-a-quarter times the neutral-fluidity level ($e^{1.18} = 3.25$) as compared with the seven-and-a-quarter times specified under the core model ($e^{1.98} = 7.24$).

In addition, though, there are two other emergent features of our Hungarian model, each prefigured in Table 5.2, that point to somewhat less predictable departures from the core-fluidity pattern. First, hierarchy effects appear as stronger in the Hungarian case than in any other, reducing mobility to less than two-fifths ($e^{-0.97} = 0.38$) of what it would otherwise be, as against a corresponding reduction under the core model of about a half. Chiefly as a result of this, Hungary several times shows up in the cross-national comparisons of Table A5.1 as having the lowest fluidity levels in transitions between classes within the non-agricultural sector. We have no readily available explanation of this feature, but Andorka has noted (1988; and cf. also Simkus *et al.* 1990) that commentators on pre-war Hungary (e.g. Keyserling 1928) emphasized the markedly hierarchical character of social relationships. And in this respect it is of interest that the other main source of difference between the parameters of our model as applied to two cohorts within the Hungarian sample is that hierarchy effects are clearly stronger in the older, that of men born between 1909 and 1928.

Secondly, and of larger consequence, it may be seen that the sectoral effect for Hungary is the next weakest after that for the FRG, implying that sectoral barriers limit mobility to about three-fifths of what it would be in their absence ($e^{-0.50} = 0.61$). Examination of Table A5.1 in turn reveals that Hungary is one of the nations for which all twenty cells entailing cross-sectoral mobilty record a value of less than 100. This means that in all these cells interaction parameters lie closer to the neutral-fluidity level (that is, with our conventions, closer to zero) than do those for the corresponding cells under the core model. And it may then be further observed that in the Hungarian case especially low values—indicating, that is, relatively high fluidity—are found in cells pertaining to mobility between the farm sector and both the skilled and non-skilled sections of the industrial working class.

These latter results would appear highly consonant with various accounts of evolving rural–urban relations in post-war Hungarian society. Thus, several authors have described how the collectivization of agriculture itself greatly encouraged the intersectoral movement of labour. It reduced the desirability of remaining on the land for peasants' sons without hope of proprietorship, while at the same time it attracted into agricultural work men from urban backgrounds with industrial training for whom 'depeasant-ization' and the increasing mechanization and scale of agricultural production provided new employment opportunities (Connor 1979: 156, 182; Andorka and Zagórski 1980; Simkus 1981; Kovács 1982; Haller, Kolosi, and Robert 1990).[10]

Furthermore, though, much attention has been given to rural–urban commuting in Hungary, which occurs on a far more extensive scale than that previously described in the FRG and far more as an unintended than a

---

[10] Within the context of an industrializing society, where major transfers of labour from the agricultural to the non-agricultural sector are occurring, it is, of course, such mobility flows 'against the tide' that are the crucial expression of low sectoral barriers.

planned consequence of Hungarian economic development. In the post-war years the rate of industrialization far outstripped that of urbanization, and an acute urban housing shortage resulted (Konrad and Szelényi 1977). Thus, many men from rural areas who took jobs in industry continued to live in their villages, and retained their ties to the land by helping their wives and kin in cultivating 'family plots' (Mód 1966; Szelényi 1988: ch. 1). These 'semi-proletarians' or 'post-peasants', who in effect straddle the agricultural and industrial sectors, have indeed been represented as performing—if often at great personal cost—a major cultural 'transmission function' within post-war Hungarian society that served to reduce differences between rural and urban values and thus to further the *rapprochement* of the 'fundamental classes' of socialist society (see, e.g., Böhm and Pál 1982; Böhm 1984; and, for a more 'pessimistic' interpretation, Volgyes 1981). However, other authors (see, esp., Szelényi 1988) have questioned whether these workers are in fact to be regarded as a merely transitional phenomenon, and envisage the 'long-term reproduction' of part-time family farming linked to industrial employment.[11]

Our national-variant model for Hungary, like that for the FRG, thus implies that fluidity both below and above core expectations is to be found in different areas of the class structure. It can, however, be added that the larger deviations from the core pattern tend to be concentrated in inter-generational transitions involving the agricultural sector and that some at least would appear to be diminishing over time.

The Republic of Ireland

The Republic of Ireland provides a further instance where the pattern of social fluidity does not conform at all closely to our core model but where the deviations that occur are fairly specific and where again, too, the most obvious relate to the agricultural sector. The modifications that we make to the core model affect four cells of the mobility table:

1. the AF2 term (positive affinity) is included in the pair of cells indicating mobility between the class of farmers, IVc, and the service class, I+II;

---

[11] In the period immediately following the 1973 Hungarian enquiry on which we draw, 'semi-proletarian' workers began to exploit the growing liberalism of the regime by orienting their family plots or 'mini-farms' increasingly towards market production. The number of such small-scale rural entrepreneurs grew steadily in the 1980s to around 1.5 million; and, in view of our finding of unusually low sectoral barriers in Hungary, it is interesting to note that their ranks were swelled by workers, both blue-collar and white-collar, who moved from the towns in order to take up family-based farming. Szelényi (1988), following the earlier writings of Erdei (see Huszár 1988), suggests that this process may be understood as the resumption of a long-term developmental tendency towards the *embourgeoisement* of the Hungarian peasantry which began in the sixteenth and seventeenth centuries during the period of Turkish occupation but was then twice interrupted: first, in the eighteenth century by the imposition of 'second feudalism' after the defeat of the Turks; and then again in the Stalinist period by the collectivization programme.

2. the AF2 term is also included in the cell indicating mobility from farm origins in Class IV*c* into the class of agricultural workers, VII*b*; and again in that indicating mobility from origins in Class VII*a*, that of non-skilled workers outside agriculture, into VII*b*.

These modifications may be seen as required by features of Ireland's large agricultural sector, which our core model in its original form is unable to accommodate. Of greatest importance is the wide variation in the size of farms. Writers from Arensberg and Kimball (1940/1968) onwards have in fact noted a tendency for two relatively distinct types of farmer to emerge and to develop as virtually separate classes in themselves: on the one hand, large farmers, operating as capitalist entrepreneurs and with various affiliations, economic and socio-cultural, to urban business and professional communities; and, on the other hand, small, often in fact marginal, farmers, seeking to follow a traditional way of life but threatened with 'proletarianization' and in many cases surviving only through social-welfare payments, remittances from emigrant kin—or indeed through periodic entries into wage-work (see, further, Jackson 1971; Hannan 1979; Peillon 1982: ch. 1; Brown 1985: ch. 8; Commins 1986). Furthermore, associated with this dualism in Irish farming, there would appear to exist a rural working class of a rather distinctive cross-sectoral form (Jackson 1971). Wage-workers on the larger farms make up a more-or-less common pool of labour with other unskilled workers—for example, roadmen and maintenance workers employed by local authorities—who are, moreover, themselves often part-time smallholders and tend in turn to merge with the marginal farmers who are forced into intermittent casual labour.

It is then these particular class linkages, deriving from the course of development of Irish agriculture, that provide the *raison d'être* for the additional positive affinities that we introduce into our variant model. And it may be seen from Table 5.3 that the AF2 term takes on a higher value in the Irish case than in any other, implying mobility at approaching twice the level that would occur in its absence ($e^{0.62} = 1.86$), as against just over one-and-a-half times ($e^{0.46} = 1.58$) under the core model. In other words, in the instances where this term applies, there is a relatively strong propensity for both hierarchical and sectoral barriers to mobility to be offset. A further consequence, observable from Table A5.1, is that the areas of white-collar and blue-collar fluidity, linking Classes I+II with III and IV*a*+*b* and Classes V+VI with VII*a*, which are largely created in the core model by the AF2 term, become most pronounced of all in the Irish case.

However, reverting to Table 5.3, it has at the same time to be recognized that alongside this strong positive affinity effect and also rather weak hierarchy effects (the HI1 term being in fact insignificant), there are other parameters returned for our Irish model that point quite unambiguously to *low* fluidity. Thus, the AF1—negative affinity—term is also stronger for

Ireland than for any other nation; and, far more consequentially, *all* inheritance effects are well above core expectations, chiefly because the basic IN1 term is again at an extreme of the variation among our nations (cf. Table 5.2). This term indicates immobility two-and-a-half times above the neutral-fluidity level ($e^{0.90} = 2.46$), as compared with one-and-a-half times ($e^{0.43} = 1.54$) under the core model. Table A5.1 then reveals values of clearly over 100 for Ireland in all diagonal cells of the mobility table—in other words, all these cells have interaction parameters further removed from neutral fluidity than with the core model. And, indeed, for Classes III, V+VI, VII*a*, and VII*b*—that is, for routine non-manual employees and all three classes of manual wage-workers— the Irish model implies a higher propensity for immobility than does any other national variant.

Findings of the kind reported above are, in fact, in close accord with several recurrent themes in historical and sociological studies of modern Ireland. For example, a number of authors have stressed the still sharp socio-cultural differentiation, especially between white-collar and blue-collar workers, that tends to reinforce lines of class division; the wide range of class-linked inequalities in incomes and living standards, little modified by redistributive social policies; and the persisting importance of personal contacts—often of limited range—in securing employment (see, e.g., Humphreys 1966; Peillon 1982, 1986; Rottman *et al.* 1982; Rottman and O'Connell 1982; Callan *et al.* 1989; Breen *et al.* 1990).

Furthermore, our representation of Irish society as displaying unusually strong tendencies towards intergenerational immobility is more directly confirmed by independent evidence for the Dublin area presented by Whelan and Whelan (1984) and Breen and Whelan (1986). In the light of their own comparative analyses, these authors concluded that the mobility experience of the Dublin population was distinctive in the propensity for class inheritance that was displayed. Marked tendencies towards immobility are also reported by Hout and Jackson (1986) and Hout (1989), who use the same data as we do but apply different analytical techniques. However, while these authors stress the importance of general hierarchical effects— whether interpreted as ones of prestige or of 'socio-economic' status—in shaping the Irish pattern of social fluidity, our model would lead us to put the emphasis rather on the more specific class affinities and disaffinities to which we have referred.[12]

---

[12] Thus, it may be pointed out that, in consequence of the relative weakness of hierarchical effects, Table A5.1 indicates that in Ireland the propensity for mobility in either direction between the service class and both the skilled and non-skilled divisions of the working class is closer to the neutral-fluidity level than under the core model. Hout (1989: 150) argues (with reference to Erikson and Goldthorpe 1987) that the conclusion to be drawn from our modelling of the Irish mobility table is not that hierarchy effects are weak but that the HI1 term in our model is not a good measure of hierarchy; with better measures, hierarchy effects, over and above those we distinguish, become of obvious importance. However, it must in this respect be noted, first, that Hout misdescribes our national variant model for Ireland (1989: 147–8 and

Northern Ireland

Unlike the last three nations considered, Northern Ireland shows a pattern of social fluidity which is in fact rather close to that of our core model. In order to obtain an acceptable variant of the model, we need make only a single modification, which bears on just two cells:

1. an additional positive affinity term (AFX in Table 5.3) is included in the pair of cells indicating mobility between the petty bourgeoisie, IV$a+b$, and the class of farmers, IVc—that is, over and above the AF2 term that already applies.

Since it was apparent from inspection of residuals that deviation from the core model was concentrated in these two cells, and that only the modification indicated was necessary in order to produce a satisfactory fit, we can in this case scarcely claim that the variant model we propose was guided by external evidence. However, we have *post factum* discovered in the relevant literature two possible explanations of the departure from core fluidity that we here encounter.

First, Mogey reports (1955: 55, 144) that in rural areas in Northern Ireland shops are often located outside settlements—for example, at country cross-roads—and that in such areas shop-keeping is often combined with farming within the same family.

Secondly, a number of authors have commented on the fact that, in the villages and small country towns in which a relatively large proportion of the Northern Irish population still live, the number of shops, public houses, and other small businesses is unusually high—and indeed the proportion of men found in Class IV$a+b$ in our Northern Irish sample is larger than in any other from a European nation (see Table 6.2). This is a result, it is then argued, of the sharp social segregation of Protestants and Roman Catholics often found in such communities, which fixes customer loyalty, restricts competition, and thus encourages the duplication of retailing and service facilities (Mogey 1955; Harris 1972: ch. 1; Aunger 1983; Hout 1986). Both of the circumstances described would, therefore, make it plausible to suppose that a high fluidity is encouraged between farmers and petty bourgeoisie, since in many parts of the Province family capital will be readily shifted, whether intergeneration-ally or otherwise, as between agricultural and other forms of small-scale enterprise.

From the parameters estimated for our accepted model, as reported in

Appendix Table A2; cf. Erikson and Goldthorpe 1987: 154–5, and text above); and, secondly, that in his own analyses he applies the model, unmodified, to a version of the Irish mobility table based on a *fourteen-category elaboration* of our class schema. If in our comparative analyses we were able to work with tables of this degree of refinement, we would then surely wish to elaborate our model correspondingly by introducing further hierarchical levels—*and* other, non-hierarchical, effects as well (cf. ch. 4 n. 17).

Table 5.3, only two points would seem to call for comment. First, the AF1 term is insignificant; and, as can then be seen from the relevant cell entries in Table A5.1, barriers to mobility between the service class and that of agricultural workers are less extreme—though of course still very high—in Northern Ireland than in most other of the nations we consider, including the Republic of Ireland. Secondly, though, the propensity for immobility among the class of farmers, as indicated by the IN3 term, is at the same high level as in the Republic; and Table A5.1 further indicates that in Northern Ireland propensities for intergenerational mobility into or from farming, except of course for exchanges with the petty bourgeoisie, fall consistently below core expectations.

However, while the pattern of social fluidity in Northern Ireland can then be regarded as largely captured by our core model, the sectarian division to which we have already referred means that a further question here arises that must, in fact, involve us in a brief excursus. The question is: are the patterns of social fluidity that prevail *within* the Protestant and Catholic communities of Northern Ireland sufficiently alike that it is appropriate to apply one model to the society as a whole?

As a first step towards an answer, we may construct mobility tables for the Protestants (N = 1,346) and Catholics (N = 686) comprised by our Northern Irish sample, and then fit to these tables the common social fluidity (CmSF) model. The result confirms that reached by earlier analysts (Bland 1980; Miller 1983) who have worked with the same data but different categories: that is, the model fits well (G^2 = 32.1, df = 36, p > 0.50). We may then say that the fluidity patterns of the two communities are indeed very similar overall. None the less, specific differences between them might remain undetected by such a global test, and one obvious way of checking on this possibility is then to apply our Northern Ireland variant of the core model to the Protestant and Catholic tables taken separately—although with full recognition that our subsample sizes are rather too small for comfort. What we find is that, while parameter estimates do not differ significantly, the model, as shown in Table 5.4, fits the Catholic table somewhat better than the Protestant one.

Finally, though, if we examine the residuals from the fit to the Protestant table, we discover that major deviations from the model occur in just two cells, IVc–I+II and IVc–VIIa: specifically, the mobility of the sons of farmers into service-class positions is underpredicted, and their mobility into non-skilled manual work is overpredicted. This finding has then to be related to the fact that, as emerges clearly from Hout's analyses (1989: ch. 7), in Northern Ireland large farms are heavily concentrated in Protestant hands. Thus, we would believe, the less good fit of our model to the Protestant mobility table chiefly reflects the differing composition of Protestant and Catholic farmers: what is shown up is not so much intrinsic differences in fluidity patterns between Protestants and Catholics as our inability, on

TABLE 5.4. *Results of fitting the national-variant model for Northern Ireland to mobility tables for Protestant and Roman Catholic subpopulations separately, and effect parameters estimated*

Subpopulation	G^2	df	p	rG^2	Δ
Protestants (N = 1,346)	48.2	28	0.01	92.8	6.1
Catholics (N = 686)	20.0	28	0.86	93.8	5.2

Effect parameters

	HI1	HI2	IN1	IN2	IN3	SE	AF1	AF2	AFX
Protestants	−0.27	−0.32	0.54	0.67	1.19	−1.16	ns	0.41	0.60
Catholics	−0.33	−0.51	0.40	0.90	1.74	−0.77	ns	0.35	0.76
All	−0.29	−0.38	0.48	0.72	1.45	−1.04	ns	0.38	0.66

which we earlier remarked, to distinguish (in a comparatively reliable way) between large farmers and small.

The conclusion to which we incline is then that the results we obtain from fitting the CmSF model are unlikely to prove misleading: patterns of social fluidity among Protestants and Catholics *are* essentially the same and may be represented by one model without undue distortion. It is, however, important that the implications of this conclusion should be correctly understood. It does *not* entail denying the well-established fact that Catholics as a whole hold less advantaged and desirable class positions than do Protestants; nor does it mean that there is no religious discrimination in employment. What is rather indicated is that, *within* each community, class operates in much the same way in structuring relative mobility chances; and thus, as Hout (1989: ch. 7) has argued, that, even though Catholics in Northern Ireland are disadvantaged overall in their employment relative to Protestants, they still do not form a more-or-less homogeneous 'underclass', for whose members the consequences of their common religious affiliation quite override the effects of their differing class origins – while, on the other hand, the presence of many disadvantaged Protestants has also to be recognized.

Poland

Poland is again a case where, to judge from the $G^2(S)$ and Δ statistics, our model of core fluidity comes relatively close to fitting, once nationally specific parameters are allowed. There are, however, still a number of deviations that can be identified and which we accommodate, so as to obtain an entirely acceptable model, by changes that affect six cells:

1. the AF2 term (positive affinity) is omitted from the pair of cells indicating mobility between the service class, I+II, and the class of routine non-manual employees, III;
2. the AF2 term is included in the pairs of cells indicating mobility between the service class and both the skilled and non-skilled divisions of the working class, V+VI and VII*a*.

These modifications find their rationale—in much the same way as those introduced in the Hungarian case—in the actions of a state socialist regime aiming at a major reconstruction of the social order. In the years following the Second World War the leaders of the new People's Republic in Poland sought in two different, and perhaps not altogether ideologically consistent, ways to give force to the official rhetoric of the regime and to advance the interests of the working class (cf. Vaughan 1971). On the one hand, they attempted to reshape traditional hierarchies of prestige and material rewards to the advantage of manual labour (Pohoski 1964); and the evidence would suggest that what was in these respects achieved was a more extensive *overlap* than is typically found in Western capitalist societies between the positions of manual workers in industry and those of white-collar employees (Parkin 1971*a*: ch. 5; Matejko 1974; Lane 1976: ch. 7; Słomczyński and Wesołowski 1978; Connor 1979: ch. 6). On the other hand, the aim was to widen the opportunities of workers, and of their children, for individual as well as for collective mobility, and specifically their opportunities to gain access to higher-level professional, administrative, and managerial positions within a new 'people's intelligentsia' (Wesołowski and Mach 1986). In the immediate post-war years, large numbers of workers were promoted directly into the party, governmental, and industrial bureaucracies; and, while subsequently demotions of these men were not infrequent and new recruits were drawn increasingly from institutions of higher education, various measures of 'positive discrimination' in favour of manual workers' children were introduced into schools and colleges in an effort to maintain the proportion of the new intelligentsia who were of working-class origin (Kolankiewicz 1973; Szczepański 1978; Adamski and Białecki 1981). In the light of these policies, there are then at least *prima facie* grounds for adapting the core model to the Polish case by changes which remove the provision for specially high fluidity between the service class and that of lower-level non-manual employees, but allow for reduced barriers to mobility between the service class and our two classes of industrial workers.

When we examine the parameters estimated for this Polish variant of our model, the most striking feature is that hierarchy effects are almost non-existent. The HI1 term is insignificant, and the HI2 term is clearly weaker than with any other nation, implying mobility at almost nine-tenths of what it would be in the absence of this effect ($e^{-0.14} = 0.87$), as compared with around a half under the core model. High fluidity is also indicated by the relatively weak SE term, Poland appearing closer to the FRG and Hungary than to other nations in its low barriers to intersectoral mobility flows. As a result, then, of these two features together, it is not only the sons of industrial workers who in Poland display unusually favourable relative chances of upward mobility but—as emerges from Table A5.1—the sons of farm workers also.

However, it must further be noted that in Poland inheritance effects are very strong, in particular the IN1 and IN2 terms. Thus, as can again be seen from Table A5.1, the propensity for immobility within both sections of the working class and the routine non-manual class is comparatively high, and in the case of the service class and the petty bourgeoisie is quite exceptional— indicating immobility at over seven times the neutral-fluidity level ($e^{1.98} = 7.24$) as against three-and-a-half times under the core model. The propensity for immobility in the two latter classes is in fact higher than that among farmers, as is shown by the negative IN3 term. It should, though, be added here that the improvement in fit of our Polish model which occurs when its parameters are allowed to vary over two birth-cohorts is due chiefly to a stronger propensity for immobility among farmers in the younger cohort, that of men born between 1928 and 1947.

The pattern of fluidity within the Polish class structure is, therefore, rather complex, and scarcely open to interpretation *simply* as one created by political intervention. Within the 'fundamental classes' of the socialist society, tendencies towards immobility would not appear to have been decisively reduced; what is distinctive about the Polish pattern is, rather, that, where mobility away from class origins *does* occur, there are strong propensities for movement of a 'long-range' kind. It has, moreover, to be kept in mind that the attempt to collectivize agriculture in Poland, which started at the end of the 1940s, was abandoned in 1956 in the face of fierce peasant opposition (Lewis 1973). Largely for this reason, one could suggest, fluidity between agricultural and non-agricultural classes, while high relative to core expectations (cf. Table 5.2)—and being again promoted by 'under-urbanization' and extensive rural–urban commuting (Pohoski 1964; Matejko 1974: ch. 4; Szczepański 1978; Zagórski 1977–8)—still does not reach the same level as in Hungary. And, finally, the urban petty bourgeoisie would seem not to have been 'marginalized' under socialism to the same extent in Poland as in Hungary. Rather, linkages have been retained with at least some 'older' professional groupings which are conducive to mobility (Vaughan 1971; Misztal 1981).

None the less, the fact remains that attempts to generate greater fluidity as between the working class and the intelligentsia do appear to have met with some degree of success; and it is then relevant to ask why, in this respect, it should be in Poland rather than in Hungary—where the attempt to create a 'people's intelligentsia' was also made (cf. Kulcsár 1984: 100–5)—that socialist policy was the more effective.[13] Part of the explanation could well be that efforts to this end were more seriously sustained in Poland. In Hungary, following 'normalization' after the 1956 uprising, the regime openly sought a *rapprochement* with the intelligentsia (in Kádár's famous words of 1962: 'Those who are not against us are with us'), which involved, among other things, an increasing disregard of students' social origins in educational selection procedures (cf. Simkus and Andorka 1982; Szelényi 1987; Andorka 1988). But a further difference that cannot be overlooked is that, during the Second World War and its aftermath, social dislocation and upheaval occurred on a yet greater scale in Poland than in any other European nation. For example, it is estimated that around a third of all Poles with secondary or higher education were killed, and post-primary educational institutions were almost totally destroyed. Again, large sections of the population were more or less coerced into mobility, both occupational and geographical, as the result of enemy occupation, deportation, and the destruction of the economy, and then in 1945 through the shifting of the national frontiers some 150 to 200 miles to the west (Vaughan 1971; Szczepański 1978).

Thus, in the post-war period policies directed towards shaping new hierarchies and patterns of mobility were able to work in Poland on a social structure already greatly 'loosened' and, one may suppose, with much reduced powers of resistance. And, if in turn the Polish case is further compared with that of the FRG, one may then suggest that the major disruptions that Olson would see as important in breaking up accumulated social rigidities and hence in promoting mobility will in fact be associated with this latter outcome only where the weakening of the social structure is actually exploited by political action that in some way has greater fluidity as its goal.[14]

[13] The major comparative study of social mobility in Hungary and Poland, that of Andorka and Zagórski (1980), does not address this issue, being primarily concerned with absolute rather than relative rates. However, a further Hungarian–Polish comparative study, carried out in 1979 and based on samples of industrial occupational groups (Akszentievics 1983), has led its author to the following conclusions which—though we would have wished to see them better documented—are, as they stand, of obvious interest in relation to our own results: (i) that mobility is greater in Poland than in Hungary primarily because of more frequent downward movement; and (ii) that the manual–non-manual distinction has more importance in patterning the choice of friends in Hungary than in Poland, where too a clearly stronger 'upward trend' in making or at least in reporting friends is present.

The further possibility should, of course, be considered that the differences shown up in our analyses are artefactual. It could, for example, be noted that our Class III is smaller in Poland than in Hungary, and, if this were the result of the dividing line btween Class I+II and Class III having been set at a lower level for Poland, then this might in turn explain the greater fluidity that is found between Class I+II and Classes V+VI and VIIa. However, what tells against such a possibility is the fact that the propensity for immobility within Class I+II is clearly higher in Poland than in Hungary—which is not what would be expected if in the Polish case these classes were more loosely defined.

[14] Preliminary results from a major study of social stratification and mobility carried out in

Scotland

Scotland is a further case where our core model needs only quite minor alteration—involving just two cells—in order to give an acceptable fit to the national mobility table.[15]

1. the IN1 term is omitted from the cells indicating immobility within Classes III and VII*b*, those of routine non-manual employees and agricultural workers.

This is a modification, like that made in the Northern Irish case, which is largely dictated by a specific feature of the residuals under the core model, and the low propensity for immobility within Classes III and VII*b* that would seem implied is in itself a feature for which we have no explanation readily to hand. However, an alternative way of interpreting the variant model is to say that inheritance effects within the two divisions of the working class, Classes V+VI and VII*a*, need to be set at a separate, higher level—and this would be consonant with one rather well-defined theme in discussion of modern Scottish society. Several authors have argued (see, e.g., Kellas and Fotheringham 1976; Harvie 1981: 84–7) that the nation's early industrialization and the predominance of heavy industry have encouraged the formation and persistence within the Scottish working class of particularly strong 'traditional' subcultures of a kind that are unlikely to favour mobility. Table 5.3 does then indeed show that the IN1 parameter for the Scottish variant model is comparatively high; and, in turn, Table A5.1 reveals propensities for immobility within the Scottish working class—that is, interaction parameters in cells indicating both immobility within and mobility between classes V+VI and VII*a*—that are in excess of the neutral-fluidity level to almost the same degree as in the Irish and Polish cases.

At the same time, though, examination of the two tables in question also reveals that, if anything, more notable departures from core fluidity come with the effects for hierarchy and, especially, for sector. From Table 5.3 it can be seen that under our Scottish model the HI1 term is omitted as insignificant, while, on the other hand, the SE term is higher than for any other nation—implying a reduction of mobility to a quarter of what it would otherwise be ($e^{-1.37} = 0.25$), as compared with the one-third reduction provided for by the core model. And the entries of Table A5.1 then indicate

---

Poland in 1984 (for which we are indebted to Zbigniew Sawiński) would indicate that the pattern of social fluidity has in fact become closer to that of the core model than it was in 1972. The trend towards a greater propensity for immobility among farmers that we have suggested is confirmed; and, moreover, the distinctively high levels of fluidity between the service class and both divisions of the working class are no longer apparent—pointing, perhaps, to a weakening of political efforts to maintain such fluidity or to greater social resistance to them.

[15] The $G^2(S)$ for the Scottish variant model is in fact somewhat over the 40 mark, but against this it should be noted that the model has 29 degrees of freedom on account of the non-significant and omitted HI1 term.

that often comparatively high propensities for mobility between classes within the non-agricultural sector (and also a high propensity for moving from agricultural wage-work into farming) coexist with consistently low propensities for *inter*sectoral mobility. In eighteen of the twenty cells entailing such mobility, the Scottish values are greater than 100.

It could then be argued that Scottish deviations from the core-fluidity pattern derive not only from the precociousness of Scottish industrialism but further from its *uneven development*. An economy has been created with a high degree of regional differentiation (Kendrick, Bechhofer, and McCrone 1985) in which industrial activity is heavily concentrated—in the central lowlands—with a resulting very wide variation in urban–rural population densities (Payne 1987: 11–14). Thus, barriers to mobility across the sectoral divide are strongly accentuated, in direct contrast with the German, Hungarian, and Polish cases previously discussed in which we have found evidence of a considerable spatial interpenetration of agricultural and non-agricultural activity, or at all events of the work-forces involved.

Our results can then lend little support to arguments for Scottish exceptionalism of the kind that we noted in Chapter 1. If any early meritocracy did indeed exist in Scotland, it has not survived, or at least not in a way that endows Scottish society with a distinctive degree of openness. Although fluidity tends in certain respects to be above core expectations, the high propensities for immobility that prevail within most classes, together with the unusually strong sectoral barriers to mobility, serve to create overall the impression of a relatively high degree of rigidity.

Sweden

As we earlier saw, Sweden is the third case, along with England and France, in which we need make no change at all to the form of our model of core social fluidity in order to obtain an acceptable fit to the national mobility data.

However, it is at once apparent from Table 5.3 that the parameters estimated for the model when it is applied to the Swedish data are not themselves in such close conformity with core expectations as was found with England and France. Although hierarchy effects are at about core level, the AF1 (negative affinity) term becomes insignificant, and the sectoral effect and all inheritance effects are much closer to the neutral-fluidity level. To revert to our cartographic metaphor, we could say that, while the contours of social fluidity in Sweden closely follow those of the core model, these contours tend to be flattened, and especially so on the diagonal 'ridge'. From Table A5.1 it may be observed that not one Swedish value exceeds 100: that is to say, for all cells of the 7×7 mobility table, the Swedish interaction parameters are either at the same distance from the neutral-fluidity level as the corresponding parameters under the core model or—as in most instances—closer to this level. In other words, the Swedish class structure may be regarded as showing a relatively high degree of openness, in that most barriers to mobility and likewise propensities for immobility tend to be weak.

Such a finding is, we may note, much in line with the results obtained by other investigators who have undertaken independent studies of Swedish mobility in comparative perspective (Pöntinen 1983; Erikson and Pöntinen 1985; Vogel 1987). It is, moreover, one that would be expected from the standpoint of those authors (e.g. Goldthorpe 1980a/1987: ch. 9) who have suggested that a positive association will prevail between equality of opportunity and equality of condition, or who have argued (Tyree, Semyonov, and Hodge 1979) that fluidity will be the greater, the more that the structure of social inequality is characterized by 'glissandos' rather than by 'gaps'. For the available evidence would suggest (cf. Erikson 1990) that in Sweden the explicitly egalitarian policies adopted by Social Democratic governments over the post-war years have met with some significant degree of success. Thus, Sweden would appear to have achieved one of the least unequal distributions of post-tax income among Western nations (Sawyer 1976; O'Higgins, Schmaus, and Stephenson 1990), and also perhaps the most comprehensive and 'vertically redistributive' social-welfare policies (Esping Andersen and Korpi 1984; Ringen 1987)—through which, it may be added, much attention has, in fact, been given to the reduction of urban–rural as well as class differences in living standards, including educational provision (Jonsson 1987, 1990).

It may, though, be further relevant to note that, over the period covered by our data, Swedish governments have also sought to maintain a full-employment economy, in large part through 'supply-side' measures. In particular, ambitious and heavily funded 'active labour market' policies have been developed, including retraining programmes and various forms of assistance for workers' geographical relocation (Rehn 1985). In other words, the question of the political generation of mobility—to which we shall return at the end of this chapter—is here again complicated by the possibility that measures not primarily or explicitly directed towards creating a greater equality of opportunity may none the less still have contributed to this end.

On the basis of our core model, we have now examined the extent and nature of variation in social fluidity across the nine European nations represented in our own data-set. However, before going on to consider the overall significance of the results we have achieved for the evaluation of the FJH hypothesis which is our ultimate concern, we take advantage, in the next section of the chapter, of mobility data for three further European nations that have been made available to us through the efforts of other researchers. By the inclusion of these data, the range of our analyses can be valuably widened.

NATIONAL VARIATION IN SOCIAL FLUIDITY: ADDITIONAL CASES

The three nations for which we have additional father–son mobility tables, constructed on the sevenfold version of our class schema, are Czechoslovakia, Italy, and the Netherlands. The Czechoslovak table derives from a major enquiry, the Social Structure Survey, carried out in 1984 by a research group from the Czechoslovak Academy of Sciences in Prague; the Italian table comes from a mobility survey jointly undertaken in 1985–6 by researchers from the Universities of Trento, Bologna, and Trieste; and for the Netherlands we have in fact two tables, both of a 'composite' kind, made up by summing three tables for 1976–7 and three for 1982–5 out of a series that have been produced by Luijkx and Ganzeboom (1989).[16]

So far as comparability with the tables in our own data-set is concerned, each of these additional tables has certain features that should be noted. First, while Luijkx and Ganzeboom in coding the Dutch data to the class schema had some consultation with us, for the other two nations this coding was carried out quite independently. However, as we have indicated earlier (p. 51), there are grounds for supposing that a high degree of reliability can be obtained in the use of the schema by investigators well acquainted with its principles—as we believe to be the case with our Czechoslovak and Italian colleagues. Secondly, it will be observed that the Czechoslovak and Italian tables are for around a decade later than those we have ourselves assembled for the 1970s. This might matter a good deal if we were here concerned with absolute rates; but we doubt if it is of much consequence in regard to relative rates, in view of the degree of temporal stability which, as we have already shown, these tend to possess. The Dutch case is of special interest in that we have data for both the 1970s and the 1980s. Thirdly, the Italian table is based on a sample (N = 1,764) that is somewhat below the minimum size of $c.2,000$ that we imposed within our own data-set. And, fourthly, there must be particular doubts about the quality of the Netherlands samples on which we draw, since, even when of similar date, statistically significant differences can be detected in their marginal distributions, and we understand that response rates were poor. These points—and especially, we believe, the last—should then be kept in mind in assessing the results that follow.

---

[16] We are extremely grateful to the researchers who have produced these tables for their generosity in making them available to us and, in particular, to Marek Boguszak, Antonio Cobalti, and Harry Ganzeboom for their help and advice. Further information on the Czechoslovak enquiry can be found in Boguszak (1989); on the Italian, in de Lillo (1988) and Cobalti (1988); and on the Dutch studies in Luijkx and Ganzeboom (1989).

TABLE 5.5. *Results of fitting the model of core social fluidity to mobility tables for three additional nations: (i) with cross-nationally common parameters; (ii) with nation-specific parameters; (ii) with effects modified or added (national-variant model)*

Nation		G^2	df	p	rG^2	Δ	$G^2(S)$ $(1,991)^*$
CZE	(i)	284.3	36	0.00	65.1	7.0	118
(N = 6,054)	(ii)	56.0	28	0.00	93.1	2.4	37
ITA	(i)	92.7	36	0.00	86.0	7.8	100
(N = 1,764)	(ii)	66.2	28	0.00	90.0	5.8	71
	(iii)	33.1	28	0.23	95.0	4.1	34
ITA–CN	(i)	48.9	36	0.07	87.9	6.8	57
(N = 1,223)†	(ii)	33.6	28	0.21	91.7	4.9	37
NET–70s	(i)	79.4	36	0.00	91.4	6.1	70
(N = 2,522)	(ii)	66.2	28	0.00	92.8	5.2	58
	(iii)	48.0	29	0.01	94.8	4.4	44
NET–80s	(i)	129.8	36	0.00	80.5	7.6	99
(N = 2,957)	(ii)	70.0	28	0.00	89.5	5.5	56
	(iii)	50.4	29	0.01	92.4	3.9	43

Notes:
   * We here retain the constant for $G^2(S)$ at 1,991, the size of the smallest sample among the nations in our own data-set.
   † ITA–CN is central and northern regions of Italy only.

In Tables 5.5 and 5.6 we show respectively—and in exactly the same way as in Tables 5.1 and 5.3 above—the results of fitting our model of core social fluidity to tables for the three additional nations and the parameter estimates for the versions of the model that we accept. We now examine the results for each case in turn.

Czechoslovakia

The fit of our core model to the Czechoslovak table has in fact already been investigated by Boguszak (1990), and in Tables 5.5 and 5.6 we essentially reproduce his findings.[17] As is indicated, the model fits adequately by the standard we have adopted—i.e. $G^2(S)$ is less than 40—once specific parameters are allowed; no modification to the form of the model is required. However, as in the similar Swedish case, the parameters estimated for the model do diverge from core expectations, and indeed do so on largely Swedish lines: that is to say, while hierarchy effects are at about core level,

---

[17] The—quite trivial—differences between our results and Boguszak's would appear to result from our standard practice of adding 0.1 to the zero cells of mobility tables.

TABLE 5.6. *Effect parameters of accepted models for three additional nations**

Nation	HI1	HI2	IN1	IN2	IN3	SE	AF1	AF2
CZE	−0.21	−0.36	0.28	0.55	ns	−0.52	−0.28	0.27
ITA	−0.14[†]	−0.74	0.25	*1.05*	*0.83*	−0.75	*−1.17*	0.11
ITA–CN	−0.14[†]	−0.61	0.28	1.15	1.01	−0.69	−1.53	0.59
NET–70s	ns	*−0.44*	0.58	0.92	*0.36*	−1.00	−0.45	0.42
NET–80s	ns	*−0.42*	0.42	0.49	*0.90*	−0.79	−0.20	0.30
CORE	−0.22	−0.42	0.43	0.81	0.96	−1.03	−0.77	0.46

Notes:
   * Parameters directly affected by modifications to the core model are in italic type; instances where a parameter initially returned a non-significant value at the 5 per cent level and has then been omitted in re-estimating the model are indicated by ns.
   † These effects are marginally short of being significant at the 5 per cent level but are retained in the model in view of the relatively small size of the Italian sample.

inheritance effects and the sector effect, as well as both positive and negative affinities, are clearly weaker. And from Table A5.1 it can be seen that for Czechoslovakia, as for Sweden, no value of above 100 is recorded. On this basis, one could then well conclude that the Czechoslovak pattern of social fluidity is best bracketed with the Swedish in that both imply an unusually high degree of openness.

It should, though, be noted that Boguszak reports that the Czechoslovak data can be still better reproduced if certain changes are in fact made to the core model, with the aim of accommodating the impact on the Czechoslovak class structure of the actions of the state socialist regime after 1948. Boguszak points in particular to the almost total 'liquidation' of both the petty bourgeoisie and the farmers—the latter in the course of a thoroughgoing collectivization of agriculture—and suggests that these two classes, whether considered as ones of origin or destination, should be relegated to the *lowest* of the three hierarchical divisions made within the class schema, with consequent changes in the HI1 and HI2 matrices. When the variant model thus produced is applied to the Czechoslovak table, a clear improvement in fit is achieved: G^2 falls by 20.7 with the same degrees of freedom. There are thus grounds for supposing that, as well as Czechoslovak society having been generally the most 'levelled' in all of post-war Eastern Europe, as several authors have suggested (Brus 1986*a*; Asselain 1987; Večerník 1987; Teichova 1988), it is further distinctive in that through political intervention self-employed groupings were not merely marginalized, as in Poland or Hungary, but systematically downgraded *en route* to their virtual extinction. It is indeed the—relatively disadvantageous—effects of petty-bourgeois *origins* that Boguszak's revised model chiefly captures, since the number of men actually found in any kind of self-employment at the time of the Czechoslovak enquiry was quite negligible.

It is also of interest to observe that, while in Czechoslovakia as in Poland (and in some contrast to Hungary) the state socialist regime sought to maintain an influence over processes of educational and occupational attainment, there is little evidence of a heightened propensity for long-range mobility between the working class and the intelligentsia of the kind that our Polish model would suggest. In Czechoslovakia, it would appear, measures aimed at encouraging such mobility were applied only 'on a relatively limited scale', and the primary objective of intervention was actually a different one: namely, the advancement of politically favoured individuals and the legitimation of this advancement by the *post factum* award of educational credentials (Gabal, Matĕjů, and Boguszak 1989: esp. 15–18). An important implication is, therefore, that, in so far as such policies were successful, the impression created from the application of our model of Czechoslovakia as a distinctively open society may be to some extent spurious: that is, because there is one important set of effects on relative mobility chances—those relating to individuals' political position and connections—that the model does not incorporate.[18]

Finally, the Czechoslovak case, like that of Northern Ireland, is of value in providing an opportunity to examine the degree of similarity in fluidity patterns between two rather distant subpopulations within the national society—that is, those of the two major regions of the Czech lands and Slovakia. Apart from their ethnic differentiation, these two regions have followed quite contrasting paths of economic development. The Czech lands became highly industrialized and urbanized during the inter-war period (cf. Smales 1986), while Slovakia remained predominantly rural. After 1948, however, the new regime sought to bring Slovak economic development up to the Czech level and intensive industrialization has been promoted, while, at least in the more recent past, the Czech lands have experienced economic stagnation.

Boguszak (1989) has shown that, if his variant Czechoslovak model is applied to separately constructed Czech and Slovak mobility tables, a very good fit is in fact obtained, even when common parameters are imposed (G^2 = 71.9, df = 64, p = 0.23). In other words, it would appear that, despite their ethnic and historical differences, the two regions have displayed largely similar fluidity patterns over recent decades—a finding which is then explored and elaborated, but essentially confirmed, in a subsequent more detailed analysis (Matĕjů and Boguszak 1989).

---

[18] This same point could indeed be taken as applying in some degree to all three state socialist societies that we consider. However, it is only in the Czechoslovak case that we are aware of evidence to suggest that political affiliations might be of some relatively large significance for the overall pattern of class mobility, as distinct from, say, individuals' promotion chances *within* professional, administrative, or managerial bureaucracies.

Italy

As is shown in Table 5.5, our core model does not give a satisfactory fit to the Italian table, even with nationally specific parameters, and a variant model is thus introduced. This entails changes affecting three cells of the table, as follows:

1. the IN2 and IN3 terms are included in the cell indicating immobility within the class of farm workers, VII*b*;
2. the AF1 term (negative affinity) is included in the pair of cells indicating mobility between the class of farm workers and that of routine non-manual employees, III.

These changes were strongly indicated by residuals under the core model, but are at the same time ones for which it is not difficult to provide a rationale. In Italy the class of agricultural wage-workers comprises, in addition to workers on family farms, a true agricultural proletariat of relatively large size, and one, moreover, whose incomes and living standards have lagged clearly behind those of other groupings (Paci 1979; Pugliese 1981). It might thus be expected that propensities for intergenerational immobility within the farm-worker class would be unusually strong in the Italian case, and likewise that severe barriers would exist to mobility between this class and lower- as well as higher-level white-collar positions.

This interpretation of our Italian variant model is in fact open to test, if only indirectly, in that the agricultural proletariat is quite heavily concentrated on the large estates of the South (de Lillo 1988). If, therefore, the interpretation has merit, it should be found that the core model fits much better when applied to a mobility table for central and northern regions of Italy only. As Table 5.5 further shows, this proves to be the case: no modification to the core model is now required. Indeed, both the fit of the model with fixed parameters and with parameters specifically estimated for the table, which are rather close to core expectations, might well lead one to regard Italy—the South apart—as being a further 'central' nation along with England and France.

On the other hand, we must, of course, recognize that, in contrast with the Czechoslovak case, we do here have evidence of regional variation in social-fluidity patterns. From this standpoint, the much discussed thesis of the 'dualism' of Italian society is amply confirmed: and, in turn, to produce a single model of social fluidity for Italy becomes somewhat problematic. Moreover, our findings could carry wider implications. If we are correct in associating the distinctive features of fluidity in the Italian South with its agrarian class structure—and, specifically, with the presence of a highly disadvantaged agricultural proletariat—then these features might be expected to recur elsewhere, in both other Southern European, and also many Third World nations. If this were to prove the case, it might then be taken to suggest that the FJH hypothesis should in fact be restricted to industrial societies instead of being extended to all those with market economies. But an alternative view would be that what is rather implied is the need to elaborate our class schema so as to distinguish within Class VII*b* between true agricultural proletarians and 'family workers' or 'relatives assisting'— the former being entirely dependent on wages, the latter often working for wages too but having the prospect or indeed expectation of inheriting land and further, perhaps, benefiting in their current level of living from their membership of a property-owning family (cf. Hout 1989: ch. 5).

The Netherlands

Table 5.5 indicates that again with the Netherlands our core model does not fit satisfactorily, without modification, to mobility data for either the 1970s or 1980s. However, we are able to produce a variant model that provides a more or less adequate fit to *both* tables by making the following changes:[19]

1. the class of routine non-manual employees, Class III, is treated as falling in the highest, rather than the intermediate, of the hierarchical levels distinguished within the class schema, and the HI1 and HI2 matrices are adjusted accordingly;
2. the IN3 term is included in the cell indicating immobility within the petty bourgeoisie, Class IV*a+b*.

These changes were again suggested by the pattern of residuals under the core model, and would appear rather extensive; the respecification of hierarchy effects itself bears on twelve cells. However, as is indicated in Table 5.6, in fitting the variant model, the HI1 term proved insignificant and was omitted; and from Table A5.1 it may then be observed that the cell-interaction parameters under the final version of this model are in general not all that far removed from those of the core pattern. Indeed, for the 1970s table, only four out of the forty-nine values reported are less than 75 or greater than 125 (these reflecting relatively strong propensities for immobility within the service class as well as the petty bourgeoisie, together with a weak negative affinity, AF1, term). It can, though, still be seen from this table that the Dutch pattern of fluidity does tend also to be distinctive—as our modification to the core model would imply—in both the high propensity for mobility between the routine non-manual and the service class and the low propensity for mobility between the routine non-manual class and the classes of non-skilled industrial and agricultural workers.

---

[19] As can be seen from Table 5.5, the $G^2(S)$ values returned are a little above the 40 mark that we have usually sought, but, as well as our variant model having here 29 degrees of freedom, we have relaxed our fitting requirement somewhat in virtue of the fact that the model is applied to two different tables.

The relatively advantaged position of routine non-manual workers that is thus indicated by our Dutch data is one for which we have no readily available explanation.[20] However, we would doubt if it is artefactual. It is unlikely to result from an unduly restrictive coding to Class III, since in the Dutch case both Class III *and* Class II are quite large (cf. Luijkx and Ganzeboom 1989). And of particular interest for present purposes is the fact that the same feature emerges in the table for the 1980s as in that for the 1970s, although, as we have noted, both are 'composites', based on three quite independent surveys. It can be seen from Table 5.6 that under the variant model the HI2 term remains virtually unchanged from the 1970s to the 1980s, even though most other effects weaken.

In this last respect we in fact confirm—accepting the Dutch data at face value—the finding of increasing fluidity within the Dutch class structure that Luijkx and Ganzeboom (1989) reach through a different analytical approach. But our model further allows us to specify the source of this increase as being in reduced propensities for immobility within the service class and all other employee classes—as distinct from the petty bourgeoisie and the farmers— and in declining sectoral and affinity effects. The distinctive Dutch hierarchical effect, which implies barriers to mobility only between Classes I+II and III, on the one hand, and Classes IVc, VIIa, and VIIb, on the other, remains unaltered. In other words, the possibility is demonstrated of a national 'peculiarity' in social fluidity persisting over time, even while some more general shift is in train.

Each of the additional cases that we have been able to consider does, then, contribute something further to our knowledge of the ways in which national patterns of social fluidity may vary. And, clearly, the more national tables that can be subsequently analysed, the better our understanding of the range and significance of this variation, relative to our core model, will become. However, we must now take the results presently available to us and turn to the question of what their larger implications would appear to be. In particular, we must ask how, in the light of these results, our ultimate evaluation of the FJH hypothesis may best be stated.

THE FJH HYPOTHESIS REASSESSED

To begin with here, we may once more rehearse the dilemma that has arisen in previous attempts at subjecting the FJH hypothesis to empirical test. If

[20] Two possibilities may, however, be suggested. One is that in the Netherlands lower-level white-collar workers have tended, following the German pattern, to enjoy employment relations more similar to those of higher-level administrative and managerial staff than to those of manual wage-workers. The second is that they have been helped in retaining this advantage by the relatively low labour-market participation rate of Dutch women, which has meant that routine non-manual work in the Netherlands has been less 'feminized' than in most other European nations (but cf. the discussion of Japan, p. 363).

the hypothesis is expressed in a strict form—as, for example, by the CmSF model—in which a complete cross-national similarity in fluidity patterns is postulated, then it undoubtedly fails: significant cross-national differences in fluidity do occur.[21] However, to demonstrate this is not, or not necessarily, to undermine the FJH hypothesis if this is taken in a less strict form in which only a 'basic' cross-national similarity is claimed. And if such a basic similarity—or large commonality—in fluidity patterns could indeed be demonstrated, the sociological interest of such a finding could scarcely be denied. But the difficulty which then arises is that of how the hypothesis in its less strict form may be expressed and modelled so that it remains open to empirical test. How is the idea of a basic cross-national similarity in social fluidity to be either established or refuted?

We have proposed that the hypothesis should be understood as claiming that cross-national differences in fluidity occur as variations on a well-defined theme. This 'theme' we have then attempted to represent by our model of core social fluidity, which can be fitted to the observed mobility data for individual nations, and which can, moreover, be modified in order to capture particular deviations in fluidity from the core pattern. The validity or otherwise of the FJH hypothesis in its less strict form is then a matter that we would wish to determine in the light of the goodness of fit of the core model *and* of the nature of the deviations from it across the nations we consider. The lack of fit of the model will undermine the hypothesis in so far as its extent makes a common theme difficult to discern; and deviations from the model will be damaging in so far as they appear better understood not as variations on a single theme but rather as differences that can be systematic-ally related to other variable attributes of national societies—as would be envisaged in certain of the theories of mobility that we earlier reviewed in Chapter 2. While, therefore, we would not pretend that in its less strict form the FJH hypothesis is open to test through any straightforward statistical operation, we do believe that, in the way we have outlined, its merits, relative to those of alternative hypotheses, can be rationally evaluated on empirical grounds.

As regards the degree of fit of the core model to the fluidity patterns of the twelve nations treated in this chapter, we may say that support for the idea of a sizable commonality does in fact emerge. It is true that the application of the model with fixed parameters leads once more, and as would be expected, to the conclusion that significant cross-national differences in fluidity do occur. But when nationally specific parameters are allowed, the performance of the model in reproducing observed mobility tables is much improved, as indicated by the Δ and rG^2 statistics; and, while the parameter estimates returned quite often show significant differences as between individual

---

[21] If we labour this point, it is because several commentators on our earlier work have represented us as giving far less qualified support to the FJH hypothesis than is in fact the case (see, e.g., Ganzeboom, Luijkx, and Treiman 1989; Kelley 1990; Wong 1990).

nations and the core model, the fact that all parameters take their expected sign is of some consequence. We can at least maintain that both the general hierarchy, inheritance, and sector effects and the more specific affinity and disaffinity effects that our model comprises do tend to operate cross-nationally in the way anticipated, even if with differing strengths.

None the less, since it remains the case that deviations from the core model are frequently revealed, it is the nature of these deviations, and of the interpretations of them that we have offered, that will be crucial to the assessment of the FJH hypothesis at which we will finally arrive. We must, therefore, consider, in the light of our previous analyses, different possible *sources* of variation in fluidity that are of differing degrees of seriousness for the hypothesis as we would construe it.

To begin with, it should be recognized that some variations in fluidity revealed in our analyses may be artefactual—that is, the result simply of defects in the original data or in our subsequent processing of them. In particular, any lack of cross-national comparability in the mobility tables that we have constructed will be likely to produce such spurious variation. Our recoding procedures were, of course, designed to minimize this problem, and, as we have earlier stated, we believe that in most instances the cross-national differences that our analyses show up can be regarded as real. But some 'charity' towards the FJH hypothesis would appear warranted in that our judgement of the quality of our data overall may be optimistic and, further, in that in certain cases we would indeed acknowledge that problems arise.

Most troublesome, perhaps, are those cases where, in collapsing categories of the class schema so as to avoid the Scylla of making non-comparable distinctions between them, we have run into the Charybdis of undue heterogeneity and misleading compositional effects. Thus, seeming national peculiarities in fluidity involving the service class, as found, for example, with the FRG, may be at least partly the result of differences in the relative sizes of the two component classes, I and II; and, likewise, we would think it highly probable that some of the deviation from core fluidity associated with the class of farmers, as, say, in the Irish case, derives from our inability to divide our Class IVc according to type of tenure or the size and value of holdings. In other words, if it were possible to work reliably with a somewhat more differentiated version of the class schema, we might well be able to produce a core model that would often perform better than our present one in fitting national mobility tables.[22]

---

[22] We should also acknowledge the possibility that, even with the version of the class schema that we use, a 'better' core model—i.e. one from which less cross-national deviation would be apparent—might be devised. While we think it unlikely that any major improvement could be achieved overall, we would note the various indications that are to be found (see, e.g., Tables 5.2 and A5.1) that the fluidity patterns of the two nations that we have taken as 'central'—and of England especially—have led us to give our core model a rather too strong sectoral effect.

It has, moreover, to be recognized that certain quite real deviations from core fluidity may be observed without any harm arising to the FJH hypothesis as we would wish to understand it: that is, deviations which are of a more-or-less transient kind, and which would thus be quite compatible with the idea of the fluidity patterns of particular nations 'oscillating' around a core pattern that is shared by all. One likely example that we can document is the unusual propensity found in the Hungarian case for mobility from farm origins into the farm-worker class. This, we have sought to show, reflects the vicissitudes of agricultural policy in the early years of the socialist regime; and it has in fact to be accommodated in modelling the Hungarian table solely on account of the mobility experience of the older men within the sample, upon whom the policy changes impacted. We have also noted that it is the experience of this cohort that chiefly lies behind the unusually strong hierarchical barriers that are revealed in the Hungarian case. And, again, it was among older men in the Polish sample that exceptionally low sectoral barriers were apparent. It would not be surprising to us if, from further research, several other national variations in fluidity that we have noted should likewise appear to be ones that are limited to, or at least especially marked in, certain periods or cohorts—for example, those associated with weak sectoral barriers in the FRG, with fluidity within the rural working class in Ireland or with propensities for immobility in Scotland.

However, we have no doubt that our analyses have also shown up deviations from the core model that are real *and* that express features of national fluidity patterns that are of a persisting rather than a passing kind. In other words, we have found evidence of cross-national variation in social fluidity that can scarcely appear congenial to the FJH hypothesis even in its less strict form. For our present purposes, though, we would still think it important to distinguish among the deviations in question according to the kind of interpretation of them that may be advanced.

Thus, in several instances, the accounts that we have given are ones referring essentially to features of national societies that are of a highly specific, historically formed character. Here the FRG provides perhaps the leading case. We have related the wide deviations from the core pattern that are found in fluidity within the German class structure to such factors as the highly institutionalized nature of differences in employment relations between manual and white-collar workers and the system of vocational training. The first of these can be traced back to the second half of the nineteenth century, being in part a consequence of Bismarckian social policy (Kocka 1981); the origins of the second are to be found even earlier, in pre-unification Germany (Lundgreen 1980–1). The fact that they remain to influence mobility patterns in the FRG in the later twentieth century—and three decades after the supposed *Stunde Null*—does, therefore, well illustrate the way in which 'the long shadow of history' (Mayer 1988) can create problems for attempts at macrosociological generalization. But what has then to be further noted is that the German case is not only problematic for the FJH hypothesis and the claim of a basic similarity in cross-national fluidity patterns; it is no less so for theories that would see these patterns as differing systematically in relation to other societal attributes. For the difficulty here is that features such as the *Angestelltenverhältnisse* or the German 'dual system' of vocational training are ones that cannot be easily subsumed under more generalized variable names, nor thus incorporated into a comparative macrosociology that pursues the Przeworski-Teune programme (see p. 60) of substituting such names for the names of nations.[23]

Furthermore, even where in seeking to explain deviations from core fluidity we have invoked such features as, say, 'sectarian cleavage' or 'uneven development', which might *prima facie* appear more amenable to treatment as variable attributes of societies, we have in fact at the same time referred to their operation within specific national contexts—that is, to *Northern Irish* sectarian cleavage or to *Scottish* uneven development. And even if, then, our interpretations in these particular cases are correct, it does not follow that a consistent cross-national effect will have been demonstrated.

Thus, the point we seek to bring out here is that evidence of cross-national variation in fluidity may, in some instances, have to be regarded as indicating the limits not just of the FJH hypothesis *per se* but of macrosociological analysis more generally. What may be revealed is the boundary at which such analysis must recognize the specificities of historical events, conjunctions, and processes as, so to speak, a 'residual category': that is, as a source of variation that lies outside its own explanatory range. And, in so far as this is the case, the possibility must in turn be recognized that the FJH hypothesis, whatever empirical qualifications to it may be necessary, does in fact sum up what is important about patterns of social fluidity from a macrosociological standpoint; or, in other words, that it is the basic cross-national similarity, rather than variation, in social fluidity that represents the appropriate focus of macrosociological attention.[24]

Finally, though, we have also advanced certain interpretations of national deviations from core fluidity which do suggest that one source of systematic variation at least is conceivable—namely, political intervention. Such interpretations have arisen, on the one hand, with the three Eastern European countries that we have considered, Hungary, Poland, and Czechoslovakia; and, on the other hand, with Sweden. And in Chapter 2 we have already outlined arguments advanced by Parkin and others on why distinctive mobility regimes might be expected in state socialist societies and likewise in liberal democracies in which social democratic parties have been politically dominant. These arguments stand in evident tension with the FJH hypothesis

---

[23] Even though the features in question might be found in some other nations—for example, Austria or Switzerland—resorting to such 'variables' as 'the German cultural area' is clearly no great advance from the Przeworski–Teune standpoint.

[24] This issue is taken up further in Chapter 11.

and, as the last, but perhaps most critical, step in our reassessment of it, we must examine just what degree of support they receive from our analyses.

As regards state socialist societies, the central argument was that of Parkin to the effect that, on account of relatively low 'normative differentiation' between classes, as well as official selection policies in education and employment, state socialist societies will display a greater propensity for *long-range* mobility than do capitalist ones. In the case of one of our Eastern European nations, Poland, this argument is strongly borne out: the Polish pattern of fluidity deviates from the core model in essentially the way that Parkin would envisage. However (as reference to Table A5.1 will show), the other two cases fail to provide any confirmation. So far as mobility between service-class and industrial working-class positions is concerned, Hungary in fact appears as one of the least open of our nations, while Czechoslovakia is in this respect close to the core pattern, although tending otherwise to show greater fluidity. Only in the relatively favourable mobility chances of agricultural workers might the three state socialist societies be said to display a common feature—and this would seem best understood as an aspect of generally low *sectoral* rather than hierarchical barriers. Moreover, while in the Hungarian and Czechoslovak cases an increase in the propensity for intersectoral mobility may be seen as a result of the collectivization of agriculture—even if not as its prime purpose—this explanation can clearly not apply to Poland; and it might be added that comparably low sectoral barriers are also found in some of our capitalist nations.

In sum, while the results and interpretations that we have presented could lend support to the claim that state socialist regimes have been able to influence fluidity, they do not suggest that, as a consequence, a *distinctive* state socialist pattern emerges. It would here seem relevant to observe that among state socialist societies, over the period to which our data relate, economic and social conditions varied widely, and that so too did the goals and priorities that their regimes adopted as well as the effectiveness of their policies. We have, for example, had occasion to refer.to various differences between, and shifts in, policies, not only towards the peasantry but likewise towards the intelligentsia and the petty bourgeoisie. Given, then, that under state socialism attempts to promote or regulate mobility by political intervention are likely yet are uncertain in their actual direction and impact, while at the same time largely unintended effects on mobility may follow from other policies, the main comparison to be drawn with capitalist societies may simply be that state socialist societies are *more* differentiated in the fluidity patterns that they display.

Turning then to the question of political influences on mobility in capitalist societies in which social democratic parties have been prominent in government, we are, of course, handicapped by the fact that Sweden is the only such case that we cover. Our finding that in Sweden a distinctively high level of fluidity prevails is certainly consistent with Parkin's expectations, and likewise with those of Stephens. We would, moreover, be ready to support the arguments of these authors further in seeing the openness of Swedish society as indeed being, in part at least, a political accomplishment because we can in fact point to specific policies and to certain empirically established consequences that would be conducive to this outcome—and going perhaps more in the direction of the generally greater equality of condition envisaged by Stephens than in that of Parkin's 'meritocratic' version of socialism.[25]

However, while it may be only social democratic governments that are likely to implement strongly egalitarian policies of the kind that are in question here, it does not follow that they will always do so. And we would, therefore, again wish to insist (cf. Erikson 1990) that it is not on the political character of regimes that attention should focus, but rather on the policies that they do actually take up and the forcefulness with which these policies are pursued. In those cases where social democratic parties have quite often been in government but have not aimed at, or succeeded in, pushing through egalitarian programmes, there would seem little reason for expecting any influence on mobility to be revealed. In other words, we may recognize a *Swedish* pattern of social fluidity, and also accept the probability that this has in some degree been shaped by Swedish social democratic politics. But the idea of a generic social democratic pattern represents quite a different proposition: one which we are not ourselves in a position to test directly but which, on the grounds that we have indicated, we would none the less regard with some degree of scepticism.[26]

In the light of our results on political influences on mobility, we would then believe that the FJH hypothesis is in need of some qualification—but that this must be rather carefully stated. The way in which Featherman, Jones, and Hauser, in their original paper, limit the range of applicability of

[25] Although some evidence has been produced to indicate a slight reduction in class inequalities in educational opportunity in Sweden during the 1960s (Jonsson 1990, 1991), it is, as we have earlier suggested, the evidence of the egalitarian redistribution of material resources, via fiscal and social policies, that in comparative perspective is most impressive. It might be added here that Pöntinen (1983: ch. 8) finds that Norway, the other capitalist nation within which some degree of social democratic hegemony might be claimed, has, if anything, a yet higher level of fluidity than Sweden. And support for the general proposition that equality of condition and of opportunity are positively associated can further be derived from the European case that stands in perhaps greatest contrast with the Scandinavian social democracies, namely, that of Ireland (see further Goldthorpe 1980a/1987: 320–1).

[26] Hauser and Grusky (1988; and cf. also Grusky and Hauser 1984) have claimed a social democratic effect on relative mobility chances, using mobility data from twenty-two nations and a measure of 'social democratic policies' which in fact refers to 'the proportion of seats in the national legislature held by socialist or "social democratic" parties averaged over the elections immediately preceding and following 1960' (1988: 739). However, even though this claim is more modest than one of a distinctive social democratic pattern of fluidity, questions about its validity can still be raised, which pertain not only to data comparability but further to the fact that no processes are spelt out that actually link numbers of seats in legislatures with differences in fluidity. As argued elsewhere, it would seem dangerous from the point of view of model specification simply to assume 'that the proportion of parliamentarians belonging to similarly denominated parties is monotonically related to policies intended to influence the class structure and thereby to rates of social fluidity' (Erikson 1990).

their hypothesis is, in our view, significant. As we earlier noted, they intend it to apply to all societies 'with a market economy and a nuclear family system' (1975: 340). Although the reasons for this limitation are not spelt out in any detail, we would take the underlying assumption to be that it is economic and familial institutions—the two great pillars of 'civil society'—that primarily determine relative chances of social mobility from one generation to the next. Thus, provided that these institutions have a basically similar form, so too, it may be expected, will the pattern that such mobility chances display. What is left out of the formulation of the hypothesis is any reference to the part that may be played in shaping social fluidity by political institutions or, more precisely, by purposive action taken through such institutions. In other words, no reference is made to the possible role of the *state* as an agency of intervention in, and against, the processes of 'civil society' through which inequalities of opportunity are 'spontaneously' generated and perpetuated.

We would, therefore, suggest that the FJH hypothesis might be refined in such a way as to acknowledge this point. That is to say, its conformity with empirical results would at all events be closer if it were to claim that a basic similarity will be found in patterns of social fluidity across industrial societies—and, we would add, following the operation of factors expressed in our core model—*to the extent that* no sustained effort has been made to use the power of a modern state apparatus in order to modify the processes, or the outcomes of the processes, through which class inequalities are produced and intergenerationally reproduced.

However, in arguing thus we do not wish to imply that one could actually construct macrosociological variables that would characterize political regimes or state structures by their ideological or institutional features and that would then provide the key to a sytematic explanation of difference in fluidity patterns. We have presented clear evidence against the idea of a typical state socialist pattern, and reasons for supposing that a typical social democratic one might prove no less difficult to find. One may identify the kinds of regime that are likely to have the will and the potential to influence mobility processes and, in turn, societies in which relatively wide deviations from core fluidity may be expected. But it is another matter to predict just what the extent and nature of these deviations will actually be. Political intervention, we would argue, has to be regarded as a factor which, by its very nature—by its voluntarism, by the diversity of the particular goals to which it may be directed (even under the same ideological banner), and, above all, by the uncertainty of its outcomes—is more useful in helping to account for variation in fluidity patterns after the fact than in a predictive mode.

Finally, we may suggest that the qualification to the FJH hypothesis that we have put forward leads to at least part of an answer to the question we earlier recognized of why it should be England and France that stand as our two 'central' nations: those, we have thus assumed, that provide the closest empirical approximation to the core pattern of fluidity or, that is, to the theme around which we would see cross-national variation as occurring. England and France, it could be said, are two nations which have moved towards mature industrialism as independent political entities and which, as well as following a capitalist path, have for the most part been characterized by political conditions under which the processes of 'civil society' that shape fluidity patterns have been allowed to operate with a minimum of intervention via the state.

This is not, we would stress, to represent these nations as being in some way archetypes of 'liberal' capitalism, and still less to suppose that they share in similar 'state traditions'—which they clearly do not. What, rather, we would see as crucial is that in England and France not only has the increase or repatterning of social mobility been rarely, if at all, an immediate policy objective, as it has in state socialist societies, but further no serious, and certainly no successful, attempt has been made to use the apparatus of the state to reduce the overall extent of class inequalities, as, say, under Swedish social democracy. Further still, in the course of industrialization, relatively little political effort was given to influencing the form of employment relations—and hence the class locations—of new groupings emerging within the changing occupational structure, as occurred, most obviously, in the German case. Thus, for example, as Kocka (1980*a*: ch. 5) has pointed out, while from the end of the nineteenth century the division between 'white-collar' and 'blue-collar' workers became strongly embedded in German public law, it achieved very little legal significance in England, and less in France than in most other continental European nations. In other words, what is important here is not the general question of whether or how far the English or French states should be seen as 'weak' or 'strong', but that of the specific ends towards which in these nations the power of the state has—or rather has *not*—been politically directed.[27]

To summarize, then, we have in the course of this chapter identified two main sources of cross-national variation in social fluidity that might appear threatening to the FJH hypothesis even in its less strict form. First, highly specific, historically formed features of national societies—usually, it would seem, of an institutional rather than of a more diffuse cultural kind—may create a distinctiveness in their fluidity patterns that cannot be dismissed as merely transient. Secondly, political intervention into social structures and processes is also capable of modifying fluidity patterns, even though the

[27] It should in particular be noted that French *étatisme* has always been highly selective in its scope and especially in regard to economic relations (cf. Hoffman 1963).

We say that we provide here only part of an answer to the question of why England and France should be central nations, since it is evident from what has gone before that deviations from core fluidity may result from a great diversity of circumstance. However, we would believe that non-intervention by the state may be taken as being a necessary, if not a sufficient, condition of 'centrality'. See further, on the US case, Chapter 9, p. 321 and n. 11.

degree of its effectiveness must always be regarded as problematic. The cross-national variation deriving from these sources is by no means sociologically negligible, and, at least in comparing national cases pairwise, one might often be more impressed by the contrasts between them than by their conformity to any standard pattern (cf. Müller 1986; Goldthorpe 1980*a*/1987: ch. 11).

However, our results would at the same time allow two important points to be advanced in favour of the FJH hypothesis. First, the 'theme', or commonality, in social-fluidity patterns that we have represented by our core model never disappears from sight—the effects that it postulates are generally present and indeed account for a large proportion of the total cross-national variation in association between class origins and destinations; and, secondly, the cross-national differences in fluidity that do show up as deviations from this model are not, at least in any obvious way, systematic. Thus, the argument may be made that these differences will in fact be more accurately understood, not as variation that occurs in relation to that among other generalizable attributes of national societies, but rather as 'variation on a theme' that is induced by more specific—institutional or political—factors that can at best be only partially brought within the scope of comparative macrosociological, as distinct from historical analysis.

This is in fact the argument that we would regard as most tenable in the light of the results that we—and indeed other investigators—have thus far presented. While it acknowledges that cross-national differences in fluidity are indeed apparent, it leads to an acceptance of the FJH hypothesis, construed and qualified on lines that we have indicated, as being still preferable in its claim of a 'basic' similarity to rival hypotheses that would imply more sociologically ambitious attempts at explanation of these differences, whether in terms either of 'types' or of 'trends'.[28] We may indeed here return to our suggestion made at the end of Chapter 3 that it is the degree of cross-national commonality in relative mobility rates that is chiefly reflected in their evident temporal constancy. As we have made clear, we would not wish to regard all variation in social fluidity that shows up cross-nationally as reflecting no more than transient departures from a core pattern that will tend always to reassert itself; there are strong indications that some aspects of national distinctiveness are of a more lasting kind. None the less, it remains, in our view, a reasonable supposition that, if effects can be identified—as in our core model—that give rise to a cross-national commonality, these same effects will also operate to restrict the degree and the direction of changes over time in the fluidity patterns that particular nations display.

---

[28] Since it was the main focus of the analyses of Chapter 3, we have not here returned explicitly to the liberal claim of a positive association between level of industrial development and level of fluidity. But it is fairly apparent that our case-by-case analyses of European nations lend no more support to it from a cross-sectional standpoint than did the cohort analyses previously presented. A more systematic comparative analysis is undertaken in Chapter 11.

ANNEX: Comparing Cell-Interaction Parameters under Different Versions of the Core Model

As we observe in Chapter 5, it is difficult to interpret, and thus to compare, the *absolute* values of the cell-interaction parameters that are produced under different versions of the core model. This is so because such values reflect the constraints that need to be imposed on the log-linear model in order to make the estimation of parameters possible, and because different sets of constraints can be chosen (Holt 1979). As noted in Chapter 4, we ourselves work with the system of parameter estimation of the GLIM program, not because this can claim any objective superiority but because it would appear to be that most apt to our substantive concerns (cf. Wilson 1979).

With the GLIM system, the parameter for the first level of each term in a model is set at zero, and parameters for other levels are estimated relative to this on the log scale. Thus, under our core model, a zero interaction parameter can be given to all cells at the 'neutral-fluidity' level—that is, to all cells in which no hierarchy, inheritance, sector, or affinity effects are postulated—and other interaction levels can then be interpreted as being so much above or below neutral fluidity. Moreover, the fact that the neutral-fluidity level will remain at zero across all of our national variant models is of particular convenience to us in pursuing our comparative concerns.

This is the case because, while one cannot directly compare cell-interaction parameters estimated under these models, one *can* compare such parameters indirectly: that is, in terms of their *differences from some reference parameter*, since these differences will in fact be *in*variant to the system of parameter estimation that is applied (cf. Long 1984). It is therefore, on such differences that, for comparative purposes, our attention should be focused; and the most obvious procedure for us to follow is to make such comparisons in terms of *differences from the neutral-fluidity level*.

To illustrate, we may consider the interaction parameters in the I+II–I+II cell—i.e. that indicating immobility within the service class—that we obtain under our models for England and for France. Since for both these nations we accept the core model (with nationally specific effect parameters), the cell-interaction parameter in question is in each case given by IN1 + IN2 (cf. Table 4.3). Thus, for England, we estimate this parameter, in log-additive form, as $0.47 + 0.71 = 1.18$, and for France as $0.41 + 0.92 = 1.33$. Given, then, that, with our GLIM parameterization, the neutral-fluidity level is always 0, the foregoing values will *also* represent the differences between the English and French cell parameters and the neutral-fluidity level. However, with a different system, it should be noted, we would here obtain different estimates. With, for example, the parameterization of the LOGLIN program, the interaction parameter for the I+II–I+II cell in the English table would be 1.24, and in the French table 1.11. Thus, if we were to compare the English and French cell parameters *directly*, our results would vary from one system to the other: $1.18 - 1.33 = -0.15$ with GLIM as compared with $1.24 - 1.11 = 0.13$ with LOGLIN. But what has further to be noted is that, using LOGLIN, it will *not* be the case that cells at the neutral-fluidity level will always have an interaction parameter of 0: rather, the neutral-fluidity parameter will differ from case to case. It would in fact be 0.06 for England and -0.22 for France. It can then be seen that, if we compare the English and French parameters not directly but *in relation to neutral fluidity*, we obtain the same result, whichever parameterization is adopted—though we reach it more simply via GLIM:

$$
\begin{array}{lllll}
\text{ENG} & \text{GLIM:} & 1.18 & - & 0.00 & = 1.18 \\
& \text{LOGLIN:} & 1.24 & - & 0.06 & = 1.18 \\
\\
\text{FRA} & \text{GLIM:} & 1.33 & - & 0.00 & = 1.33 \\
& \text{LOGLIN:} & 1.11 & -(-0.22) & = 1.33
\end{array}
$$

In other words, we could say that in England the interaction level in the I+II–I+II cell—that is, the propensity for immobility within the service class—is ($e^{1.18} = 3.25$) three-and-a-quarter times greater than the neutral-fluidity level, while in France it is ($e^{1.33} = 3.78$) three-and-three-quarter times greater.

However, given that we must in fact deal with more than just two nations, it will be better to proceed not via multiple pairwise comparisons but rather by adopting a common standard against which each nation can be matched; and such a standard is of course readily provided by our core model. In Table A5.1 we thus show the results of comparing the difference between each cell parameter under each of our national variant models and the neutral-fluidity parameter with the corresponding difference under the core model. We include here results for the nine European nations represented in our data-set, for the three additional European nations that we have considered in the preceding chapter, and also for the three non-European nations whose fluidity patterns we will examine later in the book.

The comparisons made in Table A5.1 are expressed in percentage terms. Thus, a value of 100 in the table means that, in this case, the cell parameter is the same as it would be under the core model, and in turn the same 'distance' away from the neutral-fluidity level. (Values of exactly 100 are most often found in those cells which, under both the core model and most national variants, are specified as ones where neutral fluidity prevails.) Correspondingly, a value of 50 would mean that the cell parameter under a variant model is only half the distance from the neutral-fluidity level of the corresponding parameter under the core model; while a value of 200 would mean that it is twice the distance away.

If we return to our previous example of the I+II–I+II cell, for which the parameter under the core model is $0.43 + 0.81 = 1.24$, we thus obtain in the English case

$$100 \ e^{1.18 \ - \ 1.24} \approx 94$$

and in the French case

$$100 \ e^{1.33 \ - \ 1.24} \approx 110.$$

The general formula applied in Table A5.1 is

$$100 \ e^{m_{ij}(\ (I_{vij} \ - \ I_{v0}) \ - \ (I_{cij} \ - \ I_{c0}) \ )}$$

where I_{vij} is the interaction parameter in the ijth cell of a national variant model, I_{v0} is the parameter for neutral fluidity under that model, I_{cij} is the parameter in the ijth cell of the core model, and I_{c0} is the parameter for neutral fluidity under the core model. If $(I_{cij} - I_{c0}) \geq 0$, then $m_{ij} = 1$, while if $(I_{cij} - I_{c0}) < 0$, then $m_{ij} = -1$. Where the GLIM system is used and the neutral-fluidity parameter is therefore in all cases 0, the above formula can obviously be simplified.

We refer to the entries in Table A5.1 as 'percentages' in that, if parameters are taken in multiplicative form, the entries show the ratios of cell para-meters under national variant models to the corresponding neutral-fluidity parameters as percentages of the corresponding ratios under the core model. Entries that refer to cell-interaction parameters that are below the neutral-fluidity level are printed in italic, while those that refer to parameters that are at or above this level are in roman. Usually, then, all entries in a column within a panel of the table will be in either italic or roman, but some exceptions—representing major deviations from core fluidity—are to be observed.

It may incidentally be noted that the average of the forty-nine percentages for a nation shown in Table A5.1 will be highly correlated, with the β parameter for that nation estimated under a model which is the analogue of that of equation (3.2)—i.e. where k in the model stands for nation rather than for cohort and the model is thus taken as one of uniform difference among nations rather than as one of uniform change over cohorts (see pp. 91–2 above and pp. 381–2 below).

TABLE A5.1. *Differences between cell-interaction parameters under national variant models and the neutral-fluidity level compared, in percentage terms, with the corresponding differences under the core model*

		I+II	III	IV*a*+*b*	IV*c*	V+VI	VII*a*	VII*b*
I+II	ENG	94	104	104	*114*	*94*	88	*106*
	FRA	110	98	98	*89*	*102*	*107*	92
	FRG	47	84	84	*61*	*111*	*130*	54
	HUN	47	84	*56*	*66*	*112*	*140*	68
	IRL	141	147	147	*36*	80	*81*	79
	NIR	96	86	86	*108*	*107*	103	48
	POL	209	79	128	*50*	49	37	27
	SCO	133	130	130	*113*	80	71	75
	SWE	73	97	97	*63*	*94*	97	30
	CZE	66	84	84	*60*	99	94	34
	ITA	106	77	77	70	92	127	144
	ITA–CN	121	87	87	66	93	113	173
	NET–70s	130	120	120	78	80	82	58
	NET–80s	72	106	106	62	80	*80*	35
	AUS	49	84	84	73	*149*	*109*	52
	JAP	60	97	97	62	*186*	*122*	37
	USA	62	111	91	65	92	*80*	67
III	ENG	104	105	100	*121*	100	*94*	*114*
	FRA	98	98	100	87	100	*102*	89
	FRG	84	107	148	55	100	*111*	61
	HUN	84	107	100	59	100	*112*	66
	IRL	147	161	100	84	100	80	67
	NIR	86	106	100	*101*	100	*107*	108
	POL	79	138	100	62	100	80	50
	SCO	130	65	100	*141*	100	80	113
	SWE	97	86	100	67	100	*94*	63
	CZE	84	86	100	*60*	100	99	60
	ITA	77	83	100	76	100	92	226
	ITA–CN	87	86	100	71	100	93	66
	NET–70s	120	117	100	97	100	125	122
	NET–80s	106	99	100	77	100	*122*	93
	AUS	84	86	100	71	*145*	*102*	73
	JAP	97	136	100	66	100	*94*	62
	USA	111	98	100	71	100	92	65
IV*a*+*b*	ENG	104	100	94	*124*	100	*94*	*114*
	FRA	98	100	110	87	100	*102*	89
	FRG	84	148	152	59	100	*111*	61
	HUN	*56*	100	130	62	100	*112*	66

		I+II	III	IVa+b	IVc	V+VI	VIIa	VIIb
	IRL	147	100	141	*71*	100	80	*67*
	NIR	86	100	96	*56*	100	*107*	*108*
	POL	128	100	209	*60*	100	80	*50*
	SCO	130	100	133	*135*	100	80	*113*
	SWE	97	100	73	*73*	100	*94*	*63*
	CZE	84	100	66	*72*	100	*99*	*60*
	ITA	*77*	100	106	*107*	100	*92*	*70*
	ITA–CN	87	100	121	*88*	100	*93*	*66*
	NET–70s	120	100	188	*101*	100	80	*78*
	NET–80s	106	100	176	*90*	100	80	*62*
	AUS	84	100	49	*83*	100	*102*	*73*
	JAP	97	100	60	*72*	100	*94*	*62*
	USA	91	100	62	*85*	100	*92*	*65*
IVc	ENG	*107*	*114*	*117*	83	*114*	*124*	100
	FRA	*94*	*89*	*89*	111	*89*	*87*	100
	FRG	*71*	*61*	*65*	460	*61*	*59*	100
	HUN	*83*	*66*	*70*	44	*66*	*62*	244
	IRL	*36*	*67*	*57*	150	*67*	*71*	187
	NIR	*104*	*108*	*60*	146	*108*	*108*	100
	POL	*38*	*50*	*48*	69	*50*	*60*	100
	SCO	*101*	*113*	*108*	146	*113*	*135*	100
	SWE	*65*	*63*	*68*	65	*63*	*73*	100
	CZE	*56*	*60*	*72*	26	*60*	*72*	100
	ITA	*96*	*70*	*99*	101	*70*	*107*	100
	ITA–CN	*81*	*66*	*82*	145	*66*	*88*	100
	NET–70s	*80*	*122*	*81*	90	*78*	*101*	100
	NET–80s	*61*	*93*	*73*	84	*62*	*90*	100
	AUS	*78*	*73*	*85*	56	*54*	*83*	100
	JAP	*41*	*62*	*68*	55	*62*	*72*	100
	USA	*69*	*65*	*78*	63	*49*	*85*	100
V+VI	ENG	*94*	100	100	*121*	105	104	*114*
	FRA	*102*	100	100	*87*	98	98	*89*
	FRG	*111*	100	100	*55*	107	84	*61*
	HUN	*112*	100	100	*59*	107	84	*66*
	IRL	80	100	100	*84*	161	147	*67*
	NIR	*107*	100	100	*101*	106	86	*108*
	POL	49	100	100	*62*	138	128	*50*
	SCO	80	100	100	*141*	122	130	*113*
	SWE	*94*	100	100	*67*	86	97	*63*
	CZE	*99*	100	100	*60*	86	84	*60*
	ITA	*92*	100	100	*76*	83	77	*70*

TABLE A5.1. (*cont.*)

		I+II	III	IV*a+b*	IV*c*	V+VI	VII*a*	VII*b*
	ITA–CN	93	100	100	71	86	87	66
	NET–70s	80	100	100	97	117	120	78
	NET–80s	80	100	100	77	99	106	62
	AUS	102	100	100	71	86	84	73
	JAP	94	100	100	66	136	97	62
	USA	92	100	100	71	98	91	65
VII*a*	ENG	88	94	94	114	104	105	121
	FRA	107	102	102	89	98	98	87
	FRG	213	183	183	61	84	107	55
	HUN	140	112	112	66	84	107	59
	IRL	81	80	80	67	147	161	45
	NIR	103	107	107	108	86	106	101
	POL	37	80	80	50	128	138	62
	SCO	71	80	80	113	130	122	141
	SWE	97	94	94	63	97	86	67
	CZE	94	99	99	60	84	86	60
	ITA	127	92	92	70	77	83	76
	ITA–CN	113	93	93	66	87	86	71
	NET–70s	82	125	80	78	120	117	97
	NET–80s	80	122	80	62	106	99	77
	AUS	109	102	102	73	84	86	71
	JAP	62	94	94	62	97	136	66
	USA	80	92	92	65	91	98	71
VII*b*	ENG	106	114	114	94	114	124	105
	FRA	92	89	89	102	89	87	98
	FRG	54	100	100	111	61	59	107
	HUN	68	66	66	112	66	62	107
	IRL	79	67	67	80	67	71	161
	NIR	48	108	108	107	108	108	106
	POL	27	50	50	80	50	60	138
	SCO	75	113	113	80	113	135	65
	SWE	30	63	63	94	63	73	86
	CZE	34	60	60	99	60	72	86
	ITA	144	226	70	92	70	107	549
	ITA–CN	173	66	66	93	66	88	86
	NET–70s	58	122	78	80	78	101	117
	NET–80s	35	93	62	80	62	90	99
	AUS	52	73	73	102	54	83	86
	JAP	37	62	62	94	62	72	306
	USA	67	65	65	92	49	85	98

6
Absolute Rates of Class Mobility

In this chapter we return to the consideration of absolute mobility rates. In Chapter 3 we examined trends over time in absolute rates of intergenerational mobility within the nine European nations represented in our data-set. On the basis of our analyses, we were able to identify several broad regularities: a decline in immobility within the farm sector, an increase in mobility from farm origins into manual employment, and some upturn also in mobility from both farm and manual origins into service-class positions. However, we were in general more impressed by the evidence of such rates of outflow mobility moving in *different* directions, both from period to period and from nation to nation; and, moreover, no clear and cross-nationally consistent trends emerged in the case of total mobility rates. Thus, we concluded that, overall, our results gave less support to the expectation of liberal theorists of a steady and convergent rise in mobility rates as nations progressed in their industrial development than to the hypothesis advanced by Sorokin that, over time, levels of mobility would show merely 'trendless fluctuation'.

In the present chapter we begin with the question of the degree of variation that is revealed in absolute rates when these are viewed not as they change over successive birth-cohorts within our nine nations but, rather, as they are expressed in the collective mobility experience of the male populations of these nations as of the early and mid-1970s: that is, at the end of the 'long boom' of the post-war years, in the course of which, we have argued, the process of European industrialization was completed. We show that cross-national variation is in this perspective quite substantial; and, further, that such variation must indeed be expected, if only because of the very different structural contexts of mobility that our nations provide, even though all could be regarded as having entered into the industrial world.

In the second section of the chapter we then seek to develop this latter argument in a more precise way. If the FJH hypothesis could in fact stand in its strictest form—in which the pattern of relative rates is claimed to be *identical* from nation to nation—it would, of course, follow that the cross-national variation observed in absolute rates must derive *entirely* from structural effects: that is, from effects mediated through the marginal distributions of mobility tables, and reflecting differences, and changes, in the sizes of the classes on which these tables are based. However, as we have seen in the preceding chapter, the hypothesis clearly cannot be accepted in this form, but only in a weaker one in which some degree of variation in relative rates is not precluded. Thus, the question is posed—and we attempt to respond to it—of the comparative importance in generating variation in absolute mobility rates of structural effects, on the one hand, and of variation in relative rates, or, that is, in patterns of social fluidity, on the other. In the outcome, we find that structural effects are without doubt the dominant ones—and to this extent the force of the FJH hypothesis, even in the modified form that we have proposed, is underlined. But in turn we are then forced back to the issue raised earlier in our discussion of mobility trends of how far variation in absolute rates, understood as the outcome primarily of structural effects, is amenable to sociological explanation or has rather to be accepted—in view of the diversity and frequent singularity of the factors shaping structural contexts—as a matter essentially for historical description. We again find it difficult to avoid the latter view.

In the third section of the chapter we then approach the problem of generalizing about mobility at the level of absolute rates from a different and less familiar angle. That is, we take classes themselves, rather than nations, as the primary focus of our analyses. Instead of attempting to find regularities in national rates of mobility considered across classes, we seek them rather in the rates of mobility associated with particular classes considered across nations—and we include here data on intra- as well as intergenerational transitions. This approach, we seek to show, is the more sociologically promising in that it more fully reveals how the effects of the 'genotypical' commonality that, in our view, prevails in relative rates within industrial societies is expressed at the 'phenotypical' level of absolute rates—or, in other words, is expressed at the level at which mobility, or immobility, is actually experienced in the lives of the individuals involved.

CROSS-NATIONAL VARIATION IN ABSOLUTE RATES

In our conclusion to Chapter 1 we remarked that, while different and often conflicting theories of social mobility in industrial society existed in rather embarrassing profusion, one at least did now appear to be generally discounted: namely, that advanced by Lipset and Zetterberg and associated with the hypothesis that across industrial nations the overall pattern of observed—that is, absolute—mobility rates was 'much the same'. Since the time this theory was first suggested, we noted, evidence of significant cross-national variation in such rates had accumulated; and, with the formulation of the FJH hypothesis, the search for cross-national similarity in mobility patterns had been redirected from the level of absolute to that of relative rates. However, despite this lack of success of the LZ hypothesis, we wish here to take it as our starting-point: not, we hasten to add, because we seek in any way to revive it, but because we believe that it is instructive to examine the reasons for its failure in some detail.

In Table 6.1 we present various data for our nine European nations that are relevant to this purpose. In the first column of the table we show the

6. *Absolute Rates of Class Mobility*

TABLE 6.1. *Total mobility rates (TMR) as between manual (M) and non-manual (NM) classes for men of non-farm origins in non-farm destinations, manual to non-manual rates, non-manual to manual rates, proportions of national samples covered, and total mobility rates based on the sevenfold version of the class schema*

Nation	TMR (2 classes)	M to NM (% mobile)	NM to M (% mobile)	% of sample covered*	TMR (7 classes)
ENG	33	33	33	91	65
FRA	34	35	32	66	65
FRG	32	30	35	83	62
HUN	33	23	47	50	76
IRL	30	27	32	52	58
NIR	33	31	33	70	63
POL	32	25	44	41	60
SCO	32	29	36	88	64
SWE	37	36	40	67	73

Note:
* That is, after exclusion of all men of farm origins and/or farm destinations.

percentage of men in each nation who were intergenerationally mobile either from manual class origins to non-manual destinations or vice versa (using the collapse of the class schema that is given in the final column of Table 2.1). It is in fact this figure that Lipset and Zetterberg take 'in order to get some index of the total mobility in society' (1959: 24), and that which they then see as best bringing out the cross-national similarity that they claim. For those nations for which they could compute the index, they obtained a median value of 28 per cent and a range of 23–31 per cent.

From examination of the first column of Table 6.1 it might well appear that what we have managed to provide here is yet stronger confirmation of the LZ hypothesis than its authors themselves were able to do. The level of mobility indicated is somewhat higher than they found, averaging 33 per cent, but the variation is less: only one nation, Sweden, falls outside a range of 30–34 per cent.[1] Such a result, we may add, could perhaps have been

[1] The corresponding rates for the three additional nations that we included in the analyses of the previous chapter are: Czechoslovakia, 34 per cent; Italy, 38 per cent; Netherlands 1970s, 32 per cent; and Netherlands 1980s, 36 per cent. We do not, however, attempt to treat these nations systematically in the present chapter, since we have available only basic intergenerational mobility tables which, moreover, in the case of Czechoslovakia and Italy, are for a decade later than those comprised by our own data-set and, in the case of the Netherlands (where we have both 1970s and 1980s tables), have unreliable marginal distributions as a result, it would seem, of high levels of non-response. Such a defect, as we earlier noted, must be regarded as yet more serious where it is absolute rather than relative rates that are under consideration.

We may also note here that, in dealing with absolute rates in the form of percentages based on the total samples of our national enquiries, or on major divisions of these samples, we do not take up questions of the statistical significance of observed differences. In view of the size of the samples involved, it may be generally assumed that such differences that appear worthy of

anticipated from Figures 3.8 and 3.9 above, in which we showed mobility between our manual and non-manual classes as fluctuating over time in our nine nations but mostly in the range of 25–50 per cent. Why, then, it may be asked, can the LZ hypothesis not be accepted?

One difficulty, which Lipset and Zetterberg do in fact recognize from their own data, is that, if their index of total mobility is split into its two components—as is done in the second and third columns of Table 6.1—a greater degree of cross-national variation is at once revealed. That is to say, nations with very similar total rates may show clearly different 'balances' of manual-to-non-manual and non-manual-to-manual mobility: compare, for example, France and Hungary. In other words, Lipset's and Zetterberg's index—like any other 'one-number' measure of mobility—is inadequate to the examination of similarity or variation in mobility *patterns*.

However, the major objection to the index is that brought out in the fourth column of Table 6.1, in which we show for each of our nations the proportion of the total sample to which the index refers. As can be seen, these proportions vary widely, from around 90 per cent in the cases of England and Scotland to a half or less in the cases of Hungary, Ireland, and Poland. In other words, the exclusion of men of farm origins and/or destinations has, as might be expected, a strongly differential effect—and the validity of the index as a comparative measure of 'the total mobility in society' is for this reason seriously undermined. All industrial societies comprise agricultural sectors, even if in all cases contracting ones; and, further, the way in which the contraction of the agricultural sector has occurred—its speed and its phasing in relation to other aspects of structural change—is crucial in defining the different developmental paths through which industrialization has been achieved. Thus, in leaving out of account mobility that in any way involves agricultural classes, Lipset's and Zetterberg's index carries a strong, and quite inappropriate, bias in favour of the hypothesis of cross-national similarity that they seek to establish (cf. Jones 1969).[2]

In the final column of Table 6.1 we then give the total mobility rate for each nation calculated on the basis of the sevenfold version of our class schema, and thus of course applying to the whole sample in each case. The percentages are higher than those in the first column of the table, since the number of classes involved is larger, but it can also be seen that cross-national variation is now greater; and, while mobility to or from the agriculture sector is not the only source of this, it clearly plays an important

comment from a sociological standpoint will in fact be statistically significant also, and we shall in any event be mainly concerned with patterns of variation rather than with differences between particular rates.

[2] In all fairness to Lipset and Zetterberg, it should be said that they do, indeed, present analyses of national mobility rates on a threefold—manual, non-manual, farm—basis (1959: 19–21). They do not, however, appear to appreciate the—very negative—significance of these results for the central hypothesis that they advance.

part. Thus, from the earlier analyses of Chapter 3 not only do we know that the figure for Ireland and Poland of *c*.60 per cent is the outcome of a steady increase in mobility from, however, an exceptionally low level associated with extensive peasant agriculture but, further, that the figure of 76 per cent for Hungary reflects the massive political intervention in the organization of agriculture of the immediate post-war years, and that of 73 per cent for Sweden, a particulárly rapid decline in the primary sector of the economy over the period covered by our data.

Although, therefore, as we argued in Chapter 3, there may be some truth in Lipset's and Zetterberg's suggestion that a surge in mobility tends to occur at some stage in the industrialization process—though not necessarily at the same one in all nations alike—our data show that it in no way follows from this that absolute mobility rates will subsequently emerge that are of a highly standardized kind.

We noted in Chapter 1 that Lipset and Zetterberg ground their hypothesis of such cross-national similarity in the argument that variation in mobility rates derives essentially from structural effects rather than from endogenous mobility processes, and that, once industrialization has reached a certain level, these effects will become more-or-less uniform. But, whatever merit the first of these claims may possess, it is the weakness of the second that most obviously jeopardizes their position. As we earlier observed (pp. 102–4), quite extensive evidence has been produced to show that industrial societies do not in fact converge in their development on some modal occupational or class structure. Even though changes in certain directions may regularly occur, differences in their speed and timing are in themselves sufficient for structural differences still to persist, quite apart from other more specific sources of variation—such as political intervention. This point we can, in fact, well illustrate from our own data.

In Table 6.2 we give in the first two panels the distributions of origin and destination classes for the men in each of our nine national·samples and in the third panel, two half-matrices of Δ values relating to each pairwise comparison of origin and destination distributions respectively.

Starting from the Δ values, it can be seen that origin distributions display wide cross-national differences. The discrepancy is 30 per cent or over in a third of all the comparisons made and 20 per cent or over in two-thirds. Destination distributions are somewhat less dissimilar; but, even so, the discrepancy is 20 per cent or over in more than half of all the comparisons.

With origin distributions, the most marked contrasts occur between England and Scotland—and to a somewhat lesser extent the FRG—on the one hand, and Hungary, Ireland, and Poland on the other. And inspection of the detail of the distributions then reveals that the major source of these differences is that in the former group of nations a majority of men are of industrial working-class (i.e. Classes V+VI and VIIa) origin and only a small minority of farm origin (Classes IVc and VIIb), while in the latter

TABLE 6.2. *Distributions of respondents, men aged 20–64, to national mobility enquiries, by class of origin and destination, Δ values for origin and destination distributions, and Δ values for pairwise comparisons of all national distributions*

	ENG	FRA	FRG	HUN	IRL	NIR	POL	SCO	SWE
Class of origin (% by column)									
I+II	13	11	14	6	6	9	8	10	11
III	7	9	6	7	5	7	2	7	3
IVa+b	10	14	11	7	10	9	3	7	11
IVc	5	26	13	27	39	23	53	5	26
V+VI	39	19	37	14	14	21	18	39	24
VIIa	23	15	15	19	20	26	12	26	20
VIIb	4	7	3	22	7	6	4	5	5
Class of destination (% by column)									
I+II	25	21	28	15	14	18	18	21	24
III	9	10	5	7	9	9	2	9	8
IVa+b	8	10	7	2	8	10	2	6	8
IVc	2	11	4	1	22	10	25	3	5
V+VI	33	24	37	31	20	26	31	33	30
VIIa	22	21	18	30	21	24	19	25	22
VIIb	2	3	1	14	7	3	3	3	2
Δs for origin and destination distributions									
	13	23	17	37	18	17	30	13	27
Δs for pairwise comparisons of nations*									
ENG		29	11	38	36	22	40	5	23
FRA	13		22	18	17	12	27	32	10
FRG	9	20		36	34	24	41	17	20
HUN	21	26	27		15	18	32	37	20
IRL	25	14	31	29		17	20	38	16
NIR	14	5	21	22	16		30	20	10
POL	24	20	24	27	19	20		48	27
SCO	6	13	13	16	25	11	22		26
SWE	4	10	11	21	23	11	22	7	

Note:
    * Figures in upper-right triangle refer to origin distributions; figures in lower-left triangle refer to destination distributions.

group those of farm origin clearly outnumber those of working-class origin. In addition, Hungary and Ireland especially show a very small proportion of men of service-class background. However, while, as might then be expected, relatively small discrepancies arise *among* the distributions for England, Scotland, and the FRG, and also, one could add, among those for France,

Northern Ireland, and Sweden, in regard to the Hungarian, Irish, and Polish distributions the Δ values are not consistently low. This, it would appear, is chiefly the result of differences, politically as much as economically induced, in the development of the agricultural sectors of these nations.

With destination distributions, which we can take as revealing the 'shapes' of the class structures of the nine nations at the time when our mobility data were collected, it is again in comparisons between Hungary, Ireland, and Poland and our other nations that the largest Δ values occur. But these comparisons are now more-or-less equally strong with all other nations, while some differences of similar magnitude are also apparent among the latter. From the detail of the distributions, the distinctiveness of Hungary, Ireland, and Poland can be seen to lie chiefly in the fact that, while the agricultural classes of these nations remain far from negligible in size, their service classes and also their routine non-manual classes (i.e. Classes I + II and III) are comparatively small, comprising less than 25 per cent of the active male population as against 30 per cent or more in all other nations, with the exception of Northern Ireland. And, further, in Hungary and Poland the petty bourgeoisie (Class IV$a+b$) is also small. At the same time, though, it should be noted that Hungary, Ireland, and Poland again differ quite widely among themselves, and especially in the sizes of their industrial working classes. Thus, Hungary has in fact the largest working class found in any of our nine cases, while Ireland has the smallest. Among the remaining nations, the most notable variation is perhaps in the size of their non-manual classes taken together (i.e. Classes I + II, III, and IV$a+b$) *relative to* that of their industrial working classes. To take the most striking contrast, in France the non-manual classes together amount to almost 90 per cent of the size of the industrial working class, but in Scotland to little over 60 per cent.

Finally, we may note at the bottom of the second panel of Table 6.2 the Δ values that show the differences between the distributions of men in each national sample by class of origin and by class of destination. Once more quite wide variation is revealed. Thus, while in England and Scotland the discrepancy between the two distributions is only 13 per cent, the inter-generational 'redistribution' of men by class that has occurred in the Hungarian case is almost three times greater.

Given, then, the extent of cross-national differences in the structural context of mobility that is evident from the data of Table 6.2, there is, in fact, little possibility at all of the LZ hypothesis finding empirical confirmation. Significant variation in absolute rates, in which these structural differences are to a greater or lesser degree reflected, must almost necessarily follow.[3]

---

[3] The only other possibility is, of course, that, from nation to nation, the effects of relative on absolute mobility rates are such as just to counteract the variation in the latter that structural effects induce! There is, so far as we are aware, no reason, theoretical or empirical, for supposing any tendency of this kind.

This is a point on which we may elaborate in various ways in the remainder of this section, with the aid of the data at our disposal.

To begin with, we present in Table 6.3 a decomposition of the total mobility rates, derived from our 7 × 7 class mobility tables, that we reported in the last column of Table 6.1. We can exploit the hierarchical division that we have introduced into the class schema (see Table 2.2) in order to distinguish between vertical and non-vertical mobility and then, in the case of the former, between upward and downward mobility.[4]

TABLE 6.3. *Decomposition of total mobility rates* (TMR) *into total vertical* (TV) *and total non-vertical* (TNV) *mobility and of total vertical mobility into total upward* (TU) *and total downward* (TD) *mobility*

Nation	TMR	TV	TNV	TV/TNV	TU	TD	TU/TD
ENG	65	50	15	3.4	32	17	1.9
FRA	65	44	21	2.1	32	12	2.5
FRG	62	47	15	3.2	33	14	2.4
HUN	76	45	32	1.4	35	9	3.8
IRL	58	39	19	2.1	30	9	3.4
NIR	63	45	18	2.5	34	11	3.0
POL	60	43	16	2.7	35	8	4.5
SCO	64	51	13	3.9	33	18	1.8
SWE	73	54	19	2.9	42	13	3.3

If we consider the first stage of this decomposition, as shown in the second, third, and fourth columns of Table 6.3, no very evident pattern emerges from the cross-national variation displayed. But when we move on to the second stage, as shown in the fifth, sixth, and seventh columns, a somewhat clearer picture presents itself. While rates of upward class mobility do not differ greatly, except for the relatively high figure for Sweden, rates of *downward* mobility are much more variable, and in a way that is of evident interest. They are highest in England and Scotland and lowest in Hungary, Ireland, and Poland, with the four other nations in intermediate positions. In turn, then, it is in Hungary, Ireland and Poland that upward mobility most strongly preponderates over downward, being in the region of three or four times more likely, as compared with only around twice as likely in England and Scotland.

These results could then be thought rather surprising, and especially if set against the tendency of liberal theorists to see continuing industrial develop-

---

[4] It may in this connection also be found convenient to refer to the HI1 effects matrix shown on p. 124. Excepting cells on the main diagonal, those set at level 1 in this matrix imply non-vertical mobility and those set at level 2 imply vertical mobility. Further, of the latter cells, those in the first row and the last two columns of the matrix imply downward mobility, and the remainder upward mobility.

ment, and the progressive upgrading of employment that it entails, as conducive to a steadily widening experience of social ascent. As of the early and mid-1970s, the balance of upward as against downward mobility was evidently *more* favourable in the collective experience of the male work-forces of Hungary, Ireland, and Poland than in that of work-forces within our more mature industrial nations.

However, it is important that the implications of Table 6.3 should not be misunderstood. Certainly, no support should here be seen for Marxist arguments that claim, in direct opposition to the liberal view, a progressive *de*grading of employment or of the labour force. For not only does it remain the case that in *all* our nations upward mobility is more frequent than downward but, further, the essential explanation for the differences in the amounts of downward mobility that are observed is that, all other things being equal, the volume of such mobility will in fact be the greater, the more established an 'upgraded' class structure has become. In nations such as Hungary, Ireland, and Poland the overall amount of downward mobility that occurs intergenerationally is restricted because upgrading, and in particular the expansion of the service class and the skilled working class, is still relatively recent and is therefore—as Table 6.2 brings out—only weakly reflected in the origin distributions of the men in our samples. In contrast, in England and Scotland the proportions of respondents originating in these classes is larger and so too, then, are the structural possibilities for downward movement that exist. In fact, inspection of our 7×7 mobility tables percentaged by cell reveals that the differences in downward mobility rates shown in Table 6.3 can be traced back to two main sources: first, to the movement of men of service-class origins into the class of routine non-manual employees, which accounts on average for somewhat over 0.5 per cent of all cases in the Hungarian, Irish, and Polish tables but for around 1.3 per cent of all in the English and Scottish tables; and, secondly, and yet more importantly, to the intergenerational movement of men from the skilled to the non-skilled division of the working class—a transition followed by around 3 per cent of all men in the Hungarian, Irish, and Polish samples but by just under 10 per cent of all English respondents and by over 10 per cent of all Scots.[5]

From total mobility rates we turn next to absolute rates considered in inflow and outflow perspective. First, in this connection, we give some indication of the overall extent of the cross-national variation that occurs by showing in Table 6.4 the ranges and medians of the Δ values calculated for all

---

[5] Our 1980s mobility tables for Czechoslovakia and Italy give results that fit well into this pattern. For Czechoslovakia, where extensive industrial development had already occurred in the inter-war years, total upward and downward mobility rates are 36 per cent and 13 per cent respectively. For Italy, however, the corresponding figures are 41 and 8 per cent, and specific downward mobility flows are at the same low levels as those noted in the Hungarian, Irish, and Polish cases. We do not believe that such rates for the Netherlands can be reliably established, for reasons given earlier.

pairwise comparisons of inflow and outflow distributions across our nine nations. As can be seen, differences from nation to nation in inflow rates—or, in other words, in patterns of intergenerational recruitment to particular classes—are frequently substantial, except perhaps in the case of Class IV*c*, that of farmers. With outflow rates, somewhat smaller differences are revealed, which is what would be expected in view of the lower cross-national variation in destination than in origin distributions already shown in Table 6.2. None the less, it is still evident that the class distributions of men of given class origins do in many instances show dissimilarities that are of a far from negligible magnitude.

TABLE 6.4. *Ranges and medians of* Δ *values for pairwise comparisons of national inflow and outflow distributions*

Class	Inflows		Outflows	
	Range	Median	Range	Median
I+II	5–31	18	3–20	9
III	8–55	26	6–35	17
IV*a+b*	8–40	22	4–26	16
IV*c*	2–25	12	9–54	23
V+VI	5–36	19	4–20	11
VII*a*	5–48	23	1–24	11
VII*b*	5–47	24	6–30	16

To obtain a more detailed understanding of the cross-national variation to which Table 6.4 points, we must, of course, examine specific rates; and in this respect the very quantity of data that we possess poses a problem. We have, in all, nine inflow and nine outflow tables each with seven columns or rows or, that is, 126 separate distributions to consider. Rather than attempting to transmit this information in full, we seek, in Figures 6.1 and 6.2, to bring out in graphical form certain features of it that are of particular interest for our present purposes. In these two figures we show the cross-national *ranges* of the inflow and the outflow rates respectively for each of our seven classes, and in each case indicate which are the nations whose rates mark the extremes of the range.

To start with Figure 6.1, we may note first of all that the ranges depicted vary somewhat from panel to panel: for example, the lines appearing in the first or the fourth panels tend to be shorter than those in the second, indicating, that is, less cross-national variation in intergenerational recruitment to the service class or to the class of farmers in our nine nations than in such recruitment to the class of routine non-manual employees—a finding which of course also emerges from Table 6.4. However, on further examination of Figure 6.1, another, and stronger, regularity may be discerned: that

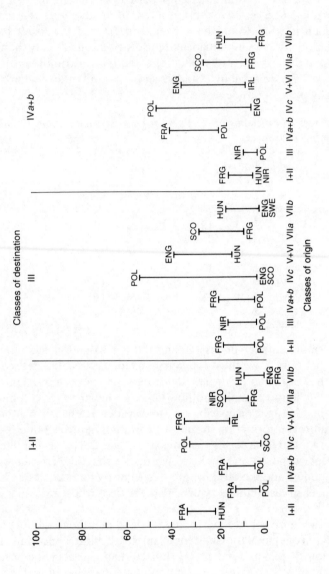

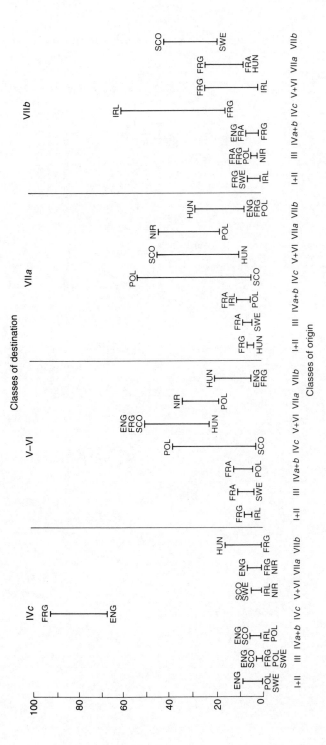

FIGURE 6.1. *Cross-national ranges of inflow rates*

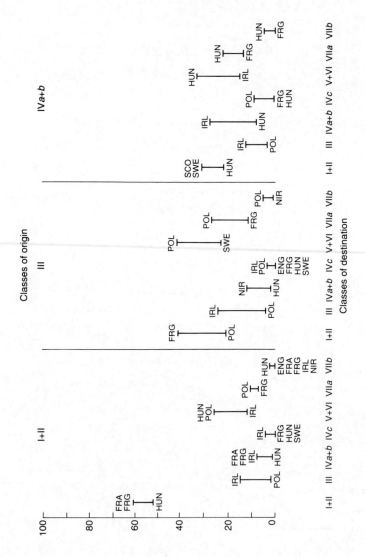

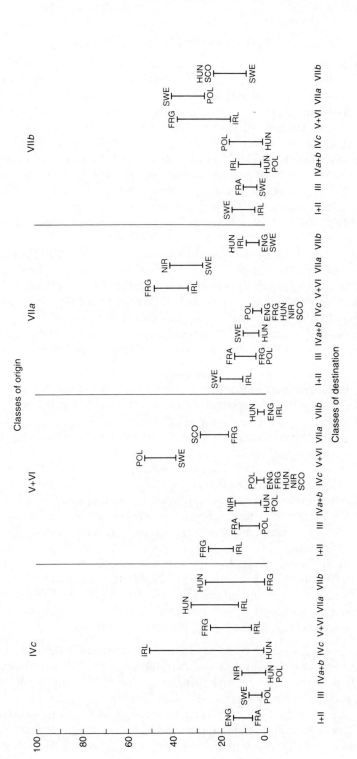

FIGURE 6.2. *Cross-national ranges of ouflow rates*

is, in the degree of variation associated with different classes of *origin*. Thus, in all panels of Figure 6.1 the longest line can be seen to be that which refers to men of Class IV*c* origins; or, in other words, for all classes of destination alike, cross-national variation is greatest in the extent to which they recruit from among the sons of farmers. Such variation tends also to be wide in regard to the recruitment of men of farm-worker (Class VII*b*) and of industrial working-class (Classes V+VI and VII*a*) origins, while it is generally least in regard to the recruitment of men from white-collar (Classes I+II and III) and petty-bourgeois (Class IV*a*+*b*) backgrounds. In sum, then, the pattern we disclose here is one that very largely corresponds to that we described earlier, on the basis of Table 6.2, in cross-national variation *in origins distributions themselves*.

Moreover, if we concentrate our attention on those origin classes that we find contribute most to differences in inflow rates—that is, Classes IV*c* and VII*b* and V+VI and VII*a*—the following more specific features of interest can also be observed from Figure 6.1; and each can likewise be related to the results of Table 6.2, in that the nations picked out as regularly lying at the extremes of the recruitment ranges will also be found to lie at the extremes of the variation in origins distributions that Table 6.2 presents.

1. In the range of recruitment from among the sons of farmers, it is the Polish rate that marks the upper limit for all five of the non-agricultural classes within our schema, and either the English or the Scottish rate that marks the lower limit.
2. As regards recruitment from among the sons of farm workers, Hungary shows the highest rate for all non-agricultural classes, as also for the class of farmers, and, for the non-agricultural classes, either England or the FRG provides the lowest rate.
3. In the range of recruitment of men from skilled working-class (Class V+VI) origins, the highest rates are shared among England, the FRG, and Scotland, while Hungary or Ireland regularly shows the lowest rates.
4. With the recruitment of men from non-skilled working-class (Class VII*a*) origins, it is the Scottish or Northern Irish rates that are highest for all non-agricultural classes, while the rate for the FRG is lowest in recruitment to the three non-manual classes and that for Poland in recruitment to Class V+VI and to Class VII*a* itself.

Overall, therefore, we could say that in the perspective of inflow mobility our nine nations prove to be most strongly differentiated in the extent to which, as of the early and mid-1970s, men of farm *or* of industrial working-class origins predominated in their class formation, and that this differentiation clearly reflects that which is likewise to be found in the structural contexts of mobility obtaining over the course of the preceding decades.

Moving on now to Figure 6.2, we can see that, with outflow rates as with inflow, differing degrees of cross-national variation are revealed from panel to panel; or, in other words, and as we also know from Table 6.4, that the dispersal of men from some classes of origin—for example, Class IVc—varies more from nation to nation than does that of men from other classes of origin—for example, Class I+II. Here again, though, there are regularities to be noted, even if less marked than with inflows, when we look at the variation associated with particular classes from panel to panel—that is, in this case, classes of *destination*. Thus, for example, across classes of origin, the variation in outflows to the two divisions of the working class (Classes V+VI and VIIa) tends to be wider than that in outflows to the class of routine non-manual employees (Class III) or to the petty bourgeoisie (Class IVa+b), as well as in outflows to the two agricultural classes which are in almost all instances very small.

Reverting to Table 6.2, it may then in turn be observed that, of the non-agricultural classes, it is Classes V+VI and VIIa that show most cross-national variation in their size as destination classes and—of particular relevance in regard to outflow rates—that, along with Class I+II, show the largest *shifts* in size as between origin and destination distributions.[6] Furthermore, in a way analogous to that seen with inflows, those nations that are here found at the extremes of structural variation are often those that in Figure 6.2 are shown as similarly distinctive where outflow rates to service-class and working-class positions are concerned. In this latter respect, we may note the following points specifically.

1. In the range of outflows of men to service-class positions, the highest rates are shared among England, France, the FRG, Scotland, and Sweden, while Hungary and Ireland account for five of the lowest rates.
2. With outflows of men to skilled working-class positions, the highest rates are shared among the FRG, Hungary, and Poland, while again in five instances the Irish rate marks the lower limit.
3. With outflows of men to non-skilled working-class positions, Hungary and Poland account for four of the highest rates, while the rate for the FRG is in four cases the lowest.

Once more, then, the influence on absolute rates of the structural context of mobility is apparent. While variation in inflows is strongly patterned by the relative importance from nation to nation of the overall distribution of men of different class origins, and especially of those of farm or of working-class backgrounds, variation in outflows is patterned by national differences in

---

[6] While in any national case the pattern of inflow rates—or, that is, of the composition of current classes according to the class of their members' fathers—will tend to reflect the development of the class structure over a period as long as, say, the preceding half-century, the pattern of outflow rates—or of the dispersal of individuals from their origins to positions within the existing class structure—is more open to influence by structural shifts of a relatively recent kind.

the distribution of different class destinations and by changes in this distribution, especially as regards the service class and the working class. In other words, cross-national variation in the mobility chances of men of all classes of origin alike clearly reflects differences in what one might call (cf. Blau and Duncan 1967: chs. 2, 7) the 'objective opportunity structures' that particular nations afford.

In sum, we have in this section sought to show not only that the LZ hypothesis of similarity in the observed mobility rates of industrial societies is invalid but, further, *that it must indeed be so* in consequence of such societies failing to display the essentially standardized structural contexts of mobility that Lipset and Zetterberg envisaged. However, while the results we have so far presented serve to demonstrate clearly enough *that* structural effects produce cross-national variation in absolute rates, they do not help us much in quantifying such effects, nor, therefore, in assessing their importance as against that of the effects of relative rates, or patterns of social fluidity, which, in the light of the preceding chapter, we must suppose also contribute in some degree to the variation that absolute rates display. We have argued that merit still attaches to the FJH hypothesis, if what this is taken as claiming is the presence of a large commonality within the patterns of social fluidity found across industrial nations. But we do by the same token also recognize that differences in national patterns occur that are of statistical, and often too of evident sociological, significance. Just what, then, is the impact of these differences in fluidity on the level of absolute rates, and especially as compared with that of structural effects? This is an issue that we must clearly address, and to which we turn in the section that follows.

STRUCTURAL EFFECTS AND SOCIAL FLUIDITY AS DETERMINANTS OF VARIATION IN ABSOLUTE RATES

In discussing our model of core social fluidity and national variants of it in Chapters 4 and 5, we focused our attention on those terms that related specifically to fluidity patterns. But terms are of course also included in the models we have developed that pertain to the effects of origin and destination distributions—that is the λ_i^O and λ_j^D terms. Thus, in considering the relative importance of structural effects and of fluidity patterns in creating cross-national variation in absolute rates, an approach that obviously suggests itself is one based on our models and the parameters that we can estimate for them.

Before attempting such an approach, however, it is of some interest to see what may be learnt from parameters for structural effects considered in themselves. For this purpose, we may usefully resort to an alternative way of treating the λ_i^O and λ_j^D terms in models such as ours that has been proposed by Sobel, Hout, and Duncan (1985). This is, in fact, a simple linear transformation of $\lambda_i^O + \lambda_j^D$ into $\lambda_i^O + \lambda_j^O + (\lambda_j^D - \lambda_j^O)$. In other words, instead of thinking of origin effects plus destination effects, we would, following Sobel, Hout, and Duncan, think in terms of the size effects of the two classes involved $(\lambda_i^O + \lambda_j^O)$ plus the marginal *shift* effect $(\lambda_j^D - \lambda_j^O)$. Shift effects can be understood as the effects of changes between origin and destination distributions which raise or lower the odds of mobility to a given destination in a uniform way—that is to say, *by the same factor across all origins alike.*[7]

As with all other parameters that we estimate from our models, those for such shift effects must be interpreted not by reference to their absolute values but rather by reference to the differences between these values. They are thus best presented in the form of a half-matrix, in which each such difference can be shown. However, rather than reporting nine arrays of this kind, one for each of our nations, we have estimated shift parameters under each of our national models, but in Table 6.5 give, in logged odds form, simply the range of each difference and indicate which are the extreme cases.

From this table, certain regularities are at once apparent. Thus, it can be seen that along the first row of the array, where the entries refer to Class I+ II, all values are positive; that is to say, in all our nations alike, shift effects favour mobility into the service class over that into any other class. Conversely, it can be seen that entries referring to Class IVc are all negative by row but positive by column; in other words, across our nations, mobility into the class of farmers is less favoured by shift effects than that into any other class. And, again, the entries referring to Class VIIb, in the last column of the array, are all positive except that in the row for Class IVc—meaning, then, that mobility into the class of farm workers is likewise generally disfavoured, except in comparison with mobility into farming.

That regularities of this kind should emerge is scarcely surprising. They might well have been predicted simply from inspection of the marginal distributions of our mobility tables, and they are consistent with general

---

[7] Sobel, Hout, and Duncan suggest their alternative parameterization in the context of a model which, as we have earlier noted (p. 59), they offer as a new way of effecting the distinction between structural and exchange mobility—but which we do not ourselves find convincing, since it requires that exchange mobility or, in our terms, the pattern of social fluidity, be symmetrical. However, their method of representing structural effects is quite detachable from their model, provided that one is ready to accept that heterogeneity in the marginal distributions of the mobility table may derive not only from structural effects but from the pattern of fluidity also—i.e. that the latter may *not* be symmetrical. Clearly, we would ourselves wish not merely to accept this point but to argue it; for neither our model of core fluidity (cf. Table 4.4) nor any of its national variants do, in fact, embody the complete symmetry which Sobel, Hout, and Duncan would have, but for which, as we have already observed, there is no evident sociological rationale. From discussion of the SHD model in the literature, it seems to be not generally appreciated that, on the condition noted, the 'size–shift' approach to treating structural effects is independent of the model, nor indeed that it entails no more than the very simple transformation of the 'origins–destination' approach (cf. Hauser 1978) that we show in the text. To argue, as do Hout and Hauser (1991), that acceptance of a symmetrical model of fluidity is essential to the estimation of structural effects seems to us quite mistaken.

TABLE 6.5. *Range of differences in shift parameters estimated under national-variant models (in logged odds form)*

	III	IVa+b	IVc	V+VI	VIIa	VIIb
I+II	0.3–1.5 IRL–POL	1.2–3.0 ENG–HUN	2.9–6.2 SCO–HUN	0.4–1.4 HUN–SCO	0.9–1.5 FRA–NIR	2.3–3.0 FRG–HUN
III		0.4–2.0 FRG–HUN	2.0–5.0 SCO–HUN	−0.7–0.6 POL–SWE	−0.4–1.0 POL–IRL	1.0–2.5 POL–SWE
IVa+b			1.5–3.2 SCO–HUN	−2.7–0.1 HUN–ENG	−1.8–0.3 HUN–NIR	0.0–1.4 HUN–NIR
IVc				−5.8–−1.5 HUN–SCO	−5.0–−1.5 HUN–SCO	−3.1–−0.6 HUN–SCO
V+VI					−0.1–0.8 SCO–HUN	0.9–2.6 SCO–HUN
VIIa						1.0–1.8 SCO–HUN

expectations concerning the course of class structural change as industrial societies develop. However, what should also be noted from Table 6.5 is that, while the tendencies in question are indeed common to all our nations, they are so in often substantially differing degrees. For example, it is evident from the ranges reported that the factor by which mobility into either of the two agricultural classes is structurally disfavoured, relative to mobility into other classes, varies enormously.[8]

Furthermore, the ways in which shift effects bear on mobility into the other classes than those we have so far mentioned do not in fact reveal any clear tendential similarities. The relevant ranges shown in Table 6.5 comprise both positive and negative values. This means, therefore, that, while in certain nations—England, Sweden, Ireland, and Northern Ireland all in some respect stand out—mobility into the routine non-manual class (III) or the petty bourgeoisie (IV$a+b$) may be structurally favoured over that into skilled or non-skilled working-class positions (Classes V+VI or VIIa), in other nations—Hungary and Poland at the extreme—the opposite tendency can be found.

In sum, we may say that the pattern of shift effects estimated under our national models of mobility regimes serves chiefly to confirm, and at the same time to give more precise expression to, what was suggested by our previous analyses in this chapter. That is, that, although the nations we consider are all industrial ones, and display what might be thought of as certain generic developmental characteristics, the structural contexts for mobility processes that they provide are none the less from case to case still clearly, and often quite strongly, differentiated.

How, then, should we seek to assess the effects of such structural differences, relative to those of differences in social fluidity, on cross-national variation in absolute mobility rates? In what follows, we make a twofold attack on this problem.

Our first line of analysis starts from the standard model of the mobility table

$$\log F_{ij} = \mu + \lambda_i^O + \lambda_j^D + \lambda_{ij}^I \tag{6.1}$$

which says that the expected frequency in cell ij of the table is determined by a scale factor and by an origin effect, a destination effect, and an interaction effect pertaining to that cell. Correspondingly, and as we show in detail in an annex to this chapter, we can then regard the variance of the expected cell values in the table (which for convenience we treat as the variance of the

---

[8] It is true that the ranges in question often show Hungary at one extreme, which, in view of its agrarian history, might be regarded as a special case. However, even if one discounts Hungary, the argument still holds. Thus, to take but one example, in Scotland, as Table 6.5 shows, mobility into the service class is structurally favoured over mobility into farming by a factor of $e^{2.9}$ or, that is, by around eighteen times; and in the FRG, the nation that stands in most marked contrast to Scotland after Hungary, the factor is still as large as $e^{4.8}$, or over 120 times!

logged odds between all pairs of values) as being partitionable into five elements: one relating to origin effects, one to destination effects, and one to interaction effects, plus two more that may be thought of as compositional effects resulting from origin and interaction effects jointly and from destination and interaction effects jointly. (We could, incidentally, here again use the parameterization of Sobel, Hout, and Duncan but choose not to do so, since in the present context it would contribute little, while entailing a partitioning of a more complex kind.)

Where, then, we are concerned with models for a number of different mobility tables—in our case, national tables—we can extend the above analysis in the following way. We can first separate the total variance in expected cell values over all tables into that occurring between different pairs of cells and that occurring among different national tables as modelled; and we can then again partition each of these components into the five elements indicated above. It will, of course, be the partitioning of the variance among the national tables that, given our present purposes, will be of major interest to us.

We may, perhaps, clarify just what is involved here if we consider, to begin with, a somewhat simplified situation: that is, one in which we take our nine national mobility tables as they would be if, while their marginal distributions remain unchanged, we represent their fluidity patterns in each case by our *core* model.[9] In this situation, the FJH hypothesis would be strictly true: all odds ratios defining relative mobility rates have been made cross-nationally identical. If we then apply to these tables the method of partitioning that we have outlined, we obtain the results that are given in the upper panel of Table 6.6. These show that, while of course all five elements are involved in the variance between pairs of cells, the variance occurring among the nine national tables modelled derives only from origin and destination effects: interaction, and hence compositional, effects are zero. In other words, since we have ensured that fluidity patterns are in all nations the same, they cannot contribute to the variation in expected cell values across nations—nor, in turn, to the variation in any absolute rates that might be calculated from these values. The structural context, as represented by origin and destination effects, is all-important.

But, we may now ask, how does the outcome differ if we move on from this contrived, and counterfactual, situation and repeat the analysis on the basis of the variants of the core model which, in Chapter 5, we have accepted as adequately reproducing our nine national mobility tables? How much difference does it make when from nation to nation fluidity patterns are seen as deviating from that defined by the core model, as the hierarchy, inheritance, sector, and affinity effects that this model comprises take on somewhat differing strengths and combinations?

---

[9] In other words, we take here the expected values produced when we fit our core model to national tables with its parameters fixed and treated in fact as 'offsets'.

TABLE 6.6. *Partitioning of variance in logged odds of expected cell frequencies under different models of national mobility tables*

Model	Variance	Variance related to			Compositional effects		Total
		Origin effects	Destination effects	Interaction effects	Origin-interaction	Destination-interaction	
Core	Pairs of cells	0.44	1.01	0.74	−0.13	0.20	2.27
	National tables	1.57	2.09	0.00	0.00	0.00	3.67
National variants	Pairs of cells	0.35	0.93	0.58	−0.07	0.12	1.92
	National tables	1.27	1.95	0.55	0.03	−0.23	3.57

The answers to these questions are to be found in the lower panel of Table 6.6. If we compare the partitioning of variance among different national models that is shown here with that shown in the upper panel, we can see that, as must of course be the case, interaction—and thus compositional—effects now do play a part. However, what we can further see is that this part is a quite minor one. Since compositional effects may, for reasons explained in the annex, become negative, we are unable to express the proportion of the total variance accounted for by different elements in a straightforward way. But from the results reported we can (as is also explained in the annex) set the contribution of interaction effects as falling within the range of 9–16 per cent. In other words, we may say that, in creating variation in expected cell values in our national mobility tables as modelled, origin and destination effects together, expressing differences in the structural contexts of mobility, heavily preponderate over the effects of interaction or, that is, of differences in fluidity patterns.

This is a conclusion that it is important to have securely established. However, it remains one that may not perhaps be found entirely satisfying in that it refers to cell values rather than to absolute rates directly. It would help us further if we could gain some understanding of just how the variation that exists in fluidity patterns—or, that is, in relative rates—actually shows up at the absolute level. It is to this end that we pursue our second line of analysis.

This starts from the counterfactual tables we previously constructed: that is, tables which suppose a world in which the FJH hypothesis holds *stricto sensu* and in which the pattern of social fluidity that prevails in all industrial societies alike is that of our core model. We may then ask how far absolute mobility rates calculated from these counterfactual tables differ either from those calculated from expected values under our national variant models or from those calculated on the basis of our observed tables.[10]

In Table 6.7 we present total mobility rates and various of their components—cf. Table 6.3—calculated in the three ways in question. The fact that the observed rates in the first column of each panel, which are reproduced from Table 6.3, are virtually the same as those derived from our national variant models in the second column should not be found greatly surprising; for we have of course sought to develop models that would give a good fit to our data. However, the degree of similarity between the rates in the first and second columns and those in the third, which derive from our counterfactual tables, is altogether more consequential. It means that if we were to form our ideas about total mobility rates in our nine nations on the assumption that the FJH hypothesis was valid and that our core model describes the

---

[10] In principle, we should, of course, work with the expected values under the models we accept rather than with the actually observed values, since the former will be less subject to sampling fluctuation. But, lest some readers should suspect statistical legerdemain, we consider rates calculated on both bases.

TABLE 6.7. *Total mobility rates, total non-vertical (TNV), total upward (TU) and total downward (TD) rates calculated from (i) observed mobility tables, (ii) tables as expected under national variant models, and (iii) tables as expected under model of core social fluidity*

Nation	TMR			TNV			TU			TD		
	(i)	(ii)	(iii)	(i)	(ii)	(iii)	(i)	(ii)	(iii)	(i)	(ii)	(iii)
ENG	65	64	64	15	14	15	33	33	32	17	17	17
FRA	65	65	66	20	20	21	32	32	32	13	13	13
FRG	62	62	63	15	15	16	33	33	33	14	14	14
HUN	76	76	74	32	32	28	35	35	36	9	9	10
IRL	58	58	60	18	18	20	31	31	31	9	9	9
NIR	63	63	65	18	18	18	34	34	35	11	11	12
POL	60	59	58	17	16	17	35	35	34	8	8	7
SCO	64	64	64	13	13	15	33	33	32	18	18	17
SWE	73	73	70	19	19	19	42	41	40	13	13	11

cross-national invariance in relative rates that this hypothesis claims, we would but rarely mislead ourselves. It may be seen that in only two instances in Table 6.7 does the 'counterfactual' rate differ by three percentage points or more from either of the two other rates. Relying on the former, we would somewhat underestimate the total mobility rate in Sweden, and likewise the amount of non-vertical mobility in Hungary. It may be recalled that our variant model for Sweden brings out unusually weak inheritance effects and low propensities for intergenerational immobility; while that for Hungary contains a special affinity term to reflect the effect of the mass collectivization of peasant farmers and also reveals weak sectoral barriers, especially to movement from farm origins into the non-skilled working class. Overall, though, the conclusion that we must draw here is that variations in social fluidity show up at the level of total mobility rates to so slight an extent as to be for the most part negligible.[11]

The rates shown in Table 6.7 are, of course, highly aggregated ones, and it is, therefore, of interest to extend our counterfactual analyses to more specific inflow and outflow rates. We have calculated such rates on the same three bases as the rates in Table 6.7, and we have then further calculated Δ values for the differences between the percentage distributions based on the counterfactual tables and on the observed tables, and again for the differences between those based on the counterfactual tables and on the expected tables under our national variant models.

---

[11] This outcome is less surprising than it may perhaps appear if one recalls (see Table 5.1) that, when our model of core fluidity was fitted to national mobility tables with fixed parameters, the highest Δ value returned—indicating the proportion of all cases misclassified—was 7.4 per cent.

In the first of these comparisons, we discover that out of a total of sixty-three inflow distributions (one for each of our seven classes in nine nations) no more than seventeen give rise to a Δ of 10 per cent or more, while, of the sixty-three outflow distributions, a difference of this magnitude occurs with only eight. Furthermore, such instances of non-negligible discrepancies are heavily concentrated among distributions with relatively small Ns, where sampling fluctuations could well inflate Δ values. And when we turn to the second comparison, where our counterfactual distributions are set against those derived from our 'modelled' tables, in which such fluctuations should be reduced, we do indeed find that Δs of 10 per cent or more now occur with only eleven inflow and three outflow distributions—that is, in little more than one in ten of all cases.

We could, then, say that, in discussing inflow and outflow rates also, we would not often be led astray if we were to work from our counterfactual tables in which all variation in social fluidity has been eliminated. For example, we would not arrive at conclusions concerning cross-national variation in inflows and outflows that departed in any serious way from those we earlier reached on the basis of either Table 6.4 or Figures 6.1 and 6.2. A majority of the instances—eight out of the fourteen—in which counterfactual rates do deviate by 10 per cent or more from both observed and modelled rates actually turn out to be of the same, rather restricted kind: that is, they are ones concerning primarily the degree of self-recruitment to agricultural classes. Thus, following our counterfactual inflow distributions, we would overestimate the extent of the self-recruitment of farmers in Hungary and Sweden, but underestimate it in Scotland; and we would overestimate self-recruitment to the class of farm workers in Hungary, Ireland, and Sweden, while underestimating it in the FRG and Poland.[12]

In the case of each of these deviations—as indeed in most of the others that are shown up—one can see reflected distinctive features of social fluidity patterns that we sought earlier to capture in our national variant models: again, for example, weak inheritance effects in Sweden, but strong ones in Poland; low sectoral barriers in Hungary, and in certain respects in Ireland, but high ones in Scotland. These differences, we believe, are real and likewise their effects. After the efforts that we have devoted to modelling them, we do not now wish to deny their sociological significance; and it should further be kept in mind that, even where an absolute rate is shifted by only a few percentage points, this will still translate into changes that bear on

[12] The other six instances where using the counterfactual tables would lead to discrepancies of 10 per cent or more are ones that would be likely to mislead us chiefly as follows. In inflow perspective, we would underestimate self-recruitment to the petty bourgeoisie in the FRG and Poland; and, also in the Polish case, the extent of the recruitment of farmers' sons to the routine non-manual class. In outflow perspective, we would underestimate immobility among the petty bourgeoisie in Poland and among farm workers in Hungary; and, again in the Polish case, the chances of the sons of routine non-manual fathers entering service-class rather than working-class positions.

large numbers of individual lives. None the less, the fact remains that for the sociologist concerned at the 'macro' level with questions of cross-national variation in absolute mobility rates—whether inflow, outflow, or total—differences in social fluidity patterns must appear as having no more than a very limited relevance. It is not at the level of social fluidity that this variation is effectively shaped.[13]

We would then see this outcome of our analyses as carrying two main implications. The first relates back to our discussion of the FJH hypothesis in the preceding chapter. We can, we believe, now provide a further way of giving meaning to this hypothesis in the weaker version that we have put forward: that is, where what is claimed is not a complete similarity in relative mobility rates or social fluidity patterns across industrial societies but rather a substantial commonality so that cross-national differences may best be understood as 'variations on a theme'. We previously argued that this version could be saved from undue vagueness and laid open to empirical evaluation by being set in contrast with rival hypotheses which claimed that national fluidity patterns fell into a series of distinctive types or, at all events, varied in some systematic fashion, in relation to other societal characteristics. In addition, we would now suggest that a pragmatic criterion for a 'substantial commonality' in fluidity patterns can be provided in terms of their impact on variation in absolute mobility rates. A substantial commonality may be said to exist to the extent that a discussion of variation in absolute rates will not differ in its sociological import whether that part of the variation due to fluidity patterns is taken into account or not. According to this criterion, we have then in this section, and especially from our counterfactual analyses, provided a good deal of further support for the FJH hypothesis in its modified form. At very least, the results we have reported must powerfully reinforce the argument that to disregard the FJH hypothesis simply because it fails in its strict version is to disregard macrosociological regularities of a rather remarkable kind.

The second implication that we would note is in effect a corollary of the foregoing: namely, that, if we wish to understand cross-national variation in absolute rates, it is on differences in the structural contexts of mobility that

---

[13] We should, of course, acknowledge that counterfactual exercises of the kind we have engaged in are not entirely unproblematic, requiring as they do strong *ceteris paribus* assumptions (cf. McClelland 1975). Specifically, we must assume that in the real world, and not just in statistical analysis, fluidity on the pattern of our core model could coexist with all of the differing structural contexts provided by our nine nations. However, since we know that their actual fluidity patterns in no case deviate very widely from our model, the assumption would in fact seem a plausible one. In an earlier counterfactual exercise Erikson (1990) produced a greater variety of counterfactual tables—seventy-two in all—by combining the fluidity pattern implied by each of our national variant models with each set of national marginals. The results essentially confirm the conclusions we reach in the text concerning the predominant importance of structural effects in creating cross-national variation. Thus, while average total mobility rates for models across marginals ranged from only 62 to 69 per cent, those for marginals across models ranged from 58 to 75 per cent.

our attention must, almost exclusively, be focused. However, once this point is recognized, a crucial issue arises that we have previously taken up in Chapter 3 in regard to trends in absolute rates and to which we must return: that is, the issue of how far there is here scope for sociological explanation as distinct from simply historical description. In Chapter 3 we were led to the conclusion that the diversity of factors influencing the context within which absolute rates evolve is such that the possibilities for generalization—other than in certain very broad terms—may prove to be quite limited. The question we must now face is, therefore, that of whether any more positive view is possible in the light of our examination of absolute rates in a cross-sectional perspective.

In fact, we would doubt if the position is greatly changed. It is true that, on the basis of the data summarized in Figures 6.1 and 6.2, certain general arguments might suggest themselves. Thus, considering inflows, we could note the tendency for the recruitment of men of farm origins into all classes of destination to be most extensive in Hungary and Poland and least so in England and Scotland, while with the recruitment of men of industrial working-class origins more or less the reverse tendency appears. And this might then lead to the idea of variation in inflow rates as being interpretable in terms of differences in the structural contexts of mobility associated with differing trajectories of industrialism, or patterns of growth, such as, say, those we pointed to among our nations with reference to Figure 3.1. England and Scotland, it will be recalled, here represent 'early' industrializing nations, whereas Hungary and Poland, along with Ireland, are cases in which decisive industrialization was 'delayed' until after the Second World War, with the remaining nations falling into an intermediate 'late' industrializing category.

From this standpoint, there are indeed certain marked contrasts in the composition of specific classes—and ones of evident sociological interest—that can be well accounted for. For example, in Poland, as of the early 1970s, men of farm and of working-class origins each made up around a third of the service class, and in Hungary from a quarter to a third; but in England and Scotland the recruitment of service-class members from men of farm origins was almost negligible and men of working-class backgrounds provided close on half. Again, while the Hungarian and the Polish industrial working classes (i.e. Classes V+VI and VIIa together) were composed in almost equal parts of men recruited from farm families and those who were themselves the sons of industrial workers, the working classes of England and Scotland were as much as three-quarters self-recruited or, that is, at least 'second-generation' urban–industrial in their composition, with 'green' recruits from the land amounting to less than 10 per cent.[14]

The relation of these patterns to differing trajectories of industrialization

[14] For further discussion of differences of this kind, see Goldthorpe (1980a/1987: ch. 11).

is then clear enough. In England and Scotland the agricultural sector was already very small, in terms of the proportion of the labour force it employed, by the end of the nineteenth century; and several decades elapsed, from, say, the 1890s through to the 1930s, before the period in which the major growth of the service class took place. At the same time, a large industrial working class developed, eventually comprising a majority of the employed male population. Thus, once the expansion of the service class began, and extensive 'recruitment from below' was required, it was perforce from the working class, rather than from the farm sector, that this recruitment was chiefly drawn. And, likewise, for the intergenerational reproduction of the working class, a large amount of self-recruitment was in these nations unavoidable. In the case of Hungary and Poland the phasing of structural change was quite different. The period of expansion of the industrial working class and that of the service class largely overlapped with each other—and with that of rapid agricultural contraction. Thus, in the years after the Second World War the working class could build up its numbers through substantial recruitment from the countryside in addition to self-recruitment, while at the same time the service class was able to draw heavily on men from working-class and farm families alike.

However, the promise that such an approach might seem to hold out is not, unfortunately, sustained: more generally applied, it leads in fact only to other features of inflow distributions having to be treated as more-or-less anomalous. For instance, since France is obviously to be placed in the intermediate category of 'late' industrializing nations, one might expect the level of working-class recruitment into its service class to lie somewhere in between that found in England and Scotland, on the one hand, and Hungary and Poland, on the other. In fact, it is still lower than in either of the two latter nations. Again, following Figure 3.1, Ireland is clearly another nation of 'delayed' industrialization, together with Hungary and Poland. But the Irish industrial working class (which in the early 1970s was the smallest in any of our nations) turns out to have a quite different composition from that of either the Hungarian or the Polish, and most notably in drawing only around a quarter of its members from farm backgrounds while almost three-fifths were self-recruited. What in both these instances would appear crucial are differences in *styles* of industrialization, quite apart from historical timing. In particular, the emphasis given in Hungary and Poland to the rapid, and, in their Stalinist phases, virtually forced transfer of manpower from agriculture into heavy manufacturing industry (Kovács 1983; and, on pre-socialist Hungary, see also Simkus *et al.* 1990) stands in marked contrast with the much more gradual processes of structural change which, out of distinctive complexes of policy choices and constraints, have charac-terized the French and Irish cases alike (cf. O'Brien and Keyder 1978; Fohlen 1976; Kennedy, Giblin, and McHugh 1988; Simkus *et al.* 1990).

Furthermore, when we turn from inflow to outflow rates, grouping our nations in the way suggested by Figure 3.1 would appear to throw little light at all on the variation they display. That is to say, although the structural contexts of mobility are of major importance in determining outflow no less than inflow rates, the structural effects that bear on outflows are not ones for which differing trajectories of industrialism can provide any ready interpretation. Rather than reflecting long-term developmental tendencies, these effects derive more from shorter-term shifts in the relative sizes of classes— affecting especially, as we have noted, the service classes and working classes of our nine nations. And these shifts would in turn appear often to be ones crucially influenced by quite specific, and diverse, historical circumstances. Thus, for instance, the fact that Poland is not so obviously placed along with the other two 'delayed' industrializers, Hungary and Ireland, as a nation in which objective opportunities for mobility into the service class are at the low end of the cross-national range has to be related to the need for the virtual reconstruction of this class following the devastation of the Polish intelligentsia during the war years (cf. p. 162). Again, in understanding the generally high outflow rates to the Hungarian and Polish working classes, as well as their distinctive composition, the political control of industrialization in these nations is once more of evident relevance; while the low outflows that are revealed to the non-skilled working class in the FRG must in part at least reflect the reduction in size of this class within the indigenous population as *Gastarbeiter* took over a large proportion of non-skilled jobs.[15]

In other words, it is here that the force becomes most apparent of the argument advanced by Featherman, Jones, and Hauser that the structural effects that shape mobility rates at the 'phenotypical' level do so by mediating a wide variety of economic, technological, demographic, and—we would wish to add—political influences that are largely exogenous to the dynamics of the process of class stratification *per se*; or, that is, to the competition that goes on among individuals as, from class origins of differing advantage, they seek to achieve class positions of differing accessibility and desirability.

Again, therefore, as in our discussion of trends, the limits on the possibility of macrosociological explanations of cross-national variation in absolute mobility rates are strongly underlined. The conclusion from which it would seem difficult to escape is that, if we are to say more of interest in regard to such rates from a macrosociological standpoint, we must be ready to redefine somewhat the problems that we address. In the final section of this chapter we seek to outline one way in which such a reorientation might be attempted and to illustrate its possibilities to the extent that the data at our disposal will allow.

---

[15] We must, of course, recognize here that whether, or in what sense, migrant workers, and especially those on fixed-term contracts, should be regarded as being themselves an element in the class structures of the nations into which they enter has proved a controversial issue. However, as already noted, they were in any event excluded from the German enquiry on which we rely.

THE MOBILITY CHARACTERISTICS OF CLASSES

In the foregoing we have followed the standard approach of comparative mobility research in taking nations as our units of analysis, and then addressing directly questions of the degree of similarity or variation in the mobility that is displayed from one such national case to another. However, in the most recent literature one may discern a shift towards a rather different approach which, so far at least as absolute rates are concerned, we would see as possessing a larger sociological potential. In this new approach, which we shall here attempt to pursue, the units of analysis are taken, in the first place, to be *classes* rather than nations, and the comparative questions that are then taken up are ones of the extent to which, from nation to nation, distinctive rates and patterns of mobility can be found associated with different classes. In other words, one could say that the aim is to explore regularities not in the mobility characteristics of nations considered across classes but, instead, in the mobility characteristics of classes considered across nations.

Two main reasons exist for supposing that to seek regularities of this kind might be rewarding. First, it would seem to be possible to think of classes within industrial societies as having their particular 'natural histories'. As we have seen, it is difficult to generalize about the development of national class structures taken overall, chiefly because the various aspects of change involved, though perhaps similar in themselves, tend from case to case to be quite differently phased relative to each other. But if we do in fact focus our attention on the trajectories of specific classes—that is, on their tendencies for growth or decline—as industrial societies emerge and continue their economic advance, a number of regularities may be claimed that are indeed of a rather commonplace kind. Secondly, we have in the preceding chapters sought to show that industrial nations do reveal a substantial commonality in their relative mobility rates; and, as our model of core social fluidity aims to bring out, this commonality can be understood in terms of the propensities for mobility, and immobility, that derive from the differing attributes of classes, considered as ones of either origin or destination.

Given the degree of regularity that is in these two respects apparent, it is not then implausible to envisage that, in turn, some regularity may also be found in certain aspects of absolute mobility rates associated with particular classes. More specifically, it may be suggested that, in inflow perspective, classes will show some consistent differentiation cross-nationally in the degree of the homogeneity (or heterogeneity) of their recruitment or, in other words, in the range of the previous experience of class membership of those individuals whom at any one time they comprise; and, in outflow perspective, in their degree of retentiveness or 'holding power' in regard to those individuals who at any point become their members, whatever their origins or previous mobility experience.

In exploring such possibilities, we would ideally wish to have data on the complete work histories of respondents in our national samples; it is, in fact, in analyses using such data that the approach we have outlined was initially taken up (cf. Goldthorpe 1980*a*/1987: ch. 5; Featherman and Selbee 1988; Featherman, Selbee, and Mayer 1989). Unfortunately, the enquiries on which our present comparative study is based did not for the most part collect information of the kind in question,[16] and the indicators of both the heterogeneity and the retentiveness of classes to which we shall resort will, therefore, be quite crude ones. However, we do have the advantage of being able to compare our own findings with those so far reported from several studies now being undertaken with more appropriate data bases, since the authors of these studies have adopted our class schema in one version or another.

The results to which our subsequent discussion will chiefly refer are presented in Tables 6.8, 6.9, and 6.10. In Table 6.8 we utilize an index of the homogeneity of classes in terms of the social origins of their members that was first proposed by Blau and Duncan (1967: 52–3). This is derived by interpreting the percentage inflow distribution for a particular class as the set of probabilities of an individual in this class being from each of the possible classes of origin and by then summing the squares of these probabilities— which is in fact equivalent to the probability that any two individuals in the class chosen at random will have the same class origins. The highest value that the index can take is 1, where all present members of a class are of the same class origin; and the lowest value will be the reciprocal of the number of classes involved in the analysis—in our case $1/7 = 0.14$—where the members of a class come from each class of origin with equal probability. In Table 6.8 we have expressed the index as a percentage of this minimum, so that, the larger the value reported, the more homogeneous a class is in its composition. The maximum value that may be recorded will then, of course, be 700.

In Tables 6.9 and 6.10 we then show measures of the retentiveness of classes that are of a simpler kind. The former table gives intergenerational stability rates for each class and the latter work-life stability rates; that is, the percentages, respectively, of men of a given class of origin and of a given class of first employment who were found in that same class at the time of the enquiry to which they responded.[17] In calculating the work-life stability rates of Table 6.10, we have restricted our attention to men aged 35–64 so as

---

[16] Complete work-history data were in fact collected only in the enquiries in Hungary, the Republic of Ireland, and Northern Ireland.

[17] We thus use 'stability' here to refer to immobility viewed in an outflow perspective. Note, however, that, since stability is here determined on the basis of only two observations, it need in no way imply *continuity* of the incumbency of a particular class position. To determine the extent of such continuity, complete work-history data are essential. For further information on the definition of 'first employment', see pp. 284–5.

TABLE 6.8. *Indices of homogeneity of classes in terms of members' class origins expressed as percentage of minimum value*

Nation	I+II	III	IV$a+b$	IVc	V+VI	VIIa	VIIb
ENG	165	167	159	339	228	206	183
FRA	143	112	159	574	137	136	229
FRG	172	152	171	613	210	160	162
HUN	112	110	142	369	129	163	286
IRL	128	119	164	599	172	157	305
NIR	131	123	142	596	166	187	267
POL	162	238	194	604	187	227	278
SCO	160	169	154	401	237	225	190
SWE	131	141	136	494	153	153	221
Range	112–172	110–238	136–194	339–613	129–237	136–227	162–305
Median	143	141	159	574	172	163	229

TABLE 6.9. *Intergenerational stability rates of classes*

Nation	Percentage of men originating in a given class found in that class at time of enquiry						
	I+II	III	IV$a+b$	IVc	V+VI	VIIa	VIIb
ENG	59	13	21	23	41	32	16
FRA	60	17	27	37	39	30	15
FRG	61	6	24	25	49	33	13
HUN	52	14	8	—*	50	38	22
IRL	55	24	28	51	47	35	21
NIR	57	22	27	39	39	39	13
POL	60	3	11	43	52	27	16
SCO	59	10	19	41	41	33	22
SWE	56	13	17	17	38	26	7
Range	52–61	3–24	8–28	17–51	38–52	26–39	7–22
Median	59	13	21	38	41	33	16

Note:
  * Hungary is here left out of account as a special case, in view of the virtually total collectivization of agriculture.

to reduce the number of those who appear as stable in their class of first employment but who have been in employment for only a short period.

In each of the three tables we give cross-national ranges and medians for the measures used as a basis for assessing the extent to which, across nations, classes do display distinctive mobility characteristics, at least so far as

TABLE 6.10. *Work-life stability rates of classes*

Nation	Percentage of men, aged 35–64, entering employment in a given class, found in that class at time of enquiry*			
	I+II	III	V+VI	VIIa
ENG	81	19	46	38
FRA	87	21	40	32
HUN	84	33	62	50
IRL	90	28	52	48
NIR	87	24	47	47
POL	84	22	63	49
SCO	73	19	49	47
SWE	88	19	49	28
Range	73–90	19–33	40–63	28–50
Median	85	22	49	47

Note:

  * Data in this table are restricted to eight nations and to four classes. As earlier noted, we do not have information on class of first employment for men in the FRG; and, further, the numbers of men entering employment via Class IV*a*+*b* are too small in any nation to permit reliable analysis, while the distinction between farmers in Class IV*c* and farm workers in Class VII*b* cannot in the case of first employment be implemented in a cross-nationally comparable way (see further, p. 285).

homogeneity and retentiveness are concerned. It can be seen that, while some amount of cross-national variation is always present, and is indeed in some instances quite wide, clear tendencies are none the less shown up for the cross-national ranges for different classes, or sets of classes, to fall within certain bands which overlap only slightly, if at all. In what follows, we will seek to elaborate on this argument, treating the classes of our schema in four separate groups.

Agricultural classes (Classes IVc and VIIb)

As industrial societies emerge and develop, agricultural classes decline in size, at varying rates but—as Figure 3.1 can serve to show—with little or no interruption. The mobility propensities of agricultural classes, as we have modelled these in Chapters 4 and 5, are dominated by sectoral effects; that is, barriers to movement between these classes and non-agricultural ones which exist quite apart from any hierarchical effects that may also apply. In addition, Class IV*c*, that of farmers, reveals an exceptionally high propensity for intergenerational immobility, associated, we have suggested, with both the inheritance of land and family traditions of work on the land. This means, therefore, that the changing structural context—cf. Table 6.5—and sectoral and inheritance effects in one respect operate conjointly: that is, in restricting the opportunities for entry into agricultural employment.

With this last point in mind, the results found in Table 6.8 can then be readily understood. Across all nations, Class IVc shows a quite exceptionally high degree of homogeneity in the social origins of its members; they are in fact overwhelmingly the sons of farmers and, to a lesser extent, of farm workers. And, while the homogeneity of Class VIIb is somewhat less pronounced—as might be expected, since inheritance effects are here weaker—this class is still in most nations more homogeneous than any other apart from IVc.

On the other hand, when we come to consider the retentiveness of agricultural classes, we must recognize that, from this point of view, structural effects run *counter to* sectoral and inheritance effects—that is, in encouraging, or indeed compelling, some amount of mobility away from agricultural work. Thus, it is not surprising to find that Table 6.9 shows levels of intergenerational stability within Class IVc that fall fairly consistently into an intermediate band (treating the Hungarian case as a special one), while those within Class VIIb now lie clearly in the lowest band.

We cannot ourselves provide any reliable measure of work-life stability within our agricultural classes, but studies based on complete work histories provide results that fit well into the foregoing account.[18] The holding power of farming appears to be generally high; that is, those men who are at any one time found as farmers show a high probability of still being farmers at later points in their lives. This result is made possible by the fact that the decline in agricultural proprietorship, other than in its most rapid phases, tends to be 'managed' far more through processes of cohort succession than of work-life mobility. However, this is not the case with agricultural labour, and in turn the retentiveness of Class VIIb is quite consistently found to be weak, and indeed to be at a lower level than that of any other class.

The petty bourgeoisie (Class IVa+b)

The petty bourgeoisie also tends to decline in size as industrial societies develop. However, it would now appear that—contrary to the suppositions

---

[18] Two research projects drawing on complete work-history data and using techniques of event-history analysis to investigate the mobility characteristics of classes distinguished in our schema have already lead to publications: those of Featherman, Selbee, and Mayer on the FRG and Norway (see Featherman and Selbee 1988; Featherman, Selbee, and Mayer 1989; Mayer *et al.* 1989), and of Hout on the Republic of Ireland and Northern Ireland (see Hout 1989). In addition, we have been given access to so far unpublished results from work by Brendan Halpin of Nuffield College, Oxford, also on the Republic of Ireland, and by Colin Mills of the University of Surrey on recently collected British data (though the latter come not from a national sample but from a number of urban labour-market areas and are thus of restricted value, especially in relation to agricultural classes). Also of relevance is the work undertaken on Swedish longitudinal data by Jonsson (1992).

of liberal and Marxist theorists alike—in the context of advanced industrialism this decline is often checked or indeed reversed (Berger and Piore 1980; Müller 1988). Table 6.5 shows that, while in some of our nations mobility into the petty bourgeoisie is less structurally favoured than mobility into the industrial working class, in others the reverse applies. Under our model of core social fluidity (and most of its national variants) the petty bourgeoisie reveals a moderately strong propensity for intergenerational immobility, which we associate with the possibility of the direct inheritance of property; but, in other respects, it must in fact be regarded as being a rather open class. Neutral fluidity prevails—cf. Table 4.3—so far as mobility between the petty bourgeoisie and both the routine non-manual class and the skilled working class is concerned, and, moreover, hierarchical and sectoral barriers to exchanges with the service class and the farm class respectively are offset by positive affinities specifically intended to reflect the possibility of transfers of property.

As these somewhat diverse influences might lead one to expect, class mobility characteristics are not always so readily specified in this case as in others. However, from Table 6.8 it can be seen that, in terms of the homogeneity of the class origins of its members, the petty bourgeoisie tends fairly consistently to fall into the lowest band—though with Poland (where, it will be recalled, inheritance effects were especially strong) as an outlying case. And from Table 6.9 it appears that, despite inheritance effects, the intergenerational stability of the petty bourgeoisie is likewise at a generally low level from nation to nation. Here the good possibilities for the sons of the petty bourgeoisie to move up into the service class, as well as their propensity to enter either routine non-manual or skilled manual positions, must be regarded as strong countervailing influences to immobility.

So far as work-life stability is concerned, we are again unable to provide useful information from our own data-set. However, analyses of complete work histories would suggest that, in this perspective, the retentiveness of petty-bourgeois positions should be seen as clearly greater. Their holding power would appear in fact to lie at an intermediate level, below that of farmers but well above that of farm workers. Furthermore, there are indications from several sources (Lafont and Leborgne 1974; Goldthorpe 1980a/1987: 128–9; Mayer 1987) that, while at any one time the petty bourgeoisie will appear to be made up of individuals with quite diverse experience of previous class memberships, a tendency does still exist for men to *return to* self-employment and small proprietorship over the course of their working lives after periods in other class locations.

The working class (Classes V+VI and VIIa)

The trajectory followed by the working classes of industrial societies is by now well established as curvilinear (see, e.g., Bell 1973; Gagliani 1985). A substantial and often rapid increase—at the expense chiefly of the declining agricultural work-force—eventually slows down into a phase of stability, which is in turn succeeded by one of incipient decline as the 'post-industrial' era is reached. Under our modelling of social fluidity patterns, both Classes V+VI and VIIa—that is, both the skilled and non-skilled divisions of the working class—display only rather weak inheritance effects. However, at the same time we see the strongest propensities for mobility as operating *between* these classes, in consequence of affinities of status offsetting hierarchical differences in material rewards and entry requirements (cf. pp. 129, 134–5). Hierarchical barriers do in general impose greater restrictions on mobility into and from Class VIIa; but, so far as the inflow of men of agricultural origins is concerned, this class is more open than Class V+VI.

One would thus anticipate, as Table 6.8 indeed largely confirms, that the homogeneity of working classes will tend to be rather low, other than in two circumstances: that is, either where, at a relatively early stage of industrialization, recruitment is overwhelmingly of men of agricultural backgrounds, which in fact explains the relatively high index for Class VIIa in Poland; or where, within a mature industrial society, both the skilled and non-skilled divisions of the working class are so large that, despite weak inheritance effects, their reproduction is still possible chiefly through self- plus inter-recruitment, which is the case, as we have in fact earlier described, in England and Scotland.

On the other hand, though, as regards the retentiveness of working classes, structural effects are more favourable. At least prior to the full emergence of 'post-industrialism', they will impose no constraints on the extent of intergenerational succession of the kind that operate in the case of agricultural classes. And from Table 6.9 it can then be seen that, while the level of intergenerational stability is in most nations somewhat higher within Class V+VI than Class VIIa—which may be taken as primarily an effect of size—both classes tend to go together with Class IVc in the intermediate band that can be distinguished.

A similar conclusion is, moreover, to be drawn from Table 6.10 in respect of work-life stability; and this would in turn appear to be generally confirmed by studies based on complete work histories, although the latter also suggest two qualifications of some interest. First, over the course of men's working lives the retentiveness of Class VI and Class VIIa does not appear to differ all that greatly, while the holding power of Class V—that of lower-grade technical and supervisory personnel, which, for reasons of comparability, we are obliged to collapse with Class VI—is clearly stronger. Secondly, though, it is usually the case that a large part of the work-life mobility experienced by men who are at any one time found in Class VI or Class VIIa is again in fact mobility *between* these two classes—in other words, between the skilled and non-skilled divisions of the working class; and thus work-life stability within the broad range of manual wage-earning positions could be regarded as quite high.

White-collar classes (Classes I+II and III)

White-collar classes are the expanding classes of industrial societies. Although from nation to nation and period to period they may grow at differing rates, and in differing relation to the trajectories followed by other classes, the long-term trend is not in question. Furthermore, it is by now clear, as we have observed in Chapter 1, that, as industrial development proceeds, expansion tends to be more sustained at the higher than the lower white-collar levels: that is, in the professional, administrative, and managerial positions of the service class, as represented by our Class I+II, rather than in the routine non-manual positions of Class III. In our modelling of the mobility propensities associated with white-collar classes, the service class appears as subject to relatively strong inheritance effects, since possibilities exist for the intergenerational transmission of both economic and cultural capital; and propensities for mobility between this class and others are quite strongly differentiated by hierarchical as well as sectoral effects. In contrast, the routine non-manual class has weak inheritance effects and is in general rather open; a high propensity exists for mobility between this class and the service class, and neutral fluidity prevails as regards exchanges with both the petty bourgeoisie and the skilled working class.

So far as the homogeneity of the service class is concerned, we may judge from Table 6.8 that the influence of structural effects is overriding. We have earlier seen from Table 6.5 that across all our nations alike these effects favour mobility into the service class over mobility into any other; and the extent of 'recruitment from below' is indeed such that, notwithstanding the wide inequalities in chances of access that exist, the homogeneity of social origins of those men found in service-class positions is consistently low. With the routine non-manual class, structural effects may be reckoned as less important than its inherent openness, but the outcome proves to be much the same. For only one nation—Poland—does homogeneity fall clearly outside the low band, as a result, in fact, of routine non-manual workers being recruited largely from among men of farm backgrounds.

When, however, we turn to their retentiveness, our two white-collar classes are quite sharply contrasted. In the case of the service class, structural effects may now be regarded as working together with inheritance, hierarch-ical, and sectoral effects so as to restrict intergenerational outflow. And from Table 6.9 it can then be seen that the level of intergenerational stability across the service classes of our nations is distinctively high. In the case of the routine non-manual class, on the other hand, such structural effects as may favour intergenerational stability are not powerful enough to offset those of fluidity patterns, and levels of stability are thus found regularly to fall within the low band.

This same contrast is again apparent in regard to work-life stability. Table 6.10 shows the holding power of Class I+II to be quite remarkably strong—reflecting, we would suggest, not only the general desirability of service-class positions but also the relative security offered by bureaucratic conditions of employment (cf. Goldthorpe 1982)—while the retentiveness of Class III is weak. And these findings are ones that work-history analyses substantially underwrite. In particular, service-class employment emerges from such analyses as that from which men are least likely to move during the course of their working lives. Routine non-manual positions are typically held for much shorter periods of time, although in full life-course perspective their holding power in some nations appears rather more comparable to that of working-class positions than our cruder analyses might suggest.

It is then possible to summarize the foregoing accounts of the mobility characteristics of the classes of our schema in the form of Table 6.11. The schematic nature of the presentation here does admittedly somewhat exaggerate the sharpness of the differences between classes in their levels of homogeneity and retentiveness from nation to nation. On the other hand, though, it serves to bring out what is not, we believe, at all an illusory finding: namely, that our classes do tend to be rather distinctive in the combination, or 'profile', of the mobility characteristics that they display overall. It would seem apparent enough that we are not dealing here with merely arbitrary categories, nor with what are simply divisions of some single underlying stratification 'dimension'. Different locations in the class structure—that is, sets of positions defined by differing employment relations—can be seen to influence in specific if quite complex ways the mobility experience of men who live out their working lives within this structure, and to do so in a broadly similar fashion across the range of industrial nations

TABLE 6.11. *Mobility characteristics of classes*

Class	Homogeneity	Retentiveness	
		Intergenerational	Work-life
I+II	low	high	high
III	low	low	low/intermediate
IVa+b	low	low	intermediate
IVc	high	intermediate	intermediate/high
V+VI	low/intermediate	intermediate	intermediate
VIIa	low/intermediate	intermediate	intermediate
VIIb	intermediate	low	low

from which our data derive. This finding we would then take as underlining the heuristic value of the general position that we have adopted throughout our work of treating social mobility within a class-structural context, as well as confirming the promise of the approach to the analysis of absolute mobility rates that we have followed in this section.

As this approach is further developed—and we would again emphasize the potential in this connection of data-sets comprising complete work histories—it should be possible to obtain both better, that is, fuller, descriptions of cross-national variation in absolute rates than we so far have available, and also a better understanding of the determinants of this variation, whether this be found at the level of macrosociological or of more specific historical analyses.

Moreover, it is, in our view, via this approach that mobility research could best proceed from the description and analysis of rates and patterns *per se*, with which we are chiefly concerned in this volume, to address the further issues of the relationship of class mobility to class formation and action that we noted at the start. Thus, to discuss the homogeneity and retentiveness of different classes is simply another way of treating the degree of their 'demographic identity' (Goldthorpe 1980a/1987: ch. 12) or, that is, the degree to which they have formed as collectivities of individuals and families identifiable through the continuity of their association with particular sets of class positions over time. And it is from such considerations that further investigation may then best proceed into the extent to which conditions exist favourable to the formation of classes as distinctive socio-cultural entities with, for example, the potential for class socialization (cf. Featherman and Spenner 1990) and, in turn, to the development of the class identities and solidarities that are essential if action aimed at realizing class interests is to be effectively pursued (cf. Wright and Shin 1988). From Table 6.11 it is evident enough that in this respect very significant differences exist across the classes that are distinguished in our schema. Thus, for example, the mobility characteristics associated with Class III are such that whether it could be said to possess a demographic identity at all has to be regarded as problematic (cf. Stewart, Prandy, and Blackburn 1980)—with damaging implications for the relevance of the entire debate that has been conducted within Marxist circles on the political potential of the 'new white-collar proletariat' or 'new petty bourgeoisie' (see, e.g., Braverman 1974; Poulantzas 1974; Crompton and Gubbay 1977; Wright 1978). Furthermore, even where mobility characteristics are more favourable to class formation at the demographic level, it is still apparent that homogeneity in recruitment and retentiveness over generations and the life-course tend to be involved in differing degree, so that the bases of class identities may in some cases lie chiefly in the experience of a shared past but in others more in the anticipation of a common future.

However, as we indicated at the outset, these are not lines of enquiry that we can ourselves seek to advance within the conception, and on the data base, of the present study. In the chapters that follow our purpose is, in fact, not so much to expand the range of our concerns as to examine further—whether to the end of consolidation or qualification—the major findings and arguments on mobility rates and patterns in industrial society that we have so far presented. In Chapter 2 we noted that the recoding exercise that we undertook of data from national mobility enquiries left us with better information on intergenerational than on work-life mobility, on men than on women, and on European than on non-European nations. We have thus given primary consideration to the intergeneration mobility of men in the nine European nations that our data-set includes. From now onwards, though, we shall address ourselves essentially to the question of how far the results that we have produced and the conclusions that we have reached on this basis might appear in need of revision if a somewhat more comprehensive view of mobility in industrial societies were to be taken. We consider in turn issues concerning the class mobility of women, the relationship between work-life and intergenerational mobility, and the possible 'exceptionalism' of mobility rates and patterns in three non-European industrial societies, the United States, Australia, and Japan.

ANNEX: Partitioning Variance in Logged Odds between Expected Cell Values

The expected logged counts from the topological model of the mobility table that we have proposed as a more structured version of that of equation (6.1) may be written as

$$\log F_{ij} = \mu + \lambda_i^O + \lambda_j^D + \lambda_{a(ij)}{}^I$$

where μ is a scale factor, λ_i^O is the parameter for the effect of the ith origin, λ_j^D is the parameter for the effect of the jth destination, and $\lambda_{a(ij)}{}^I$ is the interaction parameter of the i,jth cell, that is, the sum of the hierarchy, inheritance, sector, and affinity parameters for that cell.

To aid our exposition here, we may express the above equation, as it would refer to one of our national variant models, in the following, simplified notation

$$L_{ij} = \log F_{ij} = \mu + O_i + D_j + I_{ij} \text{ for } i,j = 1, \ldots, 7. \tag{1}$$

The logged odds of any two expected frequencies, F_{ij} and F_{kl} are then equal to

$$L_{ij} - L_{kl} = (O_i - O_k) + (D_j - D_l) + (I_{ij} - I_{kl}) \text{ for } i,j,k,l = 1, \ldots, 7. \tag{2}$$

Let $f_m = (L_{ij} - L_{kl})$, $o_m = (O_i - O_k)$, $d_m = (D_j - D_l)$ and $i_m = (I_{ij} - I_{kl})$. Then (2) can be written as

$$f_m = o_m + d_m + i_m \text{ for } m = 1, \ldots, 7^4 = 2401$$

if we include the cases where $(i,j) = (k,l)$, where the logged odds will always be equal to zero.

Note that for each m, there is some m' such that $f_m = -f_{m'}$, $o_m = -o_{m'}$, $d_m = -d_{m'}$, and $i_m = -i_{m'}$, since in the count on m each pair of cells in the mobility matrix will be included twice but with opposite signs, i.e. both $(L_{ij} - L_{kl})$ and $(L_{kl} - L_{ij})$ will be included for each (i,j,k,l). Therefore, $\Sigma f_m = \Sigma o_m = \Sigma d_m = \Sigma i_m = 0$.

The sum of the squared logged odds may be partitioned into five terms as follows:

$$\Sigma f_m^2 = \Sigma o_m^2 + \Sigma d_m^2 + \Sigma i_m^2 + 2\Sigma o_m i_m + 2\Sigma d_m i_m \tag{3}$$

where each summation is over the whole range of values of m. The third crossproduct term, $2\Sigma o_m d_m$, will be equal to zero.

For any covariate X_{ij}, let $X.. = \Sigma\Sigma X_{ij}/49$ and $S_x^2 = \Sigma\Sigma(X_{ij} - X..)^2/49$. Similarly, let $S_{xy}^2 = \Sigma\Sigma(X_{ij} - X..)(Y_{ij} - Y..)/49$. Note that if $X_{ij} = O_i$, then $X.. = \Sigma O_i/7$ and $S_O^2 = \Sigma(O_{ij} - O..)^2/7$.

It is then easily shown that

$$S_L^2 = S_O^2 + S_D^2 + S_I^2 + 2S_{OI}^2 + 2S_{DI}^2 \qquad (4)$$

because $S_{OD}^2 = 0$. Also

$$\Sigma f_m^2 = 2 \times 49^2 \times S_L^2. \qquad (5)$$

Note the structural similarity between (3) and (4). We prefer the latter, seemingly more complicated, approach for reasons that will be evident later.[1]

Σf_m^2 may be regarded as a measure of the total association in the mobility matrix. It will be zero only under the equiprobable model, that is, when expected frequencies are all equal. It will be the greater, the more the expected frequencies in the mobility matrix differ from each other. Thus, according to (3), (4), and (5), the association in a mobility matrix can be partitioned into five elements relating to origin effects, destination effects, and interaction effects, and further to compositional effects between origins and interactions and between destinations and interactions, respectively. The two latter terms may become negative, in which case we must assume that the compositional effects reduce the association produced by the main effects. That these terms may become negative also means that it is not possible to partition the variation in L into proportions accounted for by the different factors in a straightforward manner.

Consider now that we have nine national-variant models. By extension of our notation, the mth logged odds of expected values in the vth national model is f_{vm} ($v = 1, \ldots, 9$). We thus have nine logged odds for each value of m. The sum of the squared deviations from the total mean may, in standard fashion, be separated into two parts: that is, according to (i) the variation between national models in logged odds for each pair of cells in the mobility matrices, and (ii) the variation in mean logged odds between different pairs of cells, i.e.

$$\sum_m \sum_v f_{vm}^2 = \sum_m \sum_v (f_{vm} - f_{.m})^2 + 9 \sum_m (f_{.m})^2 \qquad (6)$$

---

[1] If the model is written according to Sobel, Hout, and Duncan (1985), (1) will take the form

$$L_{ij} = \mu + O_i + O_j + S_j + I_{ij}$$

where $S_j = D_j - O_j$.
Then (2) will take the form

$$L_{ij} - L_{kl} = (O_i - O_k) + (O_j - O_l) + (S_j - S_l) + (I_{ij} - I_{kl})$$

and (3) becomes

$$\Sigma f_m^2 = \Sigma o_m^2 + \Sigma c_m^2 + \Sigma s_m^2 + \Sigma i_m^2 + 2\Sigma o_m i_m + 2\Sigma c_m i_m + 2\Sigma s_m i_m + 2\Sigma c_m s_m,$$

where $c_m = (O_j - O_l)$ and $s_m = (S_j - S_l)$,
while (4) becomes

$$S_L^2 = 2S_O^2 + S_S^2 + S_I^2 + 4S_{OI}^2 + 2S_{SI}^2 + 2S_{CS}^2$$

where $f_{.m}$ is the average expected logged odds in the mth pair of cells for all national variant models.

Each element on the right-hand side of (6) may be split into constituent parts, again using what should be obvious notation:[2]

$$\sum_m \sum_v (f_{vm} - f_{.m})^2 = \sum_m \sum_v (o_{vm} - o_{.m})^2 + \sum_m \sum_v (d_{vm} - d_{.m})^2 +$$
$$\sum_m \sum_v (i_{vm} - i_{.m})^2 + 2 \sum_m \sum_v (\sum o_{vm} i_{vm} - 9 o_{.m} i_{.m}) + 2 \sum_m (\sum_v d_{vm} i_{vm} - 9 d_{.m} i_{.m}) \quad (7)$$

and

$$\Sigma f_{.m}^2 = \Sigma o_{.m}^2 + \Sigma d_{.m}^2 + \Sigma i_{.m}^2 + 2 \Sigma o_{.m} i_{.m} + 2 \Sigma d_{.m} i_{.m}. \quad (8)$$

Thus, the variation in the logged odds among all the national variant models may be partitioned into five terms related to differences between models and again into five terms related to differences between pairs of cells. The two sets of five terms may be interpreted as indicating the importance of origin parameters, destination parameters, interaction parameters, and two compositional effects for the variation between nations and between pairs of cells, respectively. Even though, because of the compositional effects, we cannot give a simple account for how much of the variation is accounted for by origins, destinations, and interactions, we can still find the range of how much each factor could possibly account for. Thus, the minimum of $\Sigma f_{.m}^2$ that, say, interaction effects could account for is $\Sigma i_{.m}^2$ plus possible negative compositional effects ($2 \Sigma o_{.m} i_{.m}$ and/or $2 \Sigma d_{.m} i_{.m}$); while the maximum is $\Sigma i_{.m}^2$ plus possible positive compositional effects.

The bottom row of Table 6.6 shows that the variance in logged odds between nations related to interaction effects, $\Sigma i_{.m}^2$, is 0.55, while the variance related to compositional effects between origins and interactions, $2 \Sigma o_{.m} i_{.m}$, is 0.03 and that related to such effects between destinations and interactions, $2 \Sigma d_{.m} i_{.m}$, is -0.23. Thus, as reported in the text, the maximum of the variance in logged odds between nations that interaction effects could account for is 16 per cent ($(0.55 + 0.03)/3.57$), while the minimum is 9 per cent ($(0.55 - 0.23)/3.57$).

---

[2] It is in order to make the partition in (9) possible that we prefer to treat the variation in our mobility tables in terms of logged odds rather than of expected values. It would be possible to partition the variation in expected values between models in a similar way to that we have proposed. However, we would then have to standardize the parameters to make their average values equal to zero, and also to make the general means in all national models the same. Thus, the more general partitioning based on logged odds appeared preferable.

7

The Class Mobility of Women

From the 1970s onwards the charge that studies of social mobility seriously neglect the experience of women became a commonplace of 'feminist' sociology (see, e.g., Acker 1973; Delphy 1981; Roberts and Woodward 1981; Allen 1982; Abbott and Sapsford 1987).[1] The charge may be disputed— and still more so the assertion usually associated with it that this neglect stems from 'entrenched androcentrism' or 'sexism' on the part of (predominantly male) mobility researchers (Goldthorpe 1980a/1987: ch. 10). However, the issues that thus arise are ones relating more to the profession of sociology and the conduct of its practitioners than to the sociology of stratification or gender *per se*; and, although we believe that these issues should certainly be taken further, this is not the place to attempt to do so.

In this chapter we shall in fact pursue questions that are directed to rather sharply defined goals. Our main objective will be to discover what can be learnt from the analysis of the data on women's social mobility that we have available to us that is of relevance to our central concern with mobility *as viewed within a class-structural context*. More specifically still, we will be interested in the extent to which, when we thus bring the experience of women within the scope of our enquiry, modifications become necessary to findings and arguments that we have previously presented on the basis of data referring to men alone.

However, to set the focus on the class mobility of women is thus at once to raise a further conceptual problem: namely, that of the appropriate unit of class composition. Is this the individual, man or woman; or, in so far as men and women live together in conjugal families, are these the units in terms of which class membership and in turn class mobility can best be treated? We would ourselves accept the latter, and reject the former position; and, in the first section of this chapter, we give our *a priori* grounds for so doing and in turn for favouring or disfavouring different research practices in regard to class allocation. At the same time, though, we also argue that it is by reference to the *empirical consequences* of different conceptual choices, and of different ways of rendering these choices operational, that their comparative evaluation must in the end be made.

[1] We here place 'feminist' in inverted commas since we would wish to question the implicit claim that only those adhering to a sociology thus styled can have a serious commitment to feminism—understood as a belief and practical concern that women should possess a full equality of opportunity with men, *de jure* and *de facto*, so far as participation in economic and public life generally is concerned. As will emerge, we believe that several lines of argument favoured by 'feminist' sociologists, as well as being mistaken in themselves, actually do a *dis*service to feminism in the above sense.

This argument becomes of particular relevance when, after reviewing in the second section of the chapter the extent of the data we have available on women's mobility, we turn in the next to our first substantive analyses. These are of major interest not within our own conceptual approach but rather within the opposing 'individual' approach in which the class position of all economically active women is seen as being determined—in just the same way as with men—by the nature of their own employment. If the results we report here were to be taken at their face value, they would indeed in certain respects point to conclusions significantly different from those we have reached in studying men's mobility only. However, their validity as data on *class* mobility is, we argue, made questionable by *other* results that must also be accepted as following from the 'individual' approach; and, in this way, a dilemma is created for its exponents which they seem so far to have tried to avoid rather than resolve. From our own standpoint, we are able to offer an alternative interpretation of the analyses in question, and one which, moreover, shows them as complementing rather than contradicting results that we have previously reported.

In the remainder of the chapter we then turn to analyses of women's class mobility on lines that our own conceptual stance would directly dictate. In the fourth section we treat women's 'marital mobility', and consider hypotheses that have been advanced to the effect that in modern societies women's chances of mobility through marriage are either better than those of men through employment—in the sense of being more likely to be upward in direction—or are less closely tied to class origins. Clearly, to the extent that such hypotheses are supported, analyses that are based on the experience of men alone may be thought likely to give an unduly limited picture of mobility opportunities.

In the fifth section we consider how, within the conceptual approach that we favour, and given the data available to us, we may best construct 'complete' mobility tables: that is, ones which refer to the total, male and female populations of national societies. In producing such tables for four of the nine European nations represented in our data-set, we apply what has become known as the 'dominance' method of determining the class position of conjugal families. We then proceed to compare results from the 'complete' tables with those from the 'men-only' tables that we have previously analysed, and on this basis seek to make some assessment of how far—and under what circumstances—our ideas about rates and patterns of class mobility derived from the latter are likely to be in need of revision.

DETERMINING THE CLASS POSITION OF WOMEN

In our view, the class position, and thus the class mobility, of women—as indeed of men also—may best be determined if the family is given priority over the individual as the unit of class composition; or, that is, if individuals living together as a family are regarded as having one and the same class location. Such a view has been that most commonly found among theorists of class from Schumpeter (1927/1951: 148–62) through to Parkin (1971*a*: 14–15), and the arguments that previous authors have advanced in its favour are ones that we would ourselves largely underwrite.[2] Two considerations would seem of particular importance.

First, in so far as members of a family live together or, that is, constitute a household, a broad similarity may be expected to prevail not only in their material conditions of life as these exist at any one time but further in a wide range of their future life-chances. The family is, in other words, the unit of class 'fate'. Secondly, the economic decision-making in which family members engage, in regard to both consumption and 'production'—especially, of course, work-force participation—is typically of a joint or interdependent kind. The family is, at the 'micro' level, a key unit of strategic action pursued within the class structure.

What it would seem here necessary to add—in view of frequent suggestions to the contrary—is that to treat the family as being 'class unitary' in these ways does *not* require that it be seen as in all respects an entity of an egalitarian and solidary kind. Thus, the possibility is in no way precluded that some inequality may exist within the general living standard of the household as between men and women—or, for that matter, as between persons in different age-groups; nor again that within decision-making processes some family members may be able to exert greater power than do others. The implication would rather be that such inequalities, where they exist, and likewise the intrafamilial conflicts to which they may give rise, should be regarded as being not ones of class, but of gender—or of age—*per se*.[3]

Indeed, far from being inattentive to differences in resources and power among family members, sociologists who would maintain the class unitary nature of the family have underlined precisely such differences in seeking to justify the practice they have most often adopted in empirical research: that of taking the class position of the conjugal family as following from that of its male 'head'. The husband/father, it has been held, is typically that member

---

[2] We refer here to the family as being the appropriate unit of class composition rather than, as previously (e.g. Goldthorpe 1983; Erikson and Goldthorpe 1988), the appropriate unit of class *analysis*. Our present usage is, we believe, more precise in that there can, in fact, be no objection, from our point of view, to taking the individual as the unit in class analysis, *provided that* members of the same conjugal family are assigned to the same class. Cf. the analogous situation in the study of income distribution, as discussed, for example, in Uusitalo (1985).

[3] We would, in addition, observe that no evidence has been produced to indicate that intrafamilial inequalities are of at all the same magnitude as those existing between families in different class positions. To investigate inequality within families is an inherently difficult task, but we would regard research thus far undertaken to this end as being conspicuously weak. Far too much weight has been tendentiously given to evidence that in fact relates to other matters—e.g. different systems of household financial management—or that comes from small samples of very questionable representativeness. Attempts to legitimize the latter approach as 'new paradigm research' (Wilson 1987: 64) are, to say the least, unfortunate.

of the family who has the fullest commitment to work-force participation; and hence it will be through his class position—his involvement in employment relations and the advantages or disadvantages, opportunities or constraints, that result—that the articulation of the family with the class structure will be crucially effected. Or, in other words, the class position of other family members may be appropriately seen as being 'derived from', or 'mediated through', that of the male head in virtue of their degree of economic dependence upon him.

It is, none the less, on the practice in question, and especially on the allocation of married women to the same class position as their husbands, that feminist criticism has focused. The chief objection raised is that, while to proceed in this way may have had some plausibility for so long as most married women were not in paid employment, it has ceased to be defensible as women's work-force participation has generally increased. In these new circumstances, in which the large majority of women enter the labour market for at least some period, or periods, of their married lives, the case for routinely deriving a wife's class position from that of her husband is regarded as no longer tenable.

As we will later show, to give due recognition to the growth in women's employment and to its consequences does not in itself require that the idea of the family as the unit of class composition should be abandoned. But this is in fact the conclusion to which most exponents of 'feminist' sociology have wished to proceed. In the present-day context, they would maintain, the class position of all individuals (or at least of all adult individuals) should be determined independently of their marital or family situation and by reference solely to their own employment—though including perhaps their *previous* employment if, as often in the case of married women, work-force participation has been discontinuous (see, e.g., Acker 1973; Delphy 1981; Stanworth 1984; Walby 1986; Abbott and Sapsford 1987).

However, despite the number of those who have declared in its favour, it is not easy to find fully worked-out statements of the case for this 'individual' approach. In part at least, its acceptance would seem motivated by extra-sociological concerns: for women to have their class positions 'derived' from those of men, rather than being treated in the same way as men, is found in itself to be morally or ideologically unacceptable. In so far as a sociological argument is also advanced, this would appear to rest—and most clearly in the writings of Marxist or *marxisant* feminists—on what might be termed (cf. Wright 1989a) a strongly 'work-centred' view of class. That is to say, class is seen as ultimately determined by the nature of the individual's involvement in relations of production or, more specifically, in the 'labour process'; and thus, the basic experience of class is taken to be that of the work-place—for example, experience of autonomy or control in work, or of authority or subordination. From this standpoint, then, if women are, or have been, in employment, it is this that must be crucial to their class allocation, while any notion of 'derived' class will obviously be problematic.

For our own part, we find little in the feminist critiques to which we have referred that would lead us to relinquish the view that lines of class division run between, but not through, families; and we would, furthermore, for several different reasons, regard the 'individual' approach to women's class allocation as being itself seriously misconceived.

First of all, most feminist authors would seem to have inadequately understood or represented just what the increased work-force participation of women has, and has not, entailed. A major change has indeed occurred with the decline in the practice of women withdrawing permanently from the labour market on marriage or after the birth of their first child; increasingly, women have returned to work following their years of 'active motherhood' or indeed for periods in between the births of children (for comparative data, see esp. Yohalem 1980; Bakker 1988). However, what has also to be recognized is that this revolution in *participation* has not for the most part been accompanied by similarly dramatic changes in other aspects of women's working lives: for example, to take up the useful categories of Rainwater, Rein, and Schwartz (1986) in their *attachment* to the work-force, in the *continuity* of their work histories or in the *contribution* that they are able to make through their employment to family incomes. Women still tend more often than men to quit the work-force—chiefly for reasons to do with child-bearing or child-care, but also on account of job changes by husbands that require the family to be geographically mobile;[4] and, in addition, women are far more likely than men to work less than full time. Consequently, women's work histories are more discontinuous than are those of men, and are also more likely to show instances of downward mobility or periods of 'under-employment' rather than steady career development (Martin and Roberts 1984; Moen 1984; Erikson 1987; König 1987). And then again, on account of the foregoing and also of persistent discrimination in job opportunities and in pay, the earnings of working wives have shown no strong tendency to increase in relation to the total income of their families—nor yet, it would seem, to offset the extent of economic inequality *among* families (Rainwater, Rein, and Schwartz 1986: chs. 4, 5; Bonney 1988a, 1988b; Björklund 1991).[5]

All these are points that one might well have expected feminists to emphasize. Yet, in their concern to make the case for determining women's class positions by reference to their own employment, exponents of 'feminist' sociology appear in fact to have been led into underestimating, or at all events understating, the degree to which married women's work, however

---

[4] Cf. Goldthorpe (1983: 475). A good indicator of women having achieved full equality with men in labour-market participation would be that husbands change employment in direct consequence of job shifts by their wives as frequently as the other way around.

[5] Also relevant here are the results of a cross-national analysis reported by Semyonov (1980) showing *higher* levels of women's work-force participation to be associated with *greater* occupational and income discrimination against women.

more extensive it has become, still fails to transform their situation of dependency. We would ourselves rather concur in what—in a different context—a feminist author, has indeed been ready to assert: namely, that 'it remains the case that over the lifetime of a marriage a woman's living standards most significantly derive [*sic*] from the status and conditions of her husband's employment, and from the level of his earnings.' (Finch 1983: 23). And for so long, then, as this dependency persists—or, one might prefer to say, a mutual but typically unequal dependency between husbands and wives—the choice of the conjugal family as the unit of class composition will remain appropriate.[6]

Secondly, as should already be apparent from Chapter 2, a work-centred view of class of the kind that apparently underpins the 'individual' approach is, for us, unduly limited. In our conception, class positions are defined in terms ultimately of employment relations in the sense we have indicated rather than of relations simply within the 'labour process'. In turn, therefore, basic class experiences will not be restricted to the work-place itself but will be ones that follow from involvement in employment relations of differing kinds, reflecting, as we have sought to show, the exigencies of both production units *and* labour markets together: for example, experiences of affluence or hardship, of economic security or insecurity, of prospects of continuing material advance, or of unyielding material constraints.[7] And these then are experiences that the members of a conjugal family will tend for the most part to share in common.

So far as the class position of married women is concerned, what is here at issue can be illustrated if we consider the case of two such women who are in identical jobs as, let us say, part-time shop assistants, but with one being married to an unskilled manual worker, and the other to a business manager. An exponent of the 'individual' approach, relying on a work-centred con-

---

[6] Other feminist authors have likewise stressed the degree of wives' dependence on lines very similar to our present argument—yet without apparently recognizing the implications for the debate on the class allocation of married women. Cf. Oakley: 'Assertions of increasing equality between the sexes are often based on employment statistics. . . . In fact the impression of convergence is illusory . . . behind these statistics of employment, the traditional differentiation between women's and men's roles endures still. . . . Women's defining role is a domestic one' (1974: 72–3). See further, for an essentially similar argument a decade and a half later, Joshi (1988).

[7] At the same time, we should note that claims such as those made by Walby to the effect that the approach we favour 'assumes a notion of class in which standard of living is the *determining* factor' (1986: 31; emphasis added) are totally mistaken—as also is Walby's further charge that this approach 'belongs to the ranking tradition [of social stratification research] rather than to the European tradition'. For us, employment relations are the crucial determinant of class position, but their implications must be seen as extending beyond the work-place to the whole of individuals' economic lives. Moreover, it is, of course, *part of* our argument that, simply because married women contribute to family income, and thus help raise family living standards, this is *not* in itself a sufficient basis on which to claim that their employment must change the class position of the family. It is surely those who maintain the opposite view who give standard of living a major role in deciding class membership.

ception of class, is obviously required to treat these women as having the same class position; their husbands' employment is irrelevant. For us, however, their class positions are clearly not the same; for we find no conceptual difficulty in recognizing the crucial—and widely differing—consequences that class relations are likely to have for the lives of these two women *via* their husbands' employment. And we may indeed ask of those who would favour the 'individual' approach: if the differences in question—in terms not only of current living standards but further of economic security and prospects—are *not* to be regarded as ones of class, just how then *are* they to be understood?

Thirdly, though, and most importantly, we would wish to return to a further point we made in Chapter 2, though in a different connection: that, in the end, different conceptual approaches must be judged by the results they produce when actually put to use. It is in fact in this respect that we find the 'individual' approach most obviously wanting. For, when applied in class analysis, it gives rise to results which, if not actually inconsistent, do none the less create serious interpretive problems, and ones moreover that are not encountered if it is the family rather than the individual that is seen as the unit of class composition. This we shall seek to demonstrate later in the chapter. For the moment, we would only add that, while conceptual approaches are not open to direct refutation in the same way as are substantive propositions, the nature of the results that follow from them can undermine their credibility—and especially so where their own exponents would appear reluctant to acknowledge *all* of the empirical consequences of the conceptual option they have taken.

On these various grounds, then, we would reject the 'individual' approach to the class allocation of women and continue to regard the conjugal family as being class unitary.[8] However, this does not necessarily mean adhering also to the practice of automatically determining the class position of the conjugal family by reference to that of the husband/father. Other ways of proceeding are in fact available that are designed to be more responsive to the decline in the number of families in which there is only one, male, 'bread-winner' and to the corresponding increase in the number of 'dual-earner' and indeed 'dual-career' families.

One possibility which has received some degree of support is that of the 'joint classification' of husbands and wives (see, esp., Britten and Heath 1983; Heath and Britten 1984). Those who would favour this approach emphasize not only the growing diversity in the economic bases of family life

[8] It is, we trust, evident that, in resting on empirical grounds of the kind indicated, our position here is entirely open to revision should certain changes occur. For example, we have no difficulty in envisaging circumstances in which we *would* think it appropriate to take over the individual approach. But our concern is with the—significantly different—circumstances that have in fact obtained—as regards this study, up to the mid-1970s—and not with predicting the future.

but, further, the likelihood of husband and wife, where both are in the work-force, having different kinds of employment. What is, therefore, proposed is that the class position of conjugal families should be determined by reference to the employment status and, where relevant, type of employment of *both* spouses. In this way, single- and dual-earner families can be distinguished, and also those in which the employment relations of husband and wife are sufficiently disparate for them to be regarded as at least potentially 'cross-class' families, in which ambivalence and tension over class identities and interests might be expected.

However, while 'joint classification' may appear attractive in principle, it does, as we have argued in detail elsewhere (Goldthorpe 1983, 1984; Erikson 1984), have major disadvantages in application. For one thing, it results in the class position of conjugal families being unduly influenced by their developmental stage. The probability of wives being in employment, or of working full rather than part time, is closely related to whether or not they have children and, if so, their number and age. Thus, in analysis, specifically class effects are likely to be confounded with those of household composition (cf. Dale 1987). Furthermore, and of greater relevance for our present purposes, 'joint classification' greatly accentuates problems of defin-ing class boundaries and tends to produce rates of class mobility that we would regard as being quite spuriously high. If, for example, families are treated as occupying a different class position every time the employment status of one or other of the spouses changes, whether through moving in or out of the labour market or between full- and part-time work, then the employment patterns of married women will themselves tend to generate levels of mobility sufficient to bring the demographic identity of all 'classes' that are distinguished close to vanishing point. And, since the very rationale of class analysis would be undermined were classes thus to appear as no more than highly unstable aggregates, one might again well ask if exponents of the approach in question would really wish to accept in full the empirical findings to which it will commit them.

An alternative way of modifying the entirely androcentric determination of the class of the conjugal family, which we would ourselves favour, is that which has become known as the 'dominance' method (Erikson 1981, 1984). In this case, the class position of the family is determined by reference to the employment of *either* husband *or* wife, depending on which may be regarded as 'dominant' in their labour-market participation according to criteria of both employment status and level of employment. In other words, the family head, through whose employment the articulation of the family unit with the class structure is chiefly made, may be male or female.

The dominance method represents a less radical departure from previous practice than either 'joint classification' or, of course, the 'individual' approach; and, for so long as wives are less likely to be in employment than their husbands, less likely to work full time, and more likely to be in lower level employment, it cannot be expected that the dominance method will produce any markedly different class distribution of conjugal families than would be obtained by taking only the husband's employment into account. On the other hand, though, it does have the merit of not generating empirical results of dubious validity by neglecting the extent to which the nature of women's work-force participation is still set apart from that of men, and further of being capable of revealing change in this situation over time, should it in fact occur.

As we have already indicated, we will use the dominance method later in this chapter in constructing for certain of our nations 'complete' mobility tables; that is, tables which relate to the mobility experience of the adult male and female populations together. At that stage we will take up the particular problems that arise in implementing the method with the data we have available to us. Our more immediate task is, however, that of describing more generally the limitations and possibilities that are to be found within our comparative data-set once we attempt to bring the class mobility of women within the scope of our enquiry.

DATA

Although the information we have relevant to the class mobility of women is less extensive than that on which we can draw in the case of men, it still allows us to carry out analyses of obvious interest for each of our nine European nations. In Table 7.1 we show just what data we can extract from each of the enquiries that are represented in our data-set.

As is indicated, in four nations—England, Ireland, Northern Ireland, and Scotland—these enquiries were restricted to the male population, and consequently the only information we have on women is that obtained from male respondents: specifically, on the employment of the respondent's wife at the time of interview (except for England), and on the employment of the respondent's wife's father at the time of her early adolescence. The other five national enquiries covered both men and women and can thus provide us with a wider range of data, including, of course, information obtained directly from female respondents. However, several important differences still arise in the coverage of these enquiries which are indicated in Table 7.1 but which should be somewhat more fully explained.

First, in the French enquiry no questions were asked about the employment of male respondents' wives, nor in fact about that of female respondents' husbands; but the latter information was subsequently added to the data-tape from the 1968 census returns—disregarding any intervening changes in marital status, on the basis of a slightly different occupational classification, and, we would suppose, with some consequent reduction in quality.[9] Secondly,

[9] To be precise, what was added was information from the census on the employment of 'heads of households'. Since, in the case of a married couple, the husband was regarded as the

TABLE 7.1. *Information available (+) and unavailable (−) in national data-sets relevant to the mobility of women*

Respondents	ENG	FRA	FRG	HUN*	IRL†	NIR†	POL*†	SCO	SWE
Female respondents									
Class via current employment	−	+	+	+	−	−	+	−	+
Father's class	−	+	+	+	−	−	+	−	+
Husband's class	−	+‡	+	+	−	−	+§	−	+
Male respondents									
Wife's class via current employment	−	−	+	+	+	+	+§	+	+
Wife's father's class	+	−	−	+	+	+	+§	+	−

Notes:

* Samples of households, not individuals. Both husband and wife were interviewed and information on class of respondent's spouse thus derives from interview with spouse.

† Information listed under 'Male respondents' is not included in the CASMIN IMS but is derived from the original surveys. In the cases of Ireland and Northern Ireland the information was kindly provided for us by Robert Miller and in the case of Poland by Bernhard Schimpl-Neimanns.

‡ Added to data-set from 1968 census returns.

§ Only members of the household currently in employment were interviewed.

both the Hungarian and Polish enquiries were based on samples of *households* in which all adults were interviewed. Thus, information on 'spouses' was in fact obtained directly from them, rather than being reported by their partners, and, while a gain in quality may thus have been achieved, married men and women cannot, of course, be regarded as independently sampled. And, thirdly, in the Polish case, interviews were carried out only with adults, men or women, who were currently in employment.

The consequence of this rather uneven data base is then that, in the analyses that follow, we will often be able to include only subsets of our nine nations, with the subset changing according to the kind of information that a particular analysis requires. The conclusions that we reach on cross-national similarities and variations in women's class mobility will thus be somewhat less well grounded than those we have earlier advanced in the case of men. However, we would still believe that the results we report mark an advance on most previous work in this area, in view especially of the high standards of cross-national comparability of data that we are able to maintain.[10] In exactly the same way as with our analyses of men's mobility, we work throughout with mobility tables that result from the recoding exercise that was described in Chapter 2: that is, with tables for persons aged 20–64 that are based on one or other version of our class schema.

It should, though, in this connection be further recalled from Chapter 2 that, in applying the schema specifically to women's employment, we make one modification. We subdivide Class III, that of routine non-manual employees, into IIIa and IIIb, with the aim of isolating in IIIb occupations which in terms of their characteristic employment relations would seem to entail straightforward wage-labour rather than displaying any of the quasi-bureaucratic features associated with the more advantaged positions within this class. The occupations most commonly found in Class IIIb, and which are in fact very largely held by women, are then those that make up the lowest grades of employment in offices, shops, and other service outlets— machine operators, counter staff, attendants, etc.; while typical of IIIa are secretaries, clerks, and other routine administrative personnel. Because the number of men in IIIb positions is in most nations quite small, our general practice in what follows, *wherever women are, or could be, included in the analysis in virtue of their own employment*, is to collapse Class IIIb with Class VIIa—that of non-skilled manual workers—for men and women alike, while treating Class IIIa as a separate category. In other analyses, however, Class III remains undivided.

'head', information was then available for the husbands of married women, but no corresponding information for the wives of married men.

[10] The only earlier studies with a similar comparative basis appear to be those of Pöntinen (1983), Roos (1985), and Portocarero (1987). This last study—of women's mobility in France and Sweden—followed on joint work with the present authors on men's mobility and is based on the same data-sets for France and Sweden as those used here, except that we have made some further minor refinements to the recoding procedures in the French case.

WOMEN'S MOBILITY VIA EMPLOYMENT

We begin our substantive analyses by examining tables that show the mobility of women from their class origins, as indexed by father's class position, to the positions they held in the work-force when interviewed in national enquiries of the early or mid-1970s. Women who were not in the labour force at the time of interview are excluded.[11] Although in these tables we use our class schema to categorize the 'present' positions of employed women, as well as their class origins, it will be evident from what we have earlier said that, so far as *married* women are concerned, we would believe that in this way a valid representation of their location within the class structure will often not be obtained. In this context, we would interpret the schema as being indicative only of women's type and level of employment and we would, therefore, define our own interest here as being primarily with the effects of *class origins* on women's *employment chances*. However, the results we report can, of course, be taken as showing how the class mobility of women appears if the 'individual' approach to their class allocation is adopted; and we shall then wish further to comment on some of the implications of opting for this interpretation.

In Table 7.2 we give origin and destination distributions for women, and also for men, in the five national samples that we can exploit for our present purposes (cf. Table 7.1): that is, those for France, the FRG, Hungary, Poland, and Sweden. As can be seen, sex differences in origin distributions are quite negligible, which may be taken as indicating that in the nations in question there was little or no 'selection' of women currently in the work-force by their class origins. In contrast, destination distributions display wide sex differences. The Δ values reported show that, across the five nations, from a quarter up to almost two-fifths of employed women would have to be reallocated in order to make their distribution the same as that of men. In other words, what is here revealed in our data is the marked sex segregation of labour markets, and thus of employment opportunities, which is by now a widely recognized feature of all industrial societies (see, e.g., Treiman and Roos 1983; Roos 1985: ch. 3).

It is also apparent from Table 7.2 that, while some amount of cross-national variation occurs, especially as regards the agricultural sector, the pattern of sex differences in employment still displays important common features. Thus, from nation to nation, women tend to be over-represented in

---

[11] In some studies of women's mobility, women not currently in the labour force have been classified according to their *last* employment. This information was not generally available in the data-sets we used, but there are in any event strong arguments against the practice in question—notably that the dating of last employment is likely to vary widely, and for some women could be up to, say, twenty years before the time of enquiry. Also, it might have been thought in this context desirable to consider mother's—present or previous—employment as well as father's as an indicator of class origins, but again the necessary information is not available (and cf. note 16 below).

TABLE 7.2. *Distribution of women* (W) *and men* (M) *by class of origin and current employment (% by column)*

Class	FRA		FRG		HUN		POL		SWE	
	W	M	W	M	W	M	W	M	W	M
	Origin									
I+II	11	11	17	14	7	6	8	7	13	11
IIIa	7	7	6	6	3	3	1	—	3	3
IVa+b	14	14	11	11	8	7	3	3	12	11
IVc	26	26	13	13	26	27	56	53	26	26
V+VI	18	19	37	37	14	14	16	18	20	24
IIIb+VIIa	18	16	13	15	22	22	13	14	23	20
VIIb	6	7	3	3	20	22	3	4	3	5
Δ	2		3		2		5		6	
	Current employment									
I+II	16	21	27	28	15	15	19	18	18	24
IIIa	21	7	14	4	17	4	8	1	22	6
IVa+b	11	9	12	7	1	2	2	2	4	8
IVc	14	10	1	4	7	1	40	25	4	5
V+VI	4	24	8	37	5	31	7	31	6	30
IIIb+VIIa	32	24	37	19	37	33	21	21	46	24
VIIb	1	3	1	1	18	14	1	3	1	2
Δ	27		33		27		25		37	

Classes IIIa and IIIb+VIIa or, that is, in routine non-manual and non-skilled manual employment, and to be under-represented in Class V+VI or, that is, in skilled manual work and in manual supervisory and lower technical grades. Moreover, if we were to separate Classes I and II (though, as we have noted, we unfortunately cannot do this in a cross-nationally comparable way), we would find that women tend to be under-represented in the higher levels of the service class and over-represented in the lower.[12] Again, then, the data of Table 7.2 reflect what other authors have been concerned to demonstrate in a more elaborate way: namely, that not only is employment markedly sex segregated but, further, the segregation is such that the opportunity structure that confronts women in the labour market, and that, as individuals, they must essentially take as given, is overall clearly less favourable than that confronting men.

---

[12] Thus, if we were to introduce our Class I/II division as it stands, the Δs in Table 7.2 would all increase by 1–5 percentage points. The proportion of employed women in Class I ranges only from 3–4 per cent, as compared with the range for men of 7–10 per cent.

When we come to examine the actual mobility tables for which Table 7.2 provides the marginal distributions, we are not, therefore, surprised to find that the types of employment engaged in by men and women of similar class origins display quite different patterns. Such differentiation may be quantified, as is shown in Table 7.3, by means of Δs calculated for outflow rates for men and women originating in each of the seven classes of our schema. It can be seen that, while only one Δ is below 20, there are several of over 40. The degree of differentiation is especially marked among the sons and daughters of skilled manual workers; and, in cross-national perspective, is somewhat greater in Sweden than in the other four nations. However, detailed inspection of the tables from which the Δs are derived reveals that the two following features tend to recur across all nations alike.

TABLE 7.3. Δ *values for men's and women's outflow rates from class origins to current employment*

Class of origin	FRA	FRG	HUN	POL	SWE
I+II	23	26	26	22	28
IIIa	30	31	23	31	44
IVa+b	27	24	36	29	38
IVc	16	39	26	25	32
V+VI	37	44	42	40	47
IIIb+VIIa	34	37	32	33	43
VIIb	27	43	24	30	38

1. Women of any class origin are more likely than men of similar origin to be found in the kinds of routine non-manual employment covered by Class IIIa of our schema, while being less likely to be found—with exceptions chiefly in the Hungarian and Polish cases—in the professional, administrative, and managerial positions of Class I+II.
2. Women of any given class origin are also more likely than men of similar origin to be found in the kinds of unskilled wage-work covered by Class IIIb+VIIa of our schema—the only exceptions arising again in the cases of Hungary and Poland—while being less likely to be found in the lower technical, manual supervisory, and skilled manual positions of Class V+VI.

In turn, if we compile summary mobility statistics for women, as in Table 7.4, and compare them with those we previously gave for men in Table 6.3 above, we can show up further differences of interest. On this basis, women appear to be somewhat more mobile than men overall, though with Hungary once more an exception; but, more significantly, they are also more often downwardly mobile and show a lower ratio of upward to downward transi-

TABLE 7.4. *Total mobility rates, total vertical* (TV), *total non-vertical* (TNV), *total upward* (TU) *and total downward* (TD) *rates for women from class origins to current employment*

Nation	TMR	TV	TNV	TV/TNV	TU*	TD*	TU/TD
FRA	67	44	23	1.9	26	18	1.4
FRG	78	58	20	2.9	27	30	0.9
HUN	75	39	36	1.1	26	14	1.9
POL	52	36	16	2.2	27	9	2.8
SWE	77	50	27	1.9	27	22	1.2

Note:
   * For definitions of upward and downward mobility, see text, p. 195.

tions. While for men this ratio ranges from 2.5 to 4.5, for women it ranges only from 0.9 to 2.8.

In sum, then, we may say that the differentiation of men's and women's mobility patterns from class origins to current employment turns out to be much on the lines that, all other things being equal, we would expect from the pattern of sex segregation that their current employment displays. This being the case, it is clearly of interest to go on to ask if, in fact, all other things *are* equal—so that differences in objective opportunity structures can indeed be regarded as the *sole* source of variation in men's and women's mobility chances; or whether differences in underlying patterns of social fluidity, that is, in the association between class origins and current employment *net* of structural effects, are also in some degree involved.

To this end, we may return to the model of common social fluidity that we have previously applied in comparing fluidity, or relative rates of mobility, across nations and also—as in the case of Northern Ireland—between subpopulations. In the present application our two subpopulations are those of men and women (aged 20–64); and in Table 7.5 we report the results of fitting the CmSF model to tables showing mobility from class origins to current employment for men and women in the five nations for which we have appropriate data.

As can be seen, for four nations out of the five—the exception being the FRG—the CmSF model, postulating identical relative rates, fits rather well. A $G^2(S)$ is returned of not greater than 51 which implies a p value of 0.05 or over, and less than 4 per cent of all cases are misclassified. However, in addition to the deviant German case, we should keep in mind that the CmSF model provides only a global test of the hypothesis of identical relative rates and that, even where it shows a satisfactory fit, certain more specific, if minor, differences in such rates could still be present.

To test for one such possibility of evident interest, namely, that women's relative rates tend overall to be more, or less, equal than those of men—or,

TABLE 7.5. *Results of fitting the CmSF model to tables on men's and women's mobility from class origins to current employment and β parameters for women from the model of uniform difference*

Model*	G^2	df	p	rG^2	Δ	$G^2(S)$ (3,650)	$\beta^\dagger$
FRA							
(N = 30,245)							
OS DS (con. ind.)	13,357	72	0.00	—	24.7	1,675	
OS DS OD (CmSF)	144.8	36	0.00	98.9	1.9	49	$-0.05^\ddagger$
FRG							
(N = 5,809)							
OS DS	1,586.5	72	0.00	—	19.0	1,024	
OS DS OD	103.4	36	0.00	93.5	4.4	78	$-0.33^\ddagger$
HUN							
(N = 22,979)							
OS DS	6,621.1	72	0.00	—	20.6	1,112	
OS DS OD	114.8	36	0.00	98.3	2.2	49	-0.01
POL							
(N = 61,541)							
OS DS	22,624	72	0.00	—	24.5	1,409	
OS DS OD	245.9	36	0.00	98.9	1.7	48	$-0.11^\ddagger$
SWE							
(N = 3,650)							
OS DS	694.9	72	0.00	—	15.5	695	
OS DS OD	50.6	36	0.05	92.7	3.3	51	-0.07

Notes:
* O = origin class; D = current employment; S = sex.
† β parameters for men set at zero.
‡ Estimated from model giving significant improvement in fit over CmSF model at 5 per cent level.

that is, to reveal greater or less fluidity—we can turn again to the model of uniform difference of equation (3.2), which we earlier introduced in investigating trends in relative rates. In the present case, the X_{ij} term will stand for the general pattern of association between class origins and current employment that is common to men and women, while the β_k term will refer to the strength of this association that is specific to one sex as against the other. When this model is applied to our data,[13] we find that it produces a significant improvement in fit over the CmSF model for the FRG and also for France and Poland, though not for Hungary or Sweden. And what further

---

[13] We estimate this model in the manner indicated in ch. 3 n. 24.

emerges, as is shown in the last column of Table 7.5, is that the β parameters that are estimated in all cases point to a level of fluidity rather higher among women than among men.

There is, in other words, some indication here that the marginally higher total mobility rates for women that are seen when Table 7.4 is compared with Table 6.3 may reflect a difference in underlying relative rates. However, it has at the same time to be recognized that, apart perhaps from in the German case, this difference could only be described, if it exists at all, as very slight indeed.[14] And the conclusion can still readily be drawn from the results of Table 7.5 taken as a whole that in all the nations represented, the FRG included, it is from the discrepant opportunity structures facing men and women that the differences in absolute rates that we have demonstrated in this section overwhelmingly derive. Our confidence in such a conclusion is, moreover, reinforced in that it is essentially the same as that reached by a series of previous investigators on the basis of quite independent analyses (see, e.g., Hauser and Featherman 1977; Pöntinen 1983: ch. 8; Erikson and Pöntinen 1985; Roos 1985: ch. 4; Dunton and Featherman 1985).[15]

In turn, then, one further question is rather directly suggested. Since we have discovered only very small differences, if any, between men's and women's fluidity patterns within nations, and since in Chapter 5 we have

---

[14] Thus, in the French and Polish cases, where the uniform-difference model also achieves a significant improvement in fit over the CmSF model, rG^2 values increase only from 98.9 to 99.0 and from 98.9 to 99.1 respectively, while the Δ value (proportion of all cases misclassified) remains unchanged for France at 1.9 and for Poland falls from 1.7 to 1.6. For the FRG, rG^2 increases from 93.5 to 95.1 and Δ falls from 4.4 to 3.6.

As regards the FRG, inspection of residuals under the CmSF model indicates that women show a lower propensity for immobility than do men within all classes other than IIIa—the most marked differences occurring within the skilled and non-skilled working classes, V+VI and VIIa. There is, however, reason to believe that what is here captured is not so much distinctive features of the fluidity patterns of German women as of German *men*—in particular, the unusually sharp differentiation of the relative chances of the sons of skilled and non-skilled manual workers that we noted earlier (pp. 149–50). When we later apply the CmSF model cross-nationally—that is, to our five women's mobility tables taken together (see Table 7.6)— inspection of residuals does not indicate that among German women the propensity for immobility is comparatively low.

[15] In so far as differences between men's and women's fluidity patterns *have* been detected in these other studies, they have tended to indicate (i) a somewhat lower propensity for immobility among women, and especially among the daughters of farmers and the petty bourgeoisie; but (ii) with the exception that the daughters of higher-level white-collar fathers show a still *stronger* propensity for immobility than do the sons of such fathers. The lower tendency towards 'inheritance' among farm and petty-bourgeois daughters does in fact rather consistently emerge in our own analyses, from inspection of residuals under the CmSF model, although the differences are slight other than in the German case. We discuss this tendency further below, when it becomes more apparent in the context of the comparison of men's mobility via employment with women's mobility via marriage. However, while the second tendency mentioned is observable in our data for Hungary, Poland, and Sweden—that is, service-class daughters have better chances relative to other women of entering service-class employment than do their 'brothers' relative to other men—it does not emerge in either the French or German cases.

argued, in support of our version of the FJH hypothesis, that a large measure of similarity prevails in men's fluidity patterns across nations, may we not expect to find cross-national similarity in women's patterns also—and further, perhaps a large commonality in such patterns when considered across the sexes and across nations alike?

TABLE 7.6. *Results of fitting the CmSF model to mobility tables for women's mobility and for women's and men's mobility from class origins to current employment for five nations*

Model*	G^2	df	p	rG^2	Δ
Women's mobility					
(N = 55,359)					
ON DN (con. ind.)	22,349	180	0.00	—	25.8
ON DN OD (CmSF)	908.0	144	0.00	95.7	3.8
Women's and men's mobility					
(N = 124,224)					
A. OSN DSN (con. ind.)	44,883	360	0.00	—	23.3
B. OSN DSN OD					
(CmSF over S and N)	2,348.5	324	0.00	94.8	4.2
C. OSN DSN ODN					
(CmSF over S)	658.5	180	0.00	98.5	2.1
D. OSN DSN ODS					
(CmSF over N)	1,815.0	288	0.00	96.0	3.7
E. OSN DSN ODN ODS	323.0	144	0.00	99.3	1.2

				G^2/df	
B–C (ODN)	1,690.0	144	0.00	11.7	
D–E (ODN)	1,492.0	144	0.00	10.4	
B–D (ODS)	533.5	36	0.00	14.8	
C–E (ODS)	335.5	36	0.00	9.3	

Note:
* O = origin class; D = current employment; S = sex; N = nation.

The analyses which this question prompts require further applications of the CmSF model, which are reported on in Table 7.6. From the results shown in the upper panel of the table, we must accept that, to judge by conventional standards, the model does not satisfactorily reproduce our cross-national data on women's mobility from class origins to current employment. That is to say, clearly significant cross-national differences are to be found in women's fluidity patterns. At the same time, though, it is also apparent that these differences are not large. The CmSF model accounts for 95 per cent of the total origins–destinations association within the five national tables, and misclassifies only about 4 per cent of all individual cases. This, it may be noted, is a finding which almost exactly replicates that which we reported in Table 4.1 above in applying the model to men's intergenerational mobility tables across nine nations.

In the lower panel of Table 7.6, where we are in effect fitting the CmSF model to an array comprising ten sex- and nation-specific mobility tables, we find results of a broadly similar kind. While, as would be expected, we cannot claim that exactly the same pattern of fluidity underlies all of these tables—as proposed by model B—we can say that among the different sex- and nation-specific patterns that obtain the presence of a substantial common element is clearly indicated. The further analyses presented on the basis of models C, D, and E would then suggest that more or less the same amount of variation occurs between the sexes as among the five nations—the ODS term is about as strong as the ODN term. But nation appears as a more important source of variation than sex if we compare the average variance in (logged) odds ratios found between sexes within nations with that found among nations within sexes (cf. p. 99): in the former case it is 0.12, in the latter, 0.50. Finally, though, we would note that the degree of overall commonality that prevails can be highlighted if we again resort to a counter-factual approach. If we were to suppose a world in which model B did indeed apply and construct the mobility tables that would be expected under this model, then results comparable to those presented in Tables 7.3 and 7.4 above derived from these tables would not lead us to modify in any way the comments we have already made on the basis of the actually observed tables regarding the salient differences in men's and women's mobility patterns that are displayed.

What, then, is the interpretation that we should give to the empirical findings so far presented? Sociologists of a feminist persuasion, who favour the 'individual' approach to the class allocation of women, would doubtless wish to concentrate their attention on the evidence of absolute rates. If the results reported in Tables 7.3 and 7.4 are regarded as providing a valid indication of women's experience of intergenerational class mobility, then it can obviously be maintained that this is far less favourable than that of men. Women can be seen as concentrated in relatively disadvantaged or 'degraded' non-manual or manual positions; and, in turn, women of all class origins alike more often appear in such positions than do men of similar origins, including where this implies downward movement relative to the class position of their fathers (cf. Abbott and Sapsford 1987: ch. 3). From this standpoint, therefore, it must surely be the case that the inclusion of women in studies of class mobility will lead to conclusions appreciably different from those arrived at where only men are considered.[16]

However, as we have earlier remarked, such an interpretation gives rise to far from negligible problems. These stem primarily from an empirical finding that has been reproduced with some consistency: namely, that not just 'sexist' sociologists but *married women themselves* tend to see their class positions as being more 'derived' from those of their husbands than determined by their own employment. More specifically, and as we have demonstrated in detail elsewhere (Erikson and Goldthorpe 1992), survey data can be assembled from a range of contemporary industrial societies to show the following.[17]

1. If both respondent and spouse within a conjugal family are assigned class positions 'individually'—that is, by reference to their own employment—a significant association exists between these positions, typically reflecting a marked tendency towards class homogamy.
2. In the case of male respondents, a significant and strong association also exists between their class position and their own, subjective, class identification. When this association and class homogamy are both controlled for, any association between husband's class identification and *wife's* class position is weak, if, in fact, it exists at all.
3. In the case of female respondents, a significant association is usually—though not always—present between class position and class identification, but this is far less strong than with male respondents. Moreover, when this association and class homogamy are controlled for, a *further* significant association still regularly occurs between wife's class identification and *husband's* class position; and, when both are considered separately, the latter association tends to be *stronger* than that between wife's class identification and her own class position.
4. Essentially the same, asymmetric, pattern of association arises if political partisanship is substituted for class identification; that is, a

---

[16] It should, however, be noted that, when authors such as Abbott and Sapsford make much of mobility tables of the kind that are in question here, they are in fact in the rather embarrassing position of trading on an application of the 'conventional' approach to the class allocation of women *so far as their class origins are concerned*. For, as we have seen, it is from the marginal discrepancies between the class distributions of fathers and their daughters that the mobility patterns they wish to emphasize predominantly derive. If they were to apply the 'individual' approach consistently, that is, to class origins as well as to destinations, they would then have to consider whether they should use fathers' or mothers' employment to determine origins. And were they to opt for the latter, one might safely predict that downward mobility would be much less prominent. See, for example, the Australian mother-by-daughter tables, based on a version of our class schema, that are given in Hayes (1990: 374–5, Tables 1, 2).

[17] We sometimes do little more here than echo the findings of earlier authors (cf., e.g., Hammond 1987; Hernes and Knudsen 1987; Marshall *et al.* 1988; Shirahase 1989). In other cases we take over data that had previously been analysed with different questions in mind; and in others still we seek to improve on analyses that would seem to us largely inadequate to the matter in hand (e.g. Abbott and Sapsford 1987: ch. 4; Leiulfsrud and Woodward 1987).

married woman's political partisanship, like her class identification, tends to be more strongly associated with her husband's class position than with her own.

What, therefore, follows for exponents of the 'individual' approach is that, if they wish to see a high proportion of married women as holding inferior class positions, and indeed as having often been downwardly mobile into such positions, they must *also* be ready to see these women as displaying a rather alarming degree of 'false consciousness'. Or, in other words, they may claim, consistently with the arguments of *marxisant* feminists noted in Chapter 1, the existence of large numbers of 'proletarian' or even 'proletarianized' women workers; but they must then recognize that many of the latter, and in particular those married to men in non-proletarian positions, are not themselves ready to accept the definition of the situation that is being imposed upon them.

While this difficulty has in fact for the most part been ignored or evaded,[18] the authors of one study at least have been prepared to spell it out. In regard to women in routine clerical and similar work, Marshall *et al.* acknowledge that

rather crucially, to the extent that these women do show evidence of proletarianization in their ideological make-up, their judgments would seem to be related to the class positions of their husbands, rather than of their own employment

and likewise that:

it is not the putatively deskilled nature of this work which best explains the voting intentions of those women who undertake it: it is rather the class situation of their husbands. (1988: 135, 136)

While Marshall and his associates make little attempt to explain the results they describe—or in turn to re-evaluate the 'individual' approach[19]—other authors who show some awareness of the embarrassment that such results threaten have resorted to largely defensive accounts in terms, for example, of 'male hegemony' and 'ideological domination within the marital relationship' (Leiulfsrud and Woodward 1987). However, against this, we would argue, on the lines of classic rejections of 'false-consciousness'

---

[18] This remains true even with recent work. See, e.g., Hayes (1990) in which the 'individual' approach to women's class allocation is apparently accepted as entirely unproblematic and women's occupational or employment mobility and their class mobility are in effect treated as equivalent. We would agree with the author that 'Naive ideological preconceptions are not a sound basis for empirically grounded research'.

[19] The reason for this may be that at one point Marshall and his associates (1988: 180–3) persuade themselves that the 'individual' approach *is* superior in displaying 'class consciousness'—as measured by a six-point scale. However (see Erikson 1989), they are here misled by a straight computational error. Correctly carried out, their analysis in fact shows the opposite of what they claim: the class consciousness of married women is more closely associated with their husbands' class than with their 'own'—as indeed the authors' previous analyses of class identification and partisanship would indicate.

arguments (cf. Lockwood 1958/1989), that, once the objective situation is adequately represented, the need to invoke such arguments in fact disappears. That is to say, once the rather limited consequences of the 'participation revolution' are recognized, and hence the differences that typically persist between spouses in work-force attachment, work-life continuity, and contribution to family income, it can be seen as quite rational and intelligible that married women *should*, even when in work themselves, still in the main regard their class interests and affiliations as being more importantly determined by their husbands' employment than by their own.[20]

From the conceptual position we ourselves take, we would, as we have already noted, wish to treat the findings presented in this section as referring *not* to women's class mobility but simply to the relationship between women's class origins and their employment chances. The conclusion then to be drawn from the analyses of absolute rates as reported in Tables 7.3 and 7.4 is indeed that women's chances are *in this respect* systematically less favourable than are those of men. And what we can then add in the light of our analyses of relative rates is that this is very largely so because of the less favourable opportunity structure within the labour market that women face, rather than on account of sex differences in fluidity patterns. From the standpoint of the present study, it is this latter point that we wish chiefly to emphasize: in the nations we consider, the relative inequalities in employment chances that are associated with differing class origins prove to be substantially *of the same extent and on the same pattern among women as among men*—just as we have previously seen such inequalities to have a broad measure of similarity across other, ethnic or regional, subpopulations of national societies or indeed across these societies themselves. However, in addition to its significance for our general concerns, the finding of a largely common pattern of fluidity for men and women underlying the mobility data that we have here considered carries certain more specific implications for the understanding of women's disadvantage in employment, and ones which, it would appear, require a fuller appreciation, not least among feminist commentators.

Thus, for example, this finding must directly undermine the suggestion made by some authors (e.g. Stanworth 1984) that, since women are subject to such a degree of shared, gender-linked, disadvantage in labour markets, there is little scope for class differences of opportunity to divide them. Even though we have found evidence for some, though not all, nations of slightly greater fluidity among women than among men, it remains evident enough that women compete for such employment opportunities as are available to

---

[20] We would see as being of further major relevance in this connection a series of results from research into class and levels of health, which consistently show (see, e.g., Arber 1989, 1991; Lundberg 1990) that greater class differences are revealed in the health of married women if their class is determined by reference to their husbands' employment than if the 'individual' approach is followed.

them under a regime of class-linked advantages and disadvantages that differs only marginally from that applying to men. Likewise, the misleading nature is also exposed of claims to the effect that, in the determination of mobility patterns, 'class background and gender *interact*' (Abbott and Sapsford 1987: 72; emphasis added). What should rather be emphasized is the very limited extent to which such interaction occurs. The forces that make for inequalities in relative mobility chances among men, stemming from the differential distribution of resources from one class origin to another, are not in any serious way modified in regard to women. And the fact that they operate in a way that is largely 'gender blind' would thus in turn suggest that, if an adequate account is to be provided of the social processes that generate sex segregation in employment—and hence women's restricted opportunities—this will, in fact, need to be one that is for the most part developed independently of class analysis.[21]

Finally, though, what is at the same time implied, and what feminists ought, presumably, to seek to stress, is that women *would* gain equality with men in their employment levels were it not for the various structural features of labour markets which amount to forms of direct or indirect discrimination against them. Or, as Dunton and Featherman have observed, it is these structural constraints and 'not the ways that females are reared—their values, attitudes, aspirations, or motivations in connection with career and marriage—or their biology that governs their mobility chances and socio-economic achievements vis-à-vis their brothers and husbands' (1985: 317).

WOMEN'S MOBILITY VIA MARRIAGE

In the foregoing we have argued that it is still the conjugal family and not the individual that should be regarded as the appropriate unit of class composition and further that, despite the increased work-force participation of married women, it is still in the majority of cases via the husband's employment that the articulation of the conjugal family with the class structure is chiefly effected. There is extensive evidence that married women tend themselves to derive their class identification from their husband's rather than from their own employment—and, in our view, with good reason. On this basis, we have therefore questioned whether, so far as married women are concerned, analyses that relate their class of origin to their own current employment are likely to provide a valid account of their rates and patterns

---

[21] In Marxist circles especially, the argument has been advanced that the sex segregation of employment must itself be explained in terms of capitalist class relations. However, we know of no attempt to formulate this argument in such a way that would make it amenable to empirically based examination. Other authors (e.g. Marshall *et al.* 1988: ch. 4; Marshall 1990) have also urged that, in some way or other, sex segregation should be brought within the scope of class analysis—but, again, performance would be more convincing than programme (see, further, McRae 1990; Goldthorpe 1990).

of intergenerational *class* mobility, however revealing they may be in other respects.

If, then, we wish to obtain a better understanding of such mobility, the logic of our position indicates clearly enough the direction that we should take. We should turn to the experience of women in 'marriage markets' rather than in labour markets; and, more specifically, we should examine their rates and patterns of 'marital mobility' or, that is, of mobility as assessed by comparing class of origin with class of spouse. It is this topic that will concern us in the present section.[22]

In previous discussion of women's marital mobility, one hypothesis has recurred. Various authors have suggested that women tend to be more mobile through marriage than are men through employment and their work careers—so that, as Heath has put it, 'in this sense a woman's "class fate" is more loosely linked to her social origins than is a man's' (1981: 114; cf., also, Glenn, Ross, and Tully 1974; Chase 1975). The main argument underlying this hypothesis would appear to be that certain attributes that can make women more or less attractive as marriage partners—that is, physical and personality attributes—are less closely associated with social origins than are those that chiefly influence men's achievements in their working lives. In other words, the processes of social selection that operate in marriage markets are different from those operating in labour markets, and tend moreover to be less restrictive. A supplementary argument that has also been deployed rests on the claim that, while unmarried women come disproportionately from more advantaged social origins, unmarried men come disproportionately from less advantaged ones. Thus, it is held, a 'discrepancy' effect is at work, increasing the likelihood of marital mobility and, in addition, favouring women's chances of 'marrying up'.

If the hypothesis in question is valid, to restrict one's attention to men's mobility alone, and to neglect women's mobility via marriage, could obviously lead one to an underestimation of the mobility opportunities that exist within a society. It is, therefore, of interest to us to investigate just how far, across the nations in our sample, women's marital mobility rates do in fact differ from men's rates of intergenerational mobility via employment. As is indicated in Table 7.1, it is in this respect that our data can provide fullest coverage. We have information on women's marital mobility for all nine of our European nations, even though that for Poland has some limitations, which we have noted, and in the cases of England, Ireland, Northern

---

[22] Heath (1981: 111) would regard the term 'marital mobility' as being 'rather unfortunate', and other writers, usually from a feminist position, have expressed still stronger disapproval. If an alternative is desired, we could perhaps suggest Pöntinen's delightful 'the social mobility of the patriarchal family in the matrilineal direction' (1983: 72). In any event, note that from one feminist perspective—that emphasizing the extent to which wives become 'incorporated' into their husbands' working lives—marital mobility must take on an evident importance (see, e.g., Finch 1983: esp. 21–3, 126–30).

Ireland, and Scotland we must rely on the reports of male respondents only.[23]

To begin with, we show in Table 7.7 the Δs that result if, for our nine nations, we compare outflow distributions from women's marital mobility tables with corresponding distributions from intergenerational class mobility tables for *married* men; or, that is, if we compare the class distributions of the husbands of married women of given classes of origin with those of married men of similar origins. It is evident that differences between the two sets of outflow rates are not very large. More often than not the Δs are less than 10, and where they rise above this figure—most often in the case of men and women of petty-bourgeois origins—few exceed 20. Northern Ireland reveals the largest dissimilarities, but otherwise there is no great amount of cross-national variation. On this basis, we would then have to conclude that women's class-mobility chances do not appear to diverge from those of men in any very systematic way.

However, in order to address more directly the issue of whether women experience more mobility through marriage than do men through employment, we may consider total mobility rates. Table 7.8 shows such rates, calculated from the same mobility tables as the Δs of Table 7.7. Again, the differences that are revealed are quite small, but it is notable that in all nine nations alike they go in the same direction: that is, they indicate that women do experience mobility away from their class of origin somewhat more often than men. From detailed inspection of the tables it emerges that the most cross-nationally consistent source of this greater mobility on the part of women is, in fact, the same as that of some of the higher Δs in Table 7.7: namely, that, with petty-bourgeois families, a lower probability exists that their daughters will marry within their class of origin than that their sons will follow in their fathers' footsteps. This pattern holds for all nine of our nations, and, it may be added, an analogous pattern is found among the sons and daughters of farm families in all nations except Hungary.

In Table 7.9 we then decompose our data on total mobility rates so as to indicate men's and women's chances of upward and downward mobility, as previously defined in Tables 6.3 and 7.4. It can be seen that, across our nations, women's rates of upward mobility via marriage do show some tendency to be higher than men's via employment—but that this is the case with their rates of downward mobility also. And, further, the ratios of the former to the latter suggest that in only one nation, the FRG, might women be regarded as being clearly at an advantage. However, far more striking than any cross-sex differences in the data of Table 7.9 is the way in which

---

[23] In examining the marital mobility of women on the basis of information obtained from male respondents, we see no reason why serious sampling problems should arise. As regards data quality, it is a moot point whether this will be better where men provide information on their own class and that of their fathers-in-law or where women provide information about the class of their husbands and fathers.

Table 7.7. *Δ values for outflow rates for marital mobility of women and intergenerational mobility of married men*

Class of origin	ENG	FRA	FRG	HUN	IRL	NIR	POL	SCO	SWE
I+II	8	11	3	8	15	16	5	11	5
III	2	6	14	3	8	15	10	4	22
IVa+b	10	10	22	11	15	14	6	9	12
IVc	11	5	20	3	9	14	2	14	8
V+VI	3	4	6	5	13	9	6	5	4
VIIa	4	5	9	5	7	13	1	4	8
VIIb	8	7	6	4	9	20	3	7	18

Table 7.8. *Total mobility rates for marital mobility of women and intergenerational mobility of married men*

Type of mobility	ENG	FRA	FRG	HUN	IRL	NIR	POL	SCO	SWE
Women's marital mobility	69	70	64	79	62	70	58	68	76
Men's intergenerational mobility	65	66	62	78	57	63	56	64	73

TABLE 7.9. *Total upward* (TU) *and total downward* (TD) *mobility rates for women's marital mobility and married men's intergenerational mobility*

Nation	Women's marital mobility			Men's intergenerational mobility		
	TU	TD	TU/TD	TU	TD	TU/TD
ENG	36	17	2.1	33	17	1.9
FRA	35	12	2.9	34	11	2.9
FRG	39	11	3.7	34	13	2.7
HUN	37	9	4.1	36	8	4.5
IRL	34	11	3.2	31	9	3.3
NIR	38	15	2.5	33	11	3.0
POL	35	7	5.0	35	6	5.5
SCO	36	18	2.0	33	18	1.9
SWE	44	11	4.1	44	11	4.0

salient features of cross-national variation in men's experience of class mobility, on which we have already commented in Chapter 6, are in fact *replicated* when women's experience of such mobility through marriage is considered. Thus, we again find a relatively low frequency of downward movement in Hungary, Ireland, and Poland, and a corresponding preponderance of upward over downward rates—which is matched only in the case of Sweden where, again as with men, it is the high frequency of upward movement that is distinctive.

So far, therefore, our findings would suggest that, when we examine women's possibilities for mobility via marriage, we are not required to see the class structures of industrial societies as being greatly more permeable than we have previously supposed, nor yet to recognize a channel of mobility that gives women generally more favourable chances for social ascent than those enjoyed by men. However, if we wish to focus our attention rather more sharply on Heath's (1981) hypothesis that a woman's 'class fate' is more loosely linked to her social origins than is a man's, we may now appropriately turn from absolute mobility rates to relative ones: that is, we may ask if, underlying the mobility tables for men and women with which we are here concerned, different patterns of social fluidity prevail which may account for the somewhat higher mobility of women that we have observed.[24]

In Table 7.10 we report the results achieved if, for each nation, we fit the CmSF model to the two mobility tables in question. It can be seen that the model reproduces the data fairly well, although not so convincingly overall

[24] One would in fact expect differences resulting from discrepant marginal distributions to be rather minor in that we are in effect comparing tables which relate class of father to class of son with those which relate class of father to class of son-in-law.

TABLE 7.10. *Results of fitting the CmSF model to tables of women's marital mobility and married men's intergenerational mobility and β parameters for women from the model of uniform difference*

Model*	G^2	df	p	rG^2	Δ	$G^2(S)$ (3,131)	$\beta^\dagger$
ENG							
(N = 15,636)							
OS DS (con. ind.)	2,738.4	72	0.00	—	13.9	606	
OS DS OD (CmSF)	109.0	36	0.00	96.0	2.4	51	$-0.30^\ddagger$
FRA							
(N = 28,715)							
OS DS	11,008	72	0.00	—	22.9	1,264	
OS DS OD	232.5	36	0.00	97.9	3.0	57	$-0.22^\ddagger$
FRG							
(N = 6,723)							
OS DS	1,924.9	72	0.00	—	20.2	935	
OS DS OD	104.3	36	0.00	94.6	3.8	68	$-0.14^\ddagger$
HUN							
(N = 18,181)							
OS DS	4,226.9	72	0.00	—	18.3	788	
OS DS OD	61.0	36	0.00	98.6	2.0	40	$-0.11^\ddagger$
IRL							
(N = 3,131)							
OS DS	1,624.2	72	0.00	—	29.3	1,624	
OS DS OD	68.0	36	0.00	95.8	4.8	68	-0.32
NIR							
(N = 3,473)							
OS DS	1,298.5	72	0.00	—	22.6	1,178	
OS DS OD	96.4	36	0.00	92.6	5.9	90	$-0.33^\ddagger$
POL							
(N = 46,714)							
OS DS	14,721	72	0.00	—	21.2	1,054	
OS DS OD	108.3	36	0.00	99.3	1.6	41	$-0.07^\ddagger$
SCO							
(N = 7,605)							
OS DS	1,886.2	72	0.00	—	15.6	819	
OS DS OD	59.5	36	0.01	96.9	2.9	46	$-0.25^\ddagger$
SWE							
(N = 3,160)							
OS DS	622.6	72	0.00	—	16.2	618	
OS DS OD	55.1	36	0.02	91.2	3.9	55	-0.17

Notes:
  * O = origin class; D = destination class; S = sex.
  † β parameters for men are set at zero.
  ‡ Estimated from model giving significant improvement in fit over CmSF model at 5 per cent level.

as in its application in Table 7.5. For four nations—England, Hungary, Poland, and Scotland—the model returns a $G^2(S)$ of 51 or less (implying $p > 0.05$), and in these cases other indicators of goodness of fit are also reassuring. But for the remaining five nations, and in the cases of the FRG, Ireland, and Northern Ireland especially, the fit of the model is clearly less than satisfactory.[25]

We have, therefore, good reason to seek to test Heath's hypothesis yet more specifically; and, for this purpose, a further application of our uniform-difference model, on the same lines as in the previous section, would appear highly appropriate. The result is, as indicated in the final column of Table 7.10, that this model produces a significant improvement in fit over the CmSF model for seven of our nine nations—Ireland and Sweden being the exceptions—but with in all cases a β parameter being returned which indicates that the association between origins and destinations does indeed tend to be weaker for women than for men.

Heath's hypothesis thus finds here some evident support. But at the same time two qualifying observations are in order. First, inspection of residuals suggests that a large part of the deviation from the CmSF model tends to follow one particular pattern. What is implied might best be summed up as follows: that as between the service class, on the one hand, and the petty bourgeoisie and farmers, on the other, daughters are 'exchanged' more readily through marriage than are sons in the course of their working lives. As was already suggested by our examination of absolute rates, a lower propensity exists for the daughters of petty-bourgeois and farming families to marry into their class of origin than for the sons of such families to retain their fathers' class position, which, of course, they may well do through inheritance of a 'direct' kind. Further, though, while petty-bourgeois and farm daughters may thus tend to be 'disinherited', this is not—as some feminist authors (e.g. Delphy and Leonard 1986) would seem to suppose—the whole of the story. For these daughters would also appear to gain an advantage from their class origins in that they show a clearly stronger tendency to marry into the service class than do their 'brothers' to enter this

---

[25] The G^2s reported in Table 7.10 for England, Ireland, Northern Ireland, and Scotland should not in fact be taken entirely at face value, since in these nations the observations for men and women are not independent of each other; as we have noted, women's marital mobility is in effect determined by relating the class of male respondents to that of their fathers-in-law. A more correct approach would therefore be to test for marginal homogeneity in a three-way table of class of respondent by class of father by class of father-in-law (cf. Bishop, Fienberg, and Holland 1975: 293). Such a test produces for England a G^2 of 125.2 with 42 df, and the corresponding G^2s for Ireland, Northern Ireland, and Scotland are 64.8, 101.1, and 77.5 respectively. The fits of the marginal homogeneity models may then be compared with those of the incorrectly specified CmSF models as reported in Table 7.10 by taking G^2/df. The pairs of values for the four nations, in the same order as above, are (CmSF model first) 2.9/3.0, 1.4/1.5, 2.6/2.4, and 1.7/1.8. The similarity here apparent suggests that we can in fact safely work from the results for the four nations reported in Table 7.10, which is an obvious advantage so far as comparisons with our other nations are concerned.

class via employment—a consequence, one may suggest, of the intergenerational transmission of cultural and social, if not of economic, resources. Conversely, then, we also find (though the differences here are rather less marked) that service-class daughters have a weaker propensity to marry within their class of origin than do service-class sons to obtain service-class employment, but at the same time show a stronger tendency to 'marry out' into the petty bourgeoisie or farming class than do their 'brothers' to enter into the kinds of proprietorial or self-employed positions that these classes comprise.

Given the degree of cross-national consistency in these deviations from the CmSF model—and also the fact that essentially similar results are reported in the one other independent enquiry of which we are aware (Handl n.d.)[26]—we would incline to believe that we do here identify real differences. It could then be that the tendency for women to show in their marital mobility a somewhat weaker association between class origins and destinations than do men in their mobility via employment reflects the experience of women of certain class origins far more than that of others. That is to say, it chiefly arises because, within service-class, petty-bourgeois, and farming families, daughters do not altogether share *in the same way* as sons in the advantages that such class origins can confer.

Secondly, it should in any event not be lost sight of that the differences that we have revealed are for the most part still quite minor.[27] And what then, in our view, should be highlighted is the rather remarkable nature of this result. Those sociologists who have hypothesized that women's marital mobility tables will reveal a different degree and pattern of fluidity from those of intergenerational class mobility tables for men can scarcely be accused of pursuing an improbable argument. Social selection in marriage markets and in labour markets could indeed be thought to involve quite different processes; and, moreover, ones which, according to standard theories of industrial society, should be displaying *divergent* tendencies. As marriage becomes less a linking of kindreds and an institution for the control of family property, and more a contract made between individuals with their personal happiness and fulfilment chiefly in view, the criteria by which partners select each other should become increasingly particularistic. In contrast, as the pressures of economic and technological rationality bear ever more closely on employing organizations, the criteria for the selection

[26] Schadee and Schizzerotto also report from an Italian study that 'the inheritance of class within the petty bourgeoisie is less for married women than for married men' (1990: 37), and attribute this to a tendency among the petty bourgeoisie to favour sons rather than daughters so far as transfers of capital are concerned. However, they do not investigate the propensities for *mobility* of petty-bourgeois daughters relative to those of petty-bourgeois sons.

[27] For the FRG, Hungary, and Poland, where the uniform-difference model gives a significantly better fit than the CmSF model, as well as for Sweden where it does not, improvement in the rG^2 and Δ values returned is still scarcely apparent; and for the remaining five nations the largest increase in rG^2 is from 96.9 to 98.2 for Scotland and the largest fall in Δ from 4.8 to 3.5 for Ireland.

of employees should become increasingly universalistic (see above, p. 6, and cf. Kerr *et al.* 1960/1973: 79–82).

And yet the evidence clearly is that both processes generate outcomes that are quite similar so far as the association of class origins and destinations is concerned. *If we know how men of a given class origin have themselves become distributed within the class structure in the course of their employment, we can predict, with no great inaccuracy, how their 'sisters' will have been distributed through marriage.* Class differences in the levels and kinds of resources that are available to individuals would in both cases appear to work to much the same effect; or, one could say, in marriage, just as in employment, men and women again act within, and are constrained by, one and the same set of class-linked inequalities.[28]

In this respect, therefore, our analyses of women's class mobility via marriage allow us to amplify and reinforce our earlier conclusions regarding the wide-ranging commonality in the patterns of fluidity that are expressed in such mobility. We can now see that this commonality extends beyond class mobility as this occurs through employment—in different periods, places, and subpopulations—to class mobility in a quite different mode. Although, as we have shown, women's marital mobility does reveal across all our nations alike certain distinctive features, and ones that are of evident sociological interest, yet greater significance must, we believe, attach to the fact that no more substantial difference from men's mobility via employment is to be observed.[29]

Before concluding this section, there is one other issue that we should consider: namely, that of how the fluidity patterns underlying women's marital mobility—or, in other words, patterns of net association between wife's father's class and husband's class—relate to married women's own employment. It could, for example, be the case that what appears as 'marital mobility' is in fact a relationship entirely mediated by the further associations that exist, on the one hand, between a woman's father's class and her own employment—that is, her own class according to the 'individual' approach—

---

[28] A pioneering study of marriage from this point of view which, unfortunately, has had few successors is Girard (1964/1974). As Thélot aptly summarizes Girard's central thesis: 'Vous n'avez pas choisi votre conjoint, dit Girard, vous l'avez trouvé, vous l'avez déniché parmi les candidats potentiels, qui dans le majorité des cas étaient en nombre limité puisqu'ils devaient être aussi proche de vous que possible' (Spouses are not chosen, says Girard, they are found, they are picked out from among potential candidates who are usually limited in number, since they must be as similar to oneself as possible) (1982: 179). Schadee and Schizzerotto (1990: 71) claim to find the similarity between mobility propensities via marriage and employment 'hardly surprising' but in seeking to justify this view give more a restatement of the similarity than an account of social processes through which it might be created.

[29] It is also of relevance to note that, in applying the same methods as with men's intergenerational mobility in Chapter 3, we are unable to detect any tendency towards greater fluidity underlying our tables of women's marital mobility. Again, the CnSF model tends to fit rather well across the birth-cohorts we distinguish, and the application of our uniform-difference model produces no instance in which the β parameters point to any steady trend, whether towards greater fluidity or less.

and, on the other hand, between her own class, thus understood, and her husband's class. Or, again, it might be that the degree and pattern of association between wife's father's class and husband's class is different depending upon wife's 'own' class—implying, that is, that an interaction effect occurs. If either of these possibilities were in fact to apply, the major importance that we have attributed to marriage as a vehicle of the class mobility of women could obviously be called into some doubt.

In order to investigate the matter, we need to organize our data in the form of three-way tables of wife's father's class by wife's class as determined by her own employment by husband's class. Reference to Table 7.1 will show that we can produce such tables for each of our nations except England and Scotland, although for Ireland and Northern Ireland we will again be reliant on information provided by male respondents. Moreover, in order to prevent too many cells in the tables from having zero or very low entries, we have to resort here to the fivefold rather than the sevenfold version of our class schema (cf. Table 2.1).

In Table 7.11 we show the results of exploring the structure of association in our three-way tables by fitting to them a series of log-linear models of increasing complexity. There are three features of these results that should be noted.

1. We cannot for any nation save Northern Ireland obtain an adequately fitting model, as indicated by a $G^2(S)$ implying a p value of greater than

TABLE 7.11. *Results of fitting models to three-way tables of wife's father's class by wife's class (via own employment) by husband's class*

Model*	$G^2(S)$ (715)							df	$G^2_{0.95}$
	FRA	FRG	HUN	IRL[†]	NIR[†]	POL	SWE		
A. O W H	1,233	680	719	1,022	736	931	531	112	138
B. OW OH	630	372	324	430	344	428	315	80	102
C. OW WH	110	213	115	116	78	112	115	80	102
D. OH WH	153	175	162	123	128	149	109	80	102
E. OW OH WH	74	113	67	48	39	65	67	64	84
B–E (WH)	556	259	257	382	305	363	256	16	26
C–E (OH)	36	100	48	68	39	47	47	16	26
D–E (OW)	79	62	95	75	89	84	50	16	26

Notes:
  * O = wife's father's class; W = wife's class via own employment; H = husband's class via own employment.
  [†] For Ireland and Northern Ireland we have assumed that farmers' wives who are not recorded as having any other employment do actually take part in work on the farm and have thus coded them as 'farmers' rather than excluding them from the analysis. (If they are excluded, then model B (OW OH) does in fact, fit the Irish data.)

0.05, without proceeding to model E, that which includes *all* two-way associations. In other words, the association between wife's father's class and husband's class (represented by the OH term) is clearly significant *net* of that between wife's father's class and wife's 'own' class (OW), and that between wife's class and husband's class (WH). And, in the Northern Irish case, where model C which omits the OH term fits the data by the criterion we adopt, adding this term still in fact produces a significant improvement in fit.

2. While the association between wife's class and husband's class (WH) is always, and by far, the strongest of the three (cf. the differences between $G^2(S)$ for models B, C, and D and for model E), the other two associations vary in their relative strengths from nation to nation. For France, Hungary, Northern Ireland, and Poland the OW term is clearly more important than the OH term; for Ireland and Sweden there is no great difference between them; and for the FRG OH is more important than OW.

3. For six out of our seven nations, model E, incorporating terms for all two-way associations, does give a satisfactory degree of fit according to our criterion, and it is only for the FRG that we need to take seriously the presence of a three-way interaction effect. This might be interpreted as one through which wife's own class creates variation in the association between wife's father's class and husband's class—but, just as plausibly, as one through which wife's father's class creates variation in the association between wife's class and husband's class.[30]

In sum, then, we may say that our arguments concerning women's marital mobility are rather little affected if married women's class as determined by their own employment is brought into the picture. It is, however, of some further interest here to note the results that are obtained if we repeat the foregoing analysis, *but from the point of view of husbands rather than of wives*: that is, if we consider three-way tables of *husband's* father's class by husband's class by wife's 'own' class. Table 7.1 indicates that we again have the data necessary to do this for seven of our nine nations, but France must now be replaced by Scotland.

Table 7.12 reports analyses of these data that are analogous to those of Table 7.11, and what can be seen is that in several respects a notably different pattern of association prevails. To begin with, there are three nations—Ireland, Northern Ireland, and Scotland—in which model D— that omitting the association between husband's father's class and wife's 'own' class (OW)—gives an adequate fit, and another, Sweden, in which it

---

[30] For example, two of the main sources of deviation from expected values under model E in the German case could be interpreted as saying that the daughters of both petty-bourgeois and farm fathers are more likely than expected to be found in 'homogeneous', white-collar (Classes I+II and IIIa) marriages.

TABLE 7.12. *Results of fitting models to three-way tables of husband's father's class by husband's class by wife's class (via own employment)*

Model*	G²(S) (715)							df	G²₀.₉₅
	FRG	HUN	IRL[†]	NIR[†]	POL	SCO	SWE		
A. O H W	718	662	1,170	841	924	347	503	112	138
B. OH OW	341	287	365	303	437	160	270	80	102
C. OW HW	172	155	254	224	130	172	141	80	102
D. OH HW	141	130	81	71	131	79	106	80	102
E. OH OW HW	79	67	53	51	65	61	65	64	84
B–E (HW)	262	220	312	252	372	99	205	16	26
C–E (OH)	93	88	201	173	65	111	76	16	26
D–E (OW)	62	63	28	20	66	18	41	16	26

Notes:
  * O = husband's father's class; H = husband's class via own employment; W = wife's class via own employment.
  [†] See note to Table 7.11.

comes very close to so doing. Furthermore, the OW association, even where significant, is still clearly less strong not only than that between husband's class and wife's class (HW) but also, in all nations but Poland, than that between husband's father's class and husband's class (OH).

These results, when set alongside those of Table 7.11, we would then see as further underlining the doubts we have earlier expressed about whether married women's employment is in fact a valid indicator of their class position. Or, at all events, we may ask those who do not share in these doubts to provide some alternative explanation for the fact that, when we control for wife's class via her own employment, we still usually find a quite strong connection between class of wife's father and class of husband, but that, when we control for husband's class, the connection between class of husband's father and wife's 'own' class becomes often a rather tenuous one.

RESULTS FROM 'COMPLETE' MOBILITY TABLES

In the foregoing we have argued that the *class* mobility of women tends to be better understood through examination of their experience in marriage markets than in labour markets. And we have then been able to show that women's rates of marital mobility, both absolute and relative, are largely similar to men's rates of intergenerational class mobility via their employment. Although some statistically and sociologically significant differences are apparent, these are rather specific and also small, and can thus give only very qualified support to claims that women are generally more likely to be mobile—or upwardly mobile—through marriage than are men through their working lives. In other words, the results we have reported would indicate that taking women's marital mobility into account, however interesting a topic it may be in its own right, is unlikely to lead us to change at all radically our assessments of the extent of the mobility opportunities or the degree of openness that characterizes the class structures of modern societies.

None the less, the possibility clearly remains that studies of mobility restricted to men could still be in some measure misleading, even if supplemented by analyses of the marital mobility of respondents' wives. Most obviously, such studies will neglect the mobility experience of *un*married (or separated) women—both those who are living singly and also those who are the 'heads' of families in which no adult male is present. And further, where men only are investigated, it has been the usual practice, as we have noted, to take the husband automatically as being the 'head' of the conjugal family. In this way however, no provision is made for those cases in which, by criteria of labour-market participation, it is the wife rather than the husband who would be better regarded as holding this position, and by reference to whom thus, following our own conceptual approach, the class allocation of the family as a unit should be made.

In this section, therefore, it is our aim to arrive at some assessment of just *how* serious such shortcomings are likely to be. To this end we produce, for those nations where our data make it at all possible, what might be termed 'complete' tables of intergenerational class mobility: that is, tables intended to display the mobility experience of national samples *which are representative of the male and female adult populations together*. We may then compare results from these tables with those we have already presented which relate to men alone.

In constructing such complete tables, we index class of origin by father's class, in the usual way, but we identify destination class differently for unmarried and married persons. The class of all unmarried persons, men and women alike, is determined by reference to their own employment— that is, according to the 'individual' approach. But the class of all married (and cohabiting) persons is determined according to the labour-market dominance of husband or wife, following the method to which we earlier referred.

In applying this method, two criteria of dominance have been proposed (Erikson 1984): those of 'work time' and 'work position'. The first, to which priority should be given, is straightforward: employment dominates non-employment and full-time employment dominates part-time. Unfortunately, though, the data at our disposal do not contain systematic information on the number of hours worked by respondents, male or female, and we can thus in this respect distinguish only between spouses in employment and those not employed—with the former being, of course, seen as dominating the latter.

The second criterion of work position requires that higher-level employment should dominate lower-level. We aim to implement this criterion via our class schema. Following the hierarchical divisions that we have already introduced, Class I+II is clearly to be placed at the head of the dominance order and Classes VIIa (plus here IIIb) and VIIb at the bottom. However, the ordering of the classes within the intermediate division is less obvious. It would seem appropriate to regard self-employment as dominating employee status, and thus to place Classes IVa+b and IVc above IIIa and V+VI; but the treatment of the latter two classes themselves is especially problematic. In fact, we have worked with two dominance orders which differ simply in that the placing of IIIa and V+VI is reversed (see below).

	Dominance 1	Dominance 2
1	I+II	I+II
2	IVa+b	IVa+b
3	IVc	IVc
4	IIIa	V+VI
5	V+VI	IIIa
6	IIIb+VIIa	IIIb+VIIa
7	VIIb	VIIb

We shall, though, in what follows, concentrate our attention on the application of 'Dominance 1', since, in privileging Class IIIa, this will maximize the number of wife-dominated couples—as also, it may be added, will our inability to relegate part-time below full-time working. We may then interpret the results we obtain on this basis as tending to show the *upper limit* of any divergence that may exist between our complete mobility tables and those that are restricted to men.

As will be evident from Table 7.1, the possibility of constructing complete tables arises with only a limited number of our nations. England, Ireland, Northern Ireland, and Scotland must be excluded from consideration, since the enquiries on which we draw did not cover women; and so too, in fact, must Poland, on account of interviews being conducted only with persons who were currently in employment. (Even though men and women not in employment would, under the dominance method, take their class from that of their spouse, they still cannot be included because we lack information on their *origins*.)

In the case of the remaining four nations, complete tables can be produced, although various difficulties still arise. Thus, for France, we have no information on male respondents' wives, and the complete table must therefore be constructed, so far as married persons are concerned, using data derived from female respondents only, with the sample being reweighted accordingly.[31] With the FRG, Hungary, and Sweden, the data available are

[31] A weight variable was introduced with a value of 0.5 for single men and single women,

in principle wholly adequate to our requirements, but in both the German and Hungarian studies certain deficiencies in coverage are in fact encountered, and in the latter case, though not the former, we have again attempted some redressment through reweighting.[32] In other words, then, the data of three of our four complete tables are more open to the possibility of inaccuracy than we would wish. However, we see no reason to suppose that any such inaccuracies will be very large, nor especially likely to introduce bias in the way that would be most damaging to our present concerns—that is, by making our complete tables *more* comparable to 'men-only' ones than would otherwise be the case.

TABLE 7.13. *Composition of complete tables: percentage distribution of types of unit represented using the dominance method (% by row)*

Nation	Single men	Single women	Couples, husband dominant*	Couples, husband and wife equal	Couples, wife dominant*
FRA	10	9	47 (48)	18	17 (15)
FRG	8	10	64 (65)	10	8 (7)
HUN	12	12	35 (38)	24	17 (14)
SWE	12	10	46 (49)	18	13 (10)

Note:
  * Unbracketed figures are for 'Dominance 1', bracketed for 'Dominance 2'.

In Table 7.13 we show the component parts, so to speak, of each of our four complete tables according to the units—individuals, or conjugal famil-ies—that are represented in the samples. It can be seen that, while in the FRG, which in the period of our enquiries had the lowest female work-force participation rate, husbands tend strongly to be dominant, this tendency is

zero for married men, and 1.0 for married women. In proceeding thus, we do of course make the assumption that no difference exists between men and women in the net association between their class origins and the class position of their families, as we would determine this. The validity of this assumption is discussed in the text, p. 273.

[32] In the Hungarian data-set information is far more often unavailable on husband's employment in cases where interviews were completed with wives than where interviews were completed with married men; and again, though to a lesser extent, on wife's employment where interviews were completed with husbands than where interviews were completed with married women. We cannot tell whether this information is unavailable because a spouse was not in paid work or because he or she was not in fact interviewed; but, from the asymmetry noted, it would seem likely that interviewers had more difficulty contacting men than women. A weight was therefore introduced aimed at reducing the number of cases where there was no information on spouse's employment—and where class position would thus be determined by the respondent's employment—to an estimate of the number of cases where spouses were in fact outside the work-force. This was done by making cases where there was no information on the employment of the husbands of interviewed women or on the wives of interviewed men equal in number to those cases where interviewed men or interviewed women respectively actually reported that they were not in employment.

rather less marked in France and Sweden, and is weakest of all in Hungary—the nation with the highest level of female participation. At the same time, though, it is evident that in all nations alike families in which the wife is dominant remain only a quite small minority.

In Tables 7.14, 7.15, and 7.16 we then present results from comparisons of our complete mobility tables with conventional, 'men-only', ones (revised, however, to follow the version of the class schema in which Class III is divided and Class IIIb combined with VIIa). Table 7.14 shows, first of all, differences in destination distributions. While these vary somewhat in their extent across the four nations, they could in no case be regarded as wide, even where 'Dominance 1' is used. It is apparent that the main sources of difference are that the complete tables imply somewhat larger white-collar classes, that is, Classes I+II and IIIa, and a smaller skilled working class, Class V+VI. This is, of course, what we might expect, given the way in which the pattern of women's employment differs from that of men (cf. Table 7.2) and, with 'Dominance 1', the ordering of the classes that is

TABLE 7.14. *Distributions of destination class from complete* (C) *mobility tables and 'men-only'* (M) *mobility tables* (% *by column*)

Class	FRA (N = 18,796)		FRG (N = 8,444)		HUN (N = 22,213)		SWE (N = 4,210)	
	C	M	C	M	C	M	C	M
Dominance 1								
I+II	21	21	32	28	20	15	28	24
IIIa	13	7	7	4	10	4	13	6
IVa+b	10	10	8	7	2	2	7	8
IVc	11	11	3	4	6	1	5	5
V+VI	18	24	32	37	21	31	23	30
IIIb+VIIa	24	24	18	19	29	33	23	24
VIIb	3	3	1	1	12	13	1	2
Δ	6		9		16		11	
Dominance 2								
I+II	21	21	32	28	20	15	28	24
IIIa	11	7	6	4	7	4	10	6
IVa+b	10	10	8	7	2	2	7	8
IVc	11	11	3	4	6	1	5	5
V+VI	21	24	33	37	24	31	26	30
IIIb+VIIa	24	24	18	19	29	33	23	24
VIIb	3	3	1	1	12	14	1	2
Δ	3		6		13		8	

TABLE 7.15. *Total mobility rates and total upward* (TU) *and total downward* (TD) *rates for complete and 'men-only' tables*

Nation	Complete tables						'Men-only' tables		
	Dominance 1			Dominance 2					
	TMR	TU	TD	TMR	TU	TD	TMR	TU	TD
FRA	69	35	14	69	35	14	65	32	14
FRG	66	37	14	65	37	14	62	33	14
HUN	77	39	8	76	39	8	76	35	9
SWE	76	44	12	75	44	12	72	41	13

adopted. Also, as might be expected from Table 7.13, it is in the case of Hungary that the differences are generally largest.

In turn, Table 7.15 presents total mobility rates and Table 7.16 Δs for outflow distributions in the two types of table. As can be seen, our complete tables tend to show higher total mobility rates than do 'men-only' ones and also, as is favoured by the expanded size of the service class, a greater amount of upward mobility. But in no case are the differences very large. Likewise, most outflow Δs are in the region of only 10–20 per cent with

TABLE 7.16. Δ *values for outflow rates from complete and 'men-only' mobility tables*

Class of origin	FRA	FRG	HUN	SWE
	Dominance 1			
I+II	11	7	16	7
IIIa	9	12	11	9
IVa+b	14	11	16	16
IVc	8	12	14	9
V+VI	11	7	21	13
IIIb+VIIa	10	10	18	11
VIIb	8	11	14	7
	Dominance 2			
I+II	9	6	11	5
IIIa	6	11	8	7
IVa+b	12	10	13	13
IVc	8	12	13	8
V+VI	7	5	15	8
IIIb+VIIa	7	9	14	7
VIIb	8	10	12	6

'Dominance 1', and are, of course, lower still with 'Dominance 2', although it may here again be noted that Hungary shows differences that are rather consistently more marked than with the other three nations. It may also be observed that Δs tend to be larger in the case of outflows from petty-bourgeois origins than from any other, but detailed inspection of the distributions reveals that in all four nations the more sizable discrepancies in particular outflows, from all origins alike, usually reflect the differences in destination distributions that were apparent in Table 7.14. That is, the larger outflows in the complete tables tend to be ones to Classes I+II and IIIa, and the smaller outflows ones to Class V+VI. The only notable variation is that the complete table for the FRG shows smaller outflows to Class IIIb+VIIa as well as to Class V+VI, while the offsetting differences are greater outflows to Classes I+II and IVa+b, the petty bourgeoisie, rather than to Classes I+II and IIIa.

It might, then, be said that the picture of class mobility—at all events at the level of absolute rates—that one obtains from complete tables does reveal some variation of a systematic kind from that obtained from tables that relate only to males. And, indeed, it could further be argued that, when the class-mobility experience of women as well as of men is in this way taken into account, chances of upward mobility, and especially into service-class positions, appear more favourable than 'men-only' tables would indicate. However, what has on the other hand to be recognized is how modest in fact are the differences that emerge, except perhaps in the Hungarian case. And it is, moreover, important here to recall that, in applying the dominance approach, we have been unable to use the work-time criterion fully. Had it been possible to allow spouses working full time to dominate those working part time, there can be little doubt that the differences shown up in Tables 7.14, 7.15, and 7.16 would have been appreciably reduced. Overall, then, and further bearing in mind the very different population coverages that are involved, one could well be more impressed with the extent of the similarities rather than of the differences that these tables display.

One other way in which it is of interest to ask whether, or how far, consideration of complete mobility tables may require us to revise ideas based on data limited to men is, of course, in regard to relative rates or patterns of social fluidity. Here, our obvious strategy is to proceed on the basis of the national variants of our model of core social fluidity that we developed, for 'men-only' tables, in Chapter 5. We may ask: do the models we have proposed for France, the FRG, Hungary, and Sweden still adequately describe patterns of social fluidity in these nations when we turn to the complete tables that we have constructed?

In Table 7.17 we report the results of fitting the models to complete tables in two different ways (confining ourselves here to complete tables based on 'Dominance 1'). First, for each of the four nations in question we have re-estimated our variant model for the 'men-only' table when this is revised

TABLE 7.17. *Results of fitting national variants of the model of core social fluidity to complete tables: (i) with parameters estimated from 'men-only' tables; (ii) with parameters being allowed to vary*

Nation	$G^2(S)$ (1991)*				rG^2		Δ	
	(i)	df	(ii)	df	(i)	(ii)	(i)	(ii)
FRA	78	36	50	28	93.2	96.4	5.2	3.8
FRG	67	36	44	28	91.6	95.1	4.5	3.1
HUN	100	36	72	28	86.8	90.8	7.1	5.0
SWE	49	36	40	29	91.1	92.7	4.1	3.3

Parameter estimates

		HI1	HI2	IN1	IN2	IN3	SE	AF1	AF2	AFX
FRA	(i)	−0.17	−0.38	0.42	0.95	0.91	−0.91	−0.82	0.44	
	(ii)	−0.15	−0.34	0.41	0.67[†]	0.89	−0.72[†]	−0.78	0.46	
FRG	(i)	−0.32	−0.56	0.49	1.16	2.26	−0.41	−0.51	0.39	
	(ii)	−0.23[†]	−0.53	0.58[†]	0.66[†]	1.69	−0.37	−0.31[†]	0.43	
HUN	(i)	−0.31	−0.56	0.54	ns	0.94	−0.50	−0.65	0.50	0.94
	(ii)	−0.38[†]	0.64[†]	0.23[†]	ns	0.56[†]	−0.67[†]	−0.51[†]	0.37[†]	0.78[†]
SWE	(i)	−0.17	−0.43	0.27	0.62	0.89	−0.62	ns	0.37	
	(ii)	−0.26[†]	−0.39	0.14	0.59	0.78	−0.58	ns	0.37	

Notes:
* We here take the constant for $G^2(S)$ as being 1991, i.e. that used in fitting the models to 'men-only' tables in Table 5.1 above.
† Differs significantly from estimate under (i).

following the division of Class III,[33] and we have then taken the resulting effect parameters as fixed in applying the model in turn to the complete table. Secondly, we have in each case fitted the national variant model to the complete table while allowing its parameters to vary.

It can be seen that, when our models are fitted with fixed parameters, the $G^2(S)$ returned is acceptable for Sweden but not for the other three nations. When parameters are allowed to vary, an adequate fit is, of course, again obtained for Sweden and very nearly so for the FRG; but the fits for France and, especially, Hungary remain unsatisfactory. We must then acknowledge that, other than in the Swedish case, the pattern of social fluidity underlying

[33] Since, as we have noted, in most of our nations there are in fact very few men in Class III*b*, this change should have no great effect on the fits of our variant models, and indeed this proved to be the case. For France, the FRG, and Sweden, the $G^2(S)$ returned remained at 40 or less, and only in the Hungarian case rose to slightly above this level. Likewise, effect parameters were very similar—as may be seen by comparing for each nation the estimates given in row (i) in the lower panel of Table 7.17 with those previously reported in Table 5.3.

complete tables differs to some significant degree from that we have modelled in our 'men-only' tables. At the same time, though, the other indicators of fit that are given would here again lead one still to emphasize how limited are the differences involved between the two sets of tables, at all events so far as France, the FRG, and Sweden are concerned. Thus, while our national variant models would need some degree of modification in order to fit complete tables, this would clearly not be such—and even in the Hungarian case—as to affect in any way our support for the version of the FJH hypothesis that we developed in Chapter 5: namely, that which claims that among industrial nations a substantial commonality in social-fluidity patterns prevails. This being the case, we believe then that the questions we may most usefully pursue arising out of the lack of fit that the variant models display are those of whether or not this has any *consistent* sources across the four nations we consider and, if so, of what implications follow.

In fact, if we examine the larger residuals from the fit of our variant models with fixed parameters, certain common features do rather readily emerge. Most obviously, with the complete tables of all four nations alike, Classes IV$a+b$ and IVc, those of the petty bourgeoisie and farmers, *show a lower propensity for intergenerational immobility than our models would predict*. And this difference, it may be noted, is also reflected in the parameters reported in the lower panel of Table 7.17: that is, when our models are fitted to complete tables with their parameters being allowed to vary, the IN2 and IN3 parameters—or, in the case of Hungary, the IN1 and IN3 parameters—are consistently lower, though not always significantly so, than when estimated for 'men-only' tables. At the same time, in the complete tables for France, the FRG, and Sweden greater fluidity than our models predict is evident between the petty bourgeoisie and farmers, on the one hand, and Class I+II, the service class, on the other; and again in all four nations there is generally greater fluidity between the petty bourgeoisie and Class IIIb+VIIa, that of non-skilled workers, and between the class of farmers and Class V+VI, that of skilled workers.

What, then, we are here observing is in some large part the differences between patterns of fluidity underlying men's mobility via employment and women's marital mobility that we have already identified in the preceding section. And what this means, therefore, is that, in one respect, our variant models must indeed be recognized as gender-specific: that is, in proposing a relatively high propensity for immobility among the petty bourgeoisie and farmers, primarily on account of the possibility of direct inheritance through the intergenerational transmission of either a 'going concern' or capital in some other form. It is apparent that this possibility is, in fact, more often realized in the case of sons than of daughters; in other words, inheritance tends in this respect to be patrilineal. Consequently, with the inclusion of women, as in our complete tables, immobility within the classes in question proves to be overestimated. However, as we have also previously noted, it cannot be supposed that the daughters of petty bourgeois and farm families are simply disadvantaged relative to sons. While, as the counterpart of their failure to inherit, they are more likely than sons to be mobile, through marriage or, it appears, through employment too, into the ranks of the skilled or non-skilled working class, they are *also* more likely to achieve upward mobility into the service class.[34]

Two further implications of these findings, one specific, the other more general, have then to be noted. The first is that, when in constructing our complete mobility table for France we relied, so far as the allocation of conjugal families was concerned, on data derived from female respondents, we are likely to have thus introduced some bias. The assumption that we make—that the net association between their class origins and the class position of their conjugal families is entirely the same for men and women—would now appear open to question; and the probable outcome is that the underlying pattern of social fluidity in the French complete table differs *more* from that of the French 'men-only' table than would have been the case if we had been able to use data derived from both female and male respondents. Thus, we would suspect, the tendency revealed in Table 7.17 for the French variant model to fit somewhat less well than the German or the Swedish is at all events exaggerated, and the real contrast to be recognized in this table is that between the French, German, and Swedish cases, on the one hand, and the Hungarian on the other.

The second, more general—and important—implication is the following: that the differences between the fluidity patterns of complete and 'men-only' tables that show up across each of our four nations alike are ones that derive not primarily from recent trends of change in rates and levels of female employment but rather from gender differences in the effects of class *origins* within what might be regarded as the more 'traditional' classes of modern industrial societies (for an earlier version of this point, cf. Erikson and Pöntinen 1985: 159). In other words, the—quite limited—difference that is made by taking women into account does not for the most part result from the inclusion of single women or from the extent to which married women are dominant. It occurs, rather, because among the women represented in the complete tables—whether via their own or their husbands' employment—are those whose class origins lie in our two self-employed, or proprietorial, classes and whose class destinations are influenced by these origins through different processes from those of their 'brothers'. From this point of view there is, therefore, little reason to suppose that as—or if—women's work-force participation continues to develop, this will in itself result in any greater divergence between their relative rates of class mobility and those of men.

---

[34] The propensity for such mobility via employment is evident when we consider, as a component of our complete tables, the still-single daughters of petty-bourgeois and farm families.

Finally, in this connection, it is also relevant to look in some more detail at the Hungarian case, in which, as we have seen, the fit of our variant model to the complete table is least satisfactory. From inspection of residuals one further notable source of this lack of fit, in addition to those discussed above, can be discovered. In Hungary, it appears, class origins have different effects for men and women on their chances of being found in Class IIIa, and especially relative to their chances of being found in the skilled or non-skilled divisions of the working class. In particular, *sector* is in this respect of much greater consequence for women than for men: the disparity between the chances of the daughters of farm or farm-worker families (Classes IVc and VIIb) being found in Class IIIa rather than in Classes V+VI or IIIb+ VIIa—whether via their own employment or marriage—and the corresponding chances of the daughters of *all* urban employee classes (i.e. Classes I+II, IIIa, V+VI, and IIIb+VIIa) is much wider than that which exists among sons. Correspondingly, one may observe from Table 7.17 that, when our Hungarian model is fitted to the complete table with its parameters being allowed to vary, a stronger sector effect is indicated than the notably low one estimated for the 'men-only' table (see p. 153).

As to the actual social processes that are reflected in these results, we can only speculate. It is possible, for example, that in farm families less importance is set on the education of daughters relative to that of sons than in urban families—with adverse implications for their chances in labour markets and marriage markets alike; or again that the daughters of farm families are less able or less motivated than sons to migrate from the countryside into the towns and cities where non-manual employment tends to be concentrated. But, for present purposes, the crucial point is that, whatever the influences that lie behind this further gender-linked variation in relative rates which sets Hungary apart, to the extent that they are grounded in rural–urban differences of some kind, they would seem more likely to diminish than to increase as the development of industrial society in Hungary proceeds.

In conclusion, then, we may say, that, if the class mobility of women is taken into account by means of the complete tables that we have constructed, the results produced do not in fact differ in any very radical way from those of 'men-only' tables. Claims made by 'feminist' sociologists to the effect that the neglect of women leads to serious distortion in accounts of the extent or pattern of mobility in modern societies or to 'an enormous limit on our understanding of mobility' (Roberts and Woodward 1981: 542) are scarcely supported. The inclusion of single women in our analyses, and the provision we have made for the class position of conjugal families to be determined by the employment of female 'heads', lead to only quite modest differences in absolute rates; most notably, outflows from all class origins to the expanded number of white-collar positions tend to increase. And at the level of relative rates the differences are still less; the modelling of our complete tables that we have undertaken would suggest little need for revision of our earlier findings on the extent of cross-national commonality in social-fluidity patterns. In so far as the lack of fit of national variants of our model of core fluidity to complete tables does reveal gender-specific features in this model, these could not be regarded as being of any great quantitative importance, except perhaps for Hungary. Further, though, the finding that is, in our view, of chief sociological interest here is that, where such features can be identified, including in the Hungarian case, they do not appear to be ones that arise out of a neglect of the trend towards women's increased work-force participation. They point, rather, to differential effects of class origins on men's and women's mobility chances in certain specific circumstances which, it would seem, in modern societies are likely to be of declining importance.

In this chapter we have addressed the question of how far bringing women within the scope of our enquiry must lead us to modify conclusions on class mobility in industrial societies that are derived from data referring only to men. The answer that we have reached may be summed up as follows. From the conceptual standpoint that we adopt throughout this study, in which the conjugal family rather than the individual is taken as the unit of class analysis, the extension of our enquiry to women does *not* point to the need for any major revision of findings or arguments previously presented. To the contrary, it could be held that the sociologically most significant outcome of our analyses both of women's marital mobility tables and of our complete tables is the evidence of how *little* women's experience of class mobility differs from that of men. To be sure, certain variations are revealed, and are of interest in their own right; but within the overall, macrosociological, picture their effect is remarkably small.[35]

A different answer may, of course, be given if, instead of the family, the individual becomes the unit of analysis and if, therefore, the practice is followed of determining the class position of all married, as well as of unmarried, women by reference to their own employment. From this standpoint, women's absolute—though not relative—rates of class mobility will be seen to diverge appreciably from those of men: in particular, women will appear more likely to experience downward mobility from their class origins into the lower levels of both non-manual and manual employment. We have, however, noted serious difficulties in the way of accepting such accounts as valid. While they have proved attractive to feminists, and

---

[35] The only other attempt of which we are aware to assess systematically the extent to which women's class mobility could be said to differ from that of men is that of Schadee and Schizzerotto (1990), based on Italian data. In this study we find a curious strain between the results of the analyses reported and the accompanying commentary and eventual conclusions drawn. We would attach more weight to the former than to the latter, which seem to us consistently to exaggerate the overall quantitative importance of the differences revealed—other than where the 'individual' approach is followed. However, Schadee and Schizzerotto, like us, regard this approach as invalid.

especially to those of a *marxisant* tendency still anxious to sustain a version of the theory of proletarianization, they would appear to call into being many proletarians of a very unconvincing kind so far at least as their class identification and political partisanship are concerned. In other words, we would find quite implausible the idea, advanced by Braverman (1974) and others, that the growth of women's employment can be seen as offsetting the long-term tendency for the working classes of industrial societies to decline in size, and that women's experience in being largely relegated to, and confined in, 'degraded' work is a potential new source of working-class organizational strength and militancy.

To the contrary, our own perspective would lead us to view the way in which women's employment has expanded as being more likely, overall, to *lessen* class-based dissent and radicalism. On the one hand, the concentration of women in lower-grade jobs, both non-manual and manual, has increased the chances of upward class mobility for men. As we have earlier observed in Chapter 3 and elsewhere, the extent and pattern of women's work-force participation must certainly be regarded as one of the exogenous factors shaping the structural context within which men's class mobility occurs. On the other hand, a sizable proportion of all women in what might be regarded as 'degraded' work are in fact married to men who hold far more advantaged positions and, as we have pointed out, tend to derive their class and political affiliations more from their husbands' employment than from their own. Braverman emphasizes the growing frequency with which women in routine non-manual jobs marry men in manual work—so that different types of proletarian are, as he sees it, increasingly 'merged within the same living family' (1974: 353). But what he crucially ignores are the numbers of such women who marry men in professional, administrative, and managerial positions, and who thus become 'merged' in families enjoying clearly non-proletarian life-chances and life-styles which they would seem unlikely to reject—even if remaining highly conscious of gender disadvantage or discrimination in the sphere of work.[36]

Many commentators, we would suggest, have in this regard been led astray by a commitment to the belief that the gender and the class inequalities to which they are alike opposed must have some close connection with each other—reflecting, say, the generally hierarchical and exploitative nature of

---

[36] We may again remark here (but we hope for the last time) that the structural implications of women's work-force participation for men's class-mobility chances, which 'feminist' sociologists and their sympathizers have recurrently emphasized, (i) were in fact from an early stage recognized by mainstream mobility researchers (e.g. Goldthorpe and Llewellyn 1977); (ii) are not (*pace* Marshall 1990) analogous with the implications of the work-force participation of blacks for whites' class-mobility chances in South Africa—since blacks do not there typically form conjugal families with whites and do not thus benefit from the improved chances that the structure of their own employment gives to whites; (iii) can, in fact, be estimated, rather than just talked about (Goldthorpe 1980a/1987: 299; McRae 1990), and, while not negligible, can scarcely be given any overriding importance among the wide range of other factors shaping the opportunity structures that men confront.

the existing social order. This is, however, a belief more readily sustained by ideology than empirical evidence. And, indeed, a clear implication of the analyses of relative mobility rates that we have reported in this chapter is that gender and class inequalities are *not* in fact of such a cognate kind. Women's mobility chances are shown to be differentiated by class on much the same pattern as we have earlier found to be persistent and prevalent among men—and even when women's experience in marriage markets as well as labour markets is examined. In other words, inequalities of gender and of class are cross-cutting in such a way as to suggest that their effects at the level of socio-political consciousness and action are as likely to offset as to reinforce each other and, further, that they are created and maintained by largely different sets of factors. Thus, as we have already argued, a convincing explanation of the gender inequalities that would appear a common feature of modern industrial societies will need to be developed for the most part outside the scope of class analysis; and, by the same token, the introduction of considerations of gender into the study of class inequalities will prove far less revelatory than it has of late been fashionable to suppose.

8

Work-Life and Intergenerational Class Mobility

In this chapter we continue with our examination of aspects of class mobility that our previous analyses largely neglected by considering such mobility— so far as we are able—in a work-life as well as an intergenerational perspective. To begin with, we review arguments recently advanced to the effect that intergenerational mobility can be properly understood only if it is recognized as a continuous, 'life-course' process, and that standard 'father-to-son' (or 'parent-to-child') mobility tables of the kind on which we have so far relied give a very imperfect basis for its investigation. We recognize that these arguments carry force, and that in regard to many issues in mobility research detailed information on individual work histories will indeed be the most appropriate data with which to work. However, we still find the critique of standard mobility tables from a 'life-course' standpoint in certain respects unconvincing, since it would appear to suppose a view of the relationship between work-life and intergenerational mobility that is not the only one possible, nor, we believe, one that should be accepted without question. Our central concern in this chapter is thus to see how far we may use the comparative material that we have available to us in order to analyse this relationship more fully.

In the second section of the chapter we discuss the various problems of data that we encounter: in particular, those resulting from our wish to work for the most part with 'three-way' mobility tables, which bring together information on men's class of origin, their class at their first entry into the labour market, and their 'present' or destination class. In consequence of these problems, we are in fact lead to concentrate our attention on just four of the nine European nations that are represented in our data-set. In the third section we then go on to report, for these nations, largely descriptive findings derived from three-way tables. When absolute rates of mobility from origins to destinations are thus considered—that is, as involving transitions *via* an 'entry' class—they do, perhaps not surprisingly, tend to display still more cross-national variation than standard tables can make apparent and, moreover, of a kind that is not so readily viewed as the outcome essentially of structural effects.

However, when in the fourth section of the chapter we turn to the relative rates, or patterns of social fluidity, that are implicit in our three-way tables, the findings that emerge are rather double-edged so far as the life-course approach is concerned. On the one hand, greater cross-national variation is indeed again found, and especially in the transition from entry class to class of destination. In other words, the degree of cross-national commonality in fluidity patterns that we have previously shown to underlie intergenerational class mobility could scarcely be claimed across the two component transitions of this process that our three-way tables enable us to distinguish. But, on the other hand, this result is itself, we seek to argue, one which within the life-course approach must be regarded as puzzling, and for which no very satisfactory explanation is provided.

In the final section of the chapter we then attempt to develop a more adequate account than this approach can offer of how our findings on work-life and intergenerational mobility may be seen as connecting. This aims to do justice to the fact that the intergenerational mobility that is represented in our standard tables does indeed come about from the actions of parents and of their children over the course of their lifetimes, while, however, giving recognition to the important macrosociological regularities that the analysis of such tables reveals, and in this way avoiding what could be regarded as the excessive voluntarism of the life-course approach, at least in its more unconsidered versions.

THE LIFE-COURSE APPROACH AND THE CRITIQUE OF STANDARD MOBILITY TABLES

During the 1980s many of the more notable contributions to mobility research came from the analysis of data-sets containing information on the complete work histories of individuals sampled from national populations. By exploiting such material—and often through the application of advanced techniques of dynamic modelling—investigators have been able to trace out the temporal, life-course aspects of social mobility in far more detail and with far greater accuracy than would be conceivable on the basis of the data that standard mobility tables comprise (see, e.g., Carroll and Mayer 1986; Blossfeld 1986; Mayer and Carroll 1987; Featherman, Selbee, and Mayer 1989). It is, therefore, not altogether surprising that among exponents of this new approach the analysis of standard tables should by now be regarded as *vieux jeu*, and indeed as a procedure which advances in data collection and analysis alike have rendered more-or-less obsolete.

The most systematic and cogent statement of this position is that made by Sørensen (1986), although many of his points are echoed elsewhere. Sørensen's central argument is that the standard table—that is, one which simply cross-classifies the social origins and destinations of the respondents to a mobility enquiry—must be seriously flawed as a source of information on mobility, since it attempts to capture in a single 'snapshot' what are in fact complex temporal sequences. Thus, the 'destinations' in such a table are just the social positions that respondents happened to hold at the time of the enquiry—and which they might well later leave; while 'origins' typically refer to the positions held by respondents' fathers at some, more-or-less arbitrarily chosen, point in *their* life-courses, which must then mean that from respondent to respondent origins will be determined at widely differing dates. In other words, the standard table 'aggregates career mobility processes for two generations' (1986: 78)—with the result that the data it contains are extremely difficult to interpret, whether considered from the point of view of individual experience or of societal attributes. On the one hand, the table is unlikely to show accurately when and where the individual mobility traject-ories that are represented by cell entries have their beginning or end—let alone what intermediate stages they have included; and, on the other hand, the structural effects that are mediated through the marginal distributions can only represent some kind of average for the period of several decades over which the events that are captured in the table will be spread.

Sørensen's conclusion is then that the future of mobility research must lie with the collection and analysis of data that have a genuinely life-course character. Only in this way will it be possible to obtain reliable estimates of the patterns of association that exist between origins and destinations and, moreover, to develop a sound understanding of the ways in which these patterns are generated. In sum—and to quote the title of a further contribu-tion (Sørensen, Allmendinger, and Sørensen 1986)—we must take the perspective of 'Intergenerational Mobility as a Life-Course Process'. Ideally, the mobility of individuals should be analysed as a series of events or 'outcomes' which carries them from their social origins, through successive life-course stages—of education, training, employment, etc.—until, pres-umably at a relatively advanced age, they could be said to have reached their destination in some more-or-less realistic sense (cf. also Allmendinger, 1989).

In addition to this critique of standard tables in principle, we should also note the attempts that have been made, from a life-course standpoint, to demonstrate their shortcomings empirically. Several authors have compared results from standard tables with those obtained from so-called 'cumulative' mobility tables utilizing complete work-history data (Featherman and Selbee 1988; Featherman, Selbee, and Mayer 1989; Mayer *et al.* 1989). In these latter tables cell entries are not, in principle, individuals, distributed accord-ing to their class origins and destinations, but rather 'class events': that is, the total number of moves between the classes defining a cell that have occurred over the lifetimes of all the individuals included in the sample. From such comparisons it has emerged that cumulative tables reveal more mobility and greater fluidity than do standard ones—as must, of course, be expected, since cases of immobility will arise only where individuals have remained in the same class throughout their lives;[1] and, further, that nations

---

[1] It has, however, to be noted that it is in this respect that the idea of treating 'class events' rather than individuals breaks down. Cells on the main diagonal of cumulative tables in fact

which from standard tables appear much alike in their patterns of mobility and fluidity may in fact show clear differences when their cumulative tables are examined. Thus, it can be maintained that standard tables are an unreliable basis for comparative mobility studies, since the very incomplete information they provide is likely to give an exaggerated idea of the extent of cross-national similarities. And it would then further follow that, where such similarities are claimed—as, for example, in the case of the FJH hypothesis—it is against the data of cumulative and not standard tables that empirical tests will most appropriately be made.[2]

In response to such attacks, it would not, in fact, be difficult to show that those who have worked with standard tables have been neither so unaware of their limitations, nor so naïve in interpreting the data they contain, as critics have sought to make out.[3] And it could in turn be observed that life-course data are also open to use in potentially highly misleading ways—not least in cumulative tables in which events and individuals tend to be in some degree confounded (cf. n. 1 to this chapter, and Tåhlin 1991) and in which, moreover, each 'class event' counts for the same, whether it refers to a shift in class position that lasted for three months or for thirty years. However, our main concern here is not with counter-arguments of this kind. We would rather wish to concur in much of the case that is advanced for the superiority of life-course data, and of the analyses that it permits, over a reliance upon standard tables. We have in fact already in Chapter 6 emphasized the importance of detailed information on individuals' work-life mobility in regard to issues of class formation; and we would see such information as being similarly important wherever the crucial questions are ones of the

record cases of individuals in whose lives no 'class event' has ever occurred—thus giving the counts of these tables a rather disturbing heterogeneity (cf. Tåhlin 1991).

[2] In the original version of Mayer *et al.* (1989), a paper presented to the Annual Convention of the American Sociological Association in 1987, the case that cumulative rather than standard tables are the appropriate basis for testing the FJH hypothesis was explicitly made; but this argument is not included in the published version.

[3] Thus, for example, problems of the aggregation of destinations can be alleviated by disaggregating tables by birth-cohort of respondent—as Sørensen indeed recognizes. He then goes on to state that such disaggregation 'is never interpreted as providing information about exposure' (i.e. to mobility processes) (1986: 77). But just such an interpretation arises with our suggestion (p. 72, and cf. Goldthorpe 1980*a*/1987: 51–2, 69–71) of a stage of 'occupational maturity', reached at about age 30–35, beyond which a clear falling-off occurs in the rate of changes in occupation or employment status that would also imply changes of class position. Work-history data would seem to lend empirical support to this idea, and Sørensen's further argument that exposure should in any event be measured by time in the labour force rather than by age can be questioned. Why should years spent in full-time education be excluded from 'exposure'? Again, while it has for long been accepted that the fathers' distribution in a standard mobility table cannot be taken as representing some previous social structural state, experience suggests that the pattern of discrepancies between this distribution and that of respondents does in fact tend to reflect rather faithfully the broad lines of structural change over recent decades, as can be established, say, from census statistics (cf. Mayer 1979). And, more importantly, we do not see the grounds for Sørensen's implied critique (1986: 78) of Duncan's (1966) proposal that the fathers' marginal distribution may be more conservatively—but still very usefully—interpreted as indexing respondents' social origins.

degree of continuity with which particular individuals hold class positions, or again of the sequences according to which they move from one position to another, or of the connection between the duration or timing of such 'class events' and other aspects of their lives. The reservations that we have on the position taken up by Sørensen and others who would see the life-course approach as having entirely superseded the analysis of standard mobility tables are in fact concentrated on just two, related points.

First, while standard tables are clearly not an adequate basis on which to treat the temporal processes through which the mobility of individuals actually occurs, they can, in our view, still be understood in a way which avoids most of the criticism that has been directed against them, and which has, in fact, led to results of major sociological interest. In the present study—and in most other work in which their analysis has had a central part—standard tables are taken as providing information *not* primarily about the mobility trajectories of particular individuals over the life-course but rather about the mobility rates and patterns displayed by societies at certain points in time: specifically, about the probabilities of individuals found in given class positions coming from different classes of origin or, alternatively, of individuals of given class origins being found in different class positions. Such probabilities will, of course, reflect *both* the frequency with which particular moves from class to class occur *and* their duration; the longer individuals of a certain origin tend to hold a certain destination position, the greater the chance of the transition thus defined being observed in the 'snapshot' that a standard table provides.

The finding of most immediate significance for present purposes which emerges from our own, as from other, analyses conducted from this standpoint is then that, when the probabilities in question are considered net of structural effects—when, that is, we think in terms of relative mobility rates or of net associations between class origins and destinations—a large degree of temporal stability is apparent. 'Snapshots' that refer to successive birth-cohorts or historical periods give in fact essentially similar results. And we have further found that relative rates tend to show strong similarities across subpopulations distinguished within national societies, and again a substantial cross-national commonality, which, we have suggested, might be seen as pointing to the source of their temporal stability. We find it difficult to envisage how such results could be merely spurious ones, deriving from the deficiencies of standard mobility tables as noted by Sørensen, and critics have indeed made no attempt to establish such a possibility. By far the more plausible view would be that the regularities displayed are manifestations of a 'social fact' of a sufficiently well-defined and obtrusive kind that the data of such tables, whatever their imperfections, could scarcely fail to reflect it.[4]

Secondly, then, although it may be that mobility at the individual, or

---

[4] It is notable that in Sørensen's (1986) paper he barely touches on the results in question.

'micro', level is most appropriately studied as a life-course process, it would seem dangerous to suppose from this that rates and patterns of intergenerational mobility as they are observed at the societal, or 'macro', level are no more than the unconstrained aggregation of so many individual mobility trajectories. In view of the degree of constancy and commonality that can be observed in relative rates, it would seem important to ask whether the outcomes of life-course mobility processes may not be in some way subject to macrolevel restrictions. However, this is a possibility that exponents of the life-course approach, in their insistence on seeing intergenerational mobility in this perspective, would appear largely to have neglected; and in turn they tend to assume, implicitly if not explicitly, a relationship between work-life and intergenerational mobility of a kind that does not necessarily apply.

In what follows we aim to explore this issue further by examining the connection that exists between work-life and intergenerational mobility on a cross-national basis. But first we must consider various problems of data that arise.

DATA

As we noted in Chapter 6, the mobility studies from which our comparative data-set derives did not in most instances collect information on respondents' work histories. We are, therefore, restricted in our treatment of work-life mobility to relating individuals' 'present', or destination, class positions to the class positions that they held in virtue of their first employment, or to what we shall refer to as their 'entry' class. However, given our concern with the connection between work-life and intergenerational mobility, we shall seek to elaborate our analysis by operating chiefly with 'three-way' mobility tables (cf. Goldthorpe 1980*a*/1987: ch. 4) through which transitions between class of first employment, or entry class, and class destinations are themselves related to class origins. One reason for so doing is, of course, the possibility of such tables revealing a three-way interaction effect, which could be taken as indicating that the association between class of first employment and present class varies with class of origin, or alternatively that the association between origin class and destination class varies with entry class.[5]

It is obviously desirable to apply here the same, sevenfold version of the class schema as we have used in our standard intergenerational tables. But three-way tables organized on this basis call for large total sample sizes if cell counts are not to become unduly sparse. And, although, for reasons we discuss below, we are, in fact, forced to collapse Classes IV*c* and VII*b* into a single 'farm' entry class, 7 × 6 × 7 tables are little less demanding in this

---

[5] The other possible specification—that the association between origin class and entry class varies with class of destination—seems somewhat less plausible, though it could still conceivably apply.

respect. Consequently, we have decided that, for the purposes of this chapter, it would be best for us to concentrate our attention on the four nations for which our source studies provide the largest sample sizes: that is, England, France, Hungary, and Poland. Among these nations, the smallest sample (for men aged 20–64) is 9,434 in the case of England, while the next largest sample among our five remaining European nations is that of 4,583 for Scotland (cf. Table 5.1).[6]

Thus reducing the number of nations that we consider will, of course, be likely to limit the conclusions that we are able to draw from our comparative analyses. But at the same time our selection of nations does happen to have certain advantages. On the one hand, England and France are the two nations that we have taken as holding 'central' positions within cross-national variation in the patterns of social fluidity that underlie intergenerational class mobility—and thus these nations provide the empirical basis for our model of core fluidity. On the other hand, Hungary and Poland are both nations that show some appreciable deviation from core fluidity, and in part at least, we have argued, as the result of policies pursued by their state socialist regimes. In other words, England, France, Hungary, and Poland are cases which we can at all events 'situate' in a fairly definite way so far as their intergenerational mobility regimes are concerned. The two former nations we would see as displaying in a rather pure form the pattern of fluidity generic to the class structures of industrial societies—that is, as this emerges where state intervention in the generative social processes is at a minimum; while the two latter illustrate how, within the context of an industrial society, this pattern of fluidity can be subject to different kinds of political modification.

In the three-way tables that we construct for England, France, Hungary, and Poland, the variables of class of origin and class of destination are exactly the same as in all previous analyses. However, rather more has, unfortunately, to be said about the variable of class of first employment or entry class.

To begin with, there is the general problem of defining 'first' employment. Should this refer literally to the first paid work that an individual ever undertook, or should certain exceptions be made—for example, for students' part-time or vacation jobs or for work done as part of, or in lieu of, military service? Each of the four national surveys on which we draw handled this problem in a different way. The definition of first employment was most restricted in the English case. Here, in fact, the reference is to first employment *after completion of full-time education* or, that is, after a period of continuous full-time education not interrupted for more than two years except by compulsory military service. Thus, all early part-time and temporary work, as well as military service itself, were in effect discounted. At the other extreme was the Hungarian survey in which, it would appear, the only qualification imposed was that military service was excluded from consideration when first employment was determined. The French and Polish enquiries then follow what could be regarded as intermediate strategies. In the French case, all employment undertaken while respondents were still at some 'recognized' educational stage—for example, students in higher educational institutions—was disregarded; in the Polish, a 'first' job followed by a break in employment of more than one year was ignored unless it had lasted for more than eighteen months and, otherwise, a first job had to be one that lasted for more than six months and produced a 'regular income'. It is thus apparent enough that for the variable in question the standard of comparability of our data is impaired; and there is, in fact, little that we can do about this, except of course to keep the differences in protocol much in mind in evaluating our results.

Another, more particular, problem arises in the case of those men whose first employment took the form of working in a family business or on a family farm. Following the procedures of the different national surveys and depending on the specific circumstances reported, these men could be treated as employees or as self-employed persons or, perhaps, be placed in a separate category of 'family worker' or 'family helper'. In the English and French surveys the procedures were not in fact all that different, and could be largely reconciled through our usual practice of eliminating the categories of family workers or helpers and treating all persons so coded simply as employees. In the Hungarian and Polish cases, however, the sons of self-employed men who worked with their fathers were in most instances coded from the start as being self-employed themselves.[7] So far as the sons of the petty bourgeoisie are concerned, the non-comparability that is in this way created is of no great consequence, since the numbers involved in the Hungarian and Polish cases alike are more-or-less negligible. But the same clearly cannot be said as regards such family workers in agriculture, and here the only solution available to us was to remove the distinction, for first or entry class, between farmers and farm workers. That is to say, for this variable we are obliged to reduce our sevenfold class schema to a sixfold one by collapsing Classes IV*c* and VII*b*.

One final point arising from the introduction of entry class into our analyses needs also to be made. It will, of course, sometimes occur that a respondent's present employment is his first employment, so that his entry class and present class are in effect conflated. Where such cases are ones of men in the very early stages of their working lives, as they are indeed most

---

[7] Personal communications from Rudolf Andorka and Krzysztof Zagórski.

likely to be, it could be argued that their appearance in the diagonal cells of a work-life mobility table will tend to give an exaggerated idea of the degree of immobility that prevails. Since our attention in this paper centres on cross-national similarities and differences in mobility rates rather than on their actual levels, we would be likely to face a serious problem here only if our national samples showed marked differences in their proportions of respondents in the younger age-groups—which is not, in fact, the case.[8] However, we still thought it advisable to repeat all our analyses with respondents aged 20–34 being excluded. In this way we can ensure that virtually all of the men then considered will be at least ten years on from their entry into work—although, of course, at the cost of losing information on the early work histories of the younger birth-cohorts represented in our samples. In fact, excluding these younger respondents tends to make rather little difference to our findings, and only in the few instances where this is not the case will we subsequently refer to results from the truncated samples.

ABSOLUTE RATES IN THREE-WAY TABLES

In this section we will adopt an outflow perspective; that is, we will draw on the data of our three-way tables in order to trace the patterns of dispersal of men from their class origins, via their classes of first employment, or entry classes, to their class destinations. However, in pursuing this objective, the amount and detail of the information that these tables hold—they entail across our four nations a total array of 1,176 cells—itself constitutes a problem. We shall not, therefore, attempt to comment on the tables in full, but will restrict ourselves to discussing what are in effect extracts from them, which we present in a graphical form. In Figure 8.1 we use flow charts to show the *major* transitions that are followed, by men of different class origins, between entry class and class of destination. Specifically, we depict, for men originating in each of the seven classes of our schema, all outflows to entry class *and thence* to present class which account for 5 per cent or more of the total number of men in question, and also any other outflows from origins to entry class which account for 10 per cent or more. We also indicate by minus or plus signs any sizable changes in the outflows reported which would result if men under 35 were excluded from the analysis.

The first visual impression to be gained from looking across the several panels of Figure 8.1 is, perhaps, one of a degree of 'family resemblance' in the patterns that are shown up. Thus, for example, in all four nations alike men originating in the two agricultural classes of our schema, IVc and VIIb, reveal a similar tendency to enter first into farm work, but subsequently to move on in large numbers to manual wage-earning jobs outside agriculture in Classes V+VI and VIIa. Again, it may be noted that in the non-

---

[8] Men aged under 35 in the English, French, Hungarian, and Polish samples amount, respectively, to 35, 40, 39, and 36 per cent of all aged 20–64.

agricultural sector it is men originating within the 'intermediate' classes of our schema, that is, Classes III, IVa+b, and V+VI, who generally show the widest range of dispersion to entry classes and, in turn, the most diverse paths to destination positions. In contrast, men from both the most and the least advantaged origins—that is, from Class I+II on the one hand and Class VIIa on the other—are far more concentrated in the classes through which they first enter employment. And further, as well as showing relatively high work-life immobility, it is they, along with men of Class V+VI origins, who most regularly follow major *counter-mobile* trajectories (indicated in Figure 8.1 by heavy lines). That is to say, it is these men who appear most likely to experience work-life mobility which *returns them to* the same class as that in which they originated, after an initial movement away from it on their entry into work (cf. Girod 1971: ch. 2).

One further cross-national similarity that can be discerned from Figure 8.1 does in fact relate to the effect of class origins on work-life mobility in a more general way. As we have already discussed in Chapter 6, it is possible to distinguish the classes of our schema according to their 'mobility characteristics', including the degree of their retentiveness or holding power. So far as their retentiveness considered as entry classes is concerned, Figure 8.1 essentially recapitulates the results presented earlier in Table 6.10; but what can now further be seen is the extent of the difference that is made in this respect by individuals' class origins. Across our four nations, this difference turns out to be least with the two classes that were found to contrast most sharply in their holding power: the service class, Class I+II, in which work-life stability is highest, and the class of routine non-manual employees, Class III, in which it is lowest. But class origins would seem to have a clearly greater influence on the work-life holding power of the farm-entry class, IVc+VIIb, in that it is farmers' sons who are most often retained in farm work of some kind (in large part, one may suppose, through inheritance) and again on that of industrial working-class positions in Classes V+VI and VIIa. In particular, it may be remarked that the sons of service-class fathers who enter employment via working-class positions are far less likely to be found in them subsequently—mainly in consequence of counter-mobility—than are the sons of men who were industrial wage-workers themselves.

We may then say that, from the data of Figure 8.1, various cross-nationally common features are apparent when patterns of mobility are traced from different class origins via class of first employment to class destinations. None the less, as exponents of the life-course approach would no doubt anticipate, elaborating on standard tables, even to this limited extent, does also increase the possibilities for observing cross-national differences. Scanning the panels of Figure 8.1, we in fact only rarely find that the major mobility flows represented are exactly the same from one nation to another: we must clearly accept that, within their 'family resemblance', each of our four nations also reveals many more distinctive features.

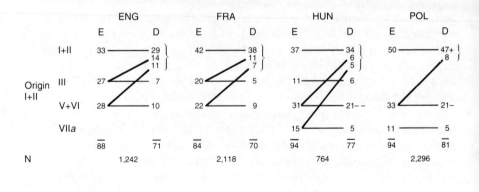

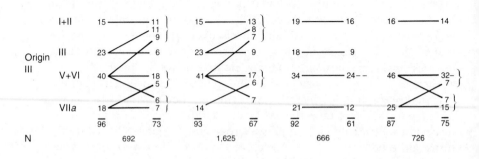

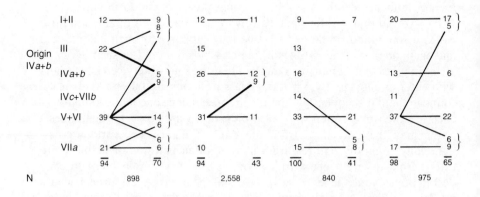

FIGURE 8.1. *Outflows to entry class and destination class by origin class, men aged 20–64; outflows of less than 10% to entry class or less than 5% to destination class omitted. (One minus or plus sign indicates that a percentage would decrease or increase by 5 percentage points or more, and two signs indicate a change of more than 10 percentage points, if men age 20–34 are excluded.)*

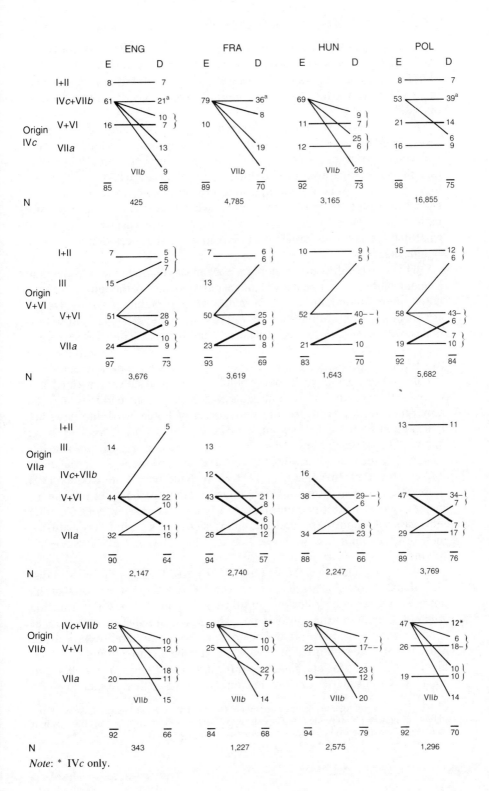

Note: * IVc only.

Furthermore, though, when we examine Figure 8.1 with an eye for differences, we may recognize, over and above those that are specific to individual nations, a number of a somewhat more systematic kind: that is, differences that set our two Eastern European nations in contrast with our two Western ones.

Most conspicuous in this respect is perhaps the tendency for flows represented by horizontal lines—that is, ones implying work-life stability—to account for larger proportions of men in the Hungarian and Polish cases than they do in the English and French. Here again we are in part rediscovering a point that was already indicated in Table 6.10: namely, that entry classes are often more retentive in the two former than in the two latter nations.[9] However, Figure 8.1 is also able to display at least two further, and what may be taken as largely complementary, differences that are also of significance.

On the one hand, counter-mobility appears as generally more frequent in England and France than it is in Hungary and Poland. Although, as we have noted, there are in all four nations major counter-mobile flows involved in creating intergenerational stability within Classes I+II, V+VI, and VIIa— that is, within the service class and the two divisions of the industrial working class—these flows are consistently stronger in the two Western than in the two Eastern European nations. Moreover, in England and France, but not in Hungary or Poland, such counter-mobile flows also show up within Class IVa+b, that of the petty bourgeoisie. On the other hand, it may be remarked that for Hungary and Poland relatively few work-life flows are indicated in Figure 8.1 which imply upward mobility into Class I+II of an 'indirect' kind; that is, upward mobility into service-class positions which is achieved in the course of working life rather than 'directly' on initial entry into employment. In England and France such indirect routes to Class I+II more often appear as major ones—most notably, perhaps, in the case of men of Class III, routine non-manual, origins—via entry in both Class III and Class V+VI positions; and in England such routes are important also for men of other intermediate-level, that is, Class IVa+b and Class V+VI, origins.

In order to check that these 'East–West' cross-national differences displayed in our flow charts are not just a product of the simplification that the latter entail, we may calculate appropriate summary measures from the *complete* data of our three-way tables. These are given in Table 8.1, and, as can be seen, they confirm that England and France do tend to have lower rates of work-life stability than Hungary and Poland, and, at the same time, higher rates of both intergenerational stability *and* upward mobility that come about through work-life movement. It is in this connection also

---

[9] It is, however, indicated by the double minus signs that in the Hungarian case work-life stability in Class V+VI is reduced to English and Polish levels for men of several class origins if those aged 20–34 are excluded from the analysis.

TABLE 8.1. *Summary measures calculated from three-way class mobility tables: rates of worklife stability, of counter-mobility, and of work-life mobility to Class I+II as percentages of all in class of origin*

	Class of origin							
	I+II	III	IVa+b	IVc	V+VI	VIIa	VIIb	All
	Work-life immobility							
ENG	49	43	34	48	46	45	43	45
FRA	56	44	42	51	44	44	36	47
HUN	69	64	45	45	65	62	52	60
POL	74	67	60	71	68	66	60	69
	Counter-mobility (excluding men of IVc and VIIb origin)							
ENG	29	7	20		13	16		15
FRA	22	8	15		14	18		11
HUN	17	5	5		10	15		6
POL	13	2	5		9	10		6
	Work-life mobility to Class I+II (excluding counter-mobility)							
ENG		23	19	9	15	11	6	14
FRA		16	10	5	13	10	4	10
HUN		12	14	6	11	7	4	8
POL		6	9	4	9	8	5	6

relevant to note that such differences are, if anything, ones more likely to be obscured than exaggerated by the problems of cross-national comparability in definitions of 'first' employment that we earlier described. It will be recalled that it was in the Hungarian case that the loosest definition was apparently allowed—and where, therefore, most spurious mobility might be expected—while the English definition was the most restrictive.

In the light of our previous analyses, and those of Chapter 6 especially, we would surely expect that the cross-national variation in mobility flows that Figure 8.1 reveals will in some substantial part derive from class-structural differences among the four nations concerned. However, it would at the same time seem rather unlikely that structural effects will here prove to be so overwhelmingly important as the source of variation in absolute rates as we found in examining our standard mobility tables. Most obviously, the line of differentiation that we have noted separating our two Eastern European from our two Western European nations is not one for which an explanation in terms of structural differences is readily apparent.[10] What would seem

[10] While it is true that in our discussion of differences in origin and destination marginals in Chapter 6 above we found contrasts between England and France, on the one hand, and

essential to this differentiation is that, with some modification according to class origins, the class in which men enter employment is more consequential in Hungary and Poland for the class positions in which they are subsequently found than it is in England and France. In the two latter nations, work-life mobility has a larger role in determining men's class destinations, whether by way of returning them to, or taking them further from, the classes in which they orginated. In other words, differences are here suggested in patterns of net association between origin, entry, and destination class; or, that is, differences not only in absolute but also in relative mobility rates within our three-way tables. It is, therefore, to the further investigation of this possibility that we turn in the section that follows.

RELATIVE RATES IN THREE TRANSITIONS

To treat cross-national variation within three-way mobility tables becomes yet more complex when the focus of attention moves from absolute to relative rates. We shall, therefore, begin our comparative analyses by considering separately the three two-way mobility tables that are involved: that is, the table which is in effect the standard intergenerational one, showing mobility from origin class to destination class (the O→D transition), plus the two tables that represent the component transitions, first from origin class to entry class (the O→E transition) and then from entry class to destination class (the E→D transition).

In Table 8.2 we show the results obtained if we take these three tables for England, France, Hungary, and Poland and for each set in turn fit the common social fluidity model. The first panel of the table, that relating to the O→D transition, has least novelty. Here we are simply repeating the initial test of the FJH hypothesis that we reported on in Table 4.1 above, but with data from only four of our nine nations.[11] And, not surprisingly, we again obtain the result that first led us to explore further the idea of a large cross-national commonality in the pattern of fluidity underlying absolute rates of intergenerational class mobility: that is, the model does not fit altogether satisfactorily but deviations from it are clearly not large.

From the second panel of the table it can then be seen that we obtain much the same kind of result when we fit the CmSF model to the tables representing

Hungary and Poland, on the other, wide differences were further apparent as between England and France and between Hungary and Poland. Moreover, so far as the distribution of entry classes is concerned, the main contrast is between England and the other three nations (with Δs in each case of over 25), resulting chiefly from the heavy concentration of men in the English sample in just three entry classes, III, V+VI, and VIIa, while in France, Hungary, and Poland alike around a third of all men entered employment via agriculture—that is, in our collapsed Class IVc + VIIb.

[11] Note, however, that the sizes of the samples here used for each of these four nations will be very slightly smaller than in Table 4.1, since men for whom we have no information on class of first employment are omitted.

TABLE 8.2. *Results of fitting the CmSF model to tables representing different transitions within three-way mobility tables for England, France, Hungary, and Poland (N = 71,616)*

Transition	Model*	G^2	df	p	rG^2	Δ	G^2/df
O→D	ON DN (con. ind.)	24,376	144	0.00	—	21.6	169.2
	ON DN OD (CmSF)	1,051.3	108	0.00	95.7	3.8	9.7
O→E	ON EN	32,006	120	0.00	—	26.2	266.7
	ON EN OE	966.5	90	0.00	97.0	3.6	10.7
E→D	EN DN	61,409	120	0.00	—	38.5	511.7
	EN DN ED	1,866.2	90	0.00	97.0	5.4	20.7

Note:

  * O = origin class; E = entry class; D = destination class; N = nation.

the O→E transition. Once more we must recognize significant cross-national differences in relative rates, although not, it appears, ones of any great magnitude. When, however, with the third panel we come to the tables for the E→D transition, the fit of the CmSF model is clearly worse. The G^2/df statistic which we report as a descriptive measure of comparative goodness of fit (cf. Hagenaars 1990) is in this case around twice as large as in the two previous tests.

Moreover, as in earlier instances where our interest has centred on the extent to which relative rates differ, we can here proceed more directly by calculating the average variance of the relevant odds ratios. If we do this on the basis of the observed cell counts in the three sets of mobility tables with which we are concerned, we find that for the O→D tables the average variance of (logged) odds ratios among nations is 0.40; for the O→E tables, 0.66; and for the E→D tables, 0.74. In other words, cross-national variation in relative mobility rates is again shown to be widest in the transition from entry class to destination class and, further, such variation in the transition from origin class to entry class appears on this basis as being also greater than that in the overall, intergenerational transition.[12]

We are thus able to confirm the supposition we made at the end of the preceding section that behind the mobility flows displayed in Figure 8.1 lies a lesser degree of cross-national similarity in fluidity patterns than is implicit in standard intergenerational tables. In addition, our examination of these flows led us to conclude that, while each of our four nations showed certain distinctive features, there were also various contrasts to be noted as between

---

[12] The difference of this result from that shown in Table 8.2 may be attributed to the fact that, as previously noted, the G^2s returned by non-fitting models will reflect not only deviations between odds ratios expected and those observed but also compositional effects related to the numbers of cases in cells involved in particular odds ratios.

the English and French cases on the one hand and the Hungarian and Polish on the other. We can then further apply the CmSF model to our data in order to test whether there is likewise a tendency at the level of relative rates for our four nations to be divided in this way. That is, we can apply the model with an additional term which restricts the requirement of common fluidity simply to tables for England and France and for Hungary and Poland while allowing variation *between* these two pairs; and we can then repeat the exercise with each of the other two possible pairwise splits of our nations.[13] The results of so doing are shown in Table 8.3.

TABLE 8.3. *Results of fitting the CmSF model to tables representing different transitions within three-way mobility tables for England, France, Hungary, and Poland with pairwise restrictions*

Pairs of nations	O→D (df = 72)			O→E (df = 60)			E→D (df = 60)		
	G^2	rG^{2*}	Δ	G^2	rG^{2*}	Δ	G^2	rG^{2*}	Δ
ENG–FRA/ HUN–POL	575.6	45.2	2.3	301.0	68.9	1.8	554.4	70.0	2.3
ENG–HUN/ FRA–POL	673.0	36.0	3.0	853.4	11.7	3.4	1,685.1	9.7	5.1
ENG–POL/ FRA–HUN	529.9	50.0	2.3	599.1	38.0	2.5	1,368.6	26.7	4.3

Note:
 * As baseline, we take here the unmodified CmSF model rather than the conditional independence model.

From the first (vertical) panel of the table where we are concerned with the O→D, intergenerational transition, it can be seen that it makes no very great difference to the fit of this modified version of the CmSF model which way our nations are divided. However, when in the second and third panels we consider the O→E and E→D transitions, the pairing of England and France as against Hungary and Poland gives clearly better fits than either of the two alternatives, and this is especially marked in the case of the E→D transition where, as we have seen, cross-national variation is greatest. If we

---

[13] The modified CmSF model for the O→D transition may be written as:

$$\log F_{ikm} = \mu + \lambda_i^O + \lambda_k^D + \lambda_m^N + \lambda_{im}^{ON} + \lambda_{km}^{DN} + \lambda_{iks}^{ODB}$$

where s = 1, 2 separates the four nations into two blocs, within which the OD interaction is set to be the same among nations, while it may differ between nations in different blocs. Thus, if for ENG and FRA s = 1, while for HUN and POL s = 2, the OD interaction is expected to be the same for the two Western European nations as also for the two Eastern European nations, while it may differ between the two blocs. The models for the O→E and E→D transitions may be written analogously.

take the unmodified CmSF model as baseline, the 'East–West' split accounts for 70 per cent of the G^2 it returns—a far higher proportion than with either of the two other pairings.

Furthermore, if we revert to the application of the CmSF model to our four national E→D tables and examine residuals, at least one major source of this divergence in fluidity patterns can readily be identified. We find that for four of the five non-agricultural classes of our schema, that is, for all except Class I+II, the model underestimates work-life immobility in Hungary and Poland while overestimating it in England and France. In other words—and again as we thought likely—the greater work-life immobility in Hungary and Poland, apparent from the flow charts of Figure 8.1, does, in part at least, reflect differences in relative rates: net of all structural effects, men in Hungary and Poland show a greater propensity to be subsequently found in the same class as that through which they first entered employment than do men in England and France.[14]

At this stage, then, we might usefully pause to take stock of what chiefly follows from the results we have so far reported for issues arising out of the critique of standard mobility tables from which we began. Most obviously, perhaps, it must be acknowledged that, to the extent that one moves away from standard tables to take up a life-course perspective on mobility, one will observe greater cross-national variation in both absolute and relative rates alike. This is apparent enough when, for our four nations, we decompose the intergenerational, O→D transition into just the two stages represented by the O→E and E→D tables. Thus, if our data had in fact allowed us to construct cumulative mobility tables, and if we had shared the enthusiasm of exponents of the life-course approach for these tables and had taken them, instead of standard ones, as the basis for our earlier analyses, then we have little doubt that we would in many respects have reached significantly different conclusions. Apart from anything else, we would think it highly unlikely that the FJH hypothesis could in this case have been sustained in any recognizable version.

However, our results do at the same time create problems for the life-course approach, and of a kind which underline the doubts we earlier expressed about the nature of the connection between work-life and inter-generational mobility that is, apparently, assumed. In particular, our finding that cross-national variation in relative rates is less in the overall O→D transition than in either of the two component transitions that we have distinguished is one for which there seems no ready explanation within a purely life-course perspective. If, underlying the mobility that is observed

---

[14] This can be readily confirmed by an application of the 'diagonal-difference' model of equation (3.3) above to our data for the E→D transition in the four nations in question. The model provides a significant improvement in fit over the CmSF model, and, with the average α parameter for the four nations set at 0, the α parameters for England, France, Hungary, and Poland respectively are -0.34, -0.27, 0.38, and 0.24.

between origin class and entry class, there are clear cross-national differences in fluidity patterns, and if such differences are yet greater in the case of work-life mobility itself, why are these differences reduced, rather than heightened, when an intergenerational view is taken? Instead of intergenerational mobility being viewed as the outcome of a quite 'open-ended' series of class events within the life-course, the possibility must be recognized that the limited degree of cross-national variation that is found in intergenerational fluidity patterns reflects constraints which are in large part common across nations, as well as constant over time, and which then react back on the way in which fluidity patterns in the transition from origin class to entry class and from entry class to destination class are related to each other.

Before seeking to elaborate further on this possibility, it may be helpful to return to our data and take up now the analysis of relative rates within our three-way tables. In fact, we proceed by combining these into a single four-way table in which nation is also a variable, and we then explore the effects that generate cell values in this array by fitting a series of models. The results of this exercise are shown in Table 8.4.

The two models in the first panel of the table are both introduced chiefly to serve as baselines. Model A is that proposing (conditional) independence of origin, entry, and destination class, and model B is the CmSF model for our three-way tables: that is to say, it proposes, via the OED term, a three-way association between origin class, entry class, and destination class that is common across our four nations. As might be expected, neither of these models fits the data at all well. But it may still be noted that the comparison of model B with model A shows that association that is cross-nationally common accounts for the very large part—almost 96 per cent—of the total association that exists within our three-way tables. In the last column of Table 8.4 we report the average variance of (logged) odds ratios among nations in the O→D tables that result from the expected values under each model fitted. For both model A and model B this variance is close to zero, since these models require complete cross-national similarity in relative rates within the O→D transition over each entry class, and variance will thus result only from compositional effects arising out of cross-national differences in entry-class distributions.

In the second panel of Table 8.4 we come to the models on which our attention will centre. Model C comprises just two three-way terms, OEN and EDN. What this model entails is that there is cross-national variation in relative rates in the O→E transition and again in the E→D transition; *but* that the association between origin class and destination class and the cross-national variation in this association derive entirely from the association, and from variation in the association, between origin class and entry class and between entry class and destination class. In other words, there is no association between origin class and destination class or variation in this association *over and above* what is produced within the two components of

TABLE 8.4. *Results of fitting models to three-way mobility tables for England, France, Hungary, and Poland* (N = 71,616)

Model*	G²	df	p	rG² (con. ind.)	rG² (CmSF)	Δ	Variance in O→D tables
A. ON EN DN (con. ind.)	99,899	1,104	0.00	—	—	45.5	0.00
B. ON EN DN OED (CmSF)	4,065.0	828	0.00	95.9	—	7.7	0.00
C. OEN EDN	6,489.8	864	0.00	93.5	—	9.0	0.13
D. OEN EDN OED	1,064.1	648	0.00	98.9	73.8	2.9	0.10
E. OEN EDN OED ODN	620.6	540	0.01	99.3	84.7	1.8	0.40
F. OEN OED ODN	2,123.5	630	0.00	97.9	47.8	5.1	0.40
G. EDN OED ODN	1,471.4	630	0.00	98.5	63.8	3.7	0.40
H. OEN EDN ODN	1,092.8	720	0.00	98.9	73.1	2.8	0.40
					G²/df		
D–E (ODN)	443.4	108	0.00		4.1		
F–E (EDN)	1,502.9	90	0.00		16.7		
G–E (OEN)	850.8	90	0.00		9.5		
H–E (OED)	472.2	180	0.00		2.6		

Note:
* O = origin class; E = entry class; D = destination class; N = nation.

the intergenerational transition. Model C, not surprisingly, does not fit our data well (in fact, it fits worse than model B). But what for present purposes is of interest is the variance in odds ratios among the intergenerational tables for our four nations that would be expected under this model. As can be seen, this is quite low: 0.13 as compared with the 0.40 which we found for our actual O→D tables and the 0.66 and 0.74 for the O→E and E→D tables respectively.

It should here be noted that what model C actually implies is that for each nation the expected O→D matrix will result from the simple multiplication of the O→E and E→D matrices.[15] And from that it will then follow that the association between origin class and destination class will be lower than that between either origin class and entry class or entry class and destination class. Moreover, since in the O→D transition all odds ratios will thus move convergently towards 1, and this movement will tend to be the more marked the further odds ratios in the component transitions are removed from 1, cross-national variation in relative rates will inevitably be less in the O→D transition than in whichever of the two component transitions it is greater. In

---

[15] To fit model C, OEN EDN, to the four-way table comprising origin class, entry class, destination class, and nation is equivalent to fitting the model OE ED to each of the national three-way tables. The expected values from this model may be written multiplicatively as

$$F_{ijk} = \eta\, \tau_i^O\, \tau_j^E\, \tau_k^D\, \tau_{ij}^{OE}\, \tau_{jk}^{ED}. \tag{1}$$

Let P_{ji} be the expected probability that a man who originated in class i entered the labour market in class j and P_{kj} and P_{ki} be the corresponding probabilities for the transitions from entries to destinations and from origins to destinations, respectively. We may then write P_{ki} as

$$P_{ki} = \sum_j F_{ijk} / \sum_k \sum_j F_{ijk}$$

which using (1) may be written as

$$P_{ki} = \sum_j \tau_j^E\, \tau_k^D\, \tau_{ij}^{OE}\, \tau_{jk}^{ED} / \sum_k \sum_j \tau_j^E\, \tau_k^D\, \tau_{ij}^{OE}\, \tau_{jk}^{ED} \tag{2}$$

Similarly

$$P_{ji} = \sum_k F_{ijk} / \sum_j \sum_k F_{ijk}$$

$$P_{ji} = \sum_k \tau_j^E\, \tau_k^D\, \tau_{ij}^{OE}\, \tau_{jk}^{ED} / \sum_k \sum_j \tau_j^E\, \tau_k^D\, \tau_{ij}^{OE}\, \tau_{jk}^{ED} \tag{3}$$

and

$$P_{kj} = \sum_i F_{ijk} / \sum_k \sum_i F_{ijk}$$

$$P_{kj} = \sum_i \tau_i^O\, \tau_k^D\, \tau_{ij}^{OE}\, \tau_{jk}^{ED} / \sum_k \sum_i \tau_i^O\, \tau_k^D\, \tau_{ij}^{OE}\, \tau_{jk}^{ED} \tag{4}$$

If the O→D matrix results from a multiplication of the O→E matrix by the E→D matrix, we should find that

$$P_{ki} = \sum_j P_{ji}\, P_{kj}$$

If we multiply (3) and (4), sum over j and simplify, the result will be equal to (2), which shows that the probabilities for the transition from origins to destinations that are expected under the OE ED model result from the multiplication of the O→E and E→D transition matrices.

fact, though, the *empirical* indication that we obtain from the fitting of model C is that, with the four national cases we consider, the pattern of relative rates in the O→E and the E→D transitions is such that the reduction in cross-national variation produced in the O→D transition is quite marked, and indeed falls well below the level of that found in *either* of the two component transitions.

We may then pursue this point with model D, which removes one of the two major restrictions imposed by model C. Through the addition of the OED term to model C, it is no longer required that the association between origin class and destination class should be simply the product of that between origin class and entry class and that between entry class and destination class. Model D provides for an association between origin class and destination class over and above that created by these two latter effects—and also for this association to vary by entry class. We would, of course, expect the inclusion of the OED term to increase the association between origin class and destination class: this need no longer be low relative to that between origin class and entry class or entry class and destination class. But, since the OED term is one that applies across nations, it remains the case that model D, like model C, allows no cross-national variation in relative rates in O→D tables other than that deriving from such variation in their constituent O→E and E→D tables.

From Table 8.4 it can then be observed that model D achieves a significant— and indeed substantial—improvement in fit over model C (G^2 falls by 5425.7 with the loss of 216 df) and that, while it cannot itself reproduce our data altogether satisfactorily, deviations from it are not large. And further, as we would anticipate, the inclusion of the OED term, representing a cross-nationally common effect, leads to little change in the cross-national variance in odds ratios within the intergenerational tables expected under model D as compared with those expected under model C. There is, in fact, a slight fall, to 0.10.

The final model that we introduce in this sequence is model E, which is model D plus the ODN term. Thus, the second of the two restrictions to which we referred in the case of model C is now also removed: through the ODN term, cross-national variation in relative rates in O→D tables is provided for in addition to that resulting from the O→E and E→D transitions. Since model D accounted for so much of the association of interest in the tables we are analysing, the improvement in fit achieved by model E cannot be a substantively large one, although it is statistically significant (G^2 falls by 443.5 with the loss of 108 df). We would, in fact, wish to take model E as adequately reproducing our data for all practical purposes, even though by conventional standards it still falls somewhat short of acceptability. It may then be further noted that, with the inclusion of the ODN term, the cross-national variance in odds ratios in the O→D tables rises from the 0.10 under model D to the 0.40 of our observed tables—which, of course, the ODN term brings into the model as fitted marginals.[16] But also of interest are the fits of the additional models, F, G, and H, shown in the third panel of Table 8.4 and, specifically, the comparisons made between, on the one hand, these models and also model D, each of which omits one of the four possible three-way terms and, on the other hand, model E, which includes all four. If we concentrate our attention on the three terms that accommodate cross-national variation in relative rates, OEN, EDN, and ODN, what we can see is that the unique contribution of ODN—that is, controlling for the contribution of the other two terms—is clearly smaller than that of either OEN or EDN.

Here, therefore, in the relative weakness of the ODN effect, we can identify one source of our finding that less cross-national variation occurs in patterns of social fluidity within our intergenerational, O→D tables than in those representing the two constituent, O→E and E→D, transitions. But we have, of course, also discovered that, despite the quite large amounts of cross-national variation that occur within these latter transitions, and in the work-life, E→D transition especially, this is to some extent of an offsetting kind, with the result that the variation that is, so to speak, transmitted through into our O→D tables, via the OEN and EDN effects, is at a much reduced level.[17]

Finally in this section, since the foregoing analyses have forced us to a rather abstract level of discussion, it may be useful if we try to illustrate *some* of the more specific patterns of fluidity that lie behind the statistical results that we have reported. To do this, we return to the inspection of residuals—that is, under model B of Table 8.4, which proposes common social fluidity within our three-way tables; and we focus, as previously, on contrasts that appear between our two Eastern and two Western European nations.

In examining residuals under the CmSF model as fitted to our four E→D tables, we found clear indications that, at least outside the agricultural sector, a stronger propensity for work-life stability prevailed in Hungary and Poland than in England and France. In turning now to the residuals under an analogous model fitted to our three-way tables, we see some evidence of this same contrast persisting when class of origin is introduced. That is to say, in

[16] The addition to model E of the four-way interaction term NOED—which would produce the saturated model—could not therefore lead to any increase in the variance in the odds ratios of the O→D tables, as collapsed over entry class.

[17] As earlier indicated, we have repeated the analyses of both Tables 8.2 and 8.4 for men in the English, French, Hungarian, and Polish samples aged 35–64 and also for men (aged 20–64) in all eight of our European nations for which we have appropriate data—although in the Irish, Northern Irish, Scottish, and Swedish cases cell counts are unduly sparse. In both respects, results on essentially the same pattern as those reported in the text are achieved. The most notable difference is that, both when we restrict the age-range of men in our four large samples and when we use all eight samples, the fit of model E in Table 8.4 becomes entirely acceptable: p = 0.19 and p = >0.50 respectively. We find it particularly reassuring that our results are little affected by the exclusion of young men, since this suggests that the relatively high degree of cross-national variation in the E→D transition is not the outcome simply of mobility processes characteristic of early life-course stages.

cells indicating stability across origin class, entry class, and destination class alike, the CmSF model gives consistent overestimates for England and France and underestimates for Hungary and Poland for Classes III, V+VI, and VII*a*. However, what can then further be noted is that, in cells indicating counter-mobile trajectories within these same classes—that is, trajectories where mobility occurring from origin class to entry class is offset by subsequent mobility from entry class to destination class—the reverse tendency is the more common: such trajectories are more likely to be underestimated for England and France and overestimated for Hungary and Poland. In particular, large residuals point to much stronger propensities in the two former nations—matched, as we have seen, in the absolute rates of Figure 8.1—for intergenerational immobility within the skilled working class to be mediated via a non-skilled entry position, and vice versa.

Likewise on the basis of our three-way tables, we can find evidence of 'East–West' contrasts in propensities for upward mobility into service-class positions via direct or indirect routes, and again corresponding to differences at the level of absolute rates on which we have already commented. Thus, in cells indicating direct mobility from working-class, Classes V+VI or VII*a*, origins into Class I+II—that is, mobility achieved in the O→E transition and confirmed by stability in the E→D transition—the CmSF model consistently overestimates for England and France and underestimates for Hungary and Poland. But residuals of the opposite sign are then to be found in various cells indicating the achievement of such mobility via indirect routes: for example, in the English case via entry into skilled working-class positions and in the French via entry into routine non-manual ones.

These features of fluidity patterns discernible within our four nations are, we must stress, here picked out with no more than an illustrative intent. Although the mobility flows to which they relate do include ones of major quantitative importance, they still, of course, represent only a small subset of all that are comprised by the three-way tables that we have constructed. We highlight these features simply to give a sharper idea of some of the many different ways in which it may come about that cross-national variation apparent among nations when mobility is viewed in a life-course perspective can, however, turn out to be contained within a more evident similarity when an intergenerational view is taken.

THE RELATION OF WORK-LIFE TO INTERGENERATIONAL MOBILITY

In the foregoing we have recognized that mobility analysts who follow a life-course approach will indeed tend to discover greater cross-national variation in both absolute and relative rates than those who rely on standard inter-generational tables. This is apparent enough when we distinguish within the life-course processes represented in such tables just the two component transitions that we can construct from the comparative data available to us. We have, however, also argued that it is not easy to produce from out of the life-course approach a ready explanation of why it should be that the relatively high degree of cross-national variation that is evident in these two component transitions is not then maintained within our intergenerational tables. And we have in turn contended that, rather than such tables being regarded as offering no more than a—distorted—summary of the outcomes of the mobility of individuals over their life-courses, the constancies and commonalities in relative rates that the tables reveal should be taken as indicative of forces operating at a macrosociological level through which individual trajectories are, in aggregate, constrained. In this final section of the chapter we seek to take our argument further by suggesting in greater detail how empirical results on the pattern that we have demonstrated for England, France, Hungary, and Poland could actually be generated as actors pursue their working lives under constraints of the kind in question but, at the same time, within the differing institutional contexts that these national societies provide.

The constraints that we wish here to invoke are the same as those to which we have in effect already alluded in developing our model of core social fluidity in Chapter 4. That is, the constraints on mobility that are created in consequence of individuals of different class origins possessing differing degrees of advantage or disadvantage—in terms of economic, cultural, and social resources—in relation to the barriers that restrict access to class positions of differing degrees of desirability. From the results of applying our model that we have reported in Chapter 5, we may claim that it captures a substantial commonality within the fluidity patterns of a range of modern industrial societies; or, in other words, our findings would indicate that, consistently with a modified version of the FJH hypothesis, class inequalities in mobility chances run on largely similar lines from one nation to another.

However, while in this respect we would place the emphasis on the extent of cross-national similarity, we would not wish to claim that such uniformity extends to the form of the institutional arrangements through which mobility processes are chiefly mediated. To the contrary, it would seem well-enough documented that modern societies display some considerable variation in, for example, the organization of their educational systems, the nature of the provision they make for vocational training, the structure of their labour markets, and, most significantly perhaps, the ways in which their education and training systems and their employment systems are articulated. Thus, if we consider the four nations on which we have concentrated our attention in this chapter, we can draw a rather clear line of contrast between our two Eastern and our two Western European cases in terms of what we might call the 'degree of specificity' of their education–employment linkages.

In Hungary and Poland educational and training systems were developed in the post-war decades in the context of a command economy, and were in fact intended to serve primarily as instruments of manpower policy. Both societies came to possess highly differentiated systems, with different types and levels of education and training being more or less explicitly related to different types and levels of employment (Andorka 1976; Simkus and Andorka 1982; Adamski and Häyrinen 1978). It became difficult to enter a certain category of employment without what were officially designated as the appropriate qualifications, while, conversely, given certain credentials, the opportunity to enter the corresponding category of employment was usually present. Not surprisingly, then, comparative studies within the 'status-attainment' tradition have revealed that, in Hungary and Poland, education and training completed prior to entry into employment have generally stronger effects in determining individuals' subsequent occupational levels than in Western societies (Andorka 1976; Słomczyński 1978; Pohoski, Pöntinen, and Zagórski 1978; Meyer, Tuma, and Zagórski 1979; Zagórski 1984).

In England and France, on the other hand, education–employment linkages have been shown to be of a notably *un*specific kind—and even in comparison with other Western nations such as the FRG and Austria (Maurice, Sorge, and Warner 1980; Maurice, Sellier, and Silvestre 1982; Haller *et al.* 1985; König and Müller 1986).[18] From the nineteenth century onwards, educational institutions and provision evolved with considerable autonomy relative to the economy, and indeed so as to be often seriously out of phase with changes in the structure of employment (Müller and Karle 1990; cf. Boudon 1974). Consequently, the allocative role of education, and especially at the stage of initial entry into work, has been relatively weak. Higher-level education completed before the start of employment has not been a prerequisite for the achievement of many higher-level positions; rather, 'alternative routes' have persisted, as, for example, via various kinds of lower-level position—whether secured on entry into work or later—which are able to provide good prospects for career advancement, aided perhaps by 'on-the-job' learning, in-house training, part-time courses, etc. (Raffe 1979; Thélot 1979, 1982: esp. ch. 6).[19]

[18] We should not, in other words, regard the contrast in education–employment linkages with which we are here concerned as being simply a correlate of that between 'command' and 'free-market' economies (cf. Mach and Peschar 1990). In particular, the latter may operate with linkages of widely varying degrees of specificity. It is also here relevant to note that in both Hungary and Poland there would appear to have been quite close connections between different types and levels of education and different categories of employment already in the period preceding communist rule—during which, of course, some of the older men in our samples would have started their working lives (see, e.g., Simkus and Andorka 1982; Adamski and Häyrinen 1978; Mach and Peschar 1990). In the Hungarian case at least, this was the direct result of the adoption of German educational ideas and institutions, at the time of the Austro-Hungarian dual monarchy.

[19] To illustrate from the English case, of men found in the service class (Class I+II) in 1972, those with a university degree or equivalent qualification amounted to only 20 per cent of all in professional or higher technical positions and to no more than 6 per cent of those in administrative and managerial positions. Moreover, while only 15 per cent of those in the

The interpretation of our empirical findings that we would offer requires then just one assumption, which we would regard as highly plausible: namely, that actors do typically possess some knowledge of how the institutions of their societies work, and tend, on the basis of this knowledge, to adapt rationally to institutional circumstances in pursuing their particular objectives. From this it will, therefore, follow that, if cross-national variation exists in the institutions through which mobility processes are mediated, corresponding differences are to be expected in what we might refer to as 'mobility strategies': that is, the strategies taken up by individuals and families in given class positions as they seek to maintain these positions or to change them for the better. From one institutional setting to another, actors will face different conditions of action, and will in turn need to apply such resources as they can command in different ways if they are to seek to realize their aspirations in the most effective manner.

Thus, where, as in Hungary and Poland, highly specific education–employment linkages exist, the best strategy for maintaining an advantaged class position, or for promoting upward mobility to such a position—and that, we suppose, most likely to be followed—is one which concentrates resources on furthering educational attainment and training at the pre-employment stage. Within the intergenerational mobility process it is the transition from origin class to entry class, as determined primarily by credentials achieved through education and training, that is crucial; that is to say, it is in the O→E transition, rather than at later stages of the life-course, that competition among individuals for different class destinations will be most decisive. Hence, we would argue, it is here that the advantages or disadvantages of class of origin will tend chiefly to be expressed.

In contrast, where, as in England and France, the linkages between education and employment are much less specific, a wider choice of mobility strategies is available. Family resources may be concentrated on pre-employment education—or, alternatively, on securing for the individual a position in a type of occupation, organization, or industry with good opportunities for subsequent work-life mobility, which family resources, whether of an economic, cultural, or social kind, can again help realize.[20] In

former group appeared to have *no* vocationally relevant qualification whatever, this proportion rose to over 40 per cent in the latter group (see, further, Goldthorpe 1982: esp. Table 2).

We would certainly expect that data relating to the experience of men entering employment in the 1970s and 1980s would in both England and France alike show education to have an increasingly important allocative role. However, it does not necessarily follow from this that differences with our two Eastern European nations would be lessened. While data for young males in Britain in 1979–80 still show substantial counter-mobility (G. Jones 1987), in Hungary and Poland the continuing decline of agriculture may be expected to result in education–employment linkages becoming yet tighter overall (cf. Meyer, Tuma, and Zagórski 1979).

[20] Family cultural resources (or 'cultural capital') tend in particular to be discussed almost exclusively in terms of the advantages they may confer in relation to children's education. But we would suggest they may be no less important in promoting work-life advancement—most obviously, perhaps, where children follow parents into entrepreneurial activity (cf. Chapter 4, pp. 125–6) or into similar areas of professional or technical employment.

these circumstances, competition for eventual class destinations, and in turn the effects of advantaged or disadvantaged class origins, will not be so sharply focused within the O→E transition; rather, they are likely to be extended much further into individuals' working lives and, therefore, to be widely expressed within the E→D transition also.[21]

It is, thus, the adoption of different mobility strategies by individuals and families acting in different institutional settings that we would wish to see as generating the relatively high degree of cross-national variation in fluidity patterns that we have observed within both the O→E and E→D transitions, and especially as between our two Eastern European and two Western European nations. For example, it is in this way that we would account, on the one hand, for the greater propensity for—and indeed actuality of—work-life stability in Hungary and Poland; and, on the other hand, for the greater importance in England and France both of counter-mobility and of 'indirect' routes of upward mobility into service-class positions.

Further, though, we would also see here the key to understanding our more general findings from the analyses reported in Table 8.4, especially as indicated by the variances in the final column: namely, that cross-national variation in fluidity in the O→E and E→D transitions is to some extent of an offsetting kind, while the degree of such variation in the O→D transition that derives other than from these two component transitions is not all that large. For what differences in mobility strategies reflect are alternative ways of applying resources in pursuit of mobility aspirations in cross-nationally differing circumstances and not, or not necessarily, cross-national differences in relative class advantages—which are, we would believe, much less than those in the institutional settings within which such advantages are exploited. Thus, while the prevalence of different strategies is likely to increase the extent of cross-national variation that is shown up in fluidity over particular stages of the life-course, such variation could be expected to appear much less marked once a longer-term, intergenerational perspective is taken within which different strategies are, so to speak, allowed time to work themselves out.

Exponents of the life-course approach do then appear to us to be in some danger of exaggerating the significance of the degree of cross-national variation in mobility and fluidity that their methods—such as cumulative tables—enable them to disclose. We would accept that, from certain standpoints, the extent to which transitions from particular origins to particular destinations are effected via different—say, more-or-less 'direct'—trajectories will be of sociological relevance. Thus, for example, we would

---

[21] In terms of the path-analytic model of status attainment research, this would imply relatively strong *direct* effects of social origins on individuals' attainment instead of such effects being largely or entirely mediated through full-time education—or, at all events, their mediation being less through education than through 'first job'. For illustrative results from a United States–Poland comparison, see Meyer, Tuma, and Zagórski (1979).

not concur with authors such as Prandy who seek to dismiss 'the apparent phenomenon of counter-mobility' as being 'no more than a typical form of occupational reproduction for which the term "mobility" is quite inappropriate' (1986: 146).[22] None the less, we would still think it important to recognize that by no means all of the cross-national variation that can be demonstrated if mobility 'events' are followed through, or aggregated over, successive stages of the life-course will be translated into variation in patterns of net association between class origins and destinations. Much of this variation will in the end turn out to express simply alternative ways of making the same overall transition under the constraints imposed by a substantial cross-national similarity in intergenerational class-mobility regimes. In short, while viewing 'intergenerational mobility as a life-course process' may in regard to certain problems be specially revealing, in treating others, including those central to the present study, greater insight may be gained from taking just the reverse perspective: life-course mobility as an intergenerational process.

We have sought in this chapter to respond to claims that the development of the life-course approach to the study of social mobility has rendered obsolete the analysis of standard mobility tables. We would ourselves regard the life-course approach as marking a major advance, and would agree with Sørensen and others that future mobility enquiries will, or at all events, should, typically collect and analyse complete work-history—together with family- and household-history—data. In addressing a range of issues that arise in mobility research, such data are highly desirable, if not essential.

At the same time, though, we have sought to argue that the critique of standard tables that has been made by exponents of the life-course approach is not as compelling as it may at first sight appear. Such tables can be—and usually have been—interpreted in a way that avoids many of the seemingly most powerful objections that are levelled against them: that is, as providing information not primarily on the mobility trajectories of individuals but rather on mobility rates and patterns understood as societal attributes. Moreover, when analysed from this point of view, standard intergenerational

---

[22] Prandy would appear here to derive his position from research previously undertaken with colleagues (Stewart, Prandy, and Blackburn 1980), which was, however, based on a sample that renders generalization on the matter in question highly problematic (that is, one of white-collar workers in South-East England in the 1960s, who could be regarded as having exceptionally good promotion chances). It must be emphasized that from more representative samples it is apparent (cf. Figure 8.1) that by no means all sons who are downwardly mobile, whether into Class III or otherwise, in fact achieve counter-mobility; and we would doubt if the degree of uncertainty here involved is unappreciated by the individuals concerned. The general position on work-life mobility that seems to be adopted by Stewart, Prandy, and Blackburn—that such mobility, properly conceptualized, will be found typically to lead towards stability and the 'reproduction' of the system of stratification—represents, in our view, the opposite extreme to the undue voluntarism that we detect in the work of some exponents of the life-course approach.

tables have yielded results of large sociological significance—but ones which do not appear to have been always fully reckoned with in either programmatic statements or empirical studies made by life-course enthusiasts: that is, results indicating, so far as relative mobility rates are concerned, not only remarkable constancy over time but further a broad commonality across different populations.

We would see these findings as pointing to constraints that operate across industrial societies and that in fact serve to impose restrictions, at the aggregate level, on the outcomes of individual mobility trajectories from class origins to destinations. Although, then, it is certainly the case that, if a life-course approach to mobility is taken—even of the very crude kind that we have been able to follow in this chapter—far more cross-national variation in absolute and relative rates alike is displayed than in standard tables, the question we have raised is that of just what social processes are here being reflected. In the light of the analyses we have presented, we would argue that what is captured is essentially the effects of differing strategies pursued by individuals and families within cross-nationally varying institutional contexts, which lead them to apply such resources as they are able to devote to enhancing their mobility chances in differing ways and at differing life-course stages. In contrast, the constancies and commonalities that the analysis of standard tables has revealed we would see as expressing the outcomes of mobility processes as shaped by differences in the class distribution of resources and in barriers to access to class positions that are far less susceptible to cross-national variation than are the institutional arrangements though which these processes are channelled. And, to the extent that it is on such regularities that attention centres, rather than on the specific mobility routes traced by individuals, variation in fluidity patterns discernible over different life-course stages may reasonably be treated as a phenomenon of only secondary interest.[23]

---

[23] In this connection it is of further interest to note that Tåhlin has recently shown (1991) that the independent variables of origin class, entry class, destination class, and education can together account for 70–90 per cent of the variance in a summary measure of total class experience over the life-course among groups of employees sampled in a Swedish city. As Tåhlin remarks, 'the proportions are not trivially high. On the contrary, the case against conventional mobility studies rests precisely on the assumption that total class experience is only weakly related to the standard class measures.' It would be of obvious interest if Tåhlin's analysis were repeated on the basis of work-history data for national populations.

9

Non-European Cases:
I. the United States and Australia

In this and the following chapter our concern is with class mobility in non-European industrial societies. As indicated in Table 2.3 above, our data-set comprises information on three such societies: the United States, Australia, and Japan. Here we will consider the two former cases, while reserving that of Japan for Chapter 10. In regard to each of these societies, the central question that we will address is the same: namely, that of how far their experience of class mobility is such as to require qualification or elaboration of arguments that we have advanced on the basis of results from the nine European nations on which our attention has so far been centred. In Chapter 1 we noted that among theories of cross-national variation in social mobility were those that claimed that certain societies were 'exceptional' in relation to supposedly general patterns or tendencies. Most often, such societies were represented as displaying unusually *high* levels of mobility or openness, as the result of distinctive, historically-formed cultural features that they were believed to possess. Although European nations were sometimes cited as instances of such 'exceptionalism', the case of the United States, followed by that of Australia, would appear to have been most widely canvassed, while, as we will describe in the following chapter, Japan has become regarded in some quarters as the emerging 'land of opportunity' of the late twentieth century. Thus, if any undue Eurocentrism does occur in the conclusions that we have drawn from our previous analyses, the examination of class mobility in the three nations in question might be thought especially likely to reveal its presence.

In the first section of this chapter we set out more fully than before the arguments that have been advanced for regarding the United States and Australia as having exceptionally mobile and open societies; and we also review the extant empirical evidence that appears relevant to these claims. In the following section we then consider the material on which we are able to draw as the basis for our own evaluations. We have earlier remarked that our initial recoding exercise left us with generally more satisfactory data for our European than for our non-European nations; and it is in fact in the US and Australian cases that the main problems of comparability within our data-set are encountered.

In the third section we begin our empirical analyses by seeking to fit our model of core fluidity to US and Australian intergenerational mobility tables. In the light of the results we obtain, we take up the question of how far relative mobility rates in these nations can be seen as sharing in the commonality that we believe to be characteristic of European industrial societies and, more specifically, of how far any deviations that are revealed are indeed ones in the direction of distinctively high fluidity or openness. In the fourth section we then turn to absolute rates, and again we concentrate on determining whether and to what extent the levels and patterns of such rates in the United States and Australia exceed the range of the European experience as we have previously been able to establish this. We should, however, point out that in regard neither to relative nor absolute rates do we try to recapitulate for the United States and Australia *all* of the analyses that in earlier chapters we have carried out for our European nations. Rather, we focus our attention on those issues that would seem most relevant to the arguments for exceptionalism that we have reviewed.

ARGUMENTS FOR AMERICAN AND AUSTRALIAN EXCEPTIONALISM

The view that American society is characterized by exceptionally high rates of social mobility is, as we earlier indicated, of long standing, and may be traced back at least to Tocqueville. In *De la démocratie en Amérique* (1835/ 1968) Tocqueville set the United States in contrast with the older nations of Europe on account not only of its democratic form of government but also of various features of the society out of which the new republic had grown. One such feature, to which he gave special emphasis, was the instability of the social position of families and, hence, the uncertainty of lines of class demarcation. Thus, he observed,

Chez les peuples aristocratiques [those of Europe] les familles restent pendant des siècles dans le même état, et souvent dans le même lieu. . . . Les classes étant fort distinctes et immobiles . . . chacune d'elles devient pour celui qui en fait partie une sorte de petite patrie. . . .

But, on the other hand,

Chez les peuples démocratiques [the Americans] de nouvelles familles sortent sans cesse du néant, d'autres y retombent sans cesse, et toutes celles qui demeurent changent de face. . . . Chaque classe venant à se rapprocher des autres et à se mêler, ses membres deviennent indifférents et commes étrangers entre eux (1835/1968: 243–4).[1]

---

[1] 'Among aristocratic peoples, families remain for centuries in the same condition, and often in the same place. . . . Since classes are highly differentiated and immobile, each becomes for its members a kind of little homeland. . . . Among democratic peoples, new families continually spring from nowhere while others disappear to nowhere, and all the rest change their complexion. . . . As every class comes more to resemble the others, and to merge with them, their members grow indistinguishable from, and unrecognisable to, each other' (authors' translation).

Over the decades following, one finds claims remarkably similar to these being maintained on various occasions in the writings of Marx and of Engels. Again, the contrast is drawn between the old world and the new—though in their case more specifically between the established capitalist societies of Europe which possess 'a developed formation of classes' and the nascent capitalist society of America in which classes 'have not yet become fixed but continually change and interchange their elements in constant flux'. In particular, in seeking to explain the weakness of organized labour in America, Marx and Engels stressed the fact that, as a result of the open frontier and the wide range of opportunities for independent entrepreneurship, America still lacked the presence of 'a permanent and hereditary proletariat'. Thus, Marx spoke of the 'continuous conversion of wage labourers into independent self-sustaining peasants', which in turn meant that 'The position of wages labourer is for the very large part of the American population but a probational state which they are sure to leave within a longer or a shorter term'; while Engels, even towards the end of the nineteenth century, saw the United States as remaining close to the ideal of a nation in which 'everyone could still become, if not a capitalist, at all events an independent man, producing or trading, with his own means, for his own account'.[2]

It was, none the less, in the way that they viewed the longer-term future of American exceptionalism that the perspectives of Tocqueville and of Marx and Engels crucially diverged. In both cases, the expectation was that this exceptionalism would diminish. But, while for Tocqueville this would come about through European societies, and polities, drawing steadily closer to the democratic model inaugurated by the United States, for Marx and Engels the United States was destined sooner or later—as the frontier closed and as large-scale enterprise developed—to become, like all other capitalist societies, one in which class divisions progressively hardened.

The issue posed by these two conflicting prognoses was then central to the debate on social mobility in the United States as this was conducted through into the twentieth century. At the same time, though, in the writings of social and political commentators, both foreign and native, the idea of a *continuing* American exceptionalism was frequently revived. While many could accept the possibility of the Marxist scenario of increasing class conflict, revolution, and the emergence of a socialist order being realized in Europe, both socialists and liberals alike found greater difficulty in envisaging a similar course of events in the United States. Thus, for example, Sombart, in his famous essay of 1906, *Warum gibt es in den Vereinigten Staaten keinen Sozialismus?* acknowledged that features of US society unfavourable to the development of a strong labour movement, including high rates of mobility,

---

[2] For the sources of these quotations and more general discussion of the views of Marx and Engels on social mobility in the United States and elsewhere, see Lipset (1977) and Goldthorpe (1980a/1987).

might well weaken with the further advance of capitalism; but he still rejected all notions of 'historical inevitability' and emphasized the pervasiveness in the United States of an individualistic and achievement-oriented ideology which could, in any event, seriously inhibit 'class' interpretations of the social structure and of the fate of individuals within it.

Furthermore, as the twentieth century wore on and socialism remained manifestly unattractive to the large majority of the American people, what appeared to Sombart as necessary qualifications to an essentially Marxist account of American society became for other observers the basis of interpretations of a quite different kind. What these shared in common was a return to the Tocquevillian position that American society, and the culture that had developed within it, were indeed *sui generis*—that is, were permanently marked by the influence of their unique historical origins; and that they could not, therefore, be adequately understood in the light of theories derived from European experience. In particular, it was questioned whether the abundant opportunity and essential 'classlessness' that characterized the early history of the republic were in fact unsustainable. Rather, it was believed, such factors as the seemingly limitless capacity of the economy for expansion, the persisting emphasis on achievement over ascription and the steady growth of educational provision would enable 'Americanism' to survive as in effect a surrogate for, or alternative to, socialism in meeting the aspirations of the mass of the population for a better life. As one author expressed it (Samson 1935: 16–21), the idea and the reality of equality of opportunity made possible 'a socialist conception of capitalism'. And as Lipset has documented (1977, 1979), a whole series of writers from Wells (1906) through to Hartz (1955, 1964) urged that the United States must be seen as representing a quite new type of society, rather than one that was simply transplanted from Europe, and one in which high levels of social mobility and the absence of 'stable hereditary class relations' were of abiding significance.[3]

Turning now to Australia, we find that arguments for exceptionalism have here both a shorter and a rather less complex history than in the US case. Encel (1970: ch. 4) cites several nineteenth- and earlier twentieth-century accounts of Australian society which saw it as highly comparable to that of the United States in offering freedom from traditional barriers to mobility— as a society in which 'ambition could rear its head from any social grade' and in which there was 'a general equality of opportunity, increased by a liberal scheme of education, that opens a career to ability, initiative and merit'. However, as Encel also observes, from the time of Hancock's classic study,

[3] The main counter-tendency, evident chiefly in the years following the Great Depression, was to be found in the views of the 'nostalgic Americans' (cf. Petersen 1953), who warned that, with the rise of 'big business' and the labour unions, the traditional openness of American society was indeed becoming threatened in the way that Marxists envisaged. It was, however, still thought possible for American exceptionalism to be preserved by a determined reassertion of the individualistic ethos.

Australia (1930), which 'did for Australia what de Tocqueville had done for America a century earlier', differences from, as well as similarities with, the United States came to be emphasized.

Hancock acknowledged that many of those who migrated to Australia went expressly in search of opportunity and indeed that they often found it. None the less, he sought to make the point (1930: 182–4) that the equality at which Australian democracy aimed was not the same as that which Tocqueville and others had described in the democracy of the United States. For, while Australians certainly opposed privilege and wished to see both the advantages and disadvantages of birth and family reduced, they were at the same time reluctant to make, in American fashion, a quite overriding commitment to equality of opportunity—and thus to accept as entirely legitimate the inequalities of condition that could in turn be generated. Rather, the tendency was to give first importance to equality of condition itself, to emphasize needs yet more than capacities—and even if this meant that merit had sometimes to 'take a place in the queue'.

Most subsequent discussion of Australian exceptionalism, and especially in comparison with the US case, has then been derivative from Hancock's argument. The contribution of academic social scientists, as they have taken up the issue (cf. Mayer 1964; Lipset 1968; Albinski 1985), has been mainly directed towards assessing the relative importance of the demographic, economic, institutional, and political aspects of the context within which the distinctive Australian egalitarian culture developed: for example, persisting labour shortages, the early growth of a strong trade union movement and Labour Party, the large involvement of the state in economic affairs and especially in labour markets, the rapid 'suburbanization' of the population, and the wide spread of home ownership. However, of chief interest for present purposes is the degree of uncertainty that has emerged over just what impact Australian egalitarianism has in the end exerted on actual mobility rates. Some commentators would evidently still support the view that Australia possesses a highly mobile and open society—in important part as a consequence of the equality that has been achieved in incomes and in standards and styles of living, together with the popular disregard for social origins and also the weak development of 'credentialism' (cf. Mayer 1964). But others would seem more to favour Hancock's own ambivalent judgement that 'Australian democracy has done much to equalise opportunities, but it has also done something to narrow them' (1930: 1893): that is, through the emphasis on equality of condition—the readiness to 'cut down the tall poppies'—which has dampened ambition and reduced the motivation to succeed.

For most of the time over which such arguments for exceptionalism were elaborated in commentary on American and Australian society, no comparative data on social mobility existed against which they could be adequately appraised. Only as national mobility studies were undertaken in the years following the Second World War, and with Lipset's and Zetterberg's attempts (1956, 1959) at synthesizing their findings, did relevant evidence become available.

As it then turned out, the main conclusion to emerge from this work, as expressed in the LZ hypothesis of similarity in mobility rates across industrial societies, was one obviously inimical to all exceptionalist positions. Indeed, as we earlier noted, Lipset and Bendix (1959: ch. 3) took it as one of the most important implications of the new comparative data that they subverted any idea of the United States as being '*the* land of opportunity'. If the United States were in any way distinctive, Lipset and Bendix argued, it was not in its actual mobility rates but rather in the way in which in American society mobility was perceived and evaluated. Americans were culturally disposed to view the amount of mobility that occurred in their society affirmatively, as indicating openness and equality of life-chances, rather than critically, as indicating the persistence of inequalities of opportunity and condition alike.

Similarly, we may note, Taft and Walker took Lipset's and Zetterberg's earlier results as a basis for rejecting Australian claims to exceptionalism. 'It is usually assumed', they wrote, 'that the opportunities offered by the open frontier of a relatively virgin continent tend rapidly to break down class differences imported from abroad. This has not been the case in Australia in the past, nor is it notably so today . . .' (1958: 142–3). Indeed, Taft and Walker went on to argue that, if the findings of a recent study of mobility in Melbourne (Oeser and Hammond 1954) were compared with those of Lipset and Zetterberg, then it appeared that in Australia *less* mobility occurred, at least from manual to non-manual occupations, than in most other modern societies. And, in Hancockian vein, they suggested that in Australia such mobility was likely to be inhibited by a lack of motivation stemming from high levels of working-class solidarity and identification.[4]

No study of comparative social mobility reported subsequently to that of Lipset and Zetterberg would appear to have given any greater degree of support to exceptionalist arguments in regard to either the United States or Australia—or, for that matter, any other nation; and indeed over recent decades such arguments have been far less fashionable than previously. However, it would, we believe, be unsafe to conclude from this that 'exceptionalism' is by now to be regarded as a completely dead issue.

To begin with, the data assembled by Lipset and Zetterberg had evident defects that have been widely recognized; and, as we have sought to show in Chapter 2, all other data-sets on comparative mobility that have been likewise constructed simply from the published data of national enquiries must be regarded as highly suspect. Further, when set against more complete

[4] Lipset and Zetterberg (1959: 29 n. 26) refer to Taft's and Walker's work and state that they 'frankly doubt' the factual claim of lower mobility in Australia that prompted these authors' psychological speculations. Lipset and Zetterberg then go on to note some major difficulties that arise in using the Oeser and Hammond study for comparative purposes.

and more reliable comparative data, the LZ hypothesis, as we have seen in Chapter 6, can scarcely be sustained. At the level of absolute—that is, total, inflow and outflow—mobility rates, we have found among the European nations that we have examined a far from negligible range of variation. Thus, the possibility of this range being, at all events, rather dramatically extended once we turn to non-European nations is one that cannot be dismissed. And finally, it may be noted that, even though full-blooded exceptionalist arguments may of late have been rather uncommon, there is, so far at least as the United States is concerned, an evident reluctance to allow the case for exceptionalism entirely to lapse.

For example, Thernstrom, in an influential work (1970), compared data from a study of mobility in Boston between 1800 and 1963 with data from studies of several European cities over the same period, and was thus led to conclude that American men *have* in fact enjoyed uniquely favourably chances of moving out of working-class positions, at least over the course of their own lifetimes. Findings such as those drawn on by Lipset and Bendix, Thernstrom later (1974) suggested, could be misleading, in that cross-nationally similar rates of *inter*generational mobility might obscure different rates of *intra*generational, or work-life, departure from particular class origins. There could thus still be force in the arguments that US rates and patterns of mobility have been historically distinctive and that this has 'a good deal to do with another fairly distinctive aspect of the American historical record—the failure of working-class-based protest movements to attract a mass following' (1974: 551).[5]

Then again, as we remarked in Chapter 1, Blau and Duncan, while rejecting the standard thesis of US exceptionalism, were still ready to maintain that in one respect at least mobility patterns in the United States did appear to stand out in cross-national comparisons: that is, in the amount of long-range upward mobility that occurred, from the lowest social strata into 'élite' positions (1967: 432–5). This feature, they held, could not be accounted for as simply the outcome of the US élite being larger than that of other nations, but had to be regarded as resulting in some part also from its greater openness. Moreover, Blau and Duncan see this 'superior opportunity for upward mobility in American society' as being of particular importance

[5] Thernstrom's argument turns on the possibility of differences in men's rates of upward work-life mobility before the birth of their children. If more men in the United States were thus mobile than elsewhere, then, he maintains, a finding of similar rates of upward and downward intergenerational mobility could be quite misleading, since the baseline from which such rates are usually computed is the occupational level of fathers at some point *subsequent to* the birth of their children. In the circumstances hypothesized,

A larger fraction of the sons of American white-collar workers *should* have been downwardly mobile, because fewer of their fathers were solidly established in the white-collar world for their full careers. Conversely, we would expect to find less upward intergenerational mobility on the part of the sons of American workers, because many of the more ambitious and intelligent workers would have been removed from the working class and drawn up into the middle class, leaving a diminished pool of talent at the working class level. (1974: 550)

in that it provides some 'existential' basis for the distinctive mobility ideology that Lipset and Bendix emphasized—the persistence of which would otherwise be puzzling. And ultimately, then, they too are drawn back to a version of the argument that high levels of mobility represent a crucial factor in preserving 'the stability of American democracy', in particular against 'extremist political movements committed to violent rebellion' (1967: 436–9).

Authors such as Blau and Duncan, we would observe, whose analyses of mobility are more or less explicitly set within the liberal theory of industrialism, do thereby come under some pressure to regard the United States as being, if not an exceptional nation in virtue of cultural features deriving from its origins, then at all events a 'vanguard' nation in consequence of its economic performance and its current economic pre-eminence. If with advancing industrialism and emergent post-industrialism, both mobility and openness increase, then the United States should, by the second half of the twentieth century, have become a more mobile and a more open society than any other.

There is a fundamental difference [Blau and Duncan write] between a stratification system that perpetuates established status distinctions between particular families over generations and one that perpetuates a structure of differentiated positions but not their inheritance. Industrial societies, *and the United States in particular*, approach the latter type . . .' (1967: 441; emphasis added)

There are, therefore, a variety of reasons why interest does still remain in an attempt to reassess arguments for American and Australian exceptionalism in the light of the comparative data that we have available to us—even though, as we shall next discuss, these data raise certain difficulties that are less tractable than we would wish.

DATA

Our mobility data for the United States (cf. Table 2.3 above) come from the study directed in 1973 by Featherman and Hauser, which was designed specifically to replicate that of Blau and Duncan carried out a decade before (Featherman and Hauser 1978). The 1973 enquiry, like its predecessor, was based on a large, well-designed sample and conducted to high professional standards. However, for our purposes, major problems derive from the fact that all occupational data were coded—as in the Blau–Duncan study—to the 1960 classificatory system of the US Bureau of the Census.

In this system—which we must rate as the least coherent of all the national occupational classifications that we have encountered—the descriptions given to the eleven 'major groups' that are recognized would suggest that the primary intention is to capture functional and/or status divisions. But, on closer inspection, the allocation of basic, 'three-digit', occupational categories to the major groups and, more seriously, the composition of these basic categories themselves would seem often to be determined as much on sectoral or 'situs' lines. Consequently, in attempting to recode the US data to our class schema, we repeatedly found that the specific occupations that made up a basic—that is, indivisible—category were ones which we would have wished to redistribute (when in combination with appropriate employment status codes) to two, or even perhaps three or four, of the different classes that we distinguish.

Thus, to take some of the most obviously disturbing cases, several of the basic categories falling within the major groups of 'Professional, Technical and Kindred Workers' and 'Managers, Officials and Proprietors' bring together occupations which clearly belong to our service class (I+II) and others which, no less clearly, should be allocated to our classes of routine non-manual employees and of skilled or indeed non-skilled manual workers. We are, for example, unable to separate from authentic scientific and higher technical staff persons working as routine testers, samplers, and other kinds of laboratory assistant, or those in a miscellany of occupations—including, *inter alia*, tracers, foresters, dental mechanics, and undertakers—which similarly have some association with professional work while not themselves typically affording professional conditions of employment. Likewise, we cannot detach from the standard categories of managers and administrators many persons holding positions that are, at best, quite marginal to managerial and administrative bureaucracies—such as, say, floorwalkers, railroad conductors and ticket collectors, and prison warders.

Conversely, within the major group of 'Sales Workers' we then find that many of the basic categories include, along with usually a majority of occupations of a routine non-manual kind, as covered by our Class III, various others of a clearly more professional or managerial (if not entrepreneurial) character, which we have in all other national cases routinely allocated to Class I+II: for example, insurance brokers and underwriters, stockbrokers, real estate brokers, advertising agents, and auctioneers.

Such problems of heterogeneity within basic occupational categories did, of course, arise in some degree in the recoding of data from all of the national enquiries that we utilize in constituting our comparative data-set. In the US case, however, they proved to be clearly more extensive and systematic than elsewhere; and, while we would not wish even then to exaggerate their quantitative impact overall, we still have no doubt that, from the standpoint of comparability, our US mobility data are the least satisfactory of all those with which we work. We treated problematic categories by giving class codings appropriate to those of their constituent occupations in which we estimated that the largest numbers of men were employed. But, inevitably, more-or-less serious misallocations were thus involved; and it can only be supposed that the effect of these will be to create some amount of mobility in the US tables that we construct that is of an artefactual kind. This defect we must simply keep in mind in interpreting the results of the analyses on which we subsequently report.

As regards our Australian data, the problem we meet is of a quite different kind and can be very shortly stated. In this case, comparability is impaired not by any particular difficulties arising from the recoding exercise but simply from the fact that in the national enquiry on which we draw—that carried out in 1973–4 as part of the Social Mobility in Australia project (Broom *et al.* 1977)—the population sampled was that of Australians *aged 30–69*. In thus excluding adults, or at all events adult males, under the age of 30, this enquiry differs from all others from which we derive our data.

There is little that we can do to overcome this—from our point of view—annoying deficiency. We might perhaps have based all comparisons involving Australia on mobility data for similarly truncated versions of other national samples; but this rather drastic recourse would in turn have left us with the wider problem of relating results from two different sets of tables. Although, then, we will take up the possibilities afforded by examining mobility rates over birth-cohorts defined within the Australian sample, we will for the most part attempt, as in the US case, to deal with questions of comparability at the stage of interpreting our empirical findings.[6]

CORE SOCIAL FLUIDITY AND THE US AND AUSTRALIAN CASES

In Chapters 4 and 5 we sought to provide a more sophisticated empirical evaluation of the FJH hypothesis than was previously available by developing a model of 'core' social fluidity and by applying this model to intergenerational mobility tables for, in all, twelve European nations. On this basis, we concluded that, while the hypothesis was clearly unsustainable in its strict form, it could none the less be defended in a somewhat weaker but still sociologically consequential version: that is, as claiming that patterns of social fluidity in industrial societies display a large commonality, variations on which tend, moreover, to be nationally specific rather than open to more systematic macrosociological explanation. If we now wish to see how far this conclusion can hold if we extend our cross-national coverage so as to take in the two putatively 'exceptional' cases of the United States and Australia, the obvious way to proceed is to fit our model of core social fluidity to intergenerational mobility tables for these two nations also.

This we do, as is indicated in Table 9.1, in the same way as for our European nations (cf. Tables 5.1 and 5.5). First of all, we apply the model with fixed parameters (that is, those that we initially estimated for it on the basis of our empirical representation of core fluidity), and from the first row of each panel of Table 9.1 it can be seen that in this case the fit achieved for

---

[6] To maintain comparability with the data of our other national enquiries, we have, of course, excluded men aged 65–69 from the Australian sample.

both the United States and Australia is quite poor. Indeed, reference back to Tables 5.1 and 5.5 will show that, for Australia, both the $G^2(S)$ and Δ values returned are greater than for any of our European nations. However, when we come, secondly, to apply the model with its parameters being allowed to vary by nation, the results given in the second row of each panel of Table 9.1 show that a substantial improvement in fit is produced. For the United States, $G^2(S)$ moves down fairly close in fact to the 40 mark that we have taken as indicating a satisfactory degree of fit, and only a little over 3 per cent of all cases are misclassified. For Australia, the fit of the model is still some way from being acceptable, but both the $G^2(S)$ and Δ values do now fall well within the European range.

TABLE 9.1. *Results of fitting the model of core social fluidity to mobility tables for the United States and Australia: (i) with cross-nationally common parameters; (ii) with nation-specific parameters; (iii) with effects modified or added (national variant model)*

Nation		G^2	df	p	rG^2	Δ	$G^2(S)$ (1,991)*
USA	(i)	737.8	36	0.00	79.6	6.7	103
(N = 20,744)	(ii)	211.8	28	0.00	94.1	3.2	46
	(iii)	180.3	27	0.00	95.0	2.9	42
AUS	(i)	155.2	36	0.00	72.8	9.4	137
(N = 2,348)	(ii)	59.8	28	0.00	89.5	4.8	55
	(iii)	40.3	28	0.06	92.9	4.0	38

Note:
   * We here retain the constant for $G^2(S)$ at 1,991, the size of the smallest sample among our nine European nations.

What is, therefore, suggested by these findings is that neither the United States nor Australia is exceptional in having a pattern of social fluidity that is quite different from that shared in by our European nations—but that they may display rather distinctive versions of this pattern: that is to say, the various effects which, under our model, generate 'core' fluidity could be unusually strong or weak.[7] To investigate this possibility further, we must then go on, again as with our European nations, to devise acceptably fitting variant models for the United States and Australia and to consider parameters estimated for these models.

[7] If, when our model is fitted in this way, we examine the differences between the effect parameters estimated and those under the core model (cf. Table 5.2 above), we find that for the United States the HI1, HI2, and SE parameters are in fact all significantly weaker, and that for Australia the IN2, SE, and AF2 parameters are significantly weaker.

With the US table, as we have seen, the core model comes close to fitting once nationally specific parameters are allowed, and we can obtain a version of this model that we would be ready to accept through changes in only two pairs of cells, both of which concern Class I+II:

1. an additional positive affinity term (AFX in Table 9.2 below) is included in the cells indicating mobility between Class I+II and Class III—that is, over and above the AF2 term already applying in these cells—and also in the cells indicating mobility between Class I+II and Class VIIa.

These changes were made in the light both of inspection of residuals *and* of arguments previously reviewed. As is shown in the third row of the first panel of Table 9.1, the $G^2(S)$ returned by this variant model is still slightly above the level that we have usually required. However, we have chosen not to introduce further modifications, since the model as it stands has the advantage of bringing out what we would regard as the key interpretive issue that arises in the US case and further changes suggested by residuals were not ones for which there was any evident external support.[8] In Table 9.2 we give the effect parameters estimated under this US variant, which may be compared with those of the core model and also, by reference back to Tables 5.3 and 5.6, with those of variant models for our European nations.

TABLE 9.2. *Effect parameters of accepted models for the United States and Australia**

Nation	HI1	HI2	IN1	IN2	IN3	SE	AF1	AF2	AFX
USA	−0.13	−0.49	0.41	0.35	0.89	−0.68	−0.74	0.28	*0.20*
AUS	−0.24	−0.49	0.28	0.25	1.11	−0.69	*−0.37*	*0.30*	
CORE	−0.22	−0.42	0.43	0.81	0.96	−1.03	−0.77	0.46	

Note:
* Parameters directly affected by modifications to the core model are in italic type.

What our US model says, in virtue of the modifications we introduce, is that the pattern of fluidity in the United States deviates from the core pattern (cf. Table 4.3) in that there is a greater propensity for mobility, in both directions, between the service class and that of routine non-manual employees (the AF2 term *and* the AFX term offset the HI1 term); and in that there is also a greater propensity for mobility, in both directions, between the service class and that of non-skilled manual workers (the AFX term offsets

[8] We could, for example, have obtained a very well-fitting model by introducing the AF2, positive affinity, term into the cell indicating mobility from farm origins (Class IVc) into the skilled working class (Class V+VI). But we could find no independent evidence to support the idea that this mobility propensity might be particularly strong in the US case.

the HI1 and HI2 terms). From Table 9.2 it may in turn be observed that, while the IN1 effect under the model is at about core level, the IN2 effect, which applies to immobility in the service class (and also the petty bourgeoisie), is much lower, indicating a propensity for immobility only a little over twice the neutral fluidity level ($e^{0.76} = 2.13$) as against three-and-a-half times under the core pattern.

If this variant model is accepted, then, in the light of our previous discussion, two main interpretations would seem possible. One is that some further support is here provided for Blau's and Duncan's view that the American mobility regime is distinctive at least in the greater openness of more advantaged class positions that it affords; the other is that the deviation from core fluidity that our model captures reflects not so much American social reality as the difficulties we faced in recoding the American data. Our own preference is strongly for the second of these interpretations: that is, we would wish to regard the additional positive affinity term in our US model as being essentially a 'correction factor' made necessary by coding error, rather than as one to which any substantive significance might safely be attached. The most worrying instances of heterogeneity in the basic categories of the US occupational classification to which we earlier referred are in fact ones likely to exaggerate the amount of mobility that is observed between the higher-level white-collar positions of the service class, on the one hand, and lower-level white-collar and manual positions, on the other.

In addition, we would note that there are good grounds for supposing that the distinctive openness of the US 'élite' that is claimed by Blau and Duncan is itself far more an outcome of the looseness of the occupational categories with which they work than of actual fluidity within the American occupational structure. Although the data of the 1973 US enquiry cannot be altogether satisfactorily recoded to our class schema, it is, on the other hand, possible to recode, with a high degree of accuracy, the data of at least one of our European enquiries—the 1972 English study—to the US classification. When this is done, it can be shown (Erikson and Goldthorpe 1985) that there is no indication whatever of 'élite' positions, on Blau's and Duncan's definition, being more open in the United States than in England. Higher rates of access to such positions from lower-level origins in the US than in the English case *can* then be attributed entirely to the larger size of the US 'élite'.[9]

---

[9] The 'élite' of Blau's and Duncan's analysis is, in fact, nothing other than the—very unsatisfactory—'Professional, Technical and Kindred Workers' category of the US Bureau of the Census, earlier discussed. Upward 'élite' mobility is defined as all mobility into this category from manual worker origins.

Wong has recently reported results from a six-nation comparative study which utilizes the 1972 English and 1973 US enquiries, and has claimed that his findings contradict those of our 1985 paper in showing that 'The complete set of odds-ratios for England and Wales is consistently higher than that for the United States' (1990: 566). However, from information provided by Wong on how he attempted to achieve comparablity of data, it is difficult to see

Finally, though, it may also be observed that, even if one were to opt for the alternative interpretation of our model, the backing that would thereby be given to Blau's and Duncan's position is still not all that impressive. From the table of differences in cell-interaction parameters under national variant models that we earlier provided (Table A5.1), it can be seen that, while in the US case propensities for mobility to and from the service class do tend overall to be comparatively closer to the neutral-fluidity level than corresponding 'core' propensities, they could still scarcely be counted as exceptional. The very most that might on this basis be said is that the United States lies towards the 'more fluid' end of the European range—as indeed could also be claimed in several other respects.[10]

In sum, then, we would maintain that, so far at least as social fluidity is concerned, no very convincing case for American exceptionalism, whether in general or in more specific terms, can be made out. Because of the problems of data that we have noted, more positive conclusions are difficult to advance with any degree of firmness. It remains possible to argue that the United States, even if in no sense exceptional, is still a more open society than most others; but, with our earlier (1985) study also in mind, we would ourselves incline towards a different judgement. We would believe that, if we could have worked with data of a more satisfactory standard of comparability, then the United States would have been found to stand rather close to England and France as in fact one of our 'central' nations—in which, again, the processes of 'civil society' that shape fluidity patterns could be regarded as operating with a large measure of freedom from direct political intervention.[11]

how he can have undertaken the radical recoding that would be necessary in order to overcome the problems with the basic categories of the Bureau of the Census occupational classification to which we have earlier referred. The strategy of our 1985 comparison had in effect to be the rather drastic one of making the English occupational categories as bad as the US ones.

[10] In one such instance, however—that is, the relatively high fluidity associated with petty-bourgeois positions—there is a yet further difficulty with the US data that has to be noted. The Bureau of the Census, which was responsible for the fieldwork for the 1973 enquiry, asked all individuals initially describing themselves as being self-employed whether their businesses were incorporated and, if so, then treated them in the 'class of worker' coding as private employees— i.e. as employees of their own businesses. This procedure is, therefore, likely to reduce the number of those counted as self-employed and, moreover, could well affect the composition of Class IVa+b in tending to filter out larger proprietors and thus, in turn, make the class appear more open than would otherwise have been the case.

[11] It has been suggested to us by Göran Ahrne that if England, France, and the United States are thus to be regarded as the three leading exemplars of the pattern of core fluidity that we propose, it might in turn be observed that these are also the three nations singled out by Moore (1966) as best characterizing a capitalist and democratic route to modernity, starting in each case from a successful bourgeois revolution—the English Civil War, the French Revolution, and the American Civil War. The idea has aesthetic and also heuristic attractions—since further related interpretations might be derived for the more deviant fluidity patterns of other nations (see, for example, the discussion of the Swedish and more general 'Scandinavian route' to modernity in Alestalo and Kuhnle 1987). None the less, it is still one which, as it stands, we would view with a good deal of scepticism, chiefly because we believe that in Moore's work the conception of 'bourgeois revolution' becomes incoherent and that, in whatever version, is far

Turning now to the Australian table, it will be recalled that the fit of the core model, once nationally specific parameters were allowed, was much improved but was still less good than for the US table. However, on inspection, the larger residuals produced in the Australian case turn out to be rather strongly patterned: that is, to be concentrated in cells relating to recruitment to Class V+VI, the class of skilled manual workers. It is then possible to obtain an acceptably fitting model by making changes that affect four of these cells:

1. the AF1 term (negative affinity) is included in the cells indicating mobility from Class I+II and Class III origins to Class V+VI;
2. the AF2 term (positive affinity) is included in the two cells indicating mobility from Class IVc and Class VIIb origins to Class V+VI (that is, paralleling the affinities already included in the core model in the cells indicating mobility from these two farm classes to Class VIIa, that of *non*-skilled manual workers).

In other words, the implication of these changes is that, in the Australian pattern of fluidity, there is a lower propensity than under the core model for men to be recruited into the skilled working class from white-collar origins but a higher propensity for them to be so recruited from farm origins.[12] In accounting for this deviation, both substantive and technical possibilities again arise, as in the US case. On the one hand, the 'excess' of mobility, relative to core expectations, from farm origins into skilled manual work can be shown to reflect the mobility patterns of immigrants. If the core model (with nationally specific parameters) is fitted to the mobility table for native-born Australian men, the 'excess' mobility in question is substantially reduced.[13] On the other hand, though, the 'shortfall' in mobility observed from white-collar origins into Class V+VI could result from the exclusion from the Australian sample of men under age 30—with a greater inflow from farm origins being then perhaps in part a compensating effect. Evidence from our other nations would indicate that skilled manual jobs are often involved in counter-mobile work-life trajectories which take men of white-

more difficult to reconcile with the historiography of the nations in question than his methodology leads him to suppose (cf. Lowental 1968; Goldthorpe 1991a).

[12] In turn, of course, it is also implied that in the Australian case there are extensive asymmetries in mobility propensities, as between Class V+VI, on the one hand, and Classes III and IVc, on the other. Comparable asymmetries, it may be noted, also show up in the modelling of the same Australian data, but on the basis of a somewhat different version of the class schema, as presented by Jones and Davis (1986: ch. 3). It is of further interest that Jones and Davis show a very close similarity between the Australian pattern of fluidity and that they find underlying mobility data for New Zealand.

[13] One may then suppose that, for some significant proportion of the sons of farmers who were found in skilled manual work, the farms in question were located outside Australia—for example, in Italy or other Mediterranean countries from which migration to Australia has been extensive; and, for such farmers' sons, to achieve a skilled manual job could be a typical aspiration.

collar origins back eventually to white-collar destinations (cf. Figure 8.1 above) and such counter-mobility would appear usually to occur while men are still in their twenties (cf. Goldthorpe, 1980*a*/1987: 25–7).

However, this Australian 'peculiarity' in recruitment to the skilled working class, in whatever way it is explained, cannot be of any major relevance to the issue of Australian exceptionalism as earlier reviewed. Rather more to the point are the parameter estimates that we can make for our national variant model. To begin with, Table 9.2 shows that, while hierarchy effects are quite close to the core level, all other effects are weaker, and the IN1 and IN2 terms especially so. The latter implies a propensity for immobility of only about one-and-three-quarter times greater than would otherwise apply ($e^{0.53} = 1.70$), as compared with three-and-a-half times greater under the core model; and the degree of fluidity thus associated with the service class and petty bourgeoisie proves to be greater in Australia than in any of our European nations except for Hungary. As might then be expected, Table A5.1 reveals that, under our Australian variant model, a majority of cell-interaction parameters come closer than under the core model to the neutral-fluidity level (i.e. values of less than 100 appear). This is in fact so with the parameters for *all* main diagonal cells, referring, that is, to class immobility; and also with those for all cells indicating mobility between agricultural and non-agricultural classes.[14]

It has then to be accepted that, on our evidence, Australia is a society in which a relatively high degree of fluidity prevails. At the same time, though, further reference to Table A5.1 will show that, in all the respects mentioned above, it is more or less matched by at least two of our European nations, Sweden and Czechoslovakia; and, moreover, that in the Australian case, in contrast to either the Swedish or Czechoslovak, there are a number of cells, the parameters for which indicate fluidity falling somewhat *further below* the neutral level than it would do if the core pattern applied. These cells are chiefly ones referring to mobility between white-collar (Classes I+II and III) and blue-collar (Classes V+VI and VIIa) positions.

Again, therefore, we must conclude that there are no strong grounds for exceptionalist claims, at least in so far as these would represent Australia as a society enjoying a degree of openness that lies quite outside the European experience. We can regard Australia with more confidence than we would the United States as showing generally higher fluidity within its class structure than do most of our European nations: the problems of comparability that arise with the age-range of the Australian sample would not seem likely to lead one to an exaggerated idea of fluidity levels—if anything, the reverse. And further, despite the indications that exist of relatively high barriers to mobility across the white-collar/blue-collar divide, we can surely

---

[14] This latter result, it may be added, is not an effect of immigration but is similarly obtained in modelling the mobility table for native-born men only.

discount the 'revisionist' view that in Australia such factors as the value-emphasis on equality of condition rather than of opportunity and the strength of working-class solidarity and identification have had a distinctively *negative* effect on mobility propensities. None the less, Australia cannot, any more than the United States, lend substance to the idea of a 'new' nation offering mobility chances of a quite different and substantially less constrained kind than are anywhere to be found within the 'class-ridden' societies of the 'old' European world. If some overall characterization of the Australian mobility regime is required, one could perhaps suggest that Australia has arrived at a version of what we have previously thought of as the Swedish pattern, although, it would need to be added, without the same degree of social-democratic political dominance.

Finally, in this section, we should consider whether our views on American or Australian exceptionalism ought in any way to be modified in the light of an examination of *trends* in relative mobility rates in these two nations. Here it will be convenient to take the Australian case first, since it would appear the more straightforward.

From the data we have available, we can find no reliable indication of directional change in the pattern of fluidity that underlies Australian inter-generational mobility. If we proceed as with our European nations in Chapter 3 and apply the CnSF model to five-class mobility tables for four successive birth-cohorts distinguished within the Australian sample—though with the youngest being necessarily limited to men born 1939–43—we discover that the model fits extremely well ($G^2 = 40.1$; df = 48; p = >0.50; $\Delta = 4.7$; N = 2,348). And if, again as in the analyses of Chapter 3, we then go beyond the CnSF model to our uniform-difference model, providing, that is, for uniform intercohort change in the net association between classes of origin and of destination, we obtain no significant improvement in fit, and the β parameters estimated indicate no weakening tendency of a consistent kind.[15] Finally, if we construct (seven-class) tables for just two broad cohorts within the Australian sample—of men born 1909–28 and 1929–43—and apply to each table our model for the Australian variant of the core fluidity pattern, we achieve no significant improvement in fit by allowing the parameters of the model to vary from one cohort to the other.

In other words, the results that these analyses produce for Australia must be seen as going along with those produced for the majority of our European nations in suggesting that patterns of social fluidity possess a large measure of stability over time. Our conclusions on the matter of Australian excep-tionalism are thus unaffected, and indeed the fact that no clear trend is

---

[15] With the parameter for the oldest cohort set at 0, the other parameters estimated, moving towards the youngest cohort, are $-0.18, 0.00$, and -0.11. A very similar result is obtained if we apply the uniform-difference model to tables for mobility from origin class to class at entry into employment. No improvement in fit over the CnSF model is produced, and the parameters corresponding to the above are $-0.08, 0.04$, and -0.04.

evident in relative rates over birth-cohorts within the Australian sample is reassuring as regards the possibility of distortions arising from its fore-shortened age-range.

In the US case, likewise, we find that mobility tables for four successive birth-cohorts within our sample are well reproduced by the CnSF model ($G^2 = 48.2$; df $= 48$; p $= 0.46$; $\Delta = 1.9$; N $= 17,782$). And, when we apply our US version of the core model of social fluidity to tables from a twofold collapse of these cohorts, a better fit is obtained with variable than with identical parameters only because the IN3 effect—referring, that is, to the distinctive propensity for immobility of farmers—is significantly stronger in the *younger* cohort. We further find that, again as in the Australian case, the CnSF model is not significantly improved on by that of uniform difference—or, that is, of uniform change over cohorts. However, in the application of this latter model to our US data it has also to be recognized that the β parameters returned are in fact such as to suggest that some shift towards greater overall fluidity *could* have occurred.[16]

This result might then be taken as lending a degree of support to the view that the United States, if not historically exceptional, is actually in process of becoming so, as that industrial nation in which the expectations of the liberal theory are being most fully realized. As we earlier remarked, Blau and Duncan would appear to have been pushed by their general acceptance of the theory—rather than by any compelling evidence—into sympathy with this view; and it should further be noted that a more recent contribution by Hout (1988) would appear to provide it with greater empirical backing. Hout observes that the 1973 repeat of the Blau–Duncan enquiry produced some indications of increasing fluidity (Featherman and Hauser 1978: 137; Hout 1984), and he then presents a further analysis, based on data from the period 1972–85, which, he believes, demonstrates more securely the existence of a secular trend towards greater openness within the American class structure—and one resulting chiefly, as the liberal theory would indeed predict, from greater 'universalism' in social, and especially educational, selection (and cf. also Semyonov and Roberts 1989). Hout goes on to comment (1988: 1390) that the conclusion reached in our own previous work (Erikson and Goldthorpe 1985; and cf. Kerckhoff, Campbell, and Wingfield-Laird 1985) that US and English patterns of social fluidity are fundamentally similar may then be suspect in neglecting the possibility that levels of association between social origins and destinations 'may change substantially over relatively short periods of time'.

Our findings reported above are consistent with Hout's in at least allowing for the possibility of some rising trend in fluidity in the United States over the middle decades of the present century. However, we would still wish to

---

[16] Again with the parameter for the oldest cohort set at 0, those for the three succeeding cohorts are -0.07, -0.04, and -0.11. However, for mobility from origin class to entry class, the three corresponding parameters are somewhat less convincing: 0.02, -0.01, and -0.04.

dissent from the judgement that the change involved has been 'substantial'—at all events if it is seen within a class-structural perspective. The goodness of fit of the CnSF model to our data, the fact that it misclassifies less than 2 per cent of the US sample and the only rather uncertain improvement that could be claimed for the uniform-difference model would all suggest that any change has, on the contrary, been rather slight. And this is, moreover, the conclusion which, in our view, could best be drawn from Hout's own data and analyses. It is important to note that the greater fluidity he emphasizes refers to only one of the 'three dimensions' of stratification that he chooses to distinguish, that of 'social status'; while in another dimension, 'autonomy'— which captures chiefly the division between the self-employed and employees and is thus of obvious relevance to class analysis—the trend is, if anything, in the *reverse* direction. Where Hout works simply with occupational groupings, he too achieves a good fit with the CnSF model and indeed remarks that, from this standpoint, there is 'even less evidence of change than Featherman and Hauser found in their 1962–73 comparison' (1988: 1374)— a finding to which, we believe, he should have given much greater weight, despite the fact that, as he is concerned to emphasize, the test of the hypothesis of constant fluidity that is involved here is a highly generalized one.[17]

A further recent study of trends in US social mobility is also of relevance here. Guest, Landale, and McCann (1989) relate intergenerational mobility data obtained from US census records for 1880 and 1900 to the results of both the 1962 and 1973 mobility enquiries, and on this basis argue that

---

[17] Hout is, of course, entirely correct in not allowing his analysis to rest with the fitting of the CnSF model alone, since this could indeed fail to show up significant shifts in certain sets of odds ratios, and perhaps ones indicative of increasing fluidity. But the question of whether any such changes as may be revealed through the application of a more refined model are to be seen as *substantial*, as well as statistically significant, is a quite separate one. Moreover, we would further note in this connection that difficulties arise with Hout's strategy of model choice. As he recognizes (1988: n. 16), the three-dimensional SAT model ('status', 'autonomy', and 'training') that he ultimately adopts does not, unlike the CnSF model, fit the data by conventional standards; and, one may add, it misclassifies *over 13 per cent* of all cases. Hout none the less opts for this model on the basis of the *bic* statistic. From reanalysis of Hout's data it can, however, be shown that, if we fit what might be regarded as the 'constant social fluidity' version of the SAT model, that is, with all parameters relating to the association between origins and destinations being constant over time, then, for men, a *yet more* satisfactory *bic* is obtained than with Hout's own version, in which parameters can of course vary. By conventional standards, the latter version gives a significant improvement in fit over the former, indicating that some change in fluidity does occur. But, if Hout wishes to uphold the *bic* criterion—and it is from a model thus chosen, it must be remembered, that the parameters crucial to his argument derive—then he should in fact take up the 'no-change' position. What is here illustrated is again (cf. our comments on the work of Ganzeboom, Treiman, and Luijkx, pp. 100–1), the perils of a reliance on *bic*. The application of our own uniform-difference model to Hout's data does indeed lend support to the argument that they show a trend towards greater fluidity—though scarcely to the further claim that this is substantial. The improvement on the fit of the CnSF model actually falls just short of significance, but, if the β parameter for the 1972–5 period is set at 0, those for the 1976–80 and 1980–5 periods are -0.04 and -0.16 respectively. As compared with the CnSF model, rG^2 increases from 82.8 to 83.2 and Δ falls from 8.3 to 8.2.

changes in fluidity have followed a *curvilinear* trend. That is, fluidity appears to have fallen from the end of the nineteenth century up to the First World War, to have remained more or less constant from then to the 1960s, and subsequently to have risen back to the nineteenth-century level.

Rather surprisingly, these authors see their results as being, as they stand, capable of supporting both Marxist arguments *and* the liberal notion of 'the logic of industrialism': 'The early drive to industrialization may have been associated with an increasingly stratified society, while later stages may evidence a looser link between fathers' and sons' occupations' (1989: 376). But, since both the Marxist and liberal positions clearly imply *uni*directional change, it would, we suggest, be more logical to regard *both* as being impugned. And, since the changes involved are again not at all large, especially in view of the quite lengthy period of time covered, the evidence of this further study of the US case—together in fact with that of Hout's analyses and of our own—could better be seen, we believe, as consistent with the hypothesis we have earlier advanced that temporal shifts in national fluidity patterns tend to occur as 'oscillations' around a core pattern, and that it is in this underlying cross-national commonality that their degree of constancy is in fact grounded.[18]

ABSOLUTE RATES IN THE UNITED STATES AND AUSTRALIA

In the foregoing section we have presented evidence to show that neither the United States nor Australia can be regarded as exceptional in the openness of their class structures or, in other words, in the degree of fluidity that underlies their observed rates of intergenerational class mobility. However, the arguments for exceptionalism that we previously reviewed were not always ones focused on fluidity rather than on observed, or absolute, mobility rates *per se*. While it is true that with many early commentators at least the distinction in question was scarcely explicit, it would seem clear enough that exceptionalism was often claimed not only in the openness— in our sense of the term—of American or Australian society but, further, in the actual volume of mobility that occurred, for example, in consequence of rapid economic expansion and associated structural change. We must, therefore, go on to consider US and Australian absolute rates, once more taking as background what we have been able to establish as the range of European experience.

In Chapter 6 we complemented our support for a modified version of the FJH hypothesis by demonstrating that cross-national differences in absolute

[18] On applying our uniform-difference model to the data in question, we obtain a significantly better fit than that given by the CnSF model over the three time points, and, with the β parameter for 1880–1900 set at 0, that for 1962 moves up to 0.24 and that for 1973 back down to 0.10—consistently with Guest's, Lansdale's, and McCann's argument of first falling, then rising, fluidity. The increase in rG^2 is from 93.8 to 94.4 and the fall in Δ from 3.4 to 3.1.

rates result overwhelmingly from variation in the structural contexts of mobility, and to only a very limited degree from variation in fluidity. Since, therefore, neither US nor Australian fluidity patterns would appear to diverge more from our core model than do those of at least some of our European nations, we may begin here with a consideration of structural factors as the most likely source of any distinctive features in absolute rates that these two nations might display.

TABLE 9.3. *Distributions of respondents to US and Australian mobility enquiries, by class of origin and destination, and corresponding ranges for European nations* (% by column)*

	Class of origin			Class of destination		
	USA	AUS	European range	USA	AUS	European range
I+II	14	14	6–14	28	27	14–28
III	8	5	2– 9	11	8	2–10
IVa+b	12	16	3–14	7	12	2–10
IVc	19	19	5–53	3	7	1–25
V+VI	19	23	14–39	24	27	20–37
VIIa	23	18	12–26	26	16	18–30
VIIb	4	5	3–22	1	2	1–14

Δs for origin and destination distributions

USA = 25, AUS = 21, European range, 13–37

Note:
  * US men aged 20–64; Australian men aged 30–64.

In Table 9.3 we show the distributions of origin and destination classes for men in our US and Australian samples, and also the highest and lowest percentages for each class that occur in the corresponding distributions for our European nations (cf. Table 6.2). What chiefly emerges is that both the United States and Australia have distributions that might be described as being at the 'post-industrial' end of the European range: that is, a relatively high proportion of men are found in service-class or in other non-manual positions, and a high proportion too are of non-manual origins. In this respect, the Australian class structure could in fact be seen as more 'evolved' than the US one. While in the US case—as, for example, in the French— men found in the three non-manual classes, I+II, III, and IVa+b, amount to around 90 per cent of those in the industrial working classes, V+VI and VIIa, there are actually *more* Australian men in non-manual than in manual employment within the non-agricultural sector. The Australian petty bour- geoisie, it may be noted, turns out to be larger than that in any other nation we consider. At the same time, though, neither the United States nor Australia could, on this evidence, be regarded as having a class structure that has developed on quite different lines from any that can be observed in Europe; and it is also of relevance that the Δs for the differences between origin and destination distributions in these two nations are not unusually high by European standards. In other words, there is no indication here of structural change of an exceptionally rapid kind.

These conclusions from the data of Table 9.3 are confirmed if we consider the parameters for structural shift effects that we can estimate from the models for US and Australian fluidity proposed in the previous section. If we set the pairwise differences among the US and Australian parameters against the ranges of corresponding differences estimated for our basic nine European nations, as given in Table 6.5 above, we find no US parameter and only one Australian which falls outside these European ranges.[19]

Given, then, that in neither the United States, nor Australia does the structural context of class mobility appear as highly distinctive, our earlier argument must lead us to expect that absolute rates should, in turn, show few extreme features. And this is indeed what we find. In Table 9.4 we report total mobility rates and various component rates in the same form as for European nations in Table 6.3 above. It can be seen that, just as there were grounds for regarding the United States and, especially, Australia as nations having relatively high fluidity *within* the range defined by the European experience, so too there are grounds for regarding them as nations of relatively high mobility. Their total mobility rates, for example, exceed those of all of the European nations covered in Table 6.3 except for Hungary and Sweden. However, only with the US rate for vertical mobility does a value reported in Table 9.4 actually fall outside—that is, above—the range established in Table 6.3, and even then the difference is marginal and could well reflect the problems of comparability that arise with the US data.[20] Moreover, as regards claims that either the United States or Australia offers distinctively favourable opportunities for social ascent, it is of particular interest to note that the preponderance of upward over downward mobility in these nations does not, in comparative perspective, appear all that impressive.

---

[19] Australia replaces Scotland as the nation in which Class VII*b*, that of farm workers, comes closest to Class IV*c*, that of farmers, as the class into which mobility is structurally least favoured.

[20] We suggested above that the modification we make to the core model in order to obtain a fitting variant for our US mobility table (i.e. introducing an additional positive affinity term in four cells) might best be interpreted as representing a 'correction factor' necessitated by some of the more severe problems of comparability that arise with the US data. Following this interpretation, we can then produce a US table that is correspondingly 'corrected' simply by dropping the additional affinity term from our variant model and re-estimating the US table from the other effect parameters. If this latter table is taken as the basis for calculating US total mobility rates as in Table 9.4, all are then found to lie within the European range, including that for vertical mobility, which falls by two percentage points.

TABLE 9.4. *Decomposition of total mobility rates* (TMR) *into total non-vertical* (TNV) *and total vertical* (TV) *mobility and of total vertical mobility into total upward* (TU) *and total downward* (TD) *mobility for the United States and Australia and ranges for European nations*

Nation	TMR	TV	TNV	TV/TNV	TU	TD	TU/TD
USA	73	55	18	3.1	40	15	2.7
AUS	70	52	18	2.9	39	13	3.0
European range	58–76	39–54	13–32	1.4–3.9	30–42	8–18	1.8–4.5

In order next to assess US and Australian inflow and outflow rates, we again follow the same approach as in Chapter 6 and resort to graphical presentation. Figures 9.1 and 9.2 are identical with Figures 6.1 and 6.2 respectively, except that we no longer indicate which European nations are at the extremes of each range of rates, but show in each case the positions of the US and Australian rates.

With inflows, it can be seen that there are only three of the forty-nine US rates and eight of the Australian that lie outside the European ranges and, moreover, that the differences involved are in most instances quite marginal. With outflows, instances of rates falling outside European ranges rise to ten for the United States, while again being eight for Australia, and these deviations are ones that, on balance, point to more rather than less mobility. But the differences remain usually small, and in the US case some of the outlying rates of most apparent interest, such as those indicating high outflows from non-skilled working-class origins to service-class positions and vice versa, would once more arouse our doubts about data comparability.[21] In the Australian case, perhaps the most notable departures from the European pattern are rates indicating unusually low intergenerational stability within both the skilled and non-skilled divisions of the working class; and also high outflows into the petty bourgeoisie (which Table 9.3 showed to be an unusually large class) from both service-class origins, on the one hand, and from working-class, especially non-skilled working-class origins, on the other.

Overall, then, the content of Figures 9.1 and 9.2 would serve to confirm our view of the United States and Australia as showing mobility which is in some respects at a higher level than in most of the European societies we have examined—but still without meriting the description of 'exceptional'.

---

[21] If outflow rates are calculated on the basis of the 'corrected' US mobility table referred to in the preceding note, three of the ten rates previously outside the European range are brought within it (including that for mobility from non-skilled manual origins into the service class) and the others move generally closer to this range.

Rather, one could say, on the evidence of their mobility rates and patterns as so far reviewed in this section, it would not be difficult for the United States and Australia to be taken as just two more European nations.

Finally, though, we should here also consider mobility from an intra- as well as from an intergenerational standpoint. Arguments for American exceptionalism, especially, have tended to emphasize the extent of opportunities for men to achieve social advancement over the course of their working lives. And, as we earlier noted, in the US case Thernstrom has sought to defend exceptionalist claims against Lipset's and Bendix's critique by arguing that this is based entirely on an examination of intergenerational mobility rates, while the historically formed distinctiveness of American society might well reside in the ease with which it allows men to move upwards during their own lifetimes from working-class to more advantaged positions.

As a basis for evaluating this dispute, we show in Table 9.5 a selection of work-life outflow rates for the United States and Australia and also for the eight of our European nations for which we have the requisite data. We consider here only men aged 35–64, so as to eliminate those who have spent only a short period of time in the labour force, and we also thus avoid problems of comparability in the Australian case.

In the upper panel of the table the rates refer to the chances of men who first entered the labour market in working-class and also in farm employment

TABLE 9.5. *Work-life outflow mobility rates between selected classes, men aged 35–64* (%)

Outflow	USA	AUS	ENG	FRA	HUN	IRL	NIR	POL	SCO	SWE
Entry in V+VI to I+II	20	18	16	15	15	8	15	12	16	22
Entry in VIIa to I+II	15	19	11	13	11	5	6	9	11	16
Entry in IVc/ VIIb to I+II	7	8	3	5	5	1	4	2	6	8
Entry in V+VI to IVa+b	11	19	10	15	5	16	13	3	7	13
Entry in VIIa to IVa+b	8	8	8	9	1	9	9	2	4	10
Origin and entry in V+VI/ VIIa to I+II	15	16	12	12	14	7	7	12	11	20
Origin and entry in IVc/ VIIb to I+II	6	7	3	3	4	1	3	2	5	6
Origin and entry in V+VI/ VIIa to IVa+b	7	14	7	10	2	4	9	2	4	8

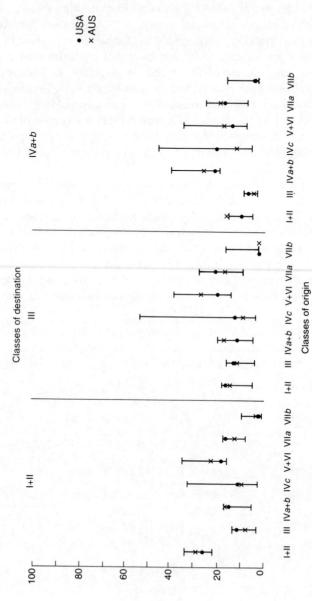

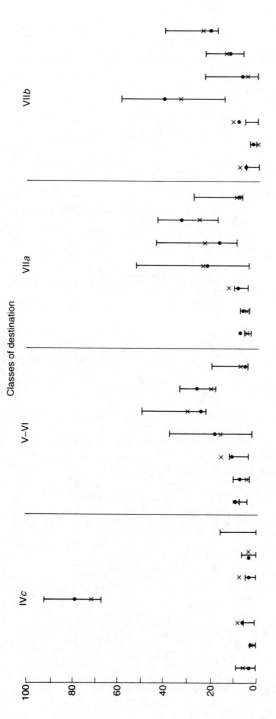

FIGURE 9.1. *European ranges of inflow rates and position of US and Australian rates*

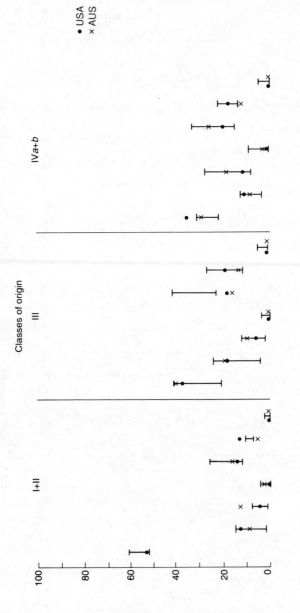

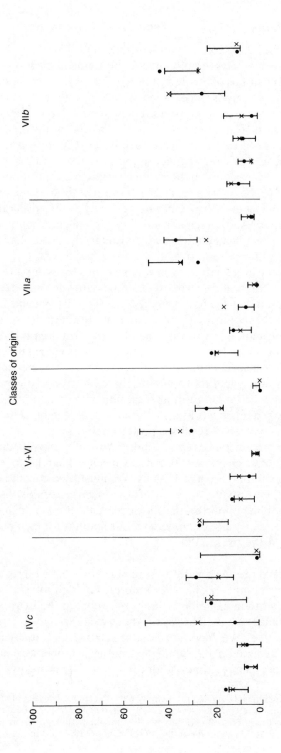

FIGURE 9.2. *European ranges of outflow rates and position of US and Australian rates*

being subsequently found in service-class positions; and also to the chances of those starting in working-class employment being found in the proprietorial or self-employed positions of the petty bourgeoisie. We include mobility of this latter kind in our analysis since the possibility of wage-workers going into business on their own account has often been referred to in arguments for American exceptionalism from Engels onwards, and has indeed been taken as a key element in the 'American Dream' (cf. Chinoy 1955). The results reported appear to give far stronger support to Lipset and Zetterberg than to Thernstrom. As regards mobility into service-class positions, US rates could, once more, be seen as relatively high yet without being exceptionally so; they are in fact in each instance exceeded by the Swedish rates as well as by the Australian. And, as regards mobility into the petty bourgeoisie, the US rates prove to be matched or exceeded again by the Australian rates and by those recorded for several of our European nations.[22]

It might, however, be argued that, even when we thus focus our attention on work-life mobility, we should also take class origins into account. It could reasonably be supposed that the real issue between Thernstrom and Lipset and Bendix concerns the mobility chances of men in working-class, or farm, employment who are, moreover, of working-class or farm *origins*—rather than the chances of men of other, more advantaged origins being upwardly mobile from initial lower-level employment as part, say, of counter-mobile trajectories. In the lower panel of Table 9.5, therefore, we give work-life outflow rates for men who on their initial entry into employment remained within either a broadly defined working or farm class. As can be seen, little change in the general pattern of results is produced. For men starting their working lives in the circumstances in question, Australia and Sweden, at least, could claim to offer chances of social advancement similar to, if not better than, those found in the United States. We must then conclude that Thernstrom's attempt to revive the idea of American exceptionalism in terms of work-life mobility opportunities, however it may fare in the light of nineteenth-century data, cannot be upheld by our findings for men born in the earlier decades of the twentieth.

In this chapter we have reviewed various arguments that have represented the United States or Australia as having exceptionally high rates of social mobility, and we have then examined these arguments in the light of the comparative data available to us. The results that we have obtained must be seen as largely negative. We have considered relative and also various absolute rates of intergenerational class mobility, and again mobility chances as viewed in work-life perspective. In none of these respects, however, could

---

[22] We would here again think it likely that problems of data may lead to US rates of mobility from working-class entry positions into the service class being somewhat exaggerated; but, on the other hand, we suspect that rates of work-life mobility into the petty bourgeoisie may be understated in view of what is said about the coding of self-employed workers in n. 10 above.

our findings for the United States or for Australia be regarded as 'exceptional' when set against those from European nations that we have previously reported. The most that might be said is that, in both the degree of fluidity and the levels of absolute mobility that they display, the United States and Australia alike are quite often found towards the 'high' end of the ranges that our European data allow us to establish. But even this conclusion, we would add, is one that we feel able to accept with greater confidence for Australia than for the United States, in view of the problems of data comparability that arise in the latter case and which seem likely to give a generally exaggerated idea of US mobility rates.

In turn, then, we may say that the analyses of this chapter give little indication that the experience of mobility in 'new nations', which have developed as leading industrial powers outside Europe, is set quite apart from that of nations of the 'old' European world, and thus threatens to undermine any conclusions regarding mobility that derive from the latter alone. No matter how distinctive the United States and Australia may be in the economic and social histories of their industrialization or in the ideas, beliefs, and values concerning mobility that are prevalent in their national cultures, it could not, on our evidence, be said that they differ more widely from European nations in their actual rates and patterns of mobility than do European nations among themselves. In the next chapter, however, we must see whether a similar judgement can be reached when we take up the further case of Japan.

10
Non-European Cases: II. Japan

In the present context, the special interest that Japan holds is not as a 'new nation', like the United States or Australia, but rather as the first nation lying outside the European cultural sphere to have attained a stage of 'mature' industrialism. On this account, the Japanese case is now in fact widely accepted among comparative sociologists as constituting an important test for all claims regarding 'generic properties' of industrial society that have been derived from the European and 'Anglo-American' experience (McCormack and Sugimoto 1988). And, as might then be expected, the question of Japanese 'uniqueness' has become the focus of a multi-faceted debate, which, while extending far beyond issues of social stratification and mobility, still involves these in a central if, as will be seen, rather complex way.

In this chapter we begin by presenting, and locating within this wider context, two arguments which lead—though via quite different routes—to exceptionalist positions in regard to stratification and, in turn, mobility in modern Japan. In the following sections we then consider, on essentially the same lines as in the previous chapter, the data that we have available for evaluating these arguments and the results that we obtain when we examine, first, Japanese relative mobility rates from the standpoint of our core model and, secondly, rates and patterns of absolute mobility. While we hope that in this way we may be able to contribute something to the debate on the nature of Japanese industrial society, we will remain chiefly concerned to ask how far the inclusion of the evidence of the Japanese case requires revision of our previous findings on social mobility as viewed in comparative perspective.[1]

ARGUMENTS FOR JAPANESE EXCEPTIONALISM

Within the debate on the nature of Japanese industrial society to which we have referred (for general reviews see Mouer and Sugimoto 1986; Dale 1986), the case for 'uniqueness' has perhaps been most vigorously presented by a number of Japanese social scientists, in more-or-less explicit reaction to what we have in this study labelled the 'liberal theory' of industrialism. As against the idea of a powerful logic of industrialism forcing all economically advanced societies on to convergent paths of development, the recurrent

---

[1] The present chapter draws extensively on Ishida, Goldthorpe, and Erikson (1991), although it should be noted that at various points new analyses are introduced which, in mostly minor ways, modify conclusions reached in this paper. We are grateful to Hiroshi Ishida for providing us with access to important literature published in Japanese.

contention of these authors has been that many of the basic forms of traditional Japanese social structure have in fact persisted in the course of industrialization and have, furthermore, found new, and by no means 'dysfunctional', expression *within* an industrial context.[2] As representative of this position, we take here the work of Nakane (1970) since—as well as being available in English—it carries a particular relevance for issues of stratification.

Nakane is in general concerned to reject the implication, which she sees as following from prevailing Western accounts of industrialism, that 'any phenomena which seem peculiar to Japan, not having been found in western society, can be labelled as "feudal" or "pre-modern" elements, and are to be regarded as contradictory or obstructive to modernisation' (1970: p. ix). As a leading illustration of her argument, she then seeks to show that in Japan characteristic modes of group formation and group relations have always been, and indeed remain, ones which serve to create a society in which the dominant structural feature is 'not that of horizontal stratification by class or caste but of vertical stratification by institutions or group of institutions'. In pre-industrial Japan the key institutions in this respect were those of family, household, and community; but, in the modern society, their role in developing basic social identities and affiliations has, in fact, been largely taken over by the new business enterprises, with their distinctive systems of 'lifetime employment' and 'company welfare'. Thus, Nakane claims, Japanese society has been able to preserve its structural distinctiveness, and without thereby incurring any obvious disadvantage. Japan has still not become a 'class' society: 'it is really not a matter of workers struggling against capitalists or managers but of Company A ranged against Company B. The protagonists do not stand in vertical relationship to each other but instead rub elbows from parallel positions' (1970: 87).[3]

What is, therefore, contended is that a theory of industrial society in which a concern with change in the class structure is central can have only doubtful relevance for Japan. As Nakane herself puts it:

Even if social classes like those in Europe can be detected in Japan, and even if something vaguely resembling those classes that are illustrated in the textbooks of western sociology can also be found in Japan, the point is that *in actual society this stratification is unlikely to function and that it does not really reflect the social structure.* (1970: 87; emphasis added)

---

[2] This body of work may be regarded as the sociological wing of, or at all events counterpart to, the indigenous genre of *nihonjinron*—an extensive literature treating questions of Japanese identity and uniqueness (see, further, Dale 1986).

[3] Such views are not, we should add, to be seen as exclusive to Japanese authors; they have also been advanced by some Western Japanologists. Cf., for example, Vogel: 'The basic cleavages in Japanese society have not been between different social classes but between one corporate group (composed of people at different positions) and other corporate groups' (1967: 108).

More specifically, then, if Nakane's argument is correct, to seek to study social mobility within a class-structural context, as we have opted to do, must be of very limited validity in the Japanese case; and thus, if the attempt is none the less made, there would seem little reason why the results produced should conform at all closely to those obtained for Western nations. In other words, one would expect Japan to appear as exceptional in its rates and patterns of mobility in consequence of a conceptual scheme that does not 'really reflect' the way in which the 'actual society' works being more or less arbitrarily imposed.

However, while the liberal theory of industrialism has in the main provoked a critical response from within Japanese sociology, this has not been invariably the case, and positions that contrast sharply with that of Nakane are also to be found. Here perhaps the best illustration can be provided by the work of Tominaga and his associates. In a number of publications (but see esp., in English, 1982), Tominaga has both criticized 'the thesis of Japanese peculiarity' and explicitly defended the applicability of the liberal theory of industrialism to the Japanese case.

In Tominaga's view, those who, like Nakane, would see Japanese society as *sui generis* quite fail to appreciate the radical nature of the socio-cultural changes that industrialization has produced and the extent to which the traditional order has been eroded, especially from the time of the post-war 'reconstruction'. Claims that traditional institutional forms are re-established within the new industrial society are, moreover, largely misconceived. Thus, for instance, Tominaga points out that the 'lifetime-employment' system, to which so much attention has been given, is *not* in fact 'traditional' (but became common only in the inter-war period), is found only in certain types of Japanese company, and must in any event be seen as differing only in degree and not in kind from employment practices that are quite widespread in many Western societies—notably, in the public services or more paternalistic private enterprises.

Moreover, for Tominaga, the nature and direction of the changes evident in present-day Japan are essentially those that the liberal theory would lead one to anticipate—and no better illustration of this could be provided than changes in social stratification. As would be predicted, industrialization has progressively undermined the traditional status order of Japanese society and has created in its place a modern form of stratification based not on the ascribed attributes of family, kinship, or locality of origin but rather on the achieved attributes of education, occupation, and income. And at the same time, and again as the theory would lead one to expect, Japan has—quite rapidly—become a more mobile and a more open society (cf. also, Tominaga 1969, 1979*b*).

Tominaga would in fact largely underwrite the argument that all industrial nations, no matter how different in culture and structure their pre-industrial societies may have been, are now set on convergent lines of social change.

Indeed, as industrialism becomes more advanced 'the pressure towards uniformity' only increases (1982: 15). Moreover, in so far as Tominaga goes beyond the liberal orthodoxy, it is in suggesting that, at least so far as social stratification is concerned, Japan may in fact have progressed *further* towards the ideal-typical industrial society on which convergence is focused than has any other nation—even the United States. Despite their very different histories, Japan and the United States are the pre-eminent 'lands of equality'; but, Tominaga argues, Japan may now display yet greater equality of both condition and opportunity than does the United States because, as well as benefiting from the 'natural' tendency towards greater equality inherent in industrialism, Japan has undertaken more extensive egalitarian social reform, notably in the immediate post-war years (1982: 30–1). In other words, Tominaga advances the idea that it is Japan, rather than the United States, that should today be seen as exceptional, at least in the sense of being the 'vanguard' nation which stands ahead of others in the industrial world and displays to them the levels of mobility and openness that they have still to attain.

In summary, then, we might say that, while Nakane is concerned to question the relevance to Japan of the liberal theory of industrial society, and especially in regard to social stratification, Tominaga, also concentrating his attention on stratification, represents the Japanese case as that in which this theory finds its apotheosis. However, one further point should here be noted: Tominaga, like Nakane, would doubt the appropriateness to Japanese society of the concept of 'class', and again on the grounds that it is too distinctively 'European' (see further Tominaga, Naoi, and Imada n.d: 1–5). When the concept is applied to European societies, it can map out 'real' social groupings; but Japan—like the United States, though for different reasons—has a history in which the idea of class did not spontaneously emerge, and thus its application to the present-day society must involve a degree of artificiality. If Japanese social stratification is to be compared with that of other societies, then, in Tominaga's view, a more 'nominalist' conceptual approach is to be preferred—as, for example, that provided by mainstream US sociology in which stratification is envisaged as a hierarchy or continuum of 'socio-economic' status groupings. In evaluating Tominaga's position in the light of our comparative data, we have, therefore, to be again ready to consider the implications of the fact that we are viewing social mobility in Japan in a different perspective from that favoured by the indigenous investigator.[4]

---

[4] Tominaga's doubts over the appropriateness of the concept of class to Japanese society would seem in part to be influenced by, and directed against, analyses of class structure that have been offered by Japanese Marxists. For an account in English, much influenced by these analyses, see Steven (1983). However, class analysis cannot, of course, be regarded as solely the preserve of Marxists.

DATA

The source of our Japanese mobility data (cf. Table 2.3 above) is the 1975 Social Stratification and Mobility National Survey, which was designed and carried out by a consortium of Japanese social scientists. The recoding of the data of this enquiry (for men aged 20–64) to the categories of our class schema proved to be in general far less problematic than might have been supposed. However Japanese social stratification may in reality differ from that of European nations, the class schema appeared to be at least formally adequate to the Japanese case—except in one respect.

The difficulty encountered concerned individuals with the employment status of 'family worker'—usually, that is, in small enterprises or on farms. Where such workers were distinguished in the European enquiries that we utilize, they were, as we have earlier noted, recoded together with 'other' employees, on the grounds that they would be typically in receipt of a wage or salary of some kind, even though they might also benefit, directly or indirectly—for example, through payments in kind—from the proceeds of the family enterprise. However, there is reason to suppose that in the Japanese case the category of 'family worker' comprises, in addition to such 'family employees', some further number of persons who do *not* have claims to a regular wage or salary but whose income derives *either* from some share in profits, and who ought, therefore, to be treated as 'partners' and given a 'self-employed' coding, *or* who receive only casual or *ad hoc* disbursements from the family head. In particular, it would appear that, until quite recent times, probably up to the early 1960s, family workers on Japanese farms, even adult and married sons, could often expect only such 'pocket-money' payments from their fathers (cf. Fukutake 1967: ch. 4).[5]

Since we were unable in any way to make further distinctions within the 'family-worker' coding, we decided to maintain our usual practice, and thus all Japanese family workers alike were allocated to 'employee' classes of our schema—that is, in fact, to Classes III, V+VI, VIIa, and VIIb. This must, however, be reckoned to involve a degree of distortion. Some of these men would have been more appropriately allocated to Classes IVa+b or IVc, while we must acknowledge that such others who were in effect in unpaid labour rather than either partners in the family enterprise or its regular employees are not satisfactorily accommodated by the schema. Fortunately, though, the problem that here arises cannot be regarded as one of major quantitative importance: the coding of 'family worker' was given *in total* to only 103 respondents and to 28 of their fathers.

---

[5] The closest European parallel to this that we have encountered occurs in Irish farming families. However, a major difference would still appear to be that in this case a son's dependence on his father, even if often protracted, would not continue after the son's marriage (cf. Hout 1989: ch. 5).

One further point regarding our treatment of the Japanese data should be noted. When the 'present' (i.e. 1975) occupational and employment status distributions of respondents to the Japanese survey were set against nominally comparable distributions from the 1975 Japanese Population Census, certain discrepancies emerged. Farmers and managers appeared somewhat over-represented at the expense mainly of manual workers in industry; and employers and self-employed men were quite clearly over-represented at the expense of employees. There is reason to believe that the main source of this latter discrepancy was that employers and the self-employed had higher response rates than employees, since they could be more readily found 'at home' by interviewers (see, further, Ando 1978; Tominaga 1979*a*). We decided, therefore, to apply a weighting factor to the sample *ex post*, which was designed to bring the employment-status distribution of respondents into line with Census data. This adjustment, it then turned out, had the effect of reducing the discrepancy in the occupational distribution also.[6]

CORE SOCIAL FLUIDITY AND THE JAPANESE CASE

We begin our empirical enquiry into exceptionalism in Japanese mobility rates and patterns, as we did previously in the cases of the United States and Australia, by considering relative rates, or patterns of social fluidity, and, specifically, by investigating the fit of our model of core fluidity to the Japanese intergenerational mobility table. The results of so doing are shown in Table 10.1.

From the first row of the table it is evident that, when our model is applied with fixed parameters, the fit is very poor; indeed, a higher $G^2(S)$ value is

TABLE 10.1. *Results of fitting the model of core social fluidity to the Japanese mobility table: (i) with cross-nationally common parameters; (ii) with nation-specific parameters; (iii) with effects modified or added (national variant model)*

Nation		G^2	df	p	rG^2	Δ	$G^2(S)$ (1,991)*
JAP	(i)	126.0	36	0.00	75.1	7.8	123
(N = 2,066)	(ii)	53.5	28	0.00	89.4	5.2	53
	(iii)	39.0	30[†]	0.10	92.3	4.4	39

Notes:
* We here retain the constant for $G^2(S)$ at 1,991, the size of the smallest sample among our nine European nations.
[†] df = 30 since the variant model omits two terms (see text).

[6] This weighting is not available in the CASMIN International Mobility Superfile, but full details of it can be obtained on request from Hiroshi Ishida, Department of Sociology, Columbia University, New York.

returned for Japan than for any European nation (cf. Tables 5.1 and 5.5) and also than for the United States, though not for Australia (cf. Table 9.1). However, when the model is applied with its parameters being allowed to vary, a rather different picture emerges. The second row of Table 10.1 indicates that, while the fit to the Japanese table is still not acceptable, the deviations from the model are much reduced, and they are now in fact of around the same order of magnitude as those we encounter in our analyses of European data: the $G^2(S)$ and Δ values fall well within the European range and the rG^2 value is on the edge. In other words, it is here indicated that—in much the same way as we found with the United States and Australia—Japan reveals a pattern of fluidity that is not set apart from that which we would see as defining a common theme among our European nations, even though certain rather distinctive features within this pattern are to be detected.[7]

Following from this, we may then aim to produce a variant of our core model which is adequate to the Japanese data while, we would hope, at the same time having some independent sociological basis. It turns out that we can in fact obtain such a model by making changes in only three cells of the mobility table—in each of which, it may be added, numbers are quite small:

1. the IN2 and IN3 terms are included in the cell indicating immobility in the class of agricultural workers, VII*b*;
2. the AF1 term (negative affinity) is included in the two cells indicating mobility from origins in the service class, I+II, to both the skilled and non-skilled divisions of the working class, V+VI and VII*a*.

The first modification of the model—in effect, the attribution to the class of farm workers of the same propensity for immobility as that of farmers— would seem chiefly required in consequence of the highly familial character of Japanese agriculture (cf. Fukutake 1967; Dore 1978). In Japan farm workers tend, to a yet greater extent than in Western societies, to be members of the farmer's own family and, moreover, sons would appear to remain in a subordinate position while their fathers are alive or at least still active. Thus, it emerges that, of those men found in the VII*b*–VII*b* cell of the Japanese mobility table, 70 per cent had fathers who were still categorized as 'family workers', even at the time of the respondent's adolescence, *and* were themselves 'family workers'—presumably waiting to inherit in turn.[8]

---

[7] When the Japanese table is modelled in this way, three of the effect parameters returned differ significantly from those estimated for the core model: the IN1 parameter is stronger, and the HI2 and IN2 parameters are weaker.

[8] For purposes of comparison, it may be reported that, in the English mobility table, only two men out of the fifty-six in the VII*b*–VII*b* cell were themselves family workers *and* also reported their fathers as being such (at respondent's age 15). It may further be noted that as many as 80 per cent of *all* Japanese respondents who were classified as farm workers, and 70 per cent of all fathers so classified, had the status of family worker. These are clearly higher percentages than any we can establish for our Western nations.

In other words, we need to adapt our model to the fact that, in the Japanese case, the large majority of men who appear as immobile farm workers are actually in the—protracted—process of succeeding their fathers as farm owners.

In addition, though, we should here recall our earlier observation about the relatively wide use made of the 'family-worker' code in the Japanese data and, in particular, our concern that it was in some instances applied to men who would in our European enquiries have been regarded as partners in family enterprises and thus as self-employed. To this extent, then, we may regard the modification that we make to the core model for the VII*b*–VII*b* cell of the Japanese table not only as reflecting a real Japanese distinctiveness in the social organization of farming but also as a correction factor; that is, one needed to allow for coding differences that bring into this cell men who in other national mobility tables would be found in the IV*c*–IV*c* or IV*c*–VII*b* cells.[9]

The second alteration that we make to the core model is required in order to accommodate an evidently very low propensity for the sons of service-class families in Japan to be downwardly mobile into the ranks of the industrial working class. This we would relate to the awareness—perhaps exaggerated awareness (cf. Ishida 1986)—of the importance of educational credentials in Japan and further to unusually low chances of work-life 'counter-mobility' back from manual employment to service-class positions, which we can, in fact, illustrate from our comparative data.[10] A particular concern may then be suggested on the part of service-class families to protect their offspring from being forced into manual jobs from which there might be no escape, and a corresponding readiness to devote resources to this end. For example, the practice would seem to have become widespread in post-war Japan of more advantaged parents buying additional private tutoring for their children in the attempt to ensure a level of educational attainment appropriate to white-collar employment (Dore 1975; Fukutake 1982: 209–11; Morishima 1982: 182–3).

When the core model with the changes indicated above is fitted to the Japanese data, an acceptable $G^2(S)$ value is produced, but it further emerges

[9] Some corresponding modification might then have been thought necessary in the IV*c*–IV*c* and IV*c*–VII*b* cells, but this proved not to be required—chiefly, we would suppose, because it is among the family workers represented in the VII*b*–VII*b* cell that the proportion of 'protracted inheritors' to true 'family employees' is greatest.

[10] The frequency of counter-mobility within the Japanese service class—as measured by the proportion of men of service-class origins who were themselves found in service-class positions after initial employment which placed them in a different class position—is in fact high: 25 per cent of all men of service-class origins, as compared with 23 per cent in England and 16 per cent in France, to take two European nations in which (cf. ch. 8) counter-mobility would seem to be institutionally favoured. However, in Japan such counter-mobility is overwhelmingly via non-manual entry positions, especially in Class III (cf. the discussion in the text, pp. 346–7). Of service-class sons who entered employment in the manual positions of Classes V+VI and VII*a*, just over a third in England and just under a third in France were subsequently found back in the service class, but in Japan the proportion is less than a sixth.

that under this variant model the HI2 and IN2 terms do not reach significance. When these terms are therefore omitted and the model re-estimated, the $G^2(S)$ and other results that are returned are as reported in the third row of Table 10.1. In Table 10.2 we show the effect parameters that are estimated under this variant model alongside those of the core model. On the basis of this table, and also of the entries for Japan in Table A5.1, it could then be said that our variant model implies deviations from core fluidity in three main respects.

TABLE 10.2. *Effect parameters of accepted model for Japan**

Nation	HI1	HI2	IN1	IN2	IN3	SE	AF1	AF2
JAP	−0.16	ns	0.73	ns	*0.81*	−0.61	*−0.68*	0.37
CORE	−0.22	−0.42	0.43	0.81	0.96	−1.03	−0.77	0.46

Note:
  * Parameters directly affected by modifications to the core model are in italic type; instances where a parameter initially returned a non-significant value at the 5 per cent level and has then been omitted are indicated by ns.

First, the fact that the AF1 term is required in the I+II–V+VI and I+II–VIIa cells of the Japanese table does, of course, imply (although being in part offset by the insignificance of the HI2 term) an *asymmetry* in propensities for mobility between service-class and working-class positions: downward movement is clearly less likely than upward.

Secondly, the inclusion of the IN2 and IN3 terms in the VIIb–VIIb cell and the subsequent dropping of the IN2 term as insignificant means that in the Japanese case only two levels of inheritance effects are distinguished: one applying to agricultural and the other to non-agricultural classes. Moreover, the IN1 effect is relatively strong, so that the propensity for immobility within Classes III, V+VI, and VIIa—those of routine non-manual employees and skilled and non-skilled industrial workers—is twice as great as it would be in the absence of this effect ($e^{0.73} = 2.08$), as against only one-and-a-half times as great under the core model; while, on the other hand, a relatively low propensity for immobility is implied within Classes I+II and IVa+b—those of the service class and the petty bourgeoisie—since the IN1 *and* IN2 terms under the core model entail an increase in this propensity of almost three-and-a-half times.

The lack of differentiation in the strength of inheritance effects as between Class I+II and Class III may be associated with the fact that the line between these classes is particularly difficult to draw in the Japanese case. This is on account of the widespread practice in business and other organizations of young entrants being required to work for an often lengthy period—possibly up to ten years—in routine clerical grades, even though they may be of graduate status and have been recruited specifically for higher level administrative or managerial positions (cf. Cole and Tominaga 1976: 74).[11] On the other hand, the propensity for immobility within Class IV$a+b$ may be depressed as a result of the role played in Japan by self-employment—especially in the form of home-working—as a response to unemployment, and also as a sequel to retirement at around age 55, which is usual in Japanese industry (cf. Steven 1983: 80–6; also Cole and Tominaga 1976: 77–8).

Thirdly, our variant model for Japan shows up a much weaker sectoral effect than does the core model—implying a reduction in the propensity for mobility between sectors to only about a half ($e^{-0.61} = 0.54$) of what it would otherwise be, as compared with a reduction to almost a third under core expectations. And from Table A5.1 it can then be seen that all Japanese entries for cells entailing cross-sectoral mobility are less than 100, implying, that is, cell-interaction parameters closer to the neutral-fluidity level than under the core pattern. In Japan farming is in fact often undertaken on a part-time basis or, alternatively, the incomes of farm families are regularly supplemented by their members engaging in various kinds of industrial wage-work (Fukutake 1967, 1982: ch. 11);[12] and, as we have previously suggested in regard to several European nations, such as the FRG, Hungary, and Poland, these are practices that typically serve to reduce the barriers to intergenerational mobility between agricultural and non-agricultural classes. Furthermore, though, with the HI2 term being dropped, the weak sectoral effect means—and again as Table A5.1 clearly reveals—that in the Japanese case propensities for mobility between both agricultural classes and the service class are especially high.

What, then, are the implications of the results we have so far presented on Japanese social fluidity for the arguments of Nakane and Tominaga that we earlier outlined? As regards Nakane's claims that the Japanese form of social stratification must be seen as quite distinct from that of Western nations, and that 'class' as understood in a Western context is 'unlikely to function' in Japanese society, our findings are scarcely supportive. It is true that our model of core social fluidity, formulated within a class-structural perspective, does not fit the Japanese mobility table without some adaptation, and we have in turn to recognize that the Japanese pattern of fluidity does display various 'peculiarities' in relation to this model. However, it has

---

[11] It might be the case that Japanese distinctiveness is here again, in part at least, no more than classificatory: young entrants are graded as clerks whose counterparts in Western nations would be more probably designated as administrative or managerial 'trainees'. Hence, the extent of Japanese deviation from core fluidity could be exaggerated.

[12] We would indeed expect that perhaps even a majority of the respondents to the Japanese survey who reported their present occupation as being that of farmer, in virtue of the fact that they did own and farm land—and who are therefore coded to Class IVc—were also engaged in some form of paid employment outside farming. Information on such 'second jobs' was unfortunately not collected in the enquiry.

also to be noted that the modification required to the form of the core model in order to obtain a fitting variant for Japan is in fact rather slight, and that, while the overall extent of Japanese deviation from the core pattern is greater than that found in *some* of the European nations that we have considered, it still could not be reckoned as in any way exceptional. Inspection of Table A5.1 will show that there are in fact only two cells of our standard intergenerational mobility table—that indicating mobility from the service class to the skilled working class and that indicating immobility within the class of farm workers—for which the Japanese propensity marks an extreme: that is, low in the first case, high in the second. In other words, the counter-argument could be made to Nakane that a model developed from the experience of European societies does in fact prove capable of reproducing Japanese mobility data to a very substantial extent, and that the Japanese peculiarities that are revealed are thus better regarded as variations on the theme that the model defines than as expressions of a national social structure which can be understood only on its own terms.

We do not, we should add, seek here to challenge the contention of Nakane, and others, that class consciousness, or even class awareness, is only rather weakly developed among the Japanese population. What we would, however, wish to maintain is, first, that sociologists need not be restricted in the concepts they apply to those that are prevalent among the 'lay members' of the societies they study; and, secondly, that class is in any event a concept relevant not only to how individuals view the social world and act within it but also to *what actually happens to them*—in the present context, that is, to what chances of mobility or immobility they have experienced or may expect.

Turning now to Tominaga's suggestion that modern Japan may be distinctive at all events in being in the van of a general movement among industrial societies towards greater openness, we must again take a negative view. On the basis of Table A5.1, Japan appears as a relatively open society overall, and it is, moreover, possible to pick out instances in which the level of fluidity within the Japanese class structure is quite unusually high: for example, in the case of transitions between the agricultural and non-agricultural sectors, and even where, in terms of our hierarchical divisions, these entail mobility of a 'long-range' kind. But at the same time there are in other respects indications of rather low fluidity: in particular, in the marked propensities for immobility that are found not only—and, as we have suggested, somewhat artificially—among farm workers, but further within both the skilled and non-skilled divisions of the industrial working class and within the class of routine non-manual employees. In showing the existence of certain strong tendencies for mobility but alongside others for class 'inheritance', our findings are, we may add, consistent with, even though more differentiated than, those reported from other comparative studies, whose authors have used the same Japanese data but have deployed different analytical techniques (see, esp., Yamaguchi 1987; Wong 1990).[13] And if, then, we bear in mind the results that we have reported for Sweden, as well as for Poland and Czechoslovakia, when comparing our European nations, or again for Australia in the preceding chapter, any claim of Japanese *pre-eminence* so far as societal openness is concerned would seem difficult to sustain.[14]

The fitting of our model of core fluidity to the Japanese mobility table does, in sum, require us to view the arguments of both Nakane and Tominaga in a very sceptical light. However, in order to guard against dismissing these arguments too readily or too comprehensively, we undertook two supplementary lines of analysis, on which, in conclusion of this section, we should also report.

To begin with, we recognized that, even if, as we would suppose, the concept of class *is* applicable to Japanese society, we might still not have implemented our class schema in the way most appropriate to the Japanese case—and that, in turn, this could conceivably have led us to understate Japanese distinctiveness in fluidity patterns. In particular, the possibility may be raised that we have not taken due account of the tendency, which Nakane along with various other commentators has emphasized, for the employment relations and conditions of Japanese workers to be influenced as much, if not more, by the type, and especially the *size*, of the organization in which they are employed as by their own occupation or skill level (see, e.g., Cole 1979; Clark 1979; and the discussion in Mouer and Sugimoto 1986: 281–8).

To explore this possibility to some extent, we modified the form of our class schema so as to provide for a distinction between employees in 'large' and 'small' establishments. The dividing line was set at three hundred employees, which is that most often used in Japanese official statistics, at least so far as manufacturing industry is concerned. Specifically, we

---

[13] Thus, Yamaguchi remarks that, overall, the Japanese pattern of social fluidity is 'closer to quasi-independence' than those of the two other nations he studies—that is, England and the United States (1987: 489). However, it may be added that, in using status rather than class categories as the basis of his analysis, Yamaguchi does not pick up the relatively low propensity for immobility among the Japanese petty bourgeoisie; nor can he observe the weak sectoral effects that operate, since he has only a single 'farm' category (which he treats as one of status). Wong claims, in a way which might at first seem supportive of Tominaga's position, that Japan and the United States 'provide images of societal openness', and especially when compared to England (1990: 570). However, in the next paragraph he also concludes that 'Japan has a very high level of inheritance'—higher in fact than that of the United States or England or indeed of any of the other nations he analyses (Brazil, Hungary, and Poland). One has then to suppose that Wong—idiosyncratically, to say the least—understands 'openness' as a concept pertaining only to the off-diagonal cells of the mobility table.

[14] In a further recent study, F. L. Jones (1987) reports on a reanalysis of the same Japanese and Australian data that we have used, but organized on an eightfold occupational classification. This also leads to the conclusion that the mobility regimes of the two nations possess 'a high degree of commonality', but that, in so far as differences do exist, the main feature to be noted is the greater propensity for immobility in Japan.

recategorized respondents' and respondents' fathers' class positions in the following ways.

1. Cases allocated to Class III but where the employing organization was large were transferred to Class I+II—on the assumption that in large organizations, even routine non-manual workers would tend to be more-or-less fully integrated, in terms of their employment relations and conditions, into administrative and managerial bureaucracies.
2. All cases allocated to Classes V+VI and VIIa were reallocated to two new classes, V–VIIa (large) and V–VIIa (small)—the assumption here being that, so far as employment relations and conditions are concerned, the division within the industrial working class by size of organization would be more consequential than that by skill.

With our mobility data reorganized on the basis of this modified version of the class schema, we then repeated the fitting of the core model, as described above. The main finding was that very little difference was made to the general pattern of our results. Once its parameters were allowed to vary, the core model fitted somewhat better than previously $(G^2(S) = 51$ as against 53), and, while our national variant model fitted less well, the difference was again not large $(G^2(S) = 45$ as against 39). We can thus at all events say that we do not find here any obvious indications that our class schema in its original form fails to give insight into some highly distinctive feature of Japanese social fluidity which attention to the size of employing organizations would reveal.[15] Rather, we are led in this respect to align ourselves with Tominaga's critique of Nakane in believing that differences in the structure of employment relations as between Japan and Western nations are in fact easily exaggerated.

The further supplementary analyses that we pursued were aimed at investigating the stability of the Japanese pattern of social fluidity, in the light especially of Tominaga's claim of a decisive shift towards greater openness. Even if Japan was not, at least by the mid-1970s, *the* land of opportunity, as Tominaga would suppose, it could still be that it was moving rapidly towards becoming so. To check on this possibility, we tested for trends in Japanese social fluidity using the same procedures as we have applied with our other nations. That is, we first of all fitted our CnSF model to five-class mobility tables constructed for four successive birth-cohorts distinguished within the Japanese sample; we then went beyond the CnSF model to that allowing for uniform intercohort differences in fluidity; and, finally, we applied our national variant model for Japan to (seven-class) tables for two broad birth-cohorts, of men born 1911–30 and 1931–50.

---

[15] In order to obtain more conclusive results in this respect, it would have been desirable also to have introduced organizational size into analyses of mobility data for our European nations. Unfortunately, however, in none of our European data-sets do we have information on this variable for both respondents *and* their fathers.

What we discover from each of these tests alike is, in fact, evidence that the Japanese mobility regime is characterized by a very high degree of temporal stability and, further, that, in so far as any changes at all are in train, they are *not* ones in the direction of generally increasing openness. Thus, the CnSF model gives a very good fit to the Japanese data ($G^2 = 52.4$; df = 48; p = 0.30; $\Delta = 3.9$; N = 1870)—upon which, moreover, the uniform-change model makes no significant improvement, though yielding β parameters to suggest that, if anything, fluidity has tended to decline, especially as between the oldest cohort and the three succeeding ones.[16] Again, although we achieve a slight improvement in fit in our national variant model for Japan if we allow its parameters to differ when applied to older and younger respondents, the significant changes that occur are that the HI1 and SE terms *strengthen* from the earlier to the later cohort, while the (extended) AF1 term weakens. In other words, the direction of change in fluidity here indicated would appear to be not so much towards greater openness as towards a closer conformity with the core pattern.

As we earlier observed, Tominaga would not himself regard a class-structural perspective as being that most suited to the analysis of stratification or mobility in the Japanese context. It is, therefore, of some importance to note that the findings we report above are in fact on much the same lines as those of several other recent studies of Japanese mobility trends that have been guided by different conceptual approaches from our own, as well as using different data-bases and techniques (see, esp., Kojima and Hamana 1984; Iwamoto 1985; Tokuyasu 1986; Yamaguchi 1987; F. L. Jones 1987).[17]

Our conclusion must then be that, rather than the Japanese case being one which provides a striking illustration of the liberal theory in action, as Tominaga would suggest, it has, on the contrary, to stand as an evident

---

[16] The β parameters estimated, with that for the oldest cohort being set at 0, are then for the three succeeding cohorts 0.23, 0.21, and 0.28. For mobility from class origins to class of first employment, on the other hand, some indication does arise of fluidity moving down over the last three cohorts closer to the relatively low level of the first, the β parameters corresponding to the above being 0.14, 0.07, and 0.03. But here again the improvement in fit of the uniform-difference model over that of the CnSF model is far from significant.

[17] Kojima and Hamana (1984), using an eightfold occupational status classification, show that the CnSF model fits well to mobility tables derived from the 1975 Japanese enquiry and from two previous enquiries undertaken in 1955 and 1965. Iwamoto (1985) and Tokuyasu (1986) find that the fit ceases to be entirely acceptable if either a fivefold or a threefold collapse of the classification is used, but we have ourselves examined the 3 × 3 tables and find that the lack of fit comes largely from one source: a decline in the propensity for immobility among manual workers as between 1955 and 1965 *only*. Even if, then, one accepts this effect as being real, it is still scarcely sufficient evidence for claiming a *general* and *continuous* increase in fluidity within the post-war Japanese occupational structure. Yamaguchi (1987), comparing results from the 1955 and 1975 studies and applying various quasi-symmetric association models to a fivefold status categorization, reports decreasing inheritance effects but a general tendency for the association between origins and destinations in off-diagonal cells to increase. Finally, F. L. Jones (1987) concludes that the degree of openness of Japanese society did not increase significantly between 1955 and 1975—contrary to what he had suggested on the basis of an earlier, but flawed, analysis (Jones 1981).

embarrassment to this theory. Over the middle decades of the twentieth century, and in the post-war years especially, Japan did indeed experience rapid industrial development, and with a concomitant transformation of many aspects of its pre-industrial society. Yet analyses of mobility data that relate to this same period reveal a large underlying constancy—and certainly point to no overall weakening—in the net association existing between class of origin and class of destination. The greater openness or, that is, greater equality in relative mobility chances which, according to the liberal theory, advancing industrialism should engender has in the Japanese case rather conspicuously failed to occur. It is thus, in this connection, of interest to recall the argument advanced by Dore that the emphasis on educationally mediated 'meritocracy' in Japanese society, *together with* the determination and capacity of more advantaged families to ensure that their children are suitably 'credentialled', could result in 'a *hereditary entrenchment* of the class division of Japanese society' (1975: 778; emphasis in original).

Our supplementary analyses can, therefore, serve only to underline our rejection of the 'exceptionalist' positions that Nakane and Tominaga may be taken to represent—so far, that is, as issues of social fluidity are concerned. We may in this respect say for Japan, as we did previously for the United States and Australia, that it does not differ any more from the European nations that we have examined than they do among themselves. The results we have reported provide, to be sure, further instances of variation on the core pattern of social fluidity that we have sought to model, but they give no indication that Japan shares in this pattern to a distinctively lesser degree than other industrial nations.

ABSOLUTE RATES IN JAPAN

In considering the issues raised by the arguments of Nakane and Tominaga, it is in fact relative rates of mobility that carry greatest relevance. None the less, it remains here of interest to examine absolute rates also. Our finding that the Japanese pattern of social fluidity cannot in itself be regarded as exceptional does not of course rule out the possibility that at the level of absolute rates the Japanese experience might still diverge significantly from the European. For this to be the case, what would be necessary would be for some marked degree of distinctiveness to exist in the structural context of mobility; and we may, therefore, begin by asking if this is indeed to be found.

In Table 10.3 we report, alongside corresponding European ranges, the distributions of origin and destination classes of the men in our Japanese sample, and the Δ for the difference between these distributions. It is at once apparent that Japan stands rather apart. The Δ of 42 for the Japanese distributions is greater than that for any European nation (or than those for the United States and Australia); and it may further be noted (cf. Table 6.2)

TABLE 10.3. *Distributions of respondents to the Japanese mobility enquiry, men aged 20–64, by class of origin and destination, and corresponding ranges for European nations (% by column)*

	Class of origin		Class of destination	
	JAP	European range	JAP	European range
I+II	14	6–14	24	14–28
III	6	2– 9	16	2–10
IVa+b	24	3–14	13	2–10
IVc	41	5–53	10	1–25
V+VI	6	14–39	20	20–37
VIIa	6	12–26	14	18–30
VIIb	3	3–22	3	1–14

Δs for origin and destination distributions

JAP = 42, European range, 13–37

that the highest European Δ of 37 is that for Hungary, which is clearly influenced by massive political intervention in the organization of agriculture, while the next highest, that for Poland, falls to 30. Moreover, the discrepancies revealed in Table 10.3 between the class origins and destinations of our Japanese respondents may be seen as reflecting more than simply the decline of agricultural classes and the growth in turn of industrial working-class and then of white-collar positions, as on the characteristic European pattern. They also show the experience of a transition made from a society based largely on small proprietorship, outside as well as within agriculture—two-thirds of all respondents had fathers in either Class IVa+b or Class IVc—to a society predominantly of employees, blue collar and white collar alike, It may, however, be further noted that, within the Japanese class destination distribution, both Class IVa+b and Class III, that of routine non-manual employees, are larger than in any of our European nations, while the size of Class V+VI, skilled industrial workers, is on the lower limit of the European range and that of Class VIIa, non-skilled workers, falls below it.

Another perspective on the structural context of Japanese mobility is provided by the parameters for structural shift effects that we can estimate under the Japanese variant of our model of core fluidity. It will be recalled from the previous chapter that, when we considered such effects under our US and Australian variant models, the European ranges, as earlier shown in Table 6.5, were in only one (Australian) instance exceeded. However, with the Japanese shift effects, we find that four fall outside the European range and that two others are on the edge. More importantly, these deviations reflect the fact that the Japanese model implies shift effects that have a quite

different pattern overall from that which emerges from our European
models. We noted in Chapter 6 that for all our European nations alike shift
effects favoured mobility into the service class over that into any other class,
while mobility into the two farm classes was consistently least favoured, with
the ordering of the other classes showing some amount of cross-national
variation. But in the Japanese case, as can be seen from Table 10.4, it is in
fact Class V+VI into which mobility is structurally most favoured, followed
by Class III and then by Class VIIa—with the service class, Class I+II,
coming in only fourth position. It should, though, be also observed from
Table 10.4 that the differences in shift effects among these four classes are
quite small, and that the major contrast arises between these classes, on the
one hand, and the three remaining classes, on the other: that is, the two
agricultural classes, IVc and VIIb together with the petty bourgeoisie, IVa+b.

TABLE 10.4. *Differences in shift parameters estimated under national variant model
for Japan (in logged odds form)*

	III	IVa+b	IVc	V+VI	VIIa	VIIb
I+II	−0.7	1.3	3.5	−0.9	−0.3	1.3
III		2.0	4.2	−0.3	0.3	2.0
IVa+b			2.2	−2.2	−1.6	0.0
IVc				−4.5	−3.9	−2.2
V+VI					0.6	2.3
VIIa						1.7

We can, therefore, say that the class-structural context of Japanese
mobility *does* display major features that are not found among our European
nations; and thus the question obviously arises of how far in fact some
correspondingly distinctive pattern of absolute mobility rates is in this way
produced.

In Table 10.5 we show for Japan the same summary measures of absolute
mobility that we have previously presented for European nations (Table
6.3) and also for the United States and Australia (Table 9.4). It can be seen

TABLE 10.5. *Decomposition of total mobility rates* (TMR) *into total non-vertical*
(TNV) *and total vertical* (TV) *mobility and of total vertical mobility into total upward*
(TU) *and total downward* (TD) *mobility for Japan and ranges for European nations*

Nation	TMR	TV	TNV	TV/TNV	TU	TD	TU/TD
JAP	73	50	23	2.2	39	12	3.3
European range	58–76	39–54	13–32	1.4–3.9	30–42	8–18	1.8–4.5

that, so far at least as these measures are concerned, Japan is in no way exceptional, even though, like the United States and Australia, it has a total mobility rate that comes towards the 'high' end of the European range. This is, in turn, associated with fairly high total vertical and total upward mobility, but it is evident that Japan could still not from this point of view, any more than in terms of social fluidity, be regarded as *the* land of opportunity. If Japanese distinctiveness at the level of absolute mobility exists, it has then to be sought in more specific, inflow and outflow rates.

In examining such rates for Japan, as against the European experience, we use the same graphical method as we did in considering the US and Australian cases. Figures 10.1 and 10.2 show the position of Japanese inflow and outflow rates respectively in relation to the European ranges earlier depicted in Figures 6.1 and 6.2. In the previous chapter we found that, although US and Australian inflow and outflow rates were not entirely contained within the European ranges, departures from these ranges were still in almost all instances quite small. From inspection of Figures 10.1 and 10.2, however, it is readily apparent that with Japan a different situation obtains: the Japanese data can scarcely be regarded as assimilable to the European pattern. For as many as nineteen of the forty-nine inflow rates represented in the first figure and sixteen of the outflow rates represented in the second, the Japanese values fall outside the European range and, not infrequently, by a widish margin.

In more detail, Figure 10.1 reveals that, of the nineteen instances of outlying Japanese inflow rates, five are ones in which inflow from Class IV$a+b$, that of the petty bourgeoisie, are greater than in any European nation, and that a further eleven are ones in which inflows from Class V + VI or Class VIIa, the two divisions of the industrial working class, are less. Of the sixteen outlying outflow rates in Figure 10.2, five prove to be ones in which outflows to Class III, that of routine non-manual employees, are above the European range, and seven more are ones in which outflows to either Class V + VI or Class VIIa are below this range. From this and other of the information contained in Figures 10.1 and 10.2 a number of further implications can then be traced for the formation, or 'reproduction', of classes in modern Japanese society and, especially, as regards the service class and the working class.

The Japanese service class is, to begin with, quite clearly set apart from those of European nations in the pattern of its recruitment. As well as comprising an exceptional proportion of men of urban petty-bourgeois origins, it tends also to recruit heavily from among the sons of farmers. Thus, of men found in Class I + II within the Japanese sample, as many as 55 per cent reported fathers who were engaged in proprietorship or self-employment of some kind—which may be set against a European range of only 12–38 per cent. Offsetting this is the very limited degree to which the Japanese service class includes men of working-class origins: only 10 per cent of its members

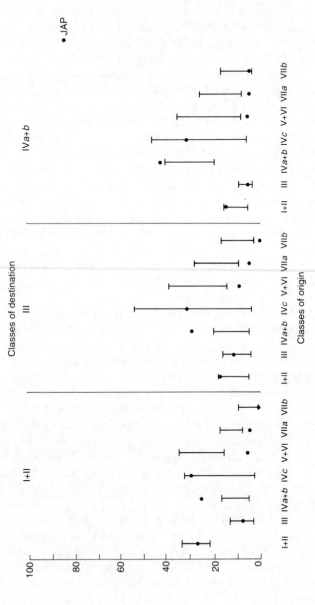

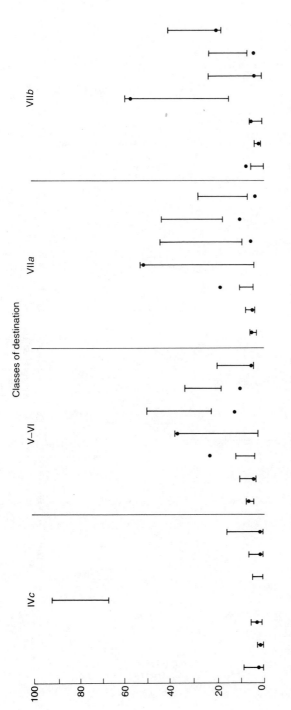

FIGURE 10.1. *European ranges of inflow rates and position of Japanese rates*

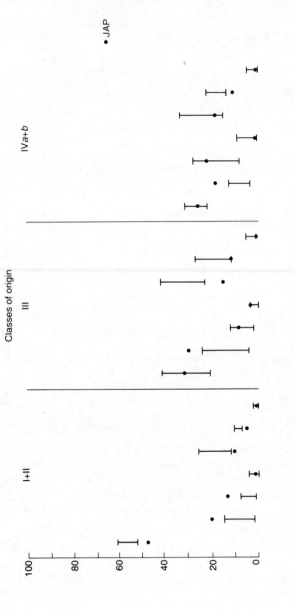

Classes of origin

Classes of destination

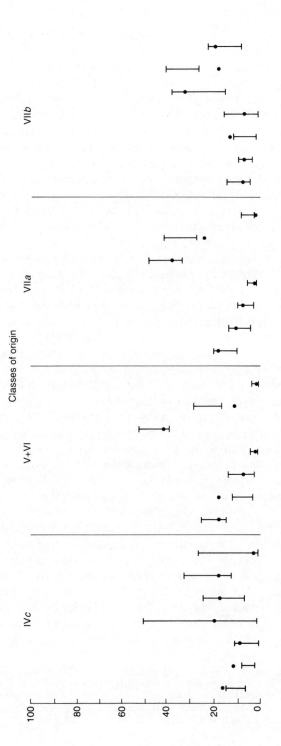

FIGURE 10.2. *European ranges of outflow rates and position of Japanese rates*

had fathers in Classes V+VI and VIIa, as compared with 28–49 per cent among our European nations.

At the same time, the intergenerational stability of the Japanese service class proves to be unusually low: only 47 per cent of the sons of service-class fathers are themselves found in service-class positions, as against a European range of 52–67 per cent. However, if, for reasons noted earlier we regard Class III as being more closely associated with Class I+II in Japan than in most of our European nations, a rather different conclusion is suggested. Intergenerational stability within the 'white-collar' bloc which is constituted by Classes I+II and III together turns out to be quite high in Japan: 65 per cent of the sons of white-collar fathers are found in white-collar positions and only 19 per cent in the working-class positions of Classes V+VI and VIIa—which may be compared with the corresponding European ranges of 52–64 per cent and 28–43 per cent respectively.[18]

Turning then to the Japanese working class, that is, Classes V+VI and VIIa taken together, the feature that most obviously calls for comment is the very low level of its *self*-recruitment. In this respect, our European nations, as we have observed in Chapter 6, themselves show wide variation: the proportions of industrial workers who are the sons of industrial workers extends from 78 down to 39 per cent. However, the Japanese figure is lower still, at only 21 per cent. In just the same way as the service class, the Japanese working class is far more extensively recruited than would seem typical in Europe from among the sons of farmers *and* of the petty bourgeoisie: 65 per cent of men in Classes V+VI and VIIa in the Japanese sample were of Classes IVa+b or IVc origins as against a European range of 7–45 per cent.

Moreover, the Japanese working class also appears unusual in its low level of intergenerational stability. In our European nations, 61–73 per cent of the sons of working-class fathers were themselves found in working-class positions; but the corresponding figure for Japan is only 56 per cent. If, then, its low self-recruitment *and* its low stability are taken together, the 'social metabolism' of the Japanese working class must be reckoned as falling clearly outside the European experience. As against a white-collar bloc which, on a comparative view, would appear to have formed as a rather stable collectivity, the working class that has emerged in modern Japan must be said to have developed, up to the mid-1970s at least, only a rather weak 'demographic identity'. And it is, thus, a rather obvious speculation that if, as several investigators have claimed (cf. Murakami 1984; Tominaga, Naoi, and Imada n.d.: 19–21), only a low level of working-class consciousness

---

[18] Similar contrasts can here be drawn between Japan and the United States and Australia. It may, however, be noted that, as regards white-collar stability, one of our 'additional' European nations, Italy, comes closer to the Japanese pattern than any of the nine covered in our own data-set—with 67 per cent of the sons of white-collar fathers being themselves found in white-collar positions and only 22 per cent in working-class ones.

exists in Japan, alongside a relatively strong 'middle-strata consciousness', one source of this is the small proportion of manual workers who could be regarded, in Sorokin's terms (1927/1959: 439), as being *both* 'hereditary' *and* 'lifetime proletarians'.[19]

Here, therefore, at the 'phenotypical' level of absolute, inflow and outflow, rates, if not at the 'genotypical' level of social fluidity, a case for Japanese distinctiveness may indeed be made out: the Japanese pattern can, at all events, be seen to diverge quite substantially from the European. And, for the most part, the differences are in fact on lines that would be expected from our previous discussion of the Japanese class-structural context. Thus, inflows from petty-bourgeois origins and outflows to routine non-manual positions tend to be greater than in our European nations, while inflows from and outflows to both divisions of the working class tend to be less— although in this latter case, it should be noted, favourable shift effects are offset by limited size. None the less, it remains of interest to enquire more directly into the importance of the structural context in shaping the distinct- iveness of Japanese inflow and outflow rates—as against any influence that might still derive from variation in fluidity.

To this end, we may resort again to the counterfactual method that we introduced in Chapter 6: that is, we may create the Japanese mobility table as it would appear if, while its marginal distributions remained unchanged, the underlying pattern of fluidity was exactly as specified by our core model. We can then compare inflow and outflow rates calculated from this table with the rates actually observed and, further, use the counterfactual rates to repeat the comparison with European ranges.

Following this procedure, what we find is, first of all, that counterfactual and observed rates do not differ all that widely in the Japanese case—any more than they did among our European nations: with only one inflow distribution (for Class VII*b*) and two outflow distributions (for Classes I+II and VIIb) does a Δ of 10 per cent or more arise. And, in turn, when we set the Japanese counterfactual rates against European ranges—whether actual or themselves counterfactual on the premiss that core fluidity prevails—the pattern of Japanese inflow and outflow rates still appears distinctive, and in essentially the same way as we have already described it. In no significant respect does our previous commentary require revision.[20]

---

[19] The Australian working class shows an even lower figure for intergenerational stability than the Japanese at only 50 per cent but, on the other hand, is also 50 per cent self-recruited. A question of obvious interest here is, then, that of how far the Japanese working class can be seen as conforming in its 'mobility characteristics' to those that we suggested in Chapter 6 might be regarded as typical. A satisfactory answer to this question would, however, require work-life mobility data, which we do not presently have available for Japan.

[20] For example, comparing the Japanese counterfactual rates against the actual European ranges, one finds that now actually twenty-one rather than nineteen Japanese inflows lie outside these ranges, while thirteen rather than sixteen outflows do so.

We may thus find confirmation here both that the peculiarities in the Japanese pattern of social fluidity that emerged from the application of our core model in the preceding section *are* reasonably treated as no more than rather slight variations on a common theme and, at the same time, that these peculiarities have little at all to do with the features of interest in Japanese absolute rates that we have subsequently demonstrated. The latter, we can now say, derive, more or less exclusively, from the shape, and from changes in the shape, of the Japanese class structure over the period to which our mobility data refer. And any deeper understanding of Japanese distinctiveness in this respect must, therefore, depend not on our analysis of social fluidity but rather on such accounts as we can offer of the course that this structural development has followed.

In Chapter 6 we argued that, while differences in the structural contexts of mobility among our European nations might in some part be open to explanation in general terms—for example, as aspects of different trajectories of industrialism or 'patterns of growth'—the limits of such explanation were still rather apparent. A wide variety of historically specific influences were also typically involved. Consideration of the Japanese case gives us little reason to alter this view.

Again, it is true that 'patterns-of-growth' analysis can provide some insights. Most obviously, perhaps, if we treat Japan as falling into a further category of nations experiencing 'late-but-rapid' industrialization, we can in this way account for the relatively small size of the Japanese working class as compared with that of its white-collar classes. As a twentieth-century 'latecomer' to the industrial world, Japan had the advantage of being able to take over advanced, labour-saving technology, in manufacturing industry especially, and was thus able to 'catch up' with the level of economic development achieved by European nations without ever needing the numbers of industrial workers that they had once required (cf. Singelmann 1978; Gagliani 1985).[21] And as, then, rising productivity also released labour from the land, a greater proportion of this surplus than in European nations was available for transfer into non-manual rather than manual employment, prompting, in fact, a rather precocious growth of large industrial and commercial bureaucracies (Dore 1973; Cole and Tominaga 1976: 76–82). However, just as with our European nations, so it would seem essential in the Japanese case also to recognize influences bearing on the class structure that are of a more specific kind than 'patterns-of-growth' analysis can capture.

---

[21] It should, however, be noted that the figures given in Table 10.3 are likely to exaggerate somewhat the differences involved, in that they refer only to men, while at least in the early decades of the twentieth century the Japanese industrial work-force comprised unusually large numbers of women—especially young unmarried women from farm families (cf. Saxenhouse 1976).

Thus, for example, the still relatively large size of the Japanese petty bourgeoisie reflects the survival, to a greater extent in Japan than in most Western industrial societies, of small-scale businesses alongside large-scale organizations, and within the manufacturing as well as the services sector of the economy (cf. Hara 1979; Patrick and Rohlen 1987). This much-discussed 'dualism' in Japanese industrial structure may in part be explained by the continuing high demand in Japanese society for traditional as well as for modern consumer goods (cf. Morishima 1982: 101–23); but more important, it would seem, is the extent to which small firms are involved in symbiotic relationships with larger ones through complex systems of subcontracting, initiated and sustained by the latter as a strategy for achieving greater operating flexibility, which draw on and at the same time sustain cultural traditions of family-based enterprise (Broadbridge 1966; Nishiguchi 1990).

Likewise, the unusually large numbers of men found in Japan in the routine non-manual positions of our Class III would appear to result not only from the pattern of Japanese economic growth but further from certain rather distinctive aspects of Japanese managerial practice. We have, in fact, already referred to the use of clerical work as a training period, of often quite lengthy duration, for recruits intended eventually for higher-level positions. But, relatedly, Japanese employers would appear to have been less ready than their Western counterparts, at least up to the mid-1970s, to accept, or to promote, the general 'feminization' of clerical or even routine sales work, with the result that at least some lower-level non-manual positions have tended to remain largely male preserves (cf. Cole and Tominaga 1976: 74–5; Shirahase 1989: chs. 3, 7).[22]

We are then led to conclude on the following lines. In so far as modern Japanese society does possess features that set it apart from the industrial societies of the Western world, their effects on mobility rates and patterns are for the most part exerted not *directly*, that is, on the Japanese mobility regime itself, but rather *indirectly* through the way in which, together with the unique course of Japanese economic history, they give distinctive shape to the structural context within which this regime operates.

In the previous chapter we considered, and found empirically unconvincing, various arguments that sought to represent the United States or Australia as having societies with exceptionally high rates of mobility, in comparison at least with those of 'older' European societies. In this chapter we have examined exceptionalist arguments advanced in the case of Japan, to the effect either that it is now Japan that should be seen as the nation furthest

---

[22] It may be added here that the 1975 Japanese enquiry did not cover women, but that a follow-up study undertaken in 1985 did so, and has been used by Shirahase (1989) in a comprehensive examination of women's mobility, in which analyses based on our class schema are included. As regards comparisons between women's and men's mobility, the results that Shirahase reports for Japan are very largely on the same lines as those we have reported for the majority of our European nations in Chapter 7.

advanced along the road towards the truly open society that the logic of industrialism is destined to create, or, in contrast, that Japan, despite its industrial development, still retains a form of social stratification that is *sui generis* and to which Western concepts and theories are inappropriate.

Once more, our empirical results have proved generally negative. The application of our model of core social fluidity to Japanese mobility data indicates that Japan does not deviate from the core pattern to any greater degree than do the European nations in our study—and certainly does not show any exceptional degree of openness; and further, since the model is capable of reproducing the Japanese data to the extent in question, this would in turn suggest that the ideas of class, and of class advantages and barriers, that it embodies are not ones quite alien to Japanese society but are in fact capable of capturing important aspects of its contemporary reality.

At the same time, though, our examination of Japanese absolute mobility rates, as viewed in inflow and outflow perspective, reveals marked departures from the European experience—and, it may be added, of a kind that previous analyses of Japanese mobility, even when undertaken within the debate on Japanese uniqueness, have rather surprisingly failed to disclose. We have, of course, earlier sought to show, in critique of the LZ hypothesis, that our European nations themselves display wide variation in their absolute rates, and that this occurs primarily because—and in direct contradiction of the LZ hypothesis—the structural contexts for mobility have not tended to become standardized from one industrial society to another. The main significance of the Japanese case lies then, in our view, in the demonstration it provides that, as one moves beyond the European cultural sphere, *this* variation can become wider still. Even if, as more nations industrialize outside this sphere, they do not breach the broad similarity in relative rates that we would believe is established at the 'genotypical' level, one could still expect to see at the 'phenotypical' level patterns of absolute rates of previously unobserved and perhaps highly divergent kinds.

11
Conclusions and Prospects

In this final chapter we seek first of all to give a summary account of the most important empirical findings to which we have been led in the course of this study, and at the same time to place them in their appropriate theoretical context. We have in fact attempted, as we have gone along, to note where our findings would appear to support, qualify, or undermine various of the theories of mobility in industrial society that we reviewed in our introductory chapter. Here, however, we shall proceed by taking each theory, or type of theory, in turn and by examining how well each fares in the light of the full range of evidence bearing upon it that we can assemble from our previous analyses.

A further, and more ambitious, aim of the chapter is then to consider the implications of our findings, not just for specific theories of mobility but, more widely, for the general prospects for comparative macrosociology in this area of enquiry. As was noted in Chapter 2, one widely held view is that the prime objective of comparative macrosociology must be to demonstrate differences in aspects of social structure or process across national societies and then to account for these differences through analyses in which, while nations serve as the basic units, the names of nations are, so far as possible, replaced by the names of variables. Such a programme must, however, rest on the assumption that the cross-national differences that are of interest are systematic ones, in the sense that they are, at least in principle, open to explanation by reference to variation in other societal attributes—of, presumably, a relatively limited and a more 'fundamental' kind. The issue does, therefore, arise of the extent to which, in any particular instance, this assumption is valid or is at all events one which could, on heuristic grounds, be reasonably maintained.

As regards absolute rates of class mobility, the results we have reported rather powerfully indicate that the cross-national variation that is displayed is *not* for the most part systematic in the above sense, and hence would seem unlikely to prove a very rewarding *explanandum* for macrosociological enquiry. As regards variation in relative rates, our findings point, at all events in our interpretation of them, to a conclusion of a rather similar kind. But here, we would acknowledge, the issue is clearly more debatable. Thus, in the second section of the chapter we report on an attempt to put the matter further to test, so far as this is possible, by actually undertaking a multivariate analysis of differences in at least one aspect of fluidity across the nations that our study has comprised.

In the outcome, the results of this analysis do not lead us to modify our position to any major extent, and in the third and final section of the chapter we seek to make out the case for some redirection of effort in the comparative study of mobility. We argue that, whatever in fact is the conclusion reached on the *nature* of variation in relative rates, its *extent* is sufficiently limited to point up the inadequacy of any macrosociology that would concentrate attention on this variation alone, to the neglect of the large measure of similarity that underlies it. The challenge of attempting to account for the degree of cross-national commonality that prevails in relative rates—and indeed for their tendency towards invariance in other respects also—cannot be avoided. We recognize the lack of paradigms and techniques for such an undertaking, but we aim at all events to provide some speculations and suggestions to help signal the problems that, in our judgement, fruitful enquiry into comparative social mobility will in future need to address.

THEORIES OF SOCIAL MOBILITY REAPPRAISED

In Chapter 1 we began by outlining a series of arguments on rates and trends of social mobility in industrial societies that derived from—and that we saw as being crucial to—what we called the liberal theory of industrialism. Having noted that this theory was elaborated chiefly with the aim of countering Marxist interpretations of the development of capitalism, we then went on to consider such arguments concerning mobility as were to be found within the Marxist response to it—essentially, as it turned out, those associated with the revival of the theory of proletarianization. Subsequently, we reviewed claims stemming from two other types of theory: first, theories that, in some contrast with those of both liberals and Marxists, focused not on general developmental patterns in mobility but rather on what were taken to be persisting differences in mobility rates evident even among national societies at similar economic levels; and, secondly, theories that came into yet sharper conflict with ones of a developmental character in emphasizing the absence of mobility trends, at all events of a directional kind, and/or the extent of similarities in mobility rates existing across nations even at different developmental stages. Here, in seeking to make some final, overall assessment of these theories on the basis of our empirical results, we will take them in the same order as before.

The liberal theory

So far as mobility is concerned, the liberal theory holds that industrial societies are both more mobile and more open than pre-industrial ones; and, further, that, as industrial development proceeds, objective opportunity structures become more favourable and social selection processes more universalistic, so that absolute rates of mobility steadily rise, with an upward bias, and relative rates steadily become more equal. In this way, then, to the extent that nations draw closer to each other in their levels of industrial development, so too will their mobility patterns tend to converge.

In the main, the results that we have reported in this study fail to support these claims of the liberal theory, and indeed go contrary to them to a degree that must bring the general cogency of the theory into serious doubt. First of all, the analyses we present in Chapter 3 of the experience of men in nine European nations provide no evidence of steadily increasing total inter-generational mobility—for a period in which the industrial development of these nations went ahead with, for the most part, no more than short-term interruptions and in which, moreover, all shared in the unprecedentedly high rates of economic growth of the long boom that followed on the Second World War. Over the years covered by our data, total mobility rates in fact move in what would appear to be an essentially directionless fashion. It is true that our results cannot preclude, and in the cases of Ireland and Poland might be taken as consistent with, the possibility that an upturn in total mobility occurs at some critical stage within the industrialization process—in the period, say, when the decline in agriculture is at its most precipitous. But even if we accept this possibility, what is implied is a once-and-for-all 'threshold' effect, of the kind suggested by Lipset and Zetterberg, rather than an effect that an inherent logic of industrialism serves to sustain over the long term, so that a secular trend of rising mobility is produced.

Secondly, we also fail to find evidence for our European nations of either convergent rates of absolute mobility or of steadily increasing rates of upward movement. The intergenerational outflow rates that we consider—including those of men from farm and working-class origins moving up into the ranks of the service class—for the most part fluctuate in a way similar to total rates, and only occasionally reveal consistent trends. Liberal expectations could be taken as to some extent borne out by our further finding, reported in Chapter 6, that in all nations in our sample upward mobility is, overall, more frequent than downward. But, contrary to these expectations, we also discover that this predominance of upward mobility is most marked in our *least* developed nations—that is, Hungary, Ireland, and Poland— chiefly because rates of downward mobility are highest in those economically more advanced nations in which an 'upgraded' class structure has been ✓ longest established.

Thirdly, our analyses of mobility in European nations do not in general support the idea that in industrial societies relative rates tend to become progressively more equal, so as to imply a growing social fluidity or openness. Our findings would indicate, rather, that relative rates possess a high degree of temporal stability. Where shifts do occur, they appear usually to follow no consistent direction and to be of very slight extent, at all events in comparison with the magnitude of the changes that are to be observed in absolute rates. Moreover, in this respect the results that we can add for our non-European nations tell further against the liberal theory. In Chapter 9 we show that there is little basis for regarding the United States as being a 'vanguard' nation that displays a distinctively high degree of social fluidity as a correlate of its economic pre-eminence, even if some tendency towards greater fluidity may be discerned over recent decades. And in Chapter 10 we show that in Japan, a nation which could claim to have achieved a more rapid and successful industrialization than any other, relative rates have remained remarkably little altered over the period of its economic transformation. Finally, our view of patterns of social fluidity as displaying considerable stability over time is also upheld by our examination in Chapter 7 of the mobility experience of women. Whether we consider women's intergenerational mobility via their own employment or via marriage, we find very few instances of significant directional change in their relative chances.

In sum, if our evidence on absolute rates goes almost entirely contrary to arguments deriving from the liberal theory, that on relative rates appears scarcely more congenial. In this latter respect, the very most that could be said for the theory is that, in those few cases where our own findings do point to a steady trend over time and are confirmed by those of other, independent studies—that is, in the cases of men in Hungary and, more arguably, in the United States and Sweden—this trend is in fact towards greater openness. However, the preponderance of counter-examples must be taken to mean that, even if those processes seen by liberal theorists as making for increased social fluidity do indeed operate, they are none the less regularly opposed and offset by other processes also at work within industrial societies, so that, more often than not, the expected tendency towards greater openness actually fails to materialize.[1] In other words, the logic of industrialism, even if we suppose that it exists, is clearly not all-powerful. Other 'logics' must also be taken into account, among which, we would suggest, one of the most obvious and important is that of the differential advantage and power that is inherent in class structures. Thus, while the functional requirements of industrialism may best be served through the development of more universalistic, achievement-oriented processes of social selection, the members of more advantaged and powerful classes can be expected still to try to maintain ascriptive elements in such processes, precisely so that they can use the superior resources they possess in order to improve the life-chances of their children. And there is then nothing whatever in the liberal theory to explain why, in the face of such opposing action, the logic of industrialism should necessarily prevail.[2]

[1] We may here reiterate that our findings of no trend in relative rates, or at least of no trend in the direction of greater fluidity, are likewise corroborated by independent studies in those national cases where these are available—for example, England and Japan. And we may add that preliminary results from studies carried out in the 1980s in Ireland and in Poland would, in this respect, tend likewise to confirm our results (personal communications from Richard Breen and Christopher Whelan, and Henryk Domański and Zbigniew Sawiński).

[2] We have here another illustration of the weakness of functionalist theory in overlooking the need to specify a 'causal feedback loop' which we discuss further, pp. 392–3.

It is, in this connection, of interest to note that, of late, not only do exponents of the liberal theory appear to have more or less abandoned attempts to validate its claims in regard to absolute rates but further, in concentrating their efforts on relative rates, have modified their position quite significantly. Thus, for example, in an early statement Treiman provided the hypothesis of a trend towards greater openness with a rationale very largely in terms of the functional exigencies of industrialism (1970: 218). However, in a more recent paper (with Yip (1989)), he puts much stronger emphasis on the part that is played in creating greater openness and equality of opportunity by the more proximate factor of greater *equality of condition*—that is, by a greater equality in the economic, cultural, and social resources that families possess. And, while it is still maintained that this increase in equality of condition itself ultimately derives from the development of industrialism, it is at the same time accepted that 'industrialization and inequality do not move in perfect concert' and, further, that *other* factors, especially political ones—for example, whether a nation has a socialist regime—may also affect the degree of inequality that exists (Treiman and Yip 1989: 376–7). That is to say, it would here seem to be recognized that, even in cases where a trend towards greater fluidity may be empirically established, this cannot be regarded as simply a matter of developmental necessity but must rather be explained as the contingent outcome of quite complex patterns of social action. And, conversely, this revised, and evidently much weaker, position is then, of course, able to accommodate the alternative possibility that, in particular instances, no trend of this kind is observed—because countervailing forces have in fact proved too strong.[3]

The Marxist response

The Marxist response to the liberal theory was chiefly based upon a direct challenge to the claim that the logic of industrialism entailed a progressive upgrading of employment, and hence of class structures. Against this claim, a new version of the theory of proletarianization was developed which contended that, under the exigencies of modern capitalism, a widespread deskilling and degrading of employment occurred, leading in turn to an expanded proletariat within which were found substantial numbers of non-skilled and entirely subordinate non-manual, as well as manual workers. So far, then, as class mobility was concerned, the main expectation was for

---

[3] This would also appear to be the position adopted by Ganzeboom, Luijkx, and Treiman (1989). Furthermore, a position even closer to our own is found in a paper by Simkus *et al.* (1990)—of which Treiman is a co-author. Here, the conclusion reached is that it is a mistake to try to test hypotheses about effects of national attributes on mobility using 'arbitrary rates or highly aggregated data' and that we cannot make 'simple assumptions about cross-national differences in mobility on the basis of differences in a single variable or attribute'. True stories may be told about, say, the consequences of industrialization or of socialism in particular cases: 'But, the closer we look at what has happened, the more the one-liners lose their punch' (1990: 72).

larger downward rather than larger upward flows, in consequence of the steady deterioration in opportunity structures that advancing capitalism entails.

However, as we already observed in Chapter 1, the new theory of proletarianization was never able to find convincing empirical support and, eventually, was abandoned even by some of those who had been among its leading exponents.[4] It cannot, then, be thought especially surprising that our own results should prove largely inimical to it. Even though our analyses of mobility trends do not provide evidence of any general and consistent increase in rates of upward mobility, neither do they point to any such increase in downward movement, at least so far as men are concerned; and indeed, among those represented in our various national samples, the experience of social ascent has clearly been more common than that of *déclassement* of any kind. Moreover, results reported in Chapter 6 and likewise in Chapter 8 underline the need for the significance of mobility into routine non-manual employment to be carefully interpreted, and especially where this occurs at a relatively early age. Thus, initial downward mobility into such employment from service-class origins is often followed by 'counter-mobility' back to a service-class position; while, for men of other class origins, entry into routine non-manual jobs appears frequently to serve as a starting-point for trajectories of upward mobility achieved over the course of their working lives.

Finally, in this connection, we may also recall that where, in Chapter 6 and subsequently, we have estimated parameters for structural shift effects from our national variant models of social fluidity, a notable uniformity has been apparent in our results. For all nations but one—Japan—such effects actually favour intergenerational mobility into the professional, administrative, and managerial positions of the service class over mobility into any other class, including, that is, those comprising routine non-manual or non-skilled manual positions.

In so far as the new theory of proletarianization was able to retain a degree of credibility, it was in a restricted version that related specifically to women. While men's mobility opportunities might appear to have been improved by upgrading, it could be argued, this was in large part because it was women entering the labour market who were predominantly channelled into the expanding forms of low-grade work. In this way, therefore, a new female proletariat was being created, which, from a socio-political standpoint, more than offset the decline in the numbers of male wage-workers.

From results that we report in Chapter 7, this position might be seen as deriving some support: it is indeed the case that, in all the nations we consider, women are more likely than men to experience downward mobility

---

[4] Here, again, one might suggest, the theory was betrayed by implicit functionalist assumptions: the supposed 'necessity' for the (net) degrading of work under the 'logic' of late capitalism simply failed to operate.

from their class origins—provided, that is, that we take their 'present' class position as being determined by their own employment. However, if this procedure is followed, we then further show that serious difficulties must be recognized, and especially from a Marxist position, so far as married women are concerned. With the latter, both their class identification and their political partisanship tend to be more strongly associated with the class character of their husband's employment than of their own. And, since, therefore, many women in low-grade work, and especially among those of more advantaged class origins, are in fact married to men in professional, administrative, or managerial employment, large numbers of the supposed female proletariat turn out to display decidedly unproletarian socio-political orientations. This finding can, of course, be explained—or explained away —in terms of massive 'false consciousness'. But it is, in our view, more realistically understood as indicating that these women have not in fact experienced downward class mobility in the way that the theory of proletarianization would imply, and that, whatever dissatisfaction with their work and with gender inequalities in employment they may feel, this is most unlikely to find expression in radical *class* action of any kind.

A different perspective is obtained, we may add, if we follow our own preferred way of bringing women's class mobility within the scope of our analysis: that is, by retaining the idea of the conjugal family as the unit of class composition and by then determining the class position of such families via the 'dominance' approach. The 'complete' mobility tables that we are able to construct on this basis for certain of our European nations do not give widely divergent results from those of 'men-only' tables. However, the size of service classes is enlarged as a result of the inclusion of families 'headed' by women in service-class employment and, chiefly for this reason, we then find that rates of upward mobility become in all cases somewhat higher.

Theories of cross-national variation in mobility

Theories of cross-national variation in mobility—or what may in some cases be little more than *ad hoc* hypotheses to this effect—reflect a belief that, even within the context of advanced industrialism, significant differentiating forces may still operate on social structures and processes, in particular, the forces of national culture and of politics.

The culturalist position has most often been expressed in the claim that a particular nation displays an 'exceptional' degree of mobility and openness on account of a distinctive historical experience that is reflected both in popular beliefs and values and in the character of its institutions. In this form, at least, culturalist arguments can derive little encouragement from our analyses. In Chapter 9 we have investigated in some detail the exceptionalist case for the United States, and also that for another 'new nation', Australia; in Chapter 10 we have further examined the possibility that, by the second half of the twentieth century, it is Japan that has emerged as the pre-eminent 'land of opportunity'. However, the conclusions that we reach are consistently negative. Although the results we report for the nations in question would place them towards the more mobile and fluid end of the range of variation displayed by our European nations, they do not in any significant respects suggest that they lie outside this range. And we have argued that, with data of a higher standard of comparability, the United States might indeed prove to be another 'central' rather than an exceptional case. Furthermore, in considering our European nations themselves, we find no support for the exceptionalist claims that have been made for Scotland, on the basis of its traditions of meritocracy, or for the FRG, on the basis of the cultural 'break' of 1945. Nor, we may add, do we find, on the other hand, any evidence to sustain Olson's hypothesis, stemming from his more general theory of social rigidities, that England has become a highly 'sclerotic' society on account of its freedom from major upheavals that might have disturbed the accumulation of privilege and organized power.

We could, therefore, say that arguments for culturally induced differentiation in mobility rates and patterns are at all events easily overstated, and we may suspect that they have more often served the cause of national mythologies than that of reliable description. At the same time, though, it is also the case that we have produced results which would indicate that to dismiss cultural influences entirely would be to go too far. In particular, in Chapter 5 and subsequently, where we have sought to account for the lack of fit of our model of common social fluidity to mobility tables for particular nations and to develop appropriate variants, we have on several occasions been led to recognize the persisting—even if quantitatively quite minor—effects of national culture on fluidity, and especially as mediated through institutional forms. Thus, what is in our view the most striking feature of the German case is the way in which, despite the political and supposed cultural disjuncture that followed on the Second World War, the mobility chances of men in the FRG in the post-war period can still be seen to display the mark of distinctive national institutions, the origins of which lie decades or even centuries in the past. But what has then further to be emphasized is that, both in the German case and in others where we have suggested that cultural influences play some part in shaping the detail of mobility regimes—for example, Hungary, Ireland, Northern Ireland, or Japan—these influences are to be seen not as making for generally greater or less openness, as exceptionalist arguments would envisage, but rather for patterns of fluidity that simply *differ* from those of other nations in certain quite specific respects.

As regards the possible effect of political intervention on variation in mobility, the argument we have been able to examine most fully is that developed chiefly by Parkin, which holds that societies under state socialist rule can be expected to show greater mobility than capitalist societies and, especially, higher rates of mobility of a long-range kind. Once more, our findings must, taken as a whole, be regarded as unsupportive. In Chapter 3 we note that, for each of the state socialist societies that we consider, the rate of upward mobility into service-class positions does rise quite sharply among the cohorts of men who reached occupational maturity during the immediate post-war period of 'socialist reconstruction'—but that, with later cohorts, the rate then falls away.[5] And although, as seen in Chapter 6, Hungary records the highest total mobility rate for men in our national samples overall, neither its total upward rate nor that for Poland or for Czechoslovakia could be reckoned as at all outstanding. Furthermore, when in Chapter 5 we examine relative mobility rates, we find that, while our national variant model for Poland does suggest unusual fluidity between service-class and working-class positions, such a pattern is much less apparent for Czechoslovakia, despite a generally high degree of openness, and is certainly not present in the Hungarian case, where hierarchical effects are strong. In other words, rather than our three state socialist nations together displaying a distinctive type of mobility regime, they reveal quite considerable variation among themselves.

However, this does not, of course, imply that political influences on mobility are absent; and, just as with cultural influences, our results do in fact point to their operation. It is, in our view, highly likely that in our state socialist societies various aspects of both absolute and relative rates *are* the more-or-less direct outcome of political action, such as the collectivization of agriculture, the suppression or disprivileging of the urban petty bourgeoisie, or measures designed to reduce inequalities of both condition and opportunity between manual and non-manual workers. But the point that must then be stressed is that such policies were not necessarily pursued in the same way, with the same goals, or with the same degree of persistence or ultimate success from one society to another. And, thus, rather than the readiness and capacity of state socialist regimes to intervene in processes of stratification being associated with one characteristic pattern of mobility, this capacity has to be seen as a source of variation that more often proves to be of a nationally specific kind.

We have also noted the argument that among capitalist societies those in which social democratic parties have been politically dominant are likely to show a greater degree of openness than others. In this respect, though, we are obviously limited in the conclusions we may seek to draw by the fact that in only one of our nations, Sweden, could social-democratic dominance be claimed. Our evidence from this single case does in fact lend support to the argument, since, as we report in Chapter 5, fluidity would appear to be at a somewhat higher level in Sweden than in the other European capitalist societies we consider, and Swedish Social Democratic governments have, moreover, pursued policies aimed, in part at least, at promoting greater

[5] As remarked in Chapter 3 (n. 17), this tendency can be documented for Czechoslovakia as well as for Hungary and Poland.

openness (Erikson 1990). However, we would at the same time readily acknowledge the possibility of social democratic parties holding power over long periods but still failing to have, or even perhaps attempting to have, any influence on mobility at all. And here again, therefore, we would wish to recognize that political intervention may be a source of cross-national differences in mobility rates and patterns—but without it necessarily being the case that the variation thus created can be systematically related to regimes or governments of differing type.[6]

Theories of 'no trend' and of cross-national similarity in mobility

Exponents of theories of cross-national variation in mobility emphasize the part that specific cultural and political factors may play in offsetting supposedly standardizing tendencies implicit in industrialism. In contrast, exponents of theories of 'no trend' or of cross-national similarity give importance to processes influencing mobility which they see as operating more widely than within industrial societies alone. Thus, Sorokin rejected the claims already current in his own day that mobility rates were set on either an indefinitely increasing or a decreasing trend, and argued that, when a broad historical view was taken, all that was observable in such rates was 'trendless fluctuation'. This came about because, while all forms of social stratification had strong self-maintaining properties—and, if anything, an inherent long-term tendency to become more rigid—they were always open to disruption by economic or political upheavals, so that from time to time periods of rising mobility would occur.

Assuming that—as would seem clearly the case—Sorokin should here be taken as referring to, in our terminology, absolute rates, then his argument is one with which our results would appear to be largely consistent. Certainly, if we consider our graphs of trends in total mobility rates (Figure 3.3), and if we keep in mind both that the period here covered is, from Sorokin's standpoint, a relatively short one and that the curves are quite heavily smoothed (so that any underlying trend has chance to show up), 'trendless fluctuation' might indeed be thought an apt summary description.

The same could, moreover, be said for many of the graphs of outflow rates that we also depict. Only in one respect do we find it necessary to suggest some qualification to Sorokin's position. At least if mobility is viewed within a class-structural perspective, certain of our broadly defined outflows would seem identifiable as ones typical of industrialism—in the sense that these rates do appear to follow a similar course across industrial societies, in

---

[6] The possibility must also, of course, be recognized that relatively high levels of openness may be created, or at least maintained, in ways other than that of direct political intervention. This possibility is currently under investigation in the case of Hong Kong in research being carried out by Tak Wing Chan at Nuffield College, Oxford. For preliminary results see Chan (1991).

association with what, in Chapter 6, we have called the 'natural history' of different classes: for example, the long-term contraction of agricultural classes, the rise and then decline of industrial working classes, and the long-term expansion of the service class. However, since wide cross-national differences can, and do, occur in the timing of these structural changes within the process of industrialization and also in the speed at which they proceed and in their phasing relative to each other, it still remains implausible to suppose that the *overall* patterns of mobility that are found in particular nations at particular times are open to interpretation as ones 'characteristic' of successive developmental stages.

Sorokin's theoretical stance led him to maintain that mobility rates in the United States were unlikely to be at a generally higher level than those of European nations. Lipset and Zetterberg started from this argument, but then went clearly beyond Sorokin with the suggestion that all industrial societies would in fact be found to show quite similar mobility levels—at least, on the basis of broad outflow comparisons. We noted already in Chapter 1 that the LZ hypothesis was rather quickly confronted with contradictory empirical evidence; and our own results, as reported chiefly in Chapter 6, provide yet further disconfirmation. We are however, able to bring out, perhaps more clearly than before, just why it is that the LZ hypothesis fails. As we have seen, our results cannot rule out, and in some cases lend support to, Lipset's and Zetterberg's claim that, as nations industrialize, their mobility rates at some stage undergo a historic upward shift; and we can, moreover, provide some justification for Lipset's and Zetterberg's scepticism concerning major cross-national differences in openness, whether culturally or otherwise induced, and their sense of underlying forces making for constancy and commonality in this respect. But, at the same time, it becomes apparent from our analyses that Lipset's and Zetterberg's assumption that industrial societies will have more-or-less uniform occupational and class structures, and thus that structural effects on mobility will *also* be cross-nationally similar, is seriously mistaken. To the contrary, the structural contexts of mobility that are created by the development of industrial societies vary substantially—and so, in turn, then do their absolute mobility rates, and even if calculated at the rather crude level at which the LZ hypothesis is posed.

In this connection, our consideration of the Japanese case in Chapter 10 is of further relevance. Although we find no grounds for regarding Japan as being in any sense 'exceptional' at the level of relative rates, the Japanese pattern of absolute rates does to a significant extent lie outside the range of European experience—in consequence, that is, of a structural context that has formed in a quite distinctive way. And what is then suggested is that we should not suppose a tendency for structural effects on mobility to appear any more uniform as the history of world industrialism proceeds; rather, as more non-European nations pursue their own paths to industrial status, yet

wider variation in these effects would seem to be the most likely outcome.

The arguments of both Sorokin and Lipset and Zetterberg contain at least
an implicit distinction between endogenous and exogenous factors bearing
on mobility rates and patterns: the former being those inherent in or
inseparable from the phenomenon of social stratification itself; the latter,
those which operate only contingently. A notable feature of the reformulation of the LZ hypothesis which was advanced by Featherman, Jones, and
Hauser is then that this distinction is made explicit. While Lipset and
Zetterberg in effect treat as endogenous simply the mobility motivations
that stem from universal needs for ego protection or enhancement, Featherman, Jones, and Hauser—more in the spirit of Sorokin—put the emphasis
on processes of competition among individuals of differing social origins to
achieve, or avoid, particular destination positions among those that are
structurally available. Moreover, although these authors do not follow
Sorokin in suggesting that all forms of stratification possess an inherent
tendency to become more rigid, they do see 'endogenous mobility regimes'
as being characterized by a large measure of temporal stability; and they
then, of course, go on to hypothesize that it is at this level of relative rates,
rather than that of observed, absolute rates, that we should find a 'basic'
cross-national similarity also. Since modern societies appear not to differ
greatly in the pattern of socio-economic inequalities that are associated with
their work organizations and occupational structures, no great difference
should be expected either in inequalities of opportunity as indicated by
relative mobility chances. With absolute rates, in contrast, cross-national
differences are to be regarded as highly probable, for such rates reflect not
only the endogenous mobility regime that underlies them but, further, a
diversity of exogenous factors—economic, technological, demographic,
etc.—that shape the structural context within which this regime operates.

In the preceding chapters we have devoted a good deal of attention to the
FJH hypothesis, in part because it is that which stands in main opposition to
the liberal claim that more advanced industrial societies will show more
equal relative rates of mobility than those less advanced, but in part too
because of its own intrinsic interest. Like virtually all other investigators, we
have discovered that, if the hypothesis is represented by a model which
proposes an identical pattern of relative rates from nation to nation, it
cannot be accepted: significant cross-national variation in relative rates or,
in other words, in social fluidity quite clearly exists. However, we have
argued that to respond to this result by simply discarding the FJH hypothesis
risks making a serious sociological misjudgement. It has to be noted that, as
initially stated, the hypothesis does in fact claim only a 'basic', and not a
complete, similarity in relative rates; and if then such a basic similarity could
be meaningfully defined and empirically established, this would be a matter
of no little sociological importance.

In Chapter 4 we therefore develop a model of a 'core' pattern of social fluidity that we would envisage as generic to the class structures of industrial societies. In Chapter 5 we apply this model to intergenerational mobility tables for men in twelve European nations, and in Chapters 9 and 10 to such tables for three industrial nations outside Europe. We find that in each of the nations we consider the model is able to account for a substantial part of the association between class origins and destinations, and that the effects specified under it generally operate in line with our theoretical expectations, albeit with varying strength. It is, however, two further findings that we would see as being of greatest consequence.

First, although for most nations statistically—and often sociologically—significant deviations from our model of core fluidity do appear, these cannot be reckoned as ones of any great quantitative importance, at all events in a macrosocial perspective. This is best brought out by the counterfactual analyses that we introduce in Chapter 6. If we construct national mobility tables as they would be if the FJH hypothesis held *stricto sensu*, so that all corresponding odds ratios are cross-nationally identical—and in fact as expected under our core model—then absolute rates calculated from these tables only rarely differ from those calculated from *actual* tables to a degree that would be worthy of sociological comment.

Secondly, deviations from our model appear, in the interpretations we have offered, to be for the most part of a nationally specific rather than of a systematic kind. This is most obviously so in those cases where we have attributed the deviant aspects of fluidity to cultural factors or to other features of national societies that are open to explanation only in terms of their distinctive historical experience. In further cases where deviations have been seen as politically induced, a systematic effect might be claimed in the sense that it is through political intervention, utilizing the apparatus of a modern state, that a modification of the social processes underlying the core pattern of fluidity is most readily and perhaps most often effected. We have indeed argued that the FJH hypothesis could usefully be qualified so as to give explicit acknowledgement to this point. However, as we have also observed, our results from the nations we consider would further indicate that the objectives and the actual outcomes of political intervention are themselves quite variable, and even under regimes of similar character, so that to seek to gain insight into cross-national differences in fluidity patterns through the development of a politically based typology would scarcely appear a promising way ahead. Finally, here, we should also note that, as might be expected from our analyses of trends, our modelling of variation in fluidity patterns among our nations reveals little to suggest an association between level of fluidity and level of industrial development. Rather than believing that such variation will express nations' differing stages of advancement along a developmental path, we would rather regard the degree of temporal constancy that fluidity patterns display as reflecting the same constraints that underlie the degree of commonality that is apparent on a cross-national view.

In the light of these findings, we are then led to the conclusion that the possibility does exist of construing the FJH hypothesis in a way which has sociological substance and at the same time a good measure of empirical support. The 'basic similarity' in relative mobility rates claimed in the original wording can, we suggest, be taken as referring to the presence of a broad cross-national commonality in such rates, deviations from which are neither so substantial that the commonality ceases to be recognizable, nor yet so systematic that they can be accounted for in terms of variation in other societal attributes so as to create the possibility of a comprehensive understanding of similarity and variation alike.

Because of the, perhaps disturbingly, heterodox character of this conclusion and of its wider implications, we shall return to it, and subject it to further examination, in the following section of this chapter. But to complete the present review, we may recall certain other results from our previous analyses that are at all events consonant with what might be regarded as the key idea informing the FJH hypothesis: namely, that mobility processes within the class structures of industrial societies are endogenously shaped so as to give outcomes on a rather persistent and pervasive pattern.

To begin with, we are able in several instances to show how mobility regimes, as well as revealing a large commonality across national societies, tend also to differ little across subpopulations distinguished within these societies. Thus, for example, in Chapter 5 we report a very close similarity between the relative mobility rates of the two ethno-religious communities co-resident in Northern Ireland, and likewise between those for the two main regional divisions of Czechoslovakia, although in the further case of Italy we must acknowledge a distinctive—perhaps in part pre-industrial—mobility regime in the South. Then in Chapter 7 we again find a high degree of similarity in the relative rates underlying men's and women's mobility from their class origins to their current employment. And of yet greater interest here is the extent of the similarity that we also find in such rates underlying two quite different types of class mobility, men's mobility via employment and women's via marriage, which occur in different kinds of market and, one might have supposed, via increasingly differentiated processes of social selection. Finally, the analyses we present in Chapter 8 indicate that cross-national commonality in relative rates of intergenerational mobility can coexist with a much greater variation in the relative chances that are involved in work-life mobility and in the institutions by which these chances are conditioned; and, we then seek to show, the nature of this variation reflects the way in which, as individuals and families pursue their mobility goals within differing institutional settings, the processes that create the intergenerational commonality ultimately constrain the aggregate outcomes of work-life trajectories.

What, in all these respects, we would see as chiefly significant is that the effects that endogenously shape mobility within class structures—that is, effects of the kind that our model of core fluidity aims to represent—are relatively little affected in their operation by *other* major sources of social differentiation within modern societies. Rather than being mitigated by, or in any way interacting with, the latter, they tend to cut more or less directly across them, so that the pattern of results produced by these effects is then found essentially replicated across a wide variety of contexts.

THE MACROSOCIOLOGY OF RELATIVE RATES: A MULTIVARIATE ANALYSIS

On the basis of the foregoing review of our empirical findings, one summary observation that could be made is that they point in quite different directions so far as absolute and relative mobility rates are concerned. As regards the former, our results are largely negative. We can give only very qualified support to the idea of directional trends, whether in relation to industrial development or otherwise; we are able firmly to reject theories of cross-national similarity; and our analyses provide little indication of cross-national variation of a systematic kind. We can, moreover, provide a good deal of evidence to suggest *why* absolute rates should prove to be thus unruly: that is, evidence of the diversity and in some cases of the highly contingent character of the effects that influence them, overwhelmingly via their impact on the structural contexts of mobility. In other words, as we have already implied in the discussion of our results in both Chapters 3 and 6, a strong case can be made out to the effect that absolute mobility rates do not constitute a very promising macrosociological *explanandum*. We do not, therefore, find it surprising (quite apart from problems of data comparability) that early attempts to account for cross-national differences in such rates via multivariate analyses (e.g. Miller and Bryce 1961; Fox and Miller 1965, 1966) should have turned out to be quite inconclusive; nor that suggestions that further attempts of this kind should be made have met with little positive response. We would suspect that mobility researchers have by now come to share largely, even if tacitly, in the view that cross-national variation in absolute rates is not usefully regarded as systematic from a macrosociological standpoint; rather, such rates call for specific, historically grounded accounts, and are in fact likely to enter into macrosociological analysis chiefly as the starting-point for comparative investigations of the *consequences* of social mobility.[7]

[7] See, for example, the discussion of 'competitive balance' in De Graaf and Ultee (1990) in the context of studies of the effects of mobility on voting behaviour. We should here make it clear that we do not wish to suggest that sociological analysis can have no useful part to play in explaining cross-national differences in absolute rates. Our position can, rather, be expressed by taking over a useful distinction from Kohn (1989): that is, we would see the potential

As regards relative rates, a clearly contrasting situation obtains. We would see our findings as contradicting liberal expectations that such rates will reveal greater openness concomitantly with industrial development, but as supporting a version of the FJH hypothesis of a basic cross-national similarity. In this version, a limited degree of cross-national variation can be accommodated by the hypothesis, especially in so far as this variation can also be regarded as being of a nationally specific kind—as might come about from distinctive cultural influences or from particular measures of political intervention. However, our view that, in the cases we have examined, cross-national variation in relative rates, as represented by national deviations from our core model, is thus specific, at least in large part, would seem far more likely to prove contentious than our argument concerning the non-systematic nature of variation in absolute rates.

For example, where authors sympathetic to the liberal theory have modified their position, as we have noted, so as to accept that forces within the logic of industrialism making for greater openness may operate less directly and consistently than was earlier implied, they evidently wish to see cross-national variation in relative rates as being open to explanation in terms of level of industrial development *taken together with* various other societal attributes that are also amenable to inclusion in multivariate analyses. And, on the other hand, authors more sceptical of the liberal theory (e.g. Tyree, Semyonov, and Hodge 1979; Grusky and Hauser 1984; Wong 1990) have likewise sought to ground their arguments in such analyses, through which they seek to show that industrialism has only weak or uncertain effects on relative rates once other, similarly generalizable but more influential, factors are taken into account.

In Chapter 2 we have set out the strong reservations that we hold concerning the kind of multivariate analysis in question, which arise from both practical and theoretical problems that it entails. Nevertheless—and with these reservations still firmly in place—we believe it appropriate here to pursue such an analysis with our own data on relative rates, if only to guard against the charge that we are claiming a lack of systematic varation without having made any serious effort to discover it. In this analysis we aim to examine variation in social fluidity across the total of fifteen nations for which we have men's intergenerational mobility tables, and in relation to the four societal attributes that previous investigators would appear most often to have considered: namely, industrial development, educational inequality, economic inequality, and political complexion of government.

As would by now be widely accepted, differences in social fluidity cannot be adequately captured by any single parameter (Grusky and Hauser 1984; Yamaguchi 1987; Wong 1990); and, if this is true where mobility is studied

contribution of sociology in this respect as coming, not from a comparative macrosociology where nations are taken as the *units* of analysis, but rather from work undertaken more at the micro- or at least the 'meso'-level, where nations serve as the given *contexts* of analysis.

within the context of a hierarchy of status or prestige, it is true *a fortiori* where the context is, as in our case, that of a class structure. We limit ourselves, therefore, to treating variation across our fifteen nations in just one aspect of fluidity, although one which has been of central theoretical interest: that is, the degree to which nations show greater or less openness overall. To estimate an appropriate parameter, we turn yet again to the model of uniform difference which we introduced in Chapter 3 in analysing trends in relative rates and which we have subsequently applied in differing forms in various other contexts. Here we may write

$$\log F_{ijk} = \mu + \lambda_i^O + \lambda_j^D + \lambda_k^N + \lambda_{ik}^{ON} + \lambda_{jk}^{DN} + \beta_k X_{ij} \qquad (11.1)$$

where, analogously with the model of equation (3.3), X_{ij} refers to a general pattern of association between class origins and destinations among our nations (and is derived initially from values expected under the CmSF model) and β_k refers to the strength of this association that is specific to the kth nation.

In the first column of Table 11.1 we show the β parameters for our fifteen nations as estimated under the model of equation (11.1). The average parameter across all nations has been set at 0; thus, in nations with positive β values, odds ratios defining the origin-destination association tend to be further from independence than under the general pattern of association,

TABLE 11.1. *Ranking of nations by overall fluidity and allocation to levels of four independent variables*

Nation	Fluidity (β value)	Industrial development (IND)	Educational inequality (EDI)	Economic inequality (ECI)	Political complexion of govt. (GOV)
SCO	0.19	3	3	2	2
NIR	0.18	2	3	2	1
IRL	0.16	1	3	1	1
NET	0.16	3	2	1	2
FRA	0.16	2	1	1	1
FRG	0.13	3	3	1	1
ITA	0.12	2	1	1	1
ENG	0.09	3	3	2	2
HUN	0.02	1	1	3	3
SWE	−0.17	3	2	3	2
POL	−0.18	1	2	3	3
USA	−0.20	3	1	2	1
JAP	−0.20	2	2	2	1
AUS	−0.23	3	2	2	1
CZE	−0.23	3	1	3	3

while in nations with negative β values these odds ratios tend to be closer to independence. The nations can then be taken as ranked in order of increasing openness, with Scotland appearing at one extreme and Australia and Czechoslovakia at the other. It will be recalled from the discussion of Chapter 3 (see, esp., n. 25) that β parameters determine the relationship between corresponding odds ratios. Thus, for example, from the βs for Scotland and Czechoslovakia of 0.19 and -0.23 respectively, we can calculate the quotient of each expected odds ratio in the Czech mobility table relative to its Scottish equivalent. And, as an indication of the range of fluidity that is implied in Table 11.2, we may note that the median of these quotients turns out to be 71 per cent.[8]

The ranking of nations is in general much as might have been expected from our case-by-case discussion of relative rates in Chapters 5, 9, and 10, although, of course, the β parameters, in giving a measure of overall fluidity, may well bracket together nations which from these earlier analyses we know have fluidity *patterns* that differ quite widely—as, say, Ireland and France or Sweden and Poland. Correspondingly, nations should not be thought of, following from their ranking, as having class structures that are more-or-less open in all respects alike. The β parameters will obviously hide differences associated with the several effects provided for under our core model; and in this regard the important part that can be played by sectoral effects—perhaps in offsetting those of inheritance or hierarchy—might most easily be forgotten. Low sectoral barriers, for instance, have much to do with Japan's ranking as one of the more fluid nations, despite quite strong propensities for class inheritance, just as high sectoral barriers have much to do with Scotland appearing as the nation with the lowest fluidity of all, despite weak hierarchical effects.

Turning now to the independent variables that we wish to include in our analysis, we can here exploit the fact that twelve of our fifteen nations are represented in the comparative study of Treiman and Yip (1989) to which we

---

[8] Again as earlier explained, differences between corresponding odds ratios will depend on the β parameters involved and *also* on the magnitude of the odds ratios in question in the X vector. As regards the significance of the reported median quotient in the Czechoslovakia–Scotland comparison for the claim of a large cross-national commonality in fluidity patterns, we would again observe that cross-national differences may well show up more strongly when nations are compared with each other rather than with the core pattern—and especially so where the nations are chosen so as to represent extreme positions in some particular aspect of fluidity. One could, of course, conversely say that, for all other pairwise comparisons based on β parameters, the median quotient of the odds ratios of the more fluid to the less fluid nation will be greater than 71 per cent.

One further point concerning the first column of Table 11.1 should be made. The β parameter for the United States is based on the actual mobility table and not on the 'corrected' version that we constructed (see ch. 9 nn. 20, 21) to try to offset problems in data comparability. We would, therefore, believe that the β reported gives an exaggerated idea of the overall level of fluidity within the American class structure, and that, in the light of our earlier analysis (Erikson and Goldthorpe 1985), the true position of the United States in the rank order should be seen as lying much closer to that of England.

have earlier referred. So far as the variables of industrial development and educational and economic inequality are concerned, we allow ourselves to be largely guided by Treiman's and Yip's measures—even though we have some misgivings about them—so that no question can arise of a tendentious choice of indicators on our part. However, because of our doubts about data quality, as indicated in Chapter 2, we have sought to avoid what we would regard as a spurious degree of precision by simply grouping our nations on each variable into three levels. In this way, it is also possible for us to deal with those of our nations not covered in Treiman's and Yip's study, and for which we could not obtain data exactly comparable to those they use.

The levels of educational and economic inequality that we distinguish are entirely consistent, for the twelve common nations, with the ordering that is given by Treiman's and Yip's measures: that is, we simply trichotomize this ordering.[9] With industrial development, we deviate from their measures—with, we believe, good reason—in just a few respects. We consider the level of industrial development of our nations *c.*1975 rather than, as in their case, *c.*1960, with the result that upward shifts occur in the relative position of two nations which developed rapidly in the intervening years, namely, Italy and Japan. Further, Treiman and Yip appear to have calculated only one industrialization measure for England and Northern Ireland together. We, however, treat them separately, and, while England obviously belongs on our highest level of industrial development, we place Northern Ireland on the intermediate level.[10] For the three of our nations not included in Treiman's and Yip's analysis—Czechoslovakia, France, and Scotland— we have produced measures as similar as possible to theirs on each of the

---

[9] Treiman and Yip (1989: 381–3) measure educational inequality with respect to the fathers' generation in their national samples, using a composite indicator that combines (i) the ratio of the mean years of schooling obtained by fathers who were high-prestige professionals to the mean years of schooling obtained by fathers who were low-prestige production workers; and (ii) the coefficient of relative variability of the years of schooling obtained by all fathers (i.e. the standard deviation divided by the mean). They then measure economic inequality by reference to the inequality of incomes and in this case, lacking good comparative data for the fathers' generation in their samples, work with a further composite indicator which combines (i) the ratio of the mean income of high-prestige professionals to the mean income of low-prestige production workers; and (ii) the proportion of income held by the top 10 per cent of all families in national income distributions.

[10] Treiman and Yip (1989: 381–3) measure level of industrialization by a further composite indicator, here combining (i) level of *per capita* energy consumption and (ii) percentage of the labour force not in agriculture—in both cases as of 1960. They would, in fact, have preferred a yet earlier date, had reliable information been available, on the grounds that 'societal forces probably have their greatest impact on career beginnings'. We have ourselves opted to measure level of industrialization as of 1975 primarily because we would think that, in periods of very rapid industrial development, such as those experienced by Italy and Japan during the 1960s, the effects on mobility might well extend beyond career beginnings. It may also be noted that the enquiries on which we draw tend overall to be of somewhat later date than those used by Treiman and Yip (by, on average, almost five years). The placing of Northern Ireland on our intermediate level of industrial development is chiefly warranted by its relatively large agricultural sector (cf. Table 6.2).

variables in question, and have allocated these nations to our levels accordingly.[11]

With the remaining independent variable, political complexion of government, which Treiman and Yip introduce only via a distinction between capitalist and state socialist nations, we follow them in distinguishing a separate level for the latter, but we further divide our capitalist nations with respect to two levels of 'left' participation in government.[12]

The second to fifth columns of Table 11.1 show the complete distribution of the fifteen nations across the levels of the independent variables. In each case, we refer to extant theory to score as level 3 that which should most favour, and as level 1 that which should least favour, greater overall fluidity.

In most attempts to explore the determinants of cross-national fluidity via multivariate analysis, regression methods in some form or other have been utilized. Here, however, we prefer to follow the lead given by Grusky and Hauser (1984) and to retain a log-linear modelling approach, although our actual procedures differ from theirs in various respects. While Grusky and Hauser introduce their independent variables as continuous 'variates', in applying our uniform-difference model we treat these variables as sets of dummies, and we then enter as a variate the general pattern of association between class origins and destinations represented by the X_{ij} term. The extended version of the model can thus be written as

$$\log F_{ijk} = \mu + \lambda_i^O + \lambda_j^D + \lambda_k^N + \lambda_{ik}^{ON} + \lambda_{jk}^{DN} + \sum_m \beta_{mn} X_{ij} \qquad (11.2)$$

where β_{mn} represents the relative strength of association between class origins and destinations that is specific and common to nations on the nth level of factor m.[13]

As a preliminary to our main modelling exercise, we report in Table 11.2 the results we obtain if we fit the simple uniform-difference model of equation (11.1) to our fifteen national mobility tables, together with the results of fitting to these tables the conditional independence model and the model of common social fluidity (these latter may be compared with the results given in Table 4.1 for our European nations only).

The G^2 for the independence model can be taken as representing the total association existing between class of origin and class of destination over the fifteen nations. The difference between this G^2 and that for the CmSF model

---

[11] In this regard, we have drawn on data on educational inequality in Kelley (1990), Matějů (1990), and Müller and Karle (1990); on income inequality in Lydall (1968); and on levels of industrialization in Taylor and Jodice (1983).

[12] We use here data generously made available to us by Walter Korpi, arising from his current research. We distinguish between nations in which left parties have, or have not, participated in government for more than 30 per cent of the period 1946–73. (The highest figure for nations in which such participation is, by the above criterion, deemed 'low' is 25 per cent, while the lowest figure for nations with 'high' left participation is 41 per cent.)

[13] We have also undertaken an OLS regression analysis with the β parameters in Table 11.1 as the dependent variable and our independent variables entered as dummies. This, in fact, produces results on essentially the same pattern as those we subsequently report in Table 11.3.

TABLE 11.2. *Results of fitting the uniform-difference, and also the conditional independence and CmSF, models to intergenerational class mobility tables for fifteen nations*

Model (N = 122,347)	G^2	df	p	rG^2	Δ
Con. ind.	36,893	540	0.00	—	19.9
CmSF	2,420.7	504	0.00	93.4	4.5
Uniform-difference	1,761.7	490	0.00	95.2	3.6

then refers to that part of the total association which is on a common pattern across all nations, and the CmSF G^2 itself refers to that part which is cross-nationally variable. In turn, the CmSF G^2 can likewise be divided. The difference between this G^2 and that for our uniform-difference model refers to that part of the cross-national variation which occurs as deviation from the common pattern in a uniform way, either towards or away from independence, while the G^2 returned by the uniform-difference model itself refers to that part of the variation which is not uniform in this sense. As is then indicated in Table 11.2, 93.4 per cent of the total association between origins and destinations is on a common pattern cross-nationally. But it may further be calculated from the results given that uniform deviation from the common pattern accounts for only 27.3 per cent—(95.2 − 93.4)/(100 − 93.4)—of the association that is cross-nationally variable. Thus, we are reminded of the fact that the aspect of cross-national variation in fluidity that we shall seek to explain—that which can be understood as implying more or less fluidity or openness overall—is only a minor part of the total variation found among our nations. The remainder is made up of differences in fluidity which do not result in the odds ratios that define the origin–destination association deviating from the common pattern so as to be, on average, either closer to or further from the value of 1 that implies independence.

In Table 11.3 we then come to the results that are, for our present purposes, of chief interest: that is, those produced by the fitting to our mobility tables of the extended uniform-difference model of equation (11.2) in which our independent variables are incorporated as factors. We show for these factors, when introduced singly and in combination, the improvement in fit that is achieved over that of the CmSF model and, most importantly, the β parameter estimates that are returned.[14]

---

[14] As will be seen, it is to these parameter estimates that we attach major importance in evaluating our findings. From a comparison of the results reported in Tables 11.2 and 11.3, it can, in fact, be shown that our four independent variables taken together account for as much as 95 per cent of the total uniform cross-national variation in fluidity levels as specified under our model. However, this is of little significance, since it must largely reflect the small number of cases involved relative to that of independent variables. *Any* set of four three-level factors

TABLE 11.3. *Improvement in fit over CmSF model produced by the extended uniform-difference model with from one to four independent variables, Δ values, and parameter estimates for levels of independent variables as differences from level 1*

Independent variable(s) included	ΔG^2	Δ	Parameter estimates for levels							
			IND		EDI		ECI		GOV	
			2	3	2	3	2	3	2	3
(df=2)										
IND	228.6	4.1	0.10	−0.15						
EDI	323.2	4.1			−0.17	0.14				
ECI	367.8	3.9					−0.24	−0.31		
GOV	195.4	4.3							0.10	−0.15
(df=4)										
IND EDI	499.7	3.8	0.18	−0.07	−0.10	0.24				
IND ECI	384.0	3.9	−0.03	−0.09			−0.20	−0.34		
IND GOV	432.0	3.9	0.09	−0.19					0.25	−0.17
EDI ECI	551.6	3.7			−0.12	0.21	−0.27	−0.17		
EDI GOV	336.9	4.1			−0.18	0.09			0.08	−0.00
ECI GOV	493.7	3.8					−0.30	−0.56	0.25	0.27
(df=6)										
IND EDI ECI	575.0	3.7	0.10	−0.02	−0.11	0.23	−0.20	−0.11		
IND EDI GOV	554.8	3.8	0.18	−0.11	−0.14	0.14			0.19	0.02
IND ECI GOV	543.7	3.7	0.02	−0.13			−0.21	−0.48	0.29	0.20
EDI ECI GOV	591.9	3.7			−0.15	0.11	−0.28	−0.33	0.18	0.17
(df=8)										
All	626.4	3.6	0.08	−0.08	−0.13	0.12	−0.20	−0.27	0.22	0.14

As is indicated, the parameters for levels 2 and 3 of each factor are reported as differences from that for level 1. Thus, given the way the factors are scored, as earlier noted, the theoretical expectation in each case is that the parameter for level 2 should take a negative value and that for level 3 a larger negative value. In other words, with each factor, the association between class of origin and destination that is specific and common to nations on level 2 should be weaker—the relevant odds ratios should be closer to independence—than the association that is specific and common to nations on level 1; and likewise with the association for nations on level 3 as compared to that for nations on level 2 (cf. ch. 3 n. 25).

If we look at the first panel of Table 11.3, where we show the results from introducing our independent variables into the model one at a time, we can see, to begin with, that the parameters for industrial development (IND) do not, in fact, follow the pattern indicated above: that is to say, fluidity does not, according to our analysis, increase steadily with industrial development. For nations on level 2 of IND, as compared with those on level 1, deviation from the general pattern of association between class origins and destinations tends to be in the direction of *less*, rather than greater, openness. Likewise, with the parameters for educational inequality (EDI), the theoretically expected ordering is not produced. Here it is nations on level 3 that are out of line, showing less fluidity than those on both levels 1 and 2. However, in the case of economic inequality (ECI), theoretical expectations are in fact met. The β parameters show increasing negative values, indicating that, across the three groupings of our nations that we distinguish, fluidity tends to be the greater, the lower the level of economic inequality (as measured, that is, by the inequality of incomes). And it may also be noted that ECI is the factor that achieves the greatest reduction in the G^2 for the CmSF model. Finally, though, with the parameters for political complexion of government (GOV), a theoretically anomalous ordering is again found. Although nations on level 3, that is, those with state socialist regimes, are shown as having greater fluidity than those on level 1, this is not so with nations on level 2. That is to say, there is no indication that among capitalist societies those in which left parties have had a relatively large share in government tend to be more open than do others.

If, then, we move on to the further panels of Table 11.3, where we give the results that follow from introducing our independent variables in combination, we can see that, for the most part, no very different impression of their effects is created. The parameters for IND still go contrary to theory for level 2 nations in all combinations except where IND is paired with ECI, when, however, the effects implied become quite weak; and the parameters for EDI remain out of line for level 3 nations in all combinations alike. On

would probably prove capable of thus 'explaining' most of the variation in question. Attention should rather focus on the extent to which parameters do or do not show values that follow theoretically expected patterns.

the other hand, the theoretically expected effects for ECI are maintained, apart from two instances where EDI is also involved, and where, one may suspect, the parameter for level 3 nations is thus depressed. The main qualification that is suggested to the results in the first panel of the table concerns GOV. It can be seen that the theoretically expected effect previously found at least for level 3, state socialist, nations entirely disappears wherever ECI is included in the model along with GOV. In other words, it would appear that, whatever increment in equality of chances in class mobility may be associated with state socialist regimes, this follows from what they achieve in reducing economic inequality of condition. And, in turn, the theoretical standing of GOV itself, at all events as a direct cause of greater fluidity, is clearly undermined.

Considered as a whole, the results of our multivariate analysis are not then such as to lead us to any radical revision of our view that cross-national variation in relative rates is of a largely non-systematic kind—that it derives more from effects specific to particular societies at particular times than from effects that can be treated as following from generalizable societal attributes. The findings we report corroborate the conclusions we have previously reached from our case-by-case analyses that, among the nations we study, there is no tendency for openness to increase with level of industrial development nor to be associated, at least in ways that theorists have suggested, with type of political regime. As regards what might be thought of as the more proximate effects on openness of aspects of inequality of condition, our evidence on the impact of educational inequality is entirely negative, and it is then only with economic inequality that we obtain results that do, in the main, point to a systematic influence. Our findings, we could say, are at all events consistent with the hypothesis that nations have more open class structures, the lower the level of economic inequality among their populations.

This hypothesis is one that we have no difficulty in accepting as plausible. It is, in fact, close to arguments that we have ourselves previously advanced (cf. Goldthorpe 1980a/1987: 320–1, 327–30; Erikson 1990) and it is one to which, as will later be seen, we believe that some special theoretical significance can be attached. However, even if we suppose that we have here produced reliable empirical support for it—a supposition, we would repeat, that must still remain questionable on grounds of data quality[15]—this is still an achievement that needs to be kept in perspective.

We must, to begin with, note the failure of the other independent variables in our analysis; and we must at the same time bear in mind that, as we earlier demonstrated, the dependent variable that we have considered

---

[15] As we have earlier implied (ch. 2 n. 35), we would, in fact, regard the indicators of income inequality on which we have drawn as being especially dubious, in the light of results from the more serious efforts now being made within the Luxembourg Income Study to improve the comparability of data in this respect.

represents just one, very partial, aspect of the total cross-national variation in fluidity that we have shown to exist. A macrosociological analysis that sought to address the full range of this variation would thus have to be of a theoretically more complex—and hence, we would believe, methodologically yet more problematic—kind than that we have essayed. And further, of course, it should be recognized that, while we cannot make any very reliable statement in this respect, our measure of inequality of condition still accounts for only some part of the variation in overall fluidity that our nations display.[16]

When, therefore, we also reflect that the total amount of the association between class origins and destinations that *is* cross-nationally variable is, in any event, only very small relative to the amount that is cross-nationally common, the case for some approach complementary, if not alternative, to that expressed via conventional multivariate analysis would appear to us to gather force. What in this regard we would wish to propose is that, rather than making the assumption that variation in relative rates is systematic and that explaining this variation represents the chief goal of macrosociological endeavour, we should suspend this assumption and, instead of concentrating so exclusively on variation, we should regard the commonality that prevails in relative rates—and their general persistence and pervasiveness—as providing the major focus for macrosociological attention. To end this chapter, and our book, we seek to elaborate on this proposal.

THE MACROSOCIOLOGY OF RELATIVE RATES: THE PROBLEM OF INVARIANCE

In a valuable but, in our view, unduly neglected discussion, Lieberson (1985/ 1987) has observed that to explain variation in a phenomenon is not, or not necessarily, to explain the phenomenon itself. As an example, Lieberson points out that one can account for the fact that a feather, a coin, and a brick will fall through the air with varying velocity by reference to differences in their density and shape. But this is not to explain why they fall at all: to do this, one would need to invoke the further factor of gravity—and, moreover,

---

[16] In any more satisfactory analysis of differences in either fluidity levels or general fluidity patterns within the class structures of industrial societies, one question that will obviously require greater attention than hitherto is that of the determinants of sectoral barriers. We have already stressed the importance of the differing strength of these barriers in the ordering of nations in the first column of Table 11.1. If we categorize our nations as having fluidity patterns with hierarchy, inheritance, and sector effects of differing strength (strong, medium, or weak), and then take these categories as independent (dummy) variables in either a log-linear analysis analogous to that described in the text or as variables in an OLS regression analysis, we can in fact show that sectoral effects account for clearly more of the cross-national variation in openness than do those of either hierarchy or inheritance. It is, however, uncertain, to say the least, whether the differing circumstances that in our case-by-case treatment we have associated with either particularly high or low sectoral barriers—uneven economic development, part-time farming, under-urbanization and worker commuting, etc.—could be effectively translated into analytical variables.

not as a variable but as a constant. In the social sciences, Lieberson argues, the techniques of statistical analysis that are applied in lieu of experimental methods actually presuppose variance in the phenomena that are treated, and this tends then to result in explanatory efforts being focused on variation rather than on its absence. However, just as in the physical example cited, the 'fundamental' cause of a phenomenon may be a constant force and hence one that is not amenable to investigation via multivariate analysis. Thus, Lieberson concludes, social scientists may often be led astray because 'we should be reasonably satisfied that we understand why an entity or a process exists to begin with *before* turning to questions about its variation' (1985/ 1987: 104).

Lieberson's remarks are, we believe, highly relevant to our present concerns. To seek to explain cross-national variation in relative rates of class mobility or, that is, variation in the pattern of net association between class origins and destinations, need not at all be the same thing as explaining why such association should exist in the first place. It is entirely possible that the fact that origins and destinations *are* associated is to be accounted for by reference to one set of 'fundamental' or primary factors, while variation in this association is to be accounted for by reference to a quite different set of secondary factors, which simply modify the operation of the primary factors and perhaps only to a quite minor extent.

If this line of argument is followed, the question that must then arise in any particular case is that of what grounds we might have for supposing that primary factors are indeed at work underlying observed variation. Lieberson suggests (1985/1987: 233–4) that what we should be alert to is evidence that the *outcomes* of a particular social process show only slight variation across a wide range of differing circumstances: that is, evidence to indicate that forces are operating through which differing conditions for, or inputs to, the process are modified, or 'transformed', in their effects, so that, in the end, much the same outcome from one case to another is still arrived at. As we have already noted, we have in fact produced evidence regarding relative rates of class mobility that is very much of the kind in question. Relative rates show only quite limited variation across the widely differing structural contexts provided by the nations we have studied and, likewise, when we view these rates over time within changing national class structures or from one national subpopulation to another. Furthermore, we would regard our findings both on the relative rates underlying women's marital mobility and on the interrelation of relative rates in work-life and intergenerational mobility as offering especially apt illustrations of cases where Lieberson would infer the presence of 'transformational' forces. *Prima facie* there would seem little reason to expect women's relative chances of class mobility via marriage to be on much the same pattern as those of men via employment, nor relative rates of intergenerational mobility to turn out much the same in nations with quite different institutional arrangements regulating the linkages between education and employment and thus characterized by quite different patterns of work-life mobility. The fact that such a similarity of outcomes is none the less apparent does, therefore, strongly underline the argument that as much, if not more, sociological interest should attach to accounting for the variation that is *not* observed in relative rates than for the fairly small amount that is.

If, then, this latter point is accepted, two further questions must in turn be faced: that of what kinds of explanation for lack of variation might here be appropriate, and that of what kind or kinds of research would be of most value both in helping the development of, and in subsequently testing, the theoretical thinking required.

As regards the first of these questions, we would wish to begin by referring to our model of core social fluidity. As we earlier argued in Chapter 4, when we choose to work within a class-structural context, more is entailed than simply the setting-up of a conceptual schema within which we are able to observe and describe mobility; we also accept the idea that positions within this structure will, as positions defined by class relations, have distinctive implications for the propensities for mobility occurring between them. In developing our model of core fluidity, we sought to spell out these propensities in terms of the relative desirability of different class positions considered as destinations, the relative advantages afforded to individuals by different class origins, and the relative barriers that face individuals in gaining access to different class positions. It was in these terms, that is, that our model, with the various effects on relative rates that it comprises, was given its theoretical rationale. In keeping with the presuppositions underlying all our previous analyses, we would then here wish to maintain that relative rates have the degree of persistence and pervasiveness that they do because the influences exerted on these rates by the class structures of industrial societies themselves vary little by time or place. In other words, although class structures may in different periods and nations provide differing contexts for mobility, in the sense of differing patterns of opportunity confronting all individuals alike, they are at the same time the source of the basic similarity in the endogenous mobility regimes operating within these contexts and through which relative mobility chances according to class origins are expressed.[17]

---

[17] Our position here comes into obvious conflict with the liberal theory of industrialism, not only on the matter of mobility trends *per se* but also on that of trends in inequality of condition. As noted in Chapter 1, the theory claims that, as industrial societies 'mature', inequalities of condition, including those associated with different class positions, tend steadily to diminish. In this respect, as in others, the influence of the development economics of the 1950s and 1960s is manifest, and in particular of Kuznets's argument (1955, 1963) that, as nations enter into the industrialization process, economic inequality first increases but subsequently follows a falling trend. In effect, then, the liberal theory also accepts that inequality of opportunity and condition are positively associated—but sees them as declining together. This view is, for example, explicit both in Treiman's early work, in which Kuznets is directly invoked (1970: 217), and again in his later work with Yip (1989), although here with the qualification we have noted that 'industrialization and inequality do not move in perfect concert'. However, we

However, to argue thus is to take matters only a little further forward. We have, of course, in turn to ask why it should be that class structures differ so little in the relative mobility rates to which they give rise or, more specifically, why from positions differently located in the class structure—that is, positions involving different kinds of employment relations—such consistent implications for desirability, advantages, and access should follow. Where, in the extant literature, such issues of invariance in class structures, or in social stratification more generally, have been addressed, two main kinds of explanation would appear to have been attempted: that is, those based, on the one hand, on functionalist theories and, on the other hand, on what might be called theories of social action.

In explanations offered from the standpoint of functionalist theory, the apparent ubiquity and degree of uniformity in inequalities associated with different class positions is accounted for as being in some way 'necessary'. Thus, in the best-known effort, that of Davis and Moore (1945), such inequalities are explained as necessary in order to motivate individuals both to enter positions to which demands and responsibilities of differing import-ance attach and to perform effectively once in these positions. Apart from the many specific criticisms that have been raised against the Davis–Moore theory (for a review, see Huaco 1966), the fundamental objection to it must remain that, like most other 'macrofunctionalist' accounts, it is crucially incomplete. That is, it does not include any specification of the 'causal feedback loop' (Elster 1979: 28–35; cf. Stinchcombe 1968: 58–9, 80–101)—analogous to that provided by natural selection in the biological world—through which the 'functionally necessary' effects of class inequalities for the societies in which they exist lead at the same time to these inequalities being maintained. Or conversely, one could say, no process is indicated which ensures that, if the degree or form of inequality in a society is *not* adequate to meeting functional exigencies, then that society, together with its defective structure, will fail to survive and will thus no longer be represented in empirical observations.

would further observe that Kuznets's hypothesis never received any decisive confirmation and that, of late, criticism of empirical work claiming to support it has mounted. Thus, re-examination of comparative data (see, esp., Anand and Kanbur 1986; also Fields and Jakubsen 1990) seriously calls into question the universality of the 'inverted-U' curve of income inequality; and attempts to establish this curve in the economic histories of particular nations have been powerfully challenged (see, for example, on the British case, J. G. Williamson 1985, and, in response, Feinstein 1988). A new interpretation of the available data would appear to be emerging which emphasizes, first, the diversity of national experience so far as the long-term relationship between economic development and inequality is concerned; and, secondly, the tendency, at least within more advanced societies, for inequality to show alternating periods of increase and decrease within, however, a distribution that retains a broadly similar form. A further point of importance is that many changes that are to be observed in the distributions of pay, total incomes, or wealth alike are ones that cannot be unequivocally described as being in the direction of greater or less equality overall, but only in certain ranges of the distribution—in other words, Lorentz curves may cross (see the classic paper by Atkinson 1970).

However, while the macrofunctionalist approach to the explanation of class inequalities would not, therefore, appear promising, some insight may still be gained from microfunctionalist theories, in particular those of work organizations. Several authors have aimed to show that certain features of work organizations can in fact be regarded as functionally necessary in a relatively rigorous sense: that is, their absence would result in a reduction in the efficiency of an organization and hence in its chances of survival, at least to the extent that a 'selective' market economy was in operation. Of greatest interest in this regard are, then, analyses such as those of O. E. Williamson (1975, 1985: ch. 9) of the rationale of hierarchy within work organizations as a means of meeting needs for both the motivation and co-ordination of work activities; and, further, more detailed studies of the nature of 'hierarchical imperatives' (e.g. Hedström 1987; le Grand 1989) which have in some cases been specifically concerned with the wider implications for class structures and associated inequalities—as, for example, through their effects in differentiating levels of both job rewards and conditions and entry requirements. The idea is, therefore, at all events plausible, and especially, of course, if we define class positions in terms of employment relations, that such hierarchical imperatives within work organizations, in so far as they exist, will be reflected in some corresponding uniformities in the desirability of different positions, in the advantages they confer upon their incumbents, and in the difficulties in gaining access to them. Or, at very least, certain limits should thus be imposed on the variation in the nature and extent of class inequalities that is empirically to be found.

At the same time, though, we would not believe that for the explanatory purposes we have in hand functionalist theory of any kind will in itself be adequate. We would, in fact, expect a more important part to be played by explanation in terms of social action: that is, explanation in terms of the consequences of individuals and groups acting purposively—though not necessarily, of course, with these same consequences actually in mind. In other words, rather than viewing the lack of variation in class inequalities as being no more than the automatic outcome of the functional viability, or non-viability, of differing structures within a selective environment, we will need to see it also as the outcome of individuals and groups acting in pursuit of their interests and goals and, in particular, of the actions of those who are relatively advantaged and powerful under the *status quo* seeking to use their power and advantage precisely in order to maintain their position.

We return here in effect to Sorokin's point that all forms of social stratification are characterized by powerful self-maintaining properties. It is, however, important to be clear about just how these operate. Lieberson argues, in a way we have, in fact, largely followed, that the 'fundamental' causes underlying social processes that produce outcomes notably lacking in variation are likely to be ones that reflect *either* some kind of functional exigency *or* the capacity of dominant actors to use their dominance to preserve an existing state of affairs. Thus, in discussing the relationship between education and occupation among blacks and whites, Lieberson emphasizes the need to recognize that this relationship 'is affected by its own consequences for the dependent variable'; it must be seen as 'holding a form and having a magnitude of consequence which is partially a consequence of what its consequences are' (1985/1987: 166–7). In other words, what the relationship is will be affected by what is implied by it for the interests of the dominant group, the whites; it will not be what it is independently of their power to influence it. Or, Lieberson concludes: '*Those who write the rules, write rules that enable them to continue to write the rules*' (1985/1987: 167; emphasis in original).

Lieberson here makes an important point in a vivid way. But we would wish to add that, at least in the case with which we are concerned, we would not suppose that the crucial action taken by dominant groups is necessarily purposive in the foresightful and concerted sense that Lieberson's final flourish might be taken to suggest. We would certainly accept that increases in equality of opportunity could, in turn, lead to increases in equality of condition, and could thus be seen as likely to undermine the *status quo*. Most importantly, as Phelps Brown has argued (1977: esp. 330–2), while *within the market* inequalities in rewards appear to be largely determined by supply and demand, supply is itself importantly determined by inequalities operating *before the market*—that is, precisely by inequalities in the economic, cultural, and social resources of families, through which children's mobility chances are already strongly conditioned prior to their first entry into employment. Thus, if such inequalities before the market were to be reduced, removing what are in effect restrictions on supply, inequalities in pay and other rewards of employment should, simply by the working of the market, also be diminished (cf. Stephens 1979: ch. 4). However, in order for a shift towards greater equality of opportunity to be prevented, it is not essential that members of more advantaged and powerful classes should in fact realize its larger consequences and act collectively against it for this reason, although they may of course to some extent do so. It can be enough that, individually, they seek, and are in sufficient numbers able, to maintain their own and their family's position by setting their superior resources strategically against whatever changes—in institutional arrangements, public policy, etc.—may appear threatening to them.

Thus, as we have earlier remarked, even though the 'logic of industrialism' may create pressures for the fuller use of a society's stock of talent through more universalistic processes of social selection, these pressures would seem more often than not to be resisted, and by opposing forces which operate chiefly at the microlevel of 'adaptive' individual and family strategies. And, as we have again argued, even though it is through the power of a modern state apparatus that such processes of 'civil society' are most likely to be modified, it is apparent that governments pursuing greater equality of opportunity as a political objective still have no guarantee of success, even in cases where political power is highly concentrated and formal limitations on state power are slight.

The foregoing, then, gives some indication of the lines on which we would wish to pursue explanations of the degree of invariance in relative rates of class mobility that we have observed.[18] The question that remains is that of through what kinds of research might such explanatory efforts be best developed and, ultimately, put to empirical test. Two approaches appear to us to hold most promise.

First, distinguishing between a suspected fundamental, or primary, cause of a phenomenon and its secondary causes is in principle best achieved, as Lieberson himself observes (1985/1987: 167), through experimental methods—which, however, are for the most part denied to the sociologist. None the less, every opportunity should, in our view, be taken of exploiting situations that have some of the characteristics of 'naturally occurring' experiments. In particular, much further attention should be given to the 'internal' analysis of those cases where, under socialist regimes, attempts have been made to modify the pattern of mobility chances to some end or other through various kinds of governmental intervention.

From the results we have reported for Hungary and Poland and also for Czechoslovakia, it would appear that such attempts introduced in the 1950s and 1960s met with varying degrees of success. It would, however, be of obvious relevance to investigate these cases more intensively, and especially in the light of studies carried out subsequent to those on which we have drawn and which can provide information on the periods in which in these nations socialist ideology and policies were weakened and socialist regimes moved into crisis and eventual collapse. In addition to discovering what changes, if any, occurred in national patterns of social fluidity—and, in the Hungarian and Polish cases, data-sets do in fact already exist that would appear adequate to this purpose[19]—more focused and detailed enquiries could also be highly rewarding. Where, for example, attempts at promoting greater fluidity through 'positive' discrimination in education or employment in favour of the children of workers and peasants failed to have their intended effects, or did so for a time but eventually faded out, it would be of evident interest to investigate how far this could in fact be related to the success of counter-strategies on the part of families with greater economic, cultural, and social resources or, perhaps, to the regime's realization of dysfunctional consequences at the level of work organizations as a result of 'hierarchical

---

[18] We should acknowledge that, as is indicated in our initial presentation of the FJH hypothesis in Chapter 1, its authors did themselves suggest a rationale for it of a broadly similar kind to our own, although only very briefly.

[19] Nationally based enquiries that allow comparisons with the results of the 1973 Hungarian and Polish surveys that we have here utilized were carried out in Hungary in 1983 (see, for some results, Andorka 1990) and in Poland in 1984.

imperatives' being breached (for suggestive comments, see Wesołowski and Mach 1986).

A further case that might in this respect prove especially revealing, though one we have been unable to cover at all, is that of Yugoslavia. Here, under a market socialist rather than a state socialist regime, the worker councils of economic enterprises have been able to act with some autonomy in distributing their 'profits', or 'net income', though subject usually to some limit on the range of pay differentials between the highest and lowest grades of worker within the enterprise. Consequently, workers of similar grade may receive widely differing levels of pay from one enterprise to another, depending not only on their own productivity but also on the favourability or otherwise of external market conditions and on the policies of their councils (cf. McFarlane 1988: esp. ch. 13). Indeed, lower-grade positions in successful enterprises may be clearly more desirable and sought after, though more difficult to obtain, than higher-grade positions in less successful ones. To the extent, therefore, that through such 'diagonal differentiation' the connection between the position of individuals in organizational hierarchies and their level of rewards is significantly weaker in Yugoslavia than in other societies—reflecting in fact a different structure of relationships within labour markets and production units—then, following the theoretical ideas we have outlined, the pattern of relative rates of class mobility should be expected to show a correspondingly wide divergence from that which our core model specifies. It seems likely that mobility data for Yugoslavia will in the near future become available that could allow this possibility to be investigated.[20]

Secondly, we would suggest that more effort should be directed specifically towards exploring the hypothesis that, within the class structures of industrial societies, inequality of opportunity will be the greater, the greater inequality of condition—as a derivative, that is, of the argument that members of more advantaged and powerful classes will seek to use their superior resources to preserve their own and their families' positions. We have already—like some, but not all, earlier investigators—found evidence to support this hypothesis from the multivariate analysis we presented earlier in this chapter; and we would propose that testing it further, with higher-quality data and on a wider range of nations, is in fact the best purpose that this type of analysis might in future serve. In other words, instead of being conceived and undertaken within a macrosociological programme that would take accounting for variation in relative rates as itself the primary goal, multivariate analyses should be carried out with the aim of evaluating possible explanations of the limited extent that such variation displays.[21]

---

[20] Of particular value should be the results of national studies of stratification and mobility in Yugoslavia currently being processed at the Institute of Sociology of the University of Ljubljana.

[21] To quote again from Lieberson:'if the goal is analytical or theoretical, it is necessary to establish the goal first and make variation fit this goal, rather than the all too common practice

In this regard, it would seem important that, as well as more than one indicator of the degree of fluidity or openness being included in the analysis, greater attention should also be given to the more comprehensive treatment of inequalities of condition. What, ideally, is needed are measures of inequality in command over economic, cultural, and social resources alike, and in each case of a wider range than those that have been previously used. Thus, little account has so far been taken of differences in wealth, in addition to those in income, or of cultural resources other than those associated with education—such as, for example, family traditions of entrepreneurship—while social resources have been almost entirely neglected, despite growing evidence of the part played by social contacts and networks in work careers (cf. Granovetter 1973, 1974, 1983; Breiger 1990).

However, attempts at investigating the hypothesis in question should by no means be limited to multivariate analyses, at least of the conventional kind. It would seem especially important to move down from the level of macrosociological relationships to study more immediately the social processes that are involved in class mobility or immobility: in particular, the various ways in which members of one generation in fact apply their resources in order to enhance the mobility chances of their successors, including such adaptive strategies as may be taken up in the face of external changes that threaten this capacity, and likewise the ways in which individuals draw on family resources in seeking advancement in their working lives or lose out where they are unable to do so. Here, we would again refer to the potential that is offered by data-sets comprising the complete work—and perhaps also family—histories of samples of national populations or of selected cohorts, on the basis of which the actual narrative structure of individuals' mobility trajectories can be analysed. We would also in this connection recognize a role for case-studies, though not ones chosen haphazardly under some kind of ethnographic licence, but rather ones locatable within the context of nationally based enquiries and selected so as to permit detailed investigation of, say, particular mobility flows, or mobility within particular milieux for which special theoretical significance can be claimed.

We well appreciate that the above suggestions are of a highly programmatic character, and that it is in their actual implementation that most of the serious effort will need to be expended. None the less, we believe that the outcome of our own work, now complete, and indeed that of the entire research tradition in which it lies, points to these as the directions in which our successors may at all events travel most hopefully, wherever they are destined ultimately to arrive.

---

of doing it the opposite way. . . . Variation will be found even when powerful forces are operating. But a different way of thinking about the matter is required. . . . So the issue is not to avoid statistical variability, but to use it properly by distinguishing its shallow applications from those where there are profoundly important regularities.' (1985/1987: 103–4)

BIBLIOGRAPHY

(For works with more than one edition, page references are to the latest edition.)

ABBOTT, P., and SAPSFORD, R. (1987), *Women and Social Class* (London: Tavistock).

ÅBERG, R. (1984), 'Teorierna om arbetets degradering och arbetsmarknadens dualisering—ett försök till empirisk prövning', *Sociologisk Forskning*, 2.

—— (1987), 'Working Conditions', in R. Erikson and R. Åberg (eds.), *Welfare in Transition: A Survey of Living Conditions in Sweden 1968–1981* (Oxford: Clarendon Press).

ACKER, J. (1973), 'Women and Social Stratification: A Case of Intellectual Sexism', *American Journal of Sociology*, 78.

ADAMSKI, W., and BIAŁECKI, I. (1981), 'Selection at School and Access to Higher Education in Poland', *European Journal of Education*, 16.

—— and HÄYRINEN, Y.-P. (1978), 'Educational Systems', in E. Allardt and W. Wesołowski (eds.), *Social Structure and Change: Finland and Poland Comparative Perspective* (Warsaw: Polish Scientific Publishers).

AKSZENTIEVICS, G. (1983), 'Mobility and Social Relations', in T. Kolosi and E. Wnuk-Lipiński (eds.), *Equality and Inequality under Socialism: Poland and Hungary Compared* (London: Sage).

ALBINSKI, H. S. (1985), 'Australia and the United States', *Daedalus* (Winter).

ALESTALO, M., and KUHNLE, S. (1987), 'The Scandinavian Route', in R. Erikson, E. J. Hansen, S. Ringen, and H. Uusitalo (eds.), *The Scandinavian Model* (Armonk, NY: Sharpe).

ALLEN, S. (1982), 'Gender Inequality and Class Formation', in A. Giddens and G. Mackenzie (eds.), *Social Class and the Division of Labour* (Cambridge: Cambridge University Press).

ALLMENDINGER, J. (1989), *Career Mobility Dynamics* (Berlin: Max-Planck-Institut für Bildungsforschung).

ANAND, S., and KANBUR, R. (1986), 'Inequality and Development: A Critique' (Yale University Economic Growth Centre).

ANDERSSON, L. (1987), 'Appendix A: Sampling and Data Collection', in R. Erikson and R. Åberg (eds.), *Welfare in Transition: A Survey of Living Conditions in Sweden, 1968–1981* (Oxford: Clarendon Press).

ANDERSSON, L.-G., ERIKSON, R., and WÄRNERYD, B. (1981), 'Att beskriva den sociala strukturen', *Statistisk Tidskrift*, 3rd ser., 19.

ANDO, B. (1978), 'Hyohon Sekkei' (Sample Design) in 1975 SSM Committee (eds.), *Shakai Kaiso to Shakai Ido* (Social Stratification and Social Mobility) (Tokyo: SSM Committee).

ANDORKA, R. (1976), 'Social Mobility in Hungary: An Analysis Applying Raymond Boudon's Models', *Social Science Information*, 15.

—— (1988), 'Comments Concerning the Results on Hungary of the CASMIN Project', Conference on 'The CASMIN Project and Comparative Sociology', Schloss Reisensburg, West Germany.

—— (1990), 'Half a Century of Trends in Social Mobility in Hungary', in J. L.

Peschar (ed.), *Social Reproduction in Eastern and Western Europe* (Nijmegen: Institute for Applied Social Sciences).

ANDORKA, R., and ZAGÓRSKI, K. (1980), *Socio-Occupational Mobility in Hungary and Poland* (Warsaw: Polish Academy of Sciences).

—— CSICSMAN, J., and KELETI A. (1982), 'Changes in the Openness of Hungarian Society', in L. Cseh-Szombathy (ed.), *Hungarian Sociology Today* (Budapest: Hungarian Sociological Association).

ARBER, S. (1989), 'Gender and Class Inequalities in Health: Understanding the Differentials', in J. Fox (ed.), *Health Inequalities in the European Countries* (Aldershot: Gower).

—— (1991), 'Class, Paid Employment and Family Roles: Making Sense of Structural Disadvantage, Gender and Health Status', *Social Science and Medicine*, 32.

ARDAGH, J. (1988), *Germany and the Germans* (London: Penguin).

ARENSBERG, C. M., and KIMBALL, S. T. (1940, 2nd edn. 1968), *Family and Community in Ireland* (Cambridge, Mass.: Harvard University Press).

ARON, R. (1962), *Dix-huit leçons sur la société industrielle* (Paris: Idées).

—— (1964), *La Lutte de classes* (Paris: Idées).

—— (1967), *The Industrial Society* (London: Weidenfeld & Nicolson).

ASSELAIN, J.-C. (1987), 'The Distribution of Income in East-Central Europe', in P. Kende and Z. Strmiska (eds.), *Equality and Inequality in Eastern Europe* (Leamington Spa: Berg).

ATKINSON, A. B. (1970), 'On the Measurement of Inequality', *Journal of Economic Theory*, 2.

AUNGER, E. A. (1983), 'Religion and Class: An Analysis of 1971 Census Data', in R. J. Cormack and R. D. Osborne (eds.), *Religion, Education and Employment: Aspects of Equal Opportunity in Northern Ireland* (Belfast: Appletree Press).

BAIROCH, P. (1968), *La Population active et sa structure* (Brussels: Éditions de l'Institut de Sociologie de l'Université Libre).

—— (1976), 'Europe's Gross National Product 1800–1974', *Journal of European Economic History*, 5.

—— (1981), 'The Main Trends in National Economic Disparities since the Industrial Revolution', in P. Bairoch and M. Lévy-Leboyer (eds.), *Disparities in Economic Development since the Industrial Revolution* (London: Macmillan).

BAKKER, I. (1988), 'Women's Employment in Comparative Perspective', in J. Jenson, E. Hagen, and C. Reddy (eds.), *Feminization of the Labor Force* (Cambridge: Polity Press).

BAUMAN, Z. (1971), 'Social Dissent in the East European Political System', *Archives européennes de sociologie*, 12.

BELL, D. (1973), *The Coming of Post-Industrial Society* (New York: Basic Books).

—— (1980), 'Liberalism in the Post-Industrial Society', in *Sociological Journeys* (London: Heinemann).

BERGER, S., and PIORE, M. (1980), *Dualism and Discontinuity in Industrial Societies* (Cambridge: Cambridge University Press).

BERTAUX, D. (1969), 'Sur l'analyse des tables de mobilité sociale', *Revue française de sociologie*, 10.

BISHOP, C. E. (1965), *Geographic and Occupational Mobility of Rural Manpower* (Paris: OECD).

—— (1969), 'The Mobility of Rural Manpower', in U. Papi and C. Nunn (eds.), *Economic Problems of Agriculture in Industrial Societies* (London: Macmillan).

BISHOP, Y. M., FIENBERG, S. E., and HOLLAND, P. W. (1975), *Discrete Multivariate Analysis* (Cambridge, Mass.: MIT Press).

BJÖRKLUND, A. (1991), 'Rising Female Labour Force Participation and the Distribution of Family Income: The Swedish Experience', (Stockholm: Swedish Institute for Social Research).

BLAND, R. (1980), 'Structural and Exchange Mobility in Northern Ireland', *Scottish Journal of Sociology*, 4.

—— ELLIOTT, B., and BECHHOFER, F. (1978), 'Social Mobility in the Petite Bourgeoisie', *Acta Sociologica*, 21.

BLAU, P. M., and DUNCAN, O. D. (1967), *The American Occupational Structure* (New York: Wiley).

BLOSSFELD, H.-P. (1986), 'Career Opportunities in the Federal Republic of Germany', *European Sociological Review*, 2.

BOGUSZAK, M. (1989), 'Transition to Socialism and Intergenerational Class Mobility: The Model of Core Social Fluidity Applied to Czechoslovakia' (Prague: Institute for Philosophy and Sociology).

—— (1990), 'Transition to Socialism and Intergenerational Class Mobility: The Model of Core Social Fluidity Applied to Czechoslovakia', in M. Haller (ed.), *Class Structure in Europe* (Armonk, NY: Sharpe).

BÖHM, A. (1984), 'Changes in the Situation of Commuters', in R. Andorka and T. Kolosi (eds.), *Stratification and Inequalities* (Budapest: Institute for Social Sciences).

—— and PÁL, L. (1982), 'Between Town and Village', in A. Böhm and T. Kolosi (eds.), *Structure and Stratification in Hungary* (Budapest: Institute for Social Sciences).

BONNEY, N. (1988a), 'Gender, Household and Social Class', *British Journal of Sociology*, 39.

—— (1988b), 'Dual Earning Couples: Trends of Change in Great Britain', *Work, Employment and Society*, 2.

BORGAN, O. (1979), 'On the Theory of Moving Average Graduation', *Scandinavian Actuarial Journal*.

BOUDON, R. (1974), *Opportunity and Social Inequality* (New York: Wiley).

BOURDIEU, P., and PASSERON, J.-C. (1964), *Les Héritiers* (Paris: Éditions de Minuit).

—— —— (1972), *La Reproduction* (Paris: Éditions de Minuit).

BOYLE, J. F. (1976), 'Analysis of the Irish Occupational Index' (Belfast: Department of Social Studies, The Queen's University).

BRAVERMAN, H. (1974), *Labor and Monopoly Capitalism* (New York: Monthly Review Press).

BREEN, R., and WHELAN, C. T. (1986), 'Vertical Mobility and Class Inheritance in the British Isles', *British Journal of Sociology*, 36.

—— HANNAN, D. F., ROTTMAN, D. B., and WHELAN, C. T. (1990), *Understanding Contemporary Ireland: State, Class and Development in the Republic of Ireland* (London: Macmillan).

BREIGER, R. L. (ed.) (1990), *Social Mobility and Social Structure* (Cambridge: Cambridge University Press).

402   *Bibliography*

BRITTEN, N., and HEATH, A. (1983), 'Women, Men and Social Class', in E.
  Gamarnikow *et al.* (eds.), *Gender, Class and Work* (London: Heinemann).
BROADBRIDGE, S. (1966), *Industrial Dualism in Japan* (London: Cass).
BROOM, L., and JONES, F. L. (1969), 'Father-to-Son Mobility: Australia in Compar-
  ative Perspective', *American Journal of Sociology*, 74.
—— DUNCAN-JONES, P., JONES, F. L., and McDONNELL, P. (1977), *Investigating
  Social Mobility* (Canberra: Research School of Social Sciences, Australian National
  University).
BROWN, T. (1985), *Ireland: A Social and Cultural History, 1922–1985* (London:
  Fontana).
BRUS, W. (1986a), 'Postwar Reconstruction and Socio-Economic Transformation',
  in M. C. Kaser and E. A. Radice (eds.), *The Economic History of Eastern Europe,
  1919–1975*, ii (Oxford: Clarendon Press).
—— (1986b), '1950 to 1953: The Peak of Stalinism', in M. C. Kaser (ed.), *The
  Economic History of Eastern Europe, 1919–1975*, iii (Oxford: Clarendon Press).
BURAWOY, M. (1977), 'Social Structure, Homogenization, and "The Process of
  Status Attainment in the United States and Great Britain" ', *American Journal of
  Sociology*, 82.
CALLAN, T., NOLAN, B., WHELAN, B. J., and HANNAN, D. F. (1989), *Poverty,
  Income and Welfare in Ireland* (Dublin: Economic and Social Research Institute).
CARCHEDI, G. (1977), *On the Economic Identification of Classes* (London: Routledge).
CARLSSON, G. (1958), *Social Mobility and Class Structure* (Lund: Gleerup).
—— (1963), 'Sorokin's Theory of Social Mobility', in P. J. Allen (ed.), *Pitirim A.
  Sorokin in Review* (Durham, NC: Duke University Press).
—— ERIKSON, R., LÖFWALL, C., and WÄRNERYD, B. (1974), 'Socio-ekonomiska
  grupperingar', *Statistisk Tidskrift*, 3rd ser., 12.
CARROLL, G., and MAYER, K.-U. (1986), 'Job-Shift Patterns in the Federal Republic
  of Germany: The Effects of Social Class, Industrial Sector and Organizational
  Size', *American Sociological Review*, 51.
CATT, C. S. (1986), 'Farmers and Factory Workers: Rural Society in Imperial
  Germany—The Example of Maudach', in R. J. Evans and W. R. Lee (eds.), *The
  German Peasantry* (London: Croom Helm).
CHAN, T. K. (1991), 'Social Mobility in Hong Kong: A Study in Comparative
  Perspective', M.Phil. Dissertation (University of Oxford).
CHASE, I. D. (1975), 'A Comparison of Men's and Women's Intergenerational
  Mobility in the United States', *American Sociological Review*, 40.
CHILD, J. (1976), 'The Industrial Supervisor', in G. Esland *et al.* (eds.), *People and
  Work* (Edinburgh: McDougall).
CHINOY, E. (1955), *Automobile Workers and the American Dream* (New York:
  Random House).
CLARK, C. (3rd edn., 1957), *The Conditions of Economic Progress* (London:
  Macmillan).
CLARK, R. (1979), *The Japanese Company* (New Haven: Yale University Press).
COBALTI, A. (1988), 'Mobili e disuguali', *Polis*, 2.
COHEN, G. A. (1978), *Karl Marx's Theory of History: A Defence* (Oxford: Clarendon
  Press).
COLE, R. E. (1979), *Work, Mobility and Participation: A Comparative Study of
  American and Japanese Industry* (Berkeley: University of California Press).

—— and Tominaga, K. (1976), 'Japan's Changing Occupational Structure and its Significance', in H. Patrick (ed.), *Japanese Industrialization and its Social Consequences* (Berkeley: University of California Press).

Commins, P. (1986), 'Rural Social Change', in P. Clancy *et al.* (eds.), *Ireland: A Sociological Profile* (Dublin: Institute of Public Administration).

Connor, W. D. (1979), *Socialism, Politics and Inequality* (New York: Columbia University Press).

Crompton, R. (1980), 'Class Mobility in Modern Britain', *Sociology*, 14.

—— and Gubbay, J. (1977), *Economy and Class Structure* (London: Macmillan).

—— and Jones, G. (1984), *White-Collar Proletariat: Deskilling and Gender in Clerical Work* (London: Macmillan).

Crossick, G., and Haupt, H.-G. (1984), *Shopkeepers and Master Artisans in Nineteenth-Century Europe* (London: Methuen).

Crozier, M. (1965), *Le Monde des employés de bureau* (Paris: Seuil).

Cutright, P. (1968), 'Occupational Inheritance: A Cross-National Analysis', *American Journal of Sociology*, 73.

Dahrendorf, R. (1959), *Class and Class Conflict in Industrial Society* (London: Routledge).

—— (1964), 'Recent Changes in the Class Structure of European Societies', *Daedalus* (Winter).

—— (1986), *Society and Democracy in Germany* (London: Weidenfeld and Nicolson).

Dale, A. (1987), 'The Effect of Life Cycle on Three Dimensions of Stratification', in A. Bryman *et al.* (eds.), *Rethinking the Life Cycle* (London: Heinemann).

Dale, P. N. (1986), *The Myth of Japanese Uniqueness* (New York: St Martin's Press).

Davis, K., and Moore, W. E. (1945), 'Some Principles of Stratification', *American Sociological Review*, 10.

De Graaf, N. D., and Ultee, W. (1990), 'Individual Preferences, Social Mobility and Electoral Outcomes', *Electoral Studies*, 9.

de Lillo, A. (1988), 'La mobilità sociale assoluta', *Polis*, 2.

—— and Schizzerotto, A. (1985), *La valutazione sociale delle occupazioni* (Bologna: Il Mulino).

Delphy, C. (1981), 'Women in Stratification Studies', in H. Roberts (ed.), *Doing Feminist Research* (London: Routledge).

—— and Leonard, D. (1986), 'Class Analysis, Gender Analysis and the Family', in R. Crompton and M. Mann (eds.), *Gender and Stratification* (Cambridge: Polity Press).

Domański, H., and Sawiński, Z. (1987), 'Dimensions of Occupational Mobility: The Empirical Invariance', *European Sociological Review*, 3.

Dore, R. P. (1973), *British Factory—Japanese Factory* (London: Allen and Unwin).

—— (1975), 'The Future of Japan's Meritocracy', *Revista internazionale di scienze economiche e commerciali*, 7–8.

—— (1978), *Shinohata* (New York: Pantheon Books).

Duncan, O. D. (1961), 'A Socioeconomic Index for all Occupations', in A. J. Reiss (ed.), *Occupations and Social Status* (New York: Free Press).

—— (1966), 'Methodological Issues in the Analysis of Social Mobility', in N. J. Smelser and S. M. Lipset (eds.), *Social Structure and Mobility in Economic Development* (London: Routledge).

DUNLOP, J. T., HARBISON, F. H., KERR, C., and MYERS, C. A. (1975), *Industrialism and Industrial Man Reconsidered* (Princeton, NJ: Inter-University Study of Human Resources in National Development).

DUNTON, N., and FEATHERMAN, D. L. (1985), 'Social Mobility through Marriage and Careers', in J. T. Spence (ed.), *Achievement and Achievement Motives* (San Francisco: W. H. Freeman).

ELSTER, J. (1979), *Ulysses and the Sirens* (Cambridge: Cambridge University Press).

—— (1985), *Making Sense of Marx* (Cambridge: Cambridge University Press).

ENCEL, S. (1970), *Equality and Authority: A Study of Class, Status and Power in Australia* (London: Tavistock).

ERIKSON, R. (1981), 'Om socio-ekonomiska indelningar av hushåll: Överväganden och ett förslag', *Statistisk Tidskrift*, 3rd ser., 19.

—— (1983), 'Changes in Social Mobility in Industrial Nations: The Case of Sweden', *Research in Social Stratification and Mobility*, 2.

—— (1984), 'Social Class of Men, Women and Families', *Sociology*, 18.

—— (1987), 'The Class Structure and its Trends', in R. Erikson and R. Åberg (eds.), *Welfare in Transition: A Survey of Living Conditions in Sweden 1968–1981* (Oxford: Clarendon Press).

—— (1989), Review of G. Marshall *et al.*, *Social Class in Modern Britain*, *European Sociological Review*, 5.

—— (1990), 'Politics and Class Mobility—Does Politics Influence Rates of Social Mobility?' in I. Persson (ed.), *Generating Equality in the Welfare State* (Oslo: Norwegian University Press).

—— and GOLDTHORPE, J. H. (1985), 'Are American Rates of Social Mobility Exceptionally High? New Evidence on an Old Issue', *European Sociological Review*, 1.

—— —— (1987), 'Commonality and Variation in Social Fluidity in Industrial Nations. Part I: A Model for Evaluating the "FJH Hypothesis"; Part II: The Model of Core Social Fluidity Applied', *European Sociological Review*, 3.

—— —— (1988), '"Woman at Class Crossroads": A Critical Note', *Sociology*, 22.

—— —— (1989), 'Is Social Mobility Best Analysed by Association Models'? (ISA Research Committee on Social Stratification, Stanford).

—— —— (1992), 'Individual or Family: Results from Two Approaches to Class Assignment', *Acta Sociologica*, 35.

—— and PÖNTINEN, S. (1985), 'Social Mobility in Finland and Sweden: A Comparison of Men and Women', in R. Alapuro *et al.* (eds.), *Small States in Comparative Perspective* (Oslo: Norwegian University Press).

—— GOLDTHORPE, J. H., and PORTOCARERO, L. (1979), 'Intergenerational Class Mobility in Three Western European Societies', *British Journal of Sociology*, 30.

—— —— —— (1982), 'Social Fluidity in Industrial Nations', *British Journal of Sociology*, 33.

—— —— —— (1983), 'Intergenerational Class Mobility and the Convergence Thesis', *British Journal of Sociology*, 34.

—— HANSEN, E. J., RINGEN, S., and UUSITALO, H. (eds.) (1987), *The Scandinavian Model* (Armonk, NY: Sharpe).

—— GOLDTHORPE, J. H., KÖNIG, W., LÜTTINGER, P., and MÜLLER, W. (1988), 'CASMIN International Mobility Superfile: Documentation' (Mannheim: Institut für Sozialwissenschaften, University of Mannheim).

ESPING ANDERSEN, G. (1985), *Politics Against Markets* (Princeton, NJ: Princeton University Press).

—— and KORPI, W. (1984), 'Social Policy as Class Politics in Post-War Capitalism', in J. H. Goldthorpe (ed.), *Order and Conflict in Contemporary Capitalism* (Oxford: Clarendon Press).

FEATHERMAN, D. L., and HAUSER, R. M. (1978), *Opportunity and Change* (New York: Academic Press).

—— and SELBEE, L. K. (1988), 'Class Formation and Class Mobility: A New Approach with Counts from Life History Data', in M. Riley and B. Huber (eds.), *Social Structure and Human Lives* (Newbury Park: Sage).

—— and SPENNER, K. I. (1990), 'Class and the Socialisation of Children: Constancy, Chance or Irrelevance?', in E. M. Hetherington, R. M. Lerner, and M. Perlmutter (eds.), *Child Development in Life-Span Perspective* (Hillsdale, NJ: Erlbaum).

—— JONES, F. L., and HAUSER, R. M. (1975), 'Assumptions of Social Mobility Research in the US: The Case of Occupational Status', *Social Science Research*, 4.

—— SELBEE, L. K., and MAYER, K.-U. (1989), 'Social Class and the Structuring of the Life Course in Norway and West Germany', in D. Kertzer, J. Meyer, and K. W. Schaie (eds.), *Social Structure and Aging* (Hillsdale, NJ: Erlbaum).

FEINSTEIN, C. (1988), 'The Rise and Fall of the Williamson Curve', *Journal of Economic History*, 48.

FIELDS, G. S., and JAKUBSEN, G. H. (1990), 'The Inequality–Development Relationship in Developing Countries' (Department of Economics, Cornell University).

FINCH, J. (1983), *Married to the Job: Wives' Incorporation into Men's Work* (London: Allen and Unwin).

FLORA, P., KRAUS, F., and PFENNING, W. (1987), *State, Economy and Society in Western Europe*, ii (Frankfurt: Campus).

FOHLEN, C. (1976), 'France 1920–1970', in C. M. Cipolla (ed.), *Fontana Economic History of Europe*, vi/i (London: Fontana).

FOX, T. G., and MILLER, S. M. (1965), 'Economic, Political and Social Determinants of Mobility', *Acta Sociologica*, 9.

—— —— (1966), 'Occupational Stratification and Mobility: Inter-Country Variations', in R. Merritt and S. Rokkan (eds.), *Comparing Nations* (New Haven: Yale University Press).

FRANKLIN, S. H. (1969), *The European Peasantry* (London: Methuen).

—— (1971), *Rural Societies* (London: Macmillan).

FRENTZEL-ZAGÓRSKA, J., and ZAGÓRSKI, K. (1989), 'East European Intellectuals on the Road to Dissent: The Old Prophecy of a New Class Re-examined', *Politics and Society*, 17.

FUKUTAKE, T. (1967), *Japanese Rural Society* (Ithaca, NY: Cornell University Press).

—— (1982), *The Japanese Social Structure* (Tokyo: University of Tokyo Press).

GABAL, I., MATĚJŮ, P., and BOGUSZAK, M. (1989), 'Stratification or De-Stratification of the Czechoslovak Society?' (Prague: Institute for Philosophy and Sociology).

GAGLIANI, G. (1985), 'Long-Term Changes in the Occupational Structure', *European Sociological Review*, 1.

GALBRAITH, J. K. (1971), *The New Industral State* (Boston: Houghton Mifflin).

GALLIE, D. (1988), 'Technological Change, Gender and Skill', Social Change and Economic Life Initiative, Working Paper 4 (London: Economic and Social Research Council).

GANZEBOOM, H., and LUIJKX, R. (1986), 'Intergenerational Occupational Mobility in Hungary between 1930 and 1982' (Working Paper Series, no. 3, Department of Sociology, Tilburg University).

—— LUIJKX, R., and TREIMAN, D. J. (1989), 'Intergenerational Class Mobility in Comparative Perspective', *Research in Social Stratification and Mobility*, 8.

GARNSEY, E. (1975), 'Occupational Stratification in Industrial Societies: Some Notes on the Convergence Thesis in the Light of Soviet Experience', *Sociology*, 9.

GARTON ASH, T. (1989), 'Reform or Revolution', in *The Uses of Adversity* (Cambridge: Granta).

GASSON, R. (1969), *Occupational Immobility of Small Farmers* (Cambridge: Cambridge University Department of Land Economy).

GEIGER, T. (1932), *Die soziale Schichtung des deutschen Volkes* (Stuttgart: Enke).

GELLNER, E. (1971), 'The Pluralist Anti-Levellers of Prague', *Archives européennes de sociologie*, 12.

GERSHUNY, J. (1983), *Social Innovation and the Division of Labour* (Oxford: Clarendon Press).

GIDDENS, A. (1973), *The Class Structure of the Advanced Societies* (London: Hutchinson).

GILBERT, N. (1981), *Modelling Society* (London: Allen and Unwin).

GIRARD, A. (1963, 2nd edn. 1974), *Le Choix du conjoint* (Paris: Presses Universitaires de France).

GIROD, R. (1971), *Mobilité sociale* (Geneva: Droz).

GLASS, D. V. (ed.) (1954), *Social Mobility in Britain* (London: Routledge).

GLENN, N. D. (1977), *Cohort Analysis* (Beverly Hills: Sage).

—— ROSS, A. A., and TULLY, J. C. (1974), 'Patterns of Intergenerational Mobility of Females through Marriage', *American Sociological Review*, 39.

GOLDTHORPE, J. H. (1971), 'Theories of Industrial Society', *Archives européennes de sociologie*, 12.

—— (1979), 'Intellectuals and the Working Class in Modern Britain' (University of Essex: Fuller Bequest Lecture).

—— (with Catriona Llewellyn and Clive Payne) (1980*a*, 2nd edn. 1987), *Social Mobility and Class Structure in Modern Britain* (Oxford: Clarendon Press).

—— (1980*b*), 'Reply to Crompton', *Sociology*, 14.

—— (1981–2), 'Social Standing, Class and Status', *SCPR Survey Methods Newsletter* (winter).

—— (1982), 'On the Service Class: Its Formation and Future', in A. Giddens and G. Mackenzie (eds.), *Social Class and the Division of Labour* (Cambridge: Cambridge University Press).

—— (1983), 'Women and Class Analysis: In Defence of the Conventional View', *Sociology*, 17.

—— (1984), 'Women and Class Analysis: A Reply to the Replies', *Sociology*, 18.

—— (1985*a*). 'Soziale Mobilität und Klassenbildung: Zur Erneuerung einer Tradition soziologischer Forschung', in H. Strasser and J. H. Goldthorpe (eds.), *Die Analyse Sozialer Ungleichheit* (Opladen: Westdeutscher Verlag).

—— (1985*b*), 'On Economic Development and Social Mobility', *British Journal of Sociology*, 36.

—— (1990), 'A Response', in J. Clark, C. Modgil, and S. Modgil (eds.), *John H. Goldthorpe: Consensus and Controversy* (London: Falmer Press).

—— (1991*a*), 'The Uses of History in Sociology', *British Journal of Sociology*, 42.

—— (1991*b*), 'Employment, Class and Mobility: A Critique of Liberal and Marxist Theories of Long-Term Change', in H. Haferkamp and N. J. Smelser (eds.), *Modernity and Social Change* (Berkeley: University of California Press).

—— and HOPE, K. (1972), 'Occupational Grading and Occupational Prestige', in K. Hope (ed.), *The Analysis of Social Mobility* (Oxford: Clarendon Press).

—— —— (1974), *The Social Grading of Occupations: A New Approach and Scale* (Oxford: Clarendon Press).

—— and LLEWELLYN, C. (1977), 'Class Mobility in Britain: Three Theses Examined', *Sociology*, 11.

—— and PAYNE, C. (1986), 'Trends in Intergenerational Class Mobility in England and Wales, 1972–1983', *Sociology*, 20.

—— and PORTOCARERO, L. (1981), 'La Mobilité sociale en France, 1953–1970: Nouvel examen', *Revue française de sociologie*, 22.

—— LOCKWOOD, D., BECHHOFER, F., and PLATT, J. (1968), *The Affluent Worker: Industrial Attitudes and Behaviour* (Cambridge: Cambridge University Press).

GOODMAN, L. A. (1972), 'A General Model for the Analysis of Surveys', *American Journal of Sociology*, 77.

—— (1979), 'Simple Models for the Analysis of Association in Cross-Classifications having Ordered Categories', *Journal of the American Statistical Association*, 74.

LE GRAND, C. (1989), *Interna arbetsmarknader, ekonomisk segmentering och social skiktning* (Stockholm: Almqvist and Wicksell).

GRANOVETTER, M. (1973), 'The Strength of Weak Ties', *American Journal of Sociology*, 78.

—— (1974) *Getting a Job* (Cambridge, Mass.: Harvard University Press).

—— (1983), 'The Strength of Weak Ties: A Network Theory Revisited' in R. Collins (ed.), *Sociological Theory 1983* (San Francisco: Jossey Bass).

GRAY, J., McPHERSON, A. F., and RAFFE, D. (1983), *Reconstructions of Secondary Education* (London: Routledge).

GRUSKY, D. B., and HAUSER, R. M. (1984), 'Comparative Social Mobility Revisited: Models of Convergence and Divergence in 16 Countries', *American Sociological Review*, 49.

GUEST, A. M., LANDALE, N. S., and McCANN, J. C. (1989), 'Intergenerational Occupational Mobility in the Late 19th Century United States', *Social Forces*, 68.

HAGENAARS, J. A. (1990), *Categorical Longitudinal Data* (London: Sage).

HALLER, M., KOLOSI, T., and ROBERT, P. (1990), 'Social Mobility in Austria, Czechoslovakia and Hungary: An Investigation of the Effects of Industrialization, Socialist Revolution and National Uniqueness', in M. Haller (ed.), *Class Structure in Europe* (Armonk, NY: Sharpe).

—— KÖNIG, W., KRAUSE, P., and KURZ, K. (1985), 'Patterns of Career Mobility and Structural Positions in Advanced Capitalist Societies: A Comparison of Men in Austria, France and the United States', *American Sociological Review*, 50.

HAMMOND, J. L. (1987), 'Wife's Status and Family Social Standing', *Sociological Perspectives*, 30.

HANCOCK, W. K. (1930), *Australia* (London: Benn).

HANDL, J. (n.d.), 'Heiratsmobilität und berufliche Mobilität von Frauen' (VASMA Project Working Paper 8; Mannheim: Institut für Sozialwissenschaften, University of Mannheim).

HANNAN, D. F. (1979), *Displacement and Development: Class, Kinship and Social Change in Irish Rural Communities* (Dublin: The Economic and Social Research Institute).

HARA, A. (1979), 'Kaikyu Kosei no Shinsuikei' (A New Estimation of Class Composition), in Y. Ando (ed.), *Ryotaisen kan no Nihon Shihonshugi* (*Japanese Capitalism in the Inter-war Years*) (Tokyo: Todai Shuppan Kai).

HARDIN, R. (1976), 'Stability of Statist Regimes: Industrialization and Institutionalization', in T. R. Burns and W. Buckley (eds.), *Power and Control* (London: Sage).

HARDY, M. A., and HAZELRIGG, L. E. (1978), 'Industrialization and the Circulatory Rate of Mobility', *Sociological Focus*, 11.

HARRIS, R. (1972), *Prejudice and Tolerance in Ulster* (Manchester: Manchester University Press).

HARTZ, L. (1955), *The Liberal Tradition in America* (New York: Harcourt Brace).

—— (1964), *The Founding of New Societies* (New York: Harcourt Brace).

HARVIE, C. (1981), *No Gods and Precious Few Heroes: Scotland 1914–1980* (London: Arnold).

HAUSER, R. M. (1978), 'A Structural Model of the Mobility Table', *Social Forces*, 56.

—— (1979), 'Some Exploratory Methods for Modeling Mobility Tables and Other Cross-Classified Data', in K. F. Schuessler (ed.), *Sociological Methodology 1980* (San Francisco: Jossey Bass).

—— (1984), 'Vertical Class Mobility in England, France and Sweden', *Acta Sociologica*, 27.

—— and FEATHERMAN, D. L. (1977), *The Process of Stratification: Trends and Analyses* (New York: Academic Press).

—— and GRUSKY, D. B. (1988), 'Cross National Variation in Occupational Distributions, Relative Mobility Chances and Intergenerational Shifts in Occupational Distributions', *American Sociological Review*, 53.

—— DICKINSON, P. J., TRAVIS, H. P., and KOFFEL, J. M. (1975), 'Temporal Change in Occupational Mobility: Evidence for Men in the United States', *American Sociological Review*, 40.

HAYES, B. C. (1990), 'Intergenerational Occupational Mobility among Employed and Non-employed Women: The Australian Case', *Australian and New Zealand Journal of Sociology*, 26.

HAZELRIGG, L. E. (1974), 'Cross-National Comparisons of Father-to-Son Occupational Mobility', in J. Lopreato and L. S. Lewis (eds.), *Social Stratification* (New York: Harper and Row).

—— and GARNIER, M. A. (1976), 'Occupational Mobility in Industrial Societies', *American Sociological Review*, 41.

HEATH, A. (1981), *Social Mobility* (London: Fontana).

—— and BRITTEN, N. (1984), 'Women's Jobs Do Make a Difference: A Reply to Goldthorpe', *Sociology*, 18.

HEDSTRÖM, P. (1987), *Structures of Inequality: A Study of Stratification within Work Organizations* (Stockholm: Swedish Institute for Social Research).

HERNES, G., and KNUDSEN, K. (1987), 'Kjønn og Klassebevissthet', in T. Colbjørnsen (ed.), *Klassesamfunnet på Hell* (Oslo: Universitetsforlaget).

HOEM, J. M. (1991), 'Fluttering Tails in Moving Average Graduation' (Stockholm: Research Reports in Demography 62; University of Stockholm).

—— and LINNEMAN, P. (1988), 'The Tails in Moving Average Graduation', *Scandinavian Actuarial Journal*.

HOFFMAN, S. (1963), 'Paradoxes of the French Political Community', in S. Hoffman *et al.*, *France: Change and Tradition* (London: Gollancz).

HOLT, D. (1979), 'Log-Linear Models for Contingency Table Analysis: On the Interpretation of Parameters', *Sociological Methods and Research*, 7.

HOUT, M. (1983), *Mobility Tables* (Beverly Hills: Sage).

—— (1984), 'Status, Autonomy and Training in Occupational Mobility', *American Journal of Sociology*, 89.

—— (1986), 'Opportunity and the Minority Middle Class: A Comparison of Blacks in the United States and Catholics in Northern Ireland', *American Sociological Review*, 51.

—— (1988), 'More Universalism, Less Structural Mobility: The American Occupational Structure in the 1980s', *American Journal of Sociology*, 93.

—— (1989), *Following in Father's Footsteps: Social Mobility in Ireland* (Cambridge, Mass.: Harvard University Press).

—— and HAUSER, R. M. (1991), 'Symmetry and Hierarchy in Social Mobility: A Methodological Analysis of the CASMIN Model of Class Mobility' (ISA Research Committee on Social Stratification, Prague).

—— and JACKSON, J. A. (1986), 'Dimensions of Occupational Mobility in the Republic of Ireland', *European Sociological Review*, 2.

HUACO, G. A. (1966), 'The Functionalist Theory of Social Stratification: Two Decades of Controversy', *Inquiry*, 9.

HUMPHREYS, A. J. (1966), *New Dubliners* (London: Routledge).

HUSZÁR, T. (ed.) (1988), *Ferenc Erdei: Selected Writings* (Budapest: Akadémiai Kiadó).

INTERNATIONAL LABOUR ORGANIZATION (ILO) (1977), *Labor Force Estimates and Projections* (2nd edn., Geneva; ILO).

ISHIDA, H. (1986), 'Educational Credentials, Class and the Labor Market: A Comparative Study of Social Mobility in Japan and the United States', (Ph.D. thesis, Harvard University).

—— GOLDTHORPE, J. H., and ERIKSON, R. (1991), 'Intergenerational Class Mobility in Post-war Japan', *American Journal of Sociology*, 96.

IWAMOTO, T. (1985), 'Sedaikan Ido no Susei Bunseki' (Trend Analysis of Intergenerational Mobility), in J. Hara and M. Umino (eds), *Suri Shakaigaku no Genzai* (*Contemporary Mathematical Sociology*) (Tokyo: Suri Shakaigaku Kenkyukai).

JACKSON, J. A. (1971), 'Ireland', in M. Archer and S. Giner (eds.), *Contemporary Europe: Class, Status and Power* (London: Weidenfeld and Nicolson).

JANOWITZ, M. (1958), 'Social Stratification and Mobility in West Germany', *American Journal of Sociology*, 64.

JENCKS, C. (and associates) (1972), *Inequality: A Reassessment of the Effect of Family and Schooling in America* (New York: Basic Books).

—— (and associates) (1979), *Who Gets Ahead? The Determinants of Economic Success in America* (New York: Basic Books).

JOHNSON, P. M. (1981), 'Changing Social Structure and the Political Role of Manual Workers', in J. F. Triska and C. Gati (eds.), *Blue-Collar Workers in Eastern Europe* (London: Allen and Unwin).

JOHNSON, T. (1977), 'What is to be Known: The Structural Determination of Social Class', *Economy and Society*, 6.

JONES, F. L. (1969), 'Social Mobility and Industrial Society: A Thesis Re-examined', *Sociological Quarterly*, 10.

—— (1981), 'Social Stratification and Mobility', in P. Drysdale and H. Kitaoji (eds.), *Japan and Australia: Two Societies and their Interaction* (Canberra: ANU Press).

—— (1987), 'Father-to-Son Mobility in Australia and Japan: A Reanalysis', *International Journal of Comparative Sociology*, 28.

—— (1991), 'Common Social Fluidity: A Comment on Some Recent Criticisms' (Research School of Social Sciences, Australian National University, Canberra).

—— and DAVIS, P. (1986), *Models of Society* (Sydney: Croom Helm).

JONES, G. (1987), 'Young Workers in the Class Structure' (London: Thomas Coram Research Unit, Institute of Education).

JONSSON, J. O. (1987), 'Class Origin, Cultural Origin and Educational Attainment: The Case of Sweden', *European Sociological Review*, 3.

—— (1990), 'Educational Reform and Changes in Inequality in Sweden', in A. Leschinsky and K.-U. Mayer (eds.), *The Comprehensive School Experiment Revisited* (Frankfurt am Main: Peter Lang).

—— (1991), 'Education, Social Mobility and Social Reproduction in Sweden: Patterns and Changes', In E. J. Hansen, S. Ringen, H. Uusitalo, and R. Erikson (eds.), *Scandinavian Trends in Welfare and Living Conditions* (Armonck, NY: Sharpe).

—— (1992), Class Formation; The Holding Power and Socio-demographic Composition of Social Classes in Sweden' (Swedish Institute for Social Research, Stockholm).

JOSHI, H. (1988), 'Changing Roles of Women in the British Labour Market and the Family' (Discussion Paper in Economics 88/13, Birkbeck College, University of London).

KAELBLE, H. (1978), 'Social Mobility in Germany, 1900–1960', *Journal of Modern History*, 50.

—— (1981), *Historical Research on Social Mobility* (London: Croom Helm).

—— (1984), 'Eras of Social Mobility in 19th and 20th Century Europe', *Journal of Social History*, 17.

KASCHUBA, W. (1986), 'Peasants and Others: The Historical Contours of Village Class Society', in R. J. Evans and W. R. Lee (eds.), *The German Peasantry* (London: Croom Helm).

KELLAS, J. G., and FOTHERINGHAM, P. (1976), 'The Political Behaviour of the Working Class', in A. A. MacLaren (ed.), *Social Class in Scotland Past and Present* (Edinburgh: John Donald).

KELLEY, J. (1990), 'The Failure of a Paradigm: Log Linear Models of Social Mobility', in J. Clark, C. Modgil, and S. Modgil (eds.), *John H. Goldthorpe: Consensus and Controversy* (London: Falmer).

KEMP, T. (1978), *Historical Patterns of Industrialization* (London: Longman).

KENDRICK, S., BECHHOFER, F., and MCCRONE, D. (1985), 'Is Scotland Different? Industrial and Occupational Change in Scotland and Britain', in H. Newby *et al.*

(eds.), *Restructuring Capital: Recession and Reorganisation in Industrial Society* (London: Macmillan).

KENNEDY, K. A., GIBLIN, T., and McHUGH, D. (1988), *The Economic Development of Ireland in the Twentieth Century* (London: Routledge).

KERCKHOFF, A. C., CAMPBELL, R. T., and WINGFIELD-LAIRD, I. (1985), 'Social Mobility in Great Britain and the United States', *American Journal of Sociology*, 90.

KERR, C. (1969), *Marshall, Marx and Modern Times* (Cambridge: Cambridge University Press).

—— (1983), *The Future of Industrial Societies* (Cambridge, Mass.: Harvard University Press).

—— DUNLOP, J. T., HARBISON, F. H., and MYERS, C. A. (1960, 2nd edn. 1973), *Industrialism and Industrial Man* (Cambridge, Mass.: Harvard University Press).

KEYSERLING, H. A. (1928), *Europe* (London: Cape).

KINDLEBERGER, C. P. (1967), *Europe's Postwar Growth: The Role of Labor Supply* (Cambridge, Mass.: Harvard University Press).

KLINGENDER, F. (1935), *The Condition of Clerical Labour in Britain* (London: Martin Lawrence).

KNOKE, D., and BURKE, P. J. (1980), *Log-linear Models* (Beverly Hills: Sage).

KOCKA, J. (1980*a*), *White-Collar Workers in America, 1890–1940* (London: Sage).

—— (1980*b*), 'The Study of Social Mobility and the Formation of the Working Class in the 19th Century', *Le Mouvement social*, 111.

—— (1981), 'Class Formation, Interest Articulation and Public Policy: The Origins of the German White-Collar Class in the Late Nineteenth and Earlier Twentieth Centuries', in S. Berger (ed.), *Organizing Interests in Western Europe* (Cambridge: Cambridge University Press).

KOHN, M. L. (1969), *Class and Conformity* (Homewood, Ill.: Dorsey).

—— (1989), 'Introduction', in M. L. Kohn (ed.), *Cross-National Research in Sociology* (Newbury Park: Sage).

KOJIMA, H., and HAMANA, A. (1984), 'Skokugyo Ido no Keiko Bunseki' (Trend Analysis of Occupational Mobility), *Ibaraki Daigaku Kyoiku Gakubu Kiyo*, 33.

KOLAKOWSKI, L. (1971), 'A Pleading for Revolution: A Rejoinder to Z. Bauman', *Archives européennes de sociologie*, 12.

KOLANKIEWICZ, G. (1973), 'The Technical Intelligentsia', in D. Lane and G. Kolankiewicz (eds.), *Social Groups in Poland* (London: Macmillan).

KÖNIG, W. (1987), 'Employment and Career Mobility of Women in France and the Federal Republic', in W. Teckenberg (ed.), *Comparative Studies of Social Structure* (New York: Sharpe).

—— and MÜLLER, W. (1986), 'Educational Systems and Labour Markets as Determinants of Worklife Mobility in France and West Germany: A Comparison of Men's Career Mobility, 1965–1970', *European Sociological Review*, 2.

KONRAD, G., and SZELÉNYI, I. (1977), 'Social Conflicts of Underurbanization', in M. Harloe (ed.), *Captive Cities* (London: Wiley).

—— —— (1979), *The Intellectuals on the Road to Class Power* (Brighton: Harvester).

KOVÁCS, F. (1982), 'Tendencies of Convergence in the Development of Social Structure', in A. Böhm and T. Kolosi (eds.), *Stratification and Inequalities* (Budapest: Institute for Social Sciences).

KOVACS, F. (1983), 'Industrialisation', in T. Kolosi and E. Wnuk-Lipiński (eds.), *Equality and Inequality under Socialism: Poland and Hungary Compared* (London: Sage).

KULCSÁR, K. (1984), *Contemporary Hungarian Society* (Budapest: Corvina).

KUZNETS, S. (1955), 'Economic Growth and Income Inequality', *American Economic Review*, 45.

—— (1963), 'Quantitative Aspects of the Economic Growth of Nations, VIII, Distribution of Income by Size', *Economic Development and Cultural Change*, 5.

—— (1966), *Modern Economic Growth* (New Haven: Yale University Press).

LAFONT, J., and LEBORGNE, D. (1974), 'L'Artisanat du bâtiment: Un monde en transition', *Economie et Statistique*, 55.

LANDES, D. S. (1957), 'Observations on France: Economy, Society and Politics', *World Politics* (April).

—— (1965, 2nd edn. 1972), *The Unbound Prometheus: Technological Change and Industrial Development in Western Europe from 1750 to the Present* (Cambridge: Cambridge University Press).

LANE, D. (1976), *The Socialist Industrial State* (London: Allen and Unwin).

LEIULFSRUD, H., and WOODWARD, A. (1987), 'Women at Class Crossroads: Repudiating Conventional Theories of Social Class', *Sociology*, 21.

LEWIS, P. (1973), 'The Peasantry', in D. Lane and G. Kolankiewicz (eds.), *Social Groups in Polish Society* (London: Macmillan).

LIEBERSON, S. (1985, 2nd edn. 1987), *Making it Count* (Berkeley: University of California Press).

LIPSET, S. M. (1960), *Political Man* (London: Heinemann).

—— (1968), 'Anglo-American Society', in D. L. Sills (ed.), *International Encyclopaedia of the Social Sciences*, i (New York: Crowell Collier and Macmillan).

—— (1977), 'Why No Socialism in the United States?', in S. Bialer and S. Sluzar (eds.), *Sources of Contemporary Radicalism* (New York: Westview Press).

—— (1979), 'American Exceptionalism', in M. Novak (ed.), *Capitalism and Socialism* (Washington DC: American Enterprise Institute).

—— (1982), 'Social Mobility in Industrial Societies', *Public Opinion*, June/July.

—— and BENDIX, R. (1959), *Social Mobility in Industrial Society* (Berkeley: University of California Press).

—— and ZETTERBERG, H. L. (1956), 'A Theory of Social Mobility', *Transactions of the Third World Congress of Sociology*, iii (London: International Sociological Association).

—— —— (1959), 'Social Mobility in Industrial Societies', in S. M. Lipset and R. Bendix, *Social Mobility in Industrial Society* (Berkeley: University of California Press).

LOCKWOOD, D. (1958, 2nd edn. 1989), *The Blackcoated Worker* (London: Allen and Unwin).

—— (1981), 'The Weakest Link in the Chain? Some Comments on the Marxist Theory of Action', *Research in the Sociology of Work*, 1.

LONG, J. S. (1984) 'Estimable Functions in Log-Linear Models', *Sociological Methods and Research*, 12.

LOW-BEER, J. R. (1978), *Protest and Participation: The New Working Class in Italy* (Cambridge: Cambridge University Press).

LOWENTAL, D. (1968), Review of B. Moore, *Social Origins of Dictatorship and Democracy*, *History and Theory*, 1.

LUIJKX, R., and GANZEBOOM, H. B. G. (1989), 'Intergenerational Class Mobility in the Netherlands between 1970 and 1986', in W. Jansen, J. Dronkers, and K. Verrips (eds.), *Similar or Different?* (Amsterdam: SISWO).

LUNDBERG, O. (1990), 'Egen klass, makes klass och skillnader i sjuklighet mellan män och kvinnor' (Stockholm: Swedish Institute for Social Research).

LUNDGREEN, P. (1980–1), *Sozialgeschichte des Deutschen Schule im Überblick* (2 vols.; Göttingen: Vandenhoek and Ruprecht).

LUTZ, B. (1984), *Der kurze Traum immerwährender Prosperität* (Frankfurt: Campus).

LYDALL, H. (1968), *The Structure of Earnings* (Oxford: Clarendon Press).

McCLELLAND, P. D. (1975), *Causal Explanation and Model Building in History, Economics and the New Economic History* (Ithaca: Cornell University Press).

McCLENDON, McK. J. (1980), 'Occupational Mobility and Economic Development', *Sociological Focus*, 13.

McCORMACK, G., and SUGIMOTO, Y. (1988), *The Japanese Trajectory: Modernization and Beyond* (Cambridge: Cambridge University Press).

McCRONE, D., BECHHOFER, F., and KENDRICK, S. (1982), 'Egalitarianism and Social Inequality in Scotland', in D. Robbins *et al.* (eds.), *Rethinking Social Inequality* (Aldershot: Gower).

MACDONALD, K. I. (1981), 'On the Formulation of a Structural Model of the Mobility Table', *Social Forces*, 60.

—— and RIDGE, J. M. (1987), 'Social Mobility', in A. H. Halsey (ed.), *British Social Trends since 1900* (London: Macmillan).

McFARLANE, B. (1988), *Yugoslavia: Politics, Economics and Society* (London: Pinter).

MACH, B. W., and WESOŁOWSKI, W. (1986), *Social Mobility and Social Structure* (London: Routledge).

—— and PESCHAR, J. L. (1990), 'On the Changing Role of Education in Social Reproduction in Different Sociopolitical Systems', in M. Haller (ed.), *Class Structure in Europe* (Armonck, NY: Sharpe).

MACLAREN, A. (ed.) (1976), *Social Class in Scotland* (Edinburgh: John Donald).

McRAE, S. (1990), 'Women and Class Analysis', in J. Clark, C. Modgil, and S. Modgil (eds.), *John H. Goldthorpe: Consensus and Controversy* (London: Falmer).

MADDISON, A. (1973), 'Economic Performance and Policy in Europe, 1913–1970', in C. M. Cipolla (ed.), *Fontana Economic History of Europe*, v/ii (London: Fontana).

MARSHALL, G. (1990), 'John Goldthorpe and Class Analysis', in J. Clark, C. Modgil, and S. Modgil (eds.), *John Goldthorpe: Consensus and Controversy* (London: Falmer).

—— and ROSE, D. (1988), 'Proletarianization in the British Class Structure?' *British Journal of Sociology*, 34.

—— —— (1990), 'Out-classed by Our Critics?', *Sociology*, 24.

—— NEWBY, H., ROSE, D., and VOGLER, C. (1988), *Social Class in Modern Britain* (London: Hutchinson).

MARTIN, J., and ROBERTS, C. (1984), *Women and Employment: A Lifetime Perspective* (London: HMSO).

MARX, K. (1958), *Selected Works* (Moscow: Foreign Languages Publishing House).

MATEJKO, A. (1974), *Social Change and Stratification in Eastern Europe* (New York: Praeger).

MATĚJŮ, P. (1990), 'Family Effect on Educational Attainment in Czechoslovakia, the Netherlands and Hungary', in J. L. Peschar (ed.), *Social Reproduction in Eastern and Western Europe* (Nijmegen: Institute for Applied Social Sciences).

MATĚJŮ, P., and BOGUSZAK, M. (1989), 'Residential and Class Mobility in Czech Lands and Slovakia' (Prague: Institute for Philosophy and Sociology).

MAURICE, M., SELLIER, F., and SILVESTRE, J.-J. (1982), *Politique d'education et organisation industrielle en France et en Allemagne* (Paris: Presses Universitaires de France).

—— SORGE, A., and WARNER, M. (1980), 'Societal Differences in Organizing Manufacturing Units: A Comparison of France, West Germany and Great Britain', *Organizational Studies*, 1.

MAYER, A. J. (1981), *The Persistence of the Old Regime: Europe to the Great War* (New York: Pantheon).

MAYER, K. (1964), 'Social Stratification in Two Equalitarian Societies: Australia and the United States', *Social Research*, 31.

MAYER, K.-U. (1979), 'Strukturwandel in Beschäftigungssystem und berufliche Mobilität zwischen Generationen', *Zeitschrift für Bevölkerungswissenschaft*, 3.

—— (1988), 'The CASMIN Results on Germany—A Comment', Conference on 'The CASMIN Project and Comparative Sociology', Schloss Reisensburg, West Germany.

—— and CARROLL, G. R. (1987), 'Jobs and Classes: Structural Constraints on Career Mobility', *European Sociological Review*, 3.

—— FEATHERMAN, D. L., SELBEE, L. K., and COLBJØRNSEN, T. (1989), 'Class Mobility During Working Life: A Comparison of Germany and Norway', in M. L. Kohn (ed.), *Cross-National Research in Sociology* (Newbury Park: Sage).

MAYER, N. (1977), 'Une filière de mobilité ouvrière: L'accès à la petite entreprise artisanale et commerciale', *Revue française de sociologie*, 18.

—— (1987), 'Small Business and Social Mobility in France', in R. Goffee and R. Scase (eds.), *Entrepreneurship in Europe: The Social Process* (London: Croom Helm).

MELLOR, R. (1978), *The Two Germanies: A Modern Geography* (New York: Harper and Row).

MENDELS, F. F. (1976), 'Social Mobility and Phases of Industrialisation', *Journal of Interdisciplinary History*, 7.

MEYER, J. M., TUMA, N. B., and ZAGÓRSKI, K. (1979), 'Education and Occupational Mobility: A Comparison of Polish and American Men', *American Journal of Sociology*, 84.

MILL, J. S. (1848), *Principles of Political Economy* (London: John W. Parker).

MILLER, D., and SWANSON, G. E. (1958), *The Changing American Parent* (New York: Wiley).

MILLER, R. L. (1983), 'Religion and Occupational Mobility', in R. J. Cormack and R. D. Osborne (eds.), *Religion, Education and Employment: Aspects of Equal Opportunity in Northern Ireland* (Belfast: Appletree Press).

—— (1986), 'Social Stratification and Social Mobility in Northern Ireland', in P. Clancy *et al.* (eds.), *The Sociology of Modern Ireland* (Dublin: Institute of Public Administration).

MILLER, S. M. (1960), 'Comparative Social Mobility', *Current Sociology*, 9.

—— and BRYCE, H. J. (1961), 'Social Mobility and Economic Growth and Structure', *Kölner Zeitschrift für Soziologie*, 13.

MILLS, C. W. (1951), *White-Collar* (New York: Oxford University Press).

MISZTAL, B. (1981), 'The Petite Bourgeoisie in Socialist Society', in F. Bechhofer and B. Elliott (eds.), *The Petite Bourgeoisie: Comparative Studies of the Uneasy Stratum* (London: St Martins Press).

MITCHELL, B. R. (1981), *European Historical Statistics, 1750–1975* (2nd edn., London: Macmillan).

MITCHELL, J. C., and CRITCHLEY, F. (1985), 'Configurational Similarity in Three Class Contexts in British Society', *Sociology*, 19.

MÓD, A. M. (1966), 'Social Stratification in Hungary' (Budapest: Hungarian Central Statistical Office).

MOEN, P. (1984), 'Continuities and Discontinuities in Women's Labor Force Activity', in G. H. Elder (ed.), *Life Course Dynamics: From 1968 to the 1980s* (Ithaca: Cornell University Press).

MOGEY, J. (1955), *Rural Life in Northern Ireland* (London: Oxford University Press).

MOORE, B. (1966), *Social Origins of Dictatorship and Democracy* (Boston: Beacon Press).

MOORE, W. E. (1963), *The Impact of Industry: Modernization of Traditional Societies* (Englewood Cliffs, NJ: Prentice-Hall).

—— (1967), *Order and Change* (New York: Wiley).

—— (1979), *World Modernization: The Limits of Convergence* (New York: Elsevier).

MORISHIMA, M. (1982), *Why Has Japan 'Succeeded'?* (Cambridge: Cambridge University Press).

MOUER, R., and SUGIMOTO, Y. (1986), *Images of Japanese Society* (London: Kegan Paul International).

MÜLLER, W. (1986), 'Soziale Mobilität: Die Bundesrespublik im Internationalen Vergleich', in M. Kaase (ed.), *Theorie und Praxis in Demokratische Regierungsweise* (Opladen: Westdeutscher Verlag).

—— (1988), 'Was bleibt von den Klassenstrukturen?', in P. Flora (ed.), *Westeuropa im Wandel* (Frankfurt: Campus).

—— and KARLE, W. (1990), 'Social Selection in Educational Systems in Europe' (ISA Research Committee on Social Stratification, Madrid).

MURAKAMI, Y. (1984), *Shin Chukan Taishu no Jidai* (*The Age of the New Middle Mass*) (Tokyo: Chuo Koronsha).

NAKANE, C. (1970), *Japanese Society* (London: Weidenfeld and Nicolson).

NAOI, A. (1979), 'Shokugyoteki Chiishakudo no Kosei' (The Construction of the Occupational Status Scale), in K. Tominaga (ed.), *Nihon no Kaiso Kozo* (*The Stratification Structure in Japan*) (Tokyo: Todai Shuppan Kai).

NEWBY, H. (1978), 'The Rural Sociology of Advanced Capitalist Societies', in H. Newby (ed.), *International Perspectives in Rural Sociology* (New York: Wiley).

NISHIGUCHI, T. (1990), 'Strategic Dualism: An Alternative in Industrial Societies', (D.Phil. thesis, University of Oxford).

OAKLEY, A. (1974), *Housewife* (Harmondsworth: Penguin).

O'BRIEN, P., and KEYDER, C. (1978), *Economic Growth in Britain and France, 1780–1914* (London: Allen and Unwin).

OECD (1970–1), *Occupational and Educational Structures of the Labour Force and Levels of Economic Development* (2 vols.; Paris: OECD).

OESER, O. A., and HAMMOND, S. B. (1954), *Social Structure and Personality in a City* (London: Routledge and Kegan Paul).

O'HIGGINS, M., SCHMAUS, G., and STEPHENSON, G. (1990), 'Income Distribution and Redistribution: A Microdata Analysis for Seven Countries,' in T. M. Smeeding, M. O'Higgins, and L. Rainwater (eds.), *Poverty, Inequality and Income Distribution in Comparative Perspective* (New York: Harvester-Wheatsheaf).

OLSON, M. (1982), *The Rise and Decline of Nations* (New Haven: Yale University Press).

O'MUIRCHEARTAIGH, C. A., and WIGGINS, R. D. (1977), 'Sample Design and Evaluation for an Occupational Mobility Study', *Economic and Social Review*, 8.

OSSOWSKI, S. (1957), 'Social Mobility Brought About by Social Revolutions' (ISA: Fourth Working Conference on Social Stratification and Mobility, Geneva).

PACI, A. (1979), 'Class Structure in Italian Society', *Archives européennes de sociologie*, 20.

PARKIN, F. (1969), 'Class Stratification in Socialist Societies', *British Journal of Sociology*, 20.

—— (1971*a*), *Class Inequality and Political Order* (London: McGibbon and Kee).

—— (1971*b*), 'Yugoslavia', in M. S. Archer and S. Giner (eds.), *Contemporary Europe: Class, Status and Power* (London: Weidenfeld and Nicolson).

PARSONS, T. (1960), *Structure and Process in Modern Societies* (Glencoe, Ill.: Free Press).

—— (1967), *Sociological Theory and Modern Society* (New York: Free Press).

—— (1971), *The System of Modern Societies* (Englewood Cliffs, NJ: Prentice-Hall).

PATRICK, H., and ROHLEN, T. (1987), 'Small-Scale Family Enterprises', in K. Yamamura and Y. Yasuba (eds.), *The Political Economy of Japan*, i. *The Domestic Transformation* (Stanford: Stanford University Press).

PAYNE, C. (1977), 'The Log-Linear Model for Contingency Tables', in C. Payne and C. A. O'Muircheartaigh (eds.), *The Analysis of Survey Data*, ii. *Model Fitting* (New York: Wiley).

PAYNE, G. (1987), *Employment and Opportunity* (London: Macmillan).

PEILLON, M. (1982), *Contemporary Irish Society* (Dublin: Gill and Macmillan).

—— (1986), 'Stratification and Class', in P. Clancy *et al.* (eds.), *Ireland: A Sociological Profile* (Dublin: Institute of Public Administration).

PETERSEN, W. (1953), 'Is America Still the Land of Opportunity?' *Commentary*, 16.

PHELPS BROWN, H. (1977), *The Inequality of Pay* (Oxford: Clarendon Press).

POHL, R., THÉLOT, C., and JOUSSET, M.-F. (1974), *L'Enquête Formation-Qualification Professionelle de 1970* (Paris: INSEE).

POHOSKI, M. (1964), 'Interrelation between Social Mobility of Individuals and Groups in the Process of Economic Growth in Poland', *Polish Sociological Bulletin*, 2.

—— PÖNTINEN, S., and ZAGÓRSKI, K. (1978), 'Social Mobility and Socio-economic Achievement', in E. Allardt and W. Wesołowski (eds.), *Social Structure and Change: Finland and Poland Comparative Perspective* (Warsaw: Polish Scientific Publishers).

POLLARD, S. (1981), *Peaceful Conquest: The Industrialization of Europe, 1760–1970* (Oxford: Oxford University Press).

PÖNTINEN, S. (1982), 'Models and Social Mobility Research', *Quality and Quantity*, 16.

—— (1983), *Social Mobility and Social Structure: A Comparison of Scandinavian Countries* (Helsinki: Societas Scientiarum Fennica).

POPPER, K. E. (1945), *The Open Society and its Enemies* (London: Routledge).

—— (1972), *Objective Knowledge* (Oxford: Clarendon Press).

PORTOCARERO, L. (1987), *Social Mobility in Industrial Societies: Women in France and Sweden* (Stockholm: Almqvist and Wicksell).

POSTAN, M. M. (1967), *An Economic History of Western Europe, 1945–64* (London: Allen and Unwin).

POULANTZAS, N. (1974), *Les Classes sociales dans le capitalisme aujourd'hui* (Paris: Seuil).

PRANDY, K. (1986), 'Similarities of Life-style and Occupations of Women', in R. Crompton and M. Mann (eds.), *Gender and Stratification* (Cambridge: Polity Press).

PRIEBE, H. (1976), 'The Changing Role of Agriculture, 1920–1970', in C. M. Cipolla (ed.), *Fontana Economic History of Europe*, v/ii (London: Fontana).

PRZEWORSKI, A., and TEUNE, H. (1970), *The Logic of Comparative Social Inquiry* (New York: Wiley).

PUGLIESE, E. (1981), 'The Mansholt Plan and the Mezzogiorno', in D. Pinto (ed.), *Contemporary Italian Sociology* (Cambridge: Cambridge University Press).

RAFFE, D. (1979), 'The "Alternative Route" Reconsidered: Part-time Further Education and Social Mobility in England and Wales', *Sociology*, 13.

RAFTERY, A. E. (1986a), 'Choosing Models for Cross-Classifications', *American Sociological Review*, 51.

—— (1986b), 'A Note on Bayes Factors for Log-Linear Contingency Table Models with Vague Prior Information', *Journal of the Royal Statistical Society*, series B, 48.

RAGIN, C. C. (1987), *The Comparative Method* (Berkeley: University of California Press).

RAINWATER, L., REIN, M., and SCHWARTZ, J. E. (1986), *Income Packaging in the Welfare State* (Oxford: Clarendon Press).

REHN, G. (1985), 'Swedish Active Labor Market Policy: Retrospect and Prospect', *Industrial Relations*, 24.

RENBORG, U. (1969), 'Tendencies towards Concentration and Specialization in Agriculture', in U. Papi and C. Nunn (eds.), *Economic Problems of Agriculture in Industrial Societies* (London: Macmillan).

RENNER, K. (1953), *Wandlungen der Modernen Gesellschaft: Zwei Abhandlungen über die Probleme der Nachkriegszeit* (Vienna: Wiener Volksbuchhandlung).

RINGEN, S. (1987), *The Possibility of Politics* (Oxford: Clarendon Press).

ROBERTS, B. C., LOVERIDGE, R., and GENNARD, J. (1972), *The Reluctant Militants* (London: Heinemann).

ROBERTS, H., and WOODWARD, D. (1981), 'Changing Patterns of Women's Employment in Sociology, 1950–1980', *British Journal of Sociology*, 32.

ROBINSON, R. V. (1984), 'Reproducing Class Relations in Industrial Capitalism', *American Sociological Review*, 49.

ROOS, P. A. (1985), *Gender and Work: A Comparative Analysis of Industrial Societies* (Albany: State University of New York Press).

ROSTOW, W. W. (1960), *The Stages of Economic Growth: A Non-Communist Manifesto* (Cambridge: Cambridge University Press).

ROTTMAN, D., and O'CONNELL, P. (1982), 'The Changing Social Structure of Ireland', in F. Litton (ed.), *Unequal Achievement: The Irish Experience, 1957–1982* (Dublin: Institute of Public Administration).

—— HANNAN, D. F., HARDIMAN, N., and WILEY, M. M. (1982), *The Distribution of Income in the Republic of Ireland: A Study in Social Class and Family-Cycle Inequalities* (Dublin: Economic and Social Research Institute).

RUNCIMAN, W. G. (1989), *A Treatise on Social Theory*, ii. *Substantive Social Theory* (Cambridge: Cambridge University Press).

—— (1990), 'How Many Classes are there in Contemporary British Society?', *Sociology*, 24.

RUTTER, A. (1986), 'Elites, Estates and Strata: Class in West Germany since 1945', in A. Marwick (ed.), *Class in the Twentieth Century* (Brighton: Harvester Press).

SAMSON, L. (1935), *Toward a United Front* (New York: Farrar and Rhinehart).

SAWIŃSKI, Z., and DOMAŃSKI, H. (1989), 'Dimensions of Social Stratification', *International Journal of Sociology*, 19.

SAWYER, M. (1976), *Income Distribution in OECD Countries* (Paris: OECD).

SAXENHOUSE, G. R. (1976), 'Country Girls and Communication among Competitors in the Japanese Cotton-spinning Industry', in H. Patrick (ed.), *Japanese Industrialization and its Social Consequences* (Berkeley: University of California Press).

SCHADEE, H. M. A., and SCHIZZEROTTO, A. (1990), *Social Mobility of Men and Women in Contemporary Italy* (Trento: Quaderno 17, Department of Social Policy, University of Trento).

SCHUMPETER, J. A. (1927, 2nd edn. 1951), 'Social Classes in an Ethnically Homogeneous Environment', in *Imperialism and Social Classes* (Oxford: Blackwell).

SCHWARTZ, J. E. (1985), 'Goodman's Coefficient of Multiple Determination: Why it is *not* Analogous to R^2' (Stockholm: Swedish Institute for Social Research).

SEMYONOV, M. (1980), 'The Comparative Context of Women's Labor Force Participation: A Comparative Analysis', *American Journal of Sociology*, 86.

—— and ROBERTS, C. W. (1989), 'Ascription and Achievement: Trends in Occupational Mobility in the United States, 1952–1984', *Research in Social Stratification and Mobility*, 8.

SHEPARD, R. N. (1972), 'Introduction' in R. N. Shepard, A. K. Romney, and S. B. Nerlove (eds.), *Multidimensional Scaling: Theory and Applications in the Behavioural Sciences* (New York: Seminar Press).

SHIRAHASE, S. (1989), 'Women in the Labour Market: Mobility and Work History of Japanese Women' (D.Phil. thesis, University of Oxford).

SIMKUS, A. A. (1981), 'Changes in Occupational Inheritance under Socialism: Hungary, 1930–1973', *Research in Social Stratification and Mobility*, 1.

—— (1984), 'Structural Transformation and Social Mobility: Hungary, 1938–1973', *American Sociological Review*, 49.

—— and ANDORKA, R. (1982), 'Inequalities in Educational Attainment in Hungary, 1923–1973', *American Sociological Review*, 47.

—— —— JACKSON, J., YIP, K.-B., and TREIMAN, D. J. (1990), 'Changes in Social Mobility in Two Societies in the Crux of Transition: A Hungarian–Irish Comparison, 1943–1973', *Research in Social Stratification and Mobility*, 9.

SINGELMANN, J. (1978), *From Agriculture to Services: The Transformation of Industrial Employment* (Beverly Hills: Sage).

—— and TIENDA, M. (1985), 'The Process of Occupational Change in a Service

Society: The Case of the United States, 1960–1980', in B. Roberts, R. Finnegan, and D. Gallie (eds.), *New Approaches to Economic Life* (Manchester: Manchester University Press).

SŁOMCZYŃSKI, K. (1978), 'The Role of Education in the Process of Social Mobility', in K. Słomczyński and T. Krauze (eds.), *Class Structure and Social Mobility in Poland* (Armonk, NY: Sharpe).

—— and WESOŁOWSKI, W. (1978), 'Reduction of Social Inequalities and Status Inconsistency', in Polish Sociological Association, *Social Structure: Polish Sociology, 1977* (Warsaw: Ossolineum).

SMALES, M. (1986), 'Class, Estate and Status in the Czech Lands, 1919–1938', in A. Marwick (ed.), *Class in the Twentieth Century* (Brighton: Harvester Press).

SMEEDING, T. M., and SCHMAUS, G. (1990), 'The LIS Database: Technical and Methodological Aspects', in T. M. Smeeding, M. O'Higgins, and L. Rainwater (eds.), *Poverty, Inequality and Income Distribution in Comparative Perspective* (New York: Harvester Wheatsheaf).

SMELSER, N. J., and LIPSET, S. M. (1966), 'Social Structure, Mobility and Development', in N. J. Smelser and S. M. Lipset (eds.), *Social Structure and Mobility in Economic Development* (London: Routledge).

SOBEL, M. E. (1983), 'Structural Mobility, Circulation Mobility and the Analysis of Occupational Mobility: A Conceptual Mismatch', *American Sociological Review*, 48.

—— HOUT, M., and DUNCAN, O. D. (1985), 'Exchange, Structure and Symmetry in Occupational Mobility', *American Journal of Sociology*, 91.

SOMBART W. (1960), *Warum gibt es in den Vereinigten Staaten keinen Sozialismus?* (Tübingen: J. C. B. Mohr).

SØRENSEN, A., ALLMENDINGER, J., and SØRENSEN, A. B. (1986), 'Intergenerational Mobility as a Life-Course Process' (Department of Sociology, Harvard University).

SØRENSEN, A. B. (1986), 'Theory and Methodology in Social Stratification', in U. Himmelstrand (ed.), *Sociology from Crisis to Science?* i (London: Sage).

SOROKIN, P. A. (1927, 2nd edn. 1959), *Social Mobility* (Glencoe, Ill.: Free Press).

SPEIER, H. (1934), 'The Salaried Employee in Modern Society', *Social Research* (February).

—— (1986), *German White-Collar Workers and the Rise of Hitler* (New Haven, Yale University Press).

STANWORTH, M. (1984), 'Women and Class Analysis: A Reply to John Goldthorpe', *Sociology*, 18.

STARSKI, S. (1982), *Class Struggles in Classless Poland* (Boston: South End Press).

STEPHENS, J. D. (1979), *The Transition from Capitalism to Socialism* (London: Macmillan).

STEVEN, R. (1983), *Classes in Contemporary Japan* (Cambridge: Cambridge University Press).

STEWART, A., PRANDY, K., and BLACKBURN, R. M. (1980), *Social Stratification and Occupations* (London: Macmillan).

STINCHCOMBE, A. L. (1961), 'Agricultural Enterprise and Rural Class Relations', *American Journal of Sociology*, 67.

—— (1968), *Constructing Social Theories* (New York: Harcourt, Brace and World).

—— (1983), *Economic Sociology* (New York: Academic Press).

STRMISKA, Z. (1987), 'Social Mobility in Soviet-type Societies in Comparative

Perspective', in P. Kende and Z. Strmiska (eds.), *Equality and Inequality in Eastern Europe* (Leamington Spa: Berg).

SVALASTOGA, K. (1959), *Prestige, Class and Mobility* (Copenhagen: Gyldendal).

—— (1965), 'Social Mobility: The Western European Model', *Acta Sociologica*, 9.

SZCZEPAŃSKI, J. (1970), *Polish Society* (New York: Random House).

—— (1978), 'Early Stages of Socialist Industrialization and Changes in Social Class Structure', in K. Słomczyński and T. Krauze (eds.), *Class Structure and Social Mobility in Poland* (Armonk, NY: Sharpe).

SZELÉNYI, I. (1987), 'The Prospects and Limits of the East European New Class Project', *Politics and Society*, 15.

—— (1988), *Socialist Entrepreneurs* (Oxford: Polity Press).

TAFT, R., and WALKER, K. F. (1958), 'Australia', in A. M. Rose (ed.), *The Institutions of Advanced Societies* (Minneapolis: University of Minnesota Press).

TÅHLIN, M. (1991), 'Class Mobility in a Swedish City', in E. J. Hansen, S. Ringen, H. Uusitalo, and R. Erikson (eds.), *Scandinavian Trends in Welfare and Living Conditions* (Armonk, NY: Sharpe).

TAYLOR, C. L., and JODICE, D. A. (1983), *World Handbook of Social and Political Indicators* (New Haven, Yale University Press).

TEICHOVA, A. (1988), *Wirtschaftsgeschichte der Tschechoslowakei 1918–1980* (Vienna: Böhlau).

THÉLOT, C. (1979), 'Les Fils de cadres qui deviennent ouvriers', *Revue française de sociologie*, 20.

—— (1982), *Tel père, tel fils?* (Paris: Dunod).

THERNSTROM, S. (1970), 'Working Class Social Mobility in Industrial America', in M. Richter (ed.), *Essays in Theory and History* (Cambridge, Mass.: Harvard University Press).

—— (1974), 'Socialism and Social Mobility', and 'Reply', in J. H. M. Laslett and S. M. Lipset (eds.), *Failure of a Dream? Essays in the History of American Socialism* (New York: Anchor Books).

THURLEY, K., and WIRDENIUS, H. (1973), *Supervision: A Reappraisal* (London: Heinemann).

TIPTON, F. B., and ALDRICH, R. (1987), *An Economic and Social History of Europe from 1939 to the Present* (London: Macmillan).

TOCQUEVILLE, A. (1835/1968), *De la démocratie en Amérique*, ed. J. P. Mayer (Paris: Gallimard).

TOKUYASU, A. (1986), 'Nihon ni okeru Sangyoka to Sedaikan no Susei Bunseki' (Industrialization and Trends in Intergenerational Mobility in Japan), in K. Tominaga (ed.), *Shakai Kaiso no Susei to Hikaku* (*Social Stratification: Trends and Comparison*) (Tokyo: SSM Committee).

TOMINAGA, K. (1969), 'Trend Analysis of Social Stratification and Social Mobility in Contemporary Japan', *Developing Economies*, 7.

—— (1979a), 'Shakai Kaiso to Shakai Ido eno Apurochi' (Approaches to Social Stratification and Mobility), in K. Tominaga (ed.), *Nihon no Kaiso Kozo* (*The Stratification Structure in Japan*) (Tokyo: Todai Shuppan Kai).

—— (1979b), 'Shakai Kaiso to Shakai Ido no Susei Bunseki' (Trend Analysis of Social Stratification and Mobility), in K. Tominaga (ed.), *Nihon no Kaiso Kozo* (*The Stratification Structure in Japan*) (Tokyo: Todai Shuppan Kai).

—— (1982), 'Problems of Viewpoint in Interpreting Japanese Society: Japan and the West' (Ostasiatisches Seminar, Freie Universität Berlin, Occasional Papers, no. 38).

—— NAOI, A., and IMADA, T. (n.d.), 'Current Trends in Studies of Social Stratification and Mobility in Japan' (University of Tokyo).

TREIMAN, D. J. (1970), 'Industrialisation and Social Stratification', in E. O. Laumann (ed.), *Social Stratification: Research and Theory for the 1970s* (Indianapolis: Bobbs Merrill).

—— (1975), 'Problems of Concept and Measurement in the Comparative Study of Occupational Mobility', *Social Science Research*, 4.

—— (1977*a*), *Occupational Prestige in Comparative Perspective* (New York: Academic Press).

—— (1977*b*), 'Toward Methods for a Quantitative Comparative Sociology: A Reply to Burawoy', *American Journal of Sociology*, 82.

—— and Roos, P. A. (1983), 'Sex and Earnings in Industrial Society: A Nine-Nation Comparison', *American Journal of Sociology*, 89.

—— and YIP, K.-B. (1989), 'Educational and Occupational Attainment in 21 Countries', in M. L. Kohn (ed.), *Cross-National Research in Sociology* (Newbury Park: Sage).

TYREE, A., SEMYONOV, M., and HODGE, R. (1979), 'Gaps and Glissandos: Inequality, Economic Development and Social Mobility in 24 Countries', *American Sociological Review*, 44.

UUSITALO, H. (1985), 'Redistribution and Inequality in the Welfare State', *European Sociological Review*, 1.

VAUGHAN, M. (1971), 'Poland', in M. Archer and S. Giner (eds.), *Contemporary Europe: Class, Status and Power* (London: Weidenfeld and Nicolson).

VEČERNÍK, J. (1987), 'Income Distribution in Czechoslovakia: Some Systemic Specificities' (Conference on 'Societies at Borderlines', University of Graz).

VOGEL, E. F. (1967), 'Kinship Structures, Migration to the City, and Modernisation', in R. P. Dore (ed.), *Aspects of Social Change in Modern Japan* (Princeton, NJ: Princeton University Press).

VOGEL, J. (1987), *Det svenska klassamhället* (Stockholm: Statistiska Centralbyrån).

VOLGYES, I. (1981), 'Hungary: The Lumpenproletarianization of the Working Class', in J. F. Triska and C. Gati (eds.), *Blue-Collar Workers in Eastern Europe* (London: Allen and Unwin).

WALBY, S. (1986), 'Gender, Class and Stratification', in R. Crompton and M. Mann (eds.), *Gender and Stratification* (Cambridge: Polity Press).

WEGENER, B. (1988), *Kritik des Prestiges* (Opladen: Westdeutscher Verlag).

WELLS, H. G. (1906), *The Future in America* (New York: Harper).

WESOŁOWSKI, W., and MACH, B. (1986), 'Unfulfilled Systemic Functions of Social Mobility', *International Sociology*, 1.

WEST, J. (1978), 'Women, Sex and Class', in A. Kuhn and A. Wolpe (eds.), *Feminism and Materialism* (London: Routledge).

WESTERGAARD, J. H., and RESLER, H. (1975), *Class in a Capitalist Society* (London: Heinemann).

WHELAN, C. T., and WHELAN, B. J. (1984), *Social Mobility in the Republic of Ireland: A Comparative Perspective* (Dublin: Economic and Social Research Institute).

WILLIAMSON, J. G. (1985), *Did British Capitalism Breed Inequality?* (Boston: Allen and Unwin).

WILLIAMSON, O. E. (1975), *Markets and Hierarchies: Analysis and Antitrust Implications* (New York: Free Press).

—— (1985), *The Economic Institutions of Capitalism* (New York: Free Press).

WILSON, G. (1987), *Money in the Family* (Aldershot: Avebury).

WILSON, T. P. (1979), 'On Not Interpreting Coefficients', *Sociological Methods and Research*, 8.

WOHL, R. (1953), 'The "Rags to Riches Story": An Episode of Secular Idealism, in S. M. Lipset and R. Bendix (eds.), *Class, Status and Power* (Glencoe, Ill.: Free Press).

WONG, R. S.-K. (1988), 'Temporal Change in Occupational Mobility in Hungary under Socialism: The Featherman–Jones–Hauser Thesis Revisited' (Department of Sociology, University of Wisconsin-Madison).

—— (1990), 'Understanding Cross-National Variation in Occupational Mobility', *American Sociological Review*, 55.

WRIGHT, E. O. (1978), *Class, Crisis and the State* (London: New Left Books).

—— (1985), *Classes* (London: Verso).

—— (1989*a*), 'Women in the Class Structure', *Politics and Society*, 17.

—— (1989*b*), 'Rethinking, Once Again, the Concept of Class Structure', in E. O. Wright (ed.), *The Debate on Classes* (London: Verso).

—— and MARTIN, B. (1987), 'The Transformation of the American Class Structure, 1960–1980', *American Journal of Sociology*, 93.

—— and SHIN, K.-Y. (1988), 'Temporality and Class Analysis: A Comparative Study of the Effects of Class Trajectory and Class Structure on Class Consciousness in Sweden and the United States', *Sociological Theory*, 6.

—— and SINGELMANN, J. (1982), 'Proletarianization in the Changing American Class Structure', *American Journal of Sociology*, 88.

WRIGLEY, E. A. (1972), 'The Process of Modernization and the Industrial Revolution in England', *Journal of Interdisciplinary History*, 3.

YAMAGUCHI, K. (1987), 'Models for Comparing Mobility Tables: Towards Parsimony and Substance', *American Sociological Review*, 52.

YOHALEM, A. M. (ed.) (1980), *Women Returning to Work* (London: Frances Pinter).

ZAGÓRSKI, K. (1977–8), 'Transformations of Social Structure and Social Mobility in Poland', *International Journal of Sociology*, 7.

—— (with ANDORKA, R., TUMA, N. B., and MEYER, J. W.) (1984), 'Comparisons of Social Mobility in Different Socio-economic Systems', in M. Niessen, J. L. Peschar, and C. Kourilsky (eds.), *International Comparative Research: Social Structures and Public Institutions in Eastern and Western Europe* (Oxford: Pergamon).

INDEX OF NAMES

SUBJECT INDEX

Name Index and Subject Index compiled by
Magnus Nermo